Atiyah and Adams' Sale of Goods

Atiyah and Adams' Sale of Goods

Fifteenth Edition

Christian Twigg-Flesner LLB, PCHE, PHD
Professor of Contract and Consumer Law, School of Law,
University of Warwick, Coventry

David Ndolo
Lecturer in Law, Coventry University.

Pearson

Harlow, England • London • New York • Boston • San Francisco • Toronto • Sydney
Dubai • Singapore • Hong Kong • Tokyo • Seoul • Taipei • New Delhi
Cape Town • São Paulo • Mexico City • Madrid • Amsterdam • Munich • Paris • Milan

PEARSON EDUCATION LIMITED
KAO Two
KAO Park
Harlow
CM17 9SR
United Kingdom
Tel: +44 (0)1279 623623
Web: www.pearson.com

First published under the Pitman imprint in Great Britain in 1957 (print)
Thirteenth edition published 2016 (print and electronic)
Fifteenth edition published 2026 (print and electronic)

ISBN: 978-1-292-73963-2 (print)
978-1-292-47163-1 (eText)
978-1-292-47162-4 (ePub)

British Library Cataloguing-in-Publication Data
A catalogue record for the print edition is available from the British Library

Library of Congress Cataloging-in-Publication Data

Names: Twigg-Flesner, Christian, 1975- author. | Canavan, Rick, author. | Atiyah, P. S., author. | Adams, John, 1939- author.
Title: Atiyah and Adams' sale of goods / Christian Twigg-Flesner, LLB, PCHE, PHD, Professor of International Commercial Law, School of Law, University of Warwick, Coventry;
Rick Canavan, Head of Faculty, Faculty of Business and Law, Manchester Metropolitan University, Manchester.
Description: Fourteenth edition. | Harlow, England ; New York : Pearson, 2021.
Identifiers: LCCN 2020011051 | ISBN 9781292251028 (print) | ISBN 9781292251042 (PDF) | ISBN 9781292251035 (ePub)
Subjects: LCSH: Sales—England. | Sales—Scotland. | Sales—European Union countries.
Classification: LCC KD1650 .A96 2020 | DDC 346.4207/2—dc23
LC record available at https://lccn.loc.gov/2020011051

10 9 8 7 6 5 4 3 2 1
30 29 28 27 26

Front cover image: DifferR/Shutterstock
Cover designed by Michelle Morgan.
Print edition typeset in Sabon MT Pro 10/12 by Straive

NOTE THAT ANY PAGE CROSS REFERENCES REFER TO THE PRINT EDITION

Contents in brief

Part VII The remedies of the buyer

Part VIII Consumer sales

Part IX Dispute resolution

Contents

Part VI
The remedies of the seller

Part VII
The remedies of the buyer

Part VIII
Consumer sales

Preface to the Fifteenth Edition

In 2016, the editorship of this long-established text passed from the late Professor John Adams to Professor Christian Twigg-Flesner and Rick Canavan. Both continued in their roles for the Fourteenth Edition, published in 2020. Since then, Rick Canavan has decided to leave academia, and he also stood down from editing this book. The task of updating any textbook is demanding and time-consuming, and it is work best shared. Professor Christian Twigg-Flesner was therefore joined by a new editor for the preparation of this fifteenth edition: Dr David Ndolo from Coventry University.

It was pleasure for both of us to work on updating this text for its 15th edition. In the previous two prefaces, the then editors noted that they tried to preserve the voices and scholarly rigour of both the original author, Professor Patrick Atiyah, and its first editor, John Adams. We have continued to approach our task in the same way, and have avoided being too radical in the changes we have made.

Our task was two-fold: ensuring that recent developments in the case law are adequately reflected in the text, and improving the flow of the discussion. The extent of the changes we have made varies from chapter to chapter, with some chapters having had a light review and others more significant changes. We hope that we have succeeded in keeping the book familiar for long-standing readers and keeping it accessible for first-time readers.

We have continued to gently insert material reflecting the growing significance of digitalisation. In particular, goods with integrated software are increasingly prevalent and we have considered some of the pertinent questions they raise in several chapters. Christian Twigg-Flesner took the lead on these matters. Eagle-eyed readers will also spot a new Chapter 22 on dispute resolution, written by David Ndolo (whose expertise includes arbitration and dispute resolution). We hope this chapter will be welcomed by readers.

The primary responsibility for updating chapters was allocated as follows: David Ndolo took the lead on chapters 1–4, 10–12, 13, 17 and 18; and Christian Twigg-Flesner led on chapters 5–9, 14–16 and 19–21, and was the overall editorial lead.

We have endeavoured to state the law as we believe it to be in December 2024.

Christian Twigg-Flesner
David Ndolo

Acknowledgements

4 The Incorporated Council of Law Reporting for England & Wales: *Bank of England* v *Vagliano Bros* [1891] AC 107, 144–5; **4 The Incorporated Council of Law Reporting for England & Wales:** *Ashington Piggeries Ltd* v *Christopher Hill Ltd* [1972] AC 441. p. 501; **15 The Incorporated Council of Law Reporting for England & Wales:** *Branwhite* v *Worcester Works Finance Ltd* [1969] 1 AC 552, per Lord Wilberforce; **20 The Incorporated Council of Law Reporting for England & Wales:** *Kingsley* v *Sterling Industrial Securities Ltd* [1967] 2 QB 747, 780; **21 The Incorporated Council of Law Reporting for England & Wales:** *Snook* v *London and West Riding Investments Ltd* [1967] 2 QB 786, 802; **30 The Incorporated Council of Law Reporting for England & Wales:** *Foley* v *Classique Coaches Ltd* [1934] 2 KB 1; **33 The Incorporated Council of Law Reporting for England & Wales:** *Campbell* v *Edwards* [1976] 1 WLR 403, 407; **42 The Incorporated Council of Law Reporting for England & Wales:** *Ingram* v *Little* [1961] 1 QB 31, At p. 48; **49 The Incorporated Council of Law Reporting for England & Wales:** *Eurodynamics Systems plc* v *General Automation Ltd* (unrep, 6 September 1988, QBD); **65 The Incorporated Council of Law Reporting for England & Wales:** *Bunge Corpn* v *Tradax* [1981] 1 WLR at 715; **74 The Incorporated Council of Law Reporting for England & Wales:** *Bell* v *Lever Bros Ltd* [1932] AC 161, at 224–5; **84 The Incorporated Council of Law Reporting for England & Wales:** *Rowland* v *Divall* [1923] 2 KB 500; **89 The Incorporated Council of Law Reporting for England & Wales:** *Mason* v *Burningham* [1949] 2 KB 545; **100 The Incorporated Council of Law Reporting for England & Wales:** *Biddell Bros Ltd* v *E Clemens Horst & Co Ltd* [1911] 1 KB 934, per Kennedy LJ at 956–7; **101 The Incorporated Council of Law Reporting for England & Wales:** Per McCardie J in *Hartley* v *Hymans* [1920] 3 KB 475, 484; **117 The Incorporated Council of Law Reporting for England & Wales:** *Hazlewood Grocery Ltd* v *Lion Foods Ltd* [2007] EWHC 1887 (QB); **118 The Incorporated Council of Law Reporting for England & Wales:** *Harlingdon & Leinster Enterprises Ltd* v *Christopher Hull Fine Art Ltd* [1991] 1 QB 564; **120 The Incorporated Council of Law Reporting for England & Wales:** *Arcos Ltd* v *E A Ronaasen & Son* [1933] AC 470, 479–80; **121 The Incorporated Council of Law Reporting for England & Wales:** Ashington Piggeries [1972] AC at pp. 503–4; **124 The Incorporated Council of Law Reporting for England & Wales:** *Varley* v *Whipp* [1900] 1 QB 513, 516 per Channel J; **124 The Incorporated Council of Law Reporting for England & Wales:** *Grant* v *Australian Knitting Mills Ltd* [1936] AC 85, 100; **127 The Incorporated Council of Law Reporting for England & Wales:** *Pinnock Bros* v *Lewis and Peat Ltd* [1923] 1 KB 690; **129 The Incorporated Council of Law Reporting for England & Wales:** *Lemy* v *Watson* [1915] 3 KB 731, 752; **140 The Incorporated Council of Law Reporting for England & Wales:** *Wilson* v *Rickett Cockerell & Co Ltd* [1954] 1 QB 598, At p. 606, 607; **152 The Incorporated Council of Law Reporting for England & Wales:** *Rogers* v *Parish (Scarborough) Ltd* [1987] QB 933; **167–168 The Incorporated Council of Law Reporting for England & Wales:**

Cammell Laird & Co Ltd v *Manganese Bronze & Brass Co Ltd* [1934] AC 402 At p. 414; **169 The Incorporated Council of Law Reporting for England & Wales:** *Grant* v *Australian Knitting Mills Ltd* [1936] AC 85, 99; **173–174 The Incorporated Council of Law Reporting for England & Wales:** *Kendall* v *Lillico* [1969] 2 AC 31, 84; **180 The Incorporated Council of Law Reporting for England & Wales:** *E & S Ruben* v *Faire Bros Ltd* [1949] 1 KB 254, 260, per Hilbery J; **184 The Incorporated Council of Law Reporting for England & Wales:** *Leaf* v *International Galleries* [1950] 2 KB 86, At p. 89; **184 The Incorporated Council of Law Reporting for England & Wales:** *Harrison & Jones* v *Bunten & Lancaster* [1953] 1 QB 646; **185 The Incorporated Council of Law Reporting for England & Wales:** *Harrison & Jones* v *Bunten & Lancaster* [1953] 1 QB 646, 654; **193 The Incorporated Council of Law Reporting for England & Wales:** *Beck & Co Ltd* v *Szymanowski & Co Ltd* [1924] AC 43; **195 The Incorporated Council of Law Reporting for England & Wales:** *McCutcheon* v *David MacBrayne Ltd* [1964] 1 WLR 125, 128, 1964 SC (HL) 28, 35 per Lord Reid; **196 The Incorporated Council of Law Reporting for England & Wales:** *Karsales* v *Wallis* [1956] 1 WLR 936, 940; **199 The Incorporated Council of Law Reporting for England & Wales:** *Lowe* v *Lombank Ltd* [1960] 1 WLR 196; **241 The Incorporated Council of Law Reporting for England & Wales:** *Weiner* v *Harris* [1910] 1 KB 285; **244 The Incorporated Council of Law Reporting for England & Wales:** Re Blyth Shipbuilding Co Ltd [1926] Ch 494, 518 per Sargant LJ; **245 The Incorporated Council of Law Reporting for England & Wales:** *Seath* v *Moore* (1886) 1 App Cas 350, 381 per Lord Watson; **246 The Incorporated Council of Law Reporting for England & Wales:** *Laing & Sons* v *Barclay, Curle & Co* [1908] AC 35 at p. 43 per Lord Halsbury; **246 The Incorporated Council of Law Reporting for England & Wales:** *McDougall* v *Aeromarine of Emsworth Ltd* [1958] 1 WLR 1126; **249 The Incorporated Council of Law Reporting for England & Wales:** Re Shipton Anderson & Co Ltd and Harrison Bros & Co Ltd [1915] 3 KB 676; **259 The Incorporated Council of Law Reporting for England & Wales:** *Tailby* v *Official Receiver* (1888) 13 App Cas 523, 533; **260 The Incorporated Council of Law Reporting for England & Wales:** Re Wait [1927] 1 Ch 606, 635–6; **263 The Incorporated Council of Law Reporting for England & Wales:** *Lord Normand in Comptoir d'Achat et de Vente SA* v *Luis de Ridder Limitada (The Julia)* [1949] AC 293 at p. 319; **269 The Incorporated Council of Law Reporting for England & Wales:** *Monkland* v *Jack Barclay Ltd* [1951] 2 KB 252, 258 per Asquith LJ; **270 The Incorporated Council of Law Reporting for England & Wales:** *Blackburn Bobbin Co Ltd* v *Allen & Son* [1918] 1 KB 540, 550; **270 The Incorporated Council of Law Reporting for England & Wales:** Court of Appeal [1918] 2 KB at p. 469; **271 The Incorporated Council of Law Reporting for England & Wales:** Re Badische Co Ltd [1921] 2 Ch at p. 382; **279 The Incorporated Council of Law Reporting for England & Wales:** *Bishopsgate Motor Finance Corpn* v *Transport Brakes Ltd* [1949] 1 KB 332, 336–7; **280 The Incorporated Council of Law Reporting for England & Wales:** *Cf. Laurie & Morewood* v *John Dudin & Sons* [1926] 1 KB 223; **281 The Incorporated Council of Law Reporting for England & Wales:** *D F Mount Ltd* v *Jay & Jay Co Ltd* [1960] 1 QB at p. 167; **285 The Incorporated Council of Law Reporting for England & Wales:** *Mercantile Bank of India Ltd* v *Central Bank of India Ltd* [1926] AC 72 at p. 303; **288 The Incorporated Council of Law Reporting for England & Wales:** *Farquharson Bros* v *King & Co Ltd* [1902] AC at 335–6 per Lord Macnaghten; **288 The Incorporated Council of Law Reporting for England & Wales:** *Lickbarrow* v *mason* (1787) 2 tr 63. Court of king's bench; **289 The Incorporated Council of Law Reporting for England & Wales:** *Mercantile Credit Co Ltd* v *Hamblin* [1965] 2 QB 242, 275; **296 The Incorporated Council of Law Reporting for England & Wales:** *National Employers Mutual General Insurance Association Ltd* v *Jones* [1990] 1 AC 24, 60 per Lord Goff; **297 The Incorporated Council of Law Reporting for England & Wales:** *Lloyds Bank* v *Bank of America* [1938] 2 KB 147, 162; **297 The Incorporated Council of Law Reporting for England & Wales:** *Pearson* v *Rose & Young* [1951] 1 KB 275, 288; **298 The Incorporated Council of Law Reporting for England & Wales:** *Oppenheimer* v *Attenborough & Sons* [1908] 1 KB 221, 230–1 per Buckley LJ; **304 The Incorporated Council of Law Reporting for England & Wales:** *Tahir Fadallah* v *John Pollak* [2013] EWHC 3159 (QB), para.47; **306 The Incorporated Council of Law Reporting for England & Wales:** *Feuer Leather Corp* v *Frank Johnstone* (1981) Com LR 251, 253 [QB]; **316 The Incorporated Council of Law Reporting for England & Wales:** *Newtons of Wembley Ltd* v *Williams* [1965] 1 QB 560, 578; **327 The Incorporated Council of Law Reporting for England & Wales:** The Albazero [1977] AC 774, 809; **329 The Incorporated Council of Law Reporting for England & Wales:** *Bunge & Co Ltd* v *Tradax England Ltd* [1975] 2 Lloyd's Rep at p. 239; **334 The Incorporated Council of Law Reporting for England & Wales:** *Smyth & Co Ltd* v *Bailey Son & Co Ltd* [1940] 3 All ER 60, 67–8; **340 The Incorporated Council of Law Reporting for England & Wales:** *Smyth & Co Ltd* v *Bailey Son & Co Ltd* [1940] 3 All ER 60, 65 per Lord Wright – above, p. 352; **341 The Incorporated Council of Law Reporting for England & Wales:** *Yangtsze Insurance Association* v *Lukmanjee* [1918] AC 585, 589 per Lord Sumner; **346 The Incorporated Council of Law Reporting for England & Wales:** *Forestal Mimosa Ltd* v *Oriental Credit Ltd* [1986] 1 WLR 631; **347 The Incorporated Council of Law Reporting for England & Wales:** *British Imex Industries Ltd* v *Midland Bank* [1958] 1 QB 542, per Salmon LJ; **348 The Incorporated Council of Law Reporting for England & Wales:** *United City Merchants (Investments) Ltd* v *Royal Bank of Canada* [1983] AC 168, 183; **349 The Incorporated Council of Law Reporting for England & Wales:** *Pavia & Co SpA* v *Thurmann-Nielsen* [1952] 2 QB 84, 88 per Denning LJ; **353 The Incorporated Council of Law Reporting for England & Wales:** See *Robinson* v *Graves* [1935] 1 KB 579; **370 The Incorporated Council of Law Reporting for England & Wales:** *Lord's Trustee* v *Great Eastern Rly* [1908] 2 KB 54, 63–4; **379 The Incorporated Council of Law Reporting for England & Wales:** *Kendall* v *Marshall, Stevens & Co Ltd* (1883) 11 QBD 356, 369 per Bowen LJ; **379 The Incorporated Council of Law Reporting for England & Wales:** *Bethell & Co Ltd* v *Clark & Co Ltd* (1888) 20 QBD 615, 617. Cf. *Lyons* v *Hoffnung* (1890) 15 App Cas 396; **381 The Incorporated Council of Law Reporting for England & Wales:** *Berndtson* v *Strang* (1868) 3 Ch App Per Lord Cairns at p. 591; **401 The Incorporated Council of Law Reporting for England & Wales:** *Johnson* v *Agnew* [1980] AC 367, at 392; **406 The Incorporated Council of Law Reporting for England & Wales:** *ABD (Metals & Waste) Ltd* v *Anglo-Chemical & Ore Co Ltd* [1955] 2 Lloyd's Rep 456; **409 The Incorporated Council of Law Reporting for England & Wales:** *AKAS Jamal* v *Moolla Dawood* [1916] 1 AC 175, 179; **420 The Incorporated Council of Law Reporting for England & Wales:** *Maple Flock Co Ltd* v *Universal Furniture Products (Wembley) Ltd* [1934] 1 KB 148, 157 per Lord Hewart CJ; **420 The Incorporated Council of Law Reporting for England & Wales:** *R A Munro & Co Ltd* v *Meyer* [1930] 2 KB 312, 331; **421 The Incorporated Council of Law Reporting for England & Wales:** *Warinco A G* v *Samor SPA* [1977] 2 Lloyd's Rep 582, at p. 588;

426 The Incorporated Council of Law Reporting for England & Wales: *Kwei Tek Chao* v *British Traders & Shippers Ltd* [1954] 2 WLR at 372, a passage omitted from the Report at [1954] 2 QB 459; **430 The Incorporated Council of Law Reporting for England & Wales:** *Kwei Tek Chao* v *British Traders & Shippers Ltd* [1954] 2 QB 459, 487; **430 The Incorporated Council of Law Reporting for England & Wales:** *British Traders & Shippers* [1954] 2 QB 459, 487–8; **436 The Incorporated Council of Law Reporting for England & Wales:** *Jackson* v *Rotax Motor & Cycle Co Ltd* [1910] 2 KB 937; **437 The Incorporated Council of Law Reporting for England & Wales:** *Kwei Tek Chao* v *British Traders & Shippers Ltd* [1954] 2 QB 459, 480 per Devlin J; **447 The Incorporated Council of Law Reporting for England & Wales:** *James Finlay & Co* v *NV Kwik Hoo Tong Handel Maatschappij* [1929] 1 KB 400, 417; **448 The Incorporated Council of Law Reporting for England & Wales:** The Arpad, 29 Jun 1934 [1934] P 189, CA; **449 The Incorporated Council of Law Reporting for England & Wales:** *Kwei Tek Chao* v *British Traders & Shippers Ltd* [1954] 2 QB 459, 489–90 per Devlin J. In *Aryeh* v *Lawrence Kostoris & Son Ltd* (see n. 37) at p. 72; **461 The Incorporated Council of Law Reporting for England & Wales:** *Kasler & Cohen* v *Slavouski* [1928] 1 KB 78, 85; **514 The Incorporated Council of Law Reporting for England & Wales:** *Junior Books* [1983] 1 AC 520, 533.

Table of statutes

Table of Treaties

Table of European Regulations and Directives

Table of International Legislation

Table of cases

Table of statutory instruments

Part I

Nature and formation of the contract of sale

1

Sources of the law of sale of goods

The previous chapter considered the extensive changes made to the consumer law landscape through the Consumer Rights Act 2015 and related legislation. This chapter concentrates on an aspect of consumer protection which was in place before the recent reforms, and considers primarily the legal obligations a manufacturer of goods may have towards consumers.

1.1 Introduction

The focus of this book is the English law on sale of goods with a particular focus on sale of goods between non-consumers. The latter distinction has for many years been of some importance as the law's approach to consumer transactions was constructed piecemeal within the Sale of Goods Act 1979. However, with the passing into law of the Consumer Rights Act 2015, a largely discrete body of law in relation to consumer sales emerged,[1] although its origins in and relationship to the old law are clear. The creation of a separate body of rules applicable to consumer sales has meant that the piecemeal additions previously made to the Sale of Goods Act 1979 (and in other related legislation such as the Unfair Contract Terms Act 1977) have now been 'peeled away', leaving, for the first time, two (almost) distinct regimes that ought to align to different perceived needs of consumers and those who buy and sell in the course of business. The Consumer Rights Act itself is considered fully in Chapter 19. The effect of the amendments made by this Act will be considered where applicable throughout the text. It should, however, be noted at this point that the Sale of Goods Act 1979 is not entirely irrelevant to consumer sales contracts; crucially, the provisions on the passing of property and title conflicts continue to apply to consumer sales contracts, at least for the time being.

1.2 The Sale of Goods Act 1979

The domestic law of sale of goods, as it applies to non-consumers, is still to be found in four main sources. The first, and still by far the most important, is the Sale of Goods Act 1979, which consolidates (with some additional amendments) the original Sale of Goods Act of 1893 and amendments to it made prior to 1979. That Act has in turn been amended by the Sale and Supply of Goods Act 1994, the Sale of Goods (Amendment) Act 1994 and the Sale of Goods (Amendment) Act 1995.

[1] Although in some instances the two regimes remain very closely linked; for example, s. 4 of the Consumer Rights Act 2015 invokes the rules on the passing of property found in the Sale of Goods Act.

Secondly, there are a number of other statutory provisions, of varying importance, some of which pre-date the Act of 1893 (such as the Factors Act 1889), but others of more recent origin, such as the Unfair Contract Terms Act 1977 and the Contracts (Rights of Third Parties) Act 1999. Thirdly, there is a considerable body of case law interpreting the Act of 1893, much of which remains relevant to the interpretation of the Act of 1979 and, of course, there is substantial case law on the 1979 Act itself. Fourthly, there is still a certain amount of relevant case law which pre-dates the Act of 1893, although, as the Act of 1893 was a codifying statute, the old case law on points dealt with by the Act is now only of marginal importance. The relationship between historic customs and practice, the law prior to 1893 and the law after 1893 is reflected in the approach taken to the interpretation of the legislation. The proper method for doing so being laid down by Lord Herschell in *Bank of England* v *Vagliano Bros.*[2]

> I think the proper course is in the first instance to examine the language of the statute and to ask what is its natural meaning, uninfluenced by any considerations derived from the previous state of the law, and not to start with inquiring how the law previously stood, and then, assuming that it was probably intended to leave it unaltered, to see if the words of the enactment will bear an interpretation in conformity with this view. If a statute, intended to embody in a code a particular branch of the law, is to be treated in this fashion, it appears to me that its utility will be almost entirely destroyed, and the very object with which it was enacted will be frustrated. The purpose of such a statute surely was that on any point specifically dealt with by it, the law should be ascertained by interpreting the language used instead of, as before, by roaming over a vast number of authorities in order to discover what the law was, extracting it by a minute critical examination of the prior decisions.

Lord Herschell then went on to observe that in exceptional cases, reference to earlier decisions may still be permissible. First, where the provisions of the Act are ambiguous, earlier cases may help to resolve the ambiguity; and, secondly, where a term has acquired a technical meaning, previous cases may be cited to illustrate this meaning. It almost goes without saying that where a point is not covered by the Act, older decisions are still binding and must be followed.

Despite this warning and its subsequent repetition in later cases, arguably, it has not always been taken to heart by courts or writers. For example, the speeches of the judges in the House of Lords in *Ashington Piggeries Ltd* v *Christopher Hill Ltd*[3] suggest that Lord Herschell's remarks may need qualification. In particular, in the interpretation of provisions of the Act relating to implied terms, Lord Diplock said that the Act 'ought not to be construed so narrowly as to force on parties to contracts for the sale of goods promises and consequences different from what they must reasonably have intended',[4] a position that is very much in evidence in the decision of the Supreme Court in *PST Energy 7 Shipping LLC* v *O W Bunker Malta Ltd.*[5] More generally, it may be said that the courts have tended to treat the provisions of the Act as though they were part of the common law, and have not generally treated cases under the Act as though they were ordinary exercises in statutory interpretation.

[2] [1891] AC 107, 144–5. These observations were made with reference to the Bills of Exchange Act 1882, but they apply to all codifying statutes alike.
[3] [1972] AC 441.
[4] At p. 501.
[5] [2016] UKSC 23.

The application of Lord Herschell's approach in some areas is, however, more controversial. For example, in the case of the former implied condition that the goods were to be of 'merchantable quality' the 1979 Act (unlike the original Act) sought to define the term 'merchantable quality',[6] but the definition appeared to provide only a framework or skeleton in which the normal processes of case law development might continue; therefore, it might have been thought that the meaning of the term 'merchantable quality' would continue to be found in the case law and there were indeed many cases which proceeded on this basis. But (as we shall see) the Court of Appeal in *Rogers* v *Parish (Scarborough) Ltd*[7] insisted that this mass of case law should be jettisoned, and the words of the 1979 Act alone looked to in the decision of cases on the meaning of the term 'merchantable quality'. The merchantable quality warranty was replaced in 1994 by the requirement that goods are to be of 'satisfactory quality[8] and the question of whether this change justified once again a fresh start was raised. For reasons given later, it seems an approach which ignores the previous case law, whether on the old merchantable quality provisions or on other parts of the Act, is likely to produce arbitrary and unpredictable decisions, and any attempt to apply Lord Herschell's approach literally must at least take account of the variety of reasons which may inspire the legislature to codify different provisions of the common law.[9]

Another problem arising from Lord Herschell's approach is that this method of interpretation is not sufficiently adaptable to be used in the interpretation of legislation which clearly departs from general common law principles. This means that every statutory amendment of the law of sale of goods either opens up a wedge between the law of sale and the law applicable to closely analogous contracts, or it has to be followed by or accompanied by parallel legislation applicable to these other contracts. But if, when this new legislation is proposed, there are second thoughts about the earlier legislation amending the law of sale, the result is likely to be yet further amendments to the law of sale. The result is that the law of sale and the law of similar contracts are engaged in a sort of leap-frog exercise which sometimes makes it difficult to identify the precise effect of modern legislation at any given moment. And it also means that arbitrary distinctions sometimes have to be drawn between cases according to the precise type of contract involved – sale of goods contracts sometimes being affected by legislation which does not apply to other closely similar transactions.

In addition to the law of sale of goods in the strict sense, there is, of course, the general body of the law against which a codifying statute has to be understood and, in particular, the general law of contract. The Sale of Goods Act makes no attempt to codify the general principles of contract law. Indeed, it expressly leaves them untouched, for s. 62(2) enacts that:

> The rules of the common law, including the law merchant except in so far as they are inconsistent with the provisions of this Act and in particular the rules relating to the law of principal and agent and the effect of fraud, misrepresentation, duress or coercion, mistake, or other invalidating cause, apply to contracts for the sale of goods.

[6] The relevant provisions first appeared in the Supply of Goods (Implied Terms) Act 1973.

[7] [1987] QB 933 –. See also *Harlingdon & Leinster Enterprises Ltd* v *Christopher Hull Fine Art* Ltd [1991] 1 QB 564. Compare the remarks of Lloyd LJ in *M/S Aswan Engineering Establishment Co* v *Lupdine Ltd* [1987] 1 WLR 1, 6 – see below.

[8] Sale and Supply of Goods Act 1994.

[9] These different approaches were thoroughly canvassed in the Law Commission's Joint Working Paper No. 85, *Sale and Supply of Goods* (1983) which explored various proposals for altering the definition of 'merchantable quality'. The Final Report of the Law Commission's *Sale and Supply of Goods* (Law Com. No. 160, Scot. Law Com. No. 104, 1987, Cm. 137) appeared to retreat somewhat from the position arrived at in the Working Paper.

Despite this section, no exposition of this subject would be complete without some account of the general rules of the law of contract insofar as they have some special bearing on the law of sale of goods.

The Sale of Goods Act was made applicable to Scotland in 1893 as a result of pressure in some commercial and legal quarters for the creation of a more uniform law of sale in the United Kingdom.[10] This was achieved with the addition of only a very few sections to the English codification statute as originally drafted. The Act is thus not a codification in any sense of the pre-existing Scots common law, but was rather a very significant change, given the Roman law roots of that law. This was particularly the case in respect of the transfer of property and, albeit to a less fundamental extent, the duties of the seller and the remedies of the buyer.[11] The Act's English terminology also caused difficulties in Scotland, although these have mostly been removed by the reforms of the Sale and Supply of Goods Act 1994, in which the Scottish Law Commission played a large part. A distinguished Scottish commentator once argued that 'the task of the Scots courts is . . . to bring the statutory provisions into harmony with the principles of our common law';[12] but this has not been the approach of the judges or of other writers in Scotland, who have preferred generally to start with the text of the statute, imperfect and sometimes difficult to understand though it may be from the perspective of Scots law.

As will appear during the course of this book, the Sale of Goods Act has not proved one of the more successful pieces of codification undertaken by Parliament towards the end of the nineteenth century.[13] The principal reason for this may well be that there has been a change in the type of sale of goods cases coming before the courts, and the types of cases, more generally, coming to legal attention. The nineteenth-century cases on which the Act was based were, in the main, sales between businessmen or organisations, that is, sales by manufacturers and suppliers. Since the passing of the 1893 Act, however, a large proportion of the cases coming before the courts appeared to be concerned with sales by retailers to the consuming public. The passing of the Consumer Rights Act 2015 (which extends to Scotland) has stemmed this flow and in any case, the volume was never great as the value of these transactions often made litigation unwarranted.[14] Even still, the increasingly vociferous demands of consumers and consumer groups have had an impact on the shape of the Act and the judicial understanding of it, not least in highlighting that the term 'merchantable quality' was not an appropriate one, and one ultimately cast aside by Sale and Supply of Goods Act 1994.

The status of the 'consumer' case law which accrued prior to the Consumer Rights Act may now be the subject of question; however, it seems unlikely that it will be cast aside. The standards which a consumer buyer might expect of a car are unlikely to be different to those expected by a commercial buyer, irrespective of whether the commercial buyer is buying for the purposes of re-sale or not.

[10] See Rodger (1992) 108 LQR 570. For the law pre-1893, see Gordon, in Reid and Zimmermann (eds), *History of Private Law in Scotland, vol. 2* (2000, Oxford University Press, Oxford).

[11] See Smith, *Property Problems in Sale* (1978, Sweet & Maxwell, London); Sutherland, 1987 JR 24.

[12] Gow, *The Mercantile and Industrial Law of Scotland* (1964, W. Green & Sons, Edinburgh), 76. Gow supported his approach by reference to what is now s. 62(2) of the Sale of Goods Act 1979 (see above).

[13] Save in terms of its widespread adoption in the jurisdictions of the Commonwealth and in the United States whose Uniform Sales Act (now replaced by Art. 2 of the Uniform Commercial Code) closely followed it.

[14] An effect of the Civil Procedure Rules 1998 seems to have been to reduce still further the trickle of reported cases. The mechanisms for redress under the new Consumer Rights Bill seem unlikely to change this.

1.3 Impact of withdrawal from the European Union ('Brexit') on English Sale of Goods Law

At the beginning of 2009, the Draft Common Frame of Reference (DCFR) was published. The text was the result of the work of a broad range of private law scholars from the member states of the European Union. It presents itself as an 'academic' document, committed to the precepts of scholarship rather than politics. The sales law aspect of the DCFR was derived in part from the Vienna Convention on International Sales of Goods (CISG), which is dealt with in Chapter 14. The sales law aspect of the DCFR emerged as the Common European Sales Law (CESL),[15] an aborted initiative by the EU to try to obviate the obvious potential difficulties of a single market with such a plurality of sales law systems. Despite its ambition, the proposal failed to gain the support of the Council of Ministers and was withdrawn.

Instead, the EU passed the Directive on Self-employed (Commercial) Agents (86/653/EEC) which had a significant impact on English agency law, and pasted all EU laws applicable to UK, including previous CJEU case law, into the domestic UK domestic law. As a result, first, UK parliament gained the ultimate power to amend and repeal any retained EU law as now UK domestic law. Secondly, the first and second instance English courts will remain bound by previous CJEU cases. The UK Supreme Court, however, via s. 6(4) of the EUWA 2018, will have the power to depart from previous CJEU decisions in the same way it can depart from its own earlier case law.

Overall, at the time of writing, Brexit has not had any significant impact on English Sale of Goods law. This is because, as mentioned above, there were very few Sale of Goods laws that resulted from EU initiatives, and for those that were, much of EU law of relevance to the sale of goods concerned consumer contracts.

On 1 May 2021, the UK–EU Trade and Cooperation Agreement (TCA) came into force providing a basic framework of trade between the UK and the EU. The specifics of this Free Trade Agreement are beyond the scope of this book. It suffices to note that it includes zero tariffs and zero quotas on trade in goods between the UK and the EU, but it does not include an agreement in relation to non-tariff barriers.

[15] See generally, Micklitz and Reich, 'The Commission proposal for a "Regulation on a Common European Sales Law (CESL)" – too broad or not broad enough?' EUI Working Papers LAW No. 2012/04 http://papers.ssrn.com/sol3/papers.cfm?abstract_id=2013183.

2

The contract of sale

2.1 Definition

Section 2(1) of the Act defines a contract of sale of goods as:

> a contract by which the seller transfers or agrees to transfer the property in goods to the buyer for a money consideration, called the price.

Subsections (3) and (4) give different names to two transactions:

> (3) Where under a contract of sale the property in the goods is transferred from the seller to the buyer the contract is called a sale.
> (4) Where under a contract of sale the transfer of the property in the goods is to take place at a future time or subject to some condition later to be fulfilled the contract is called an agreement to sell.

2.2 Sale distinguished from other contracts

A contract of sale of goods must be distinguished from other transactions which are substantially different from a sale of goods but which, in certain circumstances, may closely resemble them,[1] namely (1) a contract of barter or exchange, (2) a gift, (3) a contract of bailment, (4) a contract of hire-purchase, (5) a contract of loan on the security of goods, (6) a contract for the supply of services, (7) a contract of agency, and (8) licences of intellectual property such as 'sales' of computer software.[2] These distinctions were important as a result of s. 4 of the 1893 Act. This section, originally s. 17 of the Statute of Frauds 1677, required contracts of sale of goods of the value of £10 or more to be evidenced in writing. The other types of contract listed above were never subject to that requirement. The repeal of s. 4 of the 1893 Act by the Law Reform (Enforcement of Contracts) Act 1954, meant that this particular point ceased to be of importance in relation to domestic sales of goods[3] as no written formalities are now required, in general, for any of the above

[1] In early editions of this book, a contract for the transfer of a possessory interest in a chattel was also distinguished from a sale of goods. As a result of amendments first made by the Supply of Goods (Implied Terms) Act 1973, such a contract should be treated as a sale of goods – see Chapter 5.

[2] Which are usually licences of the copyright in the software and are independent of the media in which the software is embedded – see below. The distinction between sales and licences of intellectual property, such as computer software, is dealt with in Chapter 3.

[3] An equivalent provision is still to be found in many of the Commonwealth statutes based on the 1893 Act, however, as well as in the Uniform Commercial Code Art. 2-201. In an age of modern digital communications and the popular use of 'emojis', a formal requirement such as this can cause some difficulties, as the recent decision by the Court of Appeal of Saskatchewan in *Achter Land & Cattle Ltd.* v *South West Terminal Ltd.* [2024] SKCA 115 shows.

kinds of contracts as per s. 4 SGA 1979.[4] But it may still be necessary to decide whether a contract is a contract of sale of goods for a number of other reasons. In particular, of course, because the provisions of the Sale of Goods Act apply only to such contracts. Given that the original Act of 1893 was largely a codifying Act, however, and given the tendency to construe the Act as though it were a part of the common law, it will often be immaterial whether a particular contract is labelled a contract of sale or a contract of a different character. In particular, when a question of implication of terms arises, the law may well be the same whether or not the Act applies. Historically, there was a noticeable tendency for the courts to model the common law contracts on the Sale of Goods Act and to imply terms in these contracts very similar to those implied by the Act.[5] Parliament then followed suit, modelling the Supply of Goods and Services Act on the Sale of Goods Act and reproducing almost verbatim many of its provisions in relation to other contracts of supply.

In *Young & Marten Ltd* v *McManus Childs Ltd*,[6] the House of Lords expressed strong views on the undesirability of drawing unnecessary distinctions between different classes of contract. However, the structure of particular commercial transactions, as well as the legislative structure of the law sometimes makes this an inescapable result.

In respect of the latter, as we shall see later,[7] there are, for example, a number of provisions in the Sale of Goods Act (originating in the Factors Act 1889) enabling a person, subject to various conditions, to pass a good title to goods even if they do not own them, provided that they have agreed to buy them. This legislative formula clearly excludes cases in which the contract involves the acquisition of the goods without an agreement to buy. And we shall see recent examples of cases in which this distinction is critical to the result of a legal dispute.

Moreover, as noted above, even the most recent legislation applicable to sales and other contracts is not always, at any given moment, identical because sometimes the law applicable to one type of contract (usually sale) is amended first and the others at a later date. In any case, since the changes made by these Acts and subordinate legislation are clearly not declaratory, it is difficult to see how the courts could modify the law relating to these other contracts to keep them in line with contracts of sale. However, in the most recent updating of the legislation, care was taken to treat contracts of sale of goods and other similar transactions in the same way, subject only to necessary modifications. It is, therefore, probable that the distinction between the different types of contract will only be of practical importance in relatively unusual circumstances.

In cases under s. 4, it was necessary to draw a firm line between contracts of sale and other types of contract, but for other purposes, there seems no reason why it should not sometimes be possible to hold that a contract is partly a contract of sale and partly

[4] Assignments, though not licences, of copyright, e.g., in software, must, however, be evidenced in writing – Copyright, Designs and Patents Act 1988, s. 90(3) (and the same is true for registered intellectual property rights). Hire-purchase contracts must comply with the statutory formalities now to be found in the Consumer Credit Act 1974 and its subordinate legislation.

[5] See, e.g., *G H Myers & Co* v *Brent Cross Service Co* [1934] 1 KB 46; Samuels v Davis [1943] KB 526; *Stewart* v *Reavell's Garage* [1952] 2 QB 545; *Ingham* v *Emes* [1955] 2 QB 366. See now the Supply of Goods and Services Act 1982, below, section 2.2.6.

[6] [1969] 1 AC 454.

[7] See Chapter 15.

something else.[8] Thus a contract for the provision of a meal in a hotel is apparently a contract of sale,[9] and so is a contract for the construction of machinery.[10] Yet such contracts in some sense also involve the provision of services, and it seems clear that the law relating to the goods and the law relating to the services aspects of such a contract may differ. For instance, under the Supply of Goods and Services Act 1982 the supplier's duties as regards any goods supplied under the contract will normally be strict (i.e. it will be liable for defects in the goods even if it has not been negligent), whereas its liability in respect of services may be a liability, in effect, for negligence only. As will be seen later, this problem of distinguishing between sales and supplies of goods on the one hand, and supplies of services on the other, has historically given rise to considerable difficulties in relation to contracts for the provision of computer software.

Before considering the distinction between contracts of sale and the other types of contract mentioned above, it must be emphasised that a contract of sale must first and foremost be a contract, and that the concept of a contract under the various legislation is the same as the concept understood in the law at large, that is, a consensual transaction based on an agreement to buy and an agreement to sell.[11] Thus, for example, where an out-patient at a hospital obtains drugs at the hospital dispensary, even on payment of a statutory prescription charge, this is not a contract of sale at all. The patient has a statutory right to receive the drug and the hospital a statutory obligation to supply it.[12] It seems the position is the same with respect to drugs and other medical appliances supplied by a pharmacist under the National Health Service.[13] Since the transaction is not a sale of goods, the Sale of Goods Act cannot apply; and since it is not a contract at all, it presumably follows that the Supply of Goods and Services Act 1982 also does not apply.[14] But it is possible that the courts might still be willing to imply terms as to quality and fitness in such a transaction,[15] though this could open up an anomalous result. It would mean that an out-patient who is supplied with a drug, like a patient who obtains a National Health Service drug from a pharmacist, would be able to sue if the drug was defective even if the supplier was not guilty of negligence. On the other hand, an in-patient who is supplied with a drug as an incident to the hospital's supply of services (whether a paying patient or an NHS patient) might not be able to sue in the absence of negligence.[16] It must be noted, however, that an injured patient might well have a remedy in such cases under the Consumer Protection Act 1987.[17]

[8] See, e.g., *Hyundai Heavy Industries Co Ltd* v *Papadopoulos* [1980] 1 WLR 1129, discussed below, where this possibility is clearly recognised by the House of Lords (contract for manufacture of ship may be both contract of sale of goods and contract for services). See also *Watson* v *Buckley* [1940] 1 All ER 174; *Stocznia Gdanska SA* v *Latvian Shipping Co* [1998] UKHL 9; *Costigan* v *Cook t/a World of Heat, The Fireplace* 2005 GWD 34-637 (Sheriff W. L. Holligan).

[9] *Lockett* v *A & M Charles* Ltd [1938] 4 All ER 170. By contrast, trademark practice treats such a supply as one of services, but a take-away meal as a supply of goods.

[10] *Cammell Laird & Co Ltd* v *Manganese Bronze & Brass Co Ltd* [1934] AC 402.

[11] As emphasised by s. 62(2).

[12] *Pfizer Corpn* v *Minister of Health* [1965] AC 512.

[13] *Appleby* v *Sleep* [1968] 1 WLR 948, 954.

[14] See Chapter 3.

[15] See, e.g., *Read* v *Croydon Corpn* [1938] 4 All ER 631; PST *Energy 7 Shipping LLC* v *OW Bunker Malta Ltd* [2016] UKSC 23 at [31].

[16] In *Perlmutter* v *Beth David Hospital* 308 NY 100, 123 NE 2d 792 (1954) the Court of Appeals New York held that supplying blood in a hospital did not constitute a sale, but was merely incidental to the performing of medical services.

[17] See Chapter 20.

2.2.1 Sale and exchange

The fact that the consideration must be in money, and that the term 'goods' is defined by s. 61 so as to exclude money, serves to distinguish a sale from a contract of barter or exchange in the ordinary case. But a coin which is a collector's item may be 'goods' even though it is legal tender, and there may be a sale of such a coin. In such an event, the coin does not possess the usual negotiable qualities of money, and if the sale is by a thief they cannot pass a good title to it[18].

The position is less clear where goods on the one hand are exchanged for goods plus money on the other, as is commonly the case when a used car is traded in part exchange for a new one. Is this a contract of sale or of exchange? In *Aldridge* v *Johnson*[19] a contract for the exchange of 52 bullocks with 100 quarters of barley, the difference in value to be made up in money, was treated without argument as a contract of sale, but the case was fought on an entirely different point.[20] One view is that the answer depends upon whether the money or the goods is the substantial consideration. The decision in *Robinson* v *Graves*[21] lays down an elastic test for distinguishing contracts of sale from contracts for skill and labour, and a similar approach may sometimes be justified here. It should be noted, however, that in relation to the implied warranties,[22] Part I of the Supply of Goods and Services Act 1982 renders the distinction largely of academic importance,[23] and there is an alternative to barter as a way of analysing the used car trade-in type of transaction.[24]

Ultimately, the proper characterisation of a contract depends on the intention of the parties as long as they do not include provisions manifestly inconsistent with the intended nature of the transaction.[25] So, it may well be that, if the parties envisage the transaction as a sale, and use terminology more appropriate to a sale, the contract would be held to be such even if the substantial consideration is supplied in goods rather than money. In the motor trade, for example, a person will often 'trade in' an old car in part-exchange for a new one and, if the transaction relating to the new car is treated by the parties as a sale, it is improbable that the courts would treat it as anything else, even if the dealer's 'allowance' for the traded-in car does not fall far short of the price of the new one.[26] It seems that the transaction relating to the old car would also amount to a sale even though no money actually passes if, as is usual, the parties fix a notional price which is set off against the price of the new car. But it has been held in the Republic of

[18] *Moss* v *Hancock* [1899] 2 QB 111. But it has been held that the chips given in exchange for money in a gaming club are not 'bought' – *Lipkin Gorman* v *Karpanle* [1991] 2 AC 548. See also Chapter 15.

[19] (1857) 7 E & B 885.

[20] In *Connell Estate Agents* v *Begej* (1993) 39 EG 123 the part-exchange of a house was treated as a 'sale' so that the estate agent was entitled to commission.

[21] [1935] 1 KB 579.

[22] Though not necessarily in relation to other matters regulated by the Sale of Goods Act, so that, for example, the remedies applicable may be different.

[23] See below, section 2.2.6.

[24] See below.

[25] See *Street* v *Mountford* [1985] AC 809 and A G *Securities* v *Vaughan* [1988] 3 All ER 1058 where the House of Lords settled the approach to be adopted in the analogous case of an agreement designed to be a lease but dressed up to look like a licence.

[26] See *Sneddon v Durant* 1982 SLT (Sh Ct) 39, commented upon by Forte (1984) 101 SALJ 691. See also Smith (1974) 48 Tulane LR 1029.

Ireland that if no price is allocated to the old car, the whole transaction is one of barter, or exchange, and not sale.[27]

As noted above, a contract of exchange of goods for goods (or even of goods for some other consideration such as shares or land) is a contract for the transfer of goods within the Supply of Goods and Services Act 1982.[28] This Act incorporates into such a contract terms almost identical to those applying to a contract of sale; so if the question is one concerning the quality or fitness of goods supplied, it will be of very little importance whether the goods are supplied under a contract of sale or a contract of exchange.

2.2.2 Sale and gift

Usually, there is no difficulty in distinguishing between a sale and a gift. A gift is a transfer of property without any consideration and as such it is, of course, not binding while it remains executory unless made by deed. But difficulty may sometimes arise with regard to transactions in which a 'free' gift is offered on the condition of entering into some other transaction.

In *Esso Petroleum Ltd* v *Commissioners of Customs & Excise*,[29] filling stations advertised a 'free' gift of a commemorative coin marking the 1970 World Cup to anyone buying four gallons of fuel. It was held by the House of Lords that, although the transaction was not a gift, inasmuch as the garage was contractually bound to supply the coin to anyone buying four gallons of fuel, it was not a sale of goods either. The transaction was characterised by Lord Simon and Lord Wilberforce as one in which the garage promised to supply a coin in consideration of a customer buying the petrol. It was thus, in substance, a collateral contract existing alongside the contract for the sale of the fuel.[30] On this analysis, it would presumably be a contract for the transfer of goods within the Supply of Goods and Services Act 1982, which is dealt with later.

An unsolicited offer to sell goods, accompanied by a delivery of those goods to the offeree, may be treated as a gift in the circumstances laid down in the Unsolicited Goods and Services Act 1971.

2.2.3 Sale and bailment

A bailment is a transaction under which goods are delivered by one party (the bailor) to another (the bailee) on terms which normally require the bailee to hold the goods and ultimately to redeliver them to the bailor or in accordance with their directions. The property

[27] *Flynn* v *Mackin* [1974] IR 101, criticised in a note in (1976) 39 MLR 589. The reason why the distinction was of practical importance in this case was that it was assumed that the property passes at different times in the two transactions. But if the contract is so close to the border between two classes of contract, it would seem absurd if such consequences were held to depend on the label attached to the contract, though sometimes this may be inevitable.

[28] For examples of contracts of barter, see *Widenmeyer* v *Burn Stewart & Co* 1967 SC 85 and *Ballantyne* v *Durant* 1983 SLT (Sh Ct) 38.

[29] For examples of contracts of barter, see *Widenmeyer* v *Burn Stewart & Co* 1967 SC 85 and *Ballantyne* v *Durant* 1983 SLT (Sh Ct) 38.

[30] Lord Russell and Viscount Dilhorne held, however, that there was no intention to create legal relations. Lord Fraser held that there was a sale.

in the goods is not intended to and does not pass on delivery, though it may sometimes be the intention of the parties that it should pass in due course, as in the case of the ordinary hire-purchase contract. But where goods are delivered to another on terms which indicate that the property is to pass at once, the contract must be one of sale and not bailment. In *Chapman Bros* v *Verco Bros & Co Ltd*,[31] farmers delivered bags of wheat to a company carrying on business as millers and wheat merchants. The wheat was delivered in unidentified bags which were identical to those in which other farmers delivered wheat to the company. The terms of the transaction required the company to buy and pay for the wheat on request by the farmer or failing such a request, on a specified date, to return an equal quantity of wheat of the same type; but there was no obligation to return the identical bags. Although the contract referred to the company as 'storers', it was held by the Australian High Court that this transaction was necessarily one of sale as the property passed to the company on delivery.

Similarly, if the nature of the transaction is such that the property must pass (even if not at once) the transaction seems inconsistent with the possibility of a bailment. It will be an 'agreement to sell' within s. 2(5) of the Act. If the goods are delivered to the buyer before the property passes, they will be a 'buyer in possession' rather than a mere bailee.

As a result of the widespread use of retention of title (or *Romalpa*[32]) clauses in contracts for the supply of goods, the distinction between a sale and a bailment has gained renewed importance, particularly because there is now some uncertainty as to whether some contracts involving retention of title clauses should now be treated as *sui generis* rather than sales, at least where goods are supplied for immediate consumption.[33] These clauses take a variety of forms, but their purpose is always to allow the seller of goods to treat the goods as their property even after they have been delivered, as a sort of security for the payment of the price. In substance, these are contracts of sale in which, however, the seller claims that the delivery of the goods is, in the first instance, by way of bailment only. In some cases, the clauses go further and provide that even though the 'buyer' may deal with the goods (for instance, by using them in a process of manufacture, or by reselling them), the original supplier is to be entitled to (or to a charge upon) any goods manufactured with the goods supplied, or to (or to a charge on) the proceeds of resale when received by the 'buyer'. These clauses continue to give rise to some legal difficulty and are considered at greater length later.[34] Here it is enough to say that any bailment will be limited to the actual goods delivered. An attempt to extend the seller's security interest into goods manufactured using the goods delivered is liable to give rise to a charge registrable under the Companies Act 2006, Part 25,[35] as where resin was supplied for use in the manufacture of chipboard.[36] The result of this is that, *prima facie* at least, the seller can have no right to trace the goods

[31] (1933) 49 CLR 306; see also *South Australian Insurance Co* v *Randell* (1869) LR 3 PC 101. Distinguished in *Coleman* v *Harvey* [1989] 1 NZLR 723.

[32] See the *Romalpa case* [1976] 1 WLR 676, Chapter 15

[33] *PST Energy 7 Shipping LLC* v *O W Bunker Malta Limited* [2016] UKSC 23 (supply of fuel bunkers understood to be for consumption before full payment not a contract of sale).

[34] See Chapter 15

[35] See Chapter 15, section 15.6.

[36] *Borden (UK) Ltd* v *Scottish Timber Products Ltd* [1981] Ch 25.

supplied when they have once been used or resold. On the other hand, if the contract involves a true bailment,[37] the seller probably has rights over any goods made with the goods supplied, or over the proceeds of the sale, where they have been resold, although even this is not entirely free from doubt.[38]

A contract of hire is one species of bailment; such contracts are readily distinguishable from sales since there is no intention that property should pass in a hiring contract. The Supply of Goods and Services Act 1982 contains implied terms applicable to a contract of hire which are similar to, though not identical with, those in a contract of sale; it is also possible to exclude these terms by contrary agreement so long as they comply with the 'reasonableness' requirement under the Unfair Contracts Terms Act 1977, although this is not always possible in contracts of sale.[39]

2.2.4 Sale and hire-purchase

Contracts of hire-purchase resemble contracts of sale very closely, and, indeed, in practically all cases of hire-purchase the ultimate sale of the goods is (in a popular sense) the real object of the transaction. Nonetheless, for present purposes, the legal distinction is clear and important, though its importance has greatly diminished since the Sale of Goods (Implied Terms) Act 1973,[40] and the Consumer Credit Act 1974. A sale is a contract whereby the seller 'transfers or agrees to transfer' the property in goods to the buyer; that is to say, as soon as the contract is made the ultimate destination of the goods is determined even though the property is not to pass for some considerable time; for example, until all the instalments of the price have been paid. A contract of hire-purchase, on the other hand, is a bailment of the goods coupled with an option to purchase them, which may or may not be exercised. Only if and when the option is exercised will there be a contract of sale.

The similarity between the two transactions is accentuated by the artificial nature of most hire-purchase agreements. This is brought out by consideration of three points. First, as already observed, the real object of a contract of hire-purchase is almost invariably the ultimate sale of the goods to the hirer. Secondly, the amount which the hirer is bound to pay under the contract is usually far in excess of that which they would have had to pay if they were really hiring the goods.[41] And thirdly, the legal purchase price for which the hirer has the option to buy the goods is frequently nominal only and, in fact, is sometimes not exacted in practice. Moreover, for the purposes of the hirer claiming capital allowances, hire-purchase transactions in respect of machinery or plant are treated in the same way as outright purchases.[42]

[37] That is, not merely the use of a form to create a security interest – see Chapter 15
[38] See Chapter 15.
[39] See Chapter 8.
[40] Up to the Hire-Purchase Act 1964 there had been significant differences between the warranties in hire-purchase contracts and those in sales of goods. The relevant provisions of this Act were replaced by the Hire-Purchase Act 1965 which in turn was replaced by the 1973 Act (as amended by the Consumer Credit Act 1974, Sch. 4 and the Sale and Supply of Goods Act 1994) and see section 2.2.6 below.
[41] Because the capital cost of the goods plus interest needs to be amortised over the term. True hire, by contrast, is timeshare of an asset, e.g., short-term hire of a car.
[42] Capital Allowances Act 2001, s. 454(1).

There is a further practical complication about hire-purchase contracts which often makes them different from contracts of sale. A transaction under which a person 'buys' goods on hire-purchase is often, and in the motor trade is usually, a complex transaction involving three and not two parties. Many retailers have no wish to act as financiers themselves supplying credit to consumers. So a hire-purchase transaction often involves, first, a sale, under which the retailer sells the goods to a finance company, and then, secondly, a hire-purchase contract, under which the finance company lets the goods on hire-purchase terms to the 'buyer'. It follows that the 'buyer' has no contractual relations with the seller and this sometimes has important legal consequences, although the reality is that 'the identity or even existence of the finance company is a matter (to customers) of indifference; they look to the dealer, or their representative, as the person who fixes the payment terms and makes all the necessary arrangements'.[43] Nevertheless, it means, for instance, that the seller cannot be sued on the terms implied by the Sale of Goods Act, which create liability even in the absence of negligence,[44] although they may sometimes be liable in tort if negligence can be proved against them.[45] And if the seller gives an express warranty to the 'buyer', in consideration of which the latter enters into the contract of hire-purchase with the finance company to which the seller has sold the goods, then the seller can be held liable on this separate contract of guarantee.[46] The finance company may also be liable on the terms implied by the Supply of Goods Act 1973. Since the Consumer Credit Act 1974, it would be more correct to refer to the hirer as the debtor and to the seller as the supplier, but the principles themselves are not changed.[47]

Hire-purchase contracts were developed in England and Wales towards the end of the nineteenth century, and it is impossible to understand why they came into existence without an appreciation of the legal context which already existed. There was clearly a need for a form of contract of sale of goods on credit, under which the seller could reserve some security right to the goods. Consumers wanted to buy on credit, and financiers who were willing to supply the credit wanted security. Two obstacles existed to achieving this through the most obvious legal methods. One obvious method would have been for the seller simply to sell and deliver the goods on credit while expressly stipulating that the property in the goods should remain theirs until the buyer had paid the price. This is a conditional sale, and it does give the seller some security: it protects them against the possibility of the buyer's insolvency. But it does not protect them against the possibility that the buyer may sell the goods to a third party before they have paid the whole price. Even though the seller has reserved the property in the goods, s. 25(1) of the Sale of Goods Act

[43] *Branwhite v Worcester Works Finance Ltd* [1969] 1 AC 552, per Lord Wilberforce, foll'd *J D Williams & Co (t/a Williams Leasing) v McCauley, Parsons & Jones* [1994] CCLR 78 (CA); *Woodchester Equipment (Leasing)* v *British Association of Canned and Preserved Foods Importers and Distributors* [1995] CCLR 51.

[44] *Drury* v *Victor Buckland Ltd* [1941] 1 All ER 269. Nor, presumably, can the buyer sue the dealer under the implied terms in the Supply of Goods and Services Act 1982 because if there is no contract at all between buyer and dealer, the relationship between them can hardly amount to a 'contract for the transfer of goods' within s. 1(1) of that Act.

[45] *Herschtal* v *Stewart & Ardern* Ltd [1940] 1 KB 155.

[46] *Brown* v *Sheen & Richmond Car Sales Ltd* [1950] 1 All ER 1102.

[47] The effect of s. 56 of the Consumer Credit Act 1974 is that in regulated agreements the supplier is the agent of the finance house for all purposes connected with the transaction.

enables a person who has 'bought or agreed to buy goods' to pass a good title to a third party. In *Lee* v *Butler*,[48] the Court of Appeal held that the equivalent of this provision[49] clearly applied where the buyer was in possession of the goods under an agreement to buy the goods and pay the price in instalments. So, this obvious method of selling goods on credit failed to give the seller adequate security.

A second obvious method of achieving the desired result was for the seller to sell and deliver the goods outright to the buyer but to require the buyer to grant them a mortgage, or charge, or a right to repossess the goods in the event of the buyer's failure to pay the instalments. At common law, it was possible to create a charge of this nature on goods which would be binding even on third parties. Most probably, a legal arrangement of this nature would still have been caught by s. 25 of the Sale of Goods Act, but there was a more fundamental objection to this device. The whole essence of this scheme is that one person, the buyer (A), should have the possession of goods and be entitled to the use of them as though they were the owner, while another person, the financier (B), should actually have a charge or mortgage on the goods. This kind of transaction is not viewed favourably by the law because third parties may be induced to do business with, or give credit to, A in the belief that they are the unencumbered owner of the goods. And if A becomes insolvent, they will then find that B has a prior claim to the goods. It is generally thought to be unfair that B should be able to do this unless they have in some way publicised their transaction with A. Accordingly, the Bills of Sale Acts of 1878 and 1882 require a transaction of this kind to be made by a written instrument, called a bill of sale, which is required to be registered under the Acts.

The Bills of Sale Acts had two great disadvantages. First, they required some degree of publicity – that was their whole purpose, of course – and many borrowers disliked this requirement. But secondly, they rapidly attracted a body of extremely technical case law, and it became easy to fall foul of the Acts by accident so that the security granted (and in some cases the right to interest also) might become void.[50]

The result of these difficulties was a search for a legal form of sale which enabled the seller to retain security in the goods without falling foul of the Bills of Sale Acts and which also gave protection against bona fide purchasers from the buyer. The contract of hire-purchase was the answer, and its efficacy was upheld by the House of Lords in two cases in 1895. In *Helby* v *Matthews*,[51] it was held that a person in possession of goods under a hire-purchase agreement had not 'bought or agreed to buy' them within the meaning of s. 25(2) (now s. 25(1)) of the Sale of Goods Act. This meant that the buyer, or the 'hirer' as is now more commonly used, could not dispose of the goods to a third party in contravention of the agreement, and the seller's (or 'owner's') security was thus fully protected. And in *McEntire* v *Crossley Bros*[52] it was also held that a hire-purchase contract did not fall within the Bills of Sale Acts; those Acts, it was held, applied only

[48] [1893] 2 QB 318.
[49] Section 25(2) – see Chapter 12.
[50] The Crowther Committee 1971 (Cmnd 4596) recommended their abolition, along with the Hire-Purchase Acts and other measures, and replacement by a Lending and Security Act – see below section 2.2.5
[51] The Crowther Committee 1971 (Cmnd 4596) recommended their abolition, along with the Hire-Purchase Acts and other measures, and replacement by a Lending and Security Act – see below section 2.2.5.
[52] [1895] AC 457.

where an owner of goods granted a charge, or right to seize the goods, to another party, while in the hire-purchase contract the hirer was not owner at the time they granted the right to seize the goods.

With the blessing of the House of Lords to the legal arrangements, the way was paved for the great commercial expansion of the use of hire-purchase contracts. For the next 40 years, the use of the contract spread throughout the entire field of consumer purchasing of goods, other than purely consumable or perishable goods, and it also became relatively common in commercial situations.

As time went on, it became increasingly obvious that the contract of hire-purchase was being used as a form (in effect) of secured sale. Instead of borrowing the money to buy the goods and mortgaging the goods to the lender as a security, the consumer entered into a hire-purchase contract with the financier. While this achieved similar results from the financier's point of view, at least in the sense that it gave it the security it wanted, it created a good deal of difficulty because the legal form of the transaction did not reflect the fact that, as a sort of mortgagor (though not, of course, in strict law), the hirer had an 'equity' in the goods. In land law, it has for centuries been recognised that a mortgage is a security device (no matter what its form) and that the mortgagor has an 'equity' in the land mortgaged. This 'equity' means that for most purposes the mortgagor is treated as owner of the land and the mortgagee's interests are confined to using the land as a security for repayment of the loan. So long as the mortgagee obtains repayment, plus interest, the mortgagor is always entitled to the residuary 'equity'. These established principles of the land law were never recognised as applicable to hire-purchase contracts; and as long as total freedom of contract prevailed, the result was potential hardship for the consumer. For example, if the hirer paid 90 per cent of the price and defaulted in payment of the final instalment, the finance company might seize the goods and resell them, retaining the proceeds for itself.

Abuses of this kind led to the gradual legislative recognition of the hirer's equity, though not by that term, nor by the same methods as equity had brought to bear on mortgages of land. These reforms began with the Hire-Purchase Act 1938, and were extended and strengthened in the Hire-Purchase Acts of 1964 and 1965. However, these reforms did not address one basic problem, that the form of the hire-purchase contract created a sharp difference between a hire-purchase and a sale of goods. The law distinguished between the legal rights and duties of a consumer who borrowed money to buy goods, and one who bought them on credit, or acquired them under a hire-purchase contract.

A movement for reform began to attract support under which hire-purchase contracts, as a separate legal contract, would be abolished. If a person wanted to buy goods by instalments they would, in law, buy those goods under a contract of sale of goods; if they did not have the cash to pay the full price down, they could borrow the money from a third party (such as a finance company or a bank) or, alternatively, they could buy on credit from the actual seller. If necessary, the law could then provide some simple process to enable the buyer to 'mortgage' the goods to the lender by way of security. This movement for reform began to grow after the general adoption throughout the United States of the Uniform Commercial Code, Article 9 of which proceeded along these lines. Then in 1971, the Crowther Committee on Consumer Credit examined this problem at length as part of a general inquiry into the whole field of consumer credit.[53] This Committee proposed the abolition of hire-purchase contracts and the enactment of legislation along lines similar to those of the American Uniform Commercial Code. This recommendation was not wholly accepted by the government. Partly because there was some disagreement with the idea that a hire-purchase agreement was always based on a 'fiction', and partly because the public and the trade were familiar with the concept, it was felt to be going too far to abolish the contract altogether. Consequently, the Consumer Credit Act 1974 retained the hire-purchase contract.

It is, however, very important to appreciate that, although the name and form of hire-purchase as a distinct contract have been retained, the substance of the matter is very different. The Hire-Purchase Acts have been almost entirely repealed by the Consumer Credit Act, and the rights and duties of the parties involved in a hire-purchase contract now hardly differ from those of parties to a sale of goods in which the consumer has obtained credit, whether from the seller or a third party. The principal remaining differences are those noted at the beginning of this section.

The Crowther Committee's recommendations as to the law relating to the use of chattels as security have never been implemented, though further examination by the government did take place.[54] Today therefore, a contract of hire-purchase (or of conditional sale) remains the principal method by which a financier or seller can reserve a security interest in the goods sold; a sale on credit, without any reservation of property, means that the seller retains no security rights in the goods.

Under the provisions of the Consumer Credit Act 1974 (provisions first enacted by the Hire-Purchase Act 1965), a conditional sale agreement in which the price is payable by instalments[55] is, for most purposes, assimilated to a hire-purchase agreement, with the result that a 'sale' of goods in which the price is payable by instalments can now take only one of two forms.

1 The contract may be a genuine contract of sale in which the buyer is bound to buy and to pay the whole price, and the seller is bound to sell. The property in the goods will pass at once with a purely personal obligation to pay the price in instalments. In this case, there is an absolute contract of sale, and obviously the buyer can pass a good title to a third party; and, should they go bankrupt, the seller has no claim to the goods. The seller has no security right to the goods themselves.
2 Alternatively, the passing of the property may be made conditional on the payment of a number of instalments. Under the Hire-Purchase Act 1965, it made virtually no difference whether this transaction was drafted as a sale or in the traditional form of a contract of hire, together with an option to purchase. Since the Supply of Goods (Implied Terms) Act 1973, this has no longer been wholly true. Today the sections in the 1979 Act dealing with sales, and not those in the 1973[56] Act dealing with hire-purchase, apply to conditional sales. But this is of little moment because the wording of the two

[53] Cmnd 4596.
[54] See A. L. Diamond, *A Review of Security Interests in Property* (DTI, 1989) HMSO.
[55] But not a sale where title is reserved against payment of the price in one instalment.
[56] In fact the relevant sections derive from Sched. 4 to the Consumer Credit Act 1974, which amends the 1973 Act, and further amendments effected by the Sale and Supply of Goods Act 1994.

sets of provisions is virtually identical. It therefore remains true to say that for most purposes there is now no distinction between a conditional sale and a hire-purchase contract. In either event, the agreement takes effect as a hire-purchase agreement and the 'buyer' is unable to pass a good title to the goods should they purport to sell them before the property has vested in them. The exception for motor vehicles also applies in both cases.[57] Again, in either event, the property remains in the seller (in the one case, until the condition is satisfied; in the other, until the option is exercised) and the seller would be able to claim the goods should the buyer become bankrupt before the property has vested in them.

As mentioned above, it is common to find reservation of title clauses in sales made to commercial bodies (as distinct from consumer sales) and these clauses are, in some respects, similar (at least in general purpose though not in legal form) to hire-purchase contracts. They are similar in that their purpose is to give the seller some security where the goods are delivered before the price has been paid; this security is not as extensive as that obtained by a hire-purchase contract because it only protects the seller against the risk of the buyer's insolvency. As seen above, it does not protect the seller against the risk that the buyer may resell the goods without authority. Reservation of title clauses also differ from hire-purchase agreements in that the latter do contemplate some sort of hiring arrangement under which the hirer will be allowed to *use* the goods. Reservation of title clauses do not involve any element of hiring, though they do often contemplate that the buyer may use the goods in a different sense, that is, may use them in the course of manufacture; for example, may use leather to make handbags or may use resin to make chipboard.[58]

2.2.5 Sale and loan on security

Parties sometimes enter into, or purport to enter into, a contract to sell goods with the intention of using the goods as a security for a loan of money. If the owner of goods (A) wishes to borrow money on the security of the goods, they may charge or mortgage them to B on the understanding that (1) A will retain possession of the goods, (2) A will repay B what they have borrowed together with interest, and (3) B will have a right to take the goods from A if and only if A fails to repay the loan or interest at the agreed time. Such a transaction differs from a hire-purchase contract, which is designed to enable a person to acquire goods on credit. A loan on security is designed to enable someone who already owns goods to *borrow money* on the security of the goods.

Partly in order to evade the Bills of Sale Acts, but also for other reasons, parties sometimes enter into this kind of transaction in the form of a sale – thus A can 'sell' their goods to B, though retaining possession of them and only giving B the right to seize them in certain events. Today, this kind of transaction is almost invariably reinforced with a hire-purchase agreement, or (in commercial transactions) a 'leaseback'. A 'sells' the goods (usually a motor vehicle) to B for a cash price and then B lets the same vehicle back to A under a hire-purchase contract. Or a manufacturing company may 'sell' plant or

[57] See Chapter 12.
[58] But not a sale where title is reserved against payment of the price in one instalment – see below.

machinery to a finance company which then 'leases' the goods back to the manufacturers. Under s. 62(4) of the Sale of Goods Act:

> The provisions of this Act about contracts of sale do not apply to a transaction in the form of a contract of sale which is intended to operate by way of mortgage, pledge, charge or other security.

In analysing a transaction of this nature, the courts have always insisted that the substance of the transaction and not merely its form must be examined. If the transaction is 'really' a loan on the security of the goods the Bills of Sale Acts will apply, and if it is unregistered (as it nearly always is) the contract is void and the chargee will be unable to seize the goods or even to recover the agreed interest, though the actual loan itself will be recoverable in a restitutionary claim, formerly known as the action for money had and received.[59] If, on the other hand, the parties 'really' intend the transaction to be a genuine 'sale' followed by a genuine hire-purchase or leaseback contract, the transaction will be valid and the two contracts will take effect according to their terms. For instance, in *Kingsley* v *Sterling Industrial Securities Ltd*,[60] Winn LJ said:

> In my definite view the sole or entirely dominant question upon that part of the appeal to which I have so far adverted is whether in reality and upon a true analysis of the transactions and each of them, and having regard in particular to the intention of the parties, they constituted loans or sales. It is clear upon the authorities that if a transaction is in reality a loan of money intended to be secured by, for example, a sale and hiring agreement, the document or documents embodying the arrangement will be within the Bills of Sale Acts; it is equally clear that each case must be determined according to the proper inference to be drawn from the facts and whatever the form the transaction may take the court will decide according to its real substance.

It might have been thought that such an approach would usually lead to the transaction being struck down since in most such cases the parties do not 'really' intend the goods to be 'sold'.[61] This is borne out by the fact that the sale price will rarely be fixed by the market price of the goods but will depend on the amount of the loan the seller wishes to raise, though doubtless the market price will normally represent at least the maximum which the buyer will pay or lend. Moreover, there is never any intention in such transactions for the possession of the goods to be given unless the seller defaults in payment of the hire-purchase rental; hence the implied conditions under the Sale of Goods Act would be absurdly inappropriate. Nevertheless, the modern tendency has been to uphold the genuineness of these transactions, though judicial disagreements have been frequent.[62] The difficulty is to formulate any criterion by which the 'real intention' of the parties may be judged. In practice, there is rarely any problem about commercial sales and leasebacks, but more difficulty has often arisen with sales followed by hire-purchase contracts.

The courts tend to take at their face value the intention of the parties as expressed in the written documents which they have executed. The argument that these documents are 'shams' because they do not express the 'real intention' of the parties has been rejected

[59] *North Central Wagon Finance Co Ltd* v *Brailsford* [1962] 1 WLR 1288.

[60] [1967] 2 QB 747, 780.

[61] See Fitzpatrick [1969] J Bus Law 211.

[62] See *Stoneleigh Finance Ltd* v *Phillips* [1965] 2 QB 537; *Kingsley* v *Sterling Industrial Securities Ltd*, above; *Snook* v *London and West Riding Investments Ltd* [1967] 2 QB 786.

unless it is shown that both parties do not intend the documents to operate according to their terms. In *Snook* v *London and West Riding Investments Ltd*, Diplock LJ said:

> As regards the contention of the [plaintiff] that the transactions between himself, Auto Finance and the defendants were a 'sham', it is, I think, necessary to consider what, if any, legal concept is involved in the use of this popular and pejorative word. I apprehend that, if it has any meaning in law, it means acts done or documents executed by the parties to the 'sham' which are intended by them to give to third parties or to the court the appearance of creating between the parties legal rights and obligations different from the actual legal rights and obligations (if any) which the parties intend to create. But one thing, I think, is clear in legal principle, morality and the authorities (see *Yorkshire Railway Wagon Co* v *Maclure*[63] and *Stoneleigh Finance Ltd* v *Phillips*,[64] that for acts or documents to be a 'sham', with whatever legal consequences follow from this, all the parties thereto must have a common intention that the acts or documents are not to create the legal rights and obligations which they give the appearance of creating. No unexpressed intentions of a 'shammer' affect the rights of a party whom he deceived. There is an express finding in this case that the defendants were not parties to the alleged 'sham'. So this contention fails.[65]

Refinancing transactions are not prohibited by the Consumer Credit Act 1974, although that Act confers on the 'seller' the protection of the general provisions relating to the provision of credit. It is possible, however, that the Unfair Contract Terms Act 1977 may indirectly affect the situation. The restrictions that it places on the right of the parties to contract out of the terms as to quality and fitness imposed by that Act[66], potentially make sale and leaseback arrangements less appealing to financiers. What is more, unexpected consequences could follow if the 'seller' was held entitled to complain of defects in the goods sold and taken back on hire-purchase. So the courts would probably hold that such transactions are not genuine sales, but fall within the Bills of Sale Acts.

The question has also arisen as to whether an arrangement under which the supplier of goods to a customer acts as agent of a finance house to sell goods to the customer, and then to resell them to the finance house, creates a charge over the supplier company's assets.[67] It has been held that it does not.[68]

2.2.6 Sale of goods and supply of services

Traditionally, the law has distinguished between contracts for sale of goods and contracts for the supply of services – the distinction persists in relation to the non-consumer sales today. In older law, contracts for the supply of services were often subdivided, for instance, into contracts for skill and labour, or contracts for labour and materials, according to whether the supplier was providing services only, or materials as well. It was, however,

[63] (1882) 21 Ch D 309.
[64] [1965] 2 QB 537.
[65] [1967] 2 QB 786, 802. See also *Street* v *Mountford* [1985] AC 809 and AG *Securities* v *Vaughan* [1988] 3 All ER 1058, above, and *Re Curtain Dream plc* [1990] BCLC 925.
[66] There were, of course, similar restrictions in the previous Hire-Purchase Acts. But the current legislation makes no specific provision, as the old one did, for used or second-hand goods. It is, therefore, more likely that a refinancing transaction could involve the finance company in liability for the quality and fitness of the goods if transactions are held valid according to their terms.
[67] Which would be registrable, or void in the event of the company's insolvency – see Chapter 15
[68] See *Welsh Development Agency* v *Export Finance* [1992] BCLC 148.

generally assumed that in a contract for services the law applicable was not the law of sale of goods even though some goods might incidentally be supplied. For example, it was always said that a contract for the services of a solicitor was a contract for services, even though the solicitor might be expected to draft a document and deliver it to the client so that it would become the client's property.[69]

The first question that needs to be asked is when does it matter whether a contract is for the sale of goods or for supply of services? In many cases it will not matter at all; the applicable law will be the same. But there are some cases in which it has mattered in the past, and yet others in which it may still matter. First, as we have seen, until 1954 the law required that contracts for the sale of goods of the value of £10 or more should be evidenced in writing. No such requirement applied to contracts for the supply of services. This difference between the two kinds of contract disappeared with the repeal of the requirement of writing, but older authorities on the distinction, which may still be cited today, were often concerned with this requirement. Secondly, a contract in which a person is to manufacture goods and then supply them, or in which a person is to supply and install materials in a house or other building, may also differ from a simple contract of sale of goods in some important respects. For example, the time at which the property in the goods is to pass from the supplier to the buyer or client may differ in the two cases.[70] Thirdly, in the case of goods to be manufactured by the seller, there may sometimes be a difference between a contract under which the seller simply contracts for a result, and cases in which it actually contracts to manufacture and deliver the goods. In the former case, the contract is one of sale and nothing else, while in the latter case the contract is both for services and for the sale of goods. Important results may sometimes turn upon whether the contract falls into one class or the other. For example, a buyer who pays part of the price in advance, and then defaults, may be entitled to recover their advance payment (subject to the seller's claim for damages for the default) if the contract is a pure contract of sale,[71] while it seems that they cannot recover an advance payment if the contract is one for *manufacture and sale*.[72]

The reason for this apparently arbitrary distinction is that if the contract is a pure sale, the whole consideration for the buyer's price is the transfer of the property in the goods to the buyer: it is therefore inconsistent for the seller to claim that they need not transfer the goods to the buyer because of the buyer's default, *and* that they may retain the buyer's advance payment, which is the consideration for that transfer of the goods. On the other hand, where the contract is for the manufacture and supply of the goods, the manufacture of the goods is itself part of the consideration for the price; if the seller has devoted time and money to making the goods, any advance payment can be considered as a payment

[69] See Blackburn J in *Lee* v *Griffin* (1861) 1 B & S 272, 277–8.

[70] See *Pritchett and Gold and Electrical Power Storage Co* v *Currie* [1916] 2 Ch 515 – see Chapter 10.

[71] *Dies v British & International etc Mining Corpn* [1939] 1 KB 724 – see Chapter 18.

[72] *Hyundai Heavy Industries Co Ltd* v *Papadopoulos* [1980] 1 WLR 1129 – see below. Cf. the Fibrosa case [1943] AC 32, where nobody seems to have had any doubt that there was a total failure of consideration when a contract to manufacture machinery was frustrated before any of it was delivered. The effect of the developing law of restitution in this area should be noted, however. In *British Steel Corp* v *Cleveland Bridge Engineering* [1984] 1 All ER 504, the defendants were held liable to pay a reasonable sum to the plaintiffs for work done at their request, though no contract had been entered into. See also Jaffey [1998] NILQ 107. It is not clear that Scots law would draw these distinctions.

towards the manufacture as much as a payment towards the actual transfer of the goods. The mere fact that as a result of the buyer's default the goods will no longer be transferred to them at all does not mean that the consideration for the advance payment has wholly failed. However, despite this element of logicality, the result is far from satisfactory, and the law remains in a somewhat uncertain state.[73]

A more general reason why it may be necessary to distinguish between a contract of sale of goods and a contract for services is simply that the provisions of the Sale of Goods Act do not in general apply to contracts for services. And although in some situations there is corresponding legislation governing contracts of services – in particular, the Supply of Goods and Services Act 1982 – there are other situations in which no corresponding legislation applies. In particular situations, this may make a critical difference to the outcome of a case.[74] In the case of consumer transactions, the legal position with regards to goods to be manufactured or produced is now addressed in the Consumer Rights Act 2015.[75]

Another reason why it may be important to distinguish between a contract of sale of goods and a contract for the supply of services concerns the implied duties of the seller or supplier as to the quality and fitness of the goods or services supplied. Until the enactment of the Supply of Goods and Services Act 1982, the position was, roughly speaking, as follows:

1 If the contract was a sale of goods, the implied duties under the Sale of Goods Act were incorporated in the contract, and these duties were, and remain, *prima facie* duties of strict liability, that is to say, the seller is responsible for defects in the goods, even in the absence of negligence.
2 If the contract was for the supply of services, then, insofar as the services themselves were concerned, the supplier's duties were generally duties of due care only; but where goods were supplied incidentally as a part of such a contract, it was generally held that the supplier's duties as regards the goods so supplied were strict, at any rate in a transaction for commercial (as opposed to professional) services.[76] Although the implied terms in the Sale of Goods Act did not apply to goods supplied in the course of a contract for services the courts tended to imply terms at common law, which were more or less identical with those implied under the Act.

The Supply of Goods and Services Act 1982 in effect enacts the position as set out in paragraph 2 above. Under this Act, implied conditions as to quality and fitness, almost identical to those implied under the Sale of Goods Act, are incorporated in all contracts for the 'transfer of goods' other than contracts of sale and hire-purchase, which are already covered by other statutes.[77] Restrictions closely analogous to those governing contracts

[73] See Chapter 18.
[74] *See, e.g., Hanson (W) (Harrow)* v *Rapid Civil Engineering & Usborne Depts Ltd* (1987) 38 Build LR 106, see Chapter 12.
[75] See Chapter 19.
[76] See, e.g., *Myers* v *Brent Cross Service Co* [1934] 1 KB 46; *Watson* v *Buckley* [1940] 1 All ER 174.
[77] There are a number of other exceptions of minor importance, e.g., a gift (even if made by deed) is not covered: s. 1(1)(d) of the 1982 Act. The Law Commissions' Final Report on *Sale and Supply of Goods*, which is discussed in Chapter 9, proposed a number of important amendments to the law of sale which are also applied to other contracts for the supply of goods by the Sale and Supply of Goods Act 1994. This Act also applies to Scotland the provisions of the 1982 Act about contracts for the transfer of goods.

of sale of goods[78] are also imposed, A contract for the transfer of goods which thus falls within the 1982 Act is defined by s. 1(1) of that Act as a contract under which 'one person transfers or agrees to transfer to another the property in goods' (other than the excepted contracts, which are covered elsewhere) and s. 1(3) makes it clear that these contracts fall within the 1982 Act even if services are also provided under the contract. Then ss. 12–16 of the 1982 Act deal with contracts for the supply of services, and it is made clear that these sections apply even if goods are also to be transferred under the contract. The implied terms under these sections, however, only impose a requirement to carry out the services with reasonable care and skill (s. 13) and do not impose strict liability.

Thus, the 1982 Act clarified and simplified the law. Where a contract might be classified as a contract of sale of goods or a contract for the supply of services, the Act will often this effectively immaterial. Insofar as goods are supplied under the contract, the seller's (or supplier's) duties will normally be strict and excludable only in the limited circumstances provided for contracts for sale or supply of goods, while insofar as the contract concerns services, the supplier's duties will be duties of care, which will be excludable subject to the reasonableness requirement of the Unfair Contract Terms Act 1977. Unfortunately, the 1982 Act does not wholly succeed in separating out duties regarding goods and duties regarding services. Although the position prior to the Act was (as stated above) that normally the supplier was strictly liable as regards the goods, and only liable for negligence as regards services, there were many exceptions to this position. On the one hand, there were some cases in which goods were supplied as an incident to a contract for services in which the seller's or supplier's duties were not strict, but only duties of care; and on the other hand, there were also a number of cases (rather more in this situation than the previous one) in which the supplier's duties as regards the services were held to be strict and not just duties of care.

The first group of cases concerns contracts for professional services. These are clearly contracts for services, but in the course of some transactions of this, products may be supplied which would perhaps not be thought of as 'goods' in the ordinary way. For example, it has never been suggested in England that a doctor or hospital which supplied drugs to a patient (even a paying patient) could be held liable if the drugs, despite all reasonable care, turned out to be unfit for their purpose; nor that a patient inoculated with a contaminated vaccine could sue for breach of an implied warranty of fitness, as opposed to suing for negligence.[79] Similarly, it has never been suggested that a patient who receives a transfusion of contaminated blood could sue the supplier (even if they are a paying patient and a contract can be established) on the basis of implied warranties. In America, this possibility was specifically rejected by the decision of the New York Court of Appeals in *Perlmutter* v *Beth David Hospital*[80] in which the plaintiff was given a blood transfusion in the defendants' hospital. The blood was contaminated with jaundice viruses which, according to the expert evidence, were not detectable by any scientific tests at the time, and the plaintiff suffered injury in consequence. The plaintiff was a paying patient at the hospital and in the account rendered to him he was charged a separate sum for the cost

78 See s. 7 of the Unfair Contract Terms Act 1977, as amended by the 1982 Act, in Chapter 8.

79 See, e.g., *Roe* v *Minister of Health* [1954] 2 QB 66.

80 123 NE 2d 792 (1954). Not all US states follow this approach, but in most states where warranty liability has been recognised at common law, the result has been reversed by statute.

of the blood itself. The plaintiff claimed that the blood had been 'sold' to him and that the defendants were therefore liable for 'defects' on the basis of implied warranties.[81] But the majority of the court held that the transaction was one of services only and that the supply of the blood was merely incidental to those services, and an English court would almost certainly concur with this decision.[82]

On the other hand, in *Dodd* v *Wilson*,[83] the plaintiff contracted with a vet to inoculate his cattle with a serum, which the vet did, using vaccine which he had bought from suppliers of vaccine. It was held that this was not a contract of sale but that, nevertheless, the surgeon impliedly warranted the vaccine to be fit for the purpose for which it was supplied. Hence he was liable, despite the fact that he was not himself guilty of any negligence.

It is by no means easy to distinguish these cases. Perhaps what underlies the distinction is that human blood for transfusion is not ordinarily thought of as the subject of commerce which is bought and sold,[84] whereas cattle serum clearly is ordinarily the subject of contracts of sale. And although in *Dodd* v *Wilson* the contract between the plaintiff and the surgeon was not one of sale, the judge evidently did not wish to deprive the plaintiff of the remedy which he would undoubtedly have had if he had himself bought the serum and merely obtained the services of the defendant to inoculate his cattle with the serum. In fact, the surgeon brought in his suppliers as third parties to the case and they brought in the manufacturers as fourth parties. Since the transactions between these parties, and between the surgeon and his suppliers, were clearly contracts of sale, the liability was passed down the line to the manufacturers.

The exact effect of the 1982 Act on these problems remains unclear.[85] A literal approach would suggest that strict duties as to the quality and fitness of the goods would now apply in all these cases on the ground that they involve the transfer of goods even as an incident to a contract for services, but a court might still strive to avoid this result by holding (for instance) that human blood for transfusion is not 'goods' at all.[86] The case would be even stronger with organ transplants[87] but, on the other hand, manufactured objects which are implanted in a body (such as heart pacemakers or artificial heart valves or hip joints) would presumably be 'goods' and so could attract the strict duties of quality and fitness. Similarly, the contract in *Dodd* v *Wilson* would now seem clearly to fall within the 1982 Act.

A similar problem arises with other goods transferred as a minor incident to a contract for services. Reference has been made above to the case of a contract with a solicitor for the drafting of a legal document which is then supplied to the client becoming their property. Literal construction of the 1982 Act would suggest that the solicitor might become strictly liable if the document fails in its purpose, even if the solicitor has taken all due care; again, it does not seem likely that this result was actually intended by the Act, and a court would presumably strive to avoid it. A possible distinction which might be made is between the legal document as goods, that is, as paper and ink, and the legal effect it

[81] See Chapter 8
[82] An alternative approach is suggested at Chapter 20 et *seq*.
[83] [1946] 2 All ER 691.
[84] See Titmuss, *The Gift Relationship* (1973, Harmondsworth: Penguin).
[85] It appears to have been outside the terms of reference of the Law Commission inquiry, *Law of Contract: Implied Terms in Contracts for the Supply of Services* (Law Com. No. 156, Cmnd 9773, 1986).
[86] See Chapter 20 et *seq*.
[87] For arguably relevant dicta, see *Browne* v *Norwich Crematorium Ltd* [1967] 1 WLR 691, 695.

is intended to produce which is entirely dependent on the legal framework within which it operates.[88] An analogous distinction is between the medium upon which a painting is painted, which becomes the property of the purchaser, and the copyright in the painting, which remains vested in the artist until they assign it. A related problem arises in relation to computer software which is specially written for a customer. This question is dealt with in Chapter 3.

The second main problem raised by the 1982 Act's attempt to separate out the legal treatment of implied conditions regarding goods on the one hand and services on the other is, in a sense, the converse of the first. Prior to the Act there were some circumstances in which services were supplied as an incident to a contract for the sale (or transfer) of goods and in which the seller, or supplier, was held to the strict standard appropriate for the quality and fitness of goods, both for the goods and the services themselves. This would normally have been the case (whatever the nature of the contract) if the seller or supplier contracted to produce a result. For instance, a seller who contracted to make and deliver a machine would not normally have been able to escape liability for the machine's failure to meet the specified (or implied) quality or fitness required under the contract by pleading that they took all due care and that the resulting failure was not because the goods (or parts) were in any way defective, but because they had been defectively put together in some way not due to their negligence. Similarly, a repairer who subcontracted part of the work to competent subcontractors might have been liable for the negligence of the subcontractors on the ground that they impliedly warranted that the work under the contract would be fit for the purpose required – not just that they would do the work with due care.[89] Although the 1982 Act only implies a duty of reasonable care with regard to services (whether or not they are supplied under a contract which also involves a transfer of goods), it seems probable that the same result would still be arrived at because of s. 16(3) of the 1982 Act. This section leaves open the possibility of a court implying terms which are stricter than those of due care, so that, in effect, the implied duty that services are to be performed with reasonable care must be taken as a minimum legal requirement (subject to the possibility of valid exclusion), and not as excluding the possibility of a higher duty.

It is therefore clear that the distinction between goods and services will often remain of some importance in the law, and it will still occasionally be necessary to distinguish between a contract of sale of goods and a contract for the supply of services. The test for deciding whether a contract falls into one category or the other is to ask what is 'the substance' of the contract.[90] If the substance of the contract is the skill and labour

[88] In *Winter* v *G P Putnam's Sons* 938 F 2d 1033, 9th Cir. (1991) the plaintiffs, relying on erroneous information in a reference book, ate poisonous mushrooms and suffered serious physical injury. The court refused to hold the publishers liable on products liability theory, on the ground that the expressions and ideas contained in the book were intangible, and products liability theory is concerned with tangibles. It must be borne in mind, however, that American courts are concerned not to place restrictions on the unfettered exchange of ideas, which might run into problems with the First Amendment to the Constitution. The court distinguished the case of *Fluor Corp* v *Jeppesen & Co* 216 Cal Rptr 68 (Cal Ct of App 1985) in which the defendants were held liable on products liability theory in respect of a defective aeronautical chart. For a discussion of the question of the liability of sellers of books containing erroneous information see Lloyd [1993] JBL 48.

[89] See, e.g., *Stewart* v *Reavell's Garage* [1953] 2 QB 545.

[90] *Robinson* v *Graves* [1935] 1 KB 579.

of the supplier, then the contract is one for services, whereas if the real substance of the contract is the ultimate result – the goods to be provided – then the contract is one of sale of goods. Hence a contract for the painting of a picture is a contract for services – the skill of the artist is clearly more important than the incidental fact that the property in the completed picture (though not the copyright in it) will pass to the client.[91] *A fortiori*, on this test a contract with a professional person such as a lawyer or an accountant is a contract for services even though documents may be prepared and passed to the client so as to become their property.[92] On the other hand, a contract for the construction of two ships' propellers was held by the House of Lords in *Cammell Laird & Co Ltd* v *Manganese Bronze and Brass Co Ltd*[93] to be unquestionably a contract for the sale of goods. Similarly, a contract for the manufacture of a ship is a contract of sale of goods, but it is not necessarily a pure contract of sale:[94] if the process of manufacture itself forms part of the contract, the contract in effect consists of two sub-parts, (1) a contract under which the supplier is to make the ship – which is a contract for services – and (2) a contract under which the supplier agrees to sell the completed ship – in effect, a contract of sale of goods. A contract for the supply of a meal in a restaurant, as previously noted, seems to be a contract of sale of goods.[95]

2.2.7 Sale and agency

It may, at first sight, seem a little odd that it is thought necessary to distinguish a contract of sale of goods from a contract of agency, but in a certain type of case the distinction may well be a fine one by no means easy to draw. Where, for example, A asks B, a commission agent, to obtain goods for them from a supplier or from any other source, and B complies by sending the goods to A, it may well be a fine point whether this is a contract under which B sells the goods to A, or is a contract under which B acts as A's agent to obtain the required goods from other sources.

It is important to distinguish between the two transactions for a number of reasons. In the first place, the Commercial Agency Regulations[96] apply to many agency contracts,[97] and regulate the rights and duties of the parties in certain respects. Furthermore, if the transaction is an agency contract there may be privity of contract between the buyer and the agent's supplier which will enable action to be brought between them.[98] On the other hand, if it is a sale, there will be no privity between the buyer and the seller's own supplier.

[91] Ibid.

[92] Though in the old case of *Lee* v *Griffin* (1861) 1 B & S 272 a contract to manufacture false teeth was held to be a contract for the sale of goods – an outcome perhaps indicative of the regard in which dentists were held in the mid-nineteenth century!

[93] [1934] AC 402.

[94] *Hyundai Heavy Industries Co Ltd* v *Papadopoulos* [1980] 1 WLR 1129 – see Chapter 16

[95] *Lockett* v *A & M Charles Ltd* [1938] 4 All ER 170.

[96] SI 1993/3053, which implements then EEC Directive 86/653 of 18 December 1986. This is currently assimilated law after the UK's withdrawal from the UK, although there has been a consultation about repealing this legislation: see Department for Business and Trade, *Smarter regulation: deregulating the Commercial Agents (Council Directive) Regulations 1993* (2024).

[97] They apply in general contracts between self-employed agents and their principals – reg. 2(1), but there are certain exclusions.

[98] *Teheran-Europe Corpn Ltd* v *Belton Ltd* [1968] 2 QB 545.

Other reasons for distinguishing the relationship of agent and seller may be that the duties of a commission agent are less stringent than those of a seller and, in the event of a breach of contract, the measure of damages may also be different. Therefore, if a seller delivers less than they are bound to under the contract, the buyer can reject the whole;[99] but if, despite their best endeavours, a commission agent delivers less than their principal has ordered they have committed no breach of contract and the principal is bound to accept whatever is delivered.[100] Again, should the commission agent deliver goods of the wrong quality they will only have to pay as damages the actual loss suffered by the buyer.[101] On the other hand, should a seller be guilty of such a breach they may have to pay as damages, the buyer's probable loss of profit. Similarly, an agent who merely introduces a seller to a buyer is not necessarily warranting the seller's title to sell, whereas if the agent is buying and reselling, such a warranty is invariably implied.[102]

In *Esso Petroleum Co Ltd* v *Addison*[103] Moore-Bick J left open whether petrol station franchisees who provided customers with 'gifts'[104] in return for tokens, furnished the gifts as agents for Esso or on their own account.[105]

Where one person contracts to manufacture goods for another out of materials to be supplied by that other, it may again be doubtful whether the manufacturer is a seller or an agent.[106]

In the converse position, where a person contracts to dispose of the goods of another, it is again necessary to decide whether the relationship between the parties is that of buyer and seller or principal and agent. In the latter case, the agent is not in precisely the same position as a buyer and, for instance, cannot pass a good title to a third party without the principal's actual or apparent authority.[107] Again, where a person contracts to dispose of another's goods, it may be important to decide whether they are a buyer or an agent if they receive any payment from a third party as a result of disposing of the goods. If they are a buyer, such payment will discharge the third party, wholly or *pro tanto*. But if they are an agent and they fail to account to their principal for the money, the third party will only be discharged if the agent was authorised to receive the money.[108] The relationship between the principal and the agent depends, of course, on the terms, express or implied, of the contract between them; but in some cases where goods have been delivered to an agent for sale, the agent will have the goods on 'sale or return' or similar terms, in which case, although the transaction is not strictly a sale, some provisions of the Sale of Goods Act may apply.[109]

[99] Section 30(1) – see Chapter 7.

[100] *Ireland v Livingston* (1872) LR 5 HL 395. Similarly, in the case of late shipment: *Anglo-African Shipping Co v J Mortner Ltd* [1962] 1 Lloyd's Rep 610.

[101] *Cassaboglou* v *Gibb* (1883) 11 QBD 797.

[102] See *Warming Used Cars Ltd* v *Tucker* [1956] SASR 249, where it was held that the defendant did not warrant title although the transaction was a sale; but it seems that the defendant might more properly have been treated as a mere agent.

[103] [2003] EWHC 173.

[104] As to whether such transactions are really gifts or sales see *Esso Petroleum* v *Commissioners of Customs & Excise* [1976] 1 All ER 117 – discussed above.

[105] Id. para. 54.

[106] *Cf. Dixon v London Small Arms Co Ltd* (1876) 1 App Cas 633; *Hill & Sons* v *Edwin Showell* (1918) 87 LJKB 1106. But where consumer goods are concerned the possible effect of the consumer goods and associated guarantees directive 99/44/EC, OJ L171, 7/7/1999 needs to be considered – see section 2.2.1 *et seq*.

[107] *Edwards* v *Vaughan* (1910) 26 TLR 545.

[108] See, e.g., *Sorrell* v *Finch* [1977] AC 728 (estate agent).

[109] Section 18, Rule 4 – see Chapter 12.

2.3 Number of parties

It has been decided that the requirement that the property be transferred from one party to another means that there must be two distinct parties to a contract of sale. In *Graff* v *Evans*,[110] decided in 1882, 11 years before the original Act was passed, it was held that the transfer of intoxicating liquor by the manager of an unincorporated club to a member for money was not a 'sale' within the Licensing Act, but merely a transfer of special property. The basis of the decision was that the member was himself a part owner of the liquor and that consequently the transaction was a release of the rights of the other members to the 'purchaser'. It might have been thought, therefore, that when s. 1(1) (now s. 2(2)) of the Act specifically enacted that:

> There may be a contract of sale between one part owner and another

the basis of *Graff* v *Evans* had been swept away. But in *Davies* v *Burnett*,[111] a divisional court followed the earlier case and the Sale of Goods Act was not even referred to. This view of the law has now been accepted for so long that it is unlikely to be upset by a higher court.[112]

Although the Act contemplates two distinct parties to the contract, namely a buyer and a seller, it does not follow that the buyer cannot already be the owner of the goods, for the seller may be a person having legal authority to sell them; for example, a sheriff acting in execution of a writ of execution.[113] However, if a person contracts to buy their own goods from someone else under the mistaken impression that the goods belong to the seller, it seems clear that they can recover any price paid on the ground of total failure of consideration. *A fortiori* if they have not yet paid the price, the seller cannot sue them for it. This does not mean that such a contract is necessarily void, though it may be in some circumstances.[114]

2.4 The price

Section 8 of the Act is as follows:

> (1) The price in a contract of sale may be fixed by the contract, or may be left to be fixed in a manner agreed by the contract, or may be determined by the course of dealing between the parties.
> (2) Where the price is not determined as mentioned in subsection (1) above the buyer must pay a reasonable price.
> (3) What is a reasonable price is a question of fact dependent on the circumstances of each particular case.

We have already seen that the consideration must be paid in money and that, strictly speaking, the contract will not be a contract of sale of goods if the consideration is in some other form.[115]

[110] (1882) 8 QBD 373.
[111] [1902] 1 KB 666.
[112] In any event, the particular difficulty in question was met by legislation: see Part II of the Licensing Act 1964, now replaced by the Licensing Act 2003, which regulated the 'supply' of liquor in clubs. See also *Carlton Lodge Club* v *Customs & Excise Commissioners* [1974] 3 All ER 798. But see the discussion at Chapter 10 et *seq*.; otherwise it is questionable whether the Supply of Goods and Services Act 1982 applies to such a transaction, or whether the buyer can have any remedy in respect of defective goods under that Act or otherwise.
[113] But an argument can be made that this is not a sale at all, but a contract to release a lien – see *Hain SS Co Ltd* v *Tate & Lyle Ltd* [1936] 2 All ER 597.
[114] In *Cooper v Phibbs* (1867) LR 2 HL 149 the House of Lords held that a contract for the lease of a fishery which turned out already to belong to the lessee was voidable. It is probable, however, that it should have been held void – see *Bell* v *Lever Bros* [1932] AC 161, 218.
[115] There are dicta in *Koppel* v *Koppel* [1966] 1 WLR 802, 811, indicating that a contract to transfer goods in return for services is a sale of goods, but these seem to have been per *incuriam*.

Section 8 has given rise to more difficulty than might have been thought. The section assumes that a contract has been made by the parties and then proceeds to explain the methods by which the price can be ascertained. But the first point which must be considered in an action on the sale is whether a contract has in fact been finally agreed upon by the parties, and the absence of an agreement as to the price (or even as to the mode in which the price is to be paid)[116] may show that the parties have not yet reached a concluded contract.

Another problem concerns the question whether the parties can make a binding contract in which they agree to fix the price at some future date. When s. 8 says that the price can be 'left to be fixed in a manner agreed', does this exclude the possibility that 'the manner' may simply require the parties to agree on the price? One view is that the parties simply cannot make a binding contract for the sale of goods at prices 'to be agreed', and that s. 8 does not apply to such a case because under that section the buyer would have to pay a reasonable price, that is, a price fixed by a judge (or arbitrator) which is not the same thing as a price agreed between the parties.

There is undoubtedly some support for this view in the difficult case of *May & Butcher* v *The King*.[117] The House of Lords here held that an agreement for the sale of goods at a price to be later fixed by the parties was not, in the circumstances of the case, a concluded contract; but the later case of *Hillas & Co Ltd* v *Arcos Ltd*[118] shows that we cannot regard the earlier case as laying down any general rule and that that case is best regarded as one where the parties had not in the circumstances arrived at a concluded agreement.[119] In *Foley* v *Classique Coaches Ltd*,[120] the Court of Appeal held that an agreement to supply petrol 'at a price to be agreed by the parties' was a binding contract as the parties had clearly evinced an intention to be bound, and the contract contained, in the form of an arbitration clause, under which a reasonable price could be fixed in the event of disagreement, a means by which the uncertainty could be resolved.

On the other hand, in a number of more recent decisions, the courts have reiterated the old (but not strictly accurate) view that the law does not recognise 'an agreement to agree' as a binding contract. In *Courtney & Fairbairn Ltd* v *Tolaini Bros (Hotels) Ltd* the Court of Appeal refused recognition of a contract at a price 'to be agreed'.[121] Of course, an arbitration clause to determine the price or the relevant terms would alter the case.[122] In the Australian High Court, suggestions have also been made that s. 8 is 'anomalous' and is not to be extended,[123] and it has also been suggested in the same case that the section only applies where the goods have been delivered and accepted, and that it has no application

[116] See *Ingram* v *Little* [1961] 1 QB 31, 49, per Sellers LJ. Cf., however, *R & J Dempster Ltd* v *Motherwell Bridge & Engineering Co Ltd* 1964 SC 308; *Glynwed Distribution Ltd* v *S Koronka & Co* 1977 SC 1.

[117] [1934] 2 KB 17n.

[118] [1932] All ER Rep 494. The facts of this case illustrate the principle that parties who have had a previous course of dealings will be taken to intend the unexpressed terms of their new dealing to be those of the previous course of dealings unless a particular term is inapplicable or inappropriate to the new dealing – *Banque Paribas* v *Cargill* [1992] 1 Lloyd's Rep 96.

[119] See *Smith* v *Morgan* [1971] 2 All ER 1500; *Brown* v *Gould* [1972] Ch 53. Compare *King's Motors* v *Lax* (Oxford) *Ltd* [1970] 1 WLR 426.

[120] [1934] 2 KB 1.

[121] [1975] 1 WLR 297. Terms 'to be negotiated' would be open to the same objections.

[122] See s. 9 below,

[123] *Hall* v *Busst* (1960) 104 CLR 206.

to a purely executory contract.[124] These dicta have not been followed, even in Australia,[125] but there does seem to be good sense in distinguishing between executed and executory contracts for this purpose. If the parties have already begun to carry out the contract, it is more seemingly contrary to prevailing commercial reality as well as more unjust to declare the transaction void altogether.[126]

In *Sudbrook Trading Estate Ltd* v *Eggleton*[127] the House of Lords reviewed some similar problems which have arisen in contracts for the sale of land, which are, of course, governed by common law and equitable rules and not by the Sale of Goods Act. The case did not involve anything in the nature of an 'agreement to agree' although it did involve an option to a lessee to buy the freehold of the leased premises at a price to be fixed by valuers appointed by the two parties or, in default of agreement by the valuers, at a price to be fixed by an umpire appointed by the valuers. It was held that the failure of the lessor to appoint a valuer could not be allowed to deprive the lessee of their right to a decree of specific performance once they had exercised their option to buy. The court could direct an inquiry to ascertain the reasonable price to be paid as the lessor had waived their right to appoint a valuer. The decision does not strictly have anything to do with s. 8 of the Sale of Goods Act, but there are dicta indicating that where an agreement has been partly performed, the court will strain to find some way of enforcing the intended arrangements even in the absence of agreement on a term which might have been fatal if the whole agreement had remained executory. It seems possible, therefore, that where parties agree on a sale of goods at prices to be agreed in the future, and the goods are actually delivered and accepted, or the agreement is otherwise partly performed, the courts may now be more willing to treat this as a binding contract to sell at reasonable prices, and to provide machinery for the ascertainment of such reasonable prices, even in the absence of a provision such as an arbitration clause by which this could be done under the contract itself.

This is perhaps borne out by two Court of Appeal decisions (though these did not involve price terms) in which it was stressed that in commercial cases, it is the intention of the parties which is decisive.[128] A failure to agree even on relatively important terms is not necessarily fatal; indeed, it cannot even be said that a failure to agree on the 'essential' terms is fatal. Provided that the parties intend to be bound, and that the agreement is sufficiently complete to be enforced as a contract, it is immaterial that they have failed to agree on some term which might appear, objectively speaking, to be important or even essential.[129]

This point is emphasised in the speech of Lord Clarke giving judgement for the Supreme Court in *RTS Flexible Systems Limited* v *Molkerei Alois Muller Gmbh*,[130] a case concerning the supply and installation of defective food packaging equipment. Lord Clarke said: 'Even if certain terms of economic or other significance to the parties have not been finalised, an objective appraisal of their words and conduct may lead to the conclusion

[124] Ibid., at 234c.

[125] *Wenning* v *Robinson* (1964) 64 SR (NSW) 157.

[126] See *F & G Sykes (Wessex) Ltd* v *Fine Fare* [1967] 2 Lloyd's Rep 52, 57–8; *Avintair Ltd* v *Ryder Airline Services Ltd* 1994 SC 270

[127] [1983] 1 AC 444.

[128] *Pagnan SpA* v *Feed Products* [1987] 2 Lloyd's Rep 601; *Pagnan SpA* v *Granaria* [1986] 2 Lloyd's Rep 547.

[129] *Pagnan SpA* v *Feed Products* [1987] 2 Lloyd's Rep at 619, per Lloyd LJ.

[130] [2010] UKSC 14.

that they did not intend agreement of such terms to be a precondition to a concluded and legally binding agreement.'

While almost certainly not the last word on this matter, and mindful that each case falls to be decided to some extent on its own facts, the courts have clearly signalled that unless there is a complete absence of intention, they will strive to give effect to agreements where the parties manifestly intended to be bound by them.

The Supreme Court's decision in *Barton* v *Morris*[131] adds an interesting gloss to this discussion. Although this case relates to reasonable remuneration for providing a service under s. 15 of the Supply of Goods and Services Act 1982, the reasoning has some relevance to the implied term as to a reasonable price under s. 8(2) SGA 1979. In this case an oral contract was made between Mr Barton, and Foxpace Ltd ('Foxpace'), to sell a property in London. There was an oral agreement that Mr Barton would be paid £1.2 million if he was to secure a purchase price of at least £6.5 million. Although Mr Barton introduced a buyer willing to pay the £6.5million, the buyer later reduced their offer to £6 million. Mr Barton was refused any commission payment as a result, but claimed to be entitled to reasonable remuneration for the service he had provided instead.

A majority of the Supreme Court held that the express term as to commission for a sale of at least £6.5 million was exhaustive as far as Mr Barton's entitlement to commission was concerned, and that the default implied term as to reasonable remuneration was displaced in its entirety. The effect is that once something is said about payment, that is exhaustive. The strong dissenting judgments by Lords Burrows JSC and Leggatt JSC preferred treating the express agreement as limited to its specific conditions, with the default term continuing to apply to other circumstances (in the absence of further express provision).

One can imagine similar situations in relation to sale of goods; e.g., parties may agree a price of £100 per item if at least 1,000 items are bought, but the contract may be otherwise silent as to price. One cannot envisage a situation where the courts will allow the buyer to acquire the goods without paying at least a reasonable price for goods received. One would therefore hope that *Barton* v *Morris* will be confined to its admittedly unusual facts.[132] Nonetheless, it serves a reminder that it is important to reach agreement on fundamental aspects.

Section 9 runs as follows:

> (1) Where there is an agreement to sell goods on the terms that the price is to be fixed by the valuation of a third party, and he cannot or does not make the valuation, the agreement is avoided; but if the goods or any part of them have been delivered to and appropriated by the buyer he must pay a reasonable price for them.
> (2) Where the third party is prevented from making the valuation by the fault of the seller or buyer, the party not at fault may maintain an action for damages against the party at fault.

An agreement for the sale of goods at a valuation to be made by a third party must be distinguished from an agreement for sale at a valuation without naming any third party who is to make the valuation. In the former event, s. 9 applies, and if the third party does

[131] [2023] UKSC 3.

[132] Cf Greg Leckey, Silence can be dangerous: *Barton* v *Morris on Implied Term* (June 2023) No.5 Barristers Chambers.

not make the valuation the contract is avoided, subject to the effect of s. 9(2). But in the latter event (e.g. a sale of stock 'at valuation'), the agreement is in effect an agreement for sale at a reasonable price and, if no valuer is agreed and the parties otherwise fail to come to some arrangement for valuation, the contract will stand as a contract for sale at a reasonable price under s. 8.[133]

The sort of situation which is probably envisaged by s. 9(2) is, for example, a refusal by the seller to allow the valuer access to the goods, thereby preventing them obtaining the necessary material for making their valuation. It is a little difficult to imagine circumstances in which the buyer could prevent the valuer making their valuation, but no doubt this was inserted to meet all possible contingencies. It is, perhaps, not entirely clear whether s. 9(2) envisages a sort of action for breach of a duty of good faith, or whether it envisages that in the circumstances postulated there would be an actual contract of sale. The measure of damages could perhaps differ according to the correct answer to that question.

Where a sale at a valuation is agreed upon and a valuation is subsequently made, it cannot be upset merely because the valuer has been negligent or has gone about the valuation in an incorrect manner. As Lord Denning MR said in *Campbell* v *Edwards*:[134]

> It is simply the law of contract. If two persons agree that the price of property should be fixed by a valuer on whom they agree, and he gives that valuation honestly, they are bound by it. If there were fraud or collusion, of course, it would be very different.

It is now clear, however, that the valuer will normally be liable for negligence if it can be shown that they have adopted a wholly incorrect basis for their valuation.[135] As Lord Denning made clear in the above-cited passage, the valuation can be upset if there has been fraud or collusion. There are also some first-instance decisions holding that a valuation which sets out the basis on which it is arrived at may be open to challenge on the ground that the method disclosed is unsound in law.[136] But it cannot be assumed that the party aggrieved will always have a remedy if the valuation is made on an incorrect basis because if the basis for the valuation is not disclosed and it was made in accordance with a permissible (though wrong) professional judgment, the valuation will stand and the valuer will not be liable for negligence.

2.5 Conveyancing effect of the contract

Some comment must be made here on the words 'A contract of sale of goods is a contract by which the seller transfers . . . the property in goods' in s. 2(1). As is clearly apparent from these words, the actual contract may suffice to transfer the property in the goods,

[133] *F & G Sykes (Wessex) Ltd v Fine Fare*, above. But it may be that as a result of the Sudbrook Trading Estate case, discussed above, even the failure of a named third party to make a valuation will only avoid the contract if their identity was essential to the arrangements. Otherwise it may be held that the contract is really for sale at a reasonable price, and the naming of the third party is simply machinery which can be replaced by the court.

[134] [1976] 1 WLR 403, 407; *Baber v Kenwood* [1978] 1 Lloyd's Rep 175.

[135] *Arenson v Casson Beckman Rutley & Co* [1977] AC 405; *Arenson v Arenson* [1977] AC 747.

[136] See *Wright v Frodoor* [1967] 1 WLR 506; *Burgess v Purchase & Sons* (Farms) Ltd [1983] Ch 216. *Compare Jones v Sherwood Computer Services* [1992] 2 All ER 170.

that is to say, it may operate both as a conveyance and a contract. Attention is frequently drawn to this as though it were a remarkable rule, and a contrast is often made with the corresponding provisions of Roman law in which a sharp line was drawn between the contract and the conveyance. There is some point in this contrast, but a note of caution should be sounded against pursuing it too far, for remarkably few results follow in English law from the transfer of property by the mere agreement, which would not in any event follow from the transfer of property by delivery. This topic will be more fully examined later.[137]

It is possible that these words in s. 2(1) may also have the effect of bringing a transaction within the scope of a contract of sale even though it would be difficult to say that the object of the transaction was the transfer of the property in any goods. For example, if a person organises a party, for which they sell tickets entitling a purchaser to help themselves to drinks, it seems that a sale takes place when this happens, although it would be difficult to say that there was a contract of sale of goods arising from the mere sale of the ticket.[138] On the other hand, the courts have shown little inclination to make use of this analysis in civil cases. Thus in the case of a contract for work and materials, the courts have not said that there is a contract of sale within the Act when property in the materials eventually passes to the party ordering the work and materials.[139] And since the passing of the Supply of Goods and Services Act 1982, a court is perhaps more likely to hold that such a transaction is a contract for the transfer of goods rather than a contract for the sale of goods. But it would only be a matter of practical importance in very special circumstances.

It was alluded earlier that considerable difficulty about the scope of s. 2(1) of the Sale of Goods Act has been caused by the Supreme Court's ruling *PST Energy 7 Shipping LLC* v *OW Bunker Malta Ltd.* [140] A contract for the sale of bunkers (in a largely standard form and on standard terms), which contained a retention of title clause which also allowed the buyer (referred to as Owner) to consume the bunkers before payment became due, was construed as a 'bunker supply contract' which fell outside of the scope of s. 2. Lord Mance, who gave the judgment of the Court, said that the contract 'cannot be regarded as a straightforward agreement to transfer property in the bunkers to the Owners for a price. It was in substance an agreement with two aspects: first, to permit consumption prior to any payment and . . . without any property ever passing in the bunkers consumed; and second, but only if and so far as bunkers remained unconsumed, to transfer the property in the bunkers remaining to the Owners in return for the Owners paying the price. But in this latter connection it is to be noted that the price does not here refer to the price of the bunkers in respect of which property was passing, it refers to the price payable for all bunkers, whether consumed before or remaining at the time of payment.'[141] In Lord Mance's view, the commercial purpose of the contract was that the Owners 'should have and had the right to consume the bunkers in the vessel's propulsion as and when they did so prior to payment, and that upon payment they would acquire the property in, and thereby an absolute right to dispose of or use as they wished, any remaining bunkers.'[142]

[137] See Chapter 10.

[138] See *Doak* v *Bedford* [1964] 2 QB 587, 596, per Paull J; but cf. Lord Parker CJ at 594. An entry ticket in such cases confers a licence to enter the premises concerned – *Hurst* v *Picture Theatres Ltd* [1915] 1 KB 1 (CA).

[139] See *Young & Marten Ltd* v *McManus Childs Ltd* [1969] 1 AC 454.

[140] [2016] UKSC 23.

[141] Para [28].

[142] Para [30].

Overall, therefore, the contract 'in its essential nature, . . . offered a feature quite different from a contract of sale of goods - the liberty to consume all or any part of the bunkers supplied without acquiring property in them or having paid for them.[143]

The implications of this ruling could be far-reaching and have the effect of removing many cases hitherto regarded as contracts of sale from the scope of the Sale of Goods Act 1979. As will be discussed later,[144] many commercial contracts involve the supply of goods subject to a retention of title clause which delays the passing of property until the buyer has paid for the goods. Usually, the buyer will be permitted to use the goods before payment, which, in the case of raw-materials, will mean that the goods supplied by the seller are often 'consumed' in the sense that they cease to exist as separate and separable goods and become part of new manufactured goods. The reasoning in *PST Energy 7* would take such contracts outside the scope of the Sale of Goods Act and treat them instead as *sui generis*, governed by the common law instead, leaving few contracts within the scope of the Act.[145] Lord Mance referred to two such cases,[146] *Borden (UK) Ltd* v *Scottish Timber Products Ltd*[147] and *Armour* v *Thyssen Edelstahlwerke AG*.[148] In *Borden*, resin had become part of chipboard which meant that the retention of title to the resin was ineffective, whereas in *Armour*, steel was still within reach of the retention of title clause. *Borden* would clearly be a candidate for *PST Energy 7* re-categorisation as *sui generis*, whereas arguably in *Armour*, there was no 'consumption' as such of the steel. Lord Mance noted that these cases 'simply assumed that the transaction was one of sale' and suggested that 'even if on analysis these two cases could and should have been analysed as *sui generis*.'[149] It seems that *PST Energy 7* invites several possible interpretations. The broadest one would exclude all contracts containing a retention of title clause from the scope of the Sale of Goods Act 1979, thereby much reducing the kinds of contracts falling within the Act. Secondly, all contracts containing a retention of title clause but which envisage and permit the consumption of the goods, in the sense of losing their identity as separate goods, would no longer be within the Sale of Goods Act. On this interpretation, *Borden* would fall outside the Act but cases such as *Hendy Lennox (Industrial Engines) Ltd* v *Grahame Puttick Ltd*,[150] where components supplied subject to retention of title could easily be removed, would not. Finally, on the narrowest reading, *PST Energy 7* only applies to bunker supply contracts, leaving other contracts involving retention of title clause within the scope of the Sale of Goods Act 1979. Whilst the third interpretation would limit the effects of *PST Energy 7* to a sub-category of supply contracts, it may not be easy to support in view of Lord Mance's overall reasoning. However, the second interpretation would be sustainable even in the context of Lord Mance's analysis, which would mean that goods supplied on retention of title which are combined with or incorporated into other goods without losing their identity should still be treated as falling within the Act.[151]

[143] Para [34].
[144] See Chapter 15.
[145] See the analysis by Louise Gullifer, '"Sales" on retention of title terms: is the English law analysis broken?' (2017) 133 LQR. 244, esp. at p.259.
[146] See further Chapter 15.
[147] [1981] Ch 25.
[148] [1991] 2 AC 339.
[149] [2016] UKSC 23, para [35].
[150] [1984] 1 WLR 485.
[151] See also Djakhongir Saidov, 'Sales law post-Res Cogitans' (2019) JBL 1 at 8.

Perhaps the preferable lesson to be drawn from this case is that the time may have come to redraft the Sale of Goods Act 1979 and to follow the lead taken in the Consumer Rights Act 2015,[152] which effectively avoids the need for careful classification of supply transactions for many purposes.[153]

2.6 Formation of the contract

2.6.1 Offer and acceptance

Part II of the Act is entitled 'Formation of the Contract'; however, with the exception of s. 57 in Part VII governing the sale of goods by auction, there is nothing in it which regulates the actual formation of the contract of sale of goods.

As a result, we are left to infer from s. 62(2) that a contract of sale of goods is formed according to the ordinary principles of the common law of England and Scotland, that is to say, by offer and acceptance. As there is nothing in these rules of special significance in the law of sale of goods, this subject need not be enlarged upon here.

Apart from the Acts (and some other) provisions on auction sales,[154] only two other matters relating to formation need be dealt with here, namely the doctrine of mistake in offer and acceptance, and the special provisions relating to contracts concluded away from business premises, that is, the provisions designed to safeguard consumers against the consequences of 'doorstep selling'.

2.6.2 Auction sales

The first two subsections of s. 57 are as follows:

> (1) Where the goods are put up for sale by auction in lots, each lot is *prima facie* deemed to be the subject of a separate contract of sale.
> (2) A sale by auction is complete when the auctioneer announces its completion by the fall of the hammer, or in other customary manner, and until the announcement is made any bidder may retract his bid.

These two subsections restate the common law rules governing auction sales. Under these rules it is quite clear that the bidder is the offeror, that the auctioneer is entitled to accept or to refuse any bid,[155] and that the contract is made on the fall of the hammer. As each bidder may retract, the offeree may withdraw the article from sale even after bidding has commenced.[156] But, in practice, many auction sales are conducted under special 'Conditions of Sale' and these may sometimes affect the application of s. 57. For example, a condition justifying the auctioneer in re-opening the bidding in the event of a dispute has been applied even where the auctioneer intended to knock the goods down to the person who intended to buy them.[157]

[152] See Chapter 19.

[153] Cf. Gullifer (2017) 133 LQR 244 at 261/2. In *Wood and another* v *TUI Travel plc* [2017] EWCA Civ 11, a travel operator argued, by analogy with *PST Energy 7*, that the supply of food to a customer in a hotel restaurant did not involve any transfer of property and that the food remained the property of the hotel until it was destroyed by being consumed. The Court of Appeal rejected this argument, somewhat ridiculing 'submissions of a metaphysical nature' [26] which flowed from it.

[154] But in Scotland the common law may be that a bid cannot be retracted unless it is refused or a higher bid is made: *Cree* v *Durie*, 1 December 1810 (FC).

[155] See, e.g., *British Car Auctions* v *Wright* [1972] 3 All ER 462.

[156] *Fenwick* v *Macdonald Fraser & Co* (1904) 6 F 850.

[157] *Richards* v *Phillips* [1968] 2 All ER 859.

The next four subsections give rise to more difficulty:

(3) A sale by auction may be notified to be subject to a reserve or upset price, and a right to bid may also be reserved expressly by or on behalf of the seller.
(4) Where a sale by auction is not notified to be subject to a right to bid on behalf of the seller, it is not lawful for the seller to bid himself or to employ any person to bid at the sale, or for the auctioneer knowingly to take any bid from the seller or any such person.
(5) A sale contravening subsection (4) above may be treated as fraudulent by the buyer.
(6) Where, in respect of a sale by auction, a right to bid is expressly reserved (but not otherwise) the seller, or any one person on his behalf, may bid at the auction.

The effect of these subsections may be considered under three heads.

2.6.3 Auction sale expressly subject to reserve price or right to bid

First, where the auction is expressly advertised subject to a reserve price or to the right of the seller to bid, subss. (3) and (6) preserve the seller's right not to sell below the reserve price, or to bid themselves or to employ one (but not more than one) person to bid on their behalf, as the case may be. But as we have seen, subs. (2) preserves the common law rule that no contract of sale comes into existence until the seller accepts a bid. Subsection (3) therefore has independent force only where the auctioneer knocks the goods down below the reserve price by mistake. The effect of such a mistake was discussed in *McManus* v *Fortescue*.=[158] In that case, the printed catalogue at an auction sale stated that each lot was subject to a reserve price, but the auctioneer knocked the goods down to the plaintiff for less than the reserve price by mistake. Recollecting the reserve price, the auctioneer then refused to sign a memorandum of sale.[159] It was held by the Court of Appeal that an action against the auctioneer must fail. Since the sale was expressly subject to a reserve price, the auctioneer could not be made liable for breach of warranty of authority. An action against the owner would presumably also have failed as the auctioneer's authority was known to be limited and was in fact exceeded. It is a fair inference that had the sale not been notified to the public as being subject to a reserve price, the seller would have been liable as the buyer would have been able to rely upon the auctioneer's apparent authority.

2.6.4 Auction sale with no express statement as to reserve price or right to bid

Where nothing is said about any reserve price or right of the owner to bid, a distinction must be drawn between the two cases. In the former case, the effect of s. 57(2) is that the auctioneer is still entitled to decline to accept any bid. In the latter case, however, subs. (4) applies and the buyer may set the contract aside, or presumably may sue for damages. Even where a reserve price is notified, the owner is still not entitled to bid unless this right also is expressly reserved; and if they do so bid and the reserve price is reached, the contract may be treated as fraudulent by the buyer. If the reserve price is not reached, however, although the seller may have wrongly bid, no one will have suffered damage so as to entitle them to sue the seller.

[158] [1907] 2 KB 1.
[159] If he had signed, it seems he would have been liable – *see Fay* v *Miller* [1941] 2 All ER 18.

2.6.5 Auction sale expressly advertised without reserve

The effect of an express notification that the sale will be without reserve is left obscure by the Act. It is at any rate clear that s. 57(2) prevents any contract of sale coming into existence if the auctioneer refuses to accept a bid. There remains the possibility that the auctioneer may be held liable on the basis that they have contracted to sell the goods to the highest bidder, a device sanctioned by the Court of Exchequer Chamber in *Warlow* v *Harrison*.[160] The difficulties of this case have been explored by two learned writers.[161] Put briefly, these are (a) the fact that the highest bidder cannot be identified until the hammer has fallen, and we are postulating a case where the auctioneer has not accepted any bid and (b) the apparent lack of consideration for the auctioneer's promise. Neither of these seems to be a fatal objection, for the person who had made the highest bid when the goods were withdrawn should *prima facie* be able to claim that they were the highest bidder, and a rather generous approach to the requirement of consideration is a feature common to most cases of breach of warranty of authority by an agent, as, for example, in *Collen* v *Wright*.[162] Moreover, the decision in *Warlow* v *Harrison* has been affirmed by the Court of Appeal in *Barry* v *Heathcote Ball & Co (Commercial Auctions) Ltd*.[163]

2.6.6 Bidding agreements

Certain undesirable auction practices by buyers are dealt with by the Auctions (Bidding Agreements) Act 1969. The purpose of this Act (and the earlier Act of 1927 of the same name) is to prevent dealers from agreeing to abstain from bidding at a sale so that goods may be purchased at less than their true value if no other party is interested in bidding. Section 3 of the 1969 Act provides that where such an agreement is made the seller may avoid the contract and recover the goods or, in default, any loss they have suffered (namely the difference between the sale price and the true or fair price) from any party to the agreement. It is, however, difficult in practice to control these bidders' 'rings' because of problems of proof. Moreover, the Act does not prohibit a genuine agreement to buy the goods on joint account and, in practice, it may well be difficult to distinguish such an agreement from one whereby one dealer agrees not to bid for one item and another dealer agrees not to bid for another item.

2.7 Mistake in the offer or acceptance

2.7.1 English law

Certain kinds of mistake, although traditionally treated as part of the generic subject 'mistake' (as they were in the first edition of this book), are today often treated as part of the law of offer and acceptance. These cases, usually referred to as cases of 'mutual' and

[160] (1859) 1 E & B 309.

[161] Slade (1952) 68 LQR 238; ibid., 457; Gower (1953) 69 LQR 21.

[162] (1857) 8 E & B 647. See also *Starkey* v *Bank of England* [1903] AC 114 and *Sheffield Corpn v Barclay* [1905] AC 392, in both of which it was assumed by the House of Lords virtually without discussion that action in reliance could be treated as consideration in such cases. See also Blackpool and *Fylde Aero Club* v *Blackpool Borough Council* [1990] 3 All ER 25, discussed by Adams and Brownsword (1991) 54 MLR 281

[163] [2001] 1 All ER 944.

'unilateral' mistake, involve a denial by one of the parties that an agreement has ever been reached on the ground that the intentions of the parties, judged objectively or subjectively as the case may be, never coincided. However, the expressions 'mutual mistake' and 'unilateral mistake' are somewhat misleading. The important question is not whether a mistake is one-sided or two-sided, but whether or not the mistake has prevented an agreement from coming into existence. In deciding whether the parties have in fact agreed, or must be taken in law to have agreed, the first thing to determine is whether it is a case where the parties' intentions are to be judged objectively or subjectively, for until this is done it is obviously impossible to say whether the intentions are the same, and hence whether the parties have agreed.

Where neither party is aware of the other party's real intentions, the law is clear that the offeree is entitled to judge the offeror's intentions objectively. If, so judged, the intentions coincide, then there is an agreement, and, if the other requirements of the law are satisfied, a contract. For example, in *Tamplin* v *James*,[164] the defendant agreed to buy a public house under a mistaken impression that a certain field was included in the sale. There was nothing in the sale which should have led the buyer to make this mistake, and the seller was unaware of it. Applying the objective, 'reasonable man' test, the Court of Appeal held that the buyer was liable on the contract for the sale of the public house without the field. The objective test in these cases means no more than that the parties are bound by what a reasonable man would have regarded as their intentions.

It may happen that even on the application of the objective test it is still not possible to spell out any definite contractual agreement between the parties and in such a case there is no contract. For example, in *Raffles* v *Wichelhaus*,[165] the plaintiff agreed to sell and the defendant agreed to buy a consignment of cotton *ex Peerless* from Bombay. In fact, there were two ships of that name, one leaving Bombay in October and the other in December. The plaintiff shipped by the one leaving in December. It was pleaded by the defendant that the ship mentioned in the agreement and intended by the defendant was the one which sailed in October. The plaintiff demurred to this plea, thereby admitting the ambiguity as to which ship was intended by the agreement, and the court held that the buyer was not liable for refusing to accept the consignment arriving in the later ship.

In such circumstances, the main practical reason for holding that there is no contract is that the 'agreement' is incapable of being enforced by the courts because its meaning is not sufficiently certain. The requirement of certainty, while it may for reasons of convenience be treated independently, is really no more than a requirement that an offer must be certain in order to be capable of being converted into a contract by acceptance.[166]

It only remains to add that cases in which the contract will be held void on these grounds are necessarily rare for the application of the objective test will usually produce a definite result. The contract will nearly always be held binding on the terms intended by one party or the other. This is not always a wholly reasonable or fair result because, in

[164] (1880) 15 Ch D 215.
[165] (1864) 2 H & C 906.
[166] In *Scriven* v *Hindley* [1913] 3 KB 564, another case of sale of goods, hemp and tow was sold at an auction by the plaintiffs in bales bearing identical markings. The defendants bid an extravagant price for a lot of tow, believing it was hemp. It was held that the supposed sale could not be enforced against them.

the case of a genuine misunderstanding, there is something to be said for compromising on the terms intended by the parties.[167] But the courts rarely regard themselves as being free to achieve such results.[168]

Where, on the other hand, one party is aware, or ought reasonably to be aware, that the other party's intentions are not the same as their own, the mistaken party's intentions cannot be judged objectively and the party who is not mistaken cannot hold the other to a contract on the terms intended by them. There is no justification for permitting a person to assume that the other meant what they said where the former *knows* that the latter did *not* mean what they said. Thus in the famous case of *Smith* v *Hughes*[169] the defendant bought some oats from the plaintiff but refused to take delivery on the grounds that the oats were not old oats, as he had thought, but new oats. The judge left to the jury the question as to whether the plaintiff had believed the defendant to believe that he was contracting for old oats, and directed them that if they answered that question affirmatively, they should find for the defendant.[170] In ordering a new trial on the ground of misdirection, the court drew a distinction between these two possibilities:

1 If the defendant mistakenly thought that the goods were old then, in the absence of warranty by the plaintiff, the defendant would be bound by the contract even though the plaintiff was aware of the mistake.
2 On the other hand, if the defendant mistakenly thought that the plaintiff was offering to sell him the oats *as old oats*, and the plaintiff was aware of the mistake, then the defendant would not be liable for refusing to accept the oats.

Precisely why he would not have been liable is more difficult to say. One explanation would be that, in this event, there would have been a binding contract to sell old oats and, the oats not being old, the defendant would have been entitled to reject them. But another possibility is that in this event the agreement really would have been void.

Similar uncertainty surrounds the decision in *Hartog* v *Colin & Shields*[171] where the plaintiff snapped up an offer to sell hare skins at so much *per pound* when he must have known that the offeror really meant to offer to sell at that price *per piece*. It was held that the plaintiff could not sue on a contract at the per pound price, but it is not certain what would have happened if the offeror had tried to sue on a contract at the per piece price. The answer would presumably depend on whether the offeror had reasonably understood the offeree to be accepting their intended offer, as opposed to the erroneous offer actually stated, or written.[172]

[167] See, e.g., *Butler Machine Tool Co* v *Ex-Cell-O Corpn* [1979] 1 WLR 401, the 'battle of the forms' case – see Chapter 8

[168] But see, for some special cases, Ball (1983) 99 LQR 572.

[169] (1871) LR 6 QB 597. See also Chapter 7

[170] This complicated question is really only a reflection of the proposition that promises should be enforced in the sense in which the promisor understands the promisee to take them – *Paley's Moral Philosophy* (1809 edn), p. 101 et seq. Paley cites the case of the tyrant Temores (Tamberlance), who, having promised the inhabitants of Sebastia that if they surrendered to him no blood would be shed, buried them alive.

[171] [1939] 3 All ER 566.

[172] The courts in Singapore have grappled repeatedly with the application of mistake in the context of digital transactions. See *Chwee Kin Keong v Digilandmall.com Pte Ltd* [2005] 1 SLR 502 (pricing error on website) and *Quoine Pte Ltd* v *B2C2 Ltd* [2020] SGCA(I) 02 (pricing error in cryptocurrency trading).

The principle to be applied in cases of mistake as to the person is exactly the same, although the application of this principle in this case is more likely to make the contract void. First, a person cannot accept an offer which they know is not intended for them, but for some third person.[173] And, secondly, a person cannot hold another to an acceptance when they know that that other was intending to accept an offer not made by them, but by some third person.[174] Knowledge of the mistake by the one party is essential if the contract is to be held void. It cannot be said that one party is simply unable to accept an offer not intended for them, for a person can accept an offer not intended for them if they reasonably think it was so intended.[175]

It is also essential that there should be some identifiable third person for whom the offer or acceptance was intended if the contract is to be held void.[176] For if there is no such third person, the usual analysis is that the mistaken party does intend to contract with the other party although they are mistaken as to their attributes.[177]

These principles all go back to the late nineteenth century, if not earlier, and are well illustrated by two leading cases from that period which have caused trouble ever since. In *Cundy* v *Lindsay*,[178] a fraudster named Blenkarn ordered some goods from the plaintiffs in a letter in which he signed his name so as to resemble that of Blenkiron & Co, a firm known to the plaintiffs. Although the address of Blenkarn was not the same as that of Blenkiron & Co, they were both in the same street. The plaintiffs, without noticing the discrepancy in the street number, despatched the goods to Blenkarn, who promptly disposed of them to the defendants, who bought in good faith and for value. It was held by the House of Lords that no contract existed between the plaintiffs and Blenkarn, and the case had to be decided as though Blenkarn had stolen the goods; at no stage had the plaintiffs voluntarily decided to entrust the possession of their goods to Blenkarn. On the other hand, in *King's Norton Metal Co* v *Edridge*,[179] a fraudster ordered goods under a false name, which was not that of any identified third party, and the plaintiffs despatched these goods on credit on the strength of the order. Once again the fraudster disposed of the goods to the defendants. The Court of Appeal rejected the plaintiffs' claim on the ground that this was a simple case of a contract voidable for fraud and not a contract wholly void. It is, of course, well-established law that goods obtained under a voidable title and resold to a bona fide purchaser cannot be claimed back by the original owner. The bona fide purchaser obtains a good title, and the original owner is left to pursue their remedy against the fraudulent party, for what that is worth – which is usually very little. The distinction between these two famous cases was considered by the House of Lords in *Shogun Finance Ltd* v *Hudson*,[180] discussed below.

[173] *Boulton* v *Jones* (1857) 27 LJ Ex 117. It must be inferred that the plaintiff knew that the defendant intended to contract with Brocklehurst, and with him alone; otherwise the decision could not be supported today.

[174] *Cundy* v *Lindsay* (1878) 3 App Cas 459.

[175] *Upton RDC* v *Powell* [1942] 1 All ER 220; cf. Blackburn J in *Smith* v *Hughes* (1871) LR 6 QB 597, 607.

[176] *King's Norton Metal Co* v *Edridge* (1897) 14 TLR 98. On this point see the classic analysis of Glanville Williams in (1945) 23 Can Bar Rev 271. See also the House of Lords decision in *Shogun Finance Ltd* v *Hudson* [2003] UKHL 62 discussed below.

[177] See Unger (1955) 18 MLR 259 replying to Wilson (1954) 17 MLR 515.

[178] *Cundy* v *Lundsay* [1878 3 App Cas 459]

[179] (1897) 14 TLR 98.

[180] [2003] UKHL 62.

The application of these cases to situations where parties have dealt with each other face to face has proved particularly troublesome. In *Phillips* v *Brooks*,[181] a swindler bought some jewellery in a shop by representing himself to be 'Sir George Bullough', a real third person known by name, but not personally, to the jeweller. It was held that there was a voidable contract. On the other hand, in *Ingram* v *Little*,[182] a different result was arrived at. Here, a swindler (H) representing himself to be 'PGMH of Caterham', a real person not known personally to the plaintiffs, bought a car from them. The Court of Appeal (Devlin LJ dissenting) held that there was no contract at all between the plaintiffs and H. Sellers LJ summarised the views of the learned judge below, with which he agreed, as follows:

> The judge, treating the plaintiffs as the offerors and the rogue H as the offeree, found that the plaintiffs, in making their offer to sell the car not for cash but for a cheque . . . were under the belief that they were dealing with, and therefore making their offer to, the honest Mr PGMH of Caterham, who they had reason to believe was a man of substance and standing. H, the offeree, knew precisely what was in the minds of the two ladies [i.e. the plaintiffs] for he had put it there, and he knew that their offer was intended for Mr PGMH of Caterham, and that they were making no offer to, and had no intention to contract with him, as he was. There was no offer which he, H, could accept, and therefore there was no contract.[183]

However, in *Lewis* v *Averay*,[184] yet another case of a similar nature in which a fraudster bought a car in return for a cheque by representing himself to be a well-known actor the Court of Appeal threw doubt on *Ingram* v *Little*. In this case, the court emphasised that where parties are dealing with each other face to face there is a strong presumption that there is a contract between them. But only Lord Denning MR suggested that *Ingram* v *Little* was wrongly decided. It was also said to be surprising if the result of such cases was to turn, as suggested by Sellers LJ in *Ingram* v *Little*, on the fraudster's state of mind.

The distinctions drawn in some of these cases are very fine ones; for instance, *Ingram* v *Little* is scarcely distinguishable from *Phillips* v *Brooks* and *Lewis* v *Averay*. So too, *Cundy* v *Lindsay* is barely distinguishable from *King's Norton Metal Co* v *Edridge*. Of course, fine distinctions do not necessarily mean that the distinctions are unsound. It is the job of the law to draw distinctions and fine distinctions are often a necessary consequence. But these cases involve fine distinctions which are based on abstract concepts rather than on real social or commercial distinctions. It is, of course, clear that the only purpose of drawing these distinctions is to decide whether the contract is void or voidable and hence whether or not a bona fide purchaser should be protected. But whether or not the bona fide purchaser should be protected should depend on more substantial considerations than those which decide these cases. It is true that distinctions can be drawn between these cases which to some degree are more real than those which the courts drew. For instance, in *Phillips* v *Brooks*, the plaintiff was a shopkeeper who dealt in jewellery, whereas in *Ingram* v *Little*, the plaintiffs were two private sellers. Plainly, a shopkeeper who sells goods on credit to someone not known to them by sight and accepts a cheque in return is, in many respects, in a very different situation from a private seller. On the other hand, the plaintiff in *Lewis* v *Averay* was also a private seller and yet he was held not protected. Equally, in

[181] [1919] 2 KB 243
[182] [1961] 1 QB 31.
[183] Ibid At p. 44.
[184] [1972] 3 All ER 907. See also *Whittaker* v *Campbell* [1983] 3 All ER 582.

comparing *Cundy* v *Lindsay* with the *King's Norton* case, it is clear that the sellers in the latter case consciously took a much greater commercial risk than the sellers in the former case. In the *King's Norton* case, the sellers fulfilled an order by delivering goods on credit to a company of whom they had never heard and without any attempt to secure payment in advance. In *Cundy* v *Lindsay*, the sellers did at least think they were dealing with buyers known to them by repute. These distinctions may well be valid and they may even have influenced the actual decisions, but they are not the distinctions drawn by the courts.[185]

These cases were reviewed by the House of Lords in *Shogun Finance Ltd* v *Hudson*,[186] in which the authority of *Cundy* v *Lindsay*[187] was affirmed in a majority decision. In that case, a rogue, who had stolen the identity of a real person, a Mr Patel, purported to enter into a hire-purchase agreement in Mr Patel's name to finance the purchase of a motor car, with the plaintiff finance company. The plaintiffs carried out the usual credit status checks on Mr Patel, and accepted the purported proposal of Mr Patel. The dealer then allowed the rogue to take possession of the vehicle, and the rogue sold it to the defendant, who bought it in good faith and without notice. It was held by the majority that there was no contract between the rogue and the finance company; the only agreement that could have been in existence was the purported one between the finance company and Mr Patel. Accordingly, the defendant could not acquire title under s. 27 of the Hire-Purchase Act 1964.[188] Lord Nicholls and Lord Millett delivered strong dissenting speeches, and considered the decisions in *Phillips* v *Brooks Ltd* and *Lewis* v *Averay* preferable to that in *Cundy* v *Lindsay*. Lord Millett would have been prepared to overrule *Cundy* v *Lindsay*, *Ingram* v *Little* and the rather unsatisfactory decision in *Hector* v *Lyons*.[189] The result of the majority holding is that the law of mistake in England and Wales requires a distinction to be drawn between dealings in writing, and face-to-face dealings.

Proposals were made to abolish the distinction between void and voidable contracts, and to protect the bona fide purchaser in both cases alike.[190] But these proposals were not implemented, and, even if they had been, it is not clear that they would wholly dispose of the difficulties. So long as a person from whom goods are *stolen* is to be entitled to recover their goods even from a bona fide purchaser to whom the thief may resell them, it will be necessary to distinguish between cases where the goods have been so stolen and cases where the original owner has been deprived of the goods by fraud or deception of some kind. Frauds and deceptions take a very large variety of forms, and it will almost certainly remain necessary to draw fine distinctions between fraud which does not, and fraud which does, totally negative the owner's consent to parting with the goods. It is true that the line between the cases could be drawn a little beyond where it is now drawn; it could (for instance) be so drawn that a bona fide purchaser obtains title where the owner has *voluntarily entrusted* the goods to the fraudster, or where they have *voluntarily parted*

[185] The HL decision in *Shogun Finance* v *Hudson* [2003] UKHL 62 has scarcely improved matters. Though it does seem that *Lewis v Averay* may have been wrongly decided as *Cundy* v *Lindsay* (a HL decision) was not cited.

[186] [2003] UKHL 62.

[187] (1878) 3 App Cas 459.

[188] As to which see Chapter 12.

[189] REF Unsatisfactory because the facts were unclear. The best explanation for the decision would have been the maxim 'He who comes to equity must come with clean hands' as the plaintiff, who was seeking specific performance of a contract for the purchase of a house, had forged his son's signature – see *Shogun Finance Ltd* v *Hudson*, above, per Lord Walker at [192].

with the possession of them. The second formulation would probably be wide enough to protect the third party in a *Cundy* v *Lindsay* situation, though the first might not. But it will remain necessary to distinguish cases of voluntary parting with possession from cases of fraud or deception so great that the owner is deprived of their possession without really consenting at all. Therefore, fine distinctions will almost inevitably remain here unless the law is so drastically reformed that even a bona fide purchaser from an actual thief is allowed protection, and that raises many doubts. It has never been proposed as a serious suggestion here.[191]

2.8 Formalities

2.8.1 Repeal of formal requirements

In 1954 the Law Reform (Enforcement of Contracts) Act repealed s. 4 of the 1893 Act, which had been law since the enactment of the Statute of Frauds 1677, with the result that nearly all contracts for the sale of goods can now be made orally, irrespective of the value of the goods sold.

Section 4 of the Sale of Goods Act 1979 enacts:

(1) Subject to this and any other Act, a contract of sale may be made in writing (either with or without seal), or by word of mouth, or partly in writing and partly by word of mouth, or may be implied from the conduct of the parties.
(2) Nothing in this section affects the law relating to corporations.

Since the repeal of the old s. 4, the opening words of the above section have lost any real meaning as there are no other provisions in the Act relating to formalities. The only exceptions which need to be noted to the general effect of s. 4 are contracts of hire-purchase or credit-sale, which come within the provisions of the Consumer Credit Act 1974 and contracts for the purchase of a British ship or of a share therein, which come within s. 16 of and Sched. 1, para. 2 to the Merchant Shipping Act 1995.[192]

It is possible, in principle, that a contract for the sale of goods may sometimes also be a contract for the sale of an interest in land within s. 2 of the Law of Property (Miscellaneous Provisions) Act 1989, or s. 1 of the Requirements of Writing (Scotland) Act 1995, and may therefore be void if it is not in writing.

This possibility arises from the fact that 'goods' as defined by s. 61 of the Sale of Goods Act includes 'emblements, industrial growing crops, and things attached to or forming part of the land which are agreed to be severed before sale or under the contract of sale'. There can be little doubt that this definition embraces certain goods, *fructus naturales* (wildlife and naturally occurring and cultivated crops), which at common law were regarded as being an interest in land. The fact that since 1893 these are 'goods' within the meaning of the Sale of Goods Act does not rule out the possibility that they may at the same time be land within the meaning of the Law of Property (Miscellaneous Provisions) Act.

[190] See the Twelfth Report of the Law Reform Committee, discussed in Chapter 12.
[191] But see criticism of the Sale of Goods (Amendment) Act 1994, and there is something to be said for the clarity provided by Uniform Commercial Code, Art. 2-403 (1)(a) discussed in *Shogun Finance* v *Hudson* (above) by Lord Millett at [84].
[192] Section 16 and Sch. 1, para. 2 (1).

2.9 Bills of sale

A further word needs to be said on bills of sale within the Bills of Sale Acts.[193] Strictly speaking, these Acts do not require a contract of sale to which they apply to be in writing or in any particular form. There is nothing to prevent a person buying goods under an oral contract and allowing the seller of them to remain in possession of them, so far as the Bills of Sale Acts are concerned but in practice, a buyer who does not obtain possession of the goods would almost invariably wish to have some written evidence of the sale and if the sale is in writing, or is evidenced in writing (even by a mere receipt), the Acts will apply.

Under the Act of 1878, a sale of goods which is evidenced in writing, and under which the seller remains in possession, is void against trustees in bankruptcy and persons seizing goods in judicial execution, unless the sale is made by a written instrument called a bill of sale and registered in accordance with the Act.[194] No particular form is required for a bill of sale under the Act of 1878. But a breach of this Act does not affect the validity of a sale as between the immediate parties to it; the sale itself remains completely valid between the parties.

The above provisions only apply if the first transaction is a genuine sale. If it only takes the form of a sale but is intended to operate as a security, the Sale of Goods Act does not apply at all by reason of s. 62(4). Such a transaction is covered by s. 8 of the Bills of Sale Act 1882, which makes the transaction completely void, even as between the immediate parties, unless it is made by a registered bill of sale.[195] Moreover, a bill of sale by way of security must be made in the form prescribed in the Schedule to the Act of 1882 and failure to comply again renders the bill wholly void.

The two Acts were designed for quite different purposes. The 1878 Act was designed to protect third parties, while the second Act was an early sort of consumer protection measure intended to protect needy borrowers who gave charges over household possessions and such like in the late Victorian period, often on terribly harsh terms. So the 1882 Act was a major interference with freedom of contract, which forced lenders to use the statutory form of bill of sale and so prevented them from inserting into the contract their own contractual clauses.

The two purposes of the Acts – the protection of third parties, and consumer protection – were somewhat confused by the fact that the first Act applied to outright sales, and the second to sales which were designed to be security for loans. In fact third parties require protection in both cases – indeed, more often in the second than in the first. An owner of goods who grants a charge or mortgage over them, while retaining possession, has been put in a position in which they can easily mislead third parties as to their assets, and if they become insolvent, it is often unfair that the third parties may receive nothing, while the chargee simply claims all the goods by virtue of some secret document. Because the Acts are so easily evaded, the 1878 Act really needs to be replaced by more up-to-date legislation.

[193] Noted above, at section 2.2.5 when distinguishing from contracts of sale. Note the Bills of Sale Acts have never applied in Scotland.

[194] Bills of Sale Act 1878, s. 8 of which is still in force as regards sales, despite its apparent repeal by s. 15 of the Act of 1882.

[195] Nevertheless, sums actually advanced on an unregistered bill of sale are apparently recoverable in a restitutionary claim for money had and received: *North Central Wagon Finance Co Ltd* v *Brailsford* [1962] 1 WLR 1288.

The second main purpose of the Acts – consumer protection of small borrowers and credit users – was also largely a failure, and the Acts were superseded, first by the Money-lenders Acts, and now by the Consumer Credit Act 1974 (now itself partially superseded). So far as this purpose is concerned, therefore, the Acts could now safely be repealed.

Neither Act worked well and both are largely obsolete in practice. The two Acts were found excessively technical in application, so that alternative legal methods were devised for achieving the objectives of the parties through transactions, which did not come within either of the Acts. In particular, the invention of the hire-purchase contract very soon rendered both Acts largely obsolete. In modern times, the Acts rarely apply except by accident: that is to say, parties rarely knowingly enter into a transaction intending it to be governed by the Acts, but technical infringements of the Acts remain a common legal problem.

3

Subject-matter of the contract

3.1 Meaning of 'goods'

The term 'goods' is defined by s. 61 as including 'all personal chattels other than things in action and money', or, for Scots law, 'all corporeal moveables except money'. The term includes 'emblements, industrial growing crops, and things attached to or forming part of the land which are agreed to be severed before sale or under the contract of sale'.[1]

This definition is extensive – indeed, virtually all-embracing[2] – but there are nevertheless some 'things' which do not, or may not, fall within this definition. First, the definition clearly excludes non-physical items, such as company shares, which are technically 'things in action' or incorporeal moveables and so are excluded by the plain words of the definition. Similarly, items of 'intellectual property' such as copyrights, patents and trademarks are not 'personal chattels' or corporeal moveables and so fall outside the definition, although of course goods may exist which embody these intellectual property rights.[3]

3.1.1 Digital content/software and smart goods under the Sale of Goods Act 1979

An important, and still not yet wholly resolved matter, is whether computer software and indeed 'digital content' of any kind,[4] such as music, film and applications for smartphones and tablets, constitutes or should be regarded as akin to 'goods' within the meaning of the Act. Today, the problem has two facets, the first relates to the fact that software and digital content is now predominantly 'supplied' as a download. As merely a licensed artistic work, it has none of the characteristics of a chattel and a sale of it is categorically not within the scope of the Act, even though, as will be seen below, if the same content

[1] Emblements were growing crops sown by a tenant for life which his personal representatives had the right to take. They were personal property. In Scotland see *Boskabelle Ltd* v *Laird* [2006] CSOH 173; 2006 SLT 1079.

[2] The difficult question as to whether forms of energy such as gas and electricity are goods has not come before a court in the UK. In *Singer Co, Link Simulation Systems Div* v *Baltimore Gas and Electricity Company* 558 A 2d 419 it was held that electricity in an electricity company's distribution system was not a 'good' within §2-105 of the Uniform Commercial Code (so that the company was not liable under the Sales Article for electrical failures), and this corresponds to similar decisions in other states. Given that the definition of 'goods' in the above section is if anything broader than that in the Sale of Goods Act, it could well be that a court in the UK would come to a similar conclusion.

[3] By contrast, for the purposes of the Law of Property Act 1925 'property' is defined so as to include intellectual property – s. 205(1)(xx).

[4] *See Southwark London Borough Council* v *IBM UK Ltd* [2011] EWHC 549 (TCC) in which Akenhead J expressed that all such content could be regarded as sufficiently similar in nature to be treated in a like manner.

were acquired on physical media, this would be regarded as a sale of goods within the scope of the Act. This disparity leaves the buyer of digital content with potentially little protection beyond that afforded by the contract under which the content, or the licence to it, is acquired. The rapid obsolescence of physical media has led to special provisions for consumer contracts in respect of digital content being included in the Consumer Rights Act 2015.[5] However, the position in respect of a non-consumer buyer of digital content remains unchanged and the disparity in protection, which is elaborated below, is of some concern.

The other, now largely historical, facet of the problem concerns software and other 'digital content' supplied on some form of durable media, such as a CD or DVD or solid state drive. Software supplied in this way is usually a 'composite' of intellectual property (the code that comprises software is protected as a literary work by the law of copyright)[6] and the physical media or components on which the software was stored/supplied, which could be regarded as goods. The copyright in the software, which represented the majority of the value paid for the software by the buyer/licensee, was merely licensed by the developer to make working copies of the physical media and to load the software onto a computer, acts which otherwise would be infringements of copyright.[7] The only sale therefore was of the physical media, which is usually of nominal value and arguably incidental to the contract for the software itself.

The question whether a sale of software sold on physical media was a sale of goods was answered both by the Outer House of the Court of Session and by the Court of Appeal, in decisions which are now of diminished importance in the light of technological advancements but which remain good law and continue to not offer a wholly satisfactory answer to the question of the status of digital content supplied in this way under the Act. In *Beta Computers (Europe) Ltd* v *Adobe Systems (Europe) Ltd*,[8] the defender had ordered from the pursuer by telephone a standard computer package to upgrade its existing software. The software was delivered in a package which bore the words 'Opening the Informix S.I. software package indicates your acceptance of these terms and conditions'. These were the terms and conditions of Informix's copyright licence, Informix being the proprietor of the software. The defender did not open the package but attempted to return it. The pursuer refused to accept its return, and sued for payment of the price. The pursuer argued that it had supplied exactly what was ordered, and that it was not concerned with the terms of the licence imposed by the authors of the software. The defender argued that acceptance of the licence conditions was an implied condition suspensive of its agreement with the pursuer. Lord Penrose held that the supply of proprietary software for a price was a single contract *sui generis* though it contained elements of contracts such as sales of goods and the grant of a licence. It was an essential feature of such a contract that the supplier undertook to make available to the purchaser *both* the medium on which the program was recorded *and* the right to access and use the software. There could be no *consensus*

[5] This is considered in detail in Chapter 19.
[6] The level of copyright protection afforded to computer software is governed by the Copyright (Computer Programs) Regulations 1992, SI 1992/3233.
[7] See Copyright, Designs and Patents Act 1988, s. 17(1) and (2).
[8] 1996 SLT 604.

ad idem until the conditions of use stipulated by the copyright owner were produced and accepted by the parties, which could not occur earlier than the tender of those conditions to the purchaser. Furthermore, whether the tender of software subject to conditions for use was regarded as a breach of a previously unconditional contract, or as being subject to a suspensive condition entitling the purchasers to reject if the conditions for use were unacceptable, or as made when there was no concluded contract, the defender was entitled to reject.[9]

In *St Albans City and District Council* v *International Computers Ltd*, both Scott Baker J at first instance and Sir Iain Glidewell in the Court of Appeal expressed the view that a computer disk is within the definition of 'goods' contained in s. 61 of the Sale of Goods Act 1979 and s. 18 of the Supply of Goods and Services Act 1982. A computer program, on the other hand, is not goods. However, when a defective program is encoded and supplied on a disk, the supplier of the disk will be in breach of the terms as to quality and fitness implied by s. 14 of the Sale of Goods Act or s. 9 of the Supply of Goods and Services Act. Accordingly, both judges were of the view that a supply of a disk carrying software is either a sale or a supply of goods. The two decisions are clearly at odds. Arguably, it is less important to worry about how digital content fits into existing legal categories, than what the respective liabilities of the creator of the content and any intermediary supplier or distributor ought to be.[10] Once the latter is decided, other questions are relatively straightforward. We return to this below.

In a crucial passage,[11] Lord Penrose criticised both the views expressed by Christopher Reed,[12] to the effect that where software is supplied on a physical medium it should be regarded as physical property like a book or a record, and the views expressed by Steyn J in *Eurodynamics Systems plc* v *General Automation Ltd*,[13] that the transfer of software is a transfer of a product. Lord Penrose said:

> This reasoning appears to me to be unattractive, at least in the context with which this case is concerned. It appears to emphasise the role of the physical medium, and to relate the transaction in the medium to sale or hire of goods. It would have the somewhat odd result that the dominant characteristic of the complex product, in terms of value or of the significant interests of parties, would be subordinated to the medium by which it was transmitted to the user in analysing the true nature and effect of the contract. If one obtained computer programs by telephone, they might be introduced into one's own hardware and used as effectively as if the medium were a disk or CD or magnetic tape.

The basic argument that the rights of the parties should not depend upon the medium of supply must be right. But the point has to be made that there is the possibility that almost *any* original copyright work can, now, be delivered either on a physical medium or online, with the latter predominating. Does the fact that the contents of a book can be delivered online, or the image of a painting, mean that sales of books and paintings must now be treated as *sui generis* and therefore outside of the Sale of Goods Act? Surely

9 We deal further with this aspect of the case later – in Chapter 8

10 Even before the Supply of Goods and Services Act 1982 the courts tended to treat contracts analogous to sales of goods in the same way as sales of goods so far as the implied warranties were concerned – see *Young & Marten Ltd* v *McManus Childs Ltd* [1969] 1 AC 454.

11 At pp. 608–9.

12 *Computer Law* (2nd edn, 2004, Cambridge University Press), p. 44.

13 6 September 1988 (unreported). He does not appear to have had other English authorities cited to him.

not: it is a characteristic of many supplies of information that they can either be carried out using goods media, or supplied directly online. But, in the case of books, we distinguish the liability of the author from that of the shop and publisher. If a book has missing pages, or falls to pieces just after it is bought, the shop is clearly liable under the Sale of Goods Act quality terms, and so is the publisher who sold it to the shop. On the other hand, neither is likely to be held liable in respect of erroneous information in a reference book.[14] This is a useful starting point in considering the liability of the various undertakings in the distribution chain for software. First of all, however, it may be useful to explore where the analogy between books and software breaks down.

Clearly, in one respect digital content is analogous to a book, and if it is physically defective, the seller should be liable in the same way as the seller of a physically defective book. But there is an important difference when we consider the contents. However defective the content of a book, it is unlikely to harm its physical environment.[15] Software, on the other hand, may cause harm, and the probability of this occurring (although small) is not insignificant. Defective software which is unreliable or causes data to be lost can do considerable damage.[16] It has been suggested that an analogy can be drawn between a reference work, such as a DIY manual, and software, since software is commonly described as a 'set of instructions to a computer'.[17] The analogy is false, however. A computer cannot, for now at least, 'understand' in any epistemological sense: it is a machine, and simply follows instructions.[18] This would argue for a more 'mechanical' finding of liability in the case of defective software. Equally, the rapid development of systems that utilise artificial intelligence and machine learning and goods where those systems are embedded, may challenge that position conclusion in the near future.

In those increasingly rare instances when software is sold over the counter in stores in the same way as books or music, for some sorts of defect the buyer would expect to have a remedy against the store. Equally, most stores would likely expect their liability to be the same in both cases. There are two broad types of defect where the buyer ought probably to have a remedy against the store. The first is where software contains a virus, malware or some other unwanted program (or can introduce one), or code likely to impede performance or cause damage to the user's system. Here, the supplier should incur liability equivalent to that laid down in the quality warranties of the Sale of Goods Act. The second is when the content of the physical media on which the software is supplied may simply be corrupt, just as a book with illegible printing is considered defective. Defects in the way the program itself performs, however, are more analogous to defects in the contents of a book, and liability should, in principle, be similar.

[14] See *Winter* v *G P Putnam's Sons* 938 F 2d 1033, 9th Circ (1991), where the plaintiffs suffered serious physical injury after eating poisonous mushrooms, having relied upon a reference work. The court distinguished *Fluor Corporation* v *Jeppesen & Co* 216 Cal Rptr 68 (liability of products liability theory in respect of a defective aeronautical chart). See also *Cardozo* v *True* 342 So 2d 1053. For a discussion of the liability of the sellers of books containing erroneous information, see Lloyd [1993] JBL 48.

[15] Though a book infested with bookworm could obviously do so.

[16] Though contrary to popular belief, this is rarely serious. The damage done by the vast majority of viruses can be made good in a fairly short time.

[17] MacDonald [1995] MLR 585, 590.

[18] In any event, the leading case on misleading instructions, *Wormell* v *R H M Agriculture (East) Ltd* [1987] 1 WLR 1091, is not satisfactory, especially when applied to software.

Liability for defective software should not, in principle, depend upon the carrier medium, but upon whether what is involved is mass-produced 'off-the-shelf' software, or customised software specially written for a client. It is helpful as a starting point to take an example. Suppose an accounting package for small businesses had a defect in its program which caused certain items to be under-recorded so that a false picture of the profitability of the business emerged over a period of time. Would the developer who wrote the program be liable? It might be. We might make it liable on one of two bases: negligence in writing the program; or, in the absence of negligence, loss spreading. If we adhere to the view that the software house is liable in negligence, we might want to make the seller (if any) who sold the software liable as a conduit for passing liability back up the line, and achieve this by saying there is a breach of the quality warranties of the Sale of Goods Act; but we must be clear that this is what we are doing, and that the store's liability is no greater than the ultimate liability of the supplier. We are not doing it *simply* because, if the program was off-the-shelf software, we think off-the-shelf software is goods. On the other hand, if we adopt a loss-spreading approach, we might make the store liable as the best loss spreader in the distribution chain, by making it liable under the Sale of Goods Act, but *strictly speaking* on this approach we might not want to make the software house liable at all, for the same sort of reasons that we do not make the author of a defective cookery book liable if a recipe is wrong. In the United States, where these issues have been discussed openly by the courts, there is authority for this approach.[19] This approach to the problem of product liability is probably more open than any European court would be able to stomach. They are likely to opt either for a fudge, or for what essentially boils down to negligence liability, as a basis for awarding damages.

It is now many years since the courts had the opportunity to further explore in the light of technological developments and changing user habits, the question of if and when software can amount to goods. Two recent decisions, while not directly concerned with a 'sale' suggest that this is not possible. In *Your Response Ltd* v *Datateam Business Media Ltd*[20] the Court of Appeal considered whether a lien could be exercised over a database – 'digital asset' perhaps, rather than software but still something broadly analogous. The court had little difficulty in finding that this was an intangible thing and therefore not one over which a lien could be exercised. Moore-Bick LJ drew on the House of Lords decision in *OBG Ltd* v *Allan*,[21] which upheld the 'sharp' distinction between tangible and intangible property and the rights that subsist in each.

The issue arose again in a case involving the Commercial Agents (Council Directive) Regulations 1993/3053. The Regulations, partly due to their age and partly to the EU Treaty context, refer only to contracts for goods or services, but there is no definition of 'goods'. The High Court in *Software Incubator Ltd* v *Computer Associates Ltd*[22] held that goods should be understood broadly to include software. It should be noted the English High Court was seeking to interpret the meaning of 'goods' flexibly here and to allow the meaning of 'goods' to evolve with commercial practice. However, in 2018 the Court of

[19] *Goldberg* v *Kollsman Instrument Corp* 191 NE 2d 81 (1963).
[20] [2014] EWCA Civ 281.
[21] [2007] UKHL 21.
[22] [2016] EWHC 1587.

Appeal took a different view, having reviewed both domestic and CJEU case law which has touched on this issue:

> The EU legislature has: (i) proceeded on the basis of the well-established meaning of "goods" being limited to tangible, moveable items . . . it has not adopted a wider definition of "goods" to include intangible items . . . For the purposes of my conclusion, I find it relevant that the legislature opted to create a sui generis obligation—the supply of digital content—rather than widening the meaning of "goods". The novel legislative solution demonstrates to my mind that this is clearly an area in which reform must come from the European legislature and/or the UK Parliament and not via judicial interpretation.'[23]

The matter was appealed to the Supreme Court, which agreed to make a preliminary reference to the CJEU regarding the correct interpretation of the Directive underpinning the Regulations. In its ruling, the CJEU disagreed with the Court of Appeal's analysis and concluded that 'goods' should be understood to include software/digital content.[24] The Supreme Court treated the appeal as allowed and the first instance judgment reinstated, but without handing down its own judgment.[25]

A further challenge arises in respect of so-called 'smart goods', i.e., goods which have embedded software required so the goods can perform all their functions. Many goods that might once have been purely mechanical now rely on such embedded software, including cars, household goods and machinery. Where such software is preloaded as part of the manufacturing process and not subsequently updated, one might regard the software as a component of the goods, so if the goods fail to work, the Sale of Goods Act would apply.

However, 'smart goods' are characterised by their ability to connect to a network and/or the internet, which allows such goods to exchange information with other goods, as well as to be monitored remotely and software updates and upgrades to be made.

The English Sale of Goods Act 1979 does not recognise these goods. The Court of Appeal in *St Albans City and DC* v *International Computers Ltd*[26] suggested *obiter* that a software programme contained on a physical disk was 'goods' for the purposes of the Sale of Goods Act 1979. This would lend support for the assumption that goods with preloaded software are within the definition of 'goods' in s. 61. However, it remains open whether 'smart goods' would also qualify, particularly where the software element is considerable. A more complex issue arises where there is sale of physical products which completely rely on digital software or elements to function such as internet hub/router which in comparison to the Fridge or washing machine which can function if a part of digital element is not e.g. connecting to internet or Bluetooth, but the router cannot be considered functioning without supplying internet.

However, one of the main challenges of including 'smart goods' within the notion of goods (even through legislative reform) is the complexity associated with these types of goods. For instance, such goods require frequent updates to keep the functionality of the goods updated. Often, such updates are included in the purchase price paid by the buyer in

[23] [2018] EWCA Civ 518 at para 66-67 (Gloster LJ).

[24] See Case C-410/19 *The Software Incubator Ltd* v *Computer Associates (UK)* Ltd ECLI:EU:C:2021:742.

[25] The text of the order was provided to the authors by the Supreme Court registry, but does not appear to be publicly available.

[26] [1996] 4 All E.R. 481.

advance; moreover, these updates are not usually in control of the seller and thus operation of the goods depends on actions taken by a third party not privy to the original contract.[27]

If it were accepted that 'smart goods' are included in the Sale of Goods Act, then further matters would need to be considered, not least the question of whether a transaction for smart goods could still be described as a 'sale' at all. Although the buyer will receive a physical item and almost certainly become its owner, the same cannot be said in respect of the digital content, particularly where this is controlled remotely. Indeed, that content might be disabled after several years, causing the goods to lose much, if not all, of their functionality. This would make it arguable that the transaction in question no longer involves the transfer of property as understood for the purposes of the Sale of Goods Act. It is also arguable that it still does, but that any interference with the functionality of the goods at a later time could be a breach of the implied warranty as to quiet possession.[28]

Finally, it is useful in this context to examine whether there are rational policy reasons for the liability imposed on suppliers of services such as the writing of customised software being less strict than the liability imposed on the supplier of mass-produced goods. It can be argued that there are. In the first place, the distinction can be justified in terms of a risk-spreading approach. Suppliers of expert services to individual customers in the nature of things do not have the high volumes necessary to spread the risk among a large number of customers, whereas producers of off-the-shelf software are more likely to.[29] Secondly, the customers usually deal directly with the providers of the services, and are therefore in a better position to prove negligence than is the consumer injured by a defective product.[30] Thirdly, the provider of the services and the customer are in a position to bargain for the level of liability to be undertaken. If nothing is said, the supplier's duty is only to exercise reasonable care and skill, but if a higher level of liability is accepted, as in *Saphena Computing Ltd* v *Allied Collection Agencies Ltd*,[31] then so be it. Lastly, the provider of a service which is essentially a 'one-off' is not in a position to test the software in the way in which the manufacturer of a mass-produced product is.

Conversely, the imposition of a 'strict' standard of liability on a supplier for the sort of defects in respect of which it was suggested above that a supplier of software ought to be liable in much the same way as a bookseller, would seem to be justified by precisely the considerations which apply in contracts for the sale of goods generally. Making the supplier liable is a convenient mechanism for passing liability back up the line to the person ultimately responsible for the defect, the manufacturer. But whether the manufacturer's *ultimate* liability for defects is in fact different from negligence liability in the Learned Hand sense is questionable. In *US* v *Carroll Towing Co*,[32] which we will return to later,[33] Justice Learned Hand suggested that the duty of care in negligence is a function of three variables: (1) the probability of harm; (2) the gravity of the resulting injury; and (3) the burden of

[27] Katarzyna Kryla-Cudna 'The update obligation for smart products under the EU Sale of Goods Directive: the seller's right of redress and the CISG', (2024), 29,Uniform Law Review 287–304, at 290.
[28] See Chapter 5, at section 5.2.2.
[29] See *La Rossa* v *Scientific Design Co* 402 F 2d 937, 942, 3d Circ (1968).
[30] See, for example, *Daniels* v *R W White & Sons and Tabard* [1938] 4 All ER 258.
[31] 3 May 1989 (unreported).
[32] 159 F 2d 169 (1947).
[33] See Chapter 21.

adequate precautions. If we build into (3) opportunity costs, we have a fairly good, workable formula for understanding the nature of so-called 'strict' product liability. Thus, software sold in 2020 will have technical improvements not present in equivalent software sold in 2010, yet the 2000 software is not defective even though they might have had the 2010 features had the programmers worked at it longer and the software house delayed marketing for this purpose. Little software would appear on the market if this were not the case, and the opportunity costs of doing without admittedly less than perfect software would be great.

In other words, the key to the conundrum is not to get lost in questions as to whether or not software is goods, but to focus on who is being sued in respect of what sort of defect, and to be clear as to the basis on which liability is being imposed. The imposition of liability on the basis of loss spreading is different from the imposition of liability on the basis of negligence in the special sense in which it was used above. In Europe, generally, liability in this special sense (negligence) is arguably what is accepted under the Product Liability Directive,[34] and, as suggested above, a shop's liability for defects ought not in principle to be greater than that of the ultimate manufacturer.

The question as to the warranties to be implied in software supply contracts has been explored in a number of cases. In *Watford Electronics Ltd* v *Sanderson*,[35] Judge Thornton QC held that the Sale of Goods Act was not applicable, as the software had not been sold, but merely licensed (as is usually the case). However, he held that quality warranties could be implied from two sources: there was a contract of bailment within s. 6(1) of the Supply of Goods and Services Act 1982 because the definition of 'software' in the contract meant that goods were being supplied. Possession, not ownership, of the software was being transferred subject to a use payment. This meant that the terms implied by the 1982 Act,[36] which are identical to those in sales of goods, could be implied. Given that what was being acquired was not a medium, but the software itself, this argument is somewhat difficult to follow. However, he also held that similar terms to those implied by this Act, and the Sale of Goods Act, could be implied at common law. In the light of the views expressed in *Young & Marten Ltd* v *McManus Childs Ltd*,[37] this must be correct.[38] This issue was not pursued further in the Court of Appeal.

The seller's assertions about the performance of the software will often be crucial. These representations may themselves, of course, give rise to a claim for damages for material misrepresentation.[39]

Another modern area of doubt as to the scope of the definition of 'goods' has previously been noted. It is not wholly clear whether the term 'goods' would cover human blood for transfusion or other similar items not ordinarily thought to be the subject of commerce.

[34] See Chapter 20 *et seq*.

[35] [2001] 1 All ER (Comm) 696.

[36] See 1982 Act, s. 9.

[37] [1969] 1 AC 454.

[38] *Watford Electronics* was discussed at length in the later case of *SAM Business Systems Ltd* v *Hedley & Co* [2002] EWHC 2733 (TCC) but only in relation to the application of the Unfair Contract Terms Act 1977. See also on this latter point *Horace Holman Group Ltd* v *Sherwood International Group Ltd* (TCC) 12 April 2000 (unreported).

[39] See *Eurodynamics Systems plc* v *General Automation Ltd*, 6 September 1988 (unreported) – statement by the sellers that their system supported ANSI Cobol 74 programming language. As to material misrepresentations which give rise to a claim for damages, see Chapter 4, at section 4.7.

A further point which requires comment has previously been referred to briefly, but remains to be dealt with here. This point concerns the meaning of the latter part of the statutory definition. Since the products of the soil must always be sold with a view to their ultimate severance 'under the contract of sale', it appears that, whether or not they are also land within the meaning of s. 2 of the Law of Property (Miscellaneous Provisions) Act 1989, they are now always goods within the meaning of the Sale of Goods Act. It is, however, still necessary to distinguish the products of the soil or 'things attached to or forming part of the land' on the one hand, from the actual land itself, or interests therein, on the other. The sale of sand from a quarry, for example, is not a sale of things attached to or forming part of the land, but a sale of an interest in the land itself. Thus, in *Morgan* v *Russell*,[40] it was held that the sale of cinders and slag, which were not in definite or detached heaps resting on the ground, was not a sale of goods but a sale of an interest in land and, therefore, the Sale of Goods Act did not apply. Similarly, in the Australian case of *Mills* v *Stockman*,[41] a quantity of slate which had been quarried and then left on some land as waste material for many years was held to be part of the land, and not goods. The slate was 'unwanted dross cast on one side with the intention that it should remain on the land indefinitely, and, by implication, that it should form part of the land'.[42]

3.2 Different types of goods

Section 5 of the Act is as follows:

> (1) The goods which form the subject of a contract of sale may be either existing goods, owned or possessed by the seller, or goods to be manufactured or acquired by him after the making of the contract of sale, in this Act called 'future goods'.
> (2) There may be a contract or the sale of goods, the acquisition of which by the seller depends upon a contingency which may or may not happen.
> (3) Where by a contract of sale the seller purports to effect a present sale of future goods, the contract operates as an agreement to sell the goods.

The subject-matter of the contract of sale may be either existing goods owned or possessed by the seller, or future goods, or (a possibility not mentioned by the Act) a *spes*, or chance.

3.2.1 Existing goods

Little need be said here except to point out that existing goods may be either specific or unascertained, and that important consequences follow from this distinction; for example, in relation to the application of s. 6 and in connection with the passing of the property. These will be discussed later.[143]

[40] [1909] 1 KB 357.
[41] (1966–67) 116 CLR 61.
[42] Per Barwick CJ at 71.
[43] See Chapter 5 and Chapter 10.

3.2.2 Future goods

Future goods include goods not yet in existence and goods in existence but not yet acquired by the seller. For those parts of the Act dealing with the passing of property, it is probably safe to say that future goods can never be specific goods within the meaning of the Act. There remains some doubt about a number of other sections, such as ss. 6 and 7, which apply to contracts for the sale of specific goods. In cases under s. 7 of the Act, future goods, if sufficiently identified, may be specific goods in the limited sense that their destruction may frustrate the contract. In *Howell* v *Coupland*,[44] a sale of 200 tonnes of potatoes to be grown on a particular piece of land was held to be a sale of specific goods, despite the fact that they were not existing goods, for the purpose of the common law rules of frustration. Failure of the crop was thus held to avoid the contract. Since the Act was passed, it is largely immaterial whether this result is arrived at by application of s. 7 or not because the same result may be arrived at by holding the contract to be a sale within s. 5(2) dependent upon a contingency.[45]

The most important question in connection with future goods, the passing of the property, will be dealt with later.[46]

3.2.3 A *spes*

The sale of a *spes* – a chance – must be distinguished from the contingent sale of future goods, though the distinction is not so much as to the subject-matter of the contract but as to its construction. It is possible for a person to agree to buy future goods from a particular source and to take the chance (or, in language appropriate to the sale of goods, the risk) of the goods never coming into existence. For example, a person may agree to buy whatever crop is produced from a particular field at a fixed price.

A transaction such as that in *Howell* v *Coupland* is therefore open to at least[47] three possible constructions:

1 It may be a contingent sale of goods within s. 5(2), in which case if the crop does not come into existence the contract will not become operative at all and neither party is bound.
2 Alternatively, it may be an unconditional sale – that is, the seller may absolutely undertake to deliver the goods, so that in effect he warrants that there will be a crop, in which case, if there is no crop, he will be liable for non-delivery.
3 Thirdly, it may be a sale of a mere chance – that is, the buyer may take the risk of the crop failing completely, in which case the price is still payable.

[44] (1876) 1 QBD 258. Similarly, in *Goldsborough Mort & Co Ltd* v *Carter* (1914) 19 CLR 429, the Australian High Court held (before the enactment of the Sale of Goods Act in New South Wales) that a sale of 'about' 4,000 sheep pastured on certain lands was a sale of specific goods although the sheep were not then individually identified.

[45] *Re Wait* [1927] 1 Ch 606, 631, per Atkin LJ; *H R & S Sainsbury v Street* [1972] 1 WLR 834.

[46] See Chapter 10.

[47] At least three because it is now clear that, where part only of the crop has perished, yet other possibilities are available – see *H R & S Sainsbury* v *Street*, above, discussed in more detail in Chapter 5, at section 5.1.2.

Despite the fact that s. 5, which expressly deals with the subject-matter of the contract, classifies the types of subject-matter as either existing or future goods, there is in fact a much more important classification which cuts right across this one. This is the distinction between specific and unascertained goods, which is of the greatest importance in connection with the passing of the property and risk in the contract of sale. Specific goods are goods 'identified and agreed on at the time a contract of sale is made';[48] for example, this particular car or this particular load of wheat. Unascertained goods are not defined by the Act, but they seem to fall into three main categories:

1 Goods to be manufactured or grown by the seller, which are necessarily future goods.
2 Purely generic goods; for example, 1,000 tonnes of wheat, or the like, which must also be future goods, at least where the seller does not already own sufficient goods of the description in question which can be appropriated to the contract. Where the seller does own such a quantity of the goods, but the sale is not expressed to be of those particular goods but for goods of that generic kind, it is not easy to apply the 'future goods/existing goods' distinction. In one sense, the goods appear to fall within the definition of 'existing goods' in s. 5(1) but, on the other hand, until the goods are appropriated to the contract, the mere fact that the seller has sufficient goods for that purpose seems irrelevant. In either event it seems that nothing turns on the distinction.
3 An unidentified part of a specified whole; for example, 1,000 tonnes out of a particular load of 2,000 tonnes of wheat; these may be either future or existing goods within the meaning of s. 5.

It will be seen that the distinction between the third type of unascertained goods and specific goods is only a matter of degree, and in a particular case it may be slight indeed. Therefore, if A agrees to sell to B 9,000 tonnes of the wheat on a certain ship which is carrying 10,000 tonnes in all, this is a sale of unascertained goods because they are not identified, but it is obvious that such a transaction is more akin to a sale of specific goods than with a sale of purely generic goods. It is also true, although less obviously, that the distinction between the second and third kinds of unascertained goods is only a matter of degree. The more detailed is the description of the genus, the more it comes to resemble a sale from a specified bulk or stock. It will be seen later that the failure of the Act to draw these distinctions has led to unfortunate results. In particular, the classification of the third of the above three types as unascertained has led to difficulties in connection with the passing of property and risk,[49] and also in connection with the doctrine of frustration.

[48] So defined by s. 61.
[49] See Chapter 14.

4

The types of obligation created

4.1 Fundamental terms

At the time when the old Sale of Goods Act was passed, contractual obligations in England and Wales were generally thought to fall into two principal classes, namely conditions and warranties. In addition, there existed a body of equitable rules governing mis representations; that is, statements inducing a party to enter into a contract which were not subsequently incorporated into the contract itself. In the 1950s and 1960s, it came to be suggested in a number of decisions that the distinction between a condition and a warranty was not exhaustive. This development took two forms. On the one hand, it was held that there were terms more important even than conditions – fundamental terms. On the other hand, it was also held that there was a category of terms between conditions and the warranties – innominate, or intermediate terms. Innominate terms are considered further below;[1] here we consider fundamental terms.

For most practical purposes, it mattered little whether a term was called a condition or a fundamental term. In either case, a breach of the term, however minor, justified the innocent party in repudiating their own obligations under the contract, and treating it as discharged. But the doctrine of the fundamental term was devised principally to deal with the growing problem of unfair and unreasonable exemption clauses. It was held in a large number of decisions that an exemption clause, no matter how sweeping and no matter how broadly drafted in its language, could not protect a guilty party from liability for breach of a fundamental term of the contract.

In 1967, the House of Lords cut down this doctrine in the *Suisse Atlantique* case.[2] It was held here that the doctrine of the fundamental term was nothing more than a rule of construction; an exemption clause was not to be assumed to be drafted so as to justify one party in breaking the fundamental terms of the contract. The rule of construction was, no doubt, a strong one; that is, even though the words of an exemption clause might appear to be wide enough to cover the events which had occurred, the rule would normally be applied, and the words of the exemption clause interpreted so as to cover only less drastic breaches. Nevertheless, however strong the rule of construction, the logical result of refusing to recognise it as a rule of law was that, in the last resort, the parties must be free to make their own contract, however unfair or unpalatable the terms might be. As long only as it was absolutely clear that the words of the exemption clause were designed to cover the circumstances that had occurred, no matter how fundamental, the courts were obliged to give effect to the clause.

[1] See below, section 4.3.

[2] *Suisse Atlantique Société D'Armement Maritime SA* v *Rotterdamsche Kolen Centrale* [1967] 1 AC 361.

Some inroads were made on this doctrine by subsequent decisions, but it was clear that legislative intervention was required. This came in the form of the Supply of Goods (Implied Terms) Act 1973 and later the Unfair Contract Terms Act 1977 and, later, specific regulation for consumer contracts.[3] Together, these have given the courts a substantial degree of control over unfair exemption clauses. As a result, except in relation to the limited range of agreements to which the legislation does not apply,[4] the effect of these developments is to render the distinction between fundamental terms and conditions largely insignificant. Clauses which are unreasonable can usually be struck down, and it will be less necessary for parties to try to persuade the courts to construe the exemption clause in a strict way so that it does not cover the breach of a fundamental term. However, that is not to say that the distinction is not of any importance. Given the way lawyers tend to argue cases, unless severely discouraged by the courts, they will usually try to persuade a court that (1) a clause ought not to be construed to cover the breach of a fundamental term, and that (2) even if it does cover such a breach, it should be held to be unreasonable under the 1977 Act.[5] Moreover, as noted above, a purchase of computer software or other digital product on durable media is both a sale of the disks etc. and a licence of the software. The Unfair Contract Terms Act does not apply to contracts so far as they relate to the creation or transfer of a right or interest, *inter alia*, in a copyright.[6] Control of exemption clauses in such contracts, therefore, depends on common law. It can be argued, however, that this does not prevent the Act from applying to a licence which is simply a permission[7] and does not create or transfer any interest.[8]

George Mitchell (Chesterhall) Ltd v *Finney Lock Seeds Ltd*[9] was the first case to reach the House of Lords on the reasonableness requirement. In this case, plaintiff farmers ordered from the defendants, who were seed merchants, a quantity of 'Finney's Late Dutch Special Cabbage' seeds but were unfortunately supplied instead with an inferior type of seed, which was, indeed, not a 'Late' seed at all, and proved unsuitable to the plaintiffs' needs. A clause limiting the defendants' liability was held unreasonable for reasons which are discussed later.[10] But it was also argued that the clause should not be construed to apply to the breach which had occurred because the suppliers had delivered something quite different from what had been ordered. The House of Lords rejected this argument, but in terms suggesting that if indeed the goods supplied had been of a totally different character (as where beans instead of peas are supplied) it would have been accepted.

[3] See Part 2 of the Consumer Rights Act 2015.

[4] The principal exclusions are to be found in Sched. 1 of the Unfair Contract Terms Act 1977.

[5] It must be noted, however, that in *Fastframe Ltd* v *Lohinski*, 3 March 1993 (unreported – discussed by Adams (1994) 57 MLR 960), the Court of Appeal expressed strong disapproval of this approach. That case, however, involved the construction of a 'no set-off' clause, and, as noted below, the approach may retain some life where it is arguable that the wrong goods have been supplied.

[6] Schedule I, para 1(c). There is no equivalent provision in the Scottish Part of the Act, however, although intellectual property licences are not included in the list of those contracts to which the Part applies (s. 15, as amended by the Law Reform (Miscellaneous Provisions) (Scotland) Act 1990, ss. 68 and 74 and Sched. 9).

[7] *Federal Commissioners of Taxation* v *United Aircraft Corporation* (1943) 68 CLR 525.

[8] In *Fastframe Ltd* v *Lohinski*, 3 March 1993 (unreported – discussed by Adams (1994) 57 MLR 960), the Court of Appeal applied the Act to a franchise contract, which licensed, *inter alia*, a trade name, without commenting on this point, which was raised in the appellant's skeleton arguments. See also Chapter 8.

[9] [1983] 2 AC 803.

[10] See Chapter 8.

It seems, then, that the concept of the fundamental term retains a small residuary significance.[11] Where such a term is breached, a limitation clause will not be construed to cover the breach unless this is almost unavoidable. The strong rule of construction which also continues to apply to total exclusion clauses (as opposed to limitation clauses)[12] thus seems also to continue to apply to limitation clauses which seek to protect against breach of a fundamental term and not merely a breach of condition. This is unfortunate because it means that the courts are able to draw fine and somewhat arbitrary distinctions between the 'peas and beans' type of case, on the one hand, and less drastic departures from the contract such as that between early and late cabbage seed, or good quality and cheap quality seed. Inevitably, this means that difficulties will be encountered with other cases as, for example, where a person contracts to sell cabbage seed, but supplies beetroot or carrot seed.[13] Moreover, these difficulties will be almost completely gratuitous, since drawing these distinctions will never dispose of the whole case; they will merely decide whether a rule of construction applies, and even if it does *prima facie* apply it may be displaced by other contrary indications, or the clause may be declared void under the 1977 Act.

There could be a second type of case in which it might be important to distinguish between a fundamental term and a condition. Where there is a complete non-performance of the contract, it could be argued that there could be no acceptance, and hence no loss of the right to reject goods. The decision of the Court of Appeal in *Charterhouse Credit Co Ltd* v *Tolley*,[14] initially cast doubt on this, however. In this case, it was held that the hirer of a car under a hire-purchase agreement had affirmed the contract and accepted the goods, despite a fundamental breach by the owner in supplying a car with a defective rear axle. And it seems clear that the court contemplated the possibility of a buyer 'accepting' goods delivered by the seller even where there was a delivery of goods wholly different from those sold; for example, a horse instead of a tractor.

However, the decision in *Charterhouse Credit* v *Tolly* was overruled by the House of Lords in *Photo Production* v *Securicor*[15] and as a result, the proposition previously made may now be reasserted. As will be seen in Chapter 10, there are circumstances (though they will be rare) in which a buyer can be treated as having accepted goods even though they have no knowledge of defects in them, but it is arguable that in some of these cases a buyer would be held not to have accepted the goods if there has been a breach of a fundamental term, although a breach of condition would not help them. For example, suppose that A agrees to sell peas to B but sends them beans instead. If B, in ignorance of the substitution but having had an opportunity to examine the goods, resells and delivers the goods to C, it seems that B would not be precluded from rejecting the goods. In the *Suisse Atlantique* case, Lord Reid suggested that such a delivery could not properly be

[11] On the other hand, where beans are delivered instead of peas it could simply be said that the exemption clause is inoperative on the analogy of the *Gibaud* or 'four corners' rule – see *Gibaud* v *Great Eastern Railway* [1921] 2 KB 426.

[12] See Chapter 8.

[13] In the *George Mitchell* case counsel in the lower court conceded that the limitation clause would not apply in this event, but in the House of Lords the concession was withdrawn. The House did not, however, decide whether the concession was correctly withdrawn; nor was it made clear whether (and if so, why) the 'peas and beans' case differs from the 'cabbage seed' and 'beetroot or carrot seed' case.

[14] [1963] 2 QB 683.

[15] By *Photo Production Ltd* v *Securicor* [1980] AC 827, see Chapter 8.

treated as a delivery under the original contract at all, but only as an offer to enter into a new contract.[16] On the other hand, if A had merely been guilty of a breach of condition, B would, in such circumstances, have lost his right of rejection under the law prior to 3 January 1995.[17]

Otherwise, the principal use of the expression 'fundamental term' is in written contracts where it is sometimes used in preference to 'condition' in an attempt to make it clear that *any* breach of such a term will enable the innocent party to terminate.[18]

4.2 Conditions

The term condition is not defined by the Act, but s. 11(3) states that:

> Whether a stipulation in a contract of sale is a condition, the breach of which may give rise to a right to treat the contract as repudiated, or a warranty, the breach of which may give rise to a claim for damages but not to a right to reject the goods and treat the contract as repudiated, depends in each case on the construction of the contract; and a stipulation may be a condition, though called a warranty in the contract.

This subsection therefore explains the term 'condition' by reference to its legal effect, but it does not explain how a condition is to be distinguished from a warranty. It is enough here to say that in its usual meaning a condition is a term which, without being the fundamental obligation imposed by the contract, is still of such vital importance that it goes to the root of the transaction. The importance of a condition in contracts for the sale of goods is that its breach, if committed by the seller, may give the buyer the right to reject the goods completely and to refuse to pay the price, or, if they have already paid it, to recover it.[19]

This is the usual meaning of the word 'condition'. If the term is strictly a condition, this means that its full performance is a *condition* of the other party's obligations; their duties are *conditional* on the performance of conditions. For example, the seller's statutory implied obligations as to the quality and fitness of the goods, and as to their compliance with their description, are all conditions under the Sale of Goods Act. That means that the duties must be strictly complied with by the seller and that any breach of these conditions, however trivial, *prima facie* justifies the buyer in refusing to accept the goods.[20]

Until 1962, the general opinion was that the distinction between conditions and warranties was exhaustive (at any rate leaving aside fundamental terms which were not material to this question). Thus, it was assumed that all contractual terms had to fall within one class or another and that this distinction could, in principle, be drawn at the time when the contract was made. Any term whose breach *could possibly* take a serious form naturally tended to be treated as a condition as a result of this approach. Since the distinction related to the terms of the contract and not to the consequences of the breach

16 [1967] 1 AC at 404.

17 See ss. 34 and 35 of the Act, as amended – see Chapter 17.

18 This practice has grown up since *Wickman Machine Tools Sales Ltd* v *Schuler AG* [1974] AC 235

19 The term 'condition' is used in a large number of different senses – see Stoljar, 'The Contractual Concept of Condition' (1953) 69 LQR 485; see also Montrose [1960] CLJ 72.

20 This is known as the 'perfect tender' rule, and is rather more clearly stated in Uniform Commercial Code, Art. 2-601.

and, indeed, had to be applied in theory as at the date when the contract was made, there was a tendency for many terms to be treated as conditions even though, in the result, their breach only caused minor inconvenience or loss, or even none at all. Only where it could be said at the outset that no breach of a term could ever have really serious consequences was it possible to classify the term as a warranty.

The consequence of this was that in the law of sale of goods, the duties of the seller were traditionally treated very strictly. Any deviation from the terms implied by the Act (as mentioned above) justified the buyer in rejecting the goods. But it was also widely assumed by lawyers that there was nothing peculiar in the law of sale or even in the Sale of Goods Act with respect to these questions. It was generally thought that, for example, the position was the same with respect to all the seller's duties, whether they were implied conditions under the Act or express conditions laid down by the contract.

It will be seen that this approach tended to shut out from consideration as irrelevant the actual consequences of a breach of contract. Some breaches, of course, are serious enough on any view to justify the other party in repudiating the contract; but many breaches have relatively trivial consequences and some have no ill consequences at all. Generally speaking, the law on this point as it was understood until 1962 paid little attention to the actual results of a breach of contract. This result possibly favoured the certainty which was – especially perhaps in the nineteenth century – regarded as a very important goal of the law. Particularly in commercial contracts, it was often necessary that a buyer should be in a position to make an instant decision as to whether they would accept goods (or shipping documents) delivered under a contract of sale. So long as they could reject the goods for any breach of contract (on the ground that it was a breach of condition), their position was relatively simple. They did not have to ask themselves how serious the breach was, which is problematic where the future results of the breach remained still unknown. The certainty this approach brought came at a price, undoubtedly permitting termination of a contract for what were in reality, trivial (and unjust) breaches.

4.3 Innominate terms

The early 1960s, saw something of a legal revolution on this question. The first case in the story was *Hong Kong Fir Shipping Co Ltd* v *Kawasaki Kisen Kaisha*.[21] The contract here involved a charterparty under which a ship was hired, or chartered, by the plaintiffs to the defendants. It is settled law that a charterparty imposes obligations on the owners to provide a seaworthy ship, and it is clear that a sufficiently serious breach of this term would entitle the charterer to repudiate the contract. If a ship is supplied which is manifestly not seaworthy at all, and there is no prospect of repairing it sufficiently to make it fit to sail, then it is clear that the charterer must be entitled to repudiate the charterparty altogether. But seaworthiness is, on the authorities, a comprehensive standard, and a ship may be unseaworthy in the legal sense as a result of some very minor defect which can be easily remedied. In these circumstances, it was held by the Court of Appeal that the owners' duties as to seaworthiness could not be classified at the outset as a condition or a warranty. The truth was that this was an 'innominate term' whose consequences depended

[21] [1962] 2 QB 26.

on the actual outcome of breach. The law has to have regard to the nature and gravity of the breach before it becomes possible to say whether the innocent party is entitled to repudiate a contract for breach of a term of this character.

Passing over *The Mihalis Angelos*,[22] another important decision of the Court of Appeal, which has, however, now been superseded by House of Lords authority to be discussed below, the next case in this story is *Cehave NV* v *Bremerhandelsgesellschaft*,[23] which was a case of sale of goods. This contract was for the sale of citrus pulp pellets for use in animal foods, and it was a term of the contract that the goods should be shipped 'in good condition'. It was also an implied condition under the Sale of Goods Act that the goods should be of (then) merchantable quality. The goods were damaged, though to a relatively minor degree, and in fact they were ultimately used for their intended purpose by the buyers. But the market had fallen at the time of delivery and the buyers contended that they were entitled to reject them for breach of the implied condition of merchantability[24] and also for breach of the express condition that they should be in 'good condition'. It was held that the Sale of Goods Act did not exhaustively divide all terms into conditions and warranties. Although s. 11 only talks of these two possibilities, s. 62(2) preserves the effect of common law rules save insofar as they are inconsistent with the Act. The court took the *Hong Kong Fir* case as correctly laying down the common law rules and as demonstrating the existence of the 'innominate term', breach of which may discharge the other party, but only if the nature and consequences are sufficiently serious to justify this result. The court went on to hold that such innominate terms can exist in contracts of sale of goods and that the *express* term that the goods had to be in good condition was a term of that character. However, the court also assumed that the terms under the Act, including the implied condition of merchantability, were (as they have always been thought to be) conditions in the strict sense, but in the result they held that this term was not broken. Although the actual decision in this case was undoubtedly fair, the reasoning leads to the very odd conclusion that an *implied* term of merchantability is an entirely different thing from an *express* term. If it is express, it may or may not be a condition in the strict sense, but if it is implied under the Act, then it must be (because the Act says it is) a condition – and it was assumed that this means a condition in the strict sense. In order to arrive at a reasonable result, the court had to conclude that the goods in this case were merchantable, but not 'in good condition', a somewhat contradictory holding.[25] Of course, because of the modifications made to the right to reject by the 1994 Sale and Supply of Goods Act, which inserted a new s. 15A into the 1979 Act modifying the buyer's right to reject, if similar facts were to recur in the present day, a more satisfying outcome could be reached.[26]

[22] [1971] 1 QB 164.

[23] Also known as *The Hansa Nord* [1976] QB 44.

[24] Note the modifications to the right to reject in such cases effected by the 1994 Act.

[25] But the case has been followed several times, most notably in *The Aktion* [1987] 1 Lloyd's Rep 283 (express terms on sale of ship held innominate because too severe to hold that minor mechanical or body problems which could easily be rectified were conditions). See also *The Puerto Buitrago* [1976] 1 Lloyd's Rep 250 and *Tradax International SA* v *Goldschmidt SA* [1977] 2 Lloyd's Rep 604.

[26] See Chapter 15.

The next stage in the history of this legal revolution is the decision of the House of Lords in *Reardon Smith Lines Ltd* v *Hansen Tangen*,[27] though this again was not a contract of sale of goods. In this case, a ship which was to be constructed by the plaintiffs was chartered by them to the defendants for delivery when completed. As the ship did not exist at the time when the contract was made, it was therefore described by reference to a specification which set out that it was to be built as Yard No. 354 at Osaka Zosen. In fact, it was built at another yard, owned by another shipbuilding company to whom the plaintiffs had subcontracted the work. As will be seen later in the law of sale of goods, there is an implied condition that the goods to be delivered must correspond with their description. This has always been treated as a strict condition, so that any deviation from the contractual description has been treated as a breach of condition justifying the buyer in rejecting the goods. These cases will be examined in Chapter 19. Here it is enough to say that the analogy of these cases was naturally much pressed on the House of Lords in the *Reardon Smith Lines* case. If the plaintiffs in this case had contracted to sell (rather than charter) the vessel in question, then there is no doubt that on the law as it then stood, the sellers would have been held to have breached the implied condition that the goods must correspond with their description. That argument was rejected by the House, and it is clear that some of the sale of goods cases did not find favour with their Lordships. Lord Wilberforce, who delivered the principal speech in this case, indicated that some of the leading cases on the law of sale might need reconsideration in the future.[28] In the meantime, he insisted that the general law of contract had developed along more rational lines than the strict law of sale of goods on the point. It is clear that he preferred to treat the results of a breach of contract as something to be settled *after* the breach occurred. Moreover, he approved of the decision in the *Cehave* case to treat *express* contractual conditions in a contract of sale of goods as subject to the general law of contract and not to the distinct rules laid down by the Sale of Goods Act.

The developments described above have certainly not eliminated the legal type of term known as a ‘condition’. Indeed, the terms as to quality and fitness implied under the Sale of Goods Act are all conditions, and many non-statutory terms are also conditions – for instance, stipulations as to time. However, as we will see, in the case of commercial contracts the consequences of a term being characterised as a ‘condition’ in the Sale of Goods Act etc. have been significantly modified.[29]

4.4 Stipulations as to time

There is a strong tendency to treat stipulations as to the time when some part of a contract is to be performed as conditions, breach of which is therefore a repudiation which can be instantly accepted, thereby terminating the contract while leaving open a claim for damages. This tendency is noticeable especially in commercial contracts where a contractual breach may create a situation in which the innocent party needs to know at once what

[27] [1976] 1 WLR 989.

[28] While this has not occurred as such, the modification of the right to reject effected by s. 15A (inserted by the 1994 Act) should obviate many of the difficulties created by this old case law – see Chapter 7.

[29] See Chapter 15.

their rights are; they may need to know immediately whether they are entitled to make alternative arrangements, rather than wait and see what the consequences of the breach are. In *Bunge Corpn* v *Tradax*,[30] sellers sold goods for shipment from an American port in the Gulf of Mexico, and the buyers were required to name a vessel to carry the goods. Notice of the vessel's name was to be given at latest by 13 June, but in fact the buyers failed to give the notice until 17 June by which time the sellers claimed that it was too late, and that the contract was terminated by the buyers' breach. The sale in this case was one of a 'string', that is, one of a whole series of sales of the same goods; it is commonplace in certain areas of business, particularly the commodity trades, for this to happen, and strings may involve as many as 50 or more sales. In this event, the last buyer who actually intends to have the goods shipped (rather than reselling before shipment) must give the required site notice, and each other person in the chain or string must pass the notice upwards, or ensure that it is sent direct to the first seller who is actually going to deliver the goods for shipment. It was held by the House of Lords that in cases of this nature, terms as to the time of performance of various contractual duties must be treated as conditions. It is essential that such notices be given on time, in order that they can be passed on, and so that the ultimate seller can themselves comply with their own contractual duties as regards delivering the goods to the necessary port for shipment and so on.

In deciding that the term in question was a condition in this case the House of Lords stressed a number of points of relevance when it is unclear whether a contractual term is or is not a condition. First, it was said that a term as to time can only be broken in one way (namely by delayed performance) and that such terms differ therefore from other terms which can be broken in a variety of ways, some more and some less serious. However, this is not entirely convincing because delays in performance can vary from the trivial and technical to the inordinate and substantial and, indeed, it is already established by other House of Lords decisions that a failure to perform a contractual duty on time does not always amount to a breach of condition. For example, in *Bremer Handelsgesellschaft* v *Vanden Avenne-Izegem*[31] sellers were freed from liability for non-delivery by a contractual clause concerning governmental prohibitions of export, but they were required to notify the buyers of any such prohibition 'without delay'. It was held by the House of Lords that a failure to give the notice within such a time did not prevent the sellers relying on the clause in question.

Other points stressed by the House of Lords in *Bunge Corpn* v *Tradax* may be more critical. These include such questions as: does the performance by the innocent party of their duties under the contract depend on receipt of notices in the required time? Is the contract likely to be one of a string so that many other commercial parties will be affected by delays? Would it be difficult to assess damages for breach if the term is not construed as a condition? Taking the decision as a whole, it seems reasonably clear that in ordinary commercial contracts for the sale of goods, terms as to the time of shipment, delivery, payment and the like, as well as terms as to documents to be presented and other incidental matters to be performed by either party, will still

[30] [1981] 1 WLR 711.

[31] 1978] 2 Lloyd's Rep 109. See also *United Scientific Holdings* v *Burnley BC* [1978] AC 904 as to the effect of delay in the exercise of contractual rights.

usually fall to be treated as conditions, any breach of which will justify the other party in repudiating the whole contract. These duties have always been strictly treated as conditions in the past and *Bunge Corpn* v *Tradax* did nothing to cast any doubt on the continuation of this traditional position.[32] However, 'It remains true', Lord Wilberforce insisted, 'that the courts should not be too ready to interpret contractual clauses as conditions'.[33]

But these cautionary words do not appear to have had much effect so far as stipulations as to time are concerned. In one subsequent case, for example, it was held that evidence of a 'more relaxed' attitude to punctuality in the trade was not enough to displace the presumption that a clause requiring the buyer to nominate the port of shipment 'at latest Monday 14 November' was a condition.[34] In another case, it has been held that a long course of dealing between the parties in which goods were sold under terms requiring payment by a letter of credit did not affect the rule that the time for opening the credit is a condition, even though on many previous occasions one or other party had been late in opening the credit.[35]

There are grounds for thinking that it is commercial lawyers, rather than commercial people themselves, who believe that certainty is so important in commercial transactions that these time stipulations should nearly always be treated as conditions. The truth is that reasonable commercial people rarely respond to a breach of a time stipulation by immediately tearing up the whole contract and claiming damages. Usually some attempt is made at an accommodation; some inquiry is made to find out if the other party can still perform within a reasonable period. Moreover, the law itself recognises that this is reasonable behaviour, and indeed occasionally insists upon it, even where the term broken was a condition, by penalising a party who has failed to mitigate the damage.

Although *prima facie* the innocent party is entitled to treat a contract as terminated instantly on a breach of condition, the rules as to mitigation will in some, perhaps many, cases undercut the treatment of stipulations as to time as conditions. The mitigation rules require the innocent party to take reasonable steps to mitigate or minimise the damage or loss likely to flow from the other party's breach. A contracting party who fails to perform on time but tenders, or offers to perform, very shortly after will often be able to argue that this offer ought to be accepted as it is likely that the damage done by the delay will thereby be minimised.[36] Of course, there may be answers to this: the innocent party may say that it is already too late; that, having cancelled the contract as a result of the delay, steps have been taken to obtain (or dispose of) the goods elsewhere, which are by this stage irrevocable; or they may say – with more or less plausibility depending on the facts – that they were not confident enough that the guilty party, who had already breached once, would perform as they now promised to do.

[32] See also *Toepfer* v *Lenersan-Poortman NV* [1980] 1 Lloyd's Rep 143.

[33] [1981] 1 WLR at 715.

[34] *Gill & Duffus SA* v *Société Pour L'Exportation des Sucres* [1986] 1 Lloyd's Rep 322; see also *Warde (Michael I)* v *Feedex International* [1985] 2 Lloyd's Rep 289.

[35] *Nichimen Corpn* v *Gatoil Overseas Inc* [1987] 2 Lloyd's Rep 46.

[36] See Chapter 18. Note especially *The Solholt* [1983] 1 Lloyd's Rep 605.

If the mitigation rules do not help the guilty party, the law is undoubtedly producing some very severe consequences. Not only is the innocent party entitled to treat a breach of condition as the equivalent of a repudiation justifying instant termination of the contract, it is also immaterial why the innocent party wants to behave in this way. They are not required to act reasonably, or in good faith, in exercising their rights. Indeed, usually it seems that technical breaches of condition (such as very short delays) are only treated as grounds for termination where the innocent party is seeking a way out of the contract because market conditions have changed, or for some equally irrelevant reason. In practice, it is probably quite rare that technical breaches of condition are themselves the motive (as well as the legal justification) for a claim that the contract must be treated as terminated.

4.5 Sale and Supply of Goods Act 1994

As indicated earlier, the more recent developments discussed above do not fit easily into the framework of the Sale of Goods Act itself. In particular, all the implied terms as to quality and fitness of the goods under the Act are conditions, and there is no room for treating any of these terms as innominate terms.[37] It seems clear that, as the Law Commissions suggested, if the Sale of Goods Act had not been drafted in this form, modern courts would not have arrived at this result.[38]

After a lengthy inquiry the Law Commissions published proposals for change in the law relating to conditions,[39] and the government accepted these in principle, giving effect to them in the Sale and Supply of Goods Act 1994, amending that 1979 Act. A (non-consumer) buyer no longer had the right to reject for any breach of the implied terms if the consequences and nature of the breach are so slight that rejection would be unreasonable. Consumers continued to be allowed to reject goods for breach of any condition, a position now enshrined in the Consumer Rights Act 2015.[40]

It is perhaps regrettable that the changes did not go further, allowing, for example, the reclassification of terms implied by the Act as innominate terms. Those terms remained conditions, but the remedy for breach of condition was limited. Moreover, the changes do not affect any conditions except those implied under ss. 13, 14 and 15 of the Act, and s. 30, as to delivery of the correct quantity, so that (for instance) breach of a condition as to time is not affected. This is a regrettable result of the fact that the terms of reference of the Law Commissions' inquiry were limited. A more rational change would surely have extended to all breaches of condition. The severance of consumer sales law from non-consumer sales law may yet yield an opportunity to revisit this.

[37] The Act in its body uses the word 'term' instead of 'condition' but provides in Sched. 2 that in England and Wales and Northern Ireland the implied terms are conditions (save in the case of subss. (2), (4) and (5) of s. 12). In other words, no change of substance is made to the former provisions in this regard.

[38] Law Com Working Paper No. 85, *Sale and Supply of Goods*, para. 2.30. The subsequent Final Report, *Sale and Supply of Goods* (Law Com. No. 160, Cm. 137, 1987), as to which see below, was markedly more conservative in tone than the Working Paper, and appeared to accept unreservedly the current structure of the law and the classification of contractual terms.

[39] See last note for the Final Report, *Sale and Supply of Goods*.

[40] See Chapter 19.

4.6 Warranties

The term warranty is defined by s. 61 as an:

> . . . agreement with reference to goods which are the subject of a contract of sale, but collateral to the main purpose of such contract, the breach of which gives rise to a claim for damages but not to a right to reject the goods and treat the contract as repudiated.

This definition therefore explains both the meaning and the legal effect of a warranty. The term 'collateral' is not well chosen, for it may give the impression that a warranty is a term which is somehow outside the contract, when it is in fact a term of the contract.[41] In practice, very few terms are ever classified as warranties in this narrow technical sense. It is clearly rare that one can say, at the outset, that no breach of a term can ever have such serious consequences as would justify treating the whole contract as at an end; this is (as seen above) why the courts generally classify terms as conditions. It is even doubtful whether many pure warranties ever exist as a matter of strict law, and the Law Commissions at one time appeared inclined to suggest that the whole category of warranties should be abolished.[42] But their final recommendations contained no proposals to change the situation, and the terms in contracts of sale of goods continue to be divided at common law into conditions, innominate terms and warranties.

4.7 Representations

From terms of the contract, it is necessary to distinguish mere statements or representations, which are not part of the contract but may have serious consequences, nonetheless. On the details of this topic, reference should be made to the standard works on the law of contract.[43] It is, however, necessary to say a few words on the distinction between a term and a misrepresentation because (it will be suggested later) despite the use sometimes made by the courts of s. 13,[44] the Act does in truth leave intact the established distinction between a contract term and a representation.

Whether a statement is or is not a part of the contract depends upon the intention of the parties, but this elusive concept is often of little help,[45] especially since the courts have been prepared to hold that an oral statement may override the written terms of a contract. It is probably true to say that the courts are now much readier to interpret a statement as a term of the contract than they were in the late nineteenth and early twentieth centuries. This tendency may be illustrated by contrasting the decisions in *Hopkins* v *Tanqueray*[46]

[41] See Stoljar (1952) 15 MLR 425, 430–2.

[42] Law Com Working Paper No. 85, para. 2.32. But there are statutory implied warranties in s. 12(2) of the Act. The older use of the word 'warranty' and 'to warrant' is also still often found, especially where the question is whether a statement is a contractual term or a representation. In this context the word simply means 'contractual term'. This usage is followed in this book because there is simply no alternative to the verb, 'to warrant'.

[43] See e.g., Treitel, *Law of Contract* (15th edn, 2020, Sweet & Maxwell), §6-001 *et seq*.

[44] See *Beale* v *Taylor* [1967] 1 WLR 1193, discussed in Chapter 7.

[45] Except of course where the contract in terms states that the truth of a statement is warranted by the party making it, as, e.g., in *Liverpool & County Discount Co Ltd* v *A B Motor Co (Kilburn) Ltd* [1963] 1 WLR 611.

[46] (1854) 15 CB 130. Another possible explanation of this case is given below and in *Couchman* v *Hill* [1947] KB 554.

and *Couchman* v *Hill*.[47] In the former case, the defendant, who was offering his horse for sale by auction, gave an assurance to the plaintiff on the day before the sale that the horse was perfectly sound. It was held that this statement was a mere representation and not a term of the contract. In the second case, the defendant was offering his heifer for sale by auction. In reliance on an assurance given by the defendant and also by the auctioneer that the heifer was unserved, the plaintiff bid for and bought the animal. This statement was held to be a term of the contract. In a strictly technical sense there is no conflict between these cases because questions of intention must depend upon all the circumstances of the case, and superficial similarities may hide underlying differences.[48] It would be more realistic, however, to admit to this general change of attitude on the part of the courts. It is in fact increasingly uncommon for a court to hold that a material statement made by one of the parties to a contract is only a misrepresentation.[49] This is particularly true of statements made by a seller in a contract for the sale of goods.

The tendency today often appears to be to hold a statement to be a term of the contract when it seems reasonable to impose liability in damages on the person who made it and vice versa. To attempt to decide whether a statement is a term of the contract or a mere representation without reference to the result is, in many cases, a flawed approach. On the one hand, a statement as to the quality or state of the goods by a seller will almost invariably be held to be a term of the contract if the seller is a dealer in the goods. So in *Dick Bentley (Productions) Ltd* v *Harold Smith (Motors) Ltd*,[50] where a dealer, in selling a car, told the buyer that it had done only 20,000 miles, this was held by the Court of Appeal to be a term of the contract and not a mere representation. On the other hand, in *Oscar Chess Ltd* v *Williams*,[51] where a person selling a second-hand car in part-exchange for another innocently misrepresented the age of the car (relying on the log book, which was in fact forged), the Court of Appeal held the statement to be a mere representation. It seems from these cases that, in the absence of a clear intention one way or the other, a statement is a term of the contract where the person making it had, or could reasonably have obtained, the information necessary to show whether the statement was true.

It is unnecessary here to make more than a brief reference to the possibility of a claim for negligent misrepresentation by a buyer, whether or not they are able to establish that the representation amounts to a term of the contract. Although a claim for negligent misrepresentation can lie in some circumstances even at common law[52] it will not often

[47] [1947] KB 554.

[48] The earlier case was not cited in *Couchman* v *Hill*, and in an editorial note in [1947] 1 All ER 103 it was suggested that the decision in the later case might otherwise have been different. But in *Harling* v *Eddy* [1951] 2 KB 739 the CA held the two cases to be distinguishable, though on what grounds it is not wholly clear. The correct explanation of *Hopkins* v *Tanqueray* may well be that the auction was held at Tattersalls where, by custom (as everyone knew – though not the parties it would seem), all sales were without warranty – see Greig (1971) 87 LQR 179, 183–4. See also *Schawel* v *Reade* [1913] 2 Ir R 81, a somewhat neglected authority.

[49] See also *J Evans & Son* v *Andrea Merzario* [1967] 1 WLR 1078; *Brikom Investments Ltd* v *Carr* [1979] QB 467. Some of the judgments in these cases proceed on the basis of a 'collateral contract' and some on the basis of estoppel, but these tend to be mere devices. The results are uniform.

[50] [1965] 2 All ER 65.

[51] [1957] 1 WLR 370; see also *Routledge* v *McKay* [1954] 1 WLR 615; *Hummingbird Motors Ltd* v *Hobbs* [1986] RTR 276; *Harlingdon & Leinster Enterprises Ltd* v *Christopher Hull Fine Art Ltd* [1991] 1 QB 564.

[52] *Hedley Byrne & Co Ltd* v *Heller & Partners Ltd* [1964] AC 465.

be possible for a buyer to bring such a claim in a case where the representation is not a term of the contract.[53] Today, this of little importance because under s. 2(1) of the Misrepresentation Act 1967, a contracting party is given a statutory claim for misrepresentation against the other contracting party. As the onus is placed on the party making the representation to show that they had reasonable grounds to believe, and did believe up to the time the contract was made, that the facts represented were true, this approach, however, creates an incentive for claims based on misrepresentation to be joined with claims for damages for breach of condition or warranty.[54] However, damages under the Misrepresentation Act may not be assessed in the same way as damages for breach of a term of the contract, so the distinction may still be important in some cases.

[53] But this did happen in *Esso Petroleum Ltd* v *Mardon* [1976] QB 801. See also *Howard Marine & Dredging Co Ltd* v *A Ogden & Sons (Excavations) Ltd* [1978] QB 574.

[54] But it is important that the plaintiff clearly puts his case on the grounds of negligence, at common law, or under the statute, namely that the defendant had no reasonable grounds for his belief in the facts stated; otherwise a claim based purely on non-fraudulent misrepresentation is still liable to fail: see *Hummingbird Motors Ltd* v *Hobbs* [1986] RTR 276.

Part II

The duties of the seller

5

The existence of the goods and the duty to pass a good title

5.1 No implied condition that the goods exist

It might have been thought that in a sale of specific goods, there would be an implied condition on the part of the seller that the goods were in existence at the time when the contract was made. Since the seller warrants, as we shall see below, that they have a right to sell the goods, and since they are in many cases responsible for defects in the quality of the goods, it might seem that *a fortiori* they should be liable if they had sold non-existent goods. Nevertheless, this is not generally so, for s. 6 enacts that:

> Where there is a contract for the sale of specific goods, and the goods without the knowledge of the seller have perished at the time when the contract is made, the contract is void.

This section has been commonly understood to confirm the decision of the House of Lords in *Couturier* v *Hastie*.[1] The defendant in that case was a *del credere* agent who sold, on behalf of the plaintiffs, a cargo of corn shipped from Salonika. Before the date of the sale, the cargo had been lawfully sold by the master of the ship, so that there was no corn available for delivery to the buyer; instead, the sellers tendered the usual shipping documents. These documents included an insurance policy but since the goods had been lost before the buyer had any interest in them, he would (presumably) have been unable to claim under the policy, even assuming it covered the loss. Possibly the buyer could, if he had been compelled to pay the price, have required the seller to claim under the policy and hand over the proceeds. But the buyer obviously wanted corn, not the proceeds of an insurance policy, and he refused to accept or pay for the documents. The sellers thereupon sued the agent, whose liability depended on whether the buyer would have been liable. It was held that the agent was not liable.

It was thought for many years that the case was decided in this way on the ground that the contract was void for mistake. It is, however, now widely accepted that the decision turned simply on the construction of the contract,[2] or perhaps (though this is probably saying the same thing in a different way) that the decision does no more than illustrate the well-known principle that if the seller cannot deliver the goods the buyer is (anyhow *prima facie*) not bound to pay the price, a rule affirmed by s. 28 of the Act.[3] If the buyer had brought an action for non-delivery, then the court would have had to decide a very

[1] (1856) 5 HLC 673.
[2] See Atiyah (1957) 73 LQR 349.
[3] Slade (1954) 70 LQR at 396–7.

different question. This might have been whether the contract was void for mistake, but a better approach would have been to regard it as a question of construction. In other words, the question to be decided would have been: did the defendant contract that the goods existed, or was there an implied condition that if there were no goods there would be no contract? This apparently was the view of Lord Atkin in *Bell* v *Lever Bros Ltd*,[4] for in the course of his speech in that case he said:

> This brings the discussion to the alternative mode of expressing the result of a mutual mistake . . . The proposition does not amount to more than this, that if the contract expressly or impliedly contains a term that a particular assumption is a condition of the contract, the contract is avoided if the assumption is not true.

Looking at the problem as one of interpretation, the facts of *Couturier* v *Hastie* were open to at least three possible constructions:

1 there might have been an implied condition precedent (or, in Scotland, a resolutive condition) that the goods were in existence, in which case, if they were not, neither party would be bound; or,
2 the seller might have contracted, or warranted, that the goods were in existence, in which case he would be liable for non-delivery, and the buyer would not be liable for non-acceptance; or,
3 the buyer might have taken the risk of the goods having perished, in which case he would be liable for the price even in the absence of delivery, and the seller would not, of course, be liable for non-delivery.

In *Couturier* v *Hastie*,[5] the House of Lords merely decided that the contract could not be construed in the third of the above three ways, but the House did not decide, as it was not called upon to decide, whether the proper interpretation was of the first or second types above. A decision between these two possibilities would only have been necessary if the buyer had sued for damages for non-delivery. Such a decision was necessary in *McRae* v *Commonwealth Disposals Commission*,[6] where the defendants contracted to sell to the plaintiffs a shipwrecked tanker on a certain reef. After the plaintiffs had incurred considerable expenditure in preparing a salvage expedition, it was discovered that not only was there not and had never been any tanker but also that the reef was non-existent. The High Court of Australia approached the case on the basis that the defendants were liable for breach of contract unless they could establish that there was an implied condition precedent that the ship was in existence. Manifestly, on the facts of the case, no such condition could be implied. On the contrary, the court concluded that:

> The only proper construction of the contract is that it included a promise by the Commission that there was a tanker in the position specified. The Commission contracted that there was a tanker there.[7]

[4] [1932] AC 161, at 224–5. For the modern statement, see *Great Peace Shipping Ltd* v *Tsavliris (International) Ltd* [2002] EWCA Civ 1407 at para 76 (Lord Phillips MR).

[5] (1856) 5 HLC 673.

[6] (1951) 84 CLR 377, approved in *Great Peace Shipping Ltd* v *Tsavliris (International) Ltd* [2002] EWCA Civ 1407.

[7] At p. 380. The plaintiffs could presumably have recovered the same damages on the basis of negligence since they did not claim their loss of profits, but only their reliance expenses.

In this connection, the earlier decision of the same court in *Goldsborough, Mort & Co Ltd* v *Carter*[8] is also of some interest, although this case (like *Couturier* v *Hastie*) was decided at common law. In this case, the defendant agreed to sell 'about' 4,000 sheep pastured on certain lands at a price per head. It was agreed to muster and count the sheep on a certain date and the contract also stated that, if it should be found that there were fewer than 4,000 sheep, the buyer would take and pay for the actual number delivered. In fact, there had been conditions of severe drought in the area and these were followed by cold winter rains, with the result that, on muster, only 890 acceptable sheep were found. The buyer claimed damages for the short delivery, but his claim was rejected. Griffith CJ treated the contract as one for the sale of specific goods, and said:

> It is an implied condition of such a contract that at the time of making the contract or before the time of performance the chattels are or will be in existence (*Couturier* v *Hastie*), and, further, that they shall still be existing when the time comes for performance (*Howell* v *Coupland*).

But the majority of the court held that this principle was displaced in the particular circumstances of the case on the true construction of the contract. Since the seller did not know how many sheep there were and since the buyer was aware of the possibility of shortage and had agreed to take what number were delivered, it was held that the contract was only for the sale of such sheep as existed and could be delivered on muster.

A case resembling the *McRae* case in some respects is *Associated Japanese Bank* v *Crédit du Nord SA*.[9] Here, one JB entered into a sale and leaseback transaction with the plaintiffs, under which he sold four large machines to them for over one million pounds, and they leased the machines back to him. Such a sale and leaseback transaction is simply a way of raising money on the security of goods, and is not unusual in practice; but what was unusual about this case was that the machines did not exist at all, and the whole scheme was a fraud by JB. The validity of the contract between JB and the plaintiffs did not directly arise in the action because JB was of course not worth suing, and the action was actually brought to enforce a guarantee of the transaction given by the defendants. The action failed because Steyn J held that the guarantee contract was void either for mistake or for failure of an implied condition that the goods existed. But if the plaintiffs had sued JB on the contract itself, it seems hardly credible that he could have defended the action by claiming that the contract was void because the goods did not exist – a conclusion not rendered more plausible merely because in any event JB could plainly have been sued for fraud. Obviously, the only possible construction of the sale and leaseback contract, like that in the *McRae* case, was that the seller was guaranteeing the existence of the goods.

So it seems clear that in appropriate circumstances a seller of non-existent goods may be held liable on the basis that they have impliedly or even expressly warranted that the goods do exist. The impact of s. 6 of the Act on the problem must next be considered. In terms, the section clearly contemplates a case where the goods have existed at one time, but have perished before the contract was made, so that the sales in the *McRae* case and the *Associated Japanese Bank* case would not come within it at all (in the latter case

[8] (1914) 19 CLR 429.
[9] [1988] 3 All ER 902.

a fortiori because the seller *knew* the goods did not exist). Consequently, the common law position would remain and the result should be that already suggested – the seller should be liable for breach of contract, as indeed was held in the former case by the High Court of Australia. But this does not answer the question where the goods have in fact existed but have perished before the contract was made. In such a case, it appears at first sight that the contract must be held void under s. 6, but it is difficult to believe that this can be right. If a seller, in effect, contracts that the goods are in existence, are they entitled to avoid all liability on the ground that s. 6 applies and the contract is void? This extraordinary result can, it is submitted, best be avoided by giving a liberal interpretation to s. 55(1) of the Act which now runs:

> Where any right, duty, or liability would arise under a contract of sale of goods by implication of law, it may (subject to the Unfair Contract Terms Act 1977) be negatived or varied by express agreement or by the course of dealing between the parties, or by such usage as binds both parties to the contract.

Read literally, it might appear that this section would not prevent the operation of s. 6 in a case such as that being considered, for the whole effect of the section is to prevent any right, duty or liability arising; moreover, literally construed, s. 6 prevents any contract of sale of goods coming into existence to which s. 55(1) can apply at all. But in preventing the principal obligations from arising, s. 6 may give rise to other rights and duties; for example, as to the return of the price,[10] and perhaps the reference to 'a contract of sale of goods' could generously be read as including a reference to a contract which is void under s. 6 (which does, after all, itself refer to 'a contract for the sale of goods'). In any case, the clear object of the section does seem to be to enable the parties to vary, by agreement, all those provisions of the Act which do not affect third parties.

Of course, it is clear that anomalous results would follow if s. 6 were held to be a rule of law to be applied irrespective of the intention of the parties. Since the section is limited in various ways (e.g. in that it only applies to a sale of specific goods, and only applies also where the goods perish) closely parallel cases may fall just within or just outside the section. Those outside will be settled at common law according to the true construction of the contract. It would be unfortunate if those just on the other side of the line had to be determined by a rigid application of s. 6. It is submitted, therefore, that if, on the true construction of the contract, it appears that the seller is contracting that the goods do exist, s. 6 will not apply and the seller will be liable for non-delivery.[11] (If the seller has been negligent in not discovering that the goods have perished, it may be that the better solution would often be to hold that there is no such implied exclusion of s. 6, but that the seller should be held liable for misrepresentation. In that event the buyer could obtain damages for some of his actual ('reliance') losses, but not for his expectation losses.[12]

[10] Professor Atiyah noted in earlier editions that a learned reviewer first drew his attention to this argument (see (1959) 75 LQR 417), but he had come to feel that there were difficulties with it.

[11] In *Joseph Constantine SS Ltd* v *Imperial Smelting Corpn* [1942] AC 154, 184–6, there are dicta by Lord Wright clearly showing that he at least thought that ss. 6 and 7 of the Act merely embody common law rules of construction. See also *Christopher Hill Ltd v Ashington Piggeries* [1972] AC 441, 501, where Lord Diplock says that the Act should not 'be construed so narrowly as to force on parties to contracts for the sale of goods promises and consequences different from what they must reasonably have intended'.

[12] For the difference between expectation and reliance damages, see Peel, *Treitel's Law of Contract*, (15th edn, 2020, Sweet & Maxwell), ch.20, paras 20-033-20-038.

The only effect of s. 6 is thus to give rise to a presumption, in the cases to which it applies, that the seller is not contracting that the goods exist. In effect, the section gives rise to a rule of construction rather than a rigid rule of law. Where, on the other hand, as in *McRae*, the goods have never existed at all, s. 6 cannot apply, and the presumption may be that the seller is contracting that the goods exist.

Although this problem may appear to be of greater academic than practical importance, it is perhaps unfortunate that s. 6 was written into the Act at all in its present form. It should, of course, be remembered that *Couturier* v *Hastie* was decided before the invention of modern methods of communication and on the facts of that case, in the year 1856, it might well have been reasonable to hold that the seller was not contracting that the goods were in existence. If the identical facts were to recur today, however, it is in the highest degree improbable that the seller would not be aware of the sale of the cargo by the ship's master even before it occurred, and if he were not, it would most probably be due to his own negligence. Such a possibility could today give rise to a claim for negligent misrepresentation at common law or under s. 2(1) of the Misrepresentation Act 1967. No doubt in some circumstances, this may seem a better solution than an action for breach of contract, for example, if it seems unreasonable to award damages for loss of bargain against the seller.

The sort of facts to which s. 6 may be applied today may well differ considerably from the *Couturier* v *Hastie* situation. For example, in *Barrow, Lane & Ballard Ltd* v *Phillip Phillips & Co Ltd*[13] the plaintiffs contracted to sell to the defendants 700 bags of nuts, which were believed to be lying in certain warehouses. In fact, 109 of the bags had disappeared, presumably by theft, at the time when the contract was made, and after 150 bags had been delivered about two months later, it was eventually discovered that no further bags remained. On the face of it, one would have thought this was a plain case. The sellers had sold a specific parcel of 700 bags of nuts when in fact there were only 591 to deliver. This would seem, therefore, to have been a simple case of breach of contract by the sellers. But that was not the result.

The actual claim in this case was on two bills of exchange which had been given in payment of the price of the whole of the 700 bags. In fact, the buyers obtained delivery of the 150 bags which were available when delivery was required, and they admitted their liability to pay for these bags, though, it seems, not under the contract itself. The buyers, however, refused to honour the bills of exchange, on the ground that the sellers were in breach of an implied term that the goods were in existence. This is hardly surprising because the buyers' loss was probably not covered by their insurance, while it may well have been covered by the sellers' insurance. Wright J appears to have preferred the view that the contract was void under s. 6, rather than that the sellers were in breach.[14] (But it is unsatisfactory to say that the whole contract here was void when the buyers in fact obtained delivery of 150 of the bags, and admitted their liability to pay for them. If the contract was indeed void, then some strange results would have ensued. First, the terms governing the delivery of the 150 bags would not have been the terms agreed upon by the parties, and the buyers would only have been liable for a reasonable price in a restitutionary claim. This would also have

[13] [1929] 1 KB 574.
[14] At p. 582.

ruled out any claim for breach of the statutory implied terms as to quality and fitness, which seems an extraordinary result. And finally, it would also have meant, presumably, that the sellers could have refused to deliver the 150 bags if the facts had been discovered before delivery had been required. For reasons given below this also seems wrong.

Section 6 gives rise to three other difficulties which are considered in the next three sections.

5.1.1 Meaning of 'specific goods'

'Specific goods' are defined by s. 61(1) as 'goods identified and agreed upon at the time a contract of sale is made'. In most cases this is clear enough, and serves to distinguish such cases from contracts of sale of future or generic goods. Thus, if A contracts to deliver 1,000 tonnes of wheat to B, this is not a sale of specific goods and A's obligations are unaffected by the fact that he had a particular 1,000 tonnes in mind which have, unknown to him, perished before the date of the contract. Some cases, however, are not so clear. What of a contract to sell 200 tonnes of potatoes to be grown on a particular piece of land? In *Howell* v *Coupland*[15] (a case dealing with subsequent destruction, now covered by s. 7 of the Act[16] it was held that this was a sale of specific goods for the purpose of the common law rules of frustration. However, the modern tendency appears to be to confine the meaning of 'specific goods' under the Act to cases of existing goods which have actually been identified or agreed upon. Thus in *Re Wait*,[17] a case to be considered at length later,[18] it was held that a sale of 5,000 tons out of a cargo of 10,000 tons of wheat on a particular ship was not a sale of specific or ascertained goods within the meaning of s. 52 of which specific performance could be ordered. Similarly, in *H R & S Sainsbury* v *Street*,[19] it was held that a sale of 275 tons of barley to be grown on a particular farm was not a sale of specific goods. The effect of the perishing of the goods in such circumstances must, therefore, be a matter for the common law rather than s. 6 of the Act.

5.1.2 Effect of part of goods perishing

Where there is a sale of specific goods, part of which have perished before the date of the sale, the effect of s. 6 is now somewhat obscure. In *Barrow, Lane & Ballard Ltd* v *Phillip Phillips & Co Ltd*, the facts of which have been given above, Wright J, emphasising that he regarded the 700 bags of nuts as an indivisible parcel of goods, held that the contract was avoided by s. 6, even though only 109 bags had apparently disappeared by the time the contract was made. It has been pointed out above that this decision entails some strange results. Among others, it would mean that if the sellers had refused to deliver the 150 bags which were actually available when delivery was demanded, they would not have been liable to the buyers. That conclusion would seem particularly suspect in the

[15] (1876) 1 QBD 258.
[16] See Chapter 11 at 11.3.
[17] [1927] 1 Ch 606.
[18] See Chapter 10 at 10.2.4.
[19] [1972] 1 WLR 834.

light of *H R & S Sainsbury* v *Street*.[20] In this case the defendant agreed to sell a crop of about 275 tons of barley to be grown by him on his farm. In fact, owing to general crop failure, only some 140 tons were produced, which the defendant sold and delivered to a third party at a substantially higher price. McKenna J held that, although the contract was frustrated as to that part of the crop which failed, this did not exonerate the defendant from offering the crop actually produced to the plaintiffs. Somewhat puzzlingly, he did not seem to regard the plaintiffs as being obliged to take the 140 tons,[21] which suggests that the seller but not the buyer was bound by the contract in the events which actually occurred. What is at any rate clear is that, treating the problem purely as a common law question of construction, there are three additional possible constructions of the contract to be added to those dealing with total perishing of the goods. These are that if part of the goods perish:

1 the seller may be obliged to deliver the balance and the buyer may be bound to take it; or
2 the seller may be obliged to tender delivery of the balance to the buyer who is not bound to take it; or
3 the seller is not bound to tender delivery to the buyer, but if they do so, the buyer is bound to take it.

Which of these is the correct construction of any particular contract must depend, as usual, on the terms of the contract and all the circumstances of the case.

Although *H R & S Sainsbury* v *Street* was decided at common law, it would seem very odd if, on parallel facts falling within s. 6, a different result had to be arrived at. It would seem, therefore, that the buyers in the *Barrow Lane & Ballard* case may have been entitled to insist on delivery of the 150 bags of nuts remaining, notwithstanding s. 6, which is not easy to reconcile with the idea that the contract there was actually void. While the approach in *H R & S Sainsbury* v *Street* would seem to be more in line with modern commercial expectations, it does run into difficulties because of the approach taken to s. 6 and its consequence that the entire contract is void. Perhaps the time has come to consider amending this section to ensure its application produces a result which is more acceptable from a commercial point of view.

5.1.3 Meaning of 'perish'

Barrow, Lane & Ballard Ltd v *Phillip Phillips & Co Ltd*[22] is also material on the next point, namely the meaning of the word 'perished'. Read literally, this might be thought to cover only physical destruction, but in fact it is submitted that it should be construed to cover also perishing in a commercial sense. Although this point was not argued in this case, the actual result supports this contention. There are no other English cases precisely in point under s. 6,[23] but several cases on freight and insurance law deal with a very similar

[20] Ibid.

[21] Perhaps because of s. 30(1) (which says that if the seller delivers less than he contracted to sell the buyer may reject the goods). This provision is now modified in the case of commercial buyers – see Chapter 6, 6.5.

[22] [1929] 1 KB 574.

[23] [1896] 1 QB 123, 127

question; that is, whether there has been a total loss of goods. On this topic, one cannot do better than quote the pungent observations of Lord Esher MR in *Asfar & Co Ltd* v *Blundell*:[24]

> The first point taken on behalf of the defendants, the under-writers, is that there has been no total loss of the dates . . . The ingenuity of the argument might commend itself to a body of chemists, but not to business men. We are dealing with dates as a subject matter of commerce; and it is contended that, although these dates were under water for two days, and when brought up were simply a mass of pulpy matter impregnated with sewage and in a state of fermentation, there had been no change in their nature, and they still were dates. There is a perfectly well known test which has for many years been applied to such cases as the present – that test is whether, as a matter of business, the nature of the thing has been altered.

Mutatis mutandis these remarks could apply equally to the meaning of the word 'perish' in s. 6. The only case which is inconsistent with this view is *Horn* v *Minister of Food*,[25] which was a case under s. 7 of the Act. Morris J here held that potatoes, which had so rotted as to be worthless, had not perished within the meaning of s. 7 because they were still potatoes, but in any event he held that the section did not apply because the risk in the goods had already passed to the buyer, and the section is excluded in such a case. His remarks on this point are therefore *obiter* and it is submitted that they cannot be supported.

If a wide meaning is given to the word 'perish' it becomes all the more important that s. 6 of the Act be treated only as a rule of construction. For (as will be seen later) a seller is usually under stringent obligations as to the quality and fitness of the goods to be supplied under the contract. So, for example, a seller who contracts to sell a specific load of potatoes will be liable for breach of his implied obligations if they deliver potatoes which are not of satisfactory quality, and it will be immaterial whether they were not of satisfactory quality before the contract was made. But if they can plead s. 6 of the Act they will escape all liability. Such a result was arrived at in the New Zealand case of *Turnbull* v *Rendell*[26] where the seller agreed to sell 75 tons of 'table potatoes' from a specific crop, some of which were still undug. At the time of the contract, the potatoes were so badly affected with secondary growth that they no longer answered the description 'table potatoes'. *Prima facie* one would have thought, therefore, that there was a breach of s. 13 of the Act (that the goods must answer their description)[27] but, in fact, the buyer's claim for damages was rejected. The court held that the potatoes had 'perished' within the meaning of s. 6 of the Act and the contract was therefore void. It may seem strange that the seller's position is improved in such a case where the potatoes are so rotten as to be no longer describable as 'potatoes' so that he can rely on s. 6 of the Act. But the result can be justified on the ground that in such a case the event which has occurred is so far outside the contemplation of the parties that it would be unfair to place the risk of its occurrence on either party alone. In effect, this is the justification for the doctrines of mistake and

[24] There is the New Zealand decision, however, in *Oldfield Asphalts Ltd* v *Grovedale Coolstores* (1994) Ltd [1998] 3 NZLR 479, which supports the views expressed in the text below. The court in that case also rejected the argument that the operation of s. 6 was confined to perishable goods such as foodstuffs.

[25] [1948] 2 All ER 1036.

[26] (1908) 27 NZLR 1067.

[27] See Chapter 7, at section 7.3

frustration, and of course s. 6 is a part of the former doctrine. Still, it is important that sufficient flexibility is retained in the operation of s. 6 so that it is not available as an excuse to a seller who ought plainly to be treated as warranting the quality of the goods.

At all events there seems no inclination to extend the meaning of 'perish' by analogy to cases where the seller is clearly responsible for the unavailability of the goods. Thus it has been held no defence for a seller who is sued for non-delivery to prove that, after agreeing to sell the goods to the plaintiff, they sold and delivered the goods to another buyer.[28]

Even granting that s. 6 covers perishing in a commercial sense, a difficulty still exists in the case of goods lost by theft. Suppose, for example, that A sells his car to B, which unknown to them both has just been stolen. It may be a long time before the police give up all hope of tracing the car, and until this happens the vehicle can hardly be said to have perished even in a commercial sense, but what is to happen in the meantime? The validity of the contract can hardly depend upon the activities of the police. The insurance cases are not of much assistance here because a theft can clearly be a commercial loss and, of course, this is often the whole object of the insurance, while it is not so clear that a stolen car can be said to have perished even commercially. *Barrow, Lane & Ballard Ltd* v *Phillip Phillips & Co Ltd*[29] is distinguishable from such a case because there the nuts had in all probability been dispersed by sale after the theft and, indeed, some or all of them might well have been consumed by the ultimate purchasers. Whether, and if so at what stage, a stolen article can be said to have perished, therefore, is a question which is still open and awaits solution by the courts. Perhaps the answer is to treat the question as one of fact and degree. If, as a practical matter, there is no realistic prospect of recovering the goods, they should be treated as having perished within the meaning of s. 6.

5.2 The seller's right to sell the goods

Among the most important terms implied by the Act in a contract of sale of goods are those relating to the seller's duty to pass a good title to the goods. Section 12(1) of the 1979 Act is as follows:

> In a contract of sale, other than one to which subsection (3) below applies, there is an implied condition on the part of the seller that in the case of a sale, he has a right to sell the goods, and in the case of an agreement to sell, he will have such a right at the time when the property is to pass.

It is clear that the main purpose and effect of the section is to require the seller to transfer the property or title to the goods to the buyer. Plainly, if the seller is the owner, and nobody else has any claims to the goods, the seller's property in the goods will pass to the buyer under the contract and s. 12(1) will be satisfied. But the section does not require that the seller should themselves be owner, or even that they should acquire a title to the goods before transferring them. 'A contract of sale can perfectly well be performed by a seller who never has title at any time, by causing a third party to transfer it directly to the buyer.'[30]

[28] *Goodey* v *Garriock* [1972] 2 Lloyd's Rep 369, 372.

[29] [1929] 1 KB 574.

[30] *Karlshamns Oljefabriker* v *Eastport Navigation Corp* [1982] 1 All ER 208, 215, per Mustill J.

Section 12(1) is not, however, drafted in terms of 'property' nor of 'title'.[31] What it requires is that the seller has, or should have, a 'right to sell', and this causes problems because of the inevitable ambiguity of the word 'right'. The question whether the seller has a right to sell the goods cannot be answered until it is known precisely what it is which the seller must transfer to the buyer. The Act itself does not provide a very clear answer to this problem. All we have is the statement in s. 2(1) that 'a contract for the sale of goods is a contract by which the seller transfers or agrees to transfer the property in goods to the buyer', and the definition of the term 'property' in s. 61 as 'the general property in goods and not merely a special property'. In other words, unless the seller has a right to pass the general property to the buyer, they will be in breach of s. 12(1). But what is meant by a 'right' to sell the goods? The natural and primary meaning of the word 'right' in s. 12(1) seems to be 'power'; in other words, the seller must have the *power* to vest the general property in the goods in the buyer.

In most cases, of course, the 'power' to confer a title and the 'right' to sell the goods will go together. But there are some exceptional cases in which they may be separated, and it may then be significant that the section is not drafted in terms of a 'power'. First, there are some rare cases in which a seller may have a 'right' to sell the goods, and yet may have no power to confer a good title on the buyer. For example, a debtor who sells goods which have already been seized (but not physically removed) by the sheriff under a writ of execution has a right to sell them (at least until they are sold by the sheriff) but they sell them subject to the sheriff's rights.[32] They are thus unable to confer a good title on the buyer free from the sheriff's claims. No action lies under s. 12(1) in such a case, though (as noted later) there is a remedy under s. 12(2).

The second type of exceptional case concerns the reverse situation – that is, where the seller has the power to confer a good title on the buyer, but yet no 'right to sell the goods'. It appears, for instance, from the decision in *Niblett* v *Confectioners' Materials Co*[33] that the seller may in some circumstances be guilty of a breach of s. 12(1) although they have the power to transfer the property in the goods. The facts of this case were as follows: the defendants, an American company, sold 3,000 tins of preserved milk to the plaintiffs, but when the goods arrived in England, they were detained by the customs authorities on the ground that their labels infringed the trademark of a well-known English company. It was held that as this company could have obtained an injunction to restrain the sale of the goods, the sellers had no right to sell them.[34]

Although this was an unusual case, the more recent decision in *Azzurri Communications Limited* v *International Telecommunications Equipment Limited t/a SOS Communications*[35] is similar. Here, Azzuri had supplied a large number of telephone sets for use in call centres operated by the Automobile Association Ltd. These had been obtained from two separate suppliers, one of whom being SOS Communications. Numerous handsets

[31] Compare Uniform Commercial Code, Art. 2–312(1), which imposes an obligation on the seller to pass a good title.

[32] See *Lloyds & Scottish Finance Ltd* v *Modern Cars & Caravans (Kingston) Ltd* [1966] 1 QB 764.

[33] [1921] 3 KB 387.

[34] *Cf. Sumner Permain & Co Ltd* v *Webb & Co Ltd* [1922] 1 KB 55, the facts of which are given at p. 143, where no question was raised as to the application of s. 12(1).

[35] [2013] EWPCC 17.

developed faults, and it transpired that these were all from the batch supplied by SOS. The manufacturer of the handsets then discovered that those supplied by SOS were 'grey market' imports into the European Economic Area, that SOS was not an authorised wholesaler, and that there had been a trademark infringement, which amounted to a breach of both ss.12(1) and 12(2).

These cases are on quite a specific issue, but there are many other cases, which will be fully examined later,[36] in which a person who is not the owner of goods and who sells them without the owner's authority is enabled by the Act (or by other statutes) to pass a good title to the buyer. In such cases, it seems that there is a breach of the condition implied by s. 12(1), but the buyer has in fact suffered no damage from the breach and cannot therefore maintain an action against the seller.[37] It is true that in *Niblett* v *Confectioners' Materials Co Ltd*[38] Atkin LJ thought that in such a case the condition would not be broken at all, but it is submitted that the solution given here is better because there may be circumstances in which the buyer may justifiably wish to reject the goods, even though they have acquired a good legal title. For example, it seems that the legal title which is obtained under Part III of the Hire-Purchase Act 1964, where a private purchaser buys a motor vehicle which is the subject of a hire-purchase agreement, is not in practice always a very satisfactory one. The reason for this is that if the buyer later wishes to sell or trade in the vehicle to a motor dealer, the dealer will in all probability discover the outstanding hire-purchase agreement and may well refuse to buy it. It seems, therefore, that the buyer should be entitled to reject the goods in such a case.[39] And such a result would be justifiable because even though in these cases the seller has the power to confer a title on the buyer, they do not have what the Act specifically requires them to have, namely a 'right to sell the goods'.

5.2.1 The effect of a breach of s. 12(1)

The normal remedies open to the innocent party where there is a breach of condition are (a) repudiation of the contract, and/or (b) a claim for damages, while in Scotland they may terminate the contract if the breach is material, and/or claim damages. In addition, there are in England and Wales common law remedies of a restitutionary character, such as the right to recover money paid when there is a total failure of consideration.[40] Section 54 preserves these common law rights by enacting that:

> Nothing in this Act affects the right of the buyer . . . to recover money paid where the consideration for the payment of it has failed.

In the usual case, the buyer will not stand to gain financially from choosing to repudiate the contract rather than sue for damages. The reason is that they cannot retain any

36 See Chapter 12.

37 See the Report of the Crowther Committee on Consumer Credit (Cmnd 4596), para. 5.7.32.

38 [1921] 3 KB 387, 401; and it was so held in *Anderson* v *Ryan* [1967] IR 34, though apparently without argument on this point.

39 See the interesting American case of *Jeanneret* v *Vichey* 693 F 2d 259, US Ct of Appeals, Second Circ. (1982) – purchase of a painting which the purchaser later discovered was suspected of having been exported illegally from Italy thereby destroying its resale value.

40 Scots law does not have the doctrine of total failure of consideration, and analogies with its enrichment remedy *condictio causa data causa non secuta* are not helpful. See *Connelly v Simpson* 1993 SC 391 and discussion thereof in MacQueen, 1994 JR 137.

benefit under the contract if they wish to repudiate it, nor does the restitutionary remedy preserved by s. 54 usually help because *ex hypothesi* there must have been a total failure of consideration, and the buyer cannot therefore have obtained any benefit under the contract. A fair summary of the normal position, therefore, would be that the buyer cannot both have their cake and eat it.

In the case of a breach of the condition implied by s. 12(1), however, it appears that the buyer can do just this. The leading case is *Rowland* v *Divall*.[41] The plaintiff bought a car from the defendant for £334 and resold it for £400 to a sub-buyer who used it for four months. He then discovered that the car had never belonged to the defendant, who had bought it in good faith from someone without title. The car having been claimed by the original owner, the plaintiff paid off the sub-buyer by refunding him the £400 and claimed to recover, in turn, the £334 which he had paid the defendant. It was held by the Court of Appeal that the buyer was entitled to recover the whole purchase price and that the seller was not entitled to set off anything for the four months' use of the car which the sub-buyer had enjoyed.[42] Atkin LJ observed:[43]

> The buyer has not received any part of that which he contracted to receive – namely, the property and right to possession – and, that being so, there has been a total failure of consideration.[44]

The full implications of this decision are shown by two later cases. In *Karflex Ltd* v *Poole*[45] the plaintiffs were hire-purchase dealers who bought a car from one K and hired it to the defendant with the usual option to purchase on payment of all the instalments. The defendant paid the deposit and took possession of the car, but he defaulted on the first instalment and the plaintiffs commenced proceedings against him. It then transpired that K had never been the owner of the car at all, but the plaintiffs paid off the true owner and proceeded with their action against the defendant. It was held by a Divisional Court that the action failed because the plaintiffs were in breach of an implied condition that they had a right to sell the goods, since at the date of the delivery of the car they had no such right. The defendant, therefore, who had defaulted in payment of the very first instalment was held entitled to repudiate the contract and, indeed, to recover his deposit despite the fact that he had not been evicted by the true owner, and that by the time the case came on for trial there was no possibility of eviction because the original owners had been paid off. This was not actually a case of sale but of hire-purchase, but the court regarded the principles applicable as the same. Now, the implied condition as to title in s. 12(1) of the

41 [1923] 2 KB 500.

42 It is not clear whether Scots law would reach the same result. In the only Scottish case on breach of s. 12(1) the buyer recovered the full price paid, but as damages rather than restitution (*Spink & Co v McColl* 1992 SLT 471). Thus in principle recovery should be based upon what the buyer has lost through the breach, which, being normally the value of the goods *at the date of eviction*, may be more, less, or the same as the original price. However, the seller appears to have no claim against the buyer, since the latter's enrichment through the use of the goods has been at the expense of the true owner, *not* of the seller.

43 [1923] 2 KB 500, at p. 507.

44 He also observed that 'there can be no sale . . . of goods which the seller has no right to sell' (at p. 506), a view criticised by Ho (1997) 56 CLJ 571, at pp. 582 et *seq*. The merits of the case are somewhat complicated by the fact that, in the end, the buyer was able to get the car back on payment of £260. His claim for the full £334 which he paid thus seems to have been somewhat unfair, apart altogether from the fact that no account was taken of the use made of the car by the sub-buyer.

45 [1933] 2 KB 251.

Sale of Goods Act extends to hire-purchase contracts, [46] so at least it seems clear that the same principle must apply in the two cases.[47]

The second case is *Butterworth* v *Kingsway Motors Ltd*, [48] where A took delivery of a car under a contract of hire-purchase. Mistakenly thinking that she had a right to sell it subject to her continuing to pay the instalments, she purported to sell it to B. B sold it to C, who sold it to the defendant, and the defendant sold it to the plaintiff. After the plaintiff had had the use of the car for no less than 11½ months, he received a notification from the original hire-purchase dealers, who were of course still the owners of the car, claiming the delivery up to them of the vehicle. Seeing the opportunities which presented themselves, the plaintiff lost no time in writing to the defendants, claiming the return of the entire purchase price which he had paid. Within one week of this, A paid off the balance of the hire-purchase price to the original owners. The defendant might have been forgiven for thinking that this payment removed all difficulties and closed the transaction because the payment vested the title to the car in A, and this title 'went to feed' the defective titles of the subsequent purchasers. It was held, however, that the plaintiff was entitled to recover the full purchase price of £1,275 as the defendant had been guilty of a breach of s. 12(1). As the market had dropped in the meantime, the car was worth only about £800 at the date when the plaintiff repudiated the contract. Consequently, the Act enabled him to make a handsome profit of £475, a fact which no doubt explains the learned judge's view that 'the plaintiff's position was somewhat lacking in merits'.[49]

It is indeed possible to imagine circumstances, by no means unrealistic, which are far more extreme than those in the above cases. For example, suppose that A buys a crate of whisky from B. Suppose further that after consuming the whisky, A discovers that it never belonged to B but that B had bought it in good faith from a thief. Is it to be said that A can recover the full purchase price on the ground that there has been a total failure of consideration? This suggestion is perhaps not quite so ridiculous as might appear at first sight because the consumption of the whisky lays the consumer open to an action of conversion by the true owner. There would be nothing absurd about a rule which enabled the buyer to recover the full price from the seller if they were compelled to pay the value of the goods to the true owner. But the difficulty about *Rowland* v *Divall* is that the right of the buyer to recover the full price is not made dependent on a claim by the real owner. It is quite possible, especially where stolen goods have changed hands several times, that the real owner may never be traced at all. Again, it is quite possible that the real owner may choose to sue the seller rather than the buyer for conversion. Indeed, they will probably sue the first solvent person in the chain because the damages will probably be higher. If such were to happen in the hypothetical case above, the remarkable result would seem to follow

[46] See ss. 8–11 of the Supply of Goods (Implied Terms) Act 1973.

[47] As well as to an express term – see *Barber* v *NSW Bank* plc [1996] 1 All ER 906. The same implied condition now applies, *mutatis mutandis*, in other contracts for the transfer of goods by virtue of the Supply of Goods and Services Act 1982, ss. 2 and 7. The latter section applies to cases of hire where, however, it would seem even more troublesome to apply the decision in *Rowland v Divall*.

[48] [1954] 1 WLR 1286.

[49] At p. 1291. Pearson J here left open the question whether the plaintiff would have succeeded had he not claimed the return of his money before A paid off the owners. In New South Wales it has been held that if the seller obtains title (for example, by paying off the true owner) before the buyer seeks to repudiate the contract, it will then be too late for the buyer to recover his price: *Patten* v *Thomas Motors Pty Ltd* [1965] NSWR 1457.

that B would have to pay the whole price back to A, on the one hand, and the whole value again to the true owner, while A, on the other hand, will have had a free crate of whisky.

One possible way of avoiding this result might be as follows. Normally, a party who claims to repudiate a contract must return any benefits received.[50] In *Rowland* v *Divall*, it was pointed out that the defendant could not complain that the car had not been returned to him for it was his very breach of condition that made this impossible. In the hypothetical case above, however, it might be argued that the plaintiff's inability to return the goods is due to the fact that he has consumed the whisky. This does not dispose of all difficulty, however, for if the plaintiff is to be met by this argument the injustice may well be on the other side. The true owner may yet turn up and choose to sue the buyer for conversion.[51] In this case the buyer, having failed to recover his price from the seller, may then have to pay the value of the goods to the true owner. But the solution to this difficulty in England and Wales may be to recognise the buyer's right to seek contribution or indemnity from the seller under the Civil Liability (Contribution) Act 1978.

It may thus be possible to deal with the case discussed above so as to achieve substantial justice in the end. But this does not eliminate the serious injustice of such cases as *Butterworth* v *Kingsway Motors Ltd*. Nor does it dispose of the main objection to *Rowland* v *Divall*, which is that the decision rests basically on a fallacy. The object of a contract of sale is surely to transfer to the buyer the use and enjoyment of the goods free from any adverse third-party claims. If the buyer has such use and enjoyment and no third-party claim is made against them, it seems unrealistic to talk of a total failure of consideration.

These problems have been examined by law reform agencies over a period of several years. In 1966, the Law Reform Committee recommended in their Twelfth Report[52] that the buyer should not be allowed to recover the price in full in a *Rowland* v *Divall* situation with no allowance for the use he has had of the goods.[53] Since then the Law Commission has re-examined the problem on several different occasions. At first the Law Commission, while agreeing in principle with this recommendation, pointed out a number of practical difficulties in the proposal.[54] They concluded that no satisfactory amendment of s. 12 could be proposed until a study had been made of the rules relating to the law of restitution and the 1973 Supply of Goods (Implied Terms) Act did not, therefore, deal with this question. Since then two other Law Commission papers continued to take the view that the rule in *Rowland* v *Divall* ought to be abolished, and the buyer victim of a breach of s. 12(1) should only be entitled to damages rather than the return of his whole price.[55]

[50] That is why, in *Azzurri Communications Limited* v *SOS Communications*, the only claim was one for damages once Azzuri had agreed to return all the handsets infringing the manufacturer's trademark back to the manufacturer (accepted by the judge as a commercially sensible decision) and was therefore unable to return them to SOS, the supplier.

[51] Again, a doctrine to which there is no equivalent in Scots law. It would appear, however, that the true owner might have an unjustified enrichment claim for recompense in these circumstances: see further Evans-Jones, *Unjustified Enrichment* vol 2 (2013, W Green & Son Ltd, Edinburgh), Chapter 4.

[52] Cmnd 2958, 1966, para. 36.

[53] See also Treitel (1967) 30 MLR at 146–9.

[54] Law Commission and Scottish Law Commission, *Exemption Clauses in Contracts, First Report: Amendments to the Sale of Goods Act 1893* (Law Com. No. 24 and Scot Law Com. No. 12), paras 15–16, hereafter cited as Law Commission, *Exemption Clauses*, First Report.

[55] See Law Com. No. 121, *Pecuniary Restitution on Breach of Contract* (1983) and their Working Paper No. 85, *Sale and Supply of Goods*, p. 109.

But in 1987, after still further consideration, the Law Commission finally abandoned all attempts to deal with *Rowland* v *Divall*.[56] The reasons for this change of front appear to have been twofold. First, the Commission was not satisfied that justice requires that a buyer from a seller without title should have to pay them for the use they have had of the goods. Why, asked the Commission rhetorically, should the buyer have to pay the seller for the use of someone else's goods? But the second reason appears the dominant one, and that is the sheer complexity of trying to work out a set of rules which copes adequately with the intricate relationship between s. 12(1) of the Act and the law of conversion. It is undoubtedly true that this interrelationship makes any detailed solution very hard, but the answer may well lie not in abandoning all attempt at reform, but rather in abandoning the attempt to reform the law by working out the detailed rules in advance. After all, this has never been the common law's preferred methodology, and it would surely have been possible to give the court a little discretion to adjust the normal rules as to damages under s. 12(1). It does seem lamentable to tolerate the injustice which arose in *Butterworth* v *Kingsway Motors Ltd* (and this, surely, was gross injustice, despite the Law Commission's rhetorical question) merely because the problem seems too complex to permit a detailed legislative solution in terms of rules.

This particular problem does not seem to have arisen in other contexts. It is, however, possible that a similar situation could occur where goods are rejected for breach of one of the terms as to quality or fitness. In practice, this has not hitherto been a serious problem in such cases because the buyer is usually treated as having accepted the goods after a very short period of use.[57] However, problems with title can occur after a considerable lapse of time. In the United States, the majority response to this problem seems to be to award the plaintiff the value of the goods at the time dispossession occurred, plus any incidental damages that can be proved, on the principle that the plaintiff should be compensated for what has been lost, and surely this is the value at the time of dispossession?[58]

It is not possible for the parties to contract out of s. 12(1). This had been possible under the 1893 Act – the opening words of s. 12(1) of the 1893 Act[59] originally contemplated the possibility of the parties contracting out of the implied conditions as to title. In exceptional circumstances, a person may agree to buy goods from a *bona fide* possessor expressly subject to all defects in title. Goods seized and sold under a distress warrant, for instance, are sold without any warranty of title.[60] In such a case it is usual to sell merely the 'title and interest' of the debtor, whatever that may be. This means, for example, that the buyer takes the risk that the goods may not belong to the tenant, but may be held by them under a hire-purchase agreement. Under s. 12(3) and (4) of the 1979 Act, the possibility

[56] Law Commissions Final Report, *Sale and Supply of Goods*, paras 6.1–6.5. Under these recommendations no substantial change at all is to be made to s. 12, though there are trivial changes in the terminology of the section.

[57] See Chapter 17, at section 17.2.7.

[58] See, e.g., *Metalcraft Inc v Pratt* 65 Md. App. 281, 500 A 2d 329 (1985); *Jeanneret* v *Vichey* 693 F 2d 259 (2d Cir 1982); *Menzel v List* 24 NY 2d 91, 298 NYS 2d 979, 246 NE 2d 742 (1969).

[59] Unless the circumstances of the contract are such as to show a different intention.' See on this Hudson (1957) 20 MLR 237 and (1961) 24 MLR 690; see also Reynolds (1963) 79 LQR at p. 542.

[60] See *Payne v Elsden* (1900) 17 TLR 161, *Bogestad* v *Anderson* 143 Minn. 336, 173 NW 674 (1919) and Hudson, loc. cit. See also *Warming Used Cars Ltd v Tucker* [1956] SASR 249, where it was held that in the particular circumstances of the case the condition in s. 12 was negatived by implication. It seems, however, that the 'seller' in this case was more properly a mere agent

of a sale of a limited interest is spelt out more clearly. Where the parties intend only to transfer such title as the seller (or a third party) may have, there is an implied warranty that all charges or encumbrances known to the seller and not known to the buyer have been disclosed to the buyer before the contract is made. Moreover, under ss. 6(1) and 20 of the Unfair Contract Terms Act 1977 the seller cannot contract out of this liability.[61]

One slightly odd result of these provisions seems to be that the seller cannot contract out of s. 12(1) even to the extent that this goes beyond the implication of title. In *Niblett* v *Confectioners' Materials Co*,[62] for example, (the facts of which have already been given), it appears to have been assumed by all the members of the court that the seller would not have been liable had there been a contrary intention which negatived the implication that the sale of the tins would not constitute an infringement of a trademark. This does not seem possible under s. 12(1) of the 1979 Act. Given the uncertain ambit of the rights conferred by many forms of intellectual property, especially patents, this seems unjustifiable. The only practical, if not altogether satisfactory, solution where the parties are prepared to deal on the basis that it is uncertain whether or not intellectual property rights are infringed would appear to be insurance.

One final problem arising out of *Rowland* v *Divall* concerns the relationship between the condition implied by s. 12(1) and s. 11(4). This latter clause, which has enough difficulties of its own, will be fully discussed later,[63] but something must be said about it here. This clause states that when the buyer has accepted the goods, they are no longer entitled to reject them for breach of condition but are relegated to a claim for damages. In *Rowland* v *Divall*,[64] it was contended that this clause precluded the buyer from recovering his full price, and compelled him to sue for damages, but the court rejected this argument apparently on the ground that there can be no sale at all where the seller has no right to sell the goods. This involves saying that s. 11(4) has no application at all to breaches of s. 12(1) and Atkin LJ went to the length of saying precisely that. It is, however, difficult to find any warrant for this view in the Act itself.[65]

5.2.2 Warranty of freedom from encumbrances and of quiet possession

Section 12(2) provides that (except where a limited interest is sold) there is an implied warranty that:

> (a) the goods are free, and will remain free until the time when the property is to pass, from any charge or encumbrance not disclosed or known to the buyer before the contract is made, and
> (b) the buyer will enjoy quiet possession of the goods except so far as it may be disturbed by the owner or other person entitled to the benefit of any charge or encumbrance so disclosed or known.

61 See Chapter 8 for the effect of these provisions.
62 [1921] 3 KB 387.
63 See Chapter17, at section 17.X.
64 [1923] 2 KB 500.
65 Moreover, it has been said that if the buyer is aware of the seller's lack of title there can be an acceptance within s. 11(4) (formerly s. 11(1)(c)): see per *Devlin J in Kwei Tek Chao v British Traders & Shippers* Ltd [1954] 2 WLR 365, 372, where he also points out that the contract in *Rowland v Divall* was voidable and not void. These remarks are omitted from the report at [1954] 2 QB 459. As to this, see the note in (1955) 18 MLR 496.

In *Rubicon Computer Systems Ltd* v *United Paints Ltd*,[66] a dispute arose between the parties to a contract to install a computer system. The supplier, who had access to the system after installation, wrongfully attached a time-lock to it, which when activated denied the defendants access to their own system. It was held that the claimants were in breach of s. 12(2)(b). This case is a helpful pointer as to how the law might deal with the ability to restrict the operation of goods capable of connecting to the internet to receive regular updates to their operating software ('smart goods')[67] where such an update has the effect to switching off or restricting any of the functionalities controlled by such software (sometimes referred to as 'bricking').[68] One might assume that this is a breach of s. 12(2)(b) too, but it would depend on whether the arrangement to provide updates (usually contractual) would constitute a 'charge or encumbrance' that was sufficiently disclosed (see below).

Other than in cases such as this, it is not easy to see what additional rights this confers on the buyer over and above those conferred by s. 12(1) (especially s. 12(2)(a)). At first sight it might appear that s. 12(1) was intended to give the buyer a right to recover no more than the price of the goods, whereas a breach of s. 12(2) might entitle the buyer to recover additional damages. But this explanation is untenable for, as Singleton LJ pointed out in *Mason* v *Burningham*:[69]

> In any event if there was a breach of the implied condition the [claimant] was entitled to treat that as a breach of warranty.

In this case, the claimant recovered damages under the old s. 12(2) covering the cost of repairs done to a typewriter, in addition to the price, when it appeared that the seller was not the true owner.[70] More recently, the combined breach of s. 12(1) and s. 12(2) in *Azzurri Communications Limited* v *SOS Communications* meant that Azzurri could recover not only the full cost of buying replacement handsets from an authorized wholesaler, but also the additional expenses incurred in terms of staff time for removing and replacing the affected handsets.

The scope of s. 12(2) is not entirely clear. A 'charge or encumbrance' means a proprietary or possibly a possessory right, and does not extend to a mere contractual right.[71] It seems that s. 12(2) would protect the buyer against a wrongful disturbance of their possession by the seller themselves;[72] in this situation the remedy under s. 12(2) would overlap with a right of action in tort. Where the disturbance of the buyer's possession is by a third party, the buyer may be entitled to treat this disturbance as the responsibility of the seller

[66] (2000) 2 TCLR 453.

[67] Assuming that such goods would be within the meaning of 'goods' and that the contract would be one of sale within the sale of Goods Act 1979

[68] This is a different situation from the invocation of IP rights by the software licensor, as discussed in S Thomas, 'Goods with embedded software: obligations under section 12 of the Sale of Goods Act 1979' (2012) 26 *International Review of Law, Computers & Technology* 165.

[69] [1949] 2 KB 545. And see *Stock* v *Urey* [1954] NI 71, where the buyer of a car which was seized by the customs authorities was held entitled to recover what he had to pay to secure the release of the car, although this was more than the purchase price. Cf. *Darbishire v Warran* [1963] 1 WLR 1067, a case in tort.

[70] On such facts it would now be a serious question whether the cost of the repairs would be recoverable from the seller. Under s. 6 of the Torts (Interference with Goods) Act 1977, the plaintiff should be able to keep the typewriter, merely paying its unimproved value to the owner as damages.

[71] *The Barenbels* [1985] 1 Lloyd's Rep 528.

[72] *Healing (Sales) Pty Ltd* v *Inglis Electrix Pty Ltd* (1968) 121 CLR 584; *Industria Azucarera Nacional SA* v *Exportadora de Azucar* (1982) Com LR 171.

if, as a result of any acts or defaults of the seller, some third party with whom the seller is in contractual relations asserts an encumbrance or lien on the goods.[73]

But if the third party acts independently, the buyer can probably only rely on the subsection where the third party's act was a lawful act.[74] A seller can hardly be taken to warrant that no third party will ever tortiously interfere with the buyer's possession in the future.[75] The analogous covenant for quiet possession on a sale of land did not protect a buyer in England when he was evicted by title paramount (i.e. by a party with a title superior to the seller's), but that was because of the peculiar rule that a vendor of land did not warrant that he had a good title.[76] Accordingly, this qualification seems clearly to be confirmed by the implied warranty in s. 12(2).

Even where the third party's act is a lawful one, it will not amount to a breach of s. 12(2) unless it is based on rights to the goods which subsisted at the time when they were sold to the buyer.[77] In *The Barenbels*[78] the sale of a ship was expressly guaranteed 'free from all encumbrances and maritime liens', but this express term (which obviously closely resembles the implied term in s. 12(2)) was held not broken where the ship was seized by a foreign court as a way of compelling the seller to pay debts to a creditor previously incurred in connection with the ship. Although the debts themselves preceded the contract of sale here, the creditor's actual rights in the ship itself only came from the foreign court order, and they did not pre-date the sale. So the creditor had no proprietary or even possessory rights in the ship at the time of the contract of sale, and the creditor's rights were therefore held not to be encumbrances within the express terms of the contract.[79] At first sight, it may seem difficult to distinguish this case from *Rubicon Computer Systems Ltd* v *United Paints Ltd*.[80] The difference is that the supplier of the computer system was a party to the original contract, and was performing under it when it wrongfully attached the time lock. In *The Barenbels* what was involved was third-party rights, and no third-party rights to the goods existed until the court orders were made, which was after the contract containing the above warranty was made.[81] On the other hand, in *Great Elephant Corporation* v *Trafigura Beheer B.V*,[82] a buyer successfully established that there was a breach of s. 12(2)(b) when a ship, having loaded a cargo of oil, was prevented from leaving the port.

The precise meaning of 'charge or encumbrance' may require further exploration if a case involving smart goods were to reach the courts. A contractual right to update the

[73] *The Rio Sun* [1985] 1 Lloyd's Rep 350, 361.

[74] *Niblett* v *Confectioners' Materials Co Ltd* [1921] 3 KB 387, 403.

[75] See *Stephen v Lord Advocate* (1878) 6 R 282; *Dougall v Dunfermline Magistrates* 1908 SC 151.

[76] *Bain v Fothergill* (1874) LR 7 HL 158. This case has, in any event, now been overturned by the Law of Property (Miscellaneous Provisions) Act 1989, s. 3.

[77] In *Azzurri Communications Limited* v *SOS* Communications, the trademark rights already subsisted although the violation was only discovered when faults in the handsets supplied were being investigated by the manufacturer.

[78] [1985] 1 Lloyd's Rep 528.

[79] But the buyers succeeded on a different ground, namely that the sellers had also given the buyers an indemnity which was wide enough to cover the events which had occurred.

[80] (2000) 2 TCLR 453.

[81] A more difficult decision to reconcile this case with is *Microbeads AG* v *Vinhurst Roadmarkings Ltd*, dealt with below.

[82] *Great Elephant Corporation v Trafigura Beheer B.V.* v *Vitol S.A. & Vitol Asia Pte Ltd, China Offshore Oil (Singapore) International Pte Ltd* [2013] EWCA Civ 905.

operating software of smart goods would not constitute a charge or encumbrance; even it did, the buyer would almost certainly know that smart goods are regularly updated, and might, indeed, expect this to be so these days – unless s. 12(2)(b) requires actual knowledge or express disclosure of this fact. This might be an answer insofar as updates are made to preserve functionality, but it may be a different matter where the update removes functionality.[83] One might think that this would be a disturbance of the right to quiet possession. However, if the basis for updating the software is contractual, then it would probably not be a charge or encumbrance and s. 12(2)(b) would be of no assistance.[84] On the other hand, if updates were construed as some sort of continuing proprietary interest, then disclosure of the arrangements for updates might engage the provision in s. 12(2)(b). The spread of smart goods is a good indicator for the need to consider modernization of the Sale of Goods Act, not only in respect of s. 12 but also elsewhere; s. 12(2)(b) could certainly be an important basis for dealing with some of the effects of updates of operating software on the functionalities of the goods.

There are two other possible distinctions between the effects of s. 12(1) and (2): first, time under the Limitation Act would run against the buyer from the moment of sale under subs. (1), while under subs. (2) it is now clear that there is a continuing warranty of quiet possession. Consequently, time will only run against the buyer under (2) from the time his possession is disturbed.[85] Secondly, as we have already seen, there are some rare circumstances in which a person may have a 'right to sell' goods and yet may not be able to sell them free from some third party's rights. In such a case, a buyer would have a remedy under s. 12(2) but not under s. 12(1). We have already noted the example of a debtor who sells goods which have already been 'seized' (but not physically removed) by the sheriff under a writ of execution. The debtor has a right to sell the goods (at least until they are sold by the sheriff) but they sell them subject to the sheriff's rights. If, then, the buyer has to surrender the goods, they have an action for breach of s. 12(2).[86]

The practical operation of that part of s. 12(1)(b) dealing with freedom from encumbrances is limited because the law does not generally recognise real encumbrances over chattels by a person not in possession, and even equity only does so subject to the rights of the bona fide purchaser without notice. If, therefore, the third party is not in possession of the goods, they can rarely have an encumbrance which will be binding on the purchaser; on the other hand, if they are in possession the buyer has no need to rely on this subsection because the seller will simply be unable to make delivery. The buyer, therefore, will not be bound to pay the price or, if they have already paid it, will be entitled to recover it.[87]

[83] See also S. Thomas, 'Law, smart technology, and circular economy: all watched over by machines of loving grace?' (2018) 10 *Law, Innovation and Technology* 230, pp. 249–252. Of course, a further difficulty is in determining what the relevant functionality of the goods in question is. This may be easier with machinery (e.g., a washing machine, or aircraft engine) but less so with smartphones or computers.

[84] There may be instances where the loss of functionality could constitute a wrongful interference within the Torts (Interference with Goods) Act 1977.

[85] In Scotland prescription of the obligation to make reparation for breach of s. 12 runs from the date the obligation became enforceable, which will be when the loss, injury or damage caused by the breach occurs or, where the creditor is unaware of any damage, when it does become aware or could have been so with reasonable diligence (Prescription and Limitation (Scotland) Act 1973 s.11).

[86] *Lloyds & Scottish Finance Ltd* v *Modern Cars & Caravans (Kingston) Ltd* [1966] 1 QB 764.

[87] Section 28, which makes payment and delivery concurrent conditions – see Chapter 6, section 6.2.

But there are important exceptions to this general position. In particular, charges or encumbrances on ships (and aircraft) are common, and these may be valid and binding on a subsequent owner. So a buyer of a ship may be affected by such charges or encumbrances previously created, and for this reason these are usually the subject of express terms in a contract for the sale of a ship. But even in the absence of an express term, s. 12(2) would protect a buyer. Another exceptional type of case where s. 12(2) may be useful would arise if, for example, a person pledged goods but obtained delivery from the pledgee for some limited purpose. An unauthorised sale by the pledgor would enable the buyer to invoke this part of s. 12(2) against them, although they could not allege a breach of s. 12(1) because the seller had a right to sell the goods, though subject to the rights of the pledgee.[88] Another, very exceptional, case is illustrated by the decision in *Microbeads A G* v *Vinhurst Road Markings Ltd*,[89] where the Court of Appeal awarded damages to a buyer under the old s. 12(2). In this case, the buyer's quiet possession had been disturbed by a patentee whose patent was only granted after the sale in question, so that there had been no breach of s. 12(1) at the time of the sale.[90] This decision is difficult to reconcile with *The Barenbels*, dealt with above. The difference may be this. The causal events which led to the grant of the patent were in train at the time the contract was made, though until publication of the specification neither party could know this. By contrast, the seizure of the ship was one of a number of options no doubt open to the foreign court as a way of compelling the payment of the debts in question; there was nothing at the time the contract was made which inevitably led to the seizure of the ship. However, it should be noted that the decision in *Microbeads* has been criticised.[91] However, more recently, in *Azzurri Communications Limited* v *SOS Communications*, the buyer's quiet possession had been disturbed by the identification of a trademark infringement by the manufacturer and subsequent proceedings, which were settled by delivering-up the affected handsets to the manufacturer.

[88] *See Mitchell Cotts & Co (Middle East) Ltd* v *Hairco Ltd* [1943] 2 All ER 552; *Congimex* v *Tradax* [1983] 1 Lloyd's Rep 250.

[89] [1975] 1 All ER 529.

[90] A patentee's rights accrue from the date of publication of the specification, but they can only sue in respect of infringements of them from the grant of the patent – Patents Act 1977, s. 69. In the case of trademarks the relevant date is the date of application – *Denny v United Biscuits* [1981] FSR 114; Trade Marks Act 1994, s. 9(3). In the case of registered designs, rights commence on registration – Registered Designs Act 1949, s. 7, and the same is true of plant breeders' rights – Plant Varieties and Seeds Act 1964 (as amended), s. 4.

[91] See Law Reform Commission, New South Wales, *Working Paper on the Sale of Goods*, para. 12.5 (1975).

6

The duty to deliver the goods

6.1 The duty to deliver

Under s. 27 of the Act:

> It is the duty of the seller to deliver the goods, and of the buyer to accept and pay for them, in accordance with the terms of the contract of sale.

Aside from the fact that the seller is not generally bound to 'deliver' the goods, in the sense of physically dispatching them to the buyer (although the buyer is bound to take them), the duty of the seller to deliver the goods is a somewhat ambiguous concept covering three different possibilities.

There may be a duty to deliver to the buyer goods in which the property has already passed. Here the duty is specific and, subject to the question of payment, it is a duty which will be breached should the seller fail to deliver those particular goods. If the property has already passed, there can be no question of the seller substituting some other goods without the consent of the buyer. They must deliver those particular goods and no others will do.

Alternatively, the seller's duty to deliver may be a duty to procure and supply goods to the buyer in accordance with the contract, but without designating any particular goods that are to be delivered. Therefore, in a contract for the sale of purely generic goods the seller is in one sense bound to deliver 'the goods', but there is no duty to deliver any particular lot of those goods. Until such a duty arises, the seller is free to deliver any particular quantity of goods that meet the contract description. If the seller were to procure goods corresponding to the contract description, intending to use those in performance of the contract, but changes their mind and sells them to someone else, the buyer cannot complain that the seller has broken their duty to deliver.[1] Nor can the buyer obtain a decree of specific performance in such a case.[2]

There is a third possibility mid-way between the first two. It may be that the seller is under a personal duty to deliver a particular lot of goods although the property has not yet passed to the buyer. This is always the case where there is an agreement to sell specific goods where property in them has not yet passed; here the seller cannot resell those goods without being guilty of a breach of contract. Even in the sale of unascertained goods, it is possible for the seller's duty to deliver to attach to a particular lot of goods before the property passes. This, for example, is the effect of a notice of appropriation in a c.i.f.

[1] See *Carlos Federspiel & Co SA* v *Charles Twigg & Co Ltd* [1957] 1 Lloyd's Rep 255–6, per Pearson J.

[2] Because such a decree can only be granted where the goods are 'specific or ascertained'. Specific implement in Scotland may be different.

contract which does not pass the property, but fixes the goods to be delivered. Similarly, in a f.o.b. contract where the seller ships goods but retains the bill of lading as security, the seller will come under an obligation to deliver to the buyer the actual goods shipped, though the property remains with the seller for the moment.[3]

These three possibilities are not mutually exclusive, but three stages in the performance of the contract. The duty to deliver may start by being unattached to any particular goods, may then become attached and, finally, the property may pass. On the other hand, the three stages may be merged into one, as in a sale of specific goods, or two of them may be merged, where goods are appropriated to a contract fixing the duty to deliver and passing the property at the same time.

It should also be noted that the legal meaning of 'delivery' is different from the popular meaning. In law, delivery means the 'voluntary transfer of possession', which is a different thing from the dispatch of the goods. There is, indeed, no general rule requiring the seller to dispatch the goods to the buyer, for under s. 29:

> (1) Whether it is for the buyer to take possession of the goods or for the seller to send them to the buyer is a question depending in each case on the contract, express or implied, between the parties.
> (2) Apart from any such contract, express or implied, the place of delivery is the seller's place of business, if they have one, and if not, their residence; except that, if the contract is for the sale of specific goods, which to the knowledge of the parties when the contract is made are in some other place, then that place is the place of delivery.

This section, therefore, does two things. First, it defers to the contract between the parties regarding the place of delivery. Secondly, where the contract is silent it creates a presumption (or default rules) that in a sale of specific goods, the place of delivery is the place where the goods are known to be at the time of the contract, and that in all other cases, the place of delivery is the seller's place of business and, failing that, their residence.[4] Therefore, in the absence of a contrary intention, it is the duty of the buyer to collect the goods and not of the seller to send them. However, a contrary intention will frequently and readily be inferred from the circumstances of the case, or the express terms of the contract stipulating the seller's obligation to deliver the goods to the buyer's premises, or to dispatch them by courier.

Despite the general rule laid down in s. 29 that it is not for the seller to send the goods to the buyer, it is their responsibility to see that the goods are in a 'deliverable state'. Thus s. 29(6) enacts that:

> Unless otherwise agreed, the expenses of and incidental to putting the goods into a deliverable state must be borne by the seller.

The meaning of this phrase is considered later.[5]

Where the seller is, properly speaking, under a duty to dispatch the goods to the buyer, then this duty is absolute in the absence of frustrating circumstances; that is to say, the seller cannot plead that they were unable to dispatch the goods through no fault of their

[3] See *Wait* v *Baker* (1848) 2 Ex 1, 8–9; and see s. 19(1) and (2). C.i.f. and f.o.b. contracts are described in Chapter 13.
[4] See also *Gregor Fisken Ltd* v *Bernard Carl* [2021] EWCA Civ 792, para [91].
[5] See Chapter 10, at section 10.2.2.1.

own, or that they had taken all reasonable care in dispatching them. But a duty to deliver the goods at the buyer's premises is discharged by delivery to a respectable-looking person at these premises even though it should prove that they were not authorised to take delivery on behalf of the buyer.[6]

6.2 Payment and delivery concurrent conditions

Under s. 28 of the Act:

> Unless otherwise agreed, delivery of the goods and payment of the price are concurrent conditions, that is to say, the seller must be ready and willing to give possession of the goods to the buyer in exchange for the price, and the buyer must be ready and willing to pay the price in exchange for possession of the goods.

It is not necessary for the seller actually to tender delivery before being entitled to sue for the price or for damages if it is clear that the buyer would have refused to accept the goods, but it is enough that the seller was ready and willing to do so.[7] And, similarly, a buyer need not formally tender the price before becoming entitled to sue for non-delivery provided that they were ready and willing to do so.

Although the seller does not have to make a formal tender of delivery, they must have 'not only the disposition but the capacity to perform the contract'.[8] Moreover, a party is not precluded from relying upon one ground for repudiation merely because at the time they gave another and unjustifiable reason for repudiating. So if the buyer repudiates the contract in advance, and shows that they will not accept the goods if delivered or tendered, the mere fact that they gave an unjustified reason for this will not prevent them afterwards proving that the seller could not in fact have performed the contract. This rule, however, must be reconciled with another established proposition, that if the buyer wrongfully repudiates the contract, the seller can accept the buyer's repudiation and then maintain an action even though it is shown that they did not have the capacity to perform the contract when the buyer repudiated it. If the buyer meets the seller's claim for damages by pleading that, notwithstanding that they previously gave an unjustified reason for repudiating, the seller was themselves in breach by failing to deliver at the appointed time (or, in the case of a repudiation by the buyer before the time for delivery, that the seller would not have been able to deliver at the appointed time), these two principles appear, at first sight, to conflict.

Fortunately, the difficulty in stating the law was cleared up by the House of Lords in *Fercometal SARL* v *Mediterranean Shipping Co SA*.[9] In *Fercometal*, charterers of a vessel were informed by the owners that the vessel would not arrive in time to load in accordance with the terms of the charterparty. The charterers then purported to cancel the charter, which they had no right to do, as there was at that time no right of cancellation under the charter. But the owners in any event refused to accept this repudiation and insisted that

[6] *Galbraith & Grant Ltd* v *Block* [1922] 2 KB 155; but cf. *Linden Tricotagefabrik* v *Wheat & Meacham* [1975] 1 Lloyd's Rep 384.

[7] *Levey & Co Ltd* v *Goldberg* [1922] 1 KB 688, 692.

[8] Per Lord Abinger in *De Medina* v *Norman* (1842) 9 M & W 820, 827, cited by Lord Atkinson in *British & Bennington Ltd* v *N W Cachar Tea Co Ltd* [1923] AC 48, 63.

[9] [1989] AC 788.

the vessel would, after all, be ready to load on time. These assurances were false, however, and the vessel never was ready to load on time. The charterers having persisted in their refusal to load, the owners eventually sued them for damages for breach of the charter-party, and the charterers responded by pleading that the owners were never in a position to perform the contract. This defence was upheld. The House of Lords insisted that an anticipatory repudiation must either be accepted or refused. If accepted, the contract is then terminated, and the innocent party is freed from their duty of performance. But if the repudiation is rejected, the innocent party keeps the contract alive for all purposes. Their own duty to perform is kept alive, together with the duty of the guilty party. So they then must be able to perform the contract when performance is due. There is no third alternative, by which the innocent party can keep the contract alive, while themselves being absolved from performance.

The first possibility – that the seller's duty to deliver has been terminated by acceptance of the buyer's repudiation – is illustrated by another decision of the House of Lords, namely *Gill & Duffus SA* v *Berger & Co Inc.* [10] In this case, the sellers contracted to sell 500 tons of Argentina Bolita beans and undertook to provide a certificate of quality. The goods were delivered in two loads; the first of 445 tons was covered by a certificate but the buyers wrongly rejected the certificate, and repudiated the contract. The sellers as a result failed to tender a certificate for the other 55 tons, and in the Court of Appeal it was held that this failure was fatal to the sellers' claim. But the House of Lords reversed this decision, holding that the buyer's repudiation had been accepted by the sellers before the certificate for the second load of goods was required to be presented, and that that duty accordingly never arose at all. (It does not seem to have been argued by the buyers that the failure to deliver the whole 500 tons in one load was itself a breach of contract by the sellers.)

Although *Fercometal* was not a sale of goods case, it is clear that the principles discussed there are of general application. Indeed, one of the earlier cases, *Braithwaite* v *Foreign Hardwood Co Ltd*, discussed extensively in *Fercometal*, concerned a contract for the sale of goods.[11] In *Braithwaite*, the plaintiff had agreed to sell to the defendant 100 tons of Honduras rosewood, delivery in two instalments. The plaintiff shipped about 63 tons, but the defendant then heard that the plaintiff had shipped 468 tons to another buyer, and he regarded this as a breach of a collateral oral contract. He therefore repudiated the contract, but the seller insisted that the goods were already at sea, and he was ready to deliver the bill of lading. The defendant refused to take it, and the seller eventually resold elsewhere. The defendant later discovered that part of the timber anyhow did not conform to the contract, and, when sued for damages for non-acceptance, he pleaded that the sellers could not have performed for this reason. The buyer's defence was rejected by the Court of Appeal, and for many years the basis of this decision was controversial; however, the House of Lords in the *Fercometal* case has now explained this decision as resting on the fact that although the seller first refused to accept the buyer's repudiation, he did eventually accept it. That ultimate acceptance, therefore, terminated the contract,

[10] [1984] AC 382.

[11] [1905] 2 KB 543; and see also *Taylor* v *Oakes Roncoroni & Co* (1922) 38 TLR 349, 547.

and with it the seller's duty to deliver conforming goods. Hence the buyers were no longer entitled to raise this point.

Fercometal therefore clarified the law, but to some degree the clarification of the law itself was only achieved by leaving open for solution in particular cases certain difficulties of application. Whenever a buyer wrongfully repudiates in advance and indicates that they will not take delivery and the seller at first refuses to accept this as terminating the contract, some uncertainty will remain as to the outcome if the contract remains unperformed. When the seller eventually realises that the buyer remains obdurate, clearly they are likely to take certain steps such as not appropriating goods to the contract, or arranging for their delivery, or alternatively, disposing of the goods elsewhere. Unless they can show that they did ultimately accept the repudiation they may then have to face the accusation that they did not have the capacity to perform at the time when delivery was due. This result would often seem quite unreasonable, and the House of Lords in the *Fercometal* case approved an alternative route by which the seller may succeed in such a case.

This alternative route is to hold that the seller was freed from their duty to deliver, not by the termination of the contract (i.e. by the acceptance of the repudiation) but by an estoppel or waiver. So far as the former possibility is concerned, if the buyer has clearly represented to the seller that there is no point in them attempting to deliver the goods because, come what may, they will not take them, and if the seller acts upon that representation (for instance, by not arranging for delivery or by disposing of the goods elsewhere), then the buyer will be estopped from complaining that the seller has after all failed in their duty to deliver. Therefore here (as in many other areas of contract law) a representation, followed by action in reliance, is in effect treated as an alternative ground for achieving results normally achieved by offer and acceptance, or (as here) by repudiation and acceptance.

All this is admirably clear in theory and legal principle but it seems probable that it could cause difficulties in practice because it will often be difficult to say whether a repeated repudiation which is first rejected has ultimately been accepted, or whether it gives rise to an estoppel, or whether the seller's duty to deliver remains alive. A further complicating factor, which did not arise in the *Fercometal* case, but which could often arise in contracts of sale, is that a resale of the goods by the seller, following a repudiation by the buyer, may rescind the contract under s. 48(3) or (4), whatever the general common law rules as to acceptance of a repudiation may be.

Another complicating possibility is that the seller may occasionally be able to rely on the doctrine of waiver. Under this doctrine one party may waive performance of an act which would otherwise be a condition precedent to the performance of their own obligations. In this event, the other party is entitled to sue for breach of contract even though they could not have fulfilled their own contractual duties as a result of non-performance of that condition. Clearly the doctrines of waiver and estoppel largely overlap here, as they so often do, and it is not even certain that they are really distinct doctrines.

Although the seller must normally be ready and willing to deliver before they can claim that the buyer is in breach, it must be remembered that delivery has its usual legal meaning of transfer of possession in law. The meaning of this will be examined shortly, but it must be noted that where goods are shipped, the shipping documents represent the goods, and so transfer of these transfers possession of the goods. It follows that when the seller is ready and willing to deliver the shipping documents, they are *prima facie* entitled to demand payment of the price. A provision that payment shall only be due on delivery does not alter the position because delivery of the documents *is* equivalent to delivery of the goods. This was clearly laid down in the dissenting judgment of Kennedy LJ in *Biddell Bros Ltd* v *E Clemens Horst & Co Ltd*,[12] which was upheld in the House of Lords.[13]

It must also be borne in mind that if the goods have perished after the risk has passed to the buyer, then the seller's right to receive payment ceases to depend upon their willingness to deliver the goods.[14] It is odd that s. 28 says nothing of this possibility.

One final point needs to be made about s. 28 which could otherwise be a source of confusion. The effect of the section is that, in the absence of a contrary agreement, the seller is entitled to *demand payment* when they are ready and willing to deliver. But it does not follow, if the buyer refuses to pay, and refuses to accept the proffered delivery, that the seller can sue for the price. To be entitled to demand payment of the price and to be entitled to *sue for the price* are two different things.[15] If the buyer refuses to accept a good tender of delivery, the seller can, in general, sue for damages for non-acceptance only. Their right to sue for the price normally arises only when the buyer actually accepts the delivery of the goods and the property passes to them. The point is discussed more fully at a later stage.[16]

6.3 The meaning of delivery

Section 61 defines delivery as a 'voluntary transfer of possession'. What exactly amounts to a voluntary transfer of possession is not easy to summarise, but for present purposes delivery may take one of the following forms.

There may be a physical transfer of the actual goods themselves, and although difficult questions of law may arise in deciding whether the physical transfer is enough to transfer legal possession, we will not go into these here.

Secondly, the seller may transfer possession to the buyer by handing over to them the means of control over the goods, for example the keys to the warehouse in which they are situated.[17]

Thirdly, s. 29(4) provides that:

> Where the goods at the time of sale are in the possession of a third person, there is no delivery by seller to buyer unless and until the third person acknowledges to the buyer that he holds the goods on his behalf; but nothing in this section affects the operation of the issue or transfer of any document of title to goods.

This acknowledgment is called 'attornment' in English law and is of special importance where the goods are in the custody of a warehouse or similar. Where the seller gives the

[12] [1911] 1 KB 934.
[13] [1912] AC 18.
[14] See, e.g., *McPherson, Thorn, Kettle & Co* v *Dench Bros* [1921] VLR 437, 445: 'non-delivery was here excused by the loss of the goods which at this time were at the purchaser's risk'.
[15] The majority of the CA seems to have been guilty of confusing these two things in *Damon Cia Naviera* v *Hapag-Lloyd* [1985] 1 All ER 475.
[16] See Chapter 16, at section 16.1.
[17] *Hilton* v *Tucker* (1888) 39 Ch D 669; *Dublin City Distillery Ltd* v *Doherty* [1914] AC 823; *Wrightson* v *Macarthur* [1921] 2 KB 807; *Macdougall* v *Whitelaw* (1840) 2 D 500; *Moore* v *Gledden* (1869) 7 M 1016; *Thomson v Scoular* (1882) 9 R 430; *West Lothian Oil Co* v *Mair* (1892) 20 R 64.

buyer a delivery order or warrant for goods stored in a warehouse, this does not transfer possession or property until the warehousekeeper attorns by accepting the order or warrant.[18] Receipt of the delivery order alone, without any comment does not, without more, amount to an attornment.[19]

Fourthly, the goods may be delivered by the delivery of documents of title relating to them. A document of title is defined by s. 1(4) of the Factors Act 1889 as:

> Any bill of lading, dock warrant, warehousekeeper's certificate, and warrant or order for the delivery of goods, and any other document used in the ordinary course of business as proof of the possession or control of goods, or authorising or purporting to authorise, either by endorsement or by delivery, the possessor of the documents to transfer or receive goods thereby represented.

This definition, which is quite vague, appears to cover any document showing that the holder is entitled to claim the property specified in it. The distinctive feature of documents of title is that the mere transfer or endorsement of the document, if accompanied by the necessary intention, will transfer the possession *and* the property in the goods, even without attornment. By far the most important type of document of title is the bill of lading. When goods are shipped, the shipowner or their agent delivers to the shipper a bill of lading, and this document 'in law and in fact represents the goods. Possession of the bill of lading places the goods at the disposal of the purchaser'.[20] There seem to be few other kinds of documents of title in British commercial practice today, presumably because it is not customary for warehousekeepers' receipts and similar documents to authorise or to purport to authorise the holder to claim the goods by mere endorsement or delivery of the receipt without attornment by the warehousekeeper.[21] But it has been held that a delivery order may in certain circumstances be a document of title,[22] as also may railway receipts if suitably worded.[23] Moreover, under some private Acts of Parliament, certain warehousekeepers' delivery warrants are specially made documents of title and, indeed, in some cases they are fully negotiable instruments, so that an innocent transferee obtains a good title despite the transferor's lack of title.[24] Bills of lading are not, of course, fully negotiable in this sense.[25]

[18] *Sterns Ltd* v *Vickers Ltd* [1923] 1 KB 78; *Wardar's (Import and Export) Co Ltd* v *W Norwood & Sons Ltd* [1968] 2 QB 663. Even after attornment no actual property passes if the goods are not physically segregated or otherwise ascertained, though the attornment may be enough to raise an estoppel against the warehouseman: In *re London Wine Co (Shippers) Ltd* (1986) PCC 121.

[19] *Laurie & Morewood* v *John Dudin & Sons* [1926] 1 KB 223; *D F Mount Ltd* v *Jay & Jay (Provisions) Co Ltd* [1960] 1 QB 159.

[20] *Biddell Bros Ltd* v *E Clemens Horst & Co Ltd* [1911] 1 KB 934, per Kennedy LJ at 956–7. As to the time at which a bill of lading ceases to be a document of title, see *Barclays Bank Ltd* v *Commissioners of Customs & Excise* [1963] 1 Lloyd's Rep 81.

[21] A vehicle registration document is not a document of title because it merely identifies a 'keeper' (*Joblin* v *Watkins and Roseveare (Motors) Ltd* [1949] 1 All ER 47; *Central Newbury Car Auctions Ltd* v *Unity Finance Ltd* [1957] 1 QB 371, CA).

[22] *Ant. Jurgens* v *Margarinefabrieken* v *Louis Dreyfus & Co Ltd* [1914] 3 KB 40.

[23] *Official Assignee of Madras* v *Mercantile Bank of India* [1935] AC 53.

[24] For example, Port of London Act 1968, s. 146(4).

[25] An issue that might require legislative action in the future would be if so-called 'tokenisation' of goods with the aim of utilising modern technology (e.g., distributed ledger technology, also known as 'blockchains') to trade in such tokens. At the present time, the legal effect of transferring such a token on possession or ownership are unclear.

Fifthly, the parties may agree that the seller should hold the goods as the buyer's agent or bailee. This suffices to transfer possession of the goods for present purposes; that is to say, in the absence of a contrary intention, it entitles the seller to demand payment of the price, although in other cases it is a question of the greatest difficulty whether or not the bailor with an immediate right to take the goods can be said to have legal possession of them.

Sixthly, delivery of the goods to the buyer's agent transfers possession to the buyer themselves. Moreover, delivery to a carrier is *prima facie* deemed to be delivery to the buyer. Section 32(1) of the Act says:

> Where, in pursuance of a contract of sale, the seller is authorised or required to send the goods to the buyer, delivery of the goods to a carrier (whether named by the buyer or not) for the purpose of transmission to the buyer is *prima facie* deemed to be a delivery of the goods to the buyer.

But where the carrier is an agent or servant of the seller themselves, delivery to them cannot constitute delivery to the buyer, for it is merely a delivery to the seller's alter ego.[26]

6.4 The duty to supply the goods at the right time

6.4.1 The time of delivery

Section 10, after laying down in subs. (1) that the time of payment is *prima facie* not of the essence, goes on to state in subs. (2) that:

> Whether any other stipulation as to time is of the essence of the contract or not depends on the terms of the contract.

The Act therefore declines to lay down any general rules; however, the courts have done so, and it is well settled that 'In ordinary commercial contracts for the sale of goods the rule clearly is that time is *prima facie* of the essence with respect to delivery.'[27] If the time for delivery is fixed by the contract, then failure to deliver at that time will be a breach of condition or a material breach, which justifies the buyer refusing to take the goods. This rule applies to the time of delivery in the strict legal sense. As a result, it operates not only when the seller is obliged to dispatch the goods to the buyer but also when the buyer is bound to collect the goods from the seller. As we have previously seen, the House of Lords has affirmed that this rule applies in most commercial contracts, not merely with respect to the time of delivery but also with regard to the time for the performance of many other contractual obligations, such as the giving of notices.[28] It also applies to many duties of the buyer; especially where they are interwoven with the seller's duties, such as often occurs in cases of international trade.[29] And although, strictly speaking, this chapter is concerned with the duties of the seller, some cases relating to the duties of the buyer as to the time of delivery are also dealt with here.

Where goods are to be shipped by the seller before a fixed date or within a stipulated period, it is also well established that time is of the essence, so that any deviation from

[26] *Galbraith & Grant Ltd* v *Block* [1922] 2 KB 155, 156; *Badische Anilin und Soda Fabrik* v *Basle Chemical Works* [1898] AC 200.

[27] Per McCardie J in *Hartley* v *Hymans* [1920] 3 KB 475, 484.

[28] *Bunge Corpn* v *Tradax SA* [1981] 1 WLR 711.

[29] See, e.g., *Gill & Duffus SA* v *Société Pour L'Exportation des Sucres* [1986] 1 Lloyd's Rep 322.

the stipulations of the contract justifies the other party in treating the whole contract as at an end.[30] If, as is commonly the case in commercial contracts, the seller is allowed a period within which to deliver or ship (e.g. delivery 'during March' or 'shipment January/ February'), the seller has the whole period in which to deliver or ship, as the case may be.[31] They are not in default until the period has expired.

Where the contract provides that the seller will use their best endeavours to deliver the goods by a certain date but, despite their best endeavours, they are unable to do so, they must still deliver the goods within a reasonable time after that date.[32]

Where no time has been fixed by the contract, it is provided by s. 29(3) that:

> Where under the contract of sale the seller is bound to send the goods to the buyer, but no time for sending them is fixed, the seller is bound to send them within a reasonable time.[33]

What constitutes a reasonable time will depend on the circumstances prevailing at the time of delivery; for example, bad weather preventing a ship from docking or an aircraft from landing at the designated airport. The question is, taking into account the circumstances at the time, was delivery effected in a reasonable time?[34]

Reference should also be made here to s. 29(5) which states that:

> Demand or tender of delivery may be treated as ineffectual unless made at a reasonable hour; and what is a reasonable hour is a question of fact.[35]

Presumably, as a result, the position is the same where the seller is not bound to send the goods but is only bound to have them ready for collection.

Failure to deliver within a reasonable time (like failure to deliver within a specified time) may amount to a breach of condition by the seller.[36]

A contract may stipulate that delivery will be 'as required'. This means that the buyer must give notice of their requirements to the seller, and the seller must then presumably be allowed sufficient time to make delivery (though that time may be very short in appropriate circumstances). This also means that the buyer must require delivery within a reasonable time – they cannot in effect abandon the contract, or spin things out indefinitely by not requiring delivery.[37] But it is perhaps not entirely clear whether failure to require delivery within a reasonable time is by itself enough to justify the seller in treating the contract as repudiated, or whether they in turn must give some appropriate notice or warning to that effect to the buyer.

[30] *Bowes* v *Shand* (1877) 2 App Cas 455. As this case makes clear, early shipment is just as much a breach as late shipment.

[31] But if the last day is a non-working day (e.g., a bank holiday) the seller will not have an extension of time to the next day: *Jacobson Van Den Berg & Co* v *Biba Ltd* (1977) 121 Sol Jo 333.

[32] *McDougall* v *Aeromarine of Emsworth Ltd* [1958] 1 WLR 1126.

[33] Thus delivering goods to a building site out of working hours and leaving them in an unlocked garage would not be delivery in a reasonable time – see *Ron Mead TV & Appliances* v *Legendary Homes* 746 P 2d 1163 (Okl App 1987).

[34] *SHV Gas Supply & Trading SAS* v *Naftomar Shipping & Trading Co Ltd* Inc (The 'Azur Gaz') [2005] EWHC 2528 (Comm).

[35] *See Ron Mead TV & Appliances*, 746 P 2d 1163 (Okl App 1987).

[36] *Thomas Borthwick (Glasgow) Ltd* v *Bunge & Co Ltd* [1969] 1 Lloyd's Rep 17, 28.

[37] *Jones* v *Gibbons* (1853) 8 Ex 920. See the discussion of this case in *Pearl Mill Co Ltd* v *Ivy Tannery Co Ltd* [1919] 1 KB 78 and *Allied Marine Transport Ltd* v *Vale do Rio Doce Navegaçao SA* (The Leonidas D) [1985] 2 All ER at 806–7, superseding the use made of the *Pearl Mill* case in *The Splendid Sun* [1981] QB 694.

It is important to note that as the failure of the seller to deliver on time is a breach of condition, the buyer may reject the goods although they have suffered no damage as a result of the breach. This is illustrated in the well-known case of *Bowes* v *Shand*.[38] Here the sellers agreed to ship a quantity of rice from Chennai (then Madras) during the months of March and/or April. In fact, the bulk of the rice was shipped at the end of February and only about one-eighth was shipped during March. It was held by the House of Lords that the buyers were entitled to reject the goods, although it was conceded that there was no difference between the rice actually shipped and any rice which might have been shipped in March.

The buyer may reject in such cases not because they are aggrieved by the early (or even late) shipment but because the market has fallen, and they now want to escape from a bad bargain. This will not, however, necessarily be the case where the buyer complains of the failure to give notices on time or other similar breaches. Opinions may differ as to the desirability of retaining these rules. On the one hand, it may be objected that they permit an innocent party to escape from a bad bargain as a result of a highly technical breach of contract; on the other hand, there are serious problems about allowing a party to litigation to raise issues about the motives which have led the other party to act in a certain way. Examination of such motives often leads to very serious and difficult factual disputes. There are no current proposals for amendment of the law on this question.

6.4.2 Waiver of conditions as to delivery time

Although time is therefore *prima facie* of the essence with respect to delivery, buyers do not usually refuse to accept delivery merely because it is late. Actual acceptance of a late delivery is clearly binding on the buyer, so also even an agreement to accept late delivery will normally be binding whether made with or without consideration. It seems immaterial whether such waiver or estoppel is regarded as binding at common law[39] or by virtue of s. 11(2) of the Act which states:

> Where a contract of sale is subject to any condition to be fulfilled by the seller, the buyer may waive the condition . . .

McCardie J in *Hartley* v *Hymans*[40] rested his decision on s. 11(2), while Denning LJ in *Charles Rickards Ltd* v *Oppenhaim*[41] preferred to base it on the doctrine of promissory estoppel. In modern decisions, no clear distinction appears to be drawn between waiver and estoppel in such cases,[42] even though differences can be found between the conceptual bases of the two doctrines.

In commercial transactions, some of the most difficult questions that commonly arise are those concerning pleas of waiver and estoppel. The difficulty often arises from the fact that when a breach is committed or threatened (e.g. where the seller informs the

[38] (1877) 2 App Cas 455.

[39] Either under the common law doctrine of waiver or in equity under the rule in *Hughes* v *Metropolitan Railway Co* (now usually known as promissory estoppel).

[40] [1920] 3 KB 475.

[41] [1950] 1 KB 616.

[42] See, e.g., *Finagrain SA Geneva* v *P Kruse* [1976] 2 Lloyd's Rep 508.

buyer that they cannot ship or deliver in time) it is rare that the buyer instantly breaks off negotiations and treats the contract as repudiated.[43] More commonly, messages pass between the parties as they negotiate to try to resolve their difficulties; sometimes, too, a buyer may contact their sub-buyers because their attitude to delay may be governed by their attitude. During this time, the seller may still be doing their best to arrange delivery as soon as possible. If, finally, negotiations break down, or more extensive delays ensue, it may be very difficult to say whether the buyer has waived the delay or any part of it. Although issues of waiver and estoppel can arise with regard to other matters besides stipulations as to time, these are so commonly the source of such questions that they can most conveniently be dealt with here.

The principles to be applied in these cases can be summarised as follows. First, there must be a promise or a clear and unequivocal representation that the innocent party will not insist on strict performance of the original contract according to its terms. This does not mean that the promise or waiver needs to be expressly made. As Lord Salmon said in *Bremer* v *Vanden Avenne-Izegem*,[44] a case concerned with a notice which the sellers were entitled to give extending the date for delivery, but which was given late, 'To make an unequivocal representation or waiver, it is not necessary for the buyers to say – "We hereby waive it". It is quite enough if they behave or write in such a way that reasonable sellers would be led to believe that the buyers were waiving any defect there might be in the notice and were accepting it as effectively extending the date for delivery.'

A difficult and controversial question concerns the possibility of a waiver or estoppel arising if the party against whom waiver or estoppel is pleaded did not know all the facts at the relevant time. *Prima facie*, it still seems to be the general opinion that a party cannot be taken to have waived rights which they did not know they had because (for instance) they were ignorant of the breach of contract in question.[45] And similarly, a person cannot be held to have represented that they will not enforce their rights unless they knew what rights they had. At the same time, it is clear that there can sometimes be waiver or estoppel (or some legal equivalent) even without full knowledge of all the facts. In particular, it seems from the Court of Appeal's decision in *Procter & Gamble Philippine Manufacturing Corpn* v *Peter Cremer GmbH & Co*[46] that a representation (express or implied from words or conduct) may form the basis of a promissory estoppel if the representation strongly implies that the representor did have full knowledge of the facts. Furthermore, in principle, there seems no reason to doubt that a party could make it clear by words or conduct that they do not care what the relevant facts are, but is prepared to condone a breach if there has been one.

As with the cases dealt with earlier in this chapter (such as the *Fercometal* case[47]) there is often a conflict here between two sets of principles. On the one hand, the fact that the

[43] All this applies also to breaches by the buyer, e.g., of an obligation to open a letter of credit for payment. Here, too, breach will often justify immediate repudiation in law, but the seller is more likely to respond by demanding to know why the letter of credit has not yet been opened, and perhaps to allow some extension of time.

[44] [1978] 2 Lloyd's Rep 109, 126.

[45] See *Procter & Gamble Philippine Manufacturing Corpn* v *Peter Cremer GmbH & Co (The Manila)* [1988] 3 All ER 843; see also *Bremer v Mackprang* [1979] 1 Lloyd's Rep 220; *Cerealmangini SpA* v *Alfred C Toepfer* [1981] 3 All ER 533.

[46] [1988] 3 All E.R. 843.

[47] [1989] AC 788.

buyer does not immediately complain of late delivery does not necessarily prevent them from raising this later. A party is entitled, when sued, to offer any justification for their previous conduct, even though they did not give that justification at the time. It has also been stressed that waiver of one contractual term does not necessarily preclude the innocent party insisting on other related terms. Therefore, for example, where a seller was bound to deliver goods shipped in June and give a notice of appropriation by 10 July, a waiver of the latter requirement was held not to involve a waiver of the former. It was still possible for the seller to find a June shipment to supply to the buyer, and the buyer had not waived their right to a June shipment.[48]

On the other hand, a buyer who does not complain of the relevant breach at the time it is committed, but who at that stage appears to be willing to continue with the contract, may be held bound by waiver or estoppel so as to preclude their raising that breach at a later date. The question always is whether the buyer has led the seller to believe that they do not intend to complain about the breach. So a buyer who rejects shipping documents tendered on the basis that they do not include a certificate of quality, or who rejects the goods on grounds of quality, but makes no complaint of the time of delivery, may find that an eventual attempt to raise the issue of delay in delivery is too late: they may be told that they have, in effect, waived the late delivery.

Parties who are victims of breach of contract sometimes attempt to have things both ways by 'reserving their rights', while at the same time showing willingness to continue with the contract despite the breach. Use of this or similar wording does not rule out the possibility of waiver or estoppel if the other conditions of these doctrines are satisfied.[49] The victim of a breach of condition has alternative remedies: they can either treat the contract as terminated or affirm it, but they must choose between the two. They cannot, by claiming to 'reserve their rights', demand the right to affirm the contract while keeping in reserve the possibility of treating it as terminated. At the same time the innocent party can, if they are well advised, achieve the same result by first terminating the contract, making it quite clear that they are doing so before entering into new negotiations to try to sort out the consequences of that termination, which may lead to the conclusion of a fresh contract on more favourable terms. Unfortunately, businesspeople often think they can proceed straight to this second stage, by 'reserving their rights', only to find that the courts hold this to be ineffective.

A reservation of rights may, however, be of some legal effect up to a point. For instance, the buyer may make it clear that they are reserving their right to seek damages, while not insisting on treating the breach as a breach of condition justifying termination of the contract. The case law does not cast any doubts on this possibility.

Another important question which is still not totally resolved is whether a waiver must be acted upon to the detriment or prejudice of the party in breach before they can rely upon it. In general, it seems that this is necessary: a bare waiver or representation which is instantly retracted before it is acted upon is unlikely to be held to be binding. In *Société Italo-Belge* v *Palm & Vegetable Oils*,[50] the sellers were required to make a declaration of

[48] *Finagrain SA Geneva* v *Kruse* [1976] 2 Lloyd's Rep 508.

[49] *Bremer* v *Mackprang*, above, n. 54; *Vargas Pena Apezteguia y Cia Saic* v *Peter Cremer GmbH* [1987] 1 Lloyd's Rep 394; *Nichimen Corpn* v *Gatoil Overseas Inc* [1987] 2 Lloyd's Rep 46.

[50] [1982] 1 All ER 19.

shipment as soon as possible after the vessel sailed. The declaration was made a month later but the buyers did not protest when they received it; indeed, they asked the sellers to pass the shipping documents straight to the sub-buyers. The sub-buyers rejected them because of the delay, and the buyers thereupon also claimed the right to reject them. The sellers argued that there had been an implied waiver and that they had acted upon it by delivering the documents to the sub-buyers. It was held by Robert Goff J that, although these contentions were sound, it was not inequitable for the buyer to be able to retract the waiver. Although it may not be strictly necessary to show that the representee has acted on the representation or waiver to their detriment, it is necessary to show that they have acted on it so that it would be inequitable to allow the other party to insist on the contractual delivery date, and here such a short time had elapsed since the documents had been delivered to the sub-buyers (only two days, in fact) that there was nothing inequitable in permitting the buyers to reject the documents. Moreover, the buyers here had good reason for retracting their waiver.

6.4.3 Extension of time for delivery

The seller in a contract with a fixed delivery date sometimes indicates that they will not be able to deliver by that date, and asks for an extension of time. The buyer may respond in one of two ways (assuming they do not simply reject the request). They may either grant an extension, fixing a new delivery date, in which case the new date simply replaces the old one, and if time was of the essence (as it usually is) this means that the contract continues to operate, with the delivery time being of the essence, but with the new time simply replacing the old.[51]

Alternatively, the buyer may grant the seller an extension of time without actually fixing a new date or time. If this were an alteration of the original contract, supported by new consideration, the result would presumably be a contract to deliver within a reasonable time in accordance with s. 29(3). But where a delivery date is merely waived before the goods are delivered, the buyer is entitled to give the seller reasonable notice that they will not accept delivery after a certain date. In *Charles Rickards Ltd* v *Oppenhaim*,[52] the plaintiffs agreed to supply a Rolls-Royce chassis for the defendant, to be ready at the latest on 20 March 1948. It was not ready on this day, but the defendant continued to press for delivery, thereby impliedly waiving the condition as to the delivery date. By 29 June, the defendant had lost patience and wrote to the plaintiffs informing them that he would not accept delivery after 25 July. In fact, the chassis was not ready until 18 October, and the defendant refused to accept it. The Court of Appeal held that the defendant was entitled to reject the chassis as he had given the plaintiffs reasonable notice that delivery must be made by a certain date. If this kind of waiver is an illustration of the principle of promissory estoppel, then *Charles Rickards Ltd* v *Oppenhaim* can be regarded as an illustration of the principles discussed by the House of Lords in *Tool Metal Manufacturing Co Ltd* v

[51] *Buckland v Farmar & Moody* [1979] 1 WLR 221; *Nichimen Corpn* v *Gatoil Overseas Inc*, [1987] 2 Lloyd's Rep 46.

[52] [1950] 1 KB 616.

Tungsten Electric Co Ltd[53] as to the termination of the binding effect of a promissory estoppel by reasonable notice.[54]

Where it is clear that the party that has been permitted to perform their duty at a later time could not in any event have performed the contract within a reasonable time, notice may not be necessary, and a mere intimation that the contract is regarded as cancelled may be sufficient.[55]

Although s. 11(2) only refers to a waiver of a condition by the buyer, it is clear that the principles of waiver and promissory estoppel are general principles of contract law, and apply equally to buyer and seller. So, for example, a seller who leads a buyer to suppose that a letter of credit required by the contract will not be insisted on is not thereafter entitled to plead the failure to open such a letter of credit as an answer to a claim for non-delivery.[56]

6.5 The duty to supply goods in the right quantity

6.5.1 Delivery of the right quantity

The seller must deliver the correct quantity of goods. In the first place, s. 30(1) states:

> Where the seller delivers to the buyer a quantity of goods less than he contracted to sell, the buyer may reject them, but if the buyer accepts the goods so delivered he must pay for them at the contract rate.

Moreover, the seller cannot excuse a short delivery on the grounds that they will deliver the remainder later on because s. 31(1) states that:

> Unless otherwise agreed, the buyer of goods is not bound to accept delivery thereof by instalments.

There are no doubt circumstances (e.g. where the goods are to be shipped) in which it can be inferred from the contract quantity and the time allowed for shipment that the sellers are entitled to ship in more than one load, and therefore entitled to deliver in separate loads.[57] But the general rule is that the seller must deliver in one load.

The operation of these subsections is illustrated by *Behrend & Co Ltd* v *Produce Brokers Co Ltd*,[58] where the sellers agreed to sell a quantity of cotton seed ex the *Port Inglis* in London. The ship discharged a small part of the cargo in London, and then left for Hull where she discharged other goods. Fourteen days later, she returned to London and discharged the remainder of the cotton seed which was the subject of the sale. It was held that the buyers were entitled to reject the later delivery while retaining the earlier one.

A similar case, but one with a surprising twist to its tail, is *Gill & Duffus SA* v *Berger & Co Inc*,[59] where sellers who had agreed to sell 500 tons of beans delivered them in two

[53] [1955] 1 WLR 761.

[54] For an explanation of *Charles Rickards* v *Oppenhaim* based on the doctrine of common law waiver, see Adams (1972) 36 Conv (NS) 245 at p. 251 et *seq*.

[55] *Etablissements Chainbaux SARL* v *Harbormaster Ltd* [1955] 1 Lloyd's Rep 303.

[56] *Panoutsas v Raymond Hadley Corpn of New York* [1917] 2 KB 473; *Plasticmoda Societa* v *Davidsons (Manchester)* Ltd [1952] 1 Lloyd's Rep 527.

[57] *Pagnan & Fratelli* v *Tradax Overseas SA* [1980] 1 Lloyd's Rep 665.

[58] [1920] 3 KB 530.

[59] [1983] 1 Lloyd's Rep 622.

loads or shipments, the first of 445 tons and the second of 55 tons. The buyers rejected both loads on the ground that they did not conform to the contract description. This ground was held to be good as regards the second load, but bad as regards the first. It might therefore seem that the buyers were only entitled to reject the second load, but the Court of Appeal held that in the light of s. 30 of the Act, they must be held entitled to reject both loads because 'a right of rejection limited to 55 tons was not a possible conclusion in law'.[60] It seems that even if the buyers had waived any right to object to the fact of separate deliveries, their rejection of the first delivery, which was originally wrongful, was retrospectively validated by their rightful rejection of the second. Once the buyers had rejected the second delivery, it followed that the sellers were guilty of a breach of their duty to deliver 500 tons. On the facts that was not an unreasonable result, but the implication – that the buyers could have rejected the first load after rejection of the second, *even if they had originally accepted the first load* – does seem somewhat strange. This decision was reversed by the House of Lords[61] on grounds not affecting this point, namely that the buyers did not have the right to reject the second load at all because their wrongful rejection of the first load was a complete repudiation of the contract, which had been accepted by the sellers, so no duty of delivery arose at all as regards the second load.

Where delivery in separate instalments is permissible under the contract, the question whether a shortfall in the quantity required permits the buyer to treat the whole contract as discharged is dealt with by s. 31(2) of the Act. Here it is enough to say that that subsection is not as strict in its requirements as s. 30(1), and that a shortfall in quantity in one instalment does not justify the buyer in treating the whole contract as discharged unless it is sufficiently serious to go to the root of the contract as a whole.[62] The result may seem curious at first sight. Leaving aside the effect of s. 30(2A), suppose a seller contracts to sell and deliver 62 suits to the buyer, but they only deliver 61. If the suits were to be delivered in one load, the buyer could reject the whole lot (unless the absence of one suit is merely *de minimis*, which it probably is not). But if the suits are to be delivered in separate instalments, the buyer's rights are regulated by s. 31(2) and on these facts it has been held that the shortfall of one suit was not sufficiently serious to justify the buyer in treating the contract as completely discharged.[63] The result is not as odd as it seems. Where the parties do expressly contemplate instalment deliveries, serious problems would arise if a shortfall on one instalment gave a right to reject previous instalments already accepted. So it is natural that such a right should be severely limited, and each instalment treated as a separate delivery.[64]

The counterpart of the duty not to deliver too little is the duty not to deliver too much, although it is less obvious why this should be so objectionable. At first sight, there seems

60 At p. 627.

61 [1984] AC 382.

62 It should be noted that the Uniform Commercial Code, which preserves the 'perfect tender' rule in its full rigour (see §2-601), adopts a more relaxed rule for instalment contracts – §2-612.

63 *Regent OHG Aisenstadt* v *Francesco of Jermyn Street* [1981] 3 All ER 327.

64 But if each instalment is a separate delivery under s. 30(1) it might seem that the buyer should at least be able to reject the whole of an instalment if there is any shortfall in it. In the *Francesco of Jermyn Street* case Mustill J did not consider whether the buyer was not entitled to reject the whole of the consignment which contained the short delivery. This would then have raised the further problem that the application of s. 31(2) might have had to be considered on the supposition that the seller was in breach in respect of one whole consignment, and not just one suit.

no obvious reason why the buyer should not be required to accept that part which should have been delivered, whether or not they accept the rest. But this is not the law, for s. 30(2) lays down that:

> Where the seller delivers to the buyer a quantity of goods larger than he contracted to sell, the buyer may accept the goods included in the contract and reject the rest, or he may reject the whole.

Subsection (3) then says that if the buyer accepts all the goods delivered they must pay for them at the contract rate. This subsection does not actually say when the buyer can or cannot accept any excess delivered by the seller. It simply says that if the buyer does accept any excess, it must be paid for at the contract rate. It may well have been assumed that the buyer can always accept any excess, and it certainly seems that they should usually be able to accept whatever is delivered, whether too much or too little, because the delivery would usually be treated as a counter-offer, which the buyer accepts by accepting the goods themselves.[65]

In their Working Paper on Sale and Supply of Goods, the Law Commissions raised the question whether it is right to treat an excess delivery as always amounting to an offer to sell the surplus. While this appears reasonable in the case where the seller delivers 1,004 tons of grain instead of 1,000, it is rather different where the buyer orders one item, perhaps of a special nature, and two are mistakenly delivered.[66] The answer to this seems to be that the buyer obviously cannot accept the surplus when they know the seller does not mean to make an offer to sell those goods. That is the effect of the common law rules as to mistake which are preserved by s. 62(2) of the Act, and s. 30(3) must be read subject to those common law rules. In their Final Report the Law Commissions ultimately decided to leave s. 30(3) unamended and unrepealed.[67] They concluded that while there are theoretical difficulties in deciding when a buyer can accept an excess delivered by the seller, the difficulties do not appear to be of serious practical importance, and in any event the mere repeal of s. 30(3) would not resolve those problems.

6.5.1.1 The de minimis principle

Prior to the amendments made to the Act by the Sale of Goods (Amendment) Act 1994, the law was very strict in its insistence on the correct quantity. Any shortfall or any excess, no matter how small, was a breach of the section and justified rejection of all the goods. There was, and presumably still is, however, a principle of very limited application, known by the Latin phrase *de minimis non curat lex* (the law pays no attention to trifles) which could occasionally be invoked to excuse what would otherwise have been a technical breach. To illustrate the application of this principle in the present context, two cases, one on either side of the line, may be contrasted. In *Wilensko Slaski Towarzystwo Drewno* v *Fenwick & Co Ltd*,[68] the sellers sold timber of specified measurements to the buyers.

[65] *Hart* v *Mills* (1846) 15 M & W 85.
[66] Working Paper No. 85, Consultative Memorandum No. 58, para. 6.32.
[67] See Final Report, *Sale and Supply of Goods*, para. 6.23.
[68] [1938] 3 All ER 429. See also *Regent OHG Aisenstadt* v *Francesco of Jermyn St* [1981] 3 All ER 327, where the seller's counsel declined even to argue that a failure to deliver one, out of a contract for the delivery of 62 suits, was *de minimis*.

There were certain permitted, but strictly defined, variations from these specifications. Slightly under 1 per cent of the timber failed to comply with the contract requirements. The buyers were held entitled to reject the goods. On the other hand, in *Shipton Anderson & Co Ltd* v *Weil Bros & Co Ltd*,[69] the sellers contracted to sell to the buyers 4,500 tons of wheat or 10 per cent more or less. The sellers delivered 4,950 tons (the agreed upper limit) and 55 lb, but they did not claim payment for the 55 lb. It was held that the buyers were not entitled to reject the goods. The excess over the stipulated amount being a little over 1 lb in 100 tons, the case clearly called for the application of the maxim *de minimis*. If it had not been applied in this case, the rule would have lost all commercial importance.[70]

The maxim *de minimis non curat lex* is a legal principle of general application, but its applicability to any particular case seems to be a question of fact which depends, *inter alia*, on how far precise accuracy can be obtained, or whether there are limits of accuracy which are commercially reasonable.[71] Given how the 1994 provisions restricted the right of rejection discussed in the next paragraph, the principle ought seldom to be applied to cases falling under the present provisions, for the effect of applying it is that there is no breach of warranty at all.[72]

In their Final Report on these matters, the Law Commissions recommended that the non-consumer buyer should no longer be entitled to reject the whole of the goods delivered where the shortfall or excess is so slight that it would be unreasonable to reject the whole. The buyer would remain entitled always to reject any excess and the consumer buyer would be unaffected by these changes. The position in respect of consumers is now dealt with by s. 25 of the Consumer Rights Act 2015, so that the provisions of the 1994 Act[73] now solely address commercial buyers. The 1994 Act inserted s. 30(2A) (as amended) which provides as follows:

> (2A) (a) Where the seller delivers a quantity of goods less than he contracted to sell, reject the goods under subsection (1) above, or
> (b) where the seller delivers a quantity of goods larger than he contracted to sell, reject the whole under subsection (2) above, if the shortfall or, as the case may be, excess is so slight that it would be unreasonable for him to do so.
>
> (2B) It is for the seller to show that a shortfall or excess fell within subsection (2A) above.

This brought the right of rejection for breach of the quantity provisions of the Act into line with the provisions regarding the right to reject for breach of the implied terms as to quality and fitness, and it is discussed further in the chapter on the buyer's remedies.[74]

A minor point of some doubt is whether the buyer can accept only a part of what is delivered and reject the rest, except in the one case specifically covered by s. 30(2); that is, where an excess is delivered and the buyer proposes simply to keep what should have

[69] [1912] 1 KB 574.

[70] See also *Arcos Ltd* v *E A Ronaasen* [1933] AC 470, p. 120, below, and *Payne and Routh* v *Lillico & Son* (1920) 36 TLR 569, which was much relied on in *Rapalli* v *K L Take Ltd* [1959] 2 Lloyd's Rep 469, a case of quality rather than quantity.

[71] *Margaronis Navigation Agency Ltd* v *Henry W Peabody & Co Ltd* [1965] 1 QB 300. See Chapter 13, section 13.7, for the effect of the Uniform Customs and Practice for Documentary Credits on the *de minimis rule* in contracts where the price is payable by letter of credit.

[72] See *Cehave* v *Bremerhandelsgesellschaft* [1976] QB 44. In that case the right of the buyer to recover damages for breach of warranty arose for breach of an express condition.

[73] See s. 4(2) of the Sale and Supply of Goods Act 1994.

[74] See Chapter 17.

been delivered. They obviously cannot do this if the delivery conforms to the contract in respect of quantity and quality. But if too much or too little is delivered, it seems that the buyer may accept a distinct part of the goods, rejecting the rest.[75]

In the event of a breach of s. 30 by the seller, the buyer is entitled to recover a proportionate part of what they have paid as on a total failure of consideration, notwithstanding that they may have accepted and retained a part of the goods.[76]

6.5.1.2 Relationship between the seller's duties as to quality and duties as to quantity

The fact that the buyer may be entitled to reject the whole of the goods delivered in the circumstances dealt with by s. 30 means that, in substance, the seller in such cases is treated under English law as though they commit a breach of condition by delivering the wrong quantity. In this respect, the duties of the seller are parallel to those laid down as regards sales by description. Indeed, the whole of s. 30 is merely an application of the duty to deliver goods conforming to the description imposed by s. 13, and it is one of the peculiarities of the drafting of the Act that s. 13 is dealt with under the heading ' 'Implied Terms etc.', while s. 30 is dealt with under 'Performance of the Contract'.

For a start, the buyer's *prima facie* right of rejection means that they can always convert a breach of the rules as to quality into a breach of the rules as to quantity. If the seller contracts to deliver 100 tons of wheat of a certain quality and 10 tons are not of that quality so that the buyer rejects them, then the seller will only have effectively delivered 90 tons (and the question will now be whether the shortfall is so slight that it would be unreasonable for the buyer to reject). More generally though, the rules as to quality and the rules as to quantity are very similar in their effect, even if different in form. In particular, the close resemblance between the duties created by ss. 13 and 30 is brought out all the more when they are examined in detail. In both cases, until the right of rejection was modified by the 1994 Act, the slightest deviation from the terms of the contract was (in effect) a breach of condition entitling the buyer to reject the goods. If the seller delivered goods which failed, by the slightest margin, to conform to the contract description, or if they delivered a fraction too much or too little, the buyer might reject the whole. The only qualification on this was that if the deviations were 'microscopic',[77] the seller might be able to plead *de minimis*. But this principle was, and presumably will continue to be, applied as rarely in cases of quality as in cases of quantity. In fact, as suggested above, given the provisions restricting the right of rejection that were added in 1994 it ought not to be, for the effect of applying it is that there is no breach of warranty at all. So too the former s. 30(4) interrelated with s. 14(2) and (3) because, as will be seen later, the statutory implied terms under those subsections extend to all goods delivered in purported pursuance of the contract.

[75] *Hart v Mills* (1846) 15 M & W 85; *Champion* v *Short* (1807) 1 Camp 53; see Hudson (1976) 92 Law QR 506.

[76] *Behrend & Co Ltd* v *Produce Brokers Ltd* [1920] 3 KB 530; *Biggerstaff* v *Rowlatt's Wharf Ltd* [1896] 2 Ch 93; *Ebrahim Dawood Ltd* v *Heath Ltd* [1961] 2 Lloyd's Rep 512.

[77] *Arcos* v *E A Ronaasen & Son* [1933] AC 470, 480, per Lord Atkin. But in light of the modern cases discussed in Chapter 4, at section 4.3, it may be wondered whether this famous decision, though of the highest authority, is not now somewhat suspect. Cf. *Tradax International SA* v *Goldschmidt SA* [1977] 2 Lloyd's Rep 604.

The same close relationship between the duty to deliver the right quantity and the duty to deliver the right quality will be observed when we consider instalment contracts.[78] Here too, the buyer's right to reject is the same whether the breach consists in short delivery or delivery of the wrong quality.

For these reasons, it is undesirable for the law to distinguish between breaches of ss. 13–15 and breaches of s. 30, and in general the law does not do so. So it seems clearly right that the limitation on the right to reject in (what was then) non-consumer sales introduced by the 1994 Act should apply equally to breaches of the implied terms as to quality and to breaches of s. 30.

[78] See s. 31(2) of the Act.

7

The duty to supply goods of the right quality

7.1 From caveat emptor to caveat venditor

In England, the implied terms as to quality and fitness in ss. 13–15 of the 1893 Act represented an important step in the transition from the original common law rule of *caveat emptor* – 'let the buyer beware'. The common law had itself largely softened this rule by 1893, but in several important respects the Act went further than the courts ever did before it was passed. On the other hand, in Scotland the rule until 1856 was that a fair price demanded a fair article, and the seller was therefore bound to provide goods of reasonably good quality.[1] The Mercantile Law Amendment (Scotland) Act 1856 had introduced the doctrine of *caveat emptor*, before itself being replaced by the 1893 Act. But weaknesses in the drafting of the original sections gradually became apparent, and there was also growing concern at the freedom permitted to sellers to contract out of their liabilities. The Supply of Goods (Implied Terms) Act 1973 was designed to meet these objections. This Act, largely based on the Law Commissions' recommendations,[2] remodelled ss. 13–15 of the original Act and also contained major new provisions restricting the right of a seller to contract out of the implied terms through use of exclusion clauses. The control of exclusion clauses in contracts was later taken over by the broader provisions of the Unfair Contract Terms Act 1977, which is dealt with in Chapter 10. In this chapter, the discussion will concentrate on the implied terms themselves.

Many further developments followed. The first of these was the passing of the consolidated Sale of Goods Act 1979, which incorporated the amendments made by the 1973 Act into the rest of the Sale of Goods Act with some minor alterations, but no changes of substance. The second development was that the statutory implied terms as to quality and fitness were gradually extended to other contracts for the supply of goods as well as contracts of sale. The 1973 Act itself did this for contracts of hire-purchase while the Supply of Goods and Services Act 1982 did it for other contracts for the supply of goods. These contracts are not further dealt with here although authorities on the interpretation of these terms are relevant across the whole field.

In 1979 – before the new Sale of Goods Act was passed – the Law Commissions were invited by the Lord Chancellor to consider a number of further questions relating to the implied terms in contracts of sale of goods, and to certain related matters such as the

[1] See Sutherland, 1987 JR 24.

[2] See the Law Commissions' Report, 'First Report on Exemption Clauses in Contracts (1969)', Law Com. No. 24, Scot. Law Com. No. 12 (1968–69) HC 403.

remedies available for breach of these terms. After issuing a Working Paper in 1983, which contained many provisional proposals or suggestions for reform,[3] the Law Commissions published their Final Report, *Sale and Supply of Goods*, in 1987.[4] This Report contained further proposals for change, although many commentators were unhappy with some aspects of the proposals.[5] The proposals were implemented through the Sale and Supply of Goods Act 1994. This Act brought modifications to the implied terms as to quality, amendments to the rules on acceptance and rejection, and extended the supply of Goods and Services Act 1982 to Scotland (so far as it applies to goods).

The three primary terms laid down in the Act appear in s. 13, s. 14(2) and s. 14(3), and their combined effect is to give buyers a substantial degree of protection against the risk of the goods proving to have defects of quality or fitness for purpose. Indeed, it is now unrealistic, even in a contract between two commercial parties, to treat the basic principle of the law as *caveat emptor* rather than *caveat venditor* – 'let the seller beware'.

In one sense the three main implied terms in s. 13, s. 14(2) and s. 14(3), taken in that order, lay down a series of graduated duties upon the seller. First, there is the implied term that where goods are sold by description, the goods must correspond with their description. This applies in far wider circumstances than those in which the two other terms apply but, on the other hand, it does not afford a great deal of protection to the buyer, especially where the description of the goods is not a detailed one. Obviously, for example, a car may be described as a car, potatoes as potatoes, a reaping machine as a reaping machine, but in all cases the goods may be seriously defective.

The next implied term is that the goods must be of satisfactory quality. This does not apply in all the circumstances in which the first term applies but, on the other hand, it affords the buyer a greater degree of protection, because goods that correspond with their description may not be of satisfactory quality. Even this, however, may not suffice to protect the buyer, since goods may correspond with their description and may be of satisfactory quality, and yet they may still be unsuitable for the buyer's purpose. Hence, in still more limited circumstances, the buyer may be able to rely on the third implied term, namely that the goods must be fit for the purpose for which they were sold.

Although the law was simplified by the legislative changes made between 1973 and 1994, there remains a substantial and complex body of law to consider. As will be seen, in practice, the sections frequently overlap, and the same words appear several times in different places. To make this central aspect of the law more readily comprehensible, we will break it down into the following sections:

1 express terms;
2 implied terms that the goods must correspond with their description;
3 implied terms that the goods are of satisfactory quality;
4 implied terms that the goods are fit for a particular purpose;
5 implied terms in sales by sample;
6 implied terms annexed by trade usage.

[3] Working Paper No. 85, Consultative Memorandum No. 58, *Sale and Supply of Goods*.
[4] Law Com. No. 160, Scot. Law Com. No. 104, Cm. 137 (1987).
[5] See, e.g., Adams and Brownsword (1988) 51 MLR 481.

7.1.1 Time for compliance

The goods must be compliant at the time property in them passes to the buyer. There is, however, at the outset a problem. As we will see,[6] risk generally passes with the property in the goods, so that if goods deteriorate after the property has passed to the buyer, usually the buyer will have no remedy, and vice versa if the goods deteriorate before that time. However, it is generally said that it is the duty of the seller to *deliver* goods of the right quality, which may occur *after* the property in them has passed to the buyer. One way of resolving this apparent contradiction may be as follows. Delivery can be actual or constructive. When property passes to the buyer before actual delivery, there is a constructive delivery of the goods, and that is the point at which the conformity of the goods with the contract must be judged. After that point, the seller is a bailee of the buyer, and the buyer must take the risk of deterioration, subject to the seller's duties as bailee having been complied with. Although the Act defines 'delivery' as the 'voluntary transfer of possession from one person to the other',[7] this term seems to have reference to Part III of the Act, 'Performance of the Contract', which is clearly dealing with *actual* delivery. Given the criticisms made elsewhere in this book of constructive doctrines, an alternative way of reconciling the contradiction is possible. The buyer clearly has the right to inspect the goods, and to reject them if they are defective, and this right will be exercised when the buyer takes physical delivery of the goods. If at that time they are defective, the buyer will have the right to reject them.[8] In most cases it will be difficult for the seller to show, *as a matter of evidence*, that, at the time the property passed, the goods were conforming – even if sellers did, as a matter of course, focus their minds on the time of passing of the property.[9] In f.o.b. export sales there will usually be evidence of the state of the goods at the time the risk passed,[10] and thereafter goods are at the buyer's risk, and they should insure them but in other sales, there will usually be no evidence as to the state of the goods at the time the property in them passed.

7.2 Express terms

Express terms relating to the description, quality and fitness of goods sold are, of course, relatively common in transactions involving high value or complex goods. They are less common in sales of low value, high volume and relatively simple goods, There is no doubt that, apart from the *de minimis* rule, it is still the law that any deviation from an express term, however small, is a breach of contract for which the buyer is entitled to a remedy.[11] The cases which brought about something of a legal revolution in England by recognition of the concept of an innominate term, neither condition nor warranty, have been concerned solely with the nature of the buyer's remedy, and not with the question whether they have any remedy at all. As we have seen, the position at present is that, in the absence

[6] See Chapter 11, at section 11.2
[7] Section 62(1).
[8] Unless the defects are trivial – see Chapter 17, at section 17.1.
[9] Highly unlikely.
[10] In the bill of lading bearing a form of words such as 'shipped in apparent good condition'.
[11] See, e.g., Roskill LJ in *Cehave* v *Bremer Handelsgesellschaft (The Hansa Nord)* [1976] QB 44, 69–70; Lord Denning, ibid., at 61.

of express provision as to the remedy for breach, an express term of the contract will often be treated as an innominate term, rather than a condition, unless the case is one where certainty is the paramount consideration. If it is an innominate term, breach of that term will not necessarily entitle the buyer to reject the goods and repudiate the contract. Where the nature and consequences of the breach are not of such gravity as to justify repudiation of the whole contract, they will be compelled to accept the goods. But there is no doubt of right to damages. An interesting case where the court held that a stipulation of the contract was an absolute requirement is *Hazlewood Grocery Ltd* v *Lion Foods Ltd.*[12] The claimant in that case purchased chili powder from the defendants. An express term of the contract required the powder to be free from 'foreign and extraneous matter', clearly important in the circumstances. The powder supplied was contaminated with a small amount of industrial dye. The Food Standards Agency accordingly required food products manufactured using the powder to be recalled. The court held that the express term of the contract imposed an absolute obligation.[13] It was also held that the chili was not of satisfactory quality as required by s. 14(2) or fit for its purpose as required by s. 14(3).

On the other hand, the terms as to quality and fitness implied by the Act are all conditions in English law,[14] breach of which under the Act justifies rejection of the goods except where the breach is slight (*de minimis*). Although the restrictions on the buyer's right to reject for slight defects bring the statutory implied terms closer to innominate express terms, it does not equate them.

7.3 Implied terms that the goods must correspond with their description

Sections 13(1) and (2) are as follows:

> (1) Where there is a contract for the sale of goods by description, there is an implied term that the goods correspond with the description.
> (2) If the sale is by sample, as well as by description, it is not sufficient that the bulk of the goods corresponds with the sample if the goods do not also correspond with the description.

7.3.1 The relationship between s. 13 and the common law distinction between representations and contractual terms

The first question to be examined here is the effect of s. 13 on the traditional common law distinction between mere representations on the one hand and terms of the contract on the other hand. At first blush it might seem that s. 13 does away with this distinction in the case of a sale by description since the section states that 'there is an implied term that the goods shall correspond with the description'. If the section applied only to those parts of the description which amounted to contractual terms in any event, it would seem to be performing the somewhat odd (and redundant) function of declaring that it is an implied term that the seller must comply with express terms of the contract.

[12] [2007] EWHC 1887 (QB).
[13] See *Arcos Ltd* v *Ronaasen & Son* [1933] AC 470 p. 126.
[14] 1994 Act, Sched. 2, para. 5

However, despite this oddity, the section does not seem to obliterate the distinction between mere representations and contractual terms. For instance, in *T & J Harrison* v *Knowles and Foster*,[15] the sellers sold two ships to the buyers, each of which had been stated in particulars supplied to the buyers to have a deadweight capacity of 460 tons, but no reference was made to this in the actual memorandum of sale. In fact, the capacity of each ship was only 360 tons. In one sense these ships had been sold by description and the description certainly referred to their capacity. But the Court of Appeal held that the statements about the capacity were merely representations.[16] So also in a very careful judgment in the New Zealand case of *Taylor* v *Combined Buyers Ltd*[17] – which seems to be the only case in which this question has been explicitly and fully considered – Salmond J held that the section does not affect the traditional distinction between mere representations and terms of the contract. Similarly, in the well-known case of *Oscar Chess Ltd* v *Williams*,[18] where the seller sold a car which he described as a '1948 Morris', contrary to the facts, it does not seem to have occurred to anybody that the statement could have been treated as part of the description of the car and an action brought under s. 13, unless the buyer could first establish that the statement was a term of the contract and not a mere representation. It could, no doubt, be argued that the sale in this case was not a sale by description but a sale of a specific chattel, but it would certainly be strange if this distinction were to lead to the same statement being held a representation in one case and a condition in another. In the case of *Harlingdon & Leinster Enterprises Ltd* v *Christopher Hull Fine Art Ltd*,[19] it was held that the sale of a painting as a 'Gabriele Münter' (a German expressionist painter) was not a sale by description. In this case, it was held that the fact that a description was applied to goods either in the negotiations leading up to a contract, or in the contract itself, did not necessarily make it a sale by description for the purposes of s. 13(1). For the sale to be *by* description, the description had to be influential in the sale so as to become an essential term or condition of the contract. It was possible for a description to become a term of the contract although it was not relied on, but the court had to be able to impute to the parties a common intention that it should be a term of the contract before the sale could be said to be 'by description', and in determining what the intention of the parties was, the absence of reliance on the part of the buyer was a very relevant factor. The plaintiff dealers were specialists in German expressionist paintings, and the defendant dealers were not, and the plaintiffs had inspected the painting. Nourse LJ observed:

> For all practical purposes, I would say that there cannot be a contract for the sale of goods by description where it is not within the reasonable contemplation of the parties that the buyer is relying on the description.[20]

On the other hand, in *Beale* v *Taylor*,[21] the Court of Appeal appears to have come very close to disregarding the distinction between representations and contractual terms

[15] [1918] 1 KB 608.
[16] Cf. *Howard Marine & Dredging Co* v *Ogden (Excavations) Ltd* [1978] QB 574, where, on similar facts, damages were awarded under s. 2(1) of the Misrepresentation Act 1967.
[17] [1924] NZLR 627.
[18] [1957] 1 WLR 370.
[19] [1991] 1 QB 564.
[20] At p. 574.
[21] [1967] 1 WLR 1193. See also *Fordy* v *Harwood*, 30 March 1999 (unreported).

by giving a wide application to s. 13 of the Act. In this case, the defendant advertised his car for sale as a 'Herald, convertible, white, 1961' and it was bought by the plaintiff after examination. In fact, the car was made of two parts which had been welded together, only one of which was from a 1961 model. Although the facts bore some resemblance to those in *T & J Harrison* v *Knowles and Foster* (which was not cited), the Court of Appeal here held that the words '1961 Herald' were part of the contractual description. If this case illustrates the modern trend, it seems to suggest that in practice, s. 13 makes it easier for a buyer to argue that a descriptive statement by a seller is a contractual term and not a mere representation. The decision may well reflect a trend to hold that statements about the goods by sellers are to be treated as contractual terms rather than mere representations, particularly where the buyer was reasonable in relying on the statement.[22] After all, the seller in *Beale* v *Taylor* presumably obtained a price well above the fair value of the vehicle. In the *Oscar Chess* case, by way of contrast, the decisive fact may have been that the buyer, a car dealer, was not reasonable – or had no right – to rely on what the seller, a private person, had said.[23]

However, although this question remains tantalisingly undiscussed in the cases, it seems reasonably clear from some House of Lords decisions, and the case of *Harlingdon & Leinster Enterprises Ltd* v *Christopher Hull Fine Art Ltd*,[24] that s. 13 of the Act does not automatically convert any or all descriptive words into conditions, or even terms.[25] Some descriptive words may be inserted in the contract without having any legal force at all. For example, in the *Reardon Smith Lines* case[26] where the shipbuilders contracted to build a vessel to a certain specification at Yard No. 354 at Osaka Zosen, and the ship was in fact built at another yard, it was held that these words had no legal significance at all. They were of no substantial importance to the parties, who were not concerned with where the ship was built (though it might of course have been different if that particular yard had a particular reputation among shipowners and shipbuilders); the important descriptive words were in the specification, and that specification had to be complied with. Since the words in this case described the yard where the ship was to be built and there was no suggestion that the shipbuilders had not intended to build the ship there, these words could not even have amounted to a misrepresentation. In other cases, however, descriptive words which fail to amount to an implied condition under s. 13 may simply be a misrepresentation, and may give the representee the usual remedies available for a misrepresentation.

In the *Reardon Smith Lines* case (which did not involve a contract of sale) and again in *Ashington Piggeries* v *Christopher Hill Ltd* (which did),[27] the House of Lords discussed

[22] See *Fordy* v *Harwood*, 30 March 1999 (unreported).

[23] In previous editions it was suggested that this was contrary to the orthodox view which holds that a statement is a contractual term if this is the intention of the parties, and that Australian cases seem to follow this orthodoxy more frequently than English ones – see, e.g., *J J Savage & Sons* v *Blakeney* (1970) 119 CLR 435. This may be true of Australian cases, but so far as the English courts are concerned, Oscar Chess seems to be in line with orthodox thinking – see *Harlingdon & Leinster Enterprises Ltd* v *Christopher Hull Fine Art Ltd*, above.

[24] [1991] 1 QB 564

[25] Cf. *Qatar Investment and Projects Development Holding Co* v *John Eskenazi Ltd* [2022] EWHC 3023 (Comm), where the court rejected the suggestion that an antiques dealer had contractually guaranteed the authenticity of objects more than a 1,000 years old but which turned out to be modern forgeries.

[26] [1976] 1 WLR 989.

[27] [1972] AC 441.

another question, closely related to the one above, namely whether compliance of the goods with all parts of a description is required by the implied term in s. 13, or whether parts of the description can be treated as giving rise to liability by way of a warranty or innominate term. In both cases, it seems to have been taken for granted that not all descriptive words automatically fall within s. 13; the discussion in the two cases centred round the proper test for determining which parts of the descriptive words fall within s. 13 and which do not. As regards any other words, it was stated explicitly (e.g. by Lord Diplock)[28] that these might still give rise to a warranty (or, it can be added, an innominate or intermediate term). It thus seems established that s. 13 does not override the traditional distinctions which need to be drawn between (a) descriptive words which are words of contractual obligation and those which are mere representations, or even without any legal effect, and also between (b) descriptive words which are words giving rise to liability by way of condition, on the one hand, or by way of warranty or innominate or intermediate term, on the other.[29]

The next question concerns the test by which it can be decided what words of description do fall within s. 13 and thereby give rise to liability if the description is not complied with. In this connection, some of the case law has adopted a tendency to overlook the above distinctions and treat all descriptive words as though they must create liability under s. 13. For example, in *Arcos Ltd* v *E A Ronaasen & Son*,[30] the buyers agreed to buy a quantity of staves which they required, as the sellers knew, for making cement barrels. The contract stated that the staves were to be half an inch thick. In fact, only about 5 per cent conformed to this requirement, but a large proportion was over half an inch, but not more than of an inch; some were larger than this but less than inch and a very small proportion were larger than that. It was found that the goods 'were commercially within and merchantable under the contract specification', and also that they were reasonably fit for the purpose for which they were sold. Despite these findings, it was held by the House of Lords that the buyers were entitled to reject the goods for breach of s. 13.[31] Lord Atkin said:[32]

> It was contended that in all commercial contracts the question was whether there was a 'substantial' compliance with the contract: there must always be some margin: and it is for the tribunal of fact to determine whether the margin is exceeded or not. I cannot agree. If the written contract specifies conditions of weight, measurement and the like, those conditions must be complied with. A ton does not mean about a ton, or a yard about a yard. Still less when you descend to minute measurements does 1/2 inch mean about 1/2 inch. If the seller wants a margin he must and in my experience does stipulate for it . . .
>
> No doubt there may be microscopic deviations which business men and therefore lawyers will ignore . . . But apart from this consideration the right view is that the conditions of the contract must be strictly performed. If a condition is not performed the buyer has a right to reject.[33]

[28] [1972] AC 441 at p. 503

[29] It is surprising that in the *Reardon Smith Lines* case the leading speech of Lord Wilberforce makes no reference to the *Ashington Piggeries* case (which, indeed, seems not to have been cited, somewhat astonishingly) and his words are a trifle hesitant on this last point. But if his opinion is taken together with the speeches in the *Ashington Piggeries* case, it does seem clear that the proposition stated in the text has the support of the House of Lords.

[30] [1933] AC 470. See also *Rapalli* v *K L Take* [1958] 2 Lloyd's Rep 469, a very similar case.

[31] The right to reject in such a case is modified by s. 15A, discussed in Chapter 17.

[32] [1933] AC 470, 479–80.

[33] See also *Hazlewood Grocery Ltd* v *Lion Foods Ltd* [2007] EWHC 1887 (QB), p. 122.

Perhaps the most extreme case was *Re Moore & Co Ltd and Landauer & Co Ltd*[34] where buyers agreed to buy 3,000 tins of Australian canned fruit packed in cases of 30 tins. When the goods were delivered it was found that about half the cases contained only 24 tins, although the correct total quantity was delivered altogether. The arbitrator found that there was no difference in value between tins packed 30 to a case and those packed 24 to a case, but despite this finding it was held by the Court of Appeal that the buyers were entitled to reject the whole consignment on the ground that there had been a breach of s. 13. In the *Reardon Smith Lines* case, Lord Wilberforce (speaking for a majority of the House of Lords) expressed serious doubts as to the correctness of this decision, which he found 'excessively technical'.

In the *Ashington Piggeries* case, and again in the *Reardon Smith Lines* case, the House of Lords seems to have accepted that the only descriptive words which are to be treated as the subject of s. 13 are words which identify the subject-matter of the contract. For example, in the *Ashington Piggeries* case, Lord Diplock said:[35]

> The 'description' by which unascertained goods are sold is, in my view, confined to those words in the contract which were intended by the parties to identify the kind of goods which were to be supplied. It is open to the parties to use a description as broad or as narrow as they choose. But ultimately the test is whether the buyer could fairly and reasonably refuse to accept the physical goods proffered to him on the ground that their failure to correspond with what was said about them makes them goods of a different kind from those he had agreed to buy. The key to s. 13 is identification.

The concept of words of identification is, however, more troublesome than seems to be implied. In the *Reardon Smith Lines* case, it was argued for the appellants that the words in the contract requiring the ship to be built at the particular yard specified were words of identification because it was only with the aid of these words that it was possible to identify the vessel being built at a particular yard with the vessel contemplated under the contract. This argument was rejected by the House of Lords, and Lord Wilberforce pointed out that there are two different meanings to the idea of words of 'identity' or 'identification'. It is only words whose purpose is to state or identify an essential part of the description of the goods which are words of identity in this special sense, and so attract the implied condition in s. 13. Words which merely identify the goods in the sense of pointing out where they can be found are not words of identity in this special sense. Lord Wilberforce also expressed dissatisfaction, as already noted, with the excessive technicality of some of the cases under s. 13 such as *Re Moore and Co Ltd and Landauer*,[36] and indicated that it would be better if s. 13 were confined to descriptive words which constitute a 'substantial ingredient of the "identity" of the thing sold', other words being left to give rise to liability for breach of warranty or of an intermediate or innominate term. He added, however, that a different view might still be taken of contracts for the sale of unascertained future goods (e.g. commodities – and he probably had *Arcos v E A Ronaasen* particularly in mind) where each detail of the description must be assumed to be vital.

[34] [1921] 2 KB 519.
[35] [1972] AC at pp. 503–4.
[36] [1921] 1 KB 519.

These words of Lord Wilberforce concerning the concept of words of identification are very important. Not only do they rule out the application of s. 13 to words which merely point out the goods being sold while not actually constituting a substantial ingredient of the goods, but they also help to explain why, even on a sale of specific goods, it is possible to hold that the sale is a sale by description and the descriptive words do fall within s. 13. As will be seen later, it is well established that *prima facie* the sale of manufactured goods should be treated as a sale by description if the goods are sold not as specific things, but as things answering a general description. For example, if a buyer purchases a consignment of pure cotton shirts from a seller, and the shirts are labelled 'pure cotton', it seems clear that this is a sale by description, and that the words on the label are part of the contractual description. If the shirts are not pure cotton, there will be a clear breach of s. 13 and the buyer will be entitled to reject the goods. Yet it will be seen that in such a case the words cannot be said to be words of identification in the sense that they are needed to point out which are the goods that are the subject-matter of the contract. In a sale of specific goods like this, there will be no need to identify the goods in that sense: the identity of the goods is clear. But the words on the label are still plainly enough words of identification in the other sense mentioned by Lord Wilberforce – they identify a substantial ingredient of the goods. They are, in short, words which identify, not which goods are being sold, but what the goods actually are (not just any suit – a wool suit). The actual decision in *Beale* v *Taylor*[37] could also be supported in this manner, assuming that the words in that case were indeed contractual and not just representational. The words in the advertisement, '1961 Herald', were not needed to identify which car was the subject of the sale, but they were identifying what the car was (a 1961 Herald, not just any Herald).

There are, however, a few cases, pre-dating the *Ashington Piggeries* case and the *Reardon Smith Lines* case, in which s. 13 has been applied to words which, even if they could be called words of description at all, do not appear to be words which identify a substantial (or indeed any) ingredient of the goods sold. For example, it has been held that words about the way in which the goods are packed, or even marked, may be words of description under s. 13 of the Act.[38] So also, it has been held that words describing where the goods are situated ('Afloat per *SS Morton Bay*, due London approximately June 8th') are descriptive words within the protection of s. 13.[39] Although this last case was cited without disapproval by Lord Guest in *Ashington Piggeries*, it is hard to reconcile it with Lord Wilberforce's more subtle analysis of the concept of words of identification in *Reardon Smith Lines*. The authority of decisions of this character is today somewhat doubtful.

The result of all this is of some complexity but the position can be summarised as follows:

1 Descriptive words must first be analysed to see whether they are contractual, or merely amount to representations. If they are misrepresentations only, then the normal common law and equitable rules apply, as modified by the Misrepresentation Act 1967.

[37] [1967] 1 WLR 1193.
[38] *Smith Brothers (Hull) Ltd* v *Gosta Jacobson & Co* [1961] 2 Lloyd's Rep 522.
[39] *Macpherson Train & Co* v *Howard Ross & Co* [1955] 1 WLR 640.

2 If the words are held to be contractual, it must next be seen whether there is an express term requiring compliance with the words of description. Such a term may be a condition or a warranty, but is most likely to be an innominate term, as in the *Cehave* case. The buyer's remedies for breach of such a term depend on the nature and consequences of the breach.
3 If there is nothing amounting to an express term, then the next stage is to see whether the description relates to unascertained future goods like commodities. In this event (as in the *Arcos* case), the term is a condition in English law, and strict compliance is required, though a buyer's right to reject is modified by s. 15A.
4 If the contract is of a different character, it must next be inquired whether any item in the description of the goods amounts to a 'substantial ingredient' in the identity of the thing sold. If it does, compliance with the item will again be a condition.
5 In any other case, the requirement of compliance with descriptive words is not a condition, but a bare warranty or (more probably) an intermediate or innominate term.

While the law may seem complex it does at least avoid putting the court into a strait-jacket – the courts will in effect be able to arrive at whatever decision seems appropriate in the circumstances. It will be noticed that s. 13 itself seems to have been largely forgotten in this discussion. It is almost impossible to reconcile the law as stated by Lord Wilberforce in the *Reardon Smith Lines* case with the precise words of the Act. It appears that s. 13 needs revision, if not outright repeal. Indeed, it is not clear that s. 13 actually does anything at all, since all it seems to say, as now interpreted, is that where the seller uses words of description which would otherwise amount to a condition, then it is an implied condition that the goods should comply with that description. This hardly seems worth saying, although, of course, in a true codification, propositions may be stated which are not designed in any sense to alter the law.

Prior to the passing of the 1973 Act, it was important to consider the relation between s. 13 and the doctrine of the fundamental term or fundamental breach, and older case law must be read against this background. This question is now of very little importance because the Unfair Contract Terms Act 1977 greatly restricts the power of a seller to contract out of their liability under s. 13 and the doctrine of the fundamental term and fundamental breach has essentially been killed off by *Photo Production Ltd* v *Securicor Transport Ltd*.[40] Under ss. 6 and 20 of that Act, contracting out of s. 13 is only permissible to the extent that it is 'fair and reasonable'. For example, the breach in *Arcos Ltd* v *E A Ronaasen & Son*[41] would seem on the face of it to have been one of trivial significance, and if the contract in that case had contained an exemption clause, it would have been most unreasonable to hold the seller liable for the breaches which occurred. Rules of construction, formerly widely applied to limit the operation of exemption clauses, will now be of much less importance, though doubtless they may still be used.[42] For instance,

[40] [1980] AC 827. The doctrine never applied in Scotland: see *Alexander Stephen (Forth) Ltd* v *J J Riley (UK) Ltd* 1976 SC 151. See now Unfair Contract Terms Act 1977, s. 22.

[41] [1933] AC 470.

[42] Though in *Fastframe Ltd* v *Lohinski*, 3 March 1993 (unreported), the Court of Appeal indicated that it was not prepared to countenance arguments based on the old (artificial) rules of construction – see Adams (1994) 57 MLR 960.

in *Robert A Munro & Co Ltd* v *Meyer*,[43] the defendant agreed to buy goods 'with all faults', but it was nonetheless held by Wright J that this clause did not shut out the overriding requirement that the goods should answer to their description, but only served to protect the sellers from the obligation to supply merchantable goods.[44] But insofar as the requirements of satisfactory (or formerly merchantable[45]) quality overlap with those regarding the description of the goods, it seems that a clause which validly excludes the condition that goods be of satisfactory quality (merchantable) must also protect against non-conformity with description.[46]

7.3.2 Meaning of 'sale by description'

The next question concerns the meaning of the phrase 'sale by description'. It has been held that this phrase 'must apply to all cases where the purchaser has not seen the goods but is relying on the description alone'.[47] So it follows that a sale must be by description if it is of future or unascertained goods.[48] But, in addition, the term applies in many cases even where the buyer has seen the goods. Early doubts as to whether an ordinary sale in a shop could be a sale by description were soon laid to rest.[49] To quote from Lord Wright in *Grant* v *Australian Knitting Mills Ltd*:

> It may also be pointed out that there is a sale by description even though the buyer is buying something displayed before him on the counter: a thing is sold by description, though it is specific, so long as it is sold not merely as the specific thing, but as a thing corresponding to a description, e.g. woollen undergarments, a hot-water bottle, a second-hand reaping machine, to select a few obvious illustrations.[50]

One could add to this list items on a restaurant menu,[51] though this is perhaps a less obvious illustration. It also seems to encompass photographs of the item to be supplied, e.g., a particular type of face mask; when the masks as delivered are different from the ones in the photograph, the masks fail to correspond to their description.[52] Moreover, s. 13(3), as it is now drafted, makes clear that the term 'sale by description' is wide enough to cover a sale even where the goods have been exposed for sale and selected by the buyer, as in a supermarket or department store:

> A sale of goods is not prevented from being a sale by description by reason only that, the goods being exposed for sale or hire, are selected by the buyer.

[43] 56 [1930] 2 KB 312.
[44] Cf. also *Pinnock Bros* v *Lewis & Peat Ltd* [1923] 1 KB 690; *Vigers Bros* v *Sanderson Bros* [1901] 1 KB 608.
[45] In the case of contracts made before 3 January 1995.
[46] *Toepfer* v *Continental Grain Co Ltd* [1974] 1 Lloyd's Rep 11; *Gill & Duffus SA* v *Berger & Co Inc* [1983] 1 Lloyd's Rep 622, reversed on different grounds [1984] AC 382.
[47] *Varley* v *Whipp* [1900] 1 QB 513, 516 per Channel J.
[48] *Joseph Travers & Sons Ltd* v *Longel Ltd* (1947) TLR 150, 153 per Sellers J.
[49] *Morelli* v *Fitch & Gibbons* [1928] 2 KB 636.
[50] [1936] AC 85, 100. These are 'obvious illustrations' to a lawyer because they are drawn from decided cases; otherwise the selection may have, for the reader, a somewhat surreal quality.
[51] *Wren* v *Holt* [1903] 1 KB 610.
[52] Cf. *Local Boy'z Ltd* v *Malu NV* [2021] EWHC 2439 (Comm), one of many cases arising out of events in the early phases of the Covid-19 pandemic, which started in December 2019 and had considerable impact on societies and economies around the globe well into 2023.

It had previously been held that a sale could be by description though the buyer had examined the goods with care,[53] or even where they had selected them from stock offered to them by the seller.[54] But a sale is not by description where the buyer makes it clear that they are buying a particular thing because of its unique qualities, and that no other will do, or where there is no reliance by the buyer on the description.[55] In fact, it is probably true to say that the *only* case of a sale not being by description occurs where the buyer makes it clear that they are buying a particular thing because of its unique qualities, and that no other will do.[56]

For this reason, the sale of a manufactured item will nearly always be a sale by description (except where it is second-hand) because items made to an identical design are not generally bought as unique goods but as goods corresponding to that design. So it has been held in Australia that the sale of an ordinary pair of 'walking shoes' was a sale by description, although the buyer had tried on and examined the shoes and might well have been thought to be buying the particular pair as specific goods.[57] As we have seen, even the purchase of a used car which was fully examined by the buyer was held in *Beale* v *Taylor*[58] to be a sale by description because the buyer had relied in part on a newspaper advertisement issued by the seller.

These cases suggest that the real question at issue in deciding whether the sale should be classified as a sale by description is whether, on the true construction of the contract, the buyer has agreed to buy a specific item exactly as it is to the exclusion of all liability on the part of the seller. For example, the buyer may examine a used car and the seller may offer it for sale in terms which amount to saying: 'There is the car; there is my offer; I guarantee nothing; take it or leave it.' In this event it is thought the sale would be held to be a sale of a specific thing and not a sale by description.

One of the consequences of the 1893 Act was that if the sale was held to be a sale by description there would often be an implied condition under s. 14 that the goods were merchantable. This consequence of holding a sale to be by description was so important that it seems that the courts in practice tended to interpret s. 13 with half an eye to s. 14. In other words, if the court thought that on the true construction of the contract the seller should be held to warrant the merchantability of the goods, it would tend to hold the sale to be a sale by description, but after the 1973 Act the condition of merchantability was not limited to sales by description, resulting in s. 13 being construed ever more narrowly, or having less and less practical relevance ever since.

7.3.3 The application of s. 13

Note that s. 13 (unlike s. 14) applies even though the goods are not sold by a person who sells 'in the course of a business'. Thus in *Varley* v *Whipp*,[59] the defendant agreed to buy from the plaintiff a second-hand reaping machine, which was stated to have been new the previous

[53] *Beale* v *Taylor* [1967] 1 WLR 1193.
[54] H *Beecham & Co Pty Ltd* v *Francis Howard & Co Pty Ltd* [1921] VLR 428.
[55] *Harlingdon & Leinster Ltd* v *Christopher Hull Fine Art Ltd* [1991] 1 QB 564.
[56] Ibid.
[57] *David Jones Ltd* v *Willis* (1934) 52 CLR 110.
[58] [1967] 1 WLR 1193.
[59] [1900] 1 QB 513. Note also *Beale* v *Taylor*, above (private sale of second-hand car).

year and hardly used at all. This was a gross misdescription, and the defendant declined to accept it or pay for it. The defendant could not rely on s. 14 (which imposes requirements as to quality and fitness for purpose) because the plaintiff was not a dealer in agricultural machinery, but as the goods did not correspond with the description it was held that there was a breach of s. 13. (Changes made by later legislation are immaterial to this point.)

7.3.4 The relationship between the description and the quality or fitness of the goods

As we shall see later, s. 14 deals with implied conditions as to the quality and fitness of the goods for a particular purpose. Section 13 does not on the face of it deal with quality or fitness for purpose. As we have seen from *Arcos Ltd* v *E A Ronaasen & Son*,[60] it is quite possible for goods to be of satisfactory quality and fit for their purpose and yet not correspond with their description.

Conversely, if the goods do correspond with their description, the fact that they are unsatisfactory or not fit for the purpose for which they are sold will not enable the buyer to plead a breach of s. 13. In this event the buyer will frequently be able to rely on s. 14(2) or (3), but there are some circumstances in which they may wish to use s. 13 rather than s. 14 even though their complaint may in a broad sense be said to be one of quality. First, as seen above, s. 13 applies to a sale by a private seller while s. 14 only applies to a seller who sells in the course of a business. So a person who buys from a non-business seller can only complain about quality if they can bring their case under s. 13. This explains a case like *Beale* v *Taylor*[61] where the buyer of the car obtained damages for breach of the condition implied by s. 13 – the car was wrongly described as a 1961 Herald. If the buyer had been buying from a business seller, he would probably have had a clear case for damages under s. 14 on the ground that the vehicle was not of merchantable quality (the relevant quality warranty at the time).

But secondly, the buyer may wish to rely on s. 13 because the goods are in fact of satisfactory quality in a general sense, but still do not amount to the goods they thought they were buying. In the hypothetical example given earlier, a person who buys an item of clothing described as 'pure wool' may very well want to return it if they discover that it is not, even though it may be perfectly satisfactory, and of good quality. But they can only do that under s. 13 because there would be no breach of s. 14 on these facts.

A third type of case in which a buyer might wish to rely upon s. 13, even though their complaint is in a broad sense about quality, occurs where the contract contains a clause excluding liability for matters of quality, but not for matters of description – something which could happen despite the Unfair Contract Terms Act.

Particular problems often arise where goods are described in general terms, but are adulterated or contaminated so that the goods themselves are not greatly changed but their utility is affected. The point is illustrated by the decision of the House of Lords in *Ashington Piggeries Ltd* v *Christopher Hill Ltd*[62] where herring meal contaminated with

[60] [1933] AC 470.
[61] [1967] 1 WLR 1193.
[62] [1972] AC 441.

a substance which made it unsuitable for feeding to mink was sold to the buyers for use as mink food. It was held that there was no breach of s. 13 because the goods were still properly described as 'herring meal',[63] and it was pointed out that not every statement about the quality or fitness of the goods can be treated as a part of the 'description'.

On the other hand, in *Pinnock Bros* v *Lewis and Peat Ltd*[64] the contract was for the sale of copra cake but the goods delivered were in fact a mixture of copra cake and castor beans; it was held that the goods did not correspond with their description. As Lord Wilberforce pointed out in *Ashington Piggeries*, the question of whether a substance which has added to it a contaminant or unwanted material remains in substance what it always was, though with the addition or contamination, or whether it really becomes a different substance altogether, 'may, if pressed to analysis, be a question of an Aristotelian character'. But he went on to say that the Sale of Goods Act was not intended to provoke metaphysical discussions as to the nature of what was delivered as compared with what was sold. The question of whether the goods correspond with their description is intended to be a broader, more common sense test of a commercial character. The question of whether that is what the buyer bargained for has to be answered using the tests buyers in the market would apply, leaving more delicate questions of condition, or quality, to be determined under other clauses of the contract or sections of the Act.[65]

So where there was a contract for the sale of 500 tons of Argentina Bolita beans but the goods delivered contained a small proportion of other beans, the court referred the case back to arbitrators to find whether the goods as a whole would still be called by someone in the trade 'Argentina Bolita beans'.[66]

In some cases, the description may carry with it an implication of quality of a certain kind. For instance, in the New Zealand case of *Cotter* v *Luckie*[67] the buyer bought a bull described as 'a pure bred polled Angus bull' from the seller. The bull had been wanted, as the seller knew, for breeding purposes, but it turned out to have a physical abnormality which prevented it from breeding. The court held that the sale was a sale by description and that the description implied that the bull was capable of breeding. The court said:

> The question . . . for decision is whether this was or was not a sale by a description having the effect of describing the animal as a stud bull. Both parties are farmers. The respondent could have no use for the animal save for the purpose of serving his cows, and it is to be observed that it was sold not as a bull merely, but as a pure-bred polled Angus bull. The descriptive words appear to me to be meaningless unless intended to convey the impression that the animal might be used to get this class of stock.[68]

There is another type of case which may involve the relation between s. 13 and the quality or fitness of the goods. If the contract calls for goods of a certain quality, this quality may itself become part of the contract description, but it seems that statements

[63] Lord Dilhorne dissented on this point – see ibid., pp. 484–5.

[64] [1923] 1 KB 690.

[65] [1972] AC 441, 489.

[66] *Gill & Duffus* v *Berger & Co Inc* [1981] 2 Lloyd's Rep 233, and, after the resubmission [1983] 1 Lloyd's Rep 622, reversed on different grounds [1984] AC 382.

[67] [1918] NZLR 811.

[68] At p. 813. See also some of the examples discussed by the CA in *Ashington Piggeries* [1969] 3 All ER 1496, 1512, such as the description of goods as 'oysters' which may carry the implication that they are fit for human consumption.

as to quality will not usually be treated as part of the contract description.[69] On the other hand, there are some cases in which quality and description significantly overlap. To take an example once given by Lord Denning, if the goods being sold are said to be 'new-laid eggs' this goes both to quality and description.[70] However, for most purposes such cases give rise to no special problems. Breach by the seller will normally involve liability under ss. 13 and 14, and the overlap is of no particular importance. It would only be of importance where the implied condition under s. 14 is not applicable for some reason (e.g. where the seller is not a dealer) and the buyer has to rely exclusively on s. 13. They may then argue that the term 'new-laid eggs' implies not merely that the eggs are literally new-laid, but that they are of good quality because that is the natural implication of the term. Conversely, if the buyer cannot complain about the quality (e.g. because of a valid exclusion clause) they are not entitled to raise the same complaint under the guise of a failure to conform to description.[71]

7.3.5 Compliance with s. 13

Whether goods correspond with their description will normally be a simple question of fact, but it must be stressed that the duty of the seller is very strict indeed. We have already referred to *Arcos Ltd* v *E A Ronaasen & Son* as an example of the severity of the duties which the section can place on the seller. Although some of these older cases are (as we have seen) questionable insofar as they hold trivial breaches to be breaches of conditions, that does not affect their authority as to what is a breach. It is still quite clear that any non-conformity with the contract description (so long as it is a part of the description which constitutes a term of the contract) is a breach of contract, subject only to the *de minimis* principle.

Reference has already been made to the fact that 'microscopic' deviations may be disregarded in relation to the quantity of goods delivered, in accordance with the maxim *de minimis*, and there seems no reason to doubt that the same is true of compliance with the contract description.[72] However, in *Moralice (London) Ltd* v *E D & F Man*,[73] McNair J held that where the price is payable by means of a documentary credit against shipping documents, the maxim *de minimis* has no application as between the seller and the bank: the shipping documents must comply strictly with the requirements of the letter of credit.[74] McNair J went on to suggest that in this situation it is probably a necessary inference that the *de minimis* maxim is also excluded even in the contract of sale as between buyer and seller.

[69] See the *Ashington Piggeries case* [1972] AC 441 and *Border Harvesters Ltd* v *Edwards Engineering* (Perth) Ltd 1985 SLT 128.

[70] *Toepfer* v *Continental Grain Co Ltd* [1974] 1 Lloyd's Rep 11, 13. Today, the common description 'free range eggs' might be a more pertinent example.

[71] *Toepfer* v *Continental Grain Co Ltd* [1974] 1 Lloyd's Rep 11, 13.

[72] *Arcos Ltd* v *E A Ronaasen & Son* [1933] AC 470, see above; *Margaronis Navigation Agency Ltd* v *Henry W Peabody & Co Ltd* [1965] QB 300; *Tradax International SA* v *Goldschmidt SA* [1977] 2 Lloyd's Rep 604.

[73] [1954] 2 Lloyd's Rep 526; see also *Soproma SpA* v *Marine & Animal By-Products Corpn* [1966] 1 Lloyd's Rep 367, 390.

[74] But in practice this kind of problem would in most cases now fall under the *Uniform Customs and Practice for Documentary Credits*, which has a built-in version of *de minimis*, less strict than the common law version – see Chapter 13.

In a number of more recent cases, *Arcos Ltd* v *E A Ronaasen & Son* has been distinguished by the courts. Where goods have been sold in some such terms as 'fair average quality' or the like, it has been held that this phrase must be construed as commercial people would construe it and as referring only to such qualities as are normally observable by ordinary visual examination. Therefore, goods contaminated by some undetectable substance could still be of 'fair average quality'. Similarly, in *Steel & Busks Ltd* v *Bleecker Bik &Co Ltd*[75] it was held that goods accorded with their description – which was 'quality as previously delivered' – despite the presence of some new chemical, not present in the original deliveries, which rendered the goods unfit for the buyers' purposes. Sellers J found that 'by the standard applied and accepted in the trade they complied with the description and were of the quality called for by the contract, quality not being affected by the chemical'. This decision was approved by the House of Lords in the *Ashington Piggeries*[76] case on the ground that statements of this kind are not intended to be treated as part of the contract description of the goods. They are intended to indicate the quality desired, but not to identify the goods which the contract calls for. But this does not mean that the buyer is without remedy, for they may be able to claim damages under s. 14(2) or (3).

But if the statement is part of the contract description it must be strictly complied with, though it does not follow that a description must always be taken literally. Indeed, there can be much debate over what precisely the contractual description actually means.[77] If goods have acquired a trade description they may correspond to their description even if they are not what a literal reading of the trade description suggests they are. As Darling J said in *Lemy* v *Watson*,[78] 'If anybody ordered Bombay ducks and somebody supplied him with ducks from Bombay the contract to supply Bombay ducks would not be fulfilled.'[79] Usually this approach would be adopted to protect a buyer but it may sometimes protect the seller. In *Grenfell* v *E B Meyrowitz Ltd*,[80] the defendants were held not to be in breach of s. 13 when they supplied goggles of 'safety-glass' to the plaintiff, which subsequently splintered in an accident, as it was proved that 'safety-glass' had acquired a technical trade meaning and the goggles in fact conformed to the normal design. Similarly, in *Peter Darlington Partners Ltd* v *Gosho Co Ltd*,[81] there was a contract for the sale of 50 tons of canary seed on a 'pure basis'. It was shown that there was no such thing in the trade as 100 per cent pure seed, and that the highest standard of purity was 98 per cent; it was therefore held that the buyers were in breach in refusing to accept 98 per cent pure seed.

7.3.6 Knowledge by the buyer and contracting-out

It is, perhaps, slightly odd that s. 13 says nothing about the possibility that the buyer may examine the goods and come to realise that the description is not entirely accurate, or

[75] [1956] 1 Lloyd's Rep 228; *F E Hookway & Co Ltd* v *Alfred Isaacs & Sons Ltd* [1954] 1 Lloyd's Rep 491.
[76] [1972] AC 441, 471, 514.
[77] Cf. *Brewer* v *Mann* [2012] EWCA Civ 246.
[78] [1915] 3 KB 731, 752.
[79] Bombay duck, or bummalo is, in fact, a lizard fish which is usually dried before being eaten, it does not come exclusively from Mumbai (Bombay).
[80] [1936] 2 All ER 1313. As to the meaning in the motor trade of a 'new' car, see *Morris Motors Ltd* v *Lilley* [1959] 1 WLR 1184; R v *Ford Motor Co* [1974] 1 WLR 1220.
[81] [1964] 1 Lloyd's Rep 149.

perhaps that they should have realised this. As we shall see later, there are now severe limits on the extent to which a seller can contract out of liability under s. 13, so this possibility cannot be dealt with by holding that the implied condition is excluded by a contrary intention where the buyer knows that the description is inaccurate. Nevertheless, it would be very odd to hold that the seller is liable for a breach of s. 13 in such a case, and it must be expected that the courts would strive to avoid such a result; for instance, by holding that the sale is not by description.[82]

7.4 Implied terms that the goods are of satisfactory quality

There are two distinct cases where the Act implies a term that the goods supplied are of satisfactory quality, namely s. 14(2) and s. 15(2). These state that:

> 14. (2) Where the seller sells goods in the course of a business, there is an implied term that the goods supplied under the contract are of satisfactory quality.
>
> (2A) For the purposes of this Act, goods are of satisfactory quality if they meet the standard that a reasonable person would regard as satisfactory, taking account of any description of the goods, the price (if relevant) and all the other relevant circumstances.
>
> (2B) For the purposes of this Act, the quality of goods includes their state and condition and the following (among other things) are in appropriate cases aspects of the quality of goods___
>
> (a) fitness for all the purposes for which goods of the kind in question are commonly supplied,
> (b) appearance and finish,
> (c) freedom from minor defects,
> (d) safety, and
> (e) durability.
>
> (2C) The term implied by subsection (2) does not extend to any matter making the quality of goods unsatisfactory___
>
> (a) which is specifically drawn to the buyer's attention before the contract is made,
> (b) where the buyer examines the goods before the contract is made, which that examination ought to reveal, or
> (c) in the case of a contract for sale by sample, which would have been apparent on a reasonable examination of the sample.

Section 14(6) provides that as regards England, Wales and Northern Ireland, the terms implied by subs. (2) (and subs. (3), the fitness for purpose warranty, which is dealt with below) are conditions, so that, subject to the changes noted later,[83] the effect of breach of these terms is the same as under the previous law. In Scotland, the effect of the breach depends upon its materiality.

Section 15(2) provides:

> In the case of a contract for sale by sample[84] there is an implied term:
>
> (c) that the goods shall be free from any defect, making their quality unsatisfactory, which would not be apparent on reasonable examination of the sample.

[82] See especially *Harlingdon & Leinster Ltd* v *Christopher Hull Fine Art Ltd* [1991] 1 QB 564.
[83] See below.
[84] The meaning of this term is discussed below.
[85] 1994 Act, Sched. 2, para. 5(6)(b).

Again, in England, Wales and Northern Ireland this implied term is a condition.[85] In Scotland, the effect of breach again depends on its materiality.

This implied term is in many respects the most important part of the law of sale of goods. It is here that the seller's obligations as to the quality of the goods supplied must be found, and this is the very heart of the law of sale.

Prior to the enactment of the Sale and Supply of Goods Act 1994, the relevant term was that goods had to be of 'merchantable quality'. Under the 1893 Act no attempt to define the concept of 'merchantable quality' was made, and the matter was left entirely to case law. The word 'merchantable' seemed sufficiently precise and appropriate to most lawyers and judges of the time, especially when the cases coming to their attention were mostly commercial contracts between businessmen. However, it appeared less appropriate as it became more frequently applied to consumer sales. Despite this, the word continued to be used for more than 80 years without any statutory definition. A very large body of case law eventually developed, not merely in the UK but also in other common law jurisdictions, which historically modelled their sales law on the 1893 Act. Not surprisingly, no simple or single judicial *definition* ever emerged. The contract of sale of goods covers such an extraordinarily wide range of transactions that it seems impossible that a single standard of quality could be formulated which is appropriate to all kinds of goods, extending from machinery and plant to agricultural produce, to foods and drinks, to live animals and fish, to commodities like coal or iron ore or oil sold as raw materials and goods sold for resale as well as for use.

There were many and repeated demands for a simple statutory statement of the standard of quality required of the seller, though lawyers were divided in their response to these demands. Some appear to have thought that a simple definition or statement of the seller's duties could be provided, which would be applicable over a wide range of cases, and would simplify the law and eliminate the need to consult a large body of cases. No simple statutory statement or definition of the seller's duties as regards quality could possibly cope with the wide variety of problems found in the case law, and any attempt to avoid reference to the old case law would only lead to the new statutory term becoming itself encrusted with interpretive case law.[86] There is still plenty of scope for a judge to manoeuvre, so that the outcome of particular cases will no doubt continue to be influenced by the view the judge forms of the reasonableness of the claimant's behaviour.[87]

The Supply of Goods (Implied Terms) Act 1973 first made some response to the demand for reform and simplification by providing a statutory definition of the term 'merchantable quality', and this, together with some minor amendments made by the same Act, was eventually incorporated in the 1979 consolidation as s. 14(6), which was as follows:

> Goods of any kind are of merchantable quality within the meaning of subsection (2) above if they are as fit for the purpose or purposes for which goods of that kind are commonly bought as it is reasonable to expect having regard to any description applied to them, the price (if relevant) and all the other relevant circumstances.

In addition, it is necessary to note that under s. 61 of the Act the word 'quality' was defined[88] as including 'the state or condition of the goods'.

[86] Rather than attempting a comprehensive definition, the Law Commissions might perhaps have been better advised to have provided non-exhaustive definitions and illustrative examples of when the warranty would (or would not) be broken.

[87] See, e.g., *Millars of Falkirk Ltd* v *Turpie* 1976 SLT (Notes) 66.

[88] This definition is omitted in the new provisions, and is included in the new warranty – s. 14(2B).

But this definition, which was based on the recommendations of the Law Commissions, was probably not intended to have any substantial effect on the law. The Law Commissions at that time appear to have accepted the impossibility of solving all the difficulties of application by the apparently simple process of definition.

For some years, the case law proceeded as before, despite the statutory definition. Former editions of this book continued to discuss the case law at some length, before even considering the statutory definition. Likewise, in *Aswan Engineering Establishment Co* v *Lupdine Ltd*,[89] in 1987, the Court of Appeal analysed the cases at length before proceeding to the statutory definition, and clearly thought this was the appropriate procedure. In the same year a case concerning the merchantability of a car was brought before Rougier J who was told that the motor trade was concerned at the lack of any definition of the concept in its application to vehicles.[90] Rougier J responded that it was doubtful if 'any all-embracing definition of a car of merchantable quality could ever be made',[91] and he added that the statutory definition was probably deliberately left in the widest possible terms 'in order to cater for the great variety of situations which may occur'.[92] He went on to say:

> Any attempt to forge some exhaustive, positive and specific definition of such a term, applicable in all cases, would soon be put to mockery by some new undreamt of set of circumstances.[93]

But in *Rogers* v *Parish (Scarborough) Ltd*,[94] another panel of the Court of Appeal adopted a completely different approach to the question. The court here insisted that the then fairly recent definition in s. 14(6) was in simple language which could easily be applied to a variety of circumstances without difficulty. They criticised the practice of looking at the old case law, and insisted that the new definition should be applied without reference to the prior law.

At the same time that the courts were disagreeing on their attitude to this question, the Law Commissions were re-examining the whole issue. In their Working Paper issued in 1983, the Commissions still appeared to think, as their predecessors had done, that all attempts at simple definitions were doomed to failure.[95] At the same time they thought that there would be advantages in jettisoning the term 'merchantable' and also in clarifying the law on a number of specific points which had previously given rise to doubts and difficulties. By the time of the 1987 Final Report, however, the Law Commissions appeared to have changed their stance.[96] They now appeared to think that it was possible to lay down a simple standard of 'acceptable' quality, which, when fleshed out with some supplementary provisions, would be workable and meaningful. So the draft Sale and Supply of Goods Bill recommended by the Law Commissions contained a number of new subsections designed to replace the existing s. 14(2) and the definition of merchantable

[89] [1987] 1 WLR 1.
[90] Bernstein v Pamson Motors (Golders Green) Ltd [1987] 2 All ER 220.
[91] Ibid., at p. 222.
[92] Ibid.
[93] Ibid.
[94] [1987] QB 933. The Aswan Engineering case, though decided before this case, appears to have been only reported after it, so it was apparently not cited.
[95] Sale and Supply of Goods, Law Com. Working Paper No. 85.
[96] See Law Com. Final Report, Sale and Supply of Goods, paras 3.16–3.22.

quality in s. 14(6). The 1994 Act substantially adopts these recommendations, but substitutes the words 'satisfactory quality' for the Law Commissions' 'acceptable quality'. It is not altogether easy to understand the reason for this change, as the word 'satisfactory' is often associated with mediocrity.

As might have been predicted, the old case law has continued to be well used. The views equivalent to those expressed by the Court of Appeal in *Rogers* v *Parish (Scarborough) Ltd* do not seem to have prevailed. The fundamental difficulty appears to be that the body of case law relative to the vast volume of sales contracts is actually quite small and as each case turns largely on its own facts, there is a pressing need to look at the old cases in order to determine the correct approach across as many broadly similar cases as possible. Moreover, the decision in *Pepper (Inspector of Taxes)* v *Hart*[97] would allow a court to look at the Law Commissions' Report which led to the enactment of the 1994 Act, and the views expressed there on the old cases will have some relevance to the interpretation of the new provisions. Some treatment of the old cases is justified as illustrating the wide variety of fact situations the courts may have to grapple with in applying them.[98]

But it is first necessary to start with an examination of the circumstances which give rise to the seller's obligations under s. 14(2) – whatever those obligations may be.

7.4.1 In what circumstances does the condition apply?

7.4.1.1 Where the seller sells goods in the course of a business

The implied term of satisfactory quality in s. 14(2) only applies to goods sold by the seller in the course of a business. Goods sold privately by a seller, not selling in the course of business, are therefore not within the section, though, as seen above, they are within s. 13, which requires conformity with description. Therefore, as previously seen, a person who sells a second-hand car privately as a '2017 Ford Focus' impliedly promises that it is a 2017 Ford Focus though they do not otherwise impliedly promise that it is of any particular quality.

In *Stevenson and another* v *Rogers*,[99] it was held that having regard to the changes to s. 14(2) of the Sale of Goods Act 1893 by the Supply of Goods (Implied Terms) Act 1973, now to be found in s. 14(2) of the 1979 Act, habitual dealing in the type of goods sold is not required, a 'one off' sale in the course of a business will suffice. That case involved the sale of a fishing boat by a fisherman. The judge at first instance held that this was not a sale in the course of a business because it did not have any element of regularity. The Court of Appeal, however, decided that habitual dealing in the type of goods sold was not a requirement of the section; it sufficed that the sale was in the course of a business.

[97] [1993] 1 All ER 42. Compare *Aswan Engineering Establishment Company* v *Lupdine* [1987] 1 WLR 1 where Lloyd LJ wished to look at the earlier reports dealing with the then present statutory definition of 'merchantable quality' but both counsel objected. *Pepper v Hart* has been accepted in Scotland: *Short's Tr* v *Keeper of the Registers of Scotland* 1994 SC 122, aff'd 1996 SC (HL) 14.

[98] The new provisions came into effect on 3 January 1995, and were not retrospective: the old law still applied to contracts made before that date – Sale and Supply of Goods Act 1994, s. 8(3).

[99] [1999] QB 1028.

Section 14(5) deals with the problem of a private seller who sells through an agent. This provides as follows:

> (5) The preceding provisions of this section apply to a sale by a person who in the course of a business is acting as agent for another as they apply to a sale by a principal in the course of a business, except where that other is not selling in the course of a business and either the buyer knows that fact or reasonable steps are taken to bring it to the notice of the buyer before the contract is made.

So the implied term under s. 14(2) applies if the agent is selling in the course of business unless the principal is not acting in the course of business and the buyer is aware of this, or reasonable steps are taken to bring it to the buyer's notice. So, for instance, an auctioneer acting for a private seller can exclude these sections by making it clear that the principal is a private seller. If they do not do so, the auctioneer will be liable under this section, and the owner will also be liable unless they can bring himself within the exception. In *Boyter* v *Thomson*,[100] a principal, acting privately, sold a boat through an agent acting in the course of a business, but the buyer was unaware of the principal's existence at the time of the sale. The House of Lords found the principal liable to the buyer for defects in the boat under s. 14(5) and the principle of common law of agency, that an undisclosed principal may be sued on any contract made on their behalf, to be applicable. The argument that only the agent could be liable under s. 14(5) was rejected.

Section 15(2)(c), which deals with sales by sample, contains no words corresponding to those in s. 14(2) discussed above. This is presumably recognition of the fact that a person who sells goods by sample is unlikely to be a private seller, but will almost invariably be selling in the course of business.

7.4.1.2 Previously owned goods

There was nothing in s. 14(2) as originally drafted which restricted its application to new goods, and it is well-established that sales of previously owned, used or second hand goods are within the subsection.[101] Indeed, sales of used vehicles particularly have created a rich seam of case law even before the introduction of the 'satisfactory quality' standard. The test of merchantability (as it then was) to be applied in the case of second-hand vehicles was held to be precisely the same statutory test as applied to new goods,[102] though it did not follow that goods must be held to be merchantable when sold new just because they would be regarded as satisfying the statutory test if sold as second-hand.[103]

7.4.1.3 No reliance on seller need be shown

In contrast to the implied condition as to fitness for purpose, which is contained in s. 14(3) (and which is dealt with later), the implied condition in s. 14(2) normally applied even

[100] 1995 SC (HL) 15.

[101] See, e.g., under the pre-1973 law, *Bartlett* v *Sydney Marcus* [1965] 1 WLR 1013; and since 1973, *Lee* v *York Coach & Marine* [1977] RTR 35; *Business Appliances Specialists Ltd* v *Nationwide Credit Corpn Ltd* [1988] RTR 32. On the current provision, see, for example, *Thain* v *Anniesland Trade* Centre 1997 SLT (Sh Ct) 102.

[102] See the *Business Appliances Specialists case*. See *Business Appliances Specialists Ltd* v *Nationwide Credit Corpn Ltd* [1988] RTR 32.

[103] Ibid.; see also *Bernstein* v *Pamson Motors* (Golders Green) *Ltd* [1987] 2 All ER 220, 226.

though the buyer had in no way relied on the seller's skill and judgment. The implied term was a guarantee of inherent quality, and did not depend on showing that the buyer had relied on the seller. This could lead to liability in extreme situations. For example, if a buyer ordered goods from the seller which were only made by one manufacturer so that the goods could only be obtained from that manufacturer or from someone who had bought from him, the seller would still be treated as warranting the merchantable quality of the goods.[104] In such a case, it might seem that the seller had complied with their contract simply by supplying the buyer with precisely what they had asked for, but this did not exonerate the seller from liability. The reason for this rule, which might seem hard on the seller, was that in most circumstances the seller would themselves be able to obtain an indemnity from the manufacturer on the grounds that the contract between them also included the implied term of merchantable quality.[105] The rule applied, however, even though the seller could not in the particular circumstances obtain such an indemnity; for example, because the manufacturer was insolvent or the time under the Limitation Act had run out.[106] The position has remained the same under the current law.

However, if the manufacturer was only willing to supply the goods subject to some limitation on their liability and the buyer knew this fact when they ordered the goods from the seller, it was held that this would normally negative the implied condition between buyer and seller.[107] This is also the case under the current law, but this would amount to an implied exclusion of s. 14(2) liability and must therefore satisfy the requirement of reasonableness in the Unfair Contract Terms Act 1977, but since this is an implied exclusionary term, which derives from the courts' sense of its fairness and justice, it can hardly be suggested that it would be unreasonable. If in any particular circumstances the court felt that the seller should be liable despite these facts, it would presumably refuse to imply a term excluding the application of s. 14(2) and the application of the 1977 Act just would not arise.

A similar problem would arise if the buyer ordered goods made to their own specification, and the specification was itself such that any goods made to that specification would be inherently defective or unsatisfactory. It could hardly be supposed that in such a case the buyer could sue under s. 14(2), though it is not easy to state the precise ground on which the seller could escape liability. The problem was discussed by the Court of Appeal in the *Ashington Piggeries* case[108] where a number of possible reasons were given, some of which cannot survive the House of Lords appeal in that case.[109] But one suggestion which is not inconsistent with the decision of the House of Lords, is that where the essence of the contract is the making of goods to someone else's order or specification, the seller's duty may be limited to using all reasonable skill and care in selecting materials and making the goods. But this may be criticised because the seller's duties are traditionally thought

[104] *Young & Marten Ltd* v *McManus Childs Ltd* [1969] 1 AC 454.
[105] Ibid., p. 466.
[106] Ibid., at p. 467, per Lord Reid.
[107] *Gloucestershire* CC v *Richardson* [1969] 1 AC 480, a decision at common law because the contract was strictly not a sale of goods but the House of Lords regarded the applicable law as the same. See also *Helicopter Sales (Australia) Pty Ltd* v *Rotor-Work Pty Ltd* (1974) 132 CLR 1.
[108] [1969] 3 All ER 1469 at p. 1518.
[109] [1972] AC 441.

of as warranties involving strict liability, and it could hardly be supposed that the seller would be free from liability in such a case if, despite all care and skill, they delivered goods not precisely in accordance with the specifications. It is thought that the best reason for denying liability in the case of goods made to the buyer's own specification would be that, in the circumstances given, the goods should not be treated as unsatisfactory. If the buyer got exactly what they had ordered, it is very difficult to then claim that the goods are unsatisfactory.

7.4.1.4 Defects drawn to the buyer's attention, and examination of the goods

The implied condition that the goods must be satisfactory is excluded in two cases. These exclusions are found in s. 14(2C)(a) and (b). In addition, s. 14(2C)(c) provides that in a contract for sale by sample, the condition does not extend to any matter which would have been apparent on a reasonable examination of the sample. The first excluded case concerns defects specifically drawn to the buyer's attention before the contract is made, or after the contract is made at the time the goods are delivered.[110] No difficulty arises in this regard, except that the wording of the paragraph probably does not help a seller who tries to draw the buyer's attention to defects in the goods solely by printed wording in a written contract. It is hardly to be supposed that the court would regard this as sufficient to draw the buyer's attention 'specifically' to any defects.

If, before the contract is made, the seller points out a defect to a buyer, or if the buyer discovers it for themselves, and the seller undertakes to put it right, then it will be immaterial if the implied condition under s. 14(2) is excluded as regards that defect because the seller would plainly be liable on a separate, collateral contract, or for breach of a simple express term of the contract.[111]

In addition to matters specifically drawn to the buyer's attention by the seller, it is clear that a course of dealings between the parties might affect the extent of the seller's duties, if the buyer became aware of defects in the goods but continued to order them. In such circumstances there must come a point where the buyer becomes unable to seize on the defects as a reason for rejecting the goods, or indeed for claiming damages in respect of them.

The second exclusion, concerning examination of the goods, is contained in s. 14(2C)(b). This applies where the buyer examines the goods before the contract is made and covers any matter which would render the goods unsatisfactory if *that* examination ought to reveal such matter. As drafted, this would suggest that the enquiry has to be into the examination that was actually carried out by the buyer, rather than a hypothetical examination, and an (objective) assessment of the matters which that examination ought to have revealed. If on carrying out the examination which the buyer undertook, a matter rendering the goods unsatisfactory should have been discovered, it is no answer for the buyer to claim that they did not actually discover this matter. It does matter, though, what the buyer actually did: an external inspection of a vehicle cannot possibly reveal a problem

[110] See *Clegg* v *Olle Andersson* (T/A Nordic Marine) [2003] EWCA Civ 320.
[111] Cf. *R & B Customs Brokers Co Ltd* v *United Dominions* Trust [1988] 1 All ER 847.

with the gearbox, and so that would not be caught by s. 14(2C)(b). In this regard, the Court of Appeal's observations on the scope of s. 14(2C)(b) in *Bramhill* v *Edwards*[112] are of some concern. The buyers had purchased a motor home which was wider than permitted under UK road safety regulations. The buyers carried out an internal examination of the vehicle but did not measure its dimensions externally. Auld LJ observed that 'an examination of the vehicle . . . ought to have revealed its width and that the width was not revealed simply because Mr Bramhill did not measure it'[113] and consequently s. 14(2C)(b) was engaged. This cannot be a correct application reading of s. 14(2C)(b), because, as explained, it applies only where the buyer examines goods and that examination ought to have revealed the defect. Had the buyers actually measured the width of the motor home but made a mistake in doing so, the sellers could invoke s. 14(2C)(b). However, s. 14(2C)(b) does not require buyers to examine and merely having the opportunity does not matter.[114]

In the case of a sale by sample, the effect of s. 14(2C)(c)[115] is to exclude the implied condition that the goods are satisfactory if the defect would have been apparent on a reasonable examination of the sample, *whether or not* it has in fact been examined. In a sale by sample, the seller is entitled to assume that the buyer will examine the sample, and the latter cannot complain of defects which could have been discovered by the simple process of examining the sample. *A fortiori* this is the case where the buyer does in fact examine the sample and discovers the defect, but decides to take the goods all the same. 'If there is a defect in the sample which renders the goods unmerchantable and the buyer, notwithstanding, and with knowledge of that defect in the sample, is content to take a delivery which corresponds with the sample and gets such a delivery, he has no ground of complaint.'[116]

It is not uncommon where the goods remain packaged in their original packaging and unopened throughout the transaction for the buyer to have examined an identical item beforehand, for example in a showroom or shop. If the defect is one which is present and apparent in all models of the goods, the implied condition obviously could be excluded.[117] Equally, many cases can be envisaged in which a court might be reluctant to reach this result. Either it could make the requirement that the defect be 'apparent' a stringent one or it could hold that such cases are not sales by sample at all, on the ground that they are not intended as such.

7.4.2 What is the extent of the seller's obligation?

7.4.2.1 Goods to which s. 14(2) extends

It is well established that the subsection covers not only the goods actually bought by the buyer and passing to him, but packages or containers in which the goods are sold, even

112 [2004] EWCA Civ 403.

113 Para [51].

114 Twigg-Flesner 'Examination prior to purchase: a cautionary note on s.14(2C)' (2005) 121 *Law Quarterly Review* 205–6.

115 Section 15(2)(c) of the 1979 Act.

116 *Houndsditch Warehouse Co Ltd* v *Waltex Ltd* [1944] 2 All ER 518, 519.

117 'Defect' is perhaps the wrong word in this context. If the displayed goods lack a feature which would be present in more expensive goods, and this is obvious, the buyer could scarcely complain.

if these remain the property of the seller. In *Geddling* v *Marsh*,[118] it was held that the seller's obligations covered not only goods which were the actual subject-matter of the sale, namely mineral waters, but also the bottles in which the waters were contained, even though these remained the property of the seller.[119] Consequently, the plaintiff was able to recover damages for injuries received when a defective bottle burst.

A similar point arose in *Wilson* v *Rickett Cockerell & Co Ltd*,[120] where the plaintiff ordered a consignment of Coalite (a brand of smokeless coal) from the defendants. Unknown to either party the Coalite contained an explosive substance which blew up in the plaintiff's fireplace, causing considerable damage. Referring to the words 'goods supplied under a contract of sale' (which have been replaced without significant alteration in the present sections), Lord Denning observed:

> In my opinion that means the goods delivered in purported pursuance of the contract. The section applies to all goods so delivered whether they conform to the contract or not: that is, in this case, to the whole consignment, including the offending piece, and not merely to the Coalite alone.[121]

Dealing with the defendants' argument that there was nothing wrong with the Coalite as such and that it was only the presence of the piece of explosive that made the goods dangerous, Lord Denning went on:

> Coal is not bought by the lump. It is bought by the sack or by the hundredweight or by the ton. The consignment is delivered as a whole and must be considered as a whole, not in bits. A sack of coal, which contains hidden in it a detonator, is not fit for burning and no sophistry should lead us to believe that it is fit.[122]

It might have been thought that the contrary was unarguable were it not for the decision of the Scottish Court of Session in *Duke* v *Jackson*[123] where, on the same facts, the coal merchant was held not liable on the ground that there was nothing wrong with the coal itself. The Court of Appeal, in refusing to follow this case, pointed to *Chapronière* v *Mason*,[124] where the defendant sold a bun containing a stone on which the plaintiff broke a tooth, and a verdict for the defendant was set aside by the Court of Appeal. These cases received implicit statutory confirmation in the provisions replacing them from 1973 onwards because they expressly extended the implied conditions in these subsections to the 'goods supplied under the contract'.[125] The current iteration of s. 14(2) continues to use the same words.

[118] [1920] 1 KB 668.
[119] Cf. *Beecham Foods Ltd* v *North Supplies (Edmonton) Ltd* [1959] 1 WLR 643.
[120] [1954] 1 QB 598. For similar cases under the Food and Drugs legislation (now the Food Safety Act 1990), see *Meah* v *Roberts* [1977] 1 WLR 1187; *Barton* v *Unigate Dairies* [1987] Cr L Rev 121.
[121] At p. 607.
[122] At p. 606.
[123] 1921 SC 362.
[124] (1905) 21 TLR 633.
[125] Presumably a buyer in a situation such as that in *Wilson* v *Rickett*, Cockerell & Co Ltd (though not in *Chapronière* v *Mason*) who discovered the foreign substance in the goods before damage was done would have been able to reject under s. 30(4) (now repealed), on the ground that the seller had 'delivered the goods he contracted to sell mixed with goods of a different description'.

7.4.2.2 The basic test

As seen, the basic test in s.14(2A) is that 'goods are of satisfactory quality if they meet the standard that a reasonable person would regard as satisfactory, taking account of any description of the goods, the price (if relevant) and all the other relevant circumstances.'

The test is therefore an objective one, requiring the court to put itself into the position of a reasonable buyer in the same circumstances as the actual buyer. Although the test is objective, it is not detached from the buyer's particular knowledge or expertise. In *Bramhill* v *Edwards*. [126] Auld LJ observed:

> The reasonable person must be one who is in the position of the buyer, with his knowledge; for it would not be appropriate for the test to be that of a reasonable third party observer not acquainted with the background of the transaction.[127]

This is a question of law for the judge to decide, though in appropriate cases he or she can take account of expert testimony.[128]

A buyer who claims that goods are not of satisfactory quality has the burden of proving so; this includes proving that the matters complained about existed at the time the goods were delivered, or when risk passed, to the buyer. The seller will only be liable in respect of matters rendering the goods unsatisfactory up to that point. If the buyer fails to prove that the problem existed before delivery, the claim will fail.[129]

7.4.2.3 'Quality includes state or condition'

The basic test in s. 14(2A) includes 'the state or condition' of the goods. Here, one needs to consider the goods in general. If they are clearly broken or damaged, for instance, then the state or condition of the goods is clearly such that they would not be regarded as satisfactory, except where they had deliberately been sold for scrap. Goods intended for resale should be in clean and undamaged condition, and packaged correctly.

The scope of this phrase may be wider than that. In *Niblett* v *Confectioners' Materials Co Ltd*,[130] Bankes LJ said:

> Quality includes the state or condition of the goods. The state of this condensed milk was that it was packed in tins bearing labels. The labels were as much part of the state or condition of the goods as the tins were. The state of the packing affected the merchantable quality of the goods.[131]

As this shows, the scope of phrase might extend beyond matters which would ordinarily be thought of as pertaining to quality.

In the 1994 Act, the words relating to the state or condition of the goods are transferred from s. 61 of the Act to s. 14(2B) itself. This does not appear to lead to any change in the effect of the words.

[126] [2004] EWCA Civ 403 at [39].
[127] Followed in *Cembrit Blunn Ltd, Dansk Eternit Holding A/S* v *Apex Roofing Services LLP*, Roy Alexander Leader [2007] EWHC 111 (Ch).
[128] *Friarwood Ltd* v *Champagne Cattier SA* [2006] EWCA Civ 1105.
[129] E.g., *M G Construction Ltd* v *AGD Equipment Ltd* [2020] CSOH 72.
[130] [1921] 3 KB 387.
[131] In South Australia there is specific authority holding that the goods may be unmerchantable because of bad packaging: *Gilbert Sharp & Bishop* v *Wills & Co* [1919] SASR 114.

7.4.2.4 Relevance of the price

The price at which goods are sold is often relevant in deciding what quality the buyer is entitled to expect, which is why it can be a relevant consideration for s. 14(2A). Clearly, a price which is significantly higher than the typical price for items of the same kind might increase the level of quality reasonably expected. However, sometimes, a high price might be the result of strong demand, so here the higher price might not increase quality expectations. Similarly, a discount – whether negotiated or offered as a matter of routine – need not necessarily lower quality expectations, but if the discount is offered because goods are ex-display or similar, then a lower price would be a consideration. It is also clear from pre-1994 case law, that a buyer cannot complain that the goods are unsatisfactory merely because they have paid too much for them.

Goods which are commonly sold for a variety of purposes are also commonly sold at a variety of prices. And this is not just because market prices may vary, but because some uses may require goods of better quality, and goods fit for those purposes may therefore command a premium. For example, a wrecked car might be sold as a source of spares. One would obviously expect the price to be very much lower than if the car was sold as a roadworthy vehicle for ordinary road use. Hence if the price was a normal sort of price for a roadworthy vehicle of that type, the vehicle clearly would be unsatisfactory if it was not in fact roadworthy.[132] So the price is an important indicator as to what the buyer could reasonably expect.

As the Sheriff Principal said in *Thain* v *Anniesland Trade Centre*,[133] where a second-hand car with 80,000 miles in the odometer developed a fault in the gearbox after two weeks' use:

> People who buy second-hand cars get them at less than their original price in a large part because second-hand cars have attached to them an increased risk of expensive repairs. The price of the Renault, £2,995, was considered reasonable because there was the risk of expensive repairs attached to the Renault.

If the transaction was characterised as being about the sale of a 'collector's car', the fact that it was unroadworthy might not render it unsatisfactory.[134] In short, in borderline cases of this sort, the way in which the court characterises the deal will be crucial. On the other hand, in *Harlingdon & Leinster Ltd* v *Christopher Hull Fine Art Ltd*, the facts of which were given above,[135] it was held that the fact that a painting was not the work of the artist by whom it appeared to have been painted did not make it unmerchantable, even though its value as a forgery was much lower than as the genuine article. The finding on the s. 13 issue was crucial to this determination. The Court of Appeal did not, however, endorse the judge's observation that the words 'merchantable quality' related to anything beyond the physical qualities of the goods sold.

An Australian decision of 1921 illustrates a situation where the price difference was substantial enough to lead to a finding adverse to the seller: in *H Beecham & Co Pty Ltd* v

[132] See, e.g., *Cruickshank* v *Specialist Cars* (Aberdeen) Ltd 2002 GWD 25-858 (Sheriff A. L. MacFadyen).

[133] 1997 SLT (Sh Ct) 102. Note also *Richford* v *Parks of Hamilton* (Townhead Garage) Ltd 2012 GWD 24–505 (Hamilton Sheriff Court), but contrast *MacDonald* v *Pollock* [2012] CSIH 12, 2013 SC 22.

[134] See, e.g., the Scottish case of *MacGill* v *Talbot* 2002 GWD 12-382 (Sheriff G. J. Evans).

[135] See section 7.3.1.

Francis Howard & Co Pty Ltd,[136] the defendants bought spruce timber for piano-making from the plaintiffs. The defendants themselves selected the timber from the plaintiffs' stock, but later much of it was found to be affected by dry rot, not observable on reasonable external examination. The sellers argued that the timber was merchantable because it was still saleable as timber for making boxes, which was in fact one of the uses to which spruce timber was commonly put. But the buyer paid 80 shillings per hundred feet of timber while spruce timber for box-making was only worth 30 shillings per hundred feet. It was held that the timber was not merchantable under the contract description because 'no businessman, having a contract to buy spruce timber whether for resale or for purposes of manufacture would think for a moment of accepting this timber, its condition being known, without a very large reduction upon current market prices'.

There are some kinds of goods in which the quality is almost infinitely variable, and in which it would seem that compliance with the requirements satisfactory quality, may depend almost entirely on the price. For example, if a person buys minced meat and is supplied with minced meat with a 30 per cent fat content, proof that most minced meat has a lower fat content does not necessarily mean that the goods are not of satisfactory quality. If the price is commensurate with the quality in fact supplied, the goods would be satisfactory if the price was the only basis for complaint.[137] Indeed, there would have to be a substantial disparity between the price appropriate to the quality actually supplied and the price charged before it could be said that the goods were unsatisfactory.

7.4.2.5 'Relevant circumstances'

The overriding test is that of satisfactory quality laid down in s. 14(2A). To assist with identifying some of the 'relevant circumstances' for the purposes of s. 14(2A) there are matters listed in (2B). It is important to appreciate that the items mentioned in (2B) are only indicative and to be considered in the context of the general test in (2A). So minor defects (para. (c)) or blemishes of appearance and finish (para. (b)) will only render the goods unsatisfactory if a reasonable person would regard them as rendering them unsatisfactory, having regard to the price and other circumstances. Manifestly, in some cases, such as on the purchase of a second-hand car of some age, such blemishes are almost certain to be present and no reasonable buyer would regard them as making the car unsatisfactory.[138]

The concept of 'satisfactory quality' must be fleshed out by the case law in varying circumstances as its application is fact-sensitive. We must now look at some specific aspects of the quality of the goods which may affect the application of the test, starting with the factors listed – bearing in mind that these will neither be relevant in every case, nor that a failure of the goods in respect of one or several of these will conclusively mean that the goods are not of satisfactory quality.

[136] [1921] VLR 428.

[137] See *Goldup* v *John Manson Ltd* [1981] 3 All ER 257, a case under the Food and Drugs legislation (see now the Food Safety Act 1990).

[138] See *Thain* v *Anniesland Trade Centre* 1997 SLT (Sh Ct) 102.

7.4.2.6 Fitness for all the purposes for which the goods are commonly used

The first 'relevant circumstance' is to consider whether the goods are fit for all the purposes for which goods *of the kind in question* are commonly supplied.

The word 'commonly', which is found in s. 14(2B)(a), is of course, a very difficult word to apply because all depends on the standards of comparison. Some uses, which may appear very uncommon in certain contexts, are perfectly common in a different context. To take an extreme example, the sale of unroadworthy cars for use as a source of spare parts is no doubt a relatively uncommon use in relation to the number of cars which are sold for ordinary use. But the sale of such cars as a source of spare parts is quite common if some different standard of comparison is used. Indeed, a thriving industry exists in which traders buy up old cars for this purpose, and sell spares to buyers, especially where the cars are out-of-date models. It is even more common where vintage cars are concerned.[139] But under the present law there is no doubt that a car which was only fit for use as a source of parts would not be regarded as of unsatisfactory quality if it was sold as such, either expressly or by implication.

But although fitness for purpose is a factor in the present definition of 'unsatisfactory quality', this does not require the goods to be *immediately usable*. Many goods are sold which are not intended to be fit for immediate use. If it is in the contemplation of the parties that something should be done to the goods before they are used, they will be satisfactory even if they may be, in some sense, not be fit for anything on delivery, so long as they will be so when they have been dealt with as contemplated.[140] The Law Commission gave a number of examples,[141] such as, for instance, furniture sold in kit form which has to be assembled by the buyer, or (less commonly these days) food sold in such a condition that it needs to be cooked (or to ripen) before it is edible.

There appear to be only two authorities bearing directly on this question. In *Heil* v *Hedges*[142] it was held that pork, which may be harmful if eaten when not properly cooked, is not unmerchantable if it would have been harmless when well-cooked.[143] By contrast, in *Grant* v *Australian Knitting Mills*[144] it was held that new underpants (which contained an excess of harmful chemicals) had to be fit for immediate wear and it was no defence for the seller to show that they would have been harmless if washed before use. Clearly,

139 See, e.g., the Scottish case of *MacGill* v *Talbot* 2002 GWD 12-382 (Sheriff G. J. Evans).

140 In *Underwood* v *Burgh Castle Brick and Cement Syndicate* [1922] 1 KB 343 Rowlatt J observed that the mere fact that a chattel such as a sideboard needed to be dismantled before delivery did not prevent the passing of property. This implies that he thought such goods in a deliverable state, and thus conformed to the contract. This dictum is of relevance in relation to the many items of household furniture which are sold in 'flat packs' – see below. By contrast, in that case, it was held that a condensing engine, which required much work and expense on the part of the seller to make it ready for delivery, was not in a deliverable state – as to 'deliverable state' see Chapter 10, at section 10.2.2.1.

141 Final Report, para. 3.64.

142 [1951] 1 TLR 512.

143 The pork was infected with trichinae, a common cause of infection in America where this question has given rise to much litigation: see *Williston on Sales*, vol. 1, 243a (revised edn, 1948 and 1949 Supplement).

144 [1936] AC 85.

the test to be applied is to ask whether it is in the reasonable contemplation of the parties that the goods will be treated in the suggested manner before they are used.[145]

The question arises whether there is likely to be a finding that goods are unsatisfactory where they are commonly used for a variety of purposes, but the goods supplied under the contract are fit for some of these purposes only while being unfit for others. Before the 1994 changes, in *Aswan Engineering Establishment Co* v *Lupdine Ltd*,[146] the plaintiffs bought waterproofing compound in plastic pails for export to Kuwait. When the pails were unloaded on the quayside at Kuwait, they were stacked (six pails high) in intense sun (reaching a temperature of 60 to 70 degrees Celsius) for some days. As a result, the pails collapsed under their own weight and the waterproofing compound was lost. As far as liability under the old version of s. 14(2) was concerned, the problem obviously was that the pails were fit for most purposes for which they would be used; they were just unfit to be stacked in that way in such intense heat. The Court of Appeal held that the goods satisfied the requirement that they should be of merchantable (now satisfactory) quality. It is unlikely, however, that if the facts of the *Aswan* case were to recur, and the case fell to be decided under the current provisions, the outcome would be any different, because a court could easily conclude that stacking pails in such extreme temperatures was not a common purpose.[147] Instead, the buyer should have made this use expressly known to the sellers to engage the term implied under s. 14(3).

A similar issue arose in *Henry Kendall & Sons* v *William Lillico & Sons Ltd*,[148] in which the plaintiffs bought, for their pheasants, animal feedstuff containing Brazilian groundnut (peanut) extract. The groundnut extract had been contaminated. The groundnut extract had been bought by the sellers from G who had in turn bought it from K. The sellers paid damages to the plaintiffs, and claimed those damages in turn from G, who claimed from K. G and K were held not liable under s. 14(2) on the ground that the ground nut extract was not of unmerchantable quality. The reason for this was that the extract was perfectly suitable to be used in making up animal feedstuffs for use for cattle and other animals; it was only unsatisfactory for use in making feedstuff for pheasant and partridge chicks. It was pointed out that commodities sold under a general description such as 'Brazilian groundnut extraction' may be bought by different buyers for a wide variety of uses. The House of Lords thought that it would be unreasonable to say that because the goods were unsuitable for only one of these possible uses the goods were to be treated as unmerchantable.

It is clear from their Report that the Law Commissions intended to reverse the decision in *Aswan Engineering*.[149] They took the view, though not without some doubt, that the goods should always be fit for *all* their common purposes, and that the buyer should only be compelled to fall back on s. 14(3) when their purpose is an *uncommon* one. However,

145 But it is perhaps doubtful whether *Heil* v *Hedges* would be followed today; it seems to go too far to treat the failure to cook pork thoroughly as such an unusual thing as to break the causal chain and relieve the seller of responsibility: it would depend upon the extent to which, as a matter of fact, the dangers of undercooked pork were commonly known. Where more exotic foodstuffs are concerned, the duty of the seller must surely be to warn of dangers?

146 [1987] 1 WLR 1.

147 Cf. David Edwards QC J in *Provimi France S.A.S., Cargill S.L.U., Cargill Poland SP. zo.o, Provimi Limited* v *Stour Bay Company Limited* [2022] EWHC 218 (Comm), paras 324-6.

148 [1969] 2 AC 31.

149 See Final Report, *Sale and Supply of Goods*, para 3.36.

had the issue arisen before the Court in the *Aswan Engineering* case, it might have held that the particular use to which the pails were subjected was very uncommon, and the pails might still have been found to be satisfactory.

7.4.2.7 Appearance and finish

Many goods suffer from defects which do not necessarily affect their ordinary usability, or general fitness for purpose. For example, they may be delivered scratched, dented, discoloured or dirty; they may have minor parts missing; ancillary parts may not work well, or may not be fit for their purpose even though the goods as a whole may be reasonably fit for use and so on.

The majority of the House of Lords in *Kendall* v *Lillico*[150] appeared to assume that even non-functional defects could be held to render the goods unmerchantable, and there was at least one specific Court of Appeal authority to this effect, in which it had been held that dented and scratched goods were unmerchantable, although they could have been put right by polishing.[151]

The express inclusion of 'appearance and finish' in section 14(2B) means that cosmetic blemishes can be taken into account as part of the wider consideration of whether the goods in question are of satisfactory quality. However, as with the other relevant circumstances, the existence of such blemishes does not invariably lead to the conclusion that the goods are unsatisfactory.

7.4.2.8 Freedom from minor defects

Section 14(2B)(c) requires the goods to be free from minor defects, which at first sight seems to eliminate the possibility that the seller can supply goods which are 'far from perfect' (unless they are clearly described as such and sold on that understanding).

This had, to some degree, already been established in the case law before the introduction of the 'satisfactory quality' test. In *Rogers* v *Parish (Scarborough) Ltd*,[152] the buyer had bought a new Range Rover at a cost exceeding £16,000 (equivalent to over £65,000 today), but the vehicle had many minor defects such as deterioration of the oil seals and defects in the engine and gearbox. There were also many minor defects in the bodywork. Despite numerous attempts to repair it by the dealers, these defects remained after six months' use. It was held that the vehicle was not merchantable. It was not enough, insisted the Court of Appeal, that the vehicle could still be driven on the road. Mustill LJ brought the non-functional aspects of what the buyer was entitled to expect within the statutory definition by reading it broadly:

> Starting with the purpose for which 'goods of that kind' are commonly bought, one would include in respect of any passenger vehicle not merely the buyer's purpose of driving the car from one place to another but of doing so with the appropriate degree of comfort, ease of handling and reliability and, one may add, of pride in the vehicle's outward and interior appearance.[153]

[150] [1969] 2 AC 31.
[151] *Jackson* v *Rotax Motor & Cycle Co Ltd* [1910] 2 KB 937.
[152] [1987] QB 933.
[153] At p. 944.

So far as new vehicles are concerned, it is arguable that they must be free from all defects and even that accessories and components must all be in proper working order. It does not seem enough to say that the purpose for which a buyer wants a vehicle is simply the purpose of driving it on the road, and that, so long as it can do that, it must be reasonably fit for its purpose. If that were the case, a buyer would not be able to complain under this section that (for instance) the satnav or electric windows did not work. Yet a buyer is surely entitled to say that if they bought a new car with satnav or electric windows, they must have made it clear to the seller that one of the purposes for which they bought it (even if only a minor or subsidiary purpose) is to use these amenities.

In practice, few cases are brought which deal solely with such minor defects, doubtless because buyers do not normally attempt to reject cars in these circumstances. But it may well be a serious question whether a buyer can reject, for a breach of this section, a car which suffers from a collection or series of very trivial defects. Generally, the courts have accepted the argument that a 'congeries of defects', each of which may be relatively minor in itself, may in total render a car unfit for its purpose.[154]

However, attempts by a buyer seizing on a minor defect as a pretext for avoiding what had turned out to be a bad bargain might be met robustly by the courts. In the *Cehave* case,[155] the court was prepared to find the goods (citrus pulp pellets for animal feed) to be merchantable although part of the cargo had been damaged while at sea. Roskill LJ admitted that the goods were 'far from perfect', but nevertheless held that they were merchantable. However, the facts were very peculiar, so one should not place too much weight on this decision.

Even a finding that goods are not of satisfactory quality because of the existence of minor defects might not lead to drastic consequences; although one remedy for a breach of the implied term, as a condition, is rejection of the goods, the buyer may be denied the right to reject under s. 15A.

A related issue concerns minor defects which are very easily rectifiable. Many goods, sometimes expensive and high-quality goods, may be totally unusable because of some minor defect which can be easily corrected once the source of the trouble is known. A car sold, for instance, with a missing battery lead would simply be unusable, and in the *Bernstein*[156] case Rougier J suggested that this would, strictly speaking, render the car unmerchantable. More generally, Rougier J insisted that even a very minor defect which could easily be discovered and put right would often render a new car unmerchantable.

The specific reference to 'freedom from minor defects' in s. 14(2B)(c) really only makes sense on the basis that the new Act is in accordance with the views of Rougier J and with the Law Commissions' similar views.[157] However, in *Eagan* v *Motor Services (Bath) Ltd*,[158]

[154] *Farnworth Finance Facilities* v *Attryde* [1970] 1 WLR 1053. But cf. *Porter* v *General Guarantee Corpn Ltd* [1982] RTR 384.

[155] (*The Hansa Nord*) [1976] QB 44 – see above.

[156] [1987] 2 All ER 220. See also *Lamarra* v *Capital Bank plc* 2007 SC 95.

[157] Final Report, para. 3.34. Moreover, all kinds of warning notices, labels, instructions, etc., which render goods perfectly safe and satisfactory would then, apparently, cease to be necessary. The leading case on warnings is *Wormell* v *RHM Agriculture (East) Ltd* [1987] 1 WLR 1091, which was a case under s. 14(3) and is therefore dealt with below.

[158] [2007] EWCA Civ 1002.

where the complaint was that the rear wheel of the car sold to the complainant was set out of specification, Smith LJ observed:

> [the claimant's counsel] argued that a buyer should be entitled to reject the car because, under section 14(2B)(c), goods may be of unsatisfactory quality because of minor defects. That I accept is so, but the overall test of whether goods are of satisfactory quality is to be found in section 14(2A) . . . this is an objective test and is a matter of judgment for the judge on the individual facts of the case.[159]

This is, of course, correct insofar as structure of s. 14 is concerned – the test is the one in s. 14(2A), not s.14(2B)(c). It is submitted that 'the matter of judgment' should lean towards a finding that the goods are unsatisfactory, because the limitation on the right of rejection in s. 15A serves as a sufficient counter-balance.

7.4.2.9 Safety

Prior to the enactment of the 'satisfactory quality' test, there were a number of cases, mostly dealing with motor vehicles, which made it clear that goods which could not be safely used were not merchantable.[160] Section 14(2B) (d) lists safety as one of the factors to be taken into account in deciding whether goods meet the present standard of 'satisfactory quality' under s. 14(2).

A case of the purchase of a new car, decided under the earlier merchantable quality test, was *Bernstein* v *Pamson Motors (Golders Green) Ltd.*[161] The plaintiff here bought a new car for just under £8,000, but the car broke down within three weeks, on a motorway, after doing only 140 miles. Investigation revealed that a very minor defect (the presence of a piece of sealant in the lubricating system) had caused the breakdown, but unfortunately this minor defect had caused extensive damage because it had completely blocked the oil supply, causing the camshaft to seize up. One factor appeared to have weighed with Rougier J in holding that the car was unmerchantable: the nature and consequences of the defect. Here the defect was minor, but the consequences very serious – indeed they could have been even more serious had the plaintiff not stopped in time. This car was not safe.[162]

A distinction must also be drawn between cases of hidden danger and cases of potential danger and at what point a potentially dangerous item becomes one that is unsatisfactory. This difficulty is illustrated by the decisions in *SW Tubes Ltd* v *Owen Stuart Ltd*[163] and *Medivance Instruments Ltd* v *Gaslane Pipework Services Ltd.*[164] In *SW Tubes* a used machine saw for cutting cardboard was sold to the claimant without hand guards. The rapidly moving saw blade was therefore entirely unguarded when in use. It was common ground that the machine had not caused injury to current or past users when used without

[159] Ibid., at [47].

[160] See, e.g., *Unity Finance* v *Mitford* (1965) 109 Sol Jo 70 (strictly a case of fundamental breach); *Lee* v *York Coach & Marine* [1977] RTR 35; *Bernstein* v *Pamson Motors (Golders Green) Ltd* [1987] 2 All ER 220.

[161] [1987] 2 All ER 220.

[162] See also *Lamarra* v *Capital Bank plc* 2007 SC 95: top of range vehicle with several minor cosmetic defects and one other not minor (defective differential) held unsatisfactory although defects remediable under express warranty.

[163] [2002] EWCA Civ 854.

[164] [2002] EWCA Civ 500.

guards. That did not, however, preclude the goods from being unsafe and therefore not of satisfactory quality, such was the potential to cause injury.

This decision can be compared with the decision in *Medivance* which concerned the sale of a gas-fired space heater for a factory. The space heater had a mechanism so that it would cut out should the fans which moved the air through the heater fail, but it did not have a device that prevented overheating (and a subsequent fire) should the heater be obstructed, as it was. The buyers argued, among other things, that as a result of the absence of this device, it was unsafe and therefore not of satisfactory quality; essentially, that it was potentially unsafe. The Court of Appeal found for the sellers, holding that while such a modification would have been desirable, ultimately the fire caused by the heater was caused by the carelessness of the buyer. The issues seem to be likelihood of harm and likelihood of the extent to which the buyer has brought that harm about. Where there is a very real danger that the seller can do little to obviate, the goods will not be satisfactory, whereas a potential danger which the sellers can easily mitigate will not render the goods unsatisfactory.

There remains, however, a serious problem about hidden defects which are only dangerous because they are hidden. It is quite common for goods to be sold which may be dangerous if the buyer does not have some specific piece of information about the goods but which are not at all dangerous if the facts are fully known. Many medicines and drugs, for instance, are perfectly safe if certain simple precautions are taken (such as taking them with water, or not combining them with alcohol, or not exceeding a stated dosage) but which would be potentially dangerous if these simple precautions were not observed. Such drugs and medicines therefore nearly always come with adequate information printed on the container, or on some attached leaflet. Many of them, too, are only available on prescription,[165] so that the patient will get the necessary warnings from their doctor.[166] Clearly, goods supplied with the necessary information would not be unsatisfactory merely because without it they might be dangerous or unsafe. But equally clearly, it would seem extraordinary if such goods were not regarded as unsatisfactory if they were sold without the necessary information.[167]

The problem extends far beyond the particular case of medicines and drugs. All sorts of goods are sold which require something to be done to them to make them fit for safe use. If the product was supplied without informing the buyer that this was the case, the goods might well be held unsatisfactory – although possibly this sort of knowledge might now in particular cases be attributed to the public as a whole. Any product which is supplied in a container which states, for example, 'Warning: this product is dangerous for use unless appropriate precautions are taken', would normally be regarded as satisfactory with the warning, but very likely as unsatisfactory without it. And so on.

[165] As to whether goods supplied on prescription under the National Health Service are 'sold'.

[166] The warnings are standardised within the pharmaceutical trade – see *John Richardson Computers* v *Flanders and Chemtec* [1994] FSR 144. Failure to give such a standard warning would certainly amount to negligence on the part of the pharmacist.

[167] This is expressly stated by Lord Pearce (though dissenting) in *Kendall* v *Lillico* [1969] 2 AC 31, 119. It is also supported by the decision in *Vacwell Engineering Co Ltd* v *BDH Chemicals* [1969] 3 All ER 1681. And see *Willis* v *FMC Machinery & Chemicals Ltd* (1976) 68 DLR (3rd) 127. See also, however, *Lem* v *Barotto Sports Ltd* (1976) 69 DLR (3rd) 276, 290.

All this seems a matter of common sense. But there is unfortunately a major decision in conflicting with (at least of some) of these common-sense conclusions. In *Kendall* v *Lillico*,[168] which has already been referred to, the majority of the House of Lords held that the groundnut extract involved in that case was merchantable because it was fit for its most common use, namely for making into animal feed. Any feed containing the extract was perfectly fit for use for feeding to cattle and other animals, but it was not suitable for feeding to pheasant and partridge chicks. Indeed, the animal feeds made with the groundnut extract were not merely unsuitable for feeding to pheasant and partridge chicks – they were actually dangerous or poisonous to pheasant and partridge chicks. The buyers who bought the groundnut extract for compounding into animal feedstuffs would not have been injured or damaged if they had known of this fact because they could simply have labelled the feeds produced with the extract, 'Warning: Not Suitable for Poultry',[169] for example. But the buyers did not know of the toxic quality of the extraction, and so the feedstuffs made with it were sold for general animal use, with disastrous results. A bare majority of the House of Lords held that these facts did not render the groundnut extract of unmerchantable quality.

The ground for this decision is not entirely clear, but it seems to have been based on the following reasoning. The House asked whether a buyer *with full knowledge of all the facts* would have accepted the goods in discharge of the contract without a substantial abatement of the price. The answer to that, they reasoned, was patently yes because if the buyer had had *full knowledge of all the facts* they would have known that the goods were toxic to pheasant and partridge chicks, and would still have bought them, but have labelled their products as suggested above. This reasoning appears over-logical. Where the very nature of the defect in question depends on the fact that it is hidden and unknown, it seems absurd (the word is surely not too strong) to test the question of merchantability by asking whether a buyer *with full knowledge of the facts* would have accepted them. The whole problem arose from the very fact that the buyer did not know, and had no reason to know, all the facts. In circumstances like these it is precisely the fact that the condition is hidden which constitutes the danger, and therefore the defect in the goods. If this were not held to render the goods of unmerchantable quality, it would seem to have followed that a person who bought a piece of machinery (say a car) which was in a very dangerous state, but which could be rendered perfectly satisfactory merely by tightening up a nut, could not complain that the goods were unmerchantable.[170] If this was the case there was clearly something too narrow about the concept of 'merchantability' – for what renders such a car dangerous is precisely the fact that the buyer will have no reason to know or even suspect that the car is in a dangerous condition. Under the current provisions, in answering the question whether a reasonable person would regard the goods as 'unsatisfactory', it might appear that a similar approach could be adopted to that adopted by the House of Lords in *Kendall* v *Lillico*, by positing a reasonable person with full knowledge

168 [1969] 2 AC 31.

169 In ordinary usage 'poultry' does not include game birds, but the implication of the sixth holding in the case is that such a warning ought to have sufficed.

170 See *Bernstein* v *Pamson Motors (Golders Green) Ltd* [1987] 2 All ER 220 discussed at p. 153 below. *Compare Millars of Falkirk Ltd* v *Turpie* 1976 SLT (Notes) 66 – decided under the definition of 'merchantability' contained in the 1973 Act, later re-enacted in the 1979 Act.

of the facts. Moreover, the specific reference to 'safety' does not assist in reaching a more sensible conclusion because, in a fact situation like *Kendall* v *Lillico*, a buyer with full knowledge of the facts would regard the goods as safe, and therefore satisfactory. It is not clear, however, that the approach adopted by the House of Lords would be entirely inappropriate in commercial commodity contracts – again we have the problem of trying to draft a simple statutory provision which will cover all eventualities.

There is no evidence of the approach taken here being adopted more widely and as time goes on it seems safe to conclude that it will not be. It is certainly highly unlikely that it would be in the case of unsafe goods; otherwise the Law Commissions' purpose in spelling out a requirement of safety would have been largely defeated.[171]

7.4.2.10 Durability

There was some controversy as to whether the seller's duty to supply merchantable goods implied that the goods must continue to be satisfactory for any particular length of time. In *Mash and Murrell* v *Joseph I Emmanuel*,[172] sellers in Cyprus sold potatoes c.&f. Liverpool. The potatoes, though sound when loaded, were rotten by the time the ship arrived, and it was held by Diplock J that the sellers were liable because in such a contract the goods must be loaded in 'such a state that they could endure the normal journey and be in a merchantable condition on arrival'.[173]

On the face of it this seems a reasonable decision. Indeed, it seemed inherent in the concept of merchantability that the goods would remain in a satisfactory condition for a reasonable length of time according to the circumstances of the contract and the nature of the goods. For example, if in *George Wills & Co Ltd* v *Davids Pty Ltd*,[174] the sellers had supplied beetroot canned in vinegar with a life of only a few weeks, while the normal life of beetroot canned in vinegar was 12 months, there seems no doubt that the goods would have been unmerchantable.

The current law has put the matter beyond doubt, as 'durability' is specifically mentioned in s. 14(2B)(e) as one of the aspects of the quality of the goods to which regard is to be had. It must also be noted that cases such as *Mash & Murrell* involved f.o.b. and c.i.f. contracts where risk in general passes to the buyer on loading. If the bill of lading states that the goods were 'shipped in apparent good order and condition', the assumption will tend to be that the deterioration which occurred was due to the hazards of transit, the risks of which are the buyer's. This indeed was what turned out to be the case in *Mash & Murrell* itself.[175] In short, the buyer's decision to accept or reject will, as a matter of practicality, often be determined by what is said in the bill of lading. In *VAI Industries (UK) Ltd* v *Bostock & Bramley Org*,[176] where machinery was delivered f.o.b. with an express warranty, the majority of the Court of Appeal held that a breach of this warranty occurred at the time of delivery, not at the time the breach was discovered.[177]

171 Report, para. 2.16.
172 [1961] 1 All ER 485, reversed on the facts [1962] 1 All ER 77, but followed in *The Rio Sun* [1985] 1 Lloyd's Rep 350. See also *Beer* v *Walker* (1877) 46 LJQB 677.
173 [1961] 1 All ER 485.
174 (1956–57) 98 CLR 77.
175 See [1962] 1 All ER 77.
176 [2003] EWCA Civ 1069.
177 For a useful discussion of this case and others on this point, see Twigg-Flesner (2004) 120 LQR 214.

Of course, establishing the durability period of any goods will be a question of fact which will depend on the nature of the goods and the circumstances of the case, including, no doubt, the price paid. David Edwards QC J explained it thus:

> . . . it is important to recognize that this is an inherently relative concept. One product may be better (or differently) made and, as a result, more durable or robust than another; but, bearing in mind, in particular, the price paid for the two products, both may be regarded as of satisfactory quality. Depending upon how, and in what conditions, the purchaser intends to use the product, he or she may be happy to receive a less durable or less robust product, but to pay less.'[178]

High-quality carpets sold at a price commensurate with their quality can be expected to last longer than cheaper carpets sold at a low price. It must also be appreciated that the seller's continuing obligation does not mean that the goods must remain of the same quality or in the same condition for any length of time, nor even that they must remain, strictly speaking, at the same standard of 'satisfactory quality' as they were at the time of delivery. Clearly, very few goods will remain in the same condition after delivery and especially after use, and many of them may rapidly cease to be of satisfactory quality in the relevant sense.[179] Even brand-new goods will, soon after delivery, be second-hand goods, and if delivered in *that condition* would hardly be regarded as satisfactory when a new price has been paid. But what is required is that the goods, when delivered, should have the capacity to remain reasonably fit for the purpose, and retain their non-functional attributes, for a reasonable time. Consequently, a premature failure, particularly where this has increased noticeably compared to earlier deliveries, will point to a lack of durability.[180] It must also be borne in mind that the fact that goods break down within a short time of purchase may be evidence that they were defective at the time of the sale.[181]

7.4.2.11 Knowledge, warnings, instructions, etc.

In addition to the 'relevant circumstances' enumerated in s.14(2B), other matters might be relevant. This is evident from the fact that s.14(2A) refers to '*all* the other relevant circumstances', and the factors in (2B) are relevant 'in appropriate cases' only. A judge may therefore look beyond s.14(2B) and identify other matters as relevant circumstances.

For example, many products require to be used in a particular manner, or under specified conditions, if they are to work effectively, or at all. Weedkiller, for instance, may have to be applied when the weather is not wet and garden fertiliser when it is.[182] Products of this kind which are supplied without any or without adequate instructions may be held

178 *Provimi France S.A.S., Cargill S.L.U., Cargill Poland SP. zo.o, Provimi Limited v Stour Bay Company Limited* [2022] EWHC 218 (Comm), para 312.

179 See, e.g., *Kelly* v *Andersons House Furnishers* (Inverurie) Ltd 2012 GWD 20-422 (Aberdeen Sheriff Court), where the appearance of furniture deteriorated over time but it continued to be intact and useable, and was held to be of satisfactory quality. This approach is also evident in *Peebles* v *Rembrand Builders Merchants Ltd*. [2016] SC Dun 31.

180 *Dana UK Axle Ltd* v *Freudenberg FST GmbH* [2021] EWHC 1751 (TCC).

181 *Crowther v Shannon Motor* Co [1975] 1 WLR 30, 33 per Lord Denning MR. For a critique see Hudson (1978) 94 LQR 566. Consider also the unusual facts of *O'Farrell* v *Moroney* 2008 GWD 35–533 (Sheriff F. R. Crowe), in which an expensive young peregrine falcon was held to have been conforming to contract despite its death within four weeks of purchase.

182 There are many US cases where farmers have sued the sellers of weed-killers which have failed to control the particular weed problem for which they were applied, and the result has been serious crop failure.

unsatisfactory, while if they are supplied with adequate instructions they will be perfectly satisfactory.[183]

7.4.2.12 Pre-owned goods

As we have already seen, there is nothing in the statutory provisions to exclude their application to pre-owned or second-hand goods.

But although pre-owned goods have to be satisfactory, no less than new goods, it is clear that nobody can expect pre-owned goods at a lower price to be as good as new goods at a higher price.[184] Even before the 'satisfactory quality' test was adopted, the question arose occasionally with motor vehicles, and there was a tendency then to hold that the requirement of merchantability, as it applied to pre-owned vehicles, meant that the vehicle must at least be safe and roadworthy. But in *Business Appliances Specialists Ltd* v *Nationwide Credit Corpn Ltd*,[185] the Court of Appeal rejected this approach. The requirement of merchantability extended to other matters besides safety and roadworthiness. They stressed that the statutory definition of merchantability applied also to the case of second-hand goods. Indeed, the test to be applied was precisely the same as the test to be applied for new vehicles, as discussed in *Rogers* v *Parish (Scarborough) Ltd.*[186] The question always was whether the goods were as fit for their purpose as it was reasonable to expect. But, of course, it was also clear that what it was reasonable to expect would differ according to the price, and having regard to the fact that the goods were second-hand.

A few illustrations from the case law under the former provisions reveal some variation of judicial attitudes.[187] *Crowther* v *Shannon Motor Co*[188] is, perhaps, the most favourable decision from the buyer's point of view. In this case the buyer bought a second-hand Jaguar which had done over 82,000 miles for the (at that time) fairly modest price of £390. The engine seized up after the buyer had done a further 2,000 miles in the space of three weeks; a reconditioned engine had to be fitted to the car. It was held that a breach of s. 14 had been committed because of evidence from the former owner (who had sold it to the defendants) that the engine was 'clapped out' when he sold them the car. An award of no less than £460 in damages was upheld. The plaintiff thus, in effect, obtained a Jaguar with a clapped-out engine for nothing and, in addition, received £70 towards the price of the new engine.

In *Bartlett* v *Sydney Marcus Ltd*,[189] the plaintiff bought a second-hand car from the defendant dealers for £950. The dealers informed the plaintiff that the clutch was defective and they offered either to put it right and sell it at £975 or to leave the buyer to put it

[183] See the *Wormell case*, dealt with at section 7.5.2.5.

[184] See passage from the judgment in *Thain* v *Anniesland Trade Centre*, quoted in section 7.2.4.2.4.

[185] [1988] RTR 332. See also the helpful judgment of *Carswell J in Lutton* v *Saville Tractors (Belfast) Ltd* [1986] 12 NIJB 1 (second-hand car should be 'reliable and capable of giving good service and fair performance'), but see observations at section 7.4.2.4 above.

[186] [1987] QB 933.

[187] Some of these illustrations are actually drawn from cases in which s. 14(3) was applied rather than s. 14(2) but, as already noted, there is often an overlap between these subsections, and the cases may be equally relevant to both subsections.

[188] [1975] 1 All 139. Compare *Thain* v *Anniesland Trade Centre 1997 SLT* (Sh Ct) 102 – see section 7.4.2.4.

[189] [1965] 1 WLR 1013.

right and sell for £950. The buyer chose the latter alternative, but when he came to have the clutch repaired the defect was found to be more serious than expected and the repair cost him £84. The Court of Appeal held that the car was not unmerchantable merely because the defects proved more serious than expected. There were suggestions in this case that a car which would go, even though not perfectly, might still be merchantable, but it seems clear that these remarks must be confined to the case of second-hand cars. There can, it is thought, be no doubt that if a *new* car were sold with a defective clutch, the car would be properly said to be unsatisfactory (formerly, unmerchantable). But in this case the car was sold *as second-hand with a defective clutch*. Under that description, the car could not be said to be unmerchantable merely because the defect proved more serious than expected. Equally, under the present provisions, it could not be said to be unsatisfactory.

In *Business Appliances Specialists Ltd* v *Nationwide Credit Corpn Ltd*,[190] the plaintiff bought a second-hand Mercedes, which had done some 37,000 miles, for £14,850. After a few months, and only 800 miles, serious wear in the valves, valve guides and oil seals appeared, and repairs were required costing £635. Expert evidence was produced to the effect that such wear was very unusual on a Mercedes of that age and mileage. Nevertheless, it was held that there was no breach of the requirement of merchantability.[191] Second-hand cars, it was said, must be expected to have some defects, and some ordinary wear and tear. It was a matter of degree whether the defects exceeded the expectations of the reasonable buyer. Yet this was clearly a very expensive car of extremely high quality. The case is perhaps borderline.

In *Shine* v *General Guarantee Corpn Ltd*,[192] the car turned out to have been submerged in water for 24 hours, and had been an insurance company 'write-off'. Although there were no specific defects alleged, and the car appeared to be generally usable, this was enough to persuade the Court of Appeal that the car was unmerchantable. Perhaps the decisive fact here was that a dealer gave evidence that, if the facts had been fully known, the car would have been worth £1,000 less than the price. So, clearly the buyer had hardly got 'value for money', and that was apparently enough to show a breach of the subsection.

If the same fact situations were to fall to be decided under the current law, the outcomes would no doubt be the same. In *Thain* v *Anniesland Trade Centre*,[193] decided after the 1994 changes, the pursuer purchased for £2,995 a second-hand Renault 19, which was about five years old and had done about 80,000 miles. After two weeks' use, the car developed a gearbox fault which could not be sorted economically, and the car was written off. It was held to be sufficient that the car was fit for initial use, *Crowther* being distinguished on the ground that the defect existed at the time of sale, and that the purchaser assumed the risk that a defect might emerge at any time, given the age and mileage of the car. Durability was not a quality reasonably to be expected of a second-hand car.

190 [1988] RTR 332.
191 See also *Thain* v *Anniesland Trade Centre* (above), decided under the 1994 Act.
192 [1988] 1 All ER 911.
193 1997 SLT (Sh Ct) 102.

7.4.2.13 Satisfactory quality and differing grades of quality

It is perhaps surprising how little authority there appears to have been on the relationship of the requirement of merchantability under the pre-1994 law to the possibility of different grades of quality. Obviously, many goods are sold in different grades of quality, and no doubt the price is normally commensurate with the particular quality sold. And we have seen that the price may well be relevant in deciding whether the goods are of satisfactory quality in any given case. But the price is not everything, and it might seem that a requirement of 'satisfactory quality' would have some bearing on the particular grade of quality which the buyer is entitled to receive. But it does not seem that the Sale of Goods Act requires the goods to be of any particular grade of quality. The term 'satisfactory', does not necessarily connote that the goods are of any specific grade or quality. As was said by Salmond J in the New Zealand case of *Taylor* v *Combined Buyers Ltd*:[194]

> The term 'merchantable' does not mean of good, or fair, or average quality. Goods may be of inferior or even bad quality but yet fulfil the legal requirement of merchantable quality. For goods may be in the market in any grade, good, bad or indifferent, and yet all equally merchantable. On a sale of goods there is no implied condition that they are of any particular grade or standard. If the buyer wishes to guard himself in this respect he must expressly bargain for the particular grade or standard that he requires. If he does not do so, *caveat emptor*; and he must accept the goods, however inferior in quality, so long as they conform to the description under which they were sold and are of merchantable quality – the term 'quality' including state or condition.

Similarly, Lord Reid in *Kendall* v *Lillico*[195] pointed out that where commodities are sold in the market under some general description, of which there may be several different qualities available, it is sufficient (indeed in that case it was not disputed) that the goods comply with the lowest quality under which goods of that description can commonly be sold. But again, it may be necessary to have regard to the price, for the price paid may show clearly that the buyer was entitled to something more than the lowest quality available in the market.

Again, if the goods comply with the normal condition of goods of the quality and description under which they are sold they will not be unsatisfactory merely because they are inferior to other goods of a similar type. For instance, in the Australian case of *George Wills & Co Ltd* v *Davids Pty Ltd*,[196] the defendants manufactured and sold canned beetroot. For some time it had been customary to can beetroots in brine, but the defendants then started to can them in vinegar. Such cans had a much shorter life – about 12 months – than beetroot canned in brine, or other canned foods, which keep for at least three years, but it was held by the Australian High Court that this did not render the goods unmerchantable. The court said:

> if the contract called for the supply of beetroot canned in vinegar, the parties were bound to deliver and accept goods of this description and, if the condition and quality of the goods were normal for goods of this description, the purchaser could have no complaint on the ground of their merchantability. It would be nothing to the point, on any such complaint, to show that beetroot canned in vinegar would not keep for as long a period as canned peas or canned beans

194 [1924] NZLR 627, 645.
195 [1969] 2 AC 31, 79–80.
196 (1956–57) 98 CLR 77.

or, indeed, beetroot canned in brine or for as long as other canned foodstuffs. Nor would it be material to show that a wholesaler, who had purchased such goods, might still have them in his store more than twelve months later. Indeed, evidence as to the keeping quality of the other goods and as to the practice in the wholesale grocery trade would not be admissible in such circumstances.[197]

As suggested above, it does not seem that the amendments in the present Act will have any effect on this question.

7.4.2.14 Part of goods unsatisfactory

It may happen that only part of the goods are unsatisfactory and that the rest may be satisfactory. In *Jackson* v *Rotax Motor & Cycle Co Ltd*,[198] the plaintiff supplied motor horns to the defendant. One consignment was rejected by the defendant as unmerchantable on the ground that about half the goods were dented and scratched owing to bad packing. The Court of Appeal held that the buyer was entitled to reject the whole consignment, as it was not possible in the circumstances of the case to invoke the *de minimis* rule. The requirement of merchantability obviously applied to all the goods, and if part of the goods were unmerchantable the buyer might reject the whole. No change on this point is made by the 1994 Act, though, as we will see, the right of rejection was modified.

7.4.2.15 Maintenance of spare parts and servicing facilities

It is common for a manufacturer to continue to manufacture spare parts for goods, sometimes for many years after those goods have themselves been discontinued. The manufacturer's willingness to supply servicing facilities may, in certain cases, be a matter of some importance. In the unreported Court of Appeal decision in *L Gent & Sons* v *Eastman Machine Co Ltd*,[199] it was held that there was no legal duty on the manufacturer to observe these practices, and goods could not be held to be unmerchantable merely because these facilities were not, or were no longer available.[200] The matter was discussed briefly by the Law Commissions in their Final Report, and they concluded, inevitably it would seem, that it was too complex to be dealt with by legislation.[201] Nevertheless, it will be arguable in a given case that the lack of spare parts could, in some instances, render goods unsatisfactory, particularly where such spare parts are regularly needed (e.g. belts on vacuum cleaners).

7.4.2.16 Commissioning goods

In the case of complex goods such as machinery, the seller may have a duty not merely to supply goods but also to commission them. In such cases, the seller has a reasonable

[197] At pp. 89–90.
[198] [1910] 2 KB 937.
[199] CA, 1985, cited by the Law Commissions, Final Report, *Sale and Supply of Goods*, para. 3.66.
[200] There is, of course, the possibility of other manufacturers stepping in and filling the gap by manufacturing compatible spare parts, subject to intellectual property constraints.
[201] See Final Report, *Sale and Supply of Goods*, para. 3.66. Such codes do in fact exist for particular industries.

period in which to carry out the commissioning before the buyer can reject for breach of either s. 14(2) or (3).[202] Presumably, where this is in the contemplation of the parties, the buyer cannot complain of losses consequential on the defects until after such a reasonable period has expired. If no time is specified, what amounts to a reasonable time will depend upon the facts of the particular case. In the *Burnley Engineering Products* case,[203] a 'high tech' welding machine was delivered in August 1991 and rejected on 25 September 1992. It was held that if the defects had been remedied by that date, the buyer would not have been entitled to reject.

7.4.2.17 Non-conformity with legal standards

It is common that goods must not only be of satisfactory quality for the purposes of the Act but must also comply with other legal standards. The question is whether non-compliance with these legal standards would also render them unsatisfactory for the purposes of s. 14(2)? It could be argued that in some circumstances; for example, where the goods are in all sense precisely those ordered by the buyer, free from physical defects, etc. the two are not linked; indeed this is the basis of the dispute in *Lowe* v *W Machell Joinery Ltd*.[204] In this case, the claimants had ordered a bespoke staircase at a cost of £16,000. After delivery of the staircase they sought to reject it before claiming the purchase price. The staircase was in all senses compliant with the buyers' requirements and therefore ostensibly of satisfactory quality, however, it was later argued that had it been installed, in the claimant's newly built home, it would not have complied with Building Regulations. The claimants argued that notwithstanding its conformity with their specification, it was nonetheless, as a result of this, not of satisfactory quality, thereby entitling them to reject it. The claim failed at first instance, because minor modifications would bring it within compliance with the Building Regulations, rejection was not justified.

The Court of Appeal did not find favour in this argument. Lloyd LJ stated the court's view that 'on the basis that the goods, supplied in exact conformity with the contract, could not lawfully be used for their intended purpose, known to the seller, it does not seem to me that they were reasonably fit for the purpose, nor that a reasonable buyer would find them satisfactory'.

The result of the decision is that compliance with over-arching legal standards, whether in relation to safety or otherwise will render goods unfit under s. 14(2), even where they are all in all other sense satisfactory.

It is also interesting to consider the status that soft standards would have in relation to s. 14(2). Soft standards are pervasive and are particularly important, for example, in relation to technology. Standards such as HDMI, USB, SD are just three of the hundreds of standards used for the transmission and storage of data; similar examples could be found in relation to most other types of goods. While a failure to comply with these standards may cause the goods not to function at all, in light of *Lowe* it seems possible that potentially a lack of compliance that has no impact on functionality may provide a basis for a buyer to reject goods.

[202] See *Burnley Engineering Products Ltd* v *Cambridge Vacuum Engineering Ltd* (1994) 5 Const LR 10.
[203] Above
[204] [2011] EWCA Civ 794.

7.5 Implied terms that the goods are fit for a particular purpose

Section 14(3) lays down the following condition:

> [205] Where the seller sells goods in the course of a business and the buyer, expressly or by implication, makes known—
>
> (a) to the seller, or
> (b) where the purchase price or part of it is payable by instalments and the goods were previously sold by a credit-broker to the seller, to that credit-broker, any particular purposefor which the goods are being bought, there is an implied condition that the goods supplied under the contract are reasonably fit for that purpose, whether or not that is a purpose forwhich such goods are commonly supplied, except where the circumstances show that thebuyer does not rely, or that it is unreasonable for him to rely, on the skill or judgment of theseller or credit-broker.[206]

7.5.1 In what circumstances is the condition implied?

7.5.1.1 'Particular purpose'

Although the old s. 14(1) referred to 'the particular purpose for which the goods are required' it was well settled that the word 'particular' was used in the sense of 'specified' rather than in contradistinction to 'general'.[207] The purpose may in fact be a very general purpose; for example, a car to drive on the road. In *MacGill* v *Talbot*,[208] a classic car collector advised a commercial car dealer that he wished to buy a Rolls-Royce that was reasonably fit for the purpose of economic restoration. The dealers provided a car which it was estimated would cost about £23,500 to restore; in fact it cost £85,000 to £100,000. It was held that the buyer had made known a particular purpose, in the light of previous dealings between the parties. Moreover, the word 'particular' did not exclude cases where the goods could only be used for one purpose. In *Priest* v *Last*,[209] for example, the Court of Appeal held that a hot-water bottle was required for a particular purpose within the section although it had only one purpose in the ordinary way. To quote again from Lord Wright in *Grant* v *Australian Knitting Mills Ltd*:[210]

> There is no need to specify in terms the particular purpose for which the buyer requires the goods, which is nonetheless the particular purpose within the meaning of the section, because it is the only purpose for which anyone would ordinarily want the goods.

These decisions appear to be largely confirmed by the present s. 14(3), which has substituted the words 'any particular purpose' for 'the particular purpose'.

[205] The references to credit-brokers relate to conditional sale agreements (like hire-purchase contracts), and are designed to cover the situation in which a person who acquires goods under a consumer credit contract does not deal directly with the finance company, with whom he actually contracts, but with an ordinary dealer. Such a dealer who introduces the buyer to a finance company (for instance, by getting him to fill in the appropriate forms) is called a credit-broker in the Consumer Credit Act 1974.

[206] The references to credit-brokers relate to conditional sale agreements (like hire-purchase contracts), and are designed to cover the situation in which a person who acquires goods under a consumer credit contract does not deal directly with the finance company, with whom he actually contracts, but with an ordinary dealer. Such a dealer who introduces the buyer to a finance company (for instance, by getting him to fill in the appropriate forms) is called a credit-broker in the Consumer Credit Act 1974.

[207] *Kendall* v *Lillico* [1969] 2 AC 31, 123 per Lord Wilberforce.

[208] 2002 GWD 12-382 (Sheriff G. J. Evans).

[209] [1903] 2 KB 148.

[210] [1936] AC 85, 99.

Some difficulty has arisen where the purpose for which the buyer wants the goods is made known to the seller but there is some peculiarity about the purpose of which the seller is unaware. In *Griffiths* v *Peter Conway Ltd*,[211] the plaintiff contracted dermatitis from a Harris Tweed coat which she had bought from the defendants. It was found as a fact that the plaintiff had unusually sensitive skin and that the coat would not have harmed a normal person. It was argued for the plaintiff that the case fell within the precise words of the section as the coat was not fit for the purpose for which it was required, namely her personal use. This argument was rejected by the Court of Appeal[212] on the ground that the plaintiff's sensitive skin rendered the required use so special that she had not made known to the sellers the purpose for which the coat was required in the relevant sense.[213]

In reaching this decision, the court was obliged to distinguish *Manchester Liners* v *Rea*,[214] which has been referred to above, and in which it was held that coal supplied by sellers for a particular ship was required by the section to be suitable for that ship. Lord Greene pointed out that ships differed in their types and requirements and that coal merchants knew this well enough; hence, if a merchant undertook to supply coal for a particular ship, they were bound to supply coal suitable for that ship. There was no normal or standard type of ship from which the plainitff's ship differed. But in *Griffiths* v *Peter Conway Ltd*,[215] this was the position. A normal person would have been unaffected by the coat. This does not mean that persons who are, in one sense, 'abnormal' are never protected by the subsection because there are clearly degrees of abnormality. For instance, a drug unfit for use by pregnant women would seem clearly to be unfit for its purpose if sold for use by a woman who is in fact pregnant.

In the *Ashington Piggeries* case,[216] herring meal was sold for making into animal feeds, but the meal was contaminated. This rendered the meal mildly toxic to most animals though it was only seriously dangerous to mink. It was held that the case differed from *Griffiths* v *Peter Conway Ltd*, which was a 'highly special case' because, although mink were peculiarly susceptible to the toxic element, there was evidence that this element was also harmful to other animals. Moreover, it was held that the burden of proof was on the seller to establish that the toxic element was harmless to other animals. As a result the herring meal was held to be unfit for the purpose for which it was sold (namely making into animal feeds) even though it could have been safely made into such feeds in small quantities so long as the resultant feed was sold as not fit for use by mink. But this was largely because the dangerous element in the meal was not known. If it had been known,

211 [1939] 1 All ER 685.

212 See also *Ingham* v *Emes* [1955] 2 QB 366, a case of skill and labour. It is also instructive in this connection to compare *Sumner Permain & Co Ltd* v *Webb & Co Ltd* [1922] 1 KB 55 and *Mash & Murrell* v *Joseph I Emmanuel Ltd* [1961] 1 All ER 485.

213 See also *Slater* v *Finning Ltd* [1996] 2 Lloyd's Rep 353, 1997 SC (HL) 8 – supply of camshafts for a marine engine which suffered an abnormality which created excessive torsion resonance in the shafts. The House of Lords held that the suppliers not having been made aware of the abnormality were not in a position to exercise skill and judgment for the purpose of dealing with it. In *Kelly* v *Andersons House Furnishers (Inverurie) Ltd* 2012 GWD 20-422 (Aberdeen Sheriff Court), a buyer of a three-piece suite suffered from extreme sweat excretion which caused discolouration of the suite but, having not informed the seller of his condition, was unable to show breach of s. 14(3).

214 [1922] 2 AC 74.

215 [1939] 1 All ER 685.

216 [1972] AC 441.

and the buyers had bought it all the same, then it would clearly have been fit for the purpose for which it was sold.

Resale may be a particular purpose within the meaning of the section where it is clear enough for what purposes the goods will ultimately be used. But where a buyer buys goods which have a wide variety of possible uses, the burden placed on the seller may be a heavy one. In *Kendall* v *Lillico*,[217] Brazilian groundnut extraction was sold for the purpose of compounding it into feeding-stuff for cattle and poultry, and it was held that there was a breach of the section because the extraction proved fatal to pheasant and partridge chicks, though it was not dangerous to cattle. In the *Ashington Piggeries* case (referred to above), the original suppliers were merely selling herring meal for making into animal feeds and this proved fatal to mink. Again the suppliers were held liable. It will be seen that in cases of this nature, the 'particular purpose' may be very wide indeed, and although the goods may be quite satisfactory for a wide range of uses, the seller will be liable if the goods are in fact unsuitable for any one of those uses to which the buyer puts the goods.[218] The only qualification to this is that it must be shown that the particular use to which the buyer put the goods was not unforeseeable or abnormal. It is unnecessary to show that this particular use was actually contemplated by the parties. Nor, under s. 14(3), is it necessary that the goods are commonly supplied for the purpose in question. Thus, in the *Ashington Piggeries* case it was enough to render the ultimate suppliers liable that herring meal was commonly used in feeds for mink; it was not necessary to go further and show that this was the particular purpose for which the feeding-stuff would be likely to be used.

7.5.1.2 'Where the seller sells goods in the course of a business'

As with s.14(2), s.14(3) only applies when the seller sells goods in the course of a business.[219] Whatever interpretation is given to these words, it is clear that they exclude from the operation of s. 14(3) all cases of private sales; for example, of second-hand goods, and that, in practice, only manufacturers, wholesalers, retailers and dealers will be caught by this implied condition. Since the implied condition that the goods are satisfactory is limited in the same way, as has been seen, it follows that there is still fairly wide scope for the application of the maxim *caveat emptor* in private sales. Of course, actual reliance by a buyer in such a case may justify a finding that an express warranty was given, but there is no implied term under s. 14(2) or (3).

7.5.1.3 Onus of proof

It is for the claimant to prove, on the balance of probabilities, that the defendant's product was not reasonably fit for its purpose.[220]

[217] [1969] 2 AC 31.

[218] But see below for the view of Nicholls LJ in the *Aswan Engineering case* [1987] 1 WLR 1, 27, which suggests that where the goods are sold for one broad purpose they will be reasonably fit for that purpose even though unfit for some unusual subdivisions within it.

[219] The meaning of 'in the course of a business' was discussed in *Stevenson* v *Rogers, and Buchanan-Jardine* v *Hamilink* considered above at section 7.4.1.1.

[220] *Leicester Circuits Ltd* v *Coates Brothers plc* [2003] EWCA Civ 290.

7.5.2 What is the extent of the seller's obligation?

The second question which arises under this subsection is: what is the extent of the seller's obligation? Several points arise here.

7.5.2.1 Goods to which s. 14(3) extends

The same point arises under s. 14(2) and has already been dealt with above.[221] Reference should be made to this discussion.

7.5.2.2 Triviality

As in the case of the requirement of satisfactory quality, it seems clear that the condition under s. 14(3) can be violated even though the unfitness is a trivial matter, and could easily have been rectified. In *Parsons (Livestock) Ltd* v *Uttley, Ingham & Co*,[222] it does not seem to have been seriously disputed that the sellers were in breach of s. 14(3) when they supplied an animal-food hopper to the plaintiffs, but left sealed a ventilator (which could not be seen from the ground) with ultimately disastrous results. The only thing wrong with the hopper as supplied was that the ventilator was closed, a matter which could have been easily and instantly rectified if it had been discovered.

7.5.2.3 Strictness of seller's liability

It is now beyond doubt that the defendant's obligations can extend under s. 14(3) to latent defects not discoverable by any amount of diligence or care. In *Frost* v *Aylesbury Dairy Co Ltd*,[223] the argument was pressed that the buyer 'could not be said to rely on the skill or judgment of the sellers in a case in which no skill or judgment would enable them to find out the defect' in the goods supplied. The goods in question were milk infected with typhoid against which it was not at the time practical to test. The sellers were held liable, though a reason for this appears to have been that they warranted the milk 'free from germs and disease'. In a number of American cases, the 'blood bank' cases, patients were infected by diseases in blood given in transfusions. These were such that at the time it was not feasible to test for their presence. In some cases, the courts refused to hold that there had been a sale.[224] In other cases, however, the courts held that a warranty was implied, and was breached.[225]

In *Kendall* v *Lillico*,[226] Lord Reid said:

> If the law were always logical one would suppose that a buyer who has obtained a right to rely on the seller's skill and judgment, would only obtain thereby an assurance that proper skill and judgment had been exercised, and would only be entitled to a remedy if a defect in the goods was

[221] See section 7.4.2.1

[222] [1978] QB 791.

[223] [1905] 1 KB 608.

[224] *Perlmutter* v *Beth David Hospital* 123 NE 2d 792 (1954); *Balkowitsch* v *Minneapolis War Memorial Blood Bank* 132 NW 2d 805 (1965).

[225] *Russell* v *Community Blood Bank* 185 So 2d 749 (1966); *Hansen* v *Mercy Hospital* 570 P 2d 1309 (1977).

[226] [1969] 2 AC 31, 84.

> due to failure to exercise such skill and judgment. But the law has always gone further than that. By getting the seller to undertake to use his skill and judgment the buyer gets under s. 14(1) [now s. 14(3)] an assurance that the goods will be reasonably fit for his purpose and that covers not only defects which the seller ought to have detected but also defects which are latent in the sense that even the utmost skill and judgment on the part of the seller would not have detected them.

It should be noted, however, that this remark appears to address the question of the liability of a seller, rather than that of the manufacturer or ultimate supplier. As suggested below, the liability of the latter may be less than absolute. If we regard the holding of the seller liable to be principally a device for passing back liability 'up the chain', it can be argued that the seller's liability should not be greater than that of the manufacturer or ultimate supplier, unless the seller has expressly or impliedly undertaken a greater liability. In any event, the seller's duty is only to supply goods which are 'reasonably' fit, not which are absolutely fit. This is likely to be of special importance where the relevant 'particular purpose' is very broadly stated. For if the goods are suitable for most subdivisions within a broad 'purpose', the fact that they may not be reasonably fit for some rare and improbable subdivision will not necessarily involve a breach of s. 14(3).[227] This point was discussed by Lord Pearce in *Kendall* v *Lillico*:[228]

> I would expect a tribunal of fact to decide that a car sold in this country was reasonably fit for touring even though it was not well adapted for conditions in a heat-wave: but not, if it could not cope adequately with rain. If, however, it developed some lethal or dangerous trick in very hot weather I would expect it to be found unfit. In deciding the question of fact the rarity of the unsuitability would be weighed against the gravity of its consequences. Again, if food was merely unpalatable or useless on rare occasions, it might well be reasonably suitable for food. But I should certainly not expect it to be held reasonably suitable if even on very rare occasions it killed the consumer. The question for the tribunal of fact is simply 'were these goods reasonably fit for the specified purpose?

In the *Ashington Piggeries* case,[229] which has been referred to above, the sellers sold herring meal to buyers which was suitable for inclusion in foodstuffs for most animals but was contaminated with some substance which rendered it poisonous to mink. The buyers used the meal in preparing foodstuffs which were sold to mink companies; the companies used the foodstuffs as mink food and suffered serious losses in consequence. They sued the buyers, who claimed in turn against the sellers. The buyers argued that the meal was required to be reasonably fit for inclusion in animal feeds generally; the sellers argued that the meal was only required to be reasonably fit for inclusion in feeds for pigs, poultry and cattle. It was held, in effect, that the meal was required to be fit for inclusion in feeds for any animals to which the sellers ought to have contemplated that it might be fed, and that was sufficient to impose liability on the sellers on the facts.

A slightly less stringent test was favoured in the *Aswan Engineering* case,[230] where pails bought by the plaintiffs for filling with waterproofing compound proved unfit for stacking six high in the intense heat of a Kuwaiti dockside. The Court of Appeal rejected

[227] See *Slater* v *Finning Ltd* [1996] 3 All ER 398, 1997 SC (HL) 8 – failure of camshafts on vessel due not to the camshafts themselves but to an idiosyncrasy of the appellant's vessel.
[228] [1969] 2 AC 31, 115.
[229] [1972] AC 441.
[230] [1987] 1 WLR 1.

the buyers' claim under s. 14(3) (as well as the claim under s. 14(2)). Lloyd LJ rejected the claim because he thought the plaintiffs had not relied on the sellers, but Nicholls LJ thought that such reliance had been proved on the facts. Nevertheless, he took the view that even if the particular purpose for which the goods had been required was simply 'for export', this would not have been enough to fix liability on the sellers. Where the purpose is stated as broadly as this, it adds little to the requirements of s.14(2) because it is enough to make the goods reasonably fit 'for export' that they are in fact fit for export to most parts of the world.

7.5.2.4 Fitness for purpose and unusual consequences

Where very unusual consequences follow from the use of the goods – sometimes causing unexpected accidental injury and damage and the like – it is sometimes argued that the goods were perfectly fit for all ordinary purposes, and that the unusual consequences in the particular case should not be laid at the seller's door. In *Vacwell Engineering Co Ltd* v *B D H Chemicals*,[231] the defendants sold glass ampoules containing a chemical known as boron tribromide to the buyers, who required it for use in certain manufacturing processes. The chemical, in itself, was perfectly fit for the plaintiffs' purposes but it was liable to react with great violence on contact with water, though this was unknown to the plaintiffs. The plaintiffs' process required the labels to be washed off the ampoules and this was done with water. While this was being done one of them broke, causing a reaction which shattered all the others and as a result a very violent explosion occurred. It was held that the goods were not reasonably fit for the purpose for which they were sold and the defendants were liable because they ought to have foreseen the possibility of the chemical coming into contact with water, and they had not warned the buyers of this danger.[232] Both in this case and in the *Ashington Piggeries* case, the issue under s. 14(3) was very similar to a general argument that the damage which occurred was too remote in accordance with the ordinary principles of contract law discussed by the House of Lords in the *Heron II*.[233] In this type of situation it seems that the application of these principles is, in effect, identical with the question whether the goods are reasonably fit for their purpose under s. 14(3).

This appears to be borne out also by the decision of the House of Lords in *Lambert* v *Lewis*[234] where manufacturers had made a defective towing coupling which was sold by retailers to a farmer. The farmer continued to use the coupling after it was apparent that it was in a dangerous or unfit state, and an accident resulted which led to the farmer having to pay damages to the injured plaintiffs. The farmer sought to recover these damages in an action against the retailer for breach of s. 14(3) of the Act. There clearly was such a breach because the coupling was sold in a condition in which it was not reasonably fit for its purpose (or at least was not likely to remain so fit for a reasonable time), but the House of Lords nevertheless held that the farmer could not recover from the retailer the damages he had to pay the plaintiff. The reason for this was, in effect, that the damages were too

231 [1969] 3 All ER 1681.
232 Three books in the defendants' own library warned of the danger.
233 [1969] 1 AC 350.
234 [1982] AC 225.

remote. In accordance with ordinary principles of remoteness, the farmer's own negligence in continuing to use the coupling in an obviously dangerous state was sufficient to sever the causal chain and free the retailers from liability for the farmer's own negligence.

7.5.2.5 Knowledge, warnings, instructions, etc.

Just as with the implied condition that goods are of satisfactory quality, the seller may be liable because the goods are supplied with inadequate information, warnings or instructions. The *Ashington Piggeries* case, referred to several times above, is one example of goods which were unfit for their purpose because they involved a toxic element unknown to the buyers. If the buyers (not being the ultimate users) had been warned about this element of toxicity, the goods would probably have been fit for their purpose. The *Vacwell Engineering* case, also mentioned above, is another case where the goods were probably unfit for their purpose only because the buyers had not been warned by the sellers that the chemical must on no account be allowed to come into contact with water.

More recently the Court of Appeal had to consider a case of alleged inadequate instructions for use in *Wormell* v *R H M Agriculture (East) Ltd*,[235] where the plaintiff, a farmer, had bought a weed-killer from the defendant sellers for spraying his crops. Detailed instructions were on the canisters in which the weed-killer was supplied, saying in large letters (among other things) that spraying was not recommended after a certain stage in the growth of the crops. But the claimant thought that this warning was designed to avoid the risk of damage to the crops, and he was willing to take the risk of damage. Accordingly, he used the spray even during the period not recommended, but it proved virtually worthless, and the plaintiff sued for the wasted price of the weed-killer. The trial judge found that the instructions were somewhat ambiguous and misleading, and the plaintiff had quite reasonably understood the warning to refer only to the risk of crop-damage. But the Court of Appeal reversed this decision. They insisted that there was nothing wrong with the weed-killer, which would have done its job if applied in the right conditions (and it was immaterial that those conditions had scarcely existed at all during the year in question because of the weather). The question concerned the fitness of the goods themselves, and these were (said the court) quite fit for their use if used properly. The warning on the instructions should have been heeded. It was, however, not doubted that the instructions had to be taken into account in deciding whether the goods were fit for their purpose,[236] so it seems that the court was (in effect) finding that the instructions were not misleading. It is, perhaps, not clear if the court was rejecting the usual objective methods of interpreting contractual documents because there are indications in the judgment that the sellers would not have been liable if the weed-killer had been fit for use when used as intended by the sellers, even if the buyer reasonably misunderstood their intentions because of misleading instructions. If this is the implication of the decision it is out of line with the usual principles of interpretation, and there seems no reason why these principles should not apply to warnings and instructions as much as to all other contractual documents.

[235] [1987] 1 WLR 1091. The type of fact situation in this case has given rise to much litigation in the United States – see *Durham* v *CIBA-Geigy* 315 NW 2d 696 (SD 1982) and citations therefore.

[236] At pp. 1098, 1099–1100.

7.5.2.6 Durability

The next point concerns the length of time during which the goods must remain reasonably fit for the purpose. Similar questions arise in dealing with the implied condition that the goods must be of satisfactory quality.[237] The principle is the same here and there is no reason to duplicate the above discussion. Even though the new s. 14(2B)(e) specifically covers 'durability' in the requirement that goods should be of 'satisfactory quality', and this does not extend to the implied condition under s. 14(3), there is no reason to doubt that the case law mentioned above covers this point quite adequately.

7.5.3 Reliance on the seller's skill or judgment

Under the original s. 14(1), the precursor to the current s. 14(3), the buyer had first to satisfy the court that they had expressly or by implication made known to the seller the particular purpose for which the goods were required so as to show that they relied on the seller's skill or judgment. Now, the proviso operates as a defence for the seller, in that it is for the seller to establish that the buyer has not relied on the seller's skill or judgment.

Older case law remains instructive in determining when the proviso will apply. The courts have demonstrated a willingness to look at the facts holistically and pragmatically.[238] For example, in *Grant* v *Australian Knitting Mills Ltd*,[239] Lord Wright said:

> The reliance will seldom be express: it will usually arise by implication from the circumstances; thus to take a case like that in question, of a purchase from a retailer the reliance will be in general inferred from the fact that a buyer goes to the shop in the confidence that the tradesman has selected his stock with skill and judgment.[240]

The trend of the cases was to hold that if the seller knew the purpose for which the buyer wanted the goods, the buyer would be taken to have relied on the seller's skill or judgment.[241] The present s. 14(3) largely confirms the old case law on this point, so that it is still relevant to refer to it. It is now clear that the onus on the buyer in the first instance is only to show that they have made known the purpose for which the goods are being bought. Reliance will then be presumed unless it is positively disproved, or unless the seller can show it to have been unreasonable.

Strictly speaking, of course, reliance is a question of fact, although whether reliance is unreasonable must involve an element of evaluation.[242] But a number of illustrations from

[237] See section 7.4.2.10.

[238] See, e.g., *BSS Group Plc* v *Makers (UK) Limited (t/a Allied Services)* [2011] EWCA Civ 809.

[239] [1936] AC 85, 99.

[240] See, e.g., *Godley* v *Perry* [1960] 1 WLR 9.

[241] See Lord Guest in the *Ashington Piggeries* case [1972] AC 441, 477, explaining some dicta of Lord Reid's in *Kendall* v *Lillico* [1969] 2 AC 31, 81 where Lord Reid said:I do not think that [*Manchester Liners* v *Rea* – discussed above] is any authority for the view which has sometimes been expressed that if the seller knows the purpose for which the buyer wants the goods it will be presumed that the buyer relied on their skill and judgment. Of this dictum Lord Guest observed: I do not understand my noble and learned friend, Lord Reid, to be saying that the presumption can now be drawn from the mere fact that a particular purpose is made known to the seller. He emphasizes that the question is whether in the whole circumstances the reasonable inference can properly be drawn that a reasonable man in the shoes of the seller would realise that he was being relied on.

[242] See *Jewson Ltd* v *Boyhan* [2003] EWCA Civ 1030 and the more recent decisions of BSS Group Ltd v Makers (UK) Ltd [2011] EWCA Civ. 809 and *Trebor Bassett Holdings Ltd* v *ADT Fire and Security Plc* [2011] EWHC 1936 (TCC) (on the application of the related provision in s. 4 of the Supply of Goods and Services Act).

typical cases may nonetheless be useful. The fact that both buyers and sellers are members of the same commodity market does not of itself show that the buyer does not rely on the seller, though it no doubt tends against the inference of such reliance.[243] But where one merchant has brought the goods to the attention of another and has recommended them, such reliance may be found. When the seller is also the manufacturer, the inference that the buyer has relied on the seller, at least in part, will rarely be rebutted.[244] The fact that the buyer proposes to analyse or inspect or test the goods on delivery does not mean that they are not relying on the seller.[245] Where the seller is selling for export from the United Kingdom to some country overseas, the mere fact that they know that the buyer is buying for import into a foreign country does not show that the buyer relies on the seller's skill or judgment with respect to the suitability of the goods for that particular country.[246] In such a case it is the buyer who would normally be presumed to have the necessary knowledge of the conditions in the country of import and reliance may thus be disproved or, alternatively, may be held to be unreasonable.

The concept of 'unreasonable' reliance was introduced by s. 14(3). It will, of course, be for the courts to decide what amounts to 'unreasonable reliance'. But a good case can be made for treating reliance as unreasonable where the seller in effect disclaims responsibility and merely offers their advice for what it is worth.[247]

Where the buyer's complaint is that the goods do not perform as well as had been hoped rather than that they are defective in any real sense, it may be relevant that the goods have been made to a new and experimental design. In *Dixon Kerly Ltd* v *Robinson*,[248] the defendant agreed to buy a yacht in course of construction to an untried design of the plaintiffs. Although the plaintiffs knew that the defendant wanted the boat for sea-cruising and cross-channel trips, it was held that the plaintiffs gave no warranty that the yacht would be suitable for this purpose.

It is sufficient if the buyer relies only partially on the skill or judgment of the seller. In *Cammell Laird & Co Ltd* v *Manganese Bronze & Brass Co Ltd*,[249] the defendants agreed to construct two propellers for two ships for the plaintiffs. These were to be made according to certain specifications laid down by the plaintiffs, but certain matters, and in particular the thickness of the blades, were left to the defendants. One of the propellers proved useless owing to defects in matters not laid down in the specification. It was held by the House of Lords that the defendants were liable for breach of the condition implied

[243] *Kendall* v *Lillico* [1969] 2 AC 31, 124, per Lord Wilberforce.

[244] *Kendall* v *Lillico* [1969] 2 AC 31, 84 (Lord Reid); *Aswan Engineering Co case* [1987] 1 WLR 1, 27 (Nicholls LJ), though cf. Lloyd LJ at pp. 18–19, who thought there was no reliance because the buyer had simply selected the goods from the maker's catalogue. This seems unsound. Selection of goods from a catalogue is no evidence that the buyer does not rely on the manufacturer's skill and judgment, any more than selection of the goods themselves.

[245] *Kendall* v *Lillico* at p. 95 (Lord Morris).

[246] *Teheran-Europe Corpn* v *S T Belton Ltd* [1968] 2 QB 545. This may be of some significance in the case of goods bought over the Internet. Goods which may work perfectly well in the seller's country may be quite inadequate for the conditions in the buyer's country. See Chapter 22.

[247] See Law Commissions Report, *Exemption Clauses: First Report*, para. 37. No doubt the disclaimer must be properly brought home to the buyer and not just contained in small print.

[248] [1965] 2 Lloyd's Rep 404.

[249] [1934] AC 402. But it must be the particular quality at issue in respect of which there is partial reliance – *Jewson Ltd* v *Boyhan* [2003] EWCA Civ 1030.

by the old s. 14(1) as 'there was a substantial area outside the specification which was not covered by its directions and was therefore necessarily left to the skill and judgment of the seller'.[250] But where the buyer has only relied partially on the skill or judgment of the seller, 'the reliance in question must be such as to constitute a substantial and effective inducement which leads the buyer to agree to purchase the commodity'.[251] Moreover, it must be shown that the matters of which the buyer complains were matters in respect of which they relied on the seller.[252]

If, however, the buyer is well aware that the seller can only supply them with one particular brand of the goods in question, it cannot be said that the buyer relies on the seller's skill or judgment. In *Wren* v *Holt*,[253] where the plaintiff bought beer in a public house which he knew to be tied, the Court of Appeal held that there was evidence on which the jury could find that the buyer had not relied on the seller's skill or judgment. Mere suspicion that only a certain type of goods can be supplied is not enough to exclude liability, however.

In *Manchester Liners Ltd* v *Rea*,[254] the defendants supplied coal to the plaintiffs for their ship the *Manchester Importer*. The coal was unsuitable for this ship, and the sellers were held liable under the section although the buyers had good ground for suspecting that the seller might have difficulty in supplying the right type of coal owing to a railway strike.[255]

Where the buyer has invited a third party to inspect the goods on their behalf, and the third party has reported favourably to the buyer in reliance on the seller's skill and judgment, it is an interesting question whether the buyer themselves can be regarded as having relied on the seller's skill and judgment or whether they have merely relied on the third party's report. If the third party is the buyer's employee acting in the course of their duties,[256] or perhaps if they actually pass on to the buyer what the seller has said, it seems that the buyer can invoke the section. But as we have seen above, the fact that the buyer proposes to have the goods inspected or tested *after* delivery does not rebut the inference that they are relying on the seller's skill or judgment.

Where sellers sold potatoes for export from Northern Ireland to Poland and it was shown that a clearance certificate was required from the Northern Ireland Ministry of Agriculture, it was held that the buyers relied on the certificate rather than on the sellers in respect of matters covered by the certificate.[257] However, this may have been a special case. In export sales it is common for buyers to demand certificates of quality from impartial third parties who are required to inspect the goods, or samples, prior to shipment. Buyers clearly rely substantially on such certificates because they often have to pay for the goods

[250] At p. 414, per Lord Warrington.

[251] *Medway Oil & Storage Co Ltd* v *Silica Gel Corpn* (1928) 33 Com Cas 195, 196 per Lord Sumner.

[252] *Christopher Hill Ltd* v *Ashington Piggeries* [1969] 3 All ER 1496, upheld on this point [1972] AC 441.

[253] [1903] 1 KB 610. But the implied condition of satisfactory quality still applies.

[254] [1922] 2 AC 74 – the decision in this case has been criticised, however – notably by Lord Denning MR in *Teheran-Europe Corpn* v *S T Belton Ltd*, [1968] 2 QB 545.

[255] The actual decision in this case seems to have turned on a crucial finding of fact that the coal actually delivered was not fit for an ordinary Manchester steamer (a well-known class of vessel at the time) in the hands of average officers and crew – see *Kendall* v *Lillico* [1969] 2 AC 31, 81 per Lord Reid. Given that the seller was a coal merchant, he ought to have known that the coal was unsuitable.

[256] *Ashford Shire Council* v *Dependable Motors Pty Ltd* [1961] AC 336.

[257] *Phoenix Distributors Ltd* v *L B Clarke Ltd* [1967] 1 Lloyd's Rep 518.

before they receive them, but this does not deprive them of their normal remedies against the sellers under the contract of sale itself.

7.5.4 Comparison between s. 13, s. 14(2) and (3) and s. 15(2)(c)

It is clear by now that the conditions implied by s. 13, s. 14(2), s. 14(3) and ss. 14(2C)(c) and 15(2)(c) (which apply to sales by sample) must frequently overlap in practice and, in fact, it has often happened that a claimant has succeeded under several of the corresponding sections of the original Act. It is useful to complete this examination of these implied conditions by comparing and contrasting the provisions of the various subsections.

First, both s. 14(2) and (3) only apply where the goods are supplied by a seller who sells in the course of business, and it is clear that this qualification means the same in the two cases. In sales by sample, this restriction does not apply. Nor does it apply to the requirements of s. 13.

Secondly, s. 14(3) only applies where the buyer relies on the skill or judgment of the seller,[258] whereas ss. 14(2) and 15(2)(c) apply even where this is not the case. This distinction may be more apparent than real because the most obvious way in which the buyer can show that they are not relying on the seller is to examine the goods and, if they do, s. 14(2) excludes liability for defects which ought to have been revealed by that examination. Section 15(2)(c) also excludes liability for defects discoverable by reasonable examination of a sample whether it is in fact examined or not. In one respect, however, s. 14(3) is clearly wider than the other two subsections because a person may examine the goods and still rely partly on the seller's skill or judgment. In another respect it is narrower than the other two because if an examination is taken to indicate a lack of reliance on the seller's skill or judgment it will exclude s. 14(3) altogether, whereas it will only exclude liability under s. 14(2) in respect of defects which could have been discovered by the examination, and the same is true of s. 15(2)(c). There are also other situations in which it is plain that the buyer is not relying on the seller's skill and judgment (as where they order goods only obtainable from one source) and yet s. 14(2) applies. Examination appears at first sight to be irrelevant to s. 13, and there is no doubt that the condition in s. 13 can apply even though the buyer has examined the goods. But it is also clear that examination of the goods may be a relevant factor in deciding whether the sale is a sale by description or not. Moreover, it seems unlikely that a buyer could rely on non-conformity with description where they are aware of such non-conformity from their examination of the goods.

Thirdly, s. 14(3) is wider than the other subsections in that goods may be perfectly satisfactory although not fit for the purpose for which they were bought. Indeed, in *Jewson v Boyhan*,[259] the Court of Appeal explained the dividing line between the terms implied by s. 14(2) and 14(3) in terms of s. 14(2) focusing on the intrinsic aspects of the goods, whereas s. 14(3) was concerned with their extrinsic features. In other words, the satisfactory quality standard is of a general kind, whereas the fitness for a particular purpose test covers the peculiarities of the individual case. In *Jewson*, boilers failed to provide

[258] Note the onus of proof is now on the seller to show that the buyer did not rely on the skill and judgment of the seller.

[259] [2003] EWCA Civ 1030.

acceptable energy ratings when installed in a specific building but did so when used elsewhere; the boilers were of satisfactory quality and any claim by the buyer would have had to be made on the basis of s. 14(3).[260]

On the other hand, the wider liability only attaches if the purpose is expressly or impliedly made known to the seller, while the condition as to satisfactory quality applies in any event. Section 13, as we have seen, deals with description and not quality or fitness, but in some circumstances the description includes matters of quality or fitness. Goods may comply with their description but be unsatisfactory or unfit for their purpose, but the converse is also true.

Fourthly, s. 14(2) and s. 14(3) apply to all sales whether by description or by sample, or in any other way, whereas s. 13 only applies to sales by description, and s. 15(2)(c) only to sales by sample.

7.6 Implied terms in sales by sample

The meaning of a sale by sample has been left for treatment here, where it can be most conveniently dealt with. Section 15(1) says somewhat unhelpfully:

> A contract of sale is a contract for sale by sample where there is an express or implied term to that effect in the contract.

This subsection means that just because a sample is provided for the buyer's inspection does not make the sale a sale by sample. It is only a sale by sample if there is evidence of an intention that it should be such. In this connection the parol evidence rule has given rise to some difficulty; it has been held in a number of cases[261] that, if the contract is reduced to writing, and the writing contains no reference to a sample, parol evidence is not normally admissible to show that a sample was produced to the buyer and that the sale is a sale by sample. But where the description of the goods has no common or definite trade meaning, such evidence may be admissible to identify the description with a sample. So, for instance, where sellers sold 'matchless No. 2475 39/40 white voile' under a written contract, the Australian High Court held that it was open to the buyers to identify this product by reference to a sample, though no mention of the sample was contained in the contract.[262] It has also been held in Australia that a parol collateral contract may be proved under which the goods are warranted equal to sample, even where the contract is in writing and contains no reference to a sample.[263]

The classic exposition of the effect of a sale by sample is that of Lord Macnaghten in *Drummond* v *Van Ingen*:

> The office of a sample is to present to the eye the real meaning and intention of the parties with regard to the subject matter of the contract which, owing to the imperfections of language, it may be difficult or impossible to express in words. The sample speaks for itself. But it cannot be treated as saying more than such a sample would tell a merchant of the class to which the

[260] See Twigg-Flesner, "The Relationship between satisfactory quality and fitness for purpose" [2004] *Cambridge Law Journal* 22.

[261] *Meyer* v *Everth* (1814) 4 Camp 22; *Gardiner* v *Gray* (1815) 4 Camp 144; *Ginner* v *King* (1890) 7 TLR 140.

[262] *Cameron & Co* v *Slutzkin Pty Ltd* (1923) 32 CLR 81.

[263] *L G Thorne & Co Pty Ltd* v *Thomas Borthwick & Sons Ltd* (1956) 56 SR (NSW) 81.

> buyer belongs, using due care and diligence, and appealing to it in the ordinary way and with the knowledge possessed by merchants of that class at the time. No doubt the sample might be made to say a great deal more. Pulled to pieces and examined by unusual tests which curiosity or suspicion might suggest, it would doubtless reveal every secret of its construction. But that is not the way in which business is done in this country.[264]

It follows from this, as was held by the House of Lords in this case and as s. 15(2)(c) of the Act lays down in requiring the goods to be free from any defect making their quality unsatisfactory, that the use of a sample does not protect the seller from liability in respect of defects not reasonably discoverable on examination of the sample, although the bulk may in fact correspond perfectly with it. This is clear from the current s. 14(2C)(c).

We have already dealt with the warranty of freedom from defects rendering the quality of the goods unsatisfactory in sales by sample. In addition, s.15(2)(a) requires that the bulk will correspond with the sample in quality. It has been held that 'it is no compliance with a contractual obligation for an article to be delivered which is not in accordance with the sample but which can by some simple process, no matter how simple, be turned into an article which is in accordance with the sample'.[265] But where, according to the normal usages of trade, the sample is intended merely for visual examination, the buyer cannot complain that the bulk does not correspond with it so long as, on a normal visual examination, it would appear to correspond, even though there are in fact differences, perhaps material differences. The point is that, if the sample is only intended for a simple visual examination, the buyer has in no way been misled by a sample being different from the bulk if the difference could only have been discovered by microscopic examination.[266]

It is, of course, perfectly possible for a seller to sell goods without guaranteeing that they comply with some sample provided to the buyer. The seller may require the buyer to make their own examination of the bulk, leaving them to decide how much of the bulk they will examine and whether they are prepared to take the risk of assuming that the rest of it corresponds with the sample. And in some cases (e.g. on a sale of agricultural produce yet to be grown), the parties must know that there may be variation in the quality of the crop from year to year, and the seller is unlikely to guarantee precise correspondence of the bulk with a sample. But in such a case, the sale would not be a sale by sample within the meaning of the section.[267]

Section 35(2)(b) provides:

> Where goods are delivered to the buyer, and he has not previously examined them, he is not deemed to have accepted them . . . until he has had a reasonable opportunity of examining them for the purpose— . . . (b) in the case of a contract for sale by sample, of comparing the bulk with the sample.

This is, in effect, a special instance of the general right of examination conferred by s. 34. The buyer is not to be deemed to have accepted the goods until they have had an

[264] (1887) 12 App Cas 284, 297. See also *Godley* v *Perry* [1960] 1 WLR 9. But in these days of sophisticated technological products it must sometimes happen that a sample is provided which is indeed expected to be subjected to very extensive scientific testing. In such a case, of course, this dictum would be inapplicable.

[265] *E & S Ruben* v *Faire Bros Ltd* [1949] 1 KB 254, 260, per Hilbery J.

[266] *Hookway & Co* v *Alfred Isaacs* [1954] 1 Lloyd's Rep 491; *Steels & Busks* v *Bleecker Bik & Co* [1956] 1 Lloyd's Rep 228.

[267] See the helpful article by Murdoch (1981) 44 MLR 388.

opportunity of examining them and comparing the bulk with the sample. The effect of the acceptance is that the buyer can no longer reject for breach of condition, but is relegated to their right to claim damages.[268]

It may finally be remarked here that in a sale by sample and by description, the combined effect of ss. 13 and 15 is that the goods must correspond with the sample and with the description, and (if the seller is selling in the course of business) be satisfactory. But s. 14(2)(c) still operates so as to exclude liability in respect of defects rendering goods unsatisfactory which should have been discovered on reasonable inspection of the sample.

The Act makes no provision for what might be called a 'sale by model'. It is an everyday occurrence for a buyer to purchase some product in a shop after examining an identical product. But very often they are not actually supplied with the very goods which they have examined, but with another version, still packaged, but which is believed to be identical to the one examined. This is not exactly a sale by sample (there is no 'bulk'), though it is clearly very close to a sale by sample. It seems that there should be an implied condition that the actual goods supplied will be identical with the one examined (unless any differences are expressly mentioned or brought to the buyer's attention), and no doubt such a condition can be implied as a matter of general contract law. The implied conditions under s. 14(2) and (3) are, of course, unaffected by the particular nature of such a transaction.

Having regard to what was said above, it is difficult to see what these sale by sample provisions add to ss. 13 and 14.[269]

7.7 Implied terms annexed by trade usage

Section 14(4), replacing and slightly altering the original s. 14(3), lays down that:

> An implied condition or warranty about quality or fitness for a particular purpose may be annexed to a contract of sale by usage.

This subsection sets out the general rule applicable to all contracts that the intention of the parties must be ascertained in the light of all the surrounding circumstances. Where the transaction is connected with a particular trade, the custom and usage of that trade must be considered as a part of the background against which the parties contracted. In the words of Parke B in a leading case:

> It has long been settled, that, in commercial transactions, extrinsic evidence of custom and usage is admissible to annex incidents to written contracts, in matters with respect to which they are silent.[270]

A simple illustration is provided by *Peter Darlington Partners Ltd* v *Gosho Co Ltd*,[271] which was concerned with a sale of canary seed and, according to the custom of the trade, the buyer was not entitled to reject the goods for impurities in the seed, but was entitled to a

[268] See s. 11(4), Chapter 17, at section 17.2. For possible differences between the right of examination under s. 15(2)(c) and s. 34, see Murdoch, (1981) 44 MLR 388.

[269] Article 2 of the Uniform Commercial Code has no equivalent of these provisions.

[270] *Hutton* v *Warren* (1836) 1 M & W 466, 475.

[271] [1964] 1 Lloyd's Rep 149.

rebate on the price, proportionate to the percentage of admixture in the seed. It was held that the contract was governed by this trade custom.

7.8 Other implied terms

Section 14(1) is as follows:

> Except as provided by this section, and section 15 below and subject to any other enactment, there is no implied condition or warranty about the quality or fitness for any particular purpose of goods supplied under a contract of sale.

Given that the provisions of s. 14 have been overhauled by Acts starting from the Sale of Goods (Implied Terms) Act 1973, and culminating in the 1994 Sale and Supply of Goods Act, this residual exclusion of additional implied terms is inevitable. What is perhaps surprising is that the draftsman did not see fit to relegate this clause to the end of the section rather than leave it at the head, as the extensive nature of the terms implied by s.14(2) and (3) seems to make a mockery of the sweeping claim in s.14(1).

8

Exclusion of seller's liability

8.1 Exemption clauses

Many contracts, especially 'standard-form contracts', contain exemption clauses. The purpose of these clauses is to negate terms, such as those implied in favour of the buyer by ss. 13, 14 and 15. Historically, this posed no difficulty as s. 55 of the Act (now s. 55(1))*[1] enabled the parties to negative or vary, by express agreement, any of the terms which were implied by the Act. Similarly, in hire-purchase agreements which did not fall within the ambit of the Hire-Purchase Acts, all implied conditions and warranties could be, and invariably were, excluded by the terms of the agreement. In cases governed by the Hire-Purchase Acts, however, the right to contract out of the implied terms was always severely restricted.

If a seller can freely exclude or 'contract out' of implied terms intended to improve the position of the buyer, that freedom is clearly open to abuse. Although the courts did what they could to control the more extreme forms of abuse, the position became more and more unsatisfactory, as will be seen below.[2] It became clear that the courts could not effectively control unreasonable exemption clauses and the position was radically altered, first by the Supply of Goods (Implied Terms) Act 1973, which greatly restricted the power of the seller to contract out of their liability for defective goods and also extended the restrictions formerly applicable to hire-purchase contracts. Then, secondly, in 1977 by the Unfair Contract Terms Act, which introduced more general controls on exclusion clauses and replaced the relevant provisions of the 1973 Act.

The Consumer Rights Act 2015 now incorporates a single set of rules controlling unfair terms, including exemption clauses, in consumer contracts. This aspect of the Act is considered fully in Chapter 19. The result is that the UCTA is now focused solely on commercial contracts of sale, and from it are lost the provisions which render attempts to exclude liability for the implied terms as to the quality and fitness of goods automatically ineffective,[3] although, as will be seen, these remain subject to the test of reasonableness.

Of course, the body of common law controls on exemption clauses also remains intact and while in practice, the UCTA renders these rules of much less importance, in determining whether a term is incorporated into a contract and in cases where the UCTA does not apply, it remains applicable. Accordingly, a brief statement of the broadly similar common law position in England and Wales and Scotland follows before UCTA is closely examined.

[1] See Chapter 5.

[2] See below, section 8.3 For a history of the law relating to exemption clauses in standard form contracts see Adams, *Law Litigants and the Legal Profession* (eds Ives and Manchester, 1983, Royal Historical Society), p. 39; see also Adams, 'Unconscionability and the Standard Form Contract' in Brownsword, Howells and Wilmhelmsson (eds), *Welfarism in Contract Law* (1994, Dartmouth).

[3] While not a term as to 'quality', any attempt to exclude s. 12 will continue to have no effect in a commercial sale.

If a seller relies on an exemption clause, they will first have to show that the clause was incorporated into the contract; that is, that it was part of their offer which was accepted by the buyer. This can be done in one of two ways, either by showing that the buyer has actually signed a contract incorporating the clause in question, or by showing that the clause was brought to the attention of the buyer.

In the first case, the fact that the buyer has not understood, or even read, the contract or the clause in question is immaterial.[4] Even in this case, however, there are some circumstances in which the seller may not be entitled from relying on the exemption clause. For example, if the seller has misrepresented the effect of the clause whether fraudulently or innocently, they will not be able to rely on it,[5] or, to take an example from the case law, if it is written on the reverse of the document in another language and the buyer's attention is not drawn to it.[6] So also, an express oral statement made by the seller may in some circumstances be treated as a term which overrides the terms of the written agreement.[7] Finally, there are some rare circumstances in which a party may plead that the contract was wholly void because the nature or effect of its terms were radically different from what they had supposed.[8] In the absence of fraud, this is unlikely to arise in the context of agreements for the sale of goods as it is very unlikely that a buyer (or seller) would make a mistake so fundamental as to justify holding the contract to be void.

Secondly, a party to a written contract can rely on an exemption clause, even where the other party has not signed it, if they have given reasonable notice of the existence of the clause before the contract is made, in a way that shows that they intend it to be an integral part of the contract. This is a general principle of contract law which is less important in the context of the law of sale of goods than it is in relation to certain other types of contract, and detailed consideration is outside of the scope of this book.[9]

A controversial type of exclusion of liability is the 'shrink wrap' licence commonly used in sales of computer software. As a condition for acquiring a copyright licence to enable the software to be loaded legally on to a computer, whether from some form of durable media or via download, the purchaser is required to agree to the terms set out on the packaging (which may be reinforced by assent being required by the software itself as it is loaded on to the computer). In *Beta Computers (Europe) Ltd* v *Adobe Systems (Europe) Ltd*, the facts of which were given previously,[10] Lord Penrose accepted the efficacy of the shrink wrap licence, the unusual feature of the case being that it was in the interests of the acquirer of the software to argue for this, rather than the supplier. However, his view that no contract came into existence until acceptance of the licence terms is questionable. If he

4 *L'Estrange* v *Graucob* [1934] 2 KB 394.

5 *Curtis* v *Chemical Cleaning Co & Dyeing* [1951] 1 KB 805.

6 *Harvey* v *Ventilatoren-Fabrik Oelde GmbH* [1988] BTLR 138.

7 *Couchman* v *Hill* [1947] KB 554; *Harling* v *Eddy* [1951] 2 KB 739; *City & Westminster Properties* v *Mudd* [1959] Ch 129; *J Evans & Sons (Portsmouth)* v *Andrea Merzario* [1976] 1 WLR 1078; *Brikom Investments* v *Carr* [1979] QB 467.

8 This is the plea of *non est factum*, as to which see *Saunders* v *Anglia Building Society* [1971] AC 1104; Treitel, *Law of Contract* (15th edn, 2020, Sweet & Maxwell) §7- . . . -§7- . . . ;

9 The leading cases are *Parker* v *SE Railway* (1877) 2 CPD 416; *Thompson* v *LMSR* [1930] 1 KB 41; *Chapelton* v *Barry UDC* [1940] 1 KB 532; *Thornton* v *Shoe Lane Parking* [1971] 2 QB 163; *British Crane Hire Corpn Ltd* v *Ipswich Plant Hire Ltd* [1975] QB 303; *Interfoto Picture Library Ltd* v *Stiletto Visual Programmes Ltd* [1989] QB 433.

10 1996 SLT 604.

is right, there would seem to be no good reason for confining this to supplies of software, so that in the case of *any* goods supplied with conditions attached no contract would come into existence until the terms were accepted. Yet companies that regularly order goods by telephone or email would be surprised to learn that they had no contractual right to them if conditions (of which they had no knowledge) happened to be furnished with the goods. In order to avoid the difficulty that no contract would exist until the terms of the licence were accepted or rejected, it would be better to characterise the contract as a sale on approval, permitting the acquirer to rescind the transaction if the conditions are unacceptable.[11] It should not in principle affect this analysis whether the conditions which it is sought to impose are those of the supplier or of a third party.

Lord Penrose was also of the view that when the contract on the shrink wrap terms came into existence, it created a *jus quaesitum tertio* (third party right) in favour of the software proprietor. But why? A licence is simply a permission in favour of the user to do that which would otherwise be unlawful.[12] The proprietor of the software did not need a *jus quaesitum tertio* under the licence since it had the copyright in the software.

It is also unfortunate that Lord Penrose did not address the question as to how his analysis that the licence terms constitute an offer which the defender could have accepted or rejected was consistent with the Software Directive as implemented by the Copyright (Computer Software) Regulations,[13] which amend the Copyright, Designs and Patents Act 1988. The Act gives the lawful user of a program the basic rights necessary to make use of it.[14] Since the acquirer already has those rights, why should they be supposed to surrender those rights in return for no doubt lesser rights conferred by the shrink wrap licence? There are, however, good commercial reasons for saying that shrink wrap licences *ought* to be enforceable.[15] Perhaps the solution lies in technical means of protection. New software now often requires the user to register online. A condition of permitting this is that the user is required to accept the conditions imposed by the software house. Presumably, if the acquirer is not prepared to accept those conditions, they are entitled to reject the software. In this case, Lord Penrose's analysis would be more apposite, though modified by the suggestion made above that the transaction is a sale on approval.

Difficulties can arise with regard to contracts made by business parties who use standard order forms, acknowledgments or similar documents, where the parties attempt to incorporate by reference their own standard terms – which of course invariably conflict.[16] This is the 'battle of the forms' situation, which is solved in accordance with general contractual principles,[17] though not always in a very satisfactory way. The difficulty with the usual legal solutions is that they seem to require the court to find either that there

[11] See Sale of Goods Act 1979, s. 18, Rule 4 – and see Chapter 3.

[12] *Federal Commissioner of Taxation* v *United Aircraft Corporation* (1943) 68 CLR 525.

[13] SI 1992/3233.

[14] Copyright, Designs and Patents Act 1988 (as amended), s. 50A(2).

[15] See *ProCD* v *Zeidenberg* 86 F 3d 1447, No. 96–1139 US Ct of Appeals 7th Circ (1996).

[16] Where these conflict with the provisions of a negotiated written contract, it is the terms of the written contract which prevail – *Indian Oil Corp* v *Vanol Inc* [1991] 2 Lloyd's Rep 634.

[17] See *Butler Machine Tool Co* v *Ex-Cell-O Corpn* [1979] 1 WLR 401; *Santer Automation Ltd* v *H C Goodman (Mechanical Services) Ltd* [1986] 2 FTLR 239; *Hertford Foods Ltd and anor* v *TSB Commercial Finance Ltd*, 5 November 1999 (unreported); *Uniroyal Ltd* v *Miller & Co Ltd* 1985 SLT 101; *Continental Tyre & Rubber Co Ltd* v *Trunk Trailer Co Ltd* 1987 SLT 58.

was no contract at all, or that there was a contract on one or other set of standard terms. Frequently, neither of these appears to be a fair or satisfactory result, and a better solution would be for the court to find a contract to exist (especially where performance has actually taken place), but not necessarily on either set of terms. However, this subject belongs to the general law of contract rather than to the law of sale, and it cannot be pursued here.[18]

An attempt to avoid the difficulties created by the 'battle of the forms' has been made following the adoption of the UN Convention on Contracts for International Sales of Goods by some 97 states,[19] which contains provisions which would deal with some of the battle of the forms problems in international sales of goods. Another approach is to encourage traders to use identical standard terms of trading.

8.2 Construction of exemption clauses

Where an exemption clause is incorporated into a contract, important and difficult questions of construction may arise.

The approach to such questions has varied over the years, but there is no doubt that for many years before the enactment of the Unfair Contract Terms Act 1977, the courts had tended to use strained methods of construction to avoid giving effect to what they regarded as unreasonably wide exemption clauses. The first case to reach the House of Lords after the passing of this Act, though it was in fact governed by the pre-Act law, was *Photo Production Ltd* v *Securicor Transport Ltd*.[20] In this case, the House of Lords made it clear that they did not approve of the use of such artificial methods of construction, now that legislative methods were available for striking down at least some unreasonable exemption clauses,[21] a development that freed the law of a great deal of artificiality, eliminating the fiction of 'interpreting' clauses in ways which were almost certainly contrary to their true intent, and keeping separate the two distinct questions of, on the one hand, interpretation or construction, and, on the other hand, the striking down of unfair clauses, properly interpreted.

Unfortunately, after that decision the House of Lords appeared to endorse, in *Ailsa Craig Fishing Co Ltd* v *Malvern Shipping Co Ltd*,[22] a distinction which could perpetuate these artificial modes of construction in certain cases. In the *Ailsa Craig* case, the House distinguished between a limitation clause, and a complete exemption or exclusion clause. A limitation clause is a clause which limits the liability of a contracting party (e.g. to damages not exceeding a specified figure) while an exclusion clause totally excludes any

[18] See Atiyah, *Introduction to the Law of Contract* (6th edn, 2005, Clarendon), p. 53; Adams and Brownsword, *Understanding Contract Law* (5th edn, 2007, Thomson), p. 57 *et seq*.; MacQueen and Thomson, *Contract Law in Scotland* (3rd edn, 2012, Bloomsbury Professional, Haywards Heath), paras 2.40–2.43. See Atiyah, *Introduction to the Law of Contract* (6th edn, 2005, Clarendon), p. 53; Adams and Brownsword, *Understanding Contract Law* (5th edn, 2007, Thomson), p. 57 *et seq*.

[19] The Vienna Convention (1980).

[20] [1980] AC 827.

[21] See also *Fastframe Ltd* v *Lohinski*, 3 March 1993 (unreported – discussed by Adams (1994) 57 MLR 960) in which the Court of Appeal refused to construe a 'no deduction or set-off' clause as applying only to legal, not equitable, set-off. It simply applied the Unfair Contract Terms Act 1977 to the clause. As to the application of UCTA to 'no set-off' clauses, see *Stewart Gill Ltd* v *Horatio Myer Ltd* [1992] 2 All ER 257 discussed below.

[22] [1983] 1 All ER 101, 1982 SC (HL) 14.

liability at all from arising. In the case of a limitation clause, it was stressed, the clause ought to be given its natural meaning without straining. No doubt clear words are still necessary to protect a contracting party from the normal results of a breach of contract, but 'one must not strive to create ambiguities by strained construction . . . The relevant words must be given, if possible, their natural plain meaning'.[23] On the other hand, 'Clauses of limitation are not regarded by the courts with the same hostility as clauses of exclusion: this is because they must be related to other contractual terms, in particular to the risks to which the defending party may be exposed, the remuneration which they receive, and possibly also the opportunity of the other party to insure.'[24] The implication then was that complete exclusion clauses might remain subject to stricter, and perhaps still artificial, rules of construction. However, as noted above, at least so far as the present Court of Appeal is concerned, the move is perhaps away from such artificiality.

The distinction between a limitation clause and an exclusion clause is not very satisfactory for several reasons. First, the distinction between a limitation clause and an exclusion clause is often just a matter of degree. If a clause limits a party's liability to a trivial sum which bears no relationship at all to the amount of damage actually suffered, it is surely absurd to treat this as something wholly different from an exclusion clause. Secondly, exclusion clauses and limitation clauses are often entwined together, as indeed they were in both the *Photo Production* case and the *Ailsa Craig* case. In both cases, there were clauses which protected the defendants from all liability of a certain kind, and limited their liability for other kinds of loss or damage. This is quite normal with certain kinds of exclusion/limitation clauses and once again it seems absurd to distinguish between the two effects. Thirdly, the distinction's survival simply complicates the law unnecessarily and must cause counsel to argue, in many cases, first, whether the clause is of the one kind or the other, and secondly, that different rules of construction can apply in the same words. This is unnecessary; all that is needed is for the courts to take a common sense stance that the more drastic the effects of a clause on the claimant's normal rights, the clearer its words must be if it is to affect those rights. Furthermore, the Unfair Contract Terms Act can be resorted to where appropriate.

In *George Mitchell (Chesterhall) Ltd* v *Finney Lock Seeds*,[25] which is discussed further below,[26] Lord Denning, in the Court of Appeal, pointed out the unsatisfactory nature of the distinction between limitation and exclusion clauses, and suggested indeed that there was earlier authority rejecting such a distinction. In the House of Lords, Lord Denning's judgment was in general endorsed by the Law Lords who rejected the strained and artificial construction placed on the clause in question by the majority of the Court of Appeal, but at the same time the House appears to have reaffirmed the importance of the distinction between limitation and complete exclusion clauses, without reference to Lord Denning's criticisms.[27] It seems certain that this distinction will return to haunt the Supreme Court, and it is very difficult to understand why the House of Lords allowed their own decision in the *Photo Production* case to be glossed in this way; the natural

[23] [1983] 1 All ER 101, 124, 1982 SC (HL) 14, 57 per Lord Wilberforce.

[24] Ibid.

[25] [1983] 1 All ER 108, affirmed [1983] 2 AC 803.

[26] See below, section 8.4.4.

[27] See especially the speech of Lord Bridge, with which all the other Law Lords agreed: [1983] 2 AC at 814.

implications of that decision are that all such artificial distinctions should be rejected, and contractual clauses construed naturally in accordance with their ordinary meaning.[28]

However, the distinction still exists. Perhaps it must be accepted that exclusion clauses are still to be construed more strictly against the party relying on them than limitation clauses. But the general principle that all such clauses which derogate from common law rights must be construed *contra proferentem*, that is, against the party relying on them, seems to apply to limitation clauses as well as exclusion clauses.[29] In *Stewart Gill* v *Horatio Myer*,[30] which involved a contract for the supply and installation of a conveyor system, the Court of Appeal held that the effect of UCTA, s. 13 was to extend the effect of ss. 3 and 7 (these provisions are discussed below) to catch a 'no set-off' clause. In this case, no argument seems to have been presented about the scope of the clause, but in *Fastframe Ltd* v *Lohinski*[31] the argument that the clause in question was apt to exclude equitable, but not legal, set-off (or *vice versa*)[32] was dismissed out of hand. In *Stewart Gill*, Lord Donaldson MR seems to have considered a 'no set-off' clause to be an exclusion clause because it excludes the right, or the remedy, or the procedural rules of set-off. It is submitted that the correct view is that such clauses are properly speaking exclusion clauses, as much as are 'no rejection' and 'no refund' clauses.

Beyond this, it is uncertain what remains of some of the older case law. At least three general propositions may be deduced from the great mass of authorities on the subject though it may well be that these will now only be applied to exclusion clauses and not to limitation clauses, and perhaps not very enthusiastically even then.

The first is that the courts will interpret exemption clauses strictly, and in particular they will attribute precise legal meaning to technical terms. For example, in *Wallis, Son & Wells* v *Pratt*,[33] the plaintiff bought from the defendant seeds described as 'common English sainfoin', which were, as it transpired, a different and inferior variety known as giant sainfoin. The contract contained a term excluding all warranties express or implied. The plaintiff had accepted the goods and was therefore precluded by the predecessor of s. 11(4) from rejecting them, and was compelled to treat the breach of condition as a breach of warranty. Despite this, it was held by the House of Lords that the exemption clause did not protect the sellers. The term in question was a condition and not a warranty, and its nature was not altered by the fact that the plaintiff was compelled to fall back on his remedy in damages. So also in *Baldry* v *Marshall*,[34] the defendants' obligation to deliver a car suited to the plaintiff's requirements was held to be a condition and was therefore not excluded by a clause which referred only to guarantees and warranties.[35]

[28] Since these remarks were first written in the seventh edition, the Australian High Court has rejected the *Ailsa Craig* decision, and has adopted the approach advocated here: *Darlington Futures Ltd* v *Delco Australia Pty Ltd* (1986) 161 CLR 500.

[29] See Lord Fraser in the *Ailsa Craig* case, [1983] 1 All ER 101, 105; 1982 SC (HL) 14, 60–1, a passage cited with approval by Lord Bridge in the *George Mitchell* case. Note, however, *Fastframe Ltd* v *Lohinski*, (3 March 1993, unreported).

[30] [1992] 2 All ER 257.

[31] (3 March 1993, unreported).

[32] An argument based on the analogy of the rule that if there is more than one head of liability a clause is apt to exclude only one unless it mentions both – see *White* v *John Warrick & Co Ltd* [1953] 2 All ER 1021.

[33] [1911] AC 394.

[34] [1925] 1 KB 260.

[35] See also *The Mercini Lady* [2011] 1 Lloyd's Rep 442 which shows the exact same approach continuing to be used in a contemporary context.

One of the most striking of the older cases on the construction of exemption clauses is the decision of the House of Lords in *Beck & Co Ltd* v *Szymanowski & Co Ltd*,[36] where the defendants had sold to the plaintiffs 2,000 gross six-cord sewing cotton thread reels, the length on each reel stated to be 200 yards. The contract provided that: 'The goods delivered shall be deemed to be in all respects in accordance with the contract, and the buyer shall be bound to accept and pay for the same accordingly, unless the sellers shall within fourteen days after the arrival of the goods at their destination receive from the buyers notice of any matter or thing by reason whereof they may allege that the goods are not in accordance with the contract.' The reels had only 188 yards of cotton instead of 200 but this fact was not discovered by the buyers until 18 months later. The buyers claimed damages. It was held that the above clause provided no defence to the sellers, and the ingenious reason given by their lordships for their decision was well summarised by Lord Shaw:[37]

> The damages are claimed not in respect of the goods delivered but in respect of goods which were not delivered.

This seems to have been an example of just that kind of strained and artificial construction criticised in recent cases. Such a clause now would very likely be caught by ss. 3 and 6 of UCTA as extended by s. 13.[38] The same might be said of *Minister of Materials* v *Steel Bros & Co Ltd*,[39] where a contract for the sale of goods contained a term limiting the right to complain of defects of quality to a period of 60 days after the discharge of the goods at their destination. The goods were damaged as a result of defective packing. The Court of Appeal held that the ground of complaint was not the quality of the goods within the meaning of the exemption clause. Yet in the converse position it has been held that the 'quality' of the goods within the meaning of s. 14(2) includes the state of the packing, and that if this is unsatisfactory the goods are not of merchantable quality (now satisfactory quality).[40] The case also illustrates another problem arising from the limitation/exclusion distinction because a time-limit clause of this kind (very common in certain contracts) is neither a complete exclusion clause nor is it a limitation clause. In *R W Green Ltd* v *Cade Bros Farm*,[41] the facts of which are given later,[42] Griffiths J held that it would not be fair and reasonable to allow reliance on such a clause.[43] It is highly unlikely, therefore, that today the court would attempt to limit the effect of such a clause by an artificial construction of the sort given by the court in this case. It would, no doubt, give the clause its normal construction and then apply UCTA.

In the second place, it is a general principle of construction of exemption clauses that, where a party would, apart from the particular provisions of the contract in question, be

36 [1924] AC 43.
37 At p. 50.
38 See *Stewart Gill* v *Horatio Myer* and *Fastframe Ltd* v *Lohinski* (above) – there would probably have been little room for argument on the case law on s. 13 as it had developed even before those cases: see Adams and Brownsword, 'The Unfair Contract Terms Act: A Decade of Discretion' (1988) 104 LQR 94.
39 [1952] 1 TLR 499.
40 *Niblett* v *Confectioners' Materials Co Ltd* [1921] 3 KB 387 – see Chapter 5.
41 [1978] 1 Lloyd's Rep 602.
42 See section 8.4.4 et *seq*.
43 The case was decided on the now repealed provisions of the Supply of Goods (Implied Terms) Act 1973, as to which see section 8.4.4 below.

liable in the absence of negligence, an exemption clause in general terms does not protect them from liability for negligence.[44] Negligence must be specifically covered by the clause, or at least it must be a necessary inference that it is so covered. Since a seller is liable on the implied terms under the Sale of Goods Act irrespective of negligence, an exemption clause in general terms would not exclude the liability of the seller for negligence. Again, this principle is of little importance in consumer sales as consumer goods are generally supplied complete and fully packaged to the retailer, leaving limited circumstances in which a retailer will be guilty of negligence. The liability of manufacturers etc. will now generally be dealt with under the Consumer Protection Act 1987, the provisions of which cannot be excluded, but commercial sellers of goods which are potentially hazardous or dangerous may sometimes be liable both in negligence and under the Sale of Goods Act, and in such cases this principle of construction could be important.[45] On the other hand, clear words must be applied even if the result is to protect a negligent seller from liability. If it is found that the clause clearly limits the liability of the party in breach, there is no principle which can be applied to confine the clause to breaches occurring without negligence.[46]

Lastly, mention must be made of two particular provisions in the Act bearing on the general question of construction. First, reference should be made to s. 55(2), formerly (with verbal alterations only) s. 14(4), which says:

> An express condition or warranty does not negative a condition or warranty implied by this Act unless inconsistent with it[47]

Secondly, in addition to exclusion or variation of implied terms by express agreement, s. 55(1) says that 'the course of dealing between the parties' or 'such usage as binds both parties to the contract' may have the same effect. So far as usage is concerned, nothing need be added to the observations made above dealing with the implication of terms by usage,[48] for they are equally applicable here. With regard to the expression 'course of dealing between the parties', this has been judicially explained to mean that previous dealings between the parties may raise an implication that certain terms are or are not to be included in the contract, if these have or have not been implied on previous occasions.[49] 'If two parties have made a series of similar contracts each containing certain conditions, and then they make another without expressly referring to those conditions it may be that those conditions ought to be implied.'[50] But in order to justify the implications of terms – and more particularly, it would seem, the implication of terms contrary to those normally implied – by reference to a course of dealing, it must be shown that in fact there

[44] *Rutter* v *Palmer* [1922] 2 KB 87; *Alderslade* v *Hendon Laundry* [1945] 1 All ER 245; *Smith* v *South Wales Switchgear* [1978] 1 All ER 18. But cf. clauses merely designed to adjust the incidence of insurance: *Scottish Special Housing Assoc'n* v *Wimpey Construction UK Ltd* [1986] 1 WLR 995, 1986 SLT 559.

[45] See, e.g., *Vacwell Engineering Co Ltd* v *BDH Chemicals Ltd* [1969] 3 All ER 1681 (though there was no exemption clause in this case) See, e.g., *Vacwell Engineering Co Ltd* v *BDH Chemicals Ltd* [1969] 3 All ER 1681 (though there was no exemption clause in this case).

[46] See the *George Mitchell* case [1983] 2 AC 803, 814 per Lord Bridge. Note, however, that negligence may be a relevant factor under the Unfair Contract Terms Act – see below.

[47] See, for a case where an express warranty of the capacity of a machine 'negatived' any implied term as to quality, *Border Harvesters Ltd* v *Edwards Engineering (Perth) Ltd* 1985 SLT 128.

[48] See Chapter 7.

[49] *Pocahontas Fuel Co Ltd* v *Ambatielos* (1922) 27 Com Cas 148, 152 per McCardie J.

[50] *McCutcheon* v *David MacBrayne Ltd* [1964] 1 WLR 125, 128, 1964 SC (HL) 28, 35 per Lord Reid. See also *British Crane Hire Corpn* v *Ipswich Plant Hire* [1975] QB 303.

has been a consistent course of dealing in which the same terms have been regularly if not invariably incorporated in the past.[51] For example, where over a period of years parties have regularly contracted on the basis of certain written terms for the supply of goods, the terms may be held to be incorporated in oral contracts for the supply of the same goods between the same parties.[52] In general, it seems much easier to incorporate an exemption clause from a course of dealing in commercial than in consumer transactions, especially in the case of the standard terms laid down by trade associations.[53]

8.3 Fundamental breach

In earlier editions of this work, extensive treatment was given of this body of doctrine. For some 15 or 20 years in the 1950s and 1960s, the English courts attempted to achieve some measure of protection for consumers by dealing with harsh or oppressive exemption clauses. In retrospect, it is now easy to see this judicial activity as a response to a particular social situation. With the great post-war consumer boom well under way, with the huge increase in ownership of consumer durables and above all motor vehicles, and with inflation rapidly eroding the protections afforded by the early Hire-Purchase Acts,[54] the courts began to see a steady stream of very difficult cases. Most of these cases involved contracts of hire-purchase for second-hand cars or other vehicles. Invariably, all liability for defects was excluded and frequently real hardship to the consumer was the probable result of strict adherence to the law. The courts' answer to this was the invention of the doctrines of fundamental breach[55] and fundamental terms[56] the rise and fall of which are charted in the standard texts.[57] At least in the case of the doctrine of fundamental breach, one of its legacies was the original test of reasonableness inserted in s. 55 of the Sale of Goods Act by the Supply of Goods (Implied Terms) Act 1973. This provided that a term exempting from all or any of the provisions of ss. 13, 14 and 15 of the Act was not enforceable to the extent that it was shown that it would not be fair and reasonable to allow *reliance* on the term.[58] In the event, when these provisions came to be replaced by the Unfair Contract Terms Act 1977, it was the view of the Scottish Law Commission

[51] Ibid.

[52] *Kendall* v *Lillico* [1969] 2 AC 31. Dicta of Lord Devlin in *McCutcheon* v *David MacBrayne Ltd* [1964] 1 WLR 125, 128, 1964 SC (HL) 28, 35, to the effect that actual knowledge of the terms was required before they could be incorporated into an oral contract, were disapproved in *Kendall* v *Lillico*. See also *Hertford Foods Ltd and another* v *TSB Commercial Finance Ltd*, 5 November 1999 (unreported).

[53] Compare British Crane Hire Corpn Ltd v Ipswich Plant Hire Ltd [1975] QB 303 with McCutcheon v David MacBrayne Ltd [1964] 1 WLR 124, 1964 SC (HL) 28 and with Grayston Plant Ltd v Plean Precast Ltd 1976 SC 206.

[54] The first Hire-Purchase Act of 1938 only applied where the total purchase price did not exceed £50, and this was only increased to £300 in 1951, where the figure remained until 1964.

[55] A body of doctrine which developed from the judgment of Denning LJ in *Karsales* v *Wallis* ([1956] 1 WLR 936, 940), though the term appeared in the judgment of Devlin J in *Alexander* v *Railway Executive* [1951] 2 KB 882.

[56] Insofar as this was an independent doctrine (which was not entirely clear), its origins for present purposes may be traced to the judgment of Devlin J in *Smeaton Hanscomb* v *Sassoon & Getty* [1953] 2 All ER 1471, 1473. Note that neither doctrine took root in Scotland, however: see *Alexander Stephen (Forth) Ltd* v *J J Riley (UK) Ltd* 1976 SC 151 and Unfair Contract Terms Act 1977, s. 22.

[57] Atiyah, *Introduction to the Law of Contract* (6th edn, 2005, Clarendon); Cheshire, Fifoot and Furmston, *Law of Contract* (16th edn, 2012, Butterworths); Treitel, *Law of Contract* (14th edn, 2015, Sweet & Maxwell).

[58] See also Misrepresentation Act 1967, s. 3.

which prevailed,[59] and the test is now that of the reasonableness of *incorporating* the term into the contract.[60] The second, more enduring, legacy was the approach laid down by Denning LJ in *Karsales* v *Wallis*:[61]

> The thing to do is to look at the contract apart from the exemption clause to see what are the terms, express or implied, which impose obligations on the party.

This approach is implicit in the drafting of the Unfair Contract Terms Act. It thereby rejected Professor Coote's point that in strict logic an exception clause is simply one method of defining a positive obligation.[62] Although logical, this argument paid no attention to the history of the subject,[63] and was rightly rejected.[64] In fact, this aspect of the Unfair Contract Terms Act has not, in practice, caused difficulties.[65]

8.4 The Unfair Contract Terms Act 1977

The Act is divided into three Parts: the first applying to England and Wales, the second to Scotland, and the third to the United Kingdom although the broad thrust of the provisions is very similar.

8.4.1 England and Wales

The first relevant provision applies to all contracts, not merely to contracts for the sale of goods. Section 3 states:

> (1) This section applies as between contracting parties where one of them deals on the other's written standard terms of business.
> (2) As against that party, the other cannot by reference to any contract term—
> (a) when himself in breach of contract, exclude or restrict any liability of his in respect of the breach; or
> (b) claim to be entitled—
> (i) to render a contractual performance substantially different from that which was reasonably expected of him, or
> (ii) in respect of the whole or any part of his contractual obligation, to render no performance at all, except insofar as (in any of the cases mentioned in the above sub-section) the contract term satisfies the requirement of reasonableness.

The effects of this clause are extended by s. 13 discussed below. The reasonableness test for the purposes of s. 3 is that set out in s. 11(1):

> . . . that the term shall have been a fair and reasonable one to be included having regard to the circumstances which were, or ought reasonably to have been, known to or in the contemplation of the parties when the contract was made.

59 See Unfair Contract Terms Act 1977, s. 11(1).
60 Unfair Contract Terms Act 1977, s. 11(1).
61 [1956] 1 WLR 936, 940.
62 Coote, *Exception Clauses* (Sweet & Maxwell, 1964). See also *G H Renton & Co Ltd* v *Palmyra Trading Corp of Panama* [1957] AC 194.
63 As to which see Adams in *Welfarism in Contract Law* (Brownsword, Howells and Wilmhelmsson (eds), 1994, Dartmouth).
64 See Adams (1978) 41 MLR 613.
65 Other aspects have – see Adams and Brownsword, 'UCTA: a Decade of Discretion' (1988) 104 LQR 94.

This test is in theory different from that applied in relation specifically to the sale and supply of goods provisions discussed below.[66]

By s. 6(1) of this Act, it is provided that liability in respect of breach of s. 12 of the Sale of Goods Act cannot be excluded or restricted by any contract term. Section 12 is, of course, the section containing the implied conditions as to title. Section 6(1) also applies to the corresponding implied condition in hire-purchase contracts in s. 8 of the Supply of Goods (Implied Terms) Act 1973. And s. 7 of the Unfair Contract Terms Act 1977, as subsequently amended, contains restrictions on contracting-out of the similar implied terms in all other contracts for the supply of goods, which are dealt with by the Supply of Goods and Services Act 1982.[67]

Subsection (1A) of section 6 is as follows:

> Liability for breach of the obligations arising from—
> (a) section 13, 14 or 15 of the 1979 Act (seller's implied undertakings as to conformity of goods with description or sample, or as to their quality or fitness for a particular purpose);
> (b) section 9, 10 or 11 of the 1973 Act (the corresponding things in relation to hire purchase), cannot be excluded or restricted by reference to a contract term except in so far as the term satisfies the requirement of reasonableness.[68]

Although s. 6(1) provides that there can be no contracting out of s. 12 at all. One might suggest that this is slightly misleading because s. 12 itself envisages a limited form of contracting-out in that it recognises the possibility of a sale of a limited interest in goods. Much of s. 12 hinges on the disclosure of any limitation of title or charge or encumbrance, so a seller who, for example, knows that the goods they sell are held under some hire-purchase agreement should not be allowed to conceal this fact and protect himself merely by purporting to sell only the hirer's interest in the goods..

The effect of s. 6(1A) on contracting-out of ss. 13–15 is, of course, much more dramatic and more radical. Under s. 6(1A)(a), exclusion of the seller's duties under ss. 13–15 is only permissible subject to a test of reasonableness. In evaluating the significance of these provisions, there are two important matters to be considered: first, the extent to which some limited forms of contracting-out may still be possible through the inherent operation of ss. 13–15 themselves; and, secondly, the requirement of reasonableness.

8.4.2 Limited contracting-out still possible

Despite the limitations on clauses excluding or limiting the seller's liability under ss. 13–15 of the Act, the drafting of the Unfair Contract Terms Act 1977 does not in fact prevent the intention of the parties from having some control over liability under these sections. For instance, although the seller cannot escape liability under the implied condition that the goods must correspond with their description under s. 13 if the sale is a sale by

[66] See, however, *Danka Rentals Ltd* v *Xi Software* (1998) 7 Tr LR 74, where the judge suggested it made little practical difference – see section 8.4.4.

[67] Except that the conditions as to title are subject to the reasonableness test, rather than a prohibition on their exclusion or restriction. See below, section 8.4.4 *et seq.*, as to the reasonableness test.

[68] Section 7 also contains analogous provisions to s. 6(1A) with respect to other contracts for the transfer of the possession or ownership of goods – see section 8.4.4, *Danka Rentals Ltd* v *Xi Software* (1998) 7 Tr LR 74.

description, the question of whether the sale is indeed a sale by description is presumably still for the contract itself to determine. So, as we have seen, it is still open to the court to hold that a sale is a contract for the sale of a specific unique chattel, and not a contract for sale by description. A seller may use descriptive words in selling specific goods, but if they make it clear that it is for the buyer to examine the goods and satisfy themselves of their proper description, they may escape liability on the ground that the sale is not by description at all. For instance, despite the decision in *Beale* v *Taylor*[69] about the '1961 Herald', it seems that if a seller of a second-hand car uses descriptive words, but qualifies them by saying that they do not guarantee their correctness, and makes it otherwise clear that the buyer must examine the car themselves and take it 'as is', then the seller may escape liability even under s. 13.

In a case such as this, a delicate line would, however, need to be trodden here to ensure that the courts do not seriously undermine the provisions of the Unfair Contract Terms Act. The key here, and elsewhere, to problems of this kind may lie in the concept of reasonable reliance as was suggested when we discussed *Harlingdon & Leinster Ltd* v *Christopher Hull Fine Art Ltd*.[70] If it is clear that the buyer has reasonably relied upon the words of description used by the seller, it would seem that the court ought not to allow the seller to escape liability by claiming that the sale is not really a sale by description, but if, on the other hand, a reasonable buyer would not have attached any weight to the descriptive words but would have relied entirely on their own examination of the goods, the sale may be held not to be by description and the seller may be permitted to escape liability. *A fortiori*, if the buyer actually sees that the goods do not conform with the seller's description it seems impossible that they could sue under s. 13. This still gives some weight to the Unfair Contract Terms Act; what it does, in effect, is to stress that the totality of the negotiations must be looked at, and that the seller cannot, just by procuring the buyer's signature to a document (for instance), eliminate from the picture the fact that descriptive words have been used and have been relied upon.

Similar problems may arise in relation to other implied terms. For example, under s. 14(2) the seller can point out defects to the buyer and no implied condition that the goods should be of satisfactory quality will exist as to those defects, so also, if the buyer examines the goods, there is no implied condition that the goods should be of satisfactory quality as regards defects which their examination should have revealed. These provisions enable the parties to limit the responsibility of the seller despite the Unfair Contract Terms Act, with regard to defects which the buyer knew, or clearly ought to have known of.

It is to be expected that some sellers may attempt to take advantage of these provisions by incorporating written clauses into their conditions of sale, declaring, for example, that 'all defects have been drawn to the attention of the buyer and the buyer acknowledges this fact' or that 'the seller offers no opinion as to the suitability of the goods for any particular purpose and the buyer acknowledges that he does not rely on the seller's skill or judgment'.[71] However, it is likely that such clauses would be regarded as attempts to

[69] [1967] 1 WLR 1193.

[70] See Chapter 7, section 7.3.1. Note also the case of *Smith* v *Eric S Bush* [1989] 2 All ER 514 discussed below.

[71] *Lowe* v *Lombank Ltd* [1960] 1 WLR 196, which of course was decided long before UCTA, suggests that a clause reciting that the buyer has examined the goods would be effective only if it operated to raise an estoppel against the buyer.

exclude the liability of the seller by agreement under s. 6 of the 1977 Act. For an attempt, to be successful it would have to satisfy the 'requirement of reasonableness'. Under s. 14(2) and (3) of the Sale of Goods Act, it is the *facts* which matter and not the agreement.[72] The questions under these sections will be: Were the defects *in fact* drawn to the buyer's attention? Did the buyer *in fact* rely or reasonably rely on the seller's skill or judgment?

Another way in which, despite the Unfair Contract Terms Act, the seller may be able to escape a *prima facie* liability under s. 14(2) arises from the fact that the concept of satisfactory quality is so flexible. Thus, a buyer may actually order goods from a seller which are, or would in other circumstances be, of unsatisfactory quality.[73] If the seller supplies exactly what the buyer has ordered, the buyer may be unable to complain that the goods are of unsatisfactory quality. But once again, a delicate line needs to be trodden between two types of case: on the one hand, a buyer is clearly not to be deprived of their rights under s. 14(2) if, for example, they order goods under their trade name, and the goods supplied, while complying with their trade name, happen to be defective. On the other hand, if the buyer actually provides a detailed specification to the seller and says, in effect, 'Make me these goods to this specification', and the goods are so made in all respects in accordance with the specification, it would be remarkable if the buyer could complain that the resulting goods were still not of satisfactory quality. Yet the only way to avoid this result, if in fact the goods have defects rendering them unfit for normal use, is to hold that the goods, in the particular circumstances of the case, are of satisfactory quality despite the defects. Again, the key may lie in the question of reasonable reliance: if the buyer who orders goods to be made to a particular specification knows what they are doing, and relies entirely on their own ability to draw up the specification, the goods ought to be held to be satisfactory. If, however, it is clear that the buyer is still partially at least relying on the seller, it may be that the seller ought at least to advise the buyer that the goods may turn out to be of no use if made in accordance with the buyer's instructions.

Problems can also, as already noted, arise with respect to the implied conditions in a sale by sample. As we have observed, the two most important conditions in a sale by sample are the implied condition of satisfactory quality and the implied condition that the bulk corresponds to the sample. But this does not mean that even where *prima facie* the Unfair Contract Terms Act prohibits contracting-out, there is no way in which a seller can restrict their liability. Suppose, for instance, that a buyer orders a carpet after being shown a sample of carpeting, but they are clearly told by the sellers that they do not guarantee that the colours will be identical with those on the sample. If this is actually held to be a sale by sample, the sellers will be liable for the failure of the carpet to correspond with the sample, despite the specific warning given to the buyer. However, in such circumstances, this may well be regarded as an unreasonable result,[74] and it is open to the court to hold that the sale is not strictly speaking a sale by sample at all. In that event, although the carpet must still be of satisfactory quality under s. 14(2), the implied conditions applicable to a sale by sample will not attach.

[72] See *Lutton* v *Saville Tractors (Belfast) Ltd* [1986] 12 NIJB 1, 19, where Carswell J in the High Court of Northern Ireland approved this passage, and held void a 'declaration' that the buyer did not rely on the seller as a 'transparent attempt to escape the operation of s. 6(2)(a) of the 1977 Act'.

[73] See Chapter 7.

[74] In practice slight differences of colour between the samples and the carpets supplied are very common and probably unavoidable.

Lastly, the implied condition in s. 14(3) about fitness for purpose raises similar issues. If the buyer *does* make known the purpose for which they want the goods, and *does* rely (reasonably) on the seller's skill or judgment, the seller cannot escape liability by use of an exclusion clause, but it is possible for the seller to show that they do not guarantee that the goods will be suitable for the buyer's purposes. They may simply tell the buyer that they do not know if the goods will suit the buyer's needs, or that the buyer must make up their own mind as to this. Once again, the key concept is reasonable reliance, and in this case the Act recognises this by actually introducing the concept in s. 14(3). If the seller can show that the buyer did not rely, or did not reasonably rely, upon their skill or judgment, then they are not liable at all, and the application of the Unfair Contract Terms Act does not arise. Clearly, it is once again the facts which matter. What the two Acts together rule out is the 'small print' exclusion clause, and it seems clear that it will not help the seller to replace a 'small print' exclusion clause by one declaring that the buyer has not relied on their skill or judgment, or that the seller gave no opinion on the suitability of the goods for the buyer's purposes.[75] This kind of purely formal agreement will not defeat the buyer's claims, but a real, and reasonable, agreement will show that the buyer has not relied upon the seller in such a way as to attract the implied condition in the first place.

8.4.3 Exemption clauses affected by the Unfair Contract Terms Act 1977

The question as to what precisely is an exemption clause the use of which is regulated by the Unfair Contract Terms Act is also one of no small difficulty. As we have seen, the words of s. 6 of the Unfair Contract Terms Act say that the liability of a seller under ss. 13–15 'cannot be excluded or restricted by reference to a contract term except in so far as the term satisfies the requirement of reasonableness'. Then s. 13(1) of the same Act goes on to say that the Act also prevents:

(a) making the liability or its enforcement subject to restrictive or onerous conditions;
(b) excluding or restricting any right or remedy in respect of the liability, or subjecting a person to any prejudice in consequence of his pursuing any such right or remedy;
(c) excluding or restricting rules of evidence or procedure.

Further, the section adds that it applies to 'terms and notices' which exclude or restrict liability. Section 13(2), however, makes it clear that this does not prevent the parties incorporating an arbitration clause in their contract.

Some things are reasonably clear. An outright attempt to say that implied terms do not apply or are excluded, or that some express condition is given in lieu of all statutory conditions, must be held to be reasonable; otherwise it is simply ineffective. Similarly, a clause which says that breach gives no right of rejection would be ineffective as excluding 'a remedy in respect of the liability' under s. 13(1)(b) above. So also a clause which entitles the buyer to have the goods replaced but not to recover payment of the price would be void for the same reason. So also would a clause limiting the seller's liability for damage to a specified figure, or excluding liability for consequential losses.

[75] See *South Western General Property Co Ltd* v *Marton* (1982) 263 EG 1090; *Lutton* v *Saville Tractors (Belfast) Ltd*, [1986] 12 NIJB 1.

But other points raise much more difficulty. What of a clause attempting to exclude or limit the seller's liability by claiming that a person acting on their behalf had no authority to say or do certain things? This question has arisen, and is more likely to arise, in connection with clauses attempting to limit or exclude liability for misrepresentation, which are not wholly void under s. 6 of the 1977 Act, but are subject to the test of reasonableness. But similar questions could arise under s. 6, for example where the seller's agent has offered an opinion as to the suitability for use of the goods being sold, and the seller later claims that the agent had no authority to give such an opinion. In the cases on misrepresentation, it has so far been held that clauses (or even notices) about the authority of an agent must be treated in accordance with ordinary principles of contract law, and do not fall within the Act's control of exclusion or limitation clauses.[76] Their *effect* may be to limit the liability of the seller but their validity has never been tested by asking what their effect is, but by asking whether legitimate legal means have been used to achieve this effect.[77] On the other hand, a different result has been arrived at in a somewhat comparable situation, which is where a clause provides that one party is not to rely upon any representations made by the other party but is to make their own inquiries.[78] Here again, the issue arose in the context of a misrepresentation and an attempt to exclude liability for such a misrepresentation, but the issue is closely analogous to that which arises (for instance) under s. 14(3) of the Sale of Goods Act.[79]

Many other issues still lack authority. For instance, does s. 13(1)(a) of the 1977 Act prevent a seller from requiring a claim to be made against them within some specified period, or requiring notice of defects in the goods to be given within a certain time? If the time is so short that it is not practicable for the buyer to comply with it, then the restriction is within the Act, and will be void.[80] If the period is not as short as that it might be held that this is permissible simply because this would not be a restrictive or onerous condition, or alternatively it might be held to be within the Act but valid as reasonable.

8.4.4 The requirement of reasonableness

With the exceptions noted above in relation to UCTA ss. 6(1) and 13(1), exclusion clauses are now subject to the requirement of reasonableness by s. 2 (which deals with the exclusion of negligence liability), and s. 3 set out above. As noted at the outset,[81] the requirement of reasonableness is, at least theoretically, different for clauses relating to the implied terms in contracts for the sale or supply of goods, than it is for clauses relating to other

[76] *Overbrooke Estate Ltd* v *Glencombe Properties Ltd* [1974] 1 WLR 1335, approved by the CA in *Collins* v *Howell-Jones* (1980) 259 EG 331, criticised in (1981) 97 LQR 522.

[77] Cf. *The Hollandia* [1983] 1 AC 565 where, in a different context, the HL applied an 'effects' test.

[78] See *Photo Production* v *Securicor Transport* [1980] AC 827; also *Ailsa Craig Fishing Co Ltd* v *Malvern Shipping Co Ltd* [1983] 1 All ER 101.

[79] Thus a shop which displayed notices saying, 'Assistants are not authorised to give their opinion on the suitability of goods for particular purposes', might escape liability, while a shop displaying a notice saying, 'Customers must rely on their own judgment, not that of the assistant', would not. But cf. *Smith* v *Eric S Bush* [1989] 2 All ER 514 which suggests that the first of these conclusions may now be challengeable.

[80] *R W Green Ltd* v *Cade Bros Farm* [1978] 1 Lloyd's Rep 602.

[81] See above, section 8.2

contract terms.[82] Moreover, this requirement will operate in a number of different circumstances, of which the most important for present purposes are as follows.[83]

1 First, if the exclusion clause does not relate to the implied conditions under the Sale of Goods Act, but to some express term of the contract, as, for example, a requirement that goods be 'shipped in good condition'.[84] In this case, s. 3 provides that the requirement of reasonableness applies if the buyer is dealing on the other party's 'written standard terms of business'. The same position holds if the exclusion clause relates to some other liability under the Sale of Goods Act; for instance, the quantity of the goods to be delivered.
2 Secondly, if the exclusion clause relates to the implied conditions in ss. 13–15 of the Act, the reasonableness requirement[85] will apply. It is immaterial whether the buyer is buying on the other's written standard terms of business.
3 Thirdly, the requirement of reasonableness[86] applies to any contractual term excluding business liability for negligence[87] (except for negligence leading to death or bodily injury, liability for which cannot be excluded at all).[88] In this case, it is immaterial whether the buyer is dealing on written standard terms or not. These factors may be relevant in the application of the test, but here we are only concerned with the preliminary question, whether it applies at all.
4 Fourthly, the requirement of reasonableness[89] applies to all cases where a clause relates to the effect of a misrepresentation, and, here again, it is immaterial whether the buyer is buying on written standard terms or not; indeed, the position is the same if the clause relates to the liability of the buyer rather than the seller.

In these four cases, therefore, the Unfair Contract Terms Act requires any exclusion clause to pass the appropriate test of reasonableness if it is to be upheld. However, it will be seen that a number of preliminary questions may be relevant before that test is applied to the exclusion clause. For instance, it may be necessary to decide whether the exclusion clause is incorporated into the contract and what its effect is as a matter of construction.[90] Secondly, it may be necessary to decide whether the case does indeed fall within one of the above four classes of cases – something which may not be nearly so clear as may be thought from this summary of the Act. It would be beyond the scope of this book to examine these questions in any detail, but a number of critical points must be mentioned.

The first is that there may often be problems in deciding whether a clause is indeed an exclusion clause which is caught by the Act and so (in these four classes of cases) subjected to the relevant requirement of reasonableness. The difficulty can be illustrated by considering the ordinary commercial sale where the contract allows the seller a margin of tolerance; for instance, as to the quality or quantity of the goods. If a seller contracts to deliver 5,000 tons of grain, but the contract proceeds to give the seller a tolerance by

82 But see section 8.4.1.
83 It should be stressed that the 1977 Act is a very intricate piece of legislation, and the following summary concentrates on essentials only. For details, reference to the Act itself is indispensable.
84 See *Cehave NV* v *Bremerhandelsgesellschaft*, [1976] QB 44.
85 That is, that set out in s. 11(2)
86 That is, that set out in s. 11(1).
87 Section 2(2).
88 Section 2(1).
89 That is, that set out in s. 11(1).
90 See above, section 8.1 *et seq*.

saying they may deliver 'five per cent more or less', is the seller's right to deliver five per cent less than the contract quantity an exclusion clause, or merely a clause defining their obligation? In a simple case of this kind, where tolerances are common (and where exact compliance would anyhow not always be practicable) it is surely unthinkable that the court would hold the clause to be an exclusion clause at all.

A key authority is the decision of the House of Lords in *Smith* v *Eric S Bush*[91] where a broad view was taken of the effect of the Act. Here it was held that a surveyor engaged by a mortgagee to value a house was liable for negligence even though the mortgagee had specifically declared that the valuation was only obtained on the basis that the surveyor accepted no responsibility. The argument that this was not a disclaimer subject to the 1977 Act, but a denial of responsibility which prevented a duty of care arising in the first place, was rejected by the House of Lords. So where there is or would *prima facie* be a legal liability, any clause denying that liability (no matter how phrased) would appear to be subject to the reasonableness requirements of the Act. But where there is not even a *prima facie* liability because the contract is one which does not in itself impose such a liability, this argument presumably fails, and the Act will not apply.

These problems are likely to be most important in relation to s. 3 of the 1977 Act set out above.[92] It can be seen that two alternative cases are contemplated here. Under the first, a clause is caught by the section if it excludes or restricts a liability in the ordinary way (s. 3(2)(a)). Under the second, even where this is not the case – that is, even where the clause does not appear to be an exclusion clause in the ordinary sense – the section will bite if the effect of a clause is to permit a performance substantially different from that which could reasonably be expected, or no performance at all (s. 3(2)(b)).

The next question which arises with cases falling into these four groups, that is where the test of reasonableness is to be applied, is the ordinary question of construction. For whether the clause is held inapplicable to the circumstances which have occurred as a matter of construction or whether it is held ineffective under the statute, the result will be the same. But in the present group of cases, it is to be assumed that ordinary principles of construction will remain more important, for if the exclusion clause is found not to cover the events which have occurred, then there will be no need to apply the reasonableness test at all. It is now clear that older cases on the construction of exclusion clauses are best treated as guidelines, and subject to the general approach to contract interpretation.[93] In particular, courts prefer the general rules of contract interpretation in the case of complex contracts where exclusion clauses are part of the agreed risk allocation between the parties.[94]

If, on the other hand, the construction question leads to the conclusion that the clause is intended to apply to the events which have occurred, the court must then go on to answer the reasonableness question.

The reasonableness test is itself set out in s. 11 of the 1977 Act, and as we have noted differs at least in theory according to whether the appropriate provision is s. 11(1) or s. 11(2). In relation to the latter provision, there are guidelines set out in Sched. 2.[95]

[91] [1989] 2 All ER 514.

[92] See section 8.3.

[93] *HIH Casualty & General Insurance Ltd* v *Chase Manhattan Bank* [2003] UKHL 6.

[94] e.g., *Persimmon Homes Ltd* v *Ove Arup & Partners Lotd* [2017] EWCA Civ 373.

[95] Though, as noted below, in applying the test of reasonableness under s. 11(1), courts tend to take into account the guidelines of Sched. 2.

Section 11(1) was set out above.[96] The first point to note about this section is that it requires that the term should have been fair and reasonable *at the time when it was included in the contract*. A very wide exclusion clause may easily be held to be unreasonable under the Act, even though it would have been quite reasonable to have a narrower exclusion clause which would have actually covered what has in fact happened.

The next part of s. 11 which needs to be noted is s. 11(4), which states that where an exclusion clause seeks to restrict the liability of a party to 'a specified sum of money', regard is to be had in particular to:

(a) the resources which he could expect to be available to him for the purpose of meeting the liability should it arise; and
(b) how far it was open to him to cover himself by insurance.

Section 11(5) goes on to say that the onus is on the party who claims an exclusion clause is reasonable to satisfy the court that it was.

The guidelines in Sched. 2 are more or less the same as those which were originally contained in the Supply of Goods (Implied Terms) Act, and they do not, strictly speaking, apply in all cases where the reasonableness test has to be applied but only to cases involving contracts for the sale (or supply) of goods.[97] The court must have regard to the following, where relevant:

(a) the strength of the bargaining positions of the parties relative to each other, taking into account (among other things) alternative means by which the customer's requirements could have been met;
(b) whether the customer received an inducement to agree to the term, or in accepting it had an opportunity of entering into a similar contract with other persons, but without having to accept a similar term;
(c) whether the customer knew or ought reasonably to have known of the existence and extent of the term (having regard, among other things, to any custom of the trade and any previous course of dealing between the parties);
(d) where the term excludes or restricts any relevant liability if some condition is not complied with, whether it was reasonable at the time of the contract to expect that compliance with that condition would be practicable;
(e) whether the goods were manufactured, processed or adapted to the special order of the customer.

Even now, only one sale of goods case[98] on the modern statutory control of exception and limitation clauses[99] reached the House of Lords, (none have come before the Supreme Court) and it is appropriate to begin with that case. It must be noted at the outset, however, that this case was governed by the provisions subsequently contained in the Sale of Goods Act 1979.[100] The significance of this is dealt with below. The case was *George*

[96] See section. 8.3–8.4.
[97] But they have been taken into account – see *Danka Rentals Ltd* v *Xi Software* (1998) 7 Tr LR 74; and see *Farrans Construction Ltd* v *Ready Mixed Concrete (Scotland) Ltd* 2004 GWD 13-283 (Outer House, Court of Session).
[98] Though the House of Lords has considered the application of the Unfair Contract Terms Act in a consumer credit case: *Director General of Fair Trading* v *First National Bank plc* [2002] 1 All ER 97 – see Chapter 19.
[99] There are early examples such as the Carriers Act 1830 and the Railway and Canal Traffic Act 1854.
[100] Consolidating the identical provisions of the Supply of Goods (Implied Terms) Act 1973.

Mitchell (Chesterhall) Ltd v *Finney Lock Seeds Ltd*[101] where the plaintiffs were farmers who had ordered late cabbage seed from the defendants who were seed merchants. They were supplied with an inferior seed which was not indeed a late cabbage seed at all. The plaintiffs suffered considerable losses (over £60,000) which were not (it was stressed in the House of Lords) purely losses of profit; the losses included large sums of wasted expenditure in planting and later clearing the fields where there was a total crop failure. The contract contained a clause limiting the defendants' liability to the cost of replacing or refunding the price of the seeds sold – a relatively trivial sum. It was held that, applying the ordinary meaning of the words, the limitation clause did apply to the circumstances, but it was void under the Unfair Contract Terms Act as unreasonable.

In arriving at the second part of this decision, which is the material part for present purposes, the House of Lords balanced a number of considerations. In favour of the sellers was the fact that the parties knew and understood the terms clearly enough, and also that the damages claimed were out of all proportion to the price. But, in favour of the buyers, it was pointed out that (1) all seeds were sold on these terms by seed merchants – buyers had no opportunity to pay more and obtain protection from such risks, (2) the sellers could insure against this kind of liability without a material increase in the price of seeds, (3) the sellers had been negligent in supplying the wrong kind of seed, and (4) most important of all, it was shown that seed merchants did often negotiate settlements and offer some compensation where they were convinced that claims of this kind were genuine. This last factor was considered almost decisive by the House of Lords because it demonstrated that those in the trade did not themselves think it reasonable to rely on the limitation clauses in their full rigour. It suggested rather that the purpose of the clause was to enable the sellers to decide which claims to pay and which to reject, without control from the courts. In effect, the purpose of the clause thus seems to have been to enable the sellers to be judges in their own cause, rather than to exclude or limit their liability.

Two further points should be made about the *George Mitchell* case. The first is that, as noted above, because of the time when the facts arose, the case was governed by provisions subsequently contained in the Sale of Goods Act 1979 and not by the Unfair Contract Terms Act. Although the present Act is almost identical with the 1979 Act on many points, there are a number of points of difference; for instance, the 1979 Act provided that exclusion clauses were void 'to the extent that' they did not comply with the requirement of reasonableness; the present Act declares that the implied conditions in ss. 13–15 can only be excluded by a term 'insofar as the term satisfies the requirement of reasonableness'. In the *George Mitchell* case, it was thought by the House of Lords (though no definite opinion was expressed) that the former of these provisions did not authorise a court to sever the offending part of an exclusion clause and uphold the remainder. In *Stewart Gill Ltd* v *Horatio Myer & Co Ltd*,[102] however, Lord Donaldson MR said that the issue is whether the term, the whole term, and nothing but the term, is a fair and reasonable one to have been included.

A second point of difference between the two Acts is that (as we have previously noted) in the 1979 Act the test of reasonableness was to be applied taking account of all the

[101] [1983] 2 AC 803.
[102] [1992] 2 All ER 257, 261

circumstances of the case. In *George Mitchell*, the House of Lords held that this meant that the reasonableness of a clause was to be judged having regard to the circumstances prevailing at the time of the breach rather than when the contract was made. In the 1977 Act, the requirement of reasonableness, as we have seen, is that a term shall have been a fair and reasonable one to be included having regard to the circumstances which were, or ought reasonably to have been, known to or in the contemplation of the parties *when the contract was made*. In the *George Mitchell*, case, therefore, the House of Lords took account of all the circumstances, including the fact that in the past the sellers had not relied on their limitation clause,[103] that the supply of the defective seed was due to negligence, and that the sellers could have insured against the losses. The fact of the crop failure itself was clearly a material circumstance under the 1973 Act; would it be material under UCTA? It seems unlikely that the change made by the 1977 Act would affect this because the fact of crop failure is obviously readily foreseeable if the wrong, or inferior, seeds are supplied by a seed merchant, and if the reasonableness of the term limiting liability had been considered as at the time of the making of the contract, this foreseeable result would have been just as relevant as the actual result which had to be taken into account. But in other circumstances this change made by the 1977 Act may be more significant, as already indicated. For instance, a minor breach, with small losses, might have been held to make it permissible to rely on an exclusion clause under the 1979 Act when it would no longer be held reasonable to have included the term in the contract within the 1977 Act. Even bearing in mind the differences between the two Acts with which the respective courts were concerned, it must be admitted that *George Mitchell* seems to represent a more interventionist approach to commercial contracts than the House of Lords seemed to signal in *Photo Production*.[104]

By comparison with the *George Mitchell* case, a different result was reached in *R W Green Ltd* v *Cade Bros Farm*[105] where the contract was for the sale of seed potatoes by potato merchants. Here, too, the contract excluded liability for consequential damage and limited the responsibility of the sellers to returning the price. The potatoes proved to be infected with a virus which was not detectable in advance (by sellers or buyers) and the buyers suffered loss. Thus far, the facts were very similar to those in *George Mitchell*, but one important difference was that the potatoes in question were uncertified, and hence somewhat cheaper. Certified potatoes were free from the virus infection. In the result, Griffiths J upheld the limitation clause as reasonable though he struck down as unreasonable a clause requiring the buyers to give notice of a claim within three days of delivery. This was impractical because the fault could not be discovered until the potatoes began to grow, so the clause was clearly unreasonable. This case was not mentioned in the speeches in the House of Lords in *George Mitchell*, so it is uncertain whether it survives that case, but it would seem clearly distinguishable, both on the ground that the buyer had

[103] Lord Bridge took it that this indicated that reliance on the clause would not be fair and reasonable. The clause in question was a standard in the seed trade, but on the sellers' own evidence was rarely, if ever, invoked – see [1983] 1 All ER 108, 117 per Lord Denning MR. For a critique of Lord Bridge's approach, see Adams and Brownsword (1988) 104 LQR 94.

[104] See Adams and Brownsword (1988) 104 LQR 94. *Photo Production* did not directly involve UCTA but is recognised as authoritative so far as it dealt with the Act's application.

[105] [1978] 1 Lloyd's Rep 602.

the choice to buy certified potatoes, and also on the ground that there was no negligence on the part of the sellers.

Among other decisions on the reasonableness requirement, brief mention may be made of a few. In *Stag Line Ltd* v *Tyne Repair Group Ltd ('The Zinnia')*,[106] Staughton J suggested that the fact that terms are in very small print or difficult to understand, is an argument against their reasonableness.[107] In *Rasbora Ltd* v *JCL Marine*,[108] the subject-matter of the sale was a power boat sold for some £22,000. As a result of serious electrical faults, the boat caught fire and sank on its first outing. Lawson J held that in fact the sale was a consumer sale so that the exclusion clause was void insofar as it excluded the implied conditions under the Sale of Goods Act (then applicable to consumer sales). But he went on to say that even if the sale had not been a consumer sale, he would have held the exclusion clause unreasonable inasmuch as it purported to exclude completely the implied condition of merchantability. In *R & B Customs Brokers Co Ltd* v *United Dominions Trust*,[109] where a car was bought by a company for the use of a director, on conditional sale terms excluding all liability on the part of the sellers (who were mere financiers), it was held that the sale was a consumer sale, which would now fall outside UCTA, but the court was inclined to think that if it had been a non-consumer sale the requirement of reasonableness would have been satisfied because the sellers were mere financiers who never saw the car, and the buyers were business parties not devoid of commercial experience. It is, however, somewhat strange to see it suggested that financiers can reasonably exclude their liability in credit sales when for a very long time the hire-purchase legislation has imposed liability on financiers just as though they were sellers.[110]

In the *Howard Marine* case,[111] which has been referred to previously and which involved the former s. 3 of the Misrepresentation Act, Lord Denning gave his reasons for regarding the exclusion clause as reasonable. The parties were of equal bargaining position, the representation was quite innocent and the plaintiffs (on the misrepresentation issue) could have discovered the truth themselves by further inquiry. The majority of the court held the exclusion to be unreasonable without giving any reasons for their decision, other than to say that the matter was one of discretion for the trial judge, who was entitled to find the clause unreasonable. This last point may prove to be of some importance because the House of Lords in the *George Mitchell* case has stressed that appeals on the question of reasonableness will broadly not be entertained. The decision on a reasonableness question is primarily for the trial judge and appeals will only be available where he has gone wrong in principle, or perhaps has failed to take account of the relevant considerations.[112]

Decisions on the application of the test of reasonableness have continued to be handed down relatively infrequently. A more recent illustration of the approach of the courts and an indication of their approach when the implied terms are excluded but replaced with

[106] [1984] 2 Lloyd's Rep 211, 222.
[107] Signalling theory requires that an exemption clause be 'conspicuous' – see Uniform Commercial Code, Art. 2-316, which is based on this theory.
[108] [1976] 2 Lloyd's Rep 645.
[109] [1988] 1 All ER 847.
[110] See Chapter 2 *et seq*.
[111] [1978] QB 574.
[112] As to the implications of this, see Adams and Brownsword, 'The Unfair Contract Terms Act: A Decade of Discretion' (1988) 104 LQR 94.

an alternative regime for making good defects in quality is to be found in *Air Transworld* v *Bombardier*.[113]

The next case to be mentioned concerned not a contract of sale but of hire. In *Phillips Products* v *Hyland and Hamstead Plant Hire*,[114] the claimants hired a crane and driver for a short period from the defendants. The driver, through negligence, caused damage to the claimants' own factory, but the conditions of hire excluded liability for the negligence of the driver. The condition was held to be unreasonable on the ground that the hire period was short, and the plaintiffs had little time to arrange insurance, and were not regular hirers of such equipment.[115] However, a great deal of mechanical plant is regularly hired under similar conditions to these, so further litigation on this question may be expected.[116] *Danka Rentals Ltd* v *Xi Software*[117] is a case from outside the field of mechanical plant hire. In this case, an exemption clause which purported to exclude all express and implied warranties in a lease of a photocopier, which turned out to be a 'complete disaster', was held to be too wide and therefore unreasonable.[118]

Reference may be made again to the House of Lords' decision in *Smith* v *Eric S Bush*[119] although this was not a sale of goods case. In this case, it was held that it was not reasonable under the 1977 Act for surveyors who value houses on behalf of mortgagees to disclaim all liability for negligence towards the purchaser who in reality pays the surveyor's fees, though through the mortgagee. This decision was based on the general view that purchasers (at any rate in ordinary house-purchase transactions) have little or no bargaining power on these matters, especially because the arrangements are made by the mortgagee, and that it is impractical and expensive for purchasers to protect themselves by commissioning a second survey on their own behalf. Much of this reasoning is directed to the peculiar nature of the average house-purchase transaction and is unlikely to be especially relevant to the law of sale of goods. But there is one point about the decision which may be of wider importance. It emerged during the case that some building societies actually gave the house purchaser an option between obtaining a survey with liability and obtaining a survey without liability, and it might have been thought that this at least would have been reasonable in terms of the 1977 Act. But it also emerged that the additional cost of the survey with liability was so great that few buyers took advantage of it, and the

[113] [2012] EWHC 243 (Comm).

[114] (1985) 4 Tr LR 98.

[115] The standard form clause in question, clause 8 of the Model Conditions of the Construction Plant Hire Association, was subsequently reworded to include a duty on the part of the owner to provide a competent operator. It is believed that this change was made having regard to the words of Slade LJ [1987] 2 All ER 620, 630. On these provisions generally, see Adams, *Commercial Hiring and Leasing* (1989, Butterworths), para. 6.103 *et seq*.

[116] Indeed, in two cases following soon after *Phillips* v *Hyland* – *Paul* v *Ruddle Bros* (26 April 1985, unreported) and *Thompson* v *Lohan Plant Hire Ltd* [1987] 2 All ER 631 – it was distinguished. In these latter cases, the relevant issues against which the reasonableness of the clause fell to be determined were between the owner and the hirer, rather than between either of them and the injured third party. In most such cases, the dispute is, in reality, between insurance companies.

[117] (1998) 7 Tr LR 74. See also *AEG (UK) Ltd* v *Logic Resources Ltd*, 20 October 1995 (unreported).

[118] Since the contract was on the lessor's standard terms the judge applied both ss. 3 and 7 to trigger the tests of reasonableness, and suggested that although the guidelines set out in Sched. 2 apply only in relation to the latter, it made little practical difference as there was nothing to prevent him from taking into consideration the guidelines in relation to s. 3.

[119] [1989] 2 All ER 514.

judges were clearly doubtful whether the additional charge was truly justified. So it seems that, where options of this character are offered to a buyer, it may be necessary to show that the extra charge for the option which carries liability is itself a justifiable charge if the reasonableness requirement is to be satisfied. The availability of insurance cover is a relevant consideration in determining reasonableness,[120] as the *St Albans City and District Council* case discussed in the next paragraph illustrates.

The case of *St Albans City and District Council* v *International Computers Ltd*[121] involved a number of interesting questions. The defendants had installed a computerised database for the plaintiffs' community charge register. An error in the software significantly overstated the population in the area, and as a result the plaintiffs lost £1,314,846.[122] The contract contained a clause limiting the defendants' loss to £100,000. Scott Baker J held that this term was subject to s. 3 of UCTA and that in addition either s. 6 or s. 7 applied.[123] Section 11(4) also applied because the defendants sought to restrict their liability to a specified sum. Under this latter provision, in considering the question of reasonableness, regard had to be paid to the defendants' resources to meet potential liability and how far it was open to them to obtain insurance cover. He went on to hold that the following factors had to be taken into account: that the parties were of unequal bargaining power; that the defendants had not justified the figure of £100,000, which was small in relation to the potential risk and the actual loss; that the defendants held an aggregate of £50 million insurance cover worldwide; and the practical consequences. On the last point, he went on to ask which one of the two parties was the better loss bearer. The defendants were well able to insure, and had insured and no doubt passed the premium on to their customers. If the loss were placed on the plaintiffs, it would be borne by the local population in the form of increased taxes or reduced services. These factors outweighed the fact that bodies such as the plaintiffs and the defendants should be free to make their own bargains, that the plaintiffs contracted with their eyes open, and that these limitations were common in the computer industry, which was an area of developing technology (in fact only two or three companies offered competing software packages, and each used similar terms). The burden was on the defendants to show the clause was fair and reasonable, and they had not discharged the burden.

[120] See s. 11(4)(b).

[121] [1995] FSR 686, upheld by the Court of Appeal on the points material to the present discussion [1996] 4 All ER 481. See also *Horace Holman Group Ltd* v *Sherwood International Group Ltd*, TCC, 12 April 2000 (unreported), which also involved a computer software installation, and was made between two substantial concerns, but again the Unfair Contract Terms Act 1977 was applied. It was held that the onus was on the defendants, under s. 11(5), to show that the term was reasonable and the defendant had failed to discharge the burden. Compare *SAM Business Systems Ltd* v *Hedley & Co (a firm)* [2002] EWHC 2733 (TCC), where the software installation contract provided machinery whereby the purchaser could get its money back, and the exclusion of liability for breach and misrepresentation was upheld as reasonable. In *Messer UK Ltd and anor* v *Britvic Soft Drinks Ltd and ors* [2002] EWCA Civ 548 330–1 it was pointed out that the provision of software is an exercise notoriously liable to give rise to problems, and that an ordinary supply of manufactured goods, CO2 gas, is different. Accordingly, an exemption clause in such a supply contract was held to be unreasonable – see also *Bacardi-Martini Beverages Ltd* v *Thomas Hardy Packaging Ltd* [2002] EWCA Civ 549.

[122] This amount was reduced by the Court of Appeal for reasons not germane to the present discussion.

[123] From which it appears he considered the contract in question to involve a sale or supply of *goods*– see Chapter 3 *et seq*. for a discussion as to whether a software contract involves a sale or supply of goods. On the approach taken by the judge the outcome would have been the same, however, even if no sale or supply of goods were involved – see ibid.

8.4.5 UCTA, the Reasonableness Test and contemporary commercial cases

Over the years, the trend in the case law has been a reluctance to conclude that a term within the scope of UCTA contained in a commercial contract is unreasonable, particularly where there has been negotiation of the relevant terms, including amendments to standard terms during the negotiation process, and where parties are generally of comparable bargaining strength.[124] However, a party will struggle to persuade a court that terms which have the effect of totally excluding that party's liability still satisfy the reasonableness test.[125]

Generally, courts will respect the risk allocation that is reflected in the terms of a contract and will be reluctant to interfere with this, although pre-drafted standard terms are more likely to be scrutinised, particularly where presented on a take-it-or-leave-it basis.[126] However, even where standard forms were used, a court will consider the availability of insurance; an exclusion of liability by one party for which the other party could and did, obtain insurances is more likely to pass the reasonableness test.[127]

This flurry of recent cases shows that UCTA, despite its almost 50 years on the statute book, continues to have a significant role to play in dealing with the worst (ab)uses of exclusion and limitation clauses, particularly in standard form contracts.

[124] See e.g., *Regus (UK) Ltd* v *Epcot Solutions Ltd* [2008] EWCA Civ 361; *Goodlife Foods Limited* v *Hall Fire Protection Limited* [2018] EWCA Civ 1371.

[125] *Lobster Group Ltd* v *Heidelberg Graphic Equipment Ltd; Close Asset Finance Ltd* [2009] EWHC 1919; *Last Bus Ltd* v *Dawsongroup Bus and Coach Ltd* [2023] EWCA Civ 1297.

[126] *Balmoral Group Ltd* v *Borealis (UK) Ltd and others* [2005] EWHC 1900 (Comm), paras 421–423.

[127] *Goodlife Foods Limited* v *Hall Fire Protection Limited* [2018] EWCA Civ 1371.

Part III

The duties of the buyer

9 The duties of the buyer

In this chapter, we turn to the two duties imposed on the buyer: to pay the price and to take delivery. Although both these duties may seem self-evident, they raise a number of questions about how the buyer must comply with these duties and whether and when a breach by a buyer of either duty entitles the seller to terminate the contract.

9.1 Payment of the price

It is the duty of the buyer to pay the price of the goods they have bought or agreed to buy, and, in the absence of a contrary agreement, they are not entitled to claim possession of the goods unless they are ready and willing to pay the price in accordance with the contract. Whether it is necessary that the buyer should actually have tendered the price before they can insist on delivery has been discussed earlier.[1]

If no time is fixed for payment, the price is due immediately on the conclusion of the contract, provided that the seller is ready and willing to deliver the goods. Unless otherwise agreed, the seller is not bound to accept payment in anything but cash, and if they do accept payment by bill of exchange they are entitled (in the absence of agreement to the contrary) to retain the goods until the bill is met. But if the seller accepts payment by a bill not maturing immediately, they must be taken to have agreed to allow the buyer credit and cannot claim to retain the goods.

Historically, payment by cheque was very common but, whilst they continue to be used, their prevalence has dropped to a low proportion of overall payment transactions.[2] It is nevertheless instructive to retain some discussion of the use of cheques as a payment method here. Where the seller accepts payment by cheque bill of exchange or other negotiable instrument, this is normally treated as conditional payment only[3] and, if it is not honoured, the seller may sue either on the instrument as a contract in itself (in which case they will benefit from procedural advantages)[4] or they may sue on the contract of sale for

[1] See Chapter 6, at section 6.2

[2] In a retail setting, the use of cheques has largely stopped (in 2023 it accounted for about 112 million payments): see Pay.UK, 'Annual Summary of Payment Statistics 2023', available at https://www.wearepay.uk/wp-content/uploads/2024/02/Annual-Summary-2023.pdf [accessed November 2024].

[3] In Scotland, see *Leggatt Bros* v *Gray* 1908 SC 67.

[4] In particular, the buyer cannot set up defences based on breaches of contract by the seller in respect of defects in the goods or the like; in an action on a cheque, or other bill of exchange, the buyer must first pay, and then counterclaim for damages – see, e.g., *Jade International Steel Stahl und Eisen GmbH & Co KG* v *Robert Nicholas (Steels) Ltd* [1978] QB 917.

the price of the goods.[5] It is theoretically possible for a cheque or other instrument to be accepted as absolute payment, so that the seller has no further claim if the instrument is not honoured, but an intention to accept in absolute payment must be strictly shown.[6] Similarly, agreement to furnish a letter of credit in payment for goods sold would not normally be treated as depriving the seller of his right to sue for the price if, in exceptional circumstances, the goods are delivered to the buyer but payment is not made under the credit.[7]

However, it has been held by the Court of Appeal that there is no general rule that all forms of payment deriving from a third party must be treated as conditional payments only.[8] Each method of payment must be considered in light of all the circumstances, and it was held in the same case that payment by credit card (issued by a third party)[9] is in many circumstances an absolute payment, so that the failure of the credit card company to pay the retailer does not mean that the retailer has any residuary claim against the customer. Further, the situation is not altered merely because the customer has not yet paid the credit card company in respect of the transaction in question. The card holder's liability is to pay the credit card company, and their liability is not affected by the relationship between the credit card company and the retailer.

There are several reasons why this method of payment differs in its legal results from payment by cheque. First, in the case of cheques there is no contractual relation between the seller who accepts the cheque, and the bank on which the cheque is drawn, so if the cheque is not met the seller has no redress against the bank.[10] In the case of a credit card transaction, however, there is a prior contract in existence between the seller and the credit card company under which the company accepts liability for relevant credit card transactions, subject, no doubt, to compliance with the specified conditions. Furthermore, it is the seller who chooses to do business with the credit card company, while it is the buyer who selects the bank with which they bank. Secondly, the ordinary credit card transaction

[5] By s. 38(1)(b) of the Sale of Goods Act 1979 the seller is deemed to be an 'unpaid seller' when a bill of exchange or other negotiable instrument has been received as a conditional payment, and the condition on which it was received has not been fulfilled by reason of the dishonour of the instrument, or otherwise.

[6] *Maillard* v *Argyle* (1843) 6 M & G 40.

[7] *W J Alan & Co Ltd v El Nasr Export & Import Co* [1972] 2 QB 189; *Saffron* v *Société Minière Cafrika* (1958) 100 CLR 231; *E D & F Man Ltd* v *Nigerian Sweets & Confectionery Co Ltd* [1977] 2 Lloyd's Rep 50.

[8] *Re Charge Card Services Ltd* [1988] 3 All ER 702. The analysis in this case would also, it would seem, apply where payment is by Provident 'cheque' and the like. These are treated for VAT purposes as sales at the full value of the voucher, notwithstanding that they will be discounted by the finance house – see *Kingfisher plc* v *Customs and Excise Commissioners*, 7 December 1999 (unreported). Arguably, therefore, if the finance house became insolvent, the seller would have no claim against the buyer for the price.

[9] Some retailers issue their own credit cards, which can only be used in their own stores. If the issuing company and the seller are legally the same company, the position is obviously different. Presumably, in the event of the seller's insolvency, the credit terms contained in the credit card contract would control recovery of the purchase price from the buyer.

[10] There is an important distinction between the common law rules concerning cheques and that of many civil law systems where cheques can operate as assignments of a part of the drawer's bank account so that the payee can acquire rights against the bank. In principle, there is a possibility that an equitable assignment might be found to accompany the delivery of a cheque if it could be established that that was the intention of the parties – see Farnsworth (1962) 36 Tulane LR 245. In Scotland, the presentment of a cheque for payment no longer operates as a completed assignation of any balance held by the bank to its customer's credit (Bills of Exchange Act 1882 s. 53(2) as amended by the Banking Act 2009 s. 254(4)). For background see Cusine [1977] Juridical Review 98.

leaves the seller with no record of the buyer's address, so it is a reasonable implication that the seller does not expect under any circumstances to look to the buyer for the price.[11] Thirdly, it is the clear understanding of all parties that the customer can never be expected to pay twice for such a transaction, so if they have paid the credit card company, nobody expects the customer to be liable to pay the seller merely because the credit card company fails to pay the seller. Indeed, in the case in question this point was conceded by counsel, who merely argued that if the buyer had not yet paid the credit card company the seller ought to be able to intercept the money, as it were, and obtain payment direct from the buyer. But the court found this an unacceptable implication.

Payment made by cheque backed by a bank guarantee card appears to be different from payment by credit card.[12] It is true that here also the bank accepts a direct obligation to meet the payment, assuming it falls within the terms of the bank's undertaking to honour such transactions,[13] but this obligation is clearly by way of guarantee of the buyer's obligation which remains primary.[14] But the point is anyhow of very little practical importance because the buyer can be sued on the cheque itself even if they cannot for some reason be sued on the underlying transaction.

Where payment is made by cheque and the cheque is later met, the payment relates back to the time when it was handed over.[15] Consequently, if the cheque reaches the seller on the date agreed, they cannot complain that there has been delay in payment, provided that it is met in due course. If the seller agrees that the price shall only be due on request, they are bound to afford a reasonable time to the buyer for payment after making their request,[16] and if they write to the buyer asking them for their cheque the mere posting may be a sufficient payment, even if the cheque is stolen en route and cashed by the thief.[17]

As noted, cheques are used less frequently than they once were, but they have not fallen out of use altogether yet, and credit cards remain in current use. Other payment methods which might be preferred by commercial parties are direct bank transfers or more complex payment arrangements such as letters of credit/documentary credits. Where such methods are to be used, the contract will specify so. In due course, it may well be that these payment methods will face a new rival: cryptocurrencies utilising digital distributed ledger (or 'blockchain') technology. Well-known types of cryptocurrency include Bitcoin and

[11] By contrast, when a cheque is taken which is not covered by a cheque guarantee card, the usual practice is to require the drawer buyer to write their address on the back of the cheque.

[12] See *Re Charge Card Services Ltd* [1987] Ch 150, 166 per Millett J, a point on which the Court of Appeal expressed no opinion.

[13] In *First Sport Ltd v Barclays Bank plc* [1993] 3 All ER 789 it was held that where a cheque and cheque card were presented to a retailer by a thief, who forged the account holder's signature, the bank was liable to the retailer on its undertaking to honour the cheque. The statement on the card that it could only be used by an authorised signatory did not make the offer conditional on the cheque being signed by the authorised signatory.

[14] See *Belshaw* v *Bush* (1851) 11 CB 191; *Edwards* v *Hancher* (1875) 1 CPD 111.

[15] *Marreco* v *Richardson* [1908] 2 KB 584. But as between a trustee in bankruptcy and the payee the payment is only deemed to be made when the cheque is met: In *re Hone A Bankrupt, Ex Parte the Trustee* v *Kensington BC* [1951] Ch 85; cf. *Bolt & Nut Co (Tipton) Ltd* v *Rowlands, Nichols & Co Ltd* [1964] 2 QB 10.

[16] *Brighty* v *Norman* (1862) 3 B & S 305.

[17] *Norman* v *Ricketts* (1886) 3 TLR 182; *sed qu*: it does seem strange if the mere request of the seller that the buyer should mail them a cheque puts the seller at risk of the cheque being stolen. Does a request for a cheque invite the buyer to post an uncrossed cheque? Cf. also *Comber* v *Leyland* [1898] AC 524.

Ethereum. Blockchain technology has been described as 'a powerful way to enhance – or supplant – traditional payment systems'.[18] Instead of relying on financial institutions as central intermediaries, it is based on a decentralised and disintermediated structure. Combined with the potential for the somewhat unfortunately named 'smart contracts', i.e., digital self-executing transactions on a blockchain,[19] a buyer's payment obligation might, in the future, be automated, especially for routine high-frequency transactions. Whether this will be sufficiently attractive for large-scale commercial sales remains uncertain; the fluctuations in the value of the leading cryptocurrencies against fiat currencies might make cryptocurrencies too risky a choice for regular sales contracts.

9.2 Time for payment

Section 10 of the Act says:

> (1) Unless a different intention appears from the terms of the contract, stipulations as to time of payment are not of the essence of a contract of sale . . .
> (3) In a contract of sale 'month' means *prima facie* calendar month

Although it is obviously the duty of the buyer to pay the price agreed at the appointed time (as agreed in the contract), the effect of s. 10 is to create a presumption that this duty is not a condition. In other words, a buyer who fails to pay the price on the day fixed is guilty of a breach of contract for which the seller may be able to recover damages if they have in fact suffered any, but they are not entitled to treat the contract as repudiated and resell the goods elsewhere.[20] It is always open to the parties to stipulate in their contract that the time for payment has to be of the essence, or to provide expressly for circumstances when the seller may cancel the contract for failure to pay within a certain period, irrespective of whether this would amount to a repudiatory breach.[21]

A seller can of course decline to deliver the goods until the buyer pays, and there seems no reason why the seller should be entitled to repudiate the contract merely because the buyer is late in paying the price, perhaps by only a day or two. Indeed, even repeated failure by the buyer to pay on time (e.g. in an instalment contract) may not justify repudiation by the seller, at least where there is no serious fear that the buyer will not pay at all.[22] It can make little difference to the seller in the usual way whether they are paid one day earlier or later, and if it does make a difference they should stipulate for a right of immediate termination, or of resale on default in payment by the buyer. Moreover, damages may be

[18] *De Filippi and Wright, Blockchain and the Law – The Rule of Code* (2018, Harvard University Press), p. 61.

[19] The literature on smart contracts is already vast, but interesting contributions are by Allen, Wrapped and stacked: 'Smart contracts' and the interaction of natural and formal language (2018) 14 *European Review of Contract Law* 307 and Savelyev, Contract Law 2.0: 'Smart' contracts as the beginning of the end of classic contract law (2017) 26 *Information & Communication Technology Law* 116.

[20] *Payzu Ltd* v *Saunders* [1919] 2 KB 581. An important exception to this is that where the price is to be paid by means of a letter of credit opened by the seller, the failure to open the credit on the due date justifies immediate repudiation – see Chapter 18. And see also, for a similar case, *Warde (Michael I)* v *Feedex International* [1985] 2 Lloyd's Rep 289.

[21] *Newland Shipping and Forwarding Limited* v *Toba Trading* FZC [2014] EWHC 661 (Comm).

[22] *Decro-Wall International SA* v *Practitioners in Marketing Ltd* [1971] 1 WLR 361.

obtained for the late payment where additional costs have been imposed on the seller[23] and, anyhow, interest may be awarded to the seller by a court where they have been kept out of their money.[24]

It is also relevant to note the right of an unpaid seller to re-sell the goods under s. 48(3), which provides that:

> Where the goods are of a perishable nature, or where the unpaid seller gives notice to the buyer of his intention to re-sell, and the buyer does not within a reasonable time pay or tender the price, the unpaid seller may re-sell the goods and recover from the original buyer damages for any loss occasioned by his breach of contract.

The indirect result of this subsection is to create an exception to s. 10(1) in the case of perishable goods, for in such a case the seller may resell the goods without notice to the buyer as soon as there is default in payment. As regards non-perishable goods, the period of compulsory credit can be brought to an end by the seller giving notice to the buyer of their intention to resell.

Although failure to pay the price at the appointed time is not *per se* a breach of condition or a material breach, it was at one time thought that if the delay was of inordinate length it might be possible to infer an intention to abandon the contract, so that the seller could thus be justified in reselling even without notice.[25] But it now seems established that this is not a permissible result unless there is some ground on which the court can find that the buyer has repudiated the contract, and that the seller has accepted that repudiation.[26]

It is desirable to stress again a point that has also been made before, that the mere fact that the buyer is under an obligation to pay the price of the goods does not necessarily mean that they can be *sued for the price* if they fail to pay. The seller's remedy against the buyer for non-payment of the price is often limited to an action for damages, as we shall see in Chapter 18.

9.3 The duty to take delivery

Under ss. 27 and 28 of the Act, it is the duty of the buyer to accept and pay for the goods in exchange for the delivery of the goods by the seller. We have seen that the general rule is that it is for the buyer to take delivery of the goods from the seller's place of business and not for the seller to send the goods to the buyer. We have also seen that the time of delivery of the goods by the seller, or the time at which they are to have the goods ready

[23] See *Wadsworth* v *Lydall* [1981] 1 WLR 598, approved by the HL in *President of India* v *La Pintada Compania Navigacion SA* [1985] AC 104, subject to the limitation that the damages must fall within the second rule in *Hadley* v *Baxendale* (1854) 9 Ex 341 by reason of special facts known to the defendant. In Scots law, see the authorities discussed in MacQueen, 1996 JR 295.

[24] Under s. 3 of the Law Reform (Miscellaneous Provisions) Act 1934 in English law and at common law in Scotland (following 'wrongful withholding'). There is also a right to statutory interest under the Late Payment of Commercial Debts (Interest) Act 1998 (in both England and Wales, and Scotland), which applies when both the purchaser and the supplier are acting in the course of a business – s. 2(1).

[25] See *Pearl Mill Co Ltd* v *Ivy Tannery Co Ltd* [1919] 1 KB 78 and the use made of this case in *The Splendid Sun* [1981] QB 694.

[26] See *Allied Marine Transport Ltd* v *Vale do Rio Doce* Navegaçao SA (The Leonidas D) [1985] 2 All ER 796, 806–7.

for collection, is *prima facie* of the essence, but that the time for payment is *prima facie* not of the essence. The question now has to be answered whether the buyer's duty to take delivery at a particular time is of the essence.

The general rule seems to be that this is no more of the essence than the time of payment[27] and, consequently, the buyer's failure to take delivery of the goods at the time agreed does not by itself justify the seller in forthwith disposing of them to someone else. But, in accordance with ordinary principles of contract law, if the buyer accompanies their failure to take delivery with words or conduct which justify the seller in thinking that the buyer is repudiating the whole contract, the seller may accept the repudiation, and they are then free to resell the goods and to sue the buyer for damages for non-acceptance.

Moreover, if the contract is for the sale of goods of a perishable nature,[28] the buyer's duty to take delivery at the right time is of the essence, and default by the buyer justifies the seller in reselling immediately.[29] In this respect, the position is also the same in regard to payment for, as we have seen, s. 48(3) enables the seller to resell perishable goods without notice to the buyer if the price is not paid when due.

It also seems that in a 'spot contract', that is a contract for almost immediate delivery and payment, there will be a breach of condition if the buyer fails to take delivery at the time agreed.[30] It may well be that in such a case there will be a contrary intention which makes the time of payment also of the essence.

It is important that the rules as to the times of payment and taking delivery should be the same because otherwise difficulties would arise if the seller refused to allow the buyer to take delivery on the ground of non-payment. If the seller could transform a breach of the term as to payment into a breach of condition as to taking delivery by the simple expedient of exercising their lien, this would in effect turn every agreement for time of payment into a condition. If the time of payment is not of the essence, therefore, it would seem illogical (at any rate in ordinary circumstances) to hold that the time for taking delivery is of the essence. But there is nothing to prevent an express agreement that the time for taking delivery shall not be of the essence, but that the time for payment shall be.

It must be borne in mind that even where the time of delivery is not of the essence, s. 20 casts on the buyer, where there is delay in taking delivery, the risk of accidental destruction of, or damage to, the goods which might not have occurred but for the delay.

Where a contract provides for delivery 'as required', the buyer may be under a duty to give notice of their requirements to the seller as a preliminary to actually taking delivery. Where a buyer contracts to take delivery of goods as speedily as possible although no time limit is actually imposed, they are under an obligation to remove the goods within a reasonable time.[31] And in such circumstances the measure of damages for breach may, in an appropriate case, be the benefit to the buyer rather than the loss to the seller.[32]

27 *Woolfe* v *Horn* (1877) 2 QBD 355; *Saint* v *Pilley* (1875) LR 10 Ex 137; *Kidston* v *Monceau Iron Works Co Ltd* (1902) 7 Com Cas 82.

28 This rule probably also applies to a sale of livestock: *Harrington* v *Browne* (1917) 23 CLR 297.

29 *Sharp v Christmas* (1892) 8 TLR 687.

30 *Thames Sack & Bag Co Ltd* v *Knowles* (1918) 88 LJKB 585.

31 *Penarth Dock Engineering Co Ltd* v *Pounds* [1963] 1 Lloyd's Rep 359.

32 Ibid.

If the contract provides for the delivery of the goods in instalments and the buyer wrongfully refuses to accept one or more of them, the question whether the seller may treat the whole contract as repudiated is dealt with by s. 31(2). As will be seen later,[33] this merely provides that the answer to this question depends on the terms of the contract and all the circumstances of the case. In practice, the issue usually involves breach by the seller rather than the buyer, and it has been held that the question to be considered is the gravity of the breach in relation to the whole contract and the probability of its recurrence.[34]

Where the contract does not provide for delivery by instalments, there is nothing in the Act corresponding to s. 30(1) entitling the seller to repudiate the contract if the buyer refuses to accept some part of the goods only. Whether such refusal amounts to repudiation, therefore, depends on general principles of contract law: that is, on whether the breach goes to the root of the contract. Where a buyer refused to take 728 sheep out of a total contract quantity of over 6,000, and he was entitled to refuse 448 sheep, it was held that the seller could not repudiate the whole contract.[35]

It should be noted that in some contracts, especially f.o.b. contracts, the buyer's duty to take delivery often involves many incidental obligations, for example the duty to nominate a ship for the transport of the goods, etc. Breach of these duties usually discharges the seller as a necessary consequence.[36]

[33] See Chapter 17, at section 17.1.1.

[34] *Maple Flock Co Ltd* v *Universal Furniture Products (Wembley) Ltd* [1934] 1 KB 148.

[35] *Francis* v *Lyon* (1907) 4 CLR 1023.

[36] Because it will be a breach of condition – see, e.g., *Bunge Corp* v *Tradax Export SA* [1981] 1 WLR 711. As to f.o.b. contracts, see Chapter 13.

10

The transfer of property

10.1 The meaning of 'property'

Part III of the Act is divided into two sections, headed 'Transfer of Property as Between Seller and Buyer' and 'Transfer of Title'. There is something rather curious about this terminology. The term 'property', defined by s. 61 as 'the general property in goods', is commonly used by lawyers to signify title or ownership, and in everyday usage this terminology is also applied to the sale of goods. Yet the Sale of Goods Act talks of a transfer of property as between seller and buyer, and contrasts this with the transfer of title.[1] However, the distinguishing feature of property rights is that they bind not merely the immediate parties to the transaction, but also all third parties. How, then, can there only be a transfer of property *as between seller and buyer*?[2] Either there is a transfer of rights and duties from seller to buyer, or there is a transfer of property which affects the whole world. Nor is it possible to adopt the solution of saying that 'property' is here used in its medieval sense of right to possession[3] when at least it would make sense to talk of a transfer as between seller and buyer. The Act itself precludes the adoption of this view because it lays down the clear rule that the buyer's right to possession depends either on payment of the price or on the granting of credit, not on the passing of the property. In other words, the mere fact that the property in the goods has passed to the buyer does not confer on them a title good against the whole world, nor does it confer on them the right to possession as against the seller.

This definition is also borrowed by s. 4(1) of the Consumer Rights Act 2015,[4] although that Act adopts that as the definition of 'ownership', which is presumably intended to be synonymous with 'property' for the purposes of the Sale of Goods Act, as the Consumer Rights Act also invokes ss. 17–19 and 20A&B as its regime for the transfer of property in consumer sales.

[1] For an interesting discussion of dual terms, see Ho (1997) 56 CLJ 571.

[2] See Lawson (1949) 65 LQR 362, especially at 359–60. Cf., for a different view, Battersby and Preston (1972) 35 MLR 268 and also Lin, *Does Ownership Matter in the Sale of Goods* [2011] JBL 749. See also critique in Ho, (1997) 56 CLJ 571.

[3] This is a loose translation of the complex medieval concept of 'seisin'.

[4] The Consumer Rights Act also invokes in their entirety, ss. 17–19, 20A and 20B with the result that discussion in this chapter of the passing of property remains equally applicable to consumer sales.

What, then, is this unusual legal conception which the Act calls 'the property in the goods'? The answer can only be given by considering the consequences that flow from the passing of property. What rights does the passing of the property give to the buyer?

First, what is the position of the buyer if they wish to obtain possession from the seller? The answer is that they can only do so if they pay the price, or if the seller supplies the goods on credit.[5] The buyer cannot avoid this by framing their action in tort and suing for conversion, basing the claim on the fact that the goods are now their goods because the action for conversion is only available to someone with an immediate right to possession which the buyer does not have until they tender the price.[6] Again, if the buyer resells the goods before obtaining possession, the sub-buyer can only obtain possession on the same terms as the original buyer, that is to say, by payment of the price, unless the original seller has assented to the second sale.[7] The same applies if the buyer pledges the goods instead of selling them. In all these cases, the buyer's property avails them nothing because the position would be the same even if no property had passed.

The same is true if the buyer goes bankrupt before delivery of the goods and payment of the price. The seller cannot be compelled to deliver up the goods to the trustee in bankruptcy, and be relegated to their right to prove in the bankruptcy for the price, even though the property in the goods has passed to the buyer. Indeed, quite the contrary, the law goes out of its way to protect the seller from the bankruptcy of the buyer by conferring on them the right of stoppage in transit should the buyer go bankrupt after the seller has dispatched the goods to them, but before the buyer has received them.[8]

Suppose, next, that the buyer has actually obtained the possession of the goods. Once again, the practical effect of the passing of the property is somewhat limited because s. 25(1) of the Act enables the buyer in possession to pass a good title to a third party, binding on the first seller, whether or not the property had already passed to the original buyer. Moreover, it is arguable that s. 25(1) has the strange result that the buyer, even if in possession, and even if they have the property, cannot pass a good title to a *mala fide* transferee.[9] However, it is true that if the goods are delivered to the buyer with a stipulation that the seller reserves title and property is only to pass on payment, the seller may be able to recover the goods in the event of the buyer's bankruptcy.[10] Moreover, 'reservation of title clauses' are widely used. This then is a case where the passing (or non-passing) of the property may have important practical effects, and indeed, many modern cases dealing with the passing of property hinge on these reservation of title clauses. But as we shall see later, these clauses have caused serious difficulties, some being void unless registered under

[5] Section 28 makes delivery conditional on payment of the price – see Chapter 6, section 6.2. Indeed, a buyer who takes the goods without the consent of the seller, when they have no right to possession, may well be guilty of theft. See R *v Boardman* (1987) 9 Cr App R (S) 74, where the only question was as to the suitability of a compensation order.

[6] Ibid.

[7] Section 47 – see Chapter 12. But if the buyer has passed documents of title to the third party, the seller's rights are defeated

[8] For the right of stoppage in transit, see Chapter 15.

[9] But as to this, see below, Chapter 15.

[10] *Aluminium Industrie BV* v *Romalpa Aluminium Ltd* [1976] 1 WLR 676. See further as to these reservation of title clauses – Chapter 15.

the Companies Act 2006, because they amount in substance to the grant by the buyer of a charge by way of security, falling under s. 859A(7) of that Act.[11]

What, then, is the position if the seller, being still in possession of the goods, resells them to a third party, whether rightfully or wrongfully? Again the answer is that the transfer of property has little effect, for s. 24 enables the seller who is in possession to pass a good title to a *bona fide* transferee, even though the transfer may be wrongful as against the first buyer. And since the Privy Council's decision in *Pacific Motor Auctions Pty Ltd* v *Motor Credits (Hire Finance) Ltd*,[12] it is immaterial in what capacity the seller retains possession. Of course, if the goods are actually delivered to the buyer and then returned to the seller to hold as bailee they will not be able to pass a good title to a third party, but once again the same result would follow if property passed on delivery instead of by mere agreement.

The next case to be considered is that in which goods are sold and the property passes to the buyer but the seller remains in possession. If the seller becomes insolvent, can the buyer claim the goods by virtue of their property? As against the seller, or a liquidator or receiver, the answer at common law is *prima facie*, yes, but sometimes the Bills of Sale Acts or the Companies Act operate to invalidate the sale or the buyer's rights in these circumstances.[13] So this is again a case where the passing of property may have important practical consequences. Here too, there are a number of modern cases demonstrating the important practical effects which attach to the passing of property in this situation, and the difficulties which arise when the property has not passed, or cannot pass because the goods remain in bulk, and no physical separation of the buyer's goods from the remainder has yet been effected.[14] So also, the buyer's chances of obtaining equitable or specific relief seem to be greater if property has passed to them, especially if the seller claims no proprietary or possessory rights of any kind over the goods. A buyer's right to goods of which they are the undisputed owner will be specifically enforced against a seller who proposes to convert them and pay damages in lieu.[15]

Next, reference must be made to three[16] other important results, which generally follow from the passing of property. The first of these is that the risk in the goods *prima facie* passes with the property. The second consequence is that generally speaking the seller is not entitled to sue for the price of the goods unless the property has passed. If the buyer repudiates the contract before this happens the seller's remedy is *prima facie* an action for damages for non-acceptance. Yet even here, it cannot be said that these consequences follow naturally or logically from the passing of the property. Roman law had much the

[11] See, e.g., *Re Bond Worth* [1980] Ch 228 – see Chapter 12.

[12] [1965] AC 867 – see Chapter 12.

[13] For the Bills of Sale Acts, which do not apply in Scots law, see Chapter 11. If the seller is a company rather than a private individual, the buyer's property may have to be registered under s. 859A of the Companies Act 2006 as a charge on goods within the meaning of s. 859A(7).

[14] As to bulk sales and changes effected by the Sale of Goods (Amendment) Act 1995, see Chapter 2.

[15] *Redler Grain Silos Ltd* v *BICC Ltd* [1982] 1 Lloyd's Rep 435 – see Chapter 17.

[16] Formerly, a fourth consequence was that when the property in specific goods had passed to the buyer, they could no longer reject them for breach of condition. The law on this point was altered by the Misrepresentation Act 1967, s. 4 – see Chapter 17.

same rules as English law so far as risk is concerned, yet it refused to recognise that property passed merely by virtue of a contract of sale. Nor is there any necessary or logical connection between the right to sue for the price and the passing of property. Indeed, it will be suggested later that a number of unfortunate consequences follow from the present rules on this subject.

The next consequence is that the passing of property may in some circumstances determine who is the proper claimant to sue a third party who has damaged or destroyed the goods; for example, when they are en route to the buyer. But property alone will rarely be decisive. Usually, it is combined, either with a right to possession,[17] or with a contractual right against the third party, such as a carrier. *Prima facie*, the person who is entitled to sue in respect of goods damaged at sea is usually the person who holds the bill of lading,[18] and that person has a contractual right both against the shipowner and also the property. So it is rarely necessary to ask whether it is the one or the other which gives them the right to sue. But a contractual right without property will not usually enable the claimant to sue because they will not have suffered any damage.[19] And it has been decided by the House of Lords that a right of property (or a possessory right) is necessary to establish a cause of action in tort against someone who has been responsible for damaging or destroying goods.[20] In particular, in circumstances where the buyer does not have the benefit of the Carriage of Goods by Sea Act 1992,[21] where goods are lost or damaged while en route from a seller to a buyer, the buyer will now have no right to sue the carrier in tort unless the property had passed to them before the damage or loss occurred, or they have a possessory title to the goods.[22] In most cases of carriage by sea this will not matter because the buyer will have contractual rights against the carrier, either because they made the contract of carriage (or it was made on their behalf), [23] or because the Carriage of Goods by Sea Act 1992 applies. But there are some unusual circumstances in which these contractual rights are absent, and in that case it is of considerable practical importance whether property has passed to the buyer, and, if so, when.[24]

[17] Lord v Price (1874) LR 9 Ex 54. Cf. *Lee Cooper* v *C H Jeakins & Sons Ltd* [1967] 2 QB 1.

[18] *Lord* v *Price* (1874) LR 9 Ex 54. Cf. *Lee Cooper* v *C H Jeakins & Sons Ltd* [1967] 2 QB 1.

[19] The *Albazero* [1977] AC 774. But there can be exceptional cases – see *Obestain Inc* v *National Mineral Devp't Corp Ltd* [1987] 1 Lloyd's Rep 465; *Linden Gardens Trust* v *Linesta Sludge Disposals* Ltd [1994] 1 AC 85. In both of these cases The Albazero was distinguished and the old case of *Dunlop* v *Lambert* (1839) 6 Cl & F 600 applied. *Dunlop* v *Lambert* was a Scots case, reported also at (1839) 1 Macl & Rob 663.

[20] *Leigh & Sillivan Ltd* v *Aliakmon Shipping Co Ltd* (The Aliakmon) [1986] AC 785; *Transcontainer Express Ltd* v *Custodian Security Ltd* [1988] 1 Lloyd's Rep 128. The actual outcome of Leigh & Sillivan would now be different because of the Carriage of Goods by Sea Act 1992, but the principle stated in the text is unaffected.

[21] Or the situation is not covered by one of the conventions governing international carriage by rail (COTIF Convention: CIM Rules, Art. 54), road (CMR Convention, Art. 13) and air (Amended Warsaw Convention, Arts 13, 14 and 24).

[22] *Margarine Union GmbH* v *Cambay Prince Steamship Co Ltd* (The Wear Breeze) [1969] 1 QB 1; *Transcontainer Express Ltd* v *Custodian Security Ltd* [1988] 1 Lloyd's Rep 128, 138.

[23] It is not unusual that the circumstances may indicate that the seller made the contract of carriage as agent for the buyer – see, e.g., *Texas Instruments Ltd* v *Nason (Europe) Ltd* [1991] 1 Lloyd's Rep 146.

[24] It must be noted, however, that in the international carriage of goods by rail, road and air, the relevant conventions state who is entitled to claim against the carrier, and the rights under these conventions do not depend on ownership of the goods – see, e.g., *Texas Investments Ltd* v *Nason (Europe) Ltd* [1991] 1 Lloyd's Rep 146.

To sum up, it may be said that the most important practical consequences which flow from the mere passing of the property are as follows:[25]

1 If the property in the goods has passed to the buyer they will generally have a good title to them if the seller becomes insolvent while the goods remain in the seller's possession.
2 If the goods are delivered subject to a reservation of title (or property) by the seller, the seller *may* have a good title to the goods should the buyer become insolvent.
3 The right to sue a third party for damage to, or loss of, the goods may depend on who has the property.
4 The risk passes *prima facie* when the property passes.
5 Generally speaking, the seller can only sue for the price if the property has passed.

It will be observed that only the first three of these consequences affect third parties and that, although the passing of the property may have important results as *between buyer and seller*, its effect on third parties in ordinary circumstances is minimal.[26] Still, a buyer or seller, relying on their property against an insolvent seller or buyer, may well have a title good against a liquidator or trustee in bankruptcy claiming through the seller or buyer. Of course, parties claiming through a contracting party are not treated by the law as third parties in this sense, although in another, more realistic, sense, trustees in bankruptcy and liquidators should perhaps be treated as third parties.[27] Indeed, one of the chief problems of the existing law is that matters relating to the passing of property are treated as though they only concern the parties to the contract, and can be adjusted entirely according to the intention of the contracting parties. Yet, as we have now seen, by far the most important results of the passing of property relate to the rights of trustees in bankruptcy and liquidators who in a realistic commercial sense represent third-party creditors of buyer or seller. So it is a serious question whether contracting parties should be permitted to adjust the passing (or non-passing) of the property in a contract of sale to protect themselves against the risk of the other party's insolvency, without any regard to the interests of third party creditors. At present, the rights of third parties are occasionally protected by the provisions of the Companies Act requiring the registration of charges, but the right to property under a contract of sale is not usually regarded by the law as a charge in the relevant sense.[28]

In earlier editions of this work, it was suggested that the Sale of Goods Act adopted the policy of allowing property to be transferred by contract alone, and then contained many elaborate provisions designed to reverse the practical effects of this policy. It was

[25] Another result is that in time of war, the ownership of a cargo for prize purposes depends upon the property, but this is obviously of limited application.
[26] Lawson (1949) 65 LQR 352 at 359 went so far as to say: 'If we look at the other effects [than passing of risk] of the transfer of property as between seller and buyer in the common law systems, we shall see that they are for the most part, if not entirely, illusory.' As we have seen, this was an exaggeration, and anyhow there have been marked signs of an increase in the importance attached to the passing of property in recent years.
[27] Under §544 of the US Federal Bankruptcy Code, trustees in bankruptcy are in the position of lien creditors.
[28] See Chapter 15.

also suggested that the law would have been simpler if the Sale of Goods Act had adopted the rule of Roman law that the property in the goods passes on and not before delivery. Had this been done, all the special rights of the unpaid seller might have been unnecessary, as also would ss. 24 and 25. But it is today perhaps less clear that this is so than it seemed at the time when this book was first written. The truth is that the problems concerned cannot be eliminated by changing the rules about the transfer of property. Questions will still arise (for instance) as to who is the proper claimant to sue a third person when goods are damaged en route; questions will still arise about risk, and the right to sue for the price. Above all, questions will still arise about the claims of a buyer against an insolvent seller (and those claiming through them) as well as about the claims of a seller against an insolvent buyer (and likewise those claiming through them). These claims must be disposed of by the law somehow. One way of doing it is the traditional common law way of trying to use a concept like 'property' to decide most of the problems, while recognising that many exceptions must be made. This has the disadvantage, as indicated above, that the exceptions sometimes seem to eat up the rule.

Alternatively, the law might have abandoned the 'conceptual' approach altogether and adopted the 'specific issue' approach, that is, have dealt with each specific question, such as the buyer's ability to pass title to a third party, the passing of risk, liability for the price, etc., without reference to the passing of property. This is the approach of Article 2 of the Uniform Commercial Code in the United States.[29] But the alternative approach, while it has many attractions, fails to provide answers to new problems unforeseen by the law, or indeed to problems newly created by subsequent laws. For the 'specific issue' approach avoids general solutions by use of organising concepts like property, and therefore may offer no solution at all to new problems. Professor Atiyah thought that the traditional common law approach has at least the virtue that in principle there is always a way of meeting new problems, namely by looking to see who has the property in the goods at the relevant moment, and treating that person as owner, with consequences which are assumed to meet the new problems. A good illustration of this ability of the traditional approach to meet new problems is to be found in some cases concerning conflicts over fuel oil on board chartered vessels. In *The Span Terza*,[30] the House of Lords held that a dispute between a charterer and a mortgagee of the ship in question could be resolved by simply asking whether the fuel oil (which had been bought and paid for by the charterers) had been sold to the shipowners so that property had passed to them. It was held that it had not, so that the charterers still owned the oil and had a prior right to that of the mortgagees, who could only claim through the owners.

The previous editor of this work, Professor Adams, considered that in most cases the 'specific issue' approach leads to clearer answers. After all, under the Uniform Commercial Code the issue would probably have been resolved simply by asking if thc mortgagee had a perfected security interest covering the fuel oil under Article 9. The need to resort to such devices as reservation of title clauses does not arise, for the same reason. It is the deficiencies of the law of sale of goods that make it useful to have a workhorse concept such as the 'property in goods'.

[29] It is enacted in all states except Louisiana, which adopted the Code Napoleon in the early nineteenth century.

[30] [1984] 1 Lloyd's Rep 119.

10.2 Rules on passing property

The exact moment at which the property passes depends upon whether the goods are specific or unascertained, and this distinction is so fundamental that the subject will be dealt with under two separate headings below. In general, s. 17 of the SGA 1979 allows the parties to decide when property passes, but this must be consistent with other provisions within the Act. Where clear intention can be ascertained the SGA 1979 also sets default rules to determine the exact moment property passes. As a result, in practice, these Rules assume substantial importance as the parties often do not have or express any clear intention as to the passing of the property.[31] Moreover, if the parties do express such an intention, it will have no effect if the property has already passed in accordance with the rules.

10.2.1 Passing of property and party autonomy

Section 17 of the Act is as follows:

> (1) Where there is a contract for the sale of specific or ascertained goods the property in them is transferred to the buyer at such time as the parties to the contract intend it to be transferred.
> (2) For the purpose of ascertaining the intention of the parties regard shall be had to the terms of the contract, the conduct of the parties, and the circumstances of the case.

Although this section only applies to specific or ascertained goods, it is well settled that, as a matter of general contract law, the principle expressed in subsection (2) also applies to unascertained goods.[32]

The effect of s. 17 is such that where the parties have clearly set out the intention as to when property passes, either via a term in the contract, their conduct or in consideration of the circumstances of the case, the remaining legal issue is whether that intention is consistent with other provisions, e.g. s. 16 or s. 19 discussed below. For instance, in *Re Anchor*,[33] a contract to purchase a crane contained the terms that it will be in exchange for 'a deferred purchase price' and with it having the 'entire charge and responsibility'. As per this arrangement, the buyer was to pay for the contract in annual installments. When the buyer later became insolvent, the legal issue was whether the property had passed. The court held that the default rules of passing property does not apply where there is clear intention to pass property, and in this instance there was as the conduct indicated that it was not to pass until payment of the full purchase price.

The *Re Anchor* case above also neatly shows the relationship between s. 17 and s. 19 as the former provision allows parties to decide when property passes and the latter allows the seller to 'reserve the right of disposal of the goods until certain conditions are fulfilled'. Section 19 is discussed in more detail below, but in practice, s. 19 is used by sellers to

[31] *Smyth & Co Ltd* v *Bailey Son & Co Ltd* [1940] 3 All ER 60, 67 per Lord Wright.

[32] *Ginzberg* v *Barrow Haematite Steel Co* [1966] 1 Lloyd's Rep 343. But this is subject to the qualification laid down in s. 16 – see below, at section 10.2.2–3.

[33] [1973] Ch 1 (CA)

reserve passing of property until full payment. The effect of this will normally prevent the goods from forming part of the general assets of the buyer in the event of their insolvency.

Section 18 (which applies to both specific and unascertained goods) states that:

> Unless a different intention appears, the following are rules for ascertaining the intention of the parties as to the time at which the property in the goods is to pass to the buyer.

The section then sets out five Rules for ascertaining the intention of the parties, discussed below. In practice, these Rules assume substantial importance as the parties often do not have or express any clear intention as to the passing of the property.[34] Moreover, if the parties do express such an intention, it will have no effect if the property has already passed in accordance with the rules laid down in s. 18. In *Dennant* v *Skinner and Collom*,[35] the plaintiff sold a car to X by auction. X, who was a swindler, gave a false name and address and asked to be allowed to take the car away in return for his cheque. The plaintiff allowed X to do this on obtaining his signature to a document which stated that the title to the vehicle would not pass until the cheque was met. X sold the car, which was ultimately resold to the defendant. Hallett J held that the intention of the parties as expressed in this document was too late to prevent the property from passing since it had already done so on the fall of the hammer,[36] in accordance with Rule 1 of s. 18.

10.2.2 Rules for specific goods

Section 61 SGA 1979 defines *specific goods* as, goods 'identified and agreed upon at the time a contract of sale is made'. However, as has already been observed, this term does not necessarily mean the same thing wherever it appears in the Act, despite the single definition.

The meaning of 'identified' as used under s. 61 in most cases gives rise to no difficulty – it is usually obvious enough when the goods are identified by the contract. But sometimes difficulty arises because general descriptive words are used, which are not easy to apply. In *Kursell* v *Timber Operators & Contractors Ltd*,[37] the plaintiff sold to the defendants all the trees in a Latvian forest which conformed to certain measurements on a particular date, the buyers to have 15 years in which to cut and remove the timber. Almost immediately afterwards the Latvian Assembly passed a law confiscating the forest. The Court of Appeal held that the property in the trees had not passed to the defendants as the goods were not sufficiently identified, since not all the trees were to pass, only those conforming

[34] *Smyth & Co Ltd* v *Bailey Son & Co Ltd* [1940] 3 All ER 60, 67 per Lord Wright.

[35] [1948] 2 KB 164.

[36] It is odd that the defendant did not rely on s. 25(1), which would appear to have been decisive of this part of the case. It may be that this case turned on the fact that the sale was by auction. It might, however, have been argued on behalf of the seller that the intention of the transaction was that the seller released his lien on the vehicle in consideration of the revesting of property in him – see *Hain SS Co Ltd* v *Tate & Lyle Ltd* [1936] 2 All ER 597 (as to the unpaid seller's lien). In a sale in a shop it seems that no contract is made (and hence no property passes) until the mode of payment is agreed: see *Ingram* v *Little* [1961] 1 QB 31, 49; and in a supermarket, no property passes until the price is actually paid: *Lacis* v *Cashmarts* [1969] 2 QB 400, 407; *Davies* v *Leighton* [1978] Crim LR 575.

[37] [1927] 1 KB 298. Cf. *Lord Eldon* v *Hedley Bros* [1935] 2 KB 1 – sale of haystacks held to be of specific goods though buyer not bound to take mouldy or unmerchantable hay.

to the stipulated measurements.[38] An Australian decision provides an interesting contrast to this case. In *Joseph Reid Pty Ltd* v *Schultz*,[39] a sale of all the millable or marketable hardwood timber on a certain site was held to be a sale of specific goods. In *Commissioners of Customs & Excise* v *Everwine Ltd*,[40] as liquor was delivered to a bonded warehouse it was allocated a 'rotation number'. The totality of alcohol held by the Everwine Ltd was sold by a series of contracts to a specific buyer. It was held that property had passed, applying *Wait & James* v *Midland Bank Ltd*.[41] However, where release notes did not cover all of the claimant's stock under the specified rotation numbers, the goods were unascertained and property could not pass.[42]

Where there is a sale of specific goods and the intention of the parties as to passing of property is not clear, and thus s. 17 SGA 1979 (discussed above) does not apply, then s. 18 Rules 1–4 SGA 1979 will apply, depending on the contract. Accordingly, each of these rules will be discussed below.

10.2.2.1 Rule 1

This Rule is as follows:

> Where there is an unconditional contract for the sale of specific goods, in a deliverable state, the property in the goods passes to the buyer when the contract is made, and it is immaterial whether the time of payment or the time of delivery, or both, be postponed.

This Rule gives rise to a number of difficult questions.

'Unconditional contract'

In the first place, what is an unconditional contract within the meaning of this Rule? This may mean either (a) a contract not subject to a condition precedent or subsequent ; or (b) a contract not containing any conditions in the sense of essential stipulations, the breach of which gives the buyer the right to treat the contract as repudiated. The former interpretation clearly cannot be correct. Throughout the Act, the term 'conditional contract' is used in this sense. Section 1(2) says: 'A contract of sale may be absolute or conditional', which clearly means subject to a condition precedent, for otherwise there would be no point in the contrast. Equally, Rules 2, 3 and 4 of s. 18 all deal with contracts subject to conditions precedent, so that the natural inference is that Rule 1, by contrast, deals with contracts not subject to such conditions. Furthermore, it is difficult to see how there can be any such thing as an unconditional contract if 'condition' here means 'essential stipulation'. Every contract must contain at least some essential stipulations and most contracts contain several. In every contract of sale, there must be some fundamental

[38] Note that the Sale of Goods (Amendment) Act 1995 would not affect the situation in a case like this because even if the buyer had paid for a quantity of goods, it is questionable whether the bulk was sufficiently identified to constitute an identified bulk.

[39] (1949) SR (NSW) 231.

[40] [2003] EWCA Civ 953.

[41] (1926) 24 Ll Rep 313 – see section 10.2.1 below.

[42] See also *Re Stapylton Fletcher Ltd* [1994] 1 WLR 1181, which was distinguished – see section 10.2.3 below.

conditions or obligations, namely that of the seller to deliver the goods to the buyer, and that of the buyer to accept the goods and pay the price. If the presence of these obligations makes all contracts of sale conditional within Rule 1 it can have no effect.

Despite these arguments the question has not been free from difficulty, though it is thought that it is now settled. The difficulty arose largely from s. 11(4) of the Act which, in its original form (then s. 11(1)(c) of the 1893 Act), deprived the buyer of the right to reject goods for breach of condition 'where the contract is for specific goods, the property in which has passed to the buyer'. If the term 'unconditional contract' in Rule 1 was given its natural meaning, the result appeared to be that in the vast majority of sales of specific goods there was no real right to reject for breach of condition at all. The property passed when the contract was made and at that very same time the right to reject was lost under s. 11(1)(c). This was such a startling result that the judges, consciously or unconsciously, strove to avoid it by giving a forced interpretation to the words 'unconditional contract' in Rule 1. Therefore, in *Varley* v *Whipp*,[43] discussed previously, it was held that the sale of a reaping machine was not an unconditional sale despite the fact that it was clearly not subject to any conditions precedent, but no reasons were given for this part of the decision. Similarly, in *Ollett* v *Jordan*,[44] a case dealing with the meaning of 'unconditionally appropriated' within Rule 5, it was held that the property in fish did not pass to the buyer owing to the fact that there was a breach of the implied condition that the fish was fit for human consumption, although there was no condition precedent. Finally, in *Leaf* v *International Galleries*,[45] and again in *Long* v *Lloyd*,[46] there were dicta which supported the conclusion reached in *Varley* v *Whipp*.[47] Fortunately, these difficulties now seem to be entirely historic. The Misrepresentation Act 1967, s. 4 repealed the words formerly appearing in s. 11(1)(c), 'where the contract is for specific goods the property in which has passed to the buyer'. As a result, there was then no need for judges to give an unnatural construction to the words 'unconditional contract' in s. 18, Rule 1 in order to avoid depriving a buyer of their right to reject goods.

Section 19 SGA 1979 provides an avenue to retain ownership 'until certain conditions are fulfilled' in practice the most important kind of condition which may need to be satisfied before property passes is a condition as to payment. Express terms may make the passing of property conditional on payment even after delivery.[48] Similarly, such a term may be readily implied in circumstances where payment is normally required before delivery, for example in a supermarket.[49] Other types of conditional contract are dealt with under s. 18 rules 2 and 3 below.

[43] [1900] 1 QB 513 – see Chapter 7.

[44] [1918] 2 KB 41.

[45] [1950] 2 KB 86.

[46] [1958] 1 WLR 753.

[47] [1900] 1 QB 513.

[48] *Aluminium Industrie BV* v *Romalpa Aluminium Ltd* [1976] 1 WLR 676 – see below, Chapter 15. Although generally speaking a cheque operates only as a conditional discharge for the obligation to pay the price (see Chapter 9, at section 9.1), this will not usually prevent the property passing under Rule 1 – see *Anderson* v *Havana Horse* and others, 18 August 1999 (unreported).

[49] See *Davies* v *Leighton* [1978] Crim LR 575.

Deliverable state

The next question arising out of s. 18, Rule 1, is the meaning of the term, 'deliverable state'. Under s. 61(5):

> Goods are in a 'deliverable state' within the meaning of this Act when they are in such a state that the buyer would under the contract be bound to take delivery of them.

It is to be noted that s. 61(5) does not purport to give a comprehensive definition of 'deliverable state'. In particular, it does not say that if the buyer would not be bound to take delivery of the goods, then the goods are *not* in a deliverable state. The buyer is not bound to take delivery of defective goods, but it does not follow that all defective goods are not in a deliverable state within the meaning of this provision. If this were so, property would never pass in defective goods,[50] but it seems to be generally accepted that defects do not prevent property passing. (If the buyer rejects the goods, property revests in the seller.) Section 61(5) was probably intended to cover the case where the goods could not be said to be in a deliverable state physically, yet the buyer had agreed to take delivery as they stood. This means that the words 'deliverable state' cannot be construed by reference to the definition of delivery in s. 61 as 'a voluntary transfer of possession'. The possession of goods can probably always be transferred in law if the parties intend to transfer it, no matter what the physical condition of the goods may be. If this was what 'deliverable state' meant, therefore, goods would probably always be in a deliverable state.

The authorities on this point are not of great assistance because there has been a tendency to interpret the words literally by reference to the physical moveability of the goods. In *Underwood Ltd* v *Burgh Castle Brick & Cement Syndicate*,[51] the plaintiffs sold a condensing engine to the defendants f.o.b. The engine weighed over 30 tons and was attached to the floor. The engine had to be dismantled after being detached from the floor, a task which of course fell on the sellers under the f.o.b. contract, and which was expected to take about two weeks and to cost about £100 (in 1922). It was held that the engine was not in a deliverable state and that the property had not passed when the contract was made.[52] But the judges also thought that there was anyhow a sufficient contrary intention to be inferred from the fact that clearly some element of risk was involved in the work of dismantling the engine and dispatching it to the buyer, so it seemed that the property was not intended to pass on the sale.

Philip Head & Son Ltd v *Showfronts Ltd*[53] was a case under s. 18, Rule 5(1) which also contains the phrase 'in a deliverable state'. Here the plaintiffs sold carpet to the defendants, which they were required to lay. The carpet was delivered to the defendants' premises,

[50] In the first edition Professor Atiyah argued that this was indeed so. But this argument was largely a response to the difficulties created by s. 11 of the 1893 Act, which have now been removed by s. 4 of the Misrepresentation Act 1967. See Chapter 17.

[51] [1922] 1 KB 343.

[52] *Compare Broadcrest CD Ltd* v *Ruddick and others*, 5 May 2000 (unreported), where the machines in question were not fixed, but only needed to be disconnected into their constituent parts, held to be in a deliverable state and that property had passed on payment of the price. Similarly, *Anderson* v *Havana Horse (UK) Ltd and others 31* July 1999 (unreported): Mercedes with crack in its windscreen and some scratches on its wheels (both of which were to be fixed before delivery to the buyer) in a deliverable state.

[53] [1970] 1 Lloyd's Rep 140.

but was stolen before it could be laid. It was held that the carpet was not in a deliverable state, apparently because it was a heavy bundle and difficult to move. But importance was attached to the fact that the carpet had to be laid by the sellers. This seems a better ground for holding that the property had not passed because the mere weight of the goods cannot mean they are not in a deliverable state – after all, heavy goods are commonly delivered under contracts of sale.

Perhaps a better illustration of what is meant by the term 'deliverable state' comes from the more recent decision in *Kulkarni* v *Manor Credit (Davenham) Ltd*.[54] The issue in this case was whether a brand new car which has been registered and therefore had a registration mark assigned to it but which had not had number plates attached to it, could be regarded as being in a deliverable state. The Court of Appeal held that until the number plates were attached and it could be lawfully driven by the buyer on a public road, it was not in a deliverable state. If nothing else, the decision here indicates that 'deliverable state' clearly extends beyond simply the movability of the goods.

Factors indicating a contrary intention

As we have seen, express agreement that property is not to pass, for instance, until payment, is effective in law. Although historically more common, such 'conditional sale' agreements have long been known. Where there is no express provision, it is a matter of inference whether the *prima facie* operation of Rule 1 is displaced.[55]

There is no doubt that the rule that property passes when the contract is made does not fit easily into the pattern of consumer sales as discussed below. It is therefore not surprising to see the suggestion being made that today very little is needed to rebut the inference that property passes on the making of the contract.[56] It seems that in an ordinary sale in a shop, property does not pass at least until the parties have agreed on the mode of payment;[57] and on a sale in a supermarket, property does not pass until the price is paid.[58] At a petrol station, property in the fuel passes when it is put into the vehicle's petrol tank,[59] but that is not a case of a sale of specific goods so much as of unascertained goods, so it is dealt with later.

Despite the fact that Rule 1 states that it is immaterial for purposes of passing of property whether the time of payment or the time of delivery, or both, be postponed, it is not possible to ignore such postponement completely. For if payment or delivery or both be postponed this may be some indication of a contrary intention which excludes the operation of Rule 1 altogether. In an Irish case,[60] where the plaintiff had agreed to trade in his

[54] [2010] EWCA Civ. 69.

[55] The onus is on the seller to displace the statutory presumption – *Higgins* v *Farmer*, 8 December 1999 (unreported).

[56] *R V Ward Ltd* v *Bignall* [1967] 1 QB 534, 545 per Diplock LJ.

[57] *Ingram* v *Little* [1961] 1 QB 31, 49. But this case did not concern a sale in a shop, and it is not easy to see why the contract should not be held to be made as soon as the sale is agreed, on the assumption that the basic position is that the buyer must pay cash unless the seller agrees to accept some alternative.

[58] *Lacis* v *Cashmarts* [1969] 2 QB 400, 407; *Davies* v *Leighton* [1978] Crim LR 575; cf. *Watts* v *Seymour* [1967] 2 QB 647.

[59] *Edwards* v *Ddin* [1976] 1 WLR 943; Re Charge Card Services Ltd [1988] 3 All ER 702, 706 – see Chapter 11.

[60] *Clarke* v *Michael Reilly & Sons* (1962) 96 ILTR 96.

old car with the defendants in part-exchange for a new one, and was allowed to retain and use the old one pending delivery of the new one,[61] it was held that property and risk had both passed to the defendants. The decision seems a curious one, and it is thought that on such facts a court would be fully justified in finding a contrary intention which would negative an intention to pass property before delivery.[62] It certainly seems quite wrong that the risk should be held to be on the buyer while the seller still has the use of the car.

Another factor which may point to a contrary intention is any specific agreement on the transfer of risk. As will be seen, the risk in the goods *prima facie* passes with the property. If the risk has passed, therefore, this may be some indication that the property has also passed.[63] Conversely, where the risk is still on the seller this may be evidence that the property has not passed.[64] But it is possible to draw precisely the opposite inference from the passing of risk. In *Re Anchor Line Ltd*,[65] the Court of Appeal inferred that the property in goods had not passed because there was a specific clause in the contract placing the risk upon the buyer, and (the court reasoned) if the property had passed such a clause would not have been necessary. One can only say, therefore, that the proper inference to be drawn from an agreement placing the risk on the buyer must depend on all the circumstances of the case.[66]

An obligation to insure placed upon one party by the contract is also an indication that they bear the risk,[67] and it has been said that this is an indication that they also have the property. But once again, the proper inference to be drawn must depend upon all the circumstances of the case, for it could well be that the intention is simply that one party insures the other's risk.

In trying to determine what the correct inference is to draw from a contractual provision about the transfer of risk or an obligation to insure, the following are relevant factors to consider. First, it seems that where the seller advises the buyer to insure, this is some indication that risk and property have passed to the buyer.[68] Such advice does not suggest that the seller retains any property in the goods, as might be argued if they actually stipulated for insurance. Secondly, there may be cases in which a seller may retain some interest in the goods even where the property has passed; for example, they may still have a lien or some sort of charge on the goods. In such circumstances, the seller may wish to

[61] As to whether a part-exchange is a sale at all, is dealt with in Chapter 2.

[62] The decision seems to have been influenced by an admission by the defendants that they would have regarded it as a breach of contract had the plaintiff sold his car to a third party. This may well have been correct but it does not follow that property had passed. There are good policy reasons for holding that the 'seller' in such a case bears the risk because they should have the burden of looking after the goods, and is the more likely carrier of insurance cover – see *Martin* v *Melland's* 283 NW 2d 76 (1979), a case on Art. 2 of the Uniform Commercial Code. Although the UCC is explicit on this policy consideration, the court in that case could within the terms of the Code have reached the same conclusion as the Irish court.

[63] *The Parchim* [1918] AC 157, 168. But this decision can no longer be treated as supporting any general inference that the passing of risk (especially in shipped goods) means that property has also passed: *Mitsui &Co Ltd* v *Flota Mercante Grancolombiana SA* [1989] 1 All ER 951.

[64] *Carlos Federspiel & Co SA* v *Charles Twigg & Co Ltd* [1957] 1 Lloyd's Rep 240, 255; *President of India* v *Metcalfe Shipping Co* [1970] 1 QB 289.

[65] [1937] Ch 1.

[66] For a review of some earlier conflicting cases and dicta on the inference to be drawn from such a stipulation, see the Australian case of *McPherson, Thorn, Kettle & Co v Dench Bros* [1921] VLR 437.

[67] *Allison* v *Bristol Marine Ins Co Ltd* (1876) 1 App Cas 209, 229 per Blackburn J.

[68] See, e.g., *Donaghy's Rope and Twine Co Ltd* v *Wright, Stephenson & Co* (1906) 25 NZLR 641.

require the buyer to insure the goods in order to protect their own interest, and this would be no indication that risk had not passed, although the property remained in the seller.[69] Conversely, where the contract requires the buyer to insure the goods, but the seller would have, on the face of it, no interest in the goods if the property and risk had passed from them, the correct inference may well be that property and risk have not passed.

Another kind of case in which the presumption contained in Rule 1 would normally be rebutted is a contract for the sale of goods and land together. For example, where a person contracts to sell a house together with some furnishings, the presumption that property passes on the making of the contract would be rebutted. The normal inference in such a case would be that the property is only to pass on conveyance.[70] Indeed, where (contrary to the normal English practice) the vendor is not fully paid on conveyance and the price is to be paid by instalments, the property may not even pass on delivery of possession.[71]

Where goods are to be supplied and installed or fitted by the seller in a building or construction so that the goods will become fixtures in the technical sense, the property does not normally pass until the work of installation has been completed.[72] But cases of this nature are more likely to involve unascertained goods, so this point is dealt with more fully later.[73]

10.2.2.2 Rules 2 and 3

In contrast to Rule 1, which deals with the unconditional sale of specific goods, Rules 2, 3 and 4 deal with the conditional sale of specific goods. But unlike Rule 1, which deals with all unconditional contracts, Rules 2 to 4 deal only with certain types of conditional contract, there is no general or residuary rule dealing with conditional contracts that fall outside of Rules 2, 3 or 4. (Section 19 also deals with certain conditional contracts, but as these mostly concern unascertained goods, this section is dealt with under the next heading.) So, a conditional contract which does not fall within Rules 2, 3 or 4 (or s. 19) must be dealt with under the very general terms of s. 17, which simply require the court to ascertain the presumed intention of the parties by taking account of all the circumstances of the case. Rules 2 and 3 are as follows:

> *Rule 2*. Where there is a contract for the sale of specific goods and the seller is bound to do something to the goods, for the purpose of putting them into a deliverable state, the property does not pass until the thing is done, and the buyer has notice that it has been done.
>
> *Rule 3*. Where there is a contract for the sale of specific goods in a deliverable state, but the seller is bound to weigh, measure, test, or do some other act or thing with reference to the goods for the purpose of ascertaining the price, the property does not pass until the act or thing is done, and the buyer has notice that it has been done.

[69] This is certainly the case, for example, in hire-purchase contracts. In the case of vehicles, and other expensive goods, such contracts always require the hirer to insure.

[70] *Commissioner of Stamps* v *Queensland Meat Export Co Ltd* [1917] AC 624. The same result could be arrived at by holding that the sale is conditional on conveyance and so not within Rule 1 at all.

[71] *Warren* v *Forbes* [1959] VR 14.

[72] *Clark* v *Bulmer* (1843) 11 M & W 243; *Aristoc Industries Pty Ltd* v *R A Wenham (Builders) Pty Ltd* [1965] NSWR 581.

[73] See below, section 10.2.2 below.

It is not clear why Rule 2 is confined to cases where the seller is bound to do something to put the goods 'into a deliverable state'. Therefore, it seems that the Rule would not apply where the seller has agreed to repair the goods; for example, to overhaul a second-hand car which the buyer has agreed to purchase 'as is'. On the other hand, such a sale may still be a conditional sale, but one to which none of the Rules in s. 18 would apply. In such a case, the court may simply fall back on s. 17 and hold that property is not to pass until the repairs have been done as this is the presumed intention of the parties.[74] In a Scottish case about the sale of growing potatoes, the seller undertook to lift and store the potatoes when ready and to transport them to the railway station. It was held that the goods were in a deliverable state when put into the pits for storage, the obligation to transport them related only to actual delivery.

Rule 3 requires little comment. It clearly deals with cases where the passing of the property is conditional upon the performance of some act with reference to the goods. The presumption embodied in this rule is probably somewhat weaker than those in Rules 1 and 2 because it is easy to imagine circumstances in which the parties intend the property to pass at once, especially if the price has been paid. So, for instance, where a seller sold haystacks for delivery at the buyer's convenience and the price was paid at once, though liable to adjustment when the hay was weighed on delivery, it was held that the property passed at once.[75] Similarly, it is probable that the property would be held to have passed if the goods have been delivered, although the seller has still to do something to ascertain the price; for example, to look up the list price in a catalogue. If the seller is not *bound* to do some act to the goods to ascertain the price, Rule 3 is inapplicable.[76]

At all events, Rule 3 only applies to acts to be done by the seller. In *Nanka Bruce* v *Commonwealth Trust Ltd*,[77] A sold cocoa to B at an agreed price per 60 lb, it being arranged that B would resell the goods and that the cocoa would then be weighed by the purchasers in order to ascertain the total amount due from B to A. It was held that the weighing did not make the contract conditional and that the property passed to B before the price was ascertained.

10.2.2.3 Rule 4

Rule 4 deals with two different types of transaction altogether, although they are very similar to a conditional sale and may become a sale in due course; they are:

> When goods are delivered to the buyer on approval or on sale or return or other similar terms.

There is little authority on the meaning of the terms 'sale on approval' or 'sale or return', and it has been suggested that they are very different transactions in commercial

[74] *Anderson* v *Ryan* [1967] IR 34, 37.
[75] *Lord Eldon* v *Hedley Bros* [1935] 2 KB 1. See also *Kennedy's Tr* v *Hamilton* (1897) 25 R 252. It is very common for export contracts for the sale of goods in bulk to provide for final adjustment of the price on weighing (or measuring) the goods on discharge from the vessel. It seems clear that this would not prevent property passing at the usual time, namely on transfer of the bill of lading – see Chapter 13 (These contracts would normally be for the sale of unascertained goods and so not within Rule 3, anyhow.)
[76] *Woodburn* v *Motherwell* [1917] SC 533.
[77] [1926] AC 77.

function, and perhaps also in intent.[78] One possible difference is that a sale on approval may legally amount to a contract of sale with a condition subsequent which permits the buyer to rescind the transaction if they find the goods unsuitable,[79] while a 'sale or return' transaction may not even be a contract of sale at all, but rather an offer to sell, accompanied by delivery, which must actually be accepted before it becomes a contract of sale (i.e. up to that point it is a mere bailment). The Act does not differentiate between them, however, and as the Rule also applies to transactions on 'other similar terms', it may be that no difference was intended. It has at least been held that there is no difference between a transaction where the goods are delivered to a prospective buyer who may keep or return the goods, on the one hand, and cases where the goods are delivered to a dealer who is expected either to resell or return the goods, on the other hand. Both these transactions fall within Rule 4.[80]

Rule 4, having set out the transactions to which it applies, then goes on to say that in these transactions the property passes to the buyer:

> (a) When he signifies his approval or acceptance to the seller or does any other act adopting the transaction.

It has been held that any action by the buyer inconsistent with their free power to return the goods is an act adopting the transaction within the meaning of the Rule. Thus, where a person obtains goods on sale or return or similar terms and then resells or pledges them, this is an act adopting the transaction, and the third party is therefore protected against the seller. Nor is it material that the first buyer is guilty of a criminal offence.[81] An express stipulation that the property is not to pass until the goods are paid for is effective to protect the seller because this is evidence of a contrary intention which overrides Rule 4.[82]

Rule 4 tells us what acts of the buyer cause property to pass, but it does not indicate what they must do if they decide to return the goods. Under Rule 4(b), property passes if the buyer retains the goods beyond a certain time without giving 'notice of rejection'. Clearly, this cannot be 'notice of rejection' in the same sense as this term is used in relation to defective goods, simply because in the case of sale or return contracts what suffices for this purpose will be controlled by the terms of the original contract, which will frequently spell out what is to be done, whereas when goods are rejected as defective, the contract will rarely say what is to be done. In *Atari Corporation* v *Electronics Boutique Stores*,[83] the Court of Appeal held that in the absence of a specific provision controlling the matter, in a sale or return contract any intimation to the 'seller' that the 'buyer' does not wish to

[78] See generally, Adams, ch. I, in Essays for Clive *Schmitthoff* (ed. J.N. Adams, 1983, Professional Books). Note also *Brown* v *Marr Barclay & Co* (1880) 7 R 427.

[79] But cf. *Cranston* v *Mallow* 1912 SC 112, in which it was held that when a horse was sold under a warranty and with a week's trial, the contract was not a sale on approval because the buyer's right to return the goods was not unqualified but dependent on non-fulfilment of the warranty.

[80] *Poole* v *Smith's Car Sales* (Balham) Ltd [1962] 2 All ER 482. See also *Michelin Tyre Co Ltd* v *Macfarlane* (Glasgow) Ltd 1917 2 SLT 205, HL, distinguishing between sale and return and agency.

[81] *Kirkham* v *Attenborough* [1897] 1 QB 201; *London Jewellers Ltd* v *Attenborough* [1934] 2 KB 206; *Genn* v *Winkel* (1911) 28 TLR 483. *Weiner* v *Gill* [1906] 2 KB 574; *R* v *Eaton* (1966) 50 Cr App Rep 189.

[82] [1998] 1 All ER 1010.

[83] [1998] 1 All ER 1010.

exercise their option to purchase suffices. In modern commercial conditions, where goods are bought centrally and distributed around a chain of retailers, it will often be impractical to return the goods at the time of the notice, or even to specify exactly what goods are being returned. In *Atari*, the Court of Appeal recognised this commercial reality. It is sufficient if after giving notice, the 'buyer' collects in the goods within a reasonable time so that the 'seller' can resume possession of them.[84] This case also supports the view, set out above, that sale or return contracts are contracts of bailment up to the time property passes. This is a matter of some importance because if the passing of property and time of payment are separate, the goods will remain at the seller's risk notwithstanding payment by the buyer. So if the 'buyer' must pay for the goods by 30 November, but has until 31 January to reject them,[85] the goods will remain at the 'seller's' risk until 31 January. Since these are, in reality, financing transactions, time of payment merely indicates the point of time up to which the 'seller' is prepared to finance the 'buyer's' inventory. It is submitted that Rule 4 still controls the passing of property,[86] and therefore risk, in the absence of contract provisions dealing with this.

Today, the extensive use of 'reservation of title' clauses (under which goods are delivered but the seller reserves title until they are paid[87] sometimes leads to a transaction which is rather similar to a sale on approval or a sale or return, although these are more likely to be transactions relating to unascertained goods to which, strictly, Rule 4 has no application. Where goods are delivered to a buyer under a reservation of title clause, and they are authorised by the seller to use the goods even before payment, such use may – if it deprives the goods of their identity – amount to an act which necessarily transfers the property to the buyer, despite the terms of the reservation of title clause. So, for instance, resin delivered to a buyer who used it in a matter of days in the manufacture of chipboard was held to have ceased to exist as a separate commodity, despite a reservation of title clause,[88] and a similar result was reached when leather was sold which was intended to be used in the making of handbags.[89] It was held that as soon as the buyer started to work the leather, the property passed to them, despite the reservation of title clause. These decisions can be explained by saying that the reservation of title clause must be read subject to the paramount intent of the parties that the buyer is to be entitled to use the goods in the process of their business, and that this intent is inconsistent with any real intention that property is to remain in the seller after the process has begun. None of these cases actually refers to s. 18, Rule 4, presumably because they related to unascertained goods. It was suggested in previous editions that the result in these cases is in line with Rule 4 in that they appear to be examples of acts 'adopting the transaction' under this Rule if the contracts are characterised as transactions 'on sale or return or other similar terms'. This is true in a sense, but perhaps is slightly misleading because a fundamental difference between retention of title and sale or return transactions is that usually the buyer in the

[84] Ibid., pp. 1023–4.
[85] As in *Atari*.
[86] See Adams (1998) 61 MLR 432.
[87] See Chapter 15.
[88] *Borden (UK) Ltd* v *Scottish Timber Products Ltd* [1981] Ch 25.
[89] *Re Peachdart Ltd* [1983] 3 All ER 204. But cf. *Hendy Lennox Ltd* v *Grahame Puttick Ltd* [1984] 2 All ER 152.

former type of transaction is committed to buy, whereas the whole point of the latter arrangement is that they are not. The legal basis of retention of title clauses under the Act is s. 19 (as already explained), and the rule expressed in s. 17 that property passes when the parties intend it to.

A slightly different problem arises where the buyer under a sale or return transaction sells the goods to a third party despite a clause providing that property is not to pass until payment. Although such a clause overrides s. 18, Rule 4 because it shows a contrary intention as to the time when property is to pass, there are many other ways in which the third party buyer may be protected. For example, the seller may be caught by the doctrine of estoppel,[90] or by the provisions of s. 2 of the Factors Act 1889.[91] In *Weiner* v *Harris*,[92] the plaintiff sent jewellery to F, a retailer, under a standing contract, whereby the property was to remain in the plaintiff until the goods were sold or paid for. F pledged the jewels in question with the defendant. Cozens-Hardy MR posed the following question: 'Was the transaction the ordinary well-known transaction of goods taken on sale or return, or was it a transaction under which F was constituted agent for sale, with authority to sell, and bound to account to his principal for the proceeds of such sale?' In the former case, s. 18, Rule 4 would be overridden by a contrary intention and the seller would be protected. In the latter case, F would be a mercantile agent enabled by s. 2 of the Factors Act to pass a good title to a buyer or pledgee. The Court of Appeal had no doubt that in this case F was a mercantile agent, and the defendants were protected.

It has been held that a person who has obtained goods on sale or return cannot pass a good title to a third party under s. 25(1) of the Act, if there is a contrary intention which excludes the operation of Rule 4.[93] The reason for this is not very clear, but it seems to depend on the view that such a person is not, within the meaning of s. 25(1), a person who has 'bought or agreed to buy goods'. They have an option to purchase, but that is all; until they exercise their option by accepting the goods or adopting the transaction, there is no sale. But there is one difficulty about this analysis, and that is that the buyer can 'adopt' the transaction without communicating their intention to the seller. If this were really a mere option, it would seem that the buyer would have to communicate their acceptance to the seller. It may be, therefore, that the right view is that there must actually be a contract of sale of goods and *then* an act adopting the transaction before the property passes.[94]

The second alternative given by Rule 4 is:

> (b) If he does not signify his approval or acceptance to the seller but retains the goods without giving notice of rejection, then, if a time has been fixed for the return of the goods, on the expiration of that time, and, if no time has been fixed, on the expiration of a reasonable time.

[90] On estoppel, see Chapter 12.
[91] On the Factors Act, see Chapter 12.
[92] [1910] 1 KB 285.
[93] *Edwards* v *Vaughan* (1910) 26 TLR 545.
[94] Rule 4 does not start by saying 'Where there is a contract for the sale of specific goods' etc., so it appears to apply to a delivery of the goods even where there is no contract then in being – see, generally, Adams, (1998) 61 MLR 432.

Therefore, if a time has been fixed for the return of the goods, the buyer is deemed to have exercised their option to buy them if they retain them after this time. Here again, therefore, the transaction may be completed without a communication of acceptance. It is clear that an unsolicited delivery of goods with an offer to sell them does not have this effect,[95] and it is therefore arguable that delivery on sale or return must be more than a mere option or offer to sell. The buyer may, of course, waive the time limit and accept the goods at once by so informing the seller, or by doing some act which adopts the transaction.

If the goods are not returned within a reasonable time because of the defaults of employees of the buyer, the property will be held to have passed to them even though they may have given instructions for the return of the goods.[96] But the sub-rule does not apply if the goods are detained by someone for whose acts the buyer is not responsible. Thus where goods were delivered to X on sale or return within one week, and two days later they were seized by execution creditors of X, who retained them until after the week was over, it was held that the property had not passed under Rule 4(b).[97]

10.2.3 Rules for unascertained goods

The meaning of the term 'unascertained goods' has already been discussed and it has been shown to cover three possibilities: first, goods to be manufactured or grown by the seller; secondly, purely generic goods and thirdly, an unidentified portion of a specified bulk or whole.[98] Although the Act does not distinguish between these three types of unascertained goods, the rules as to the passing of property and risk may differ in each case. In particular, the passing of risk in an unidentified portion of a specified bulk may sometimes take place at a different time from the usual. And, secondly, what amounts to an 'unconditional appropriation' – which is what is usually required to transfer the property – in one type of sale may not do so in another. The fundamental rules to passing of property for unascertained goods are set out in s. 16, 17, 18, Rule 5, 20A, although these rules must be interpreted with consideration of other provisions under the SGA 1979.

10.2.3.1 Section 16

It is clear that s. 16 must be the starting point in considering the passing of property in a sale of unascertained goods. The section states that:

> Subject to section 20A, where there is a contract for the sale of unascertained goods no property in the goods is transferred to the buyer unless and until the goods are ascertained.

95 Indeed, the goods may become the property of the buyer without payment under the Unsolicited Goods and Services Act 1971.

96 *Poole* v *Smith's Car Sales (Balham) Ltd* [1962] 2 All ER 482.

97 In *re Ferrier* [1944] Ch 295.

98 See Chapter 3.

This rule lays down the fundamental rule that subject to s. 20A, for property to transfer the goods must be ascertained. In accordance with Re Wait,[99] unascertained goods become ascertained when they are identified after the contract as goods employed for the performance of a contract. The identification of goods after contract is an important step. Lord Mustill justified this by stating that 'common sense dictates that the buyer cannot acquire the title until it is known to what goods the title relates to'.[100]

This requirement is mandatory (subject to s. 20A) and it takes precedence over the intention of the parties.[101] Thus it can be argued that it limits freedom of contract afforded by s. 17 discussed above.[102] However, s. 17 expressly provides that it only operates in a sale of 'specific or ascertained goods'. There was no provision covering the passing of property in goods which are still unascertained; the Act clearly did not contemplate this as a legal possibility. No matter what the parties may have intended property cannot pass until the goods are ascertained. As per Mustill J:

> Whatever the intentions of the parties, where there is a contract for the sale of unascertained goods, no property can pass until the goods are ascertained: see s. 16 of the Sale of Goods Act 1893.[103] Once ascertainment has taken place, the passing of property depends on the intention of the parties and the circumstances of the case: see s. 17.[104]

This rule would still apply to contracts made before 19 September 1995 when the Sale of Goods (Amendment) Act 1995 came into force, although it is almost unforeseeable that an action could still arise out of a dispute on any such contract. After that date the position is regulated by the new s. 20A, 18, Rule 5, s. (3) and (4) (discussed below in section 10.2.3), but it is submitted that the last sentence of this dictum is still relevant. We now turn to s. 18, Rule 5

10.2.3.2 Section 18, Rule 5

When goods are ascertained and the parties' intention cannot be determined, s. 18, Rule 5,[105] applies. It provides:

> Where there is a contract for the sale of unascertained or future goods by description, and goods of that description and in a deliverable state are unconditionally appropriated to the contract, either by the seller with the assent of the buyer or by the buyer with the assent of the seller, the property in the goods then passes to the buyer; and the assent may be express or implied, and may be given either before or after the appropriation is made.

99 [1927] 1 Ch 606 (CA).

100 Re Goldcorp Exchange Ltd [1995] 1 ac 74(PC).

101 Before amendment by the Sale of Goods (Amendment) Act 1995, which added s. 20A, this led to certain problems – see section 10.2.3.

102 Sinead Eaton 'Protecting Prepaying Buyers of Unascertained Goods: Why 'Pay Before You Go' May be Bad for You Protecting Prepaying Buyers of Unascertained Goods' (2007) 36 *Common Law World Review* 50.

103 Now, of course, the 1979 Act: there is no change on this point.

104 *Karlshamns Oljefabriker* v *Eastport Navigation Corp* [1982] 1 All ER 208, 212 per Mustill J. See also *Hayman & Son* v *McLintock* [1907] SC 936.

105 s. 18 Rule 5 of the Sales of Goods Act 1979.

In simple terms, it states where the goods have become ascertained but the intentions of the parties regarding the passing of property is unclear, property will pass when, goods match the contract description,[106] are in a deliverable state, and are unconditionally appropriated to the contract by one party[107] with the assent (consent)[108] of the other. The meaning of 'description' in this section is not entirely clear; it could cover descriptive words used in the contract generally, or it could be confined to the kinds of description within the scope of s. 13. A buyer of unascertained goods will often not have seen the goods to be used for the performance of the contract in advance, so it is important that the right goods have been unconditionally appropriated to the contract.

Deliverable state

The meaning of this term, which also appears in Rule 1, has already been discussed in connection with that Rule.

Unconditional appropriation

Under the terms of Rule 5, an 'unconditional appropriation' is the usual method by which the property will pass. Put very briefly, the requirement of unconditional appropriation means that some ascertained and identified goods must be irrevocably attached or earmarked for the particular contract in question.[109] Subject to the question of assent, which is dealt with below, the property in the goods will then pass to the buyer. So the first and most vital question is how do ascertained goods become unconditionally appropriated to the contract? One of the commonest and simplest ways in which this happens is by delivery. If the seller actually delivers to the buyer goods answering the contract description, this is an appropriation, which, assuming it to be unconditional and subject to the question of assent, will then pass the property to the buyer, at least if the goods are delivered to the correct destination.[110]

Rule 5(2) gives another illustration of an unconditional appropriation:

> Where, in pursuance of the contract, the seller delivers the goods to the buyer or to a carrier or other bailee . . . (whether named by the buyer or not) for the purpose of transmission to the buyer, and does not reserve the right of disposal, he is to be taken to have unconditionally appropriated the goods to the contract.[111]

This sub-rule, like the whole of s. 18, had to be read subject to the unamended s. 16 because it was clear that if the seller delivered the goods to a carrier still mixed with other

[106] Implied term that goods must match the contract description in Sale of Goods Act 1979, s. 13(1) and see *Beale* v *Taylor* [1967] 1 WLR 1193.
[107] Usually, the seller.
[108] Usually, the buyer, see *Pignataro* v *Gilroy* [1919] 1B 459 (KB).
[109] [1994] 4 All ER 714.
[110] If the goods are not delivered to the correct destination, they remain at the seller's risk – see *CTN Cash and Carry Ltd* v *Gallagher Ltd* [1994] 4 All ER 714.
[111] See also s. 32(1), but note that this latter provision does not apply in the case of consumer sales – s. 32(4).

goods, no property could pass, because the goods were still unascertained, despite what would otherwise amount to an unconditional appropriation. So, for instance, in *Healy* v *Howlett & Sons*,[112] the defendant ordered 20 boxes of mackerel from the plaintiff, a fish exporter carrying on business in Ireland. The plaintiff dispatched 190 boxes and instructed the railway officials to earmark 20 of the boxes for the defendant and the remaining boxes for two other consignees. The train was delayed before the defendant's boxes were earmarked, and by the time this was done the fish had deteriorated. It was held that the property in the fish had not passed to the defendant before the boxes were earmarked and that they were, therefore, still at the seller's risk when they deteriorated. Because it was not possible to say which of the boxes belonged to the buyer until the earmarking had been done, no identified or ascertained goods had yet been appropriated to the contracts of each individual buyer.[113]

Apart from the particular instance given in Rule 5(2), the meaning of the term 'unconditional appropriation' has been considered on many occasions by the courts. The possibility of the appropriation being conditional is discussed further below. Here we shall concentrate on the concept of appropriation itself. Despite the fact that the word 'appropriated' has been said to be 'a term of legal art [which] has a certain definite meaning',[114] it is extremely difficult to define it with precision. One thing at least was clear, that where an unidentified part of a bulk was sold there could be no appropriation until there was a severance of the part sold from the rest and thus no passing of property. *Healy* v *Howlett & Sons*[115] is one authority for this. Another is *Laurie & Morewood* v *John Dudin & Son*.[116] Here the defendants owned a warehouse and were in possession of maize belonging to A. A sold part of it to B and B resold it to the plaintiffs, who obtained a delivery order and lodged it with the defendants. A, not having been paid by B, stopped delivery, and the plaintiffs then brought an action of detinue[117] against the defendants. The Court of Appeal disposed of the case on the ground that without severance, no property could have passed to the plaintiffs because the goods were not identified. The changes brought about by the 1995 Act would almost certainly produce the same result.

The question of appropriation has arisen in a number of different situations. One common type of case concerns builders or contractors who leave a contract uncompleted (often because they have become insolvent) and disputes then arise as to the ownership of materials brought onto the site by the builder. Of course, if the site itself belongs to the builder and he has merely contracted to sell or convey the completed building, it is

[112] [1917] 1 KB 337. Conversely, if the seller delivers goods to the buyer with the intention that the goods will lose their identity by being mixed with other goods, it is almost impossible to hold that property has not passed: *Borden (UK) Ltd* v *Scottish Timber Products Ltd* [1981] Ch 25; *South Australian Insurance Co* v *Randell* (1869) LR 3 PC 101. But see below, Chapter 15, as to the *Romalpa* case.

[113] As to the passing of property in such fact situations under the Sale of Goods (Amendment) Act 1995, see section 10.2.3. Of course, what ultimately was at issue in *Healy* v *Howlett* was the passing of risk, and, for the reasons explained above, the questions of the passing of risk and passing of property need to be considered separately. It is certainly possible that had the goods been specific in *Healy* v *Howlett*, they might have travelled at the seller's risk even though property in them had passed to the buyer.

[114] *Re Blyth Shipbuilding Co Ltd* [1926] Ch 494, 518 per Sargant LJ.

[115] [1917] 1 KB 337.

[116] [1926] 1 KB 223. See also *Wardar's (Import and Export) Co Ltd* v *W Norwood & Sons Ltd* [1968] 2 QB 663.

[117] The action brought against a party who refuses to deliver up goods to a person having an immediate right of possession over them.

almost impossible that the property in such materials could pass to the client before the building is completed and the land conveyed to the buyer. But if the site is already owned by the client, or the builder is working on renovation or repairs to an existing building, the owner of the site may claim that the property in the materials has passed to them, while the builder's creditors may dispute this and claim that the property remains in the builder.

As we have already seen, where goods are to be supplied and installed or fixed by the seller in a building or construction, so that the goods will become fixtures in the technical sense becoming attached to the land or a building on the land, the general rule or presumption is that property does not pass until the work of installation has been completed, or, anyhow, until the materials are 'affixed to or in a reasonable sense made part of the corpus'.[118] This is often explained by saying that the contract is for work and materials in such a case, rather than a sale of goods. Hence, if the contract is clearly intended to be for the sale of goods to be afterwards installed,[119] even by the seller, the Sale of Goods Act will apply, and property may pass on the making of the contract under Rule 1 if the goods are specific goods. It seems best, however, to explain these differences as resting on the intention of the parties and the nature of the transaction rather than on its technical classification. Whether it is a contract for the sale of goods or for work and materials is itself immaterial.[120]

So also, an ordinary supply of goods to a building site for ultimate incorporation into a building will usually be a sale of goods, and property will normally pass on delivery, if not sooner, though subject to any express contractual conditions, which are common in such sales. For instance, in *Santer-Automation Ltd* v *H C Goodman (Mechanical Services) Ltd*[121] the plaintiffs were subcontractors who had brought materials onto a site for incorporation into a building being constructed by the defendants, the main contractors for the Property Services Agency, a public body. The main contractors became insolvent and the Agency determined the contract with them, and proposed to use the materials and equipment brought onto the site by the plaintiffs. The plaintiffs claimed that the property in these materials was still vested in them under their conditions of work, but it was held that these conditions had never been accepted, and that the Agency's conditions governed because the claimants must have known of these conditions when they contracted with the main contractors. The Agency's conditions provided that the property in materials and equipment brought onto the site vested in them, so here the question of appropriation under Rule 5 simply did not arise.[122] The passing of property was governed by express contractual provision, not by the Act.

Where a seller, who is not involved in the construction works, delivers goods to a site under a contract with a contractor, the passing of property will depend on the contract

118 *Seath* v *Moore* (1886) 1 App Cas 350, 381 per Lord Watson. Of course the installation may not involve a transfer of property at all, as where a tenant installs furniture and fittings which do not become fixtures, and so remain his property. See, e.g., *Young* v *Dalgety PLC* (1987) 281 EG 427.

119 *Pritchett and Gold and Electrical Power Storage Co* v *Currie* [1916] 2 Ch 515.

120 See *Young & Marten Ltd* v *McManus Childs* [1969] 1 AC 454.

121 [1986] 2 FTLR 239.

122 *Cf. Dawber Williamson Roofing Ltd* v *Humberside CC* (1979) 14 Build LR 70, where the subcontractor succeeded, but standard building terms have been altered since this case.

between them. *Prima facie* the delivery would be an appropriation of the goods under Rule 5, but the position is often complicated by reservation of title clauses which enable the seller to claim title until they are paid.[123] Again, therefore, the question of appropriation would not strictly arise; although it may well be that the courts would decline to uphold a reservation of title where the goods have actually been incorporated into the building works.[124]

The question of appropriation has also arisen in a number of shipbuilding cases. In these cases, as in the case of all goods to be manufactured by the seller, the general presumption is that no property is to pass until the article is completed.[125] This is still the case even if the price is to be paid by instalments during the construction of the ship.[126] But it was said 'there is no doubt that a contract might be so framed as to give the purchaser power to claim the property in those parts which, when they are put together, make the complete ship'[127] and since then it has become customary for shipbuilding contracts to do something like this where the price is payable by instalments as the work proceeds. In *Re Blyth Shipbuilding Co*,[128] A agreed to build a ship for B, the price to be paid by instalments as the work proceeded. The contract provided that on the payment of the first instalment 'the vessel and all materials and things appropriated for her should thenceforth . . . become and remain the absolute property of the purchaser'.[129] A went bankrupt before the ship was complete. An amount of worked and unworked material remained in the yard at the relevant time, some of which was ready to be incorporated into the ship. It was held by the Court of Appeal that the property in the incomplete ship had passed to the buyers, but the worked and unworked material gave rise to more difficulty. It was held that neither had been sufficiently appropriated to pass the property, mainly because they had not yet been fixed to the body of the ship. Although complete and final fixing to the body of the ship was perhaps not necessary, it was held that the goods must be substantially in position so that to remove them would have involved undoing work already done.

Another kind of case arises where a seller manufactures goods for subsequent delivery to the buyer, and the goods are completed or virtually completed and ready for delivery, and the seller then becomes bankrupt or insolvent. If the buyer has paid the price, or part of the price in advance, they may wish to claim that the property in the goods has passed to them, while the seller's creditors, or liquidator, may argue that the property was still

[123] See *Hanson (W) (Harrow) Ltd* v *Rapid Civil Engineering & Usborne Developments Ltd* (1987) 38 Build LR 106.

[124] Possibly such incorporation might amount to a wrongful conversion on the part of the building owner, and, because this is not a contract of sale, they cannot rely on s. 24 of the Act. See *Dawber Williamson Roofing Ltd* v *Humberside CC* (1979) 14 Build LR 70

[125] *Reid* v *Macbeth* [1904] AC 223.

[126] *Laing & Sons* v *Barclay, Curle & Co* [1908] AC 35.

[127] Ibid., at p. 43 per Lord Halsbury.

[128] [1926] Ch 494. Strictly speaking, this case did not involve the meaning of a statutory 'appropriation' within Rule 5, but since the contract itself used the same term, the decision would seem an authority on the application of Rule 5.

[129] A clause of this kind does not deprive the buyer of any right of rejection they may have when the vessel is completed: *McDougall* v *Aeromarine of Emsworth Ltd* [1958] 1 WLR 1126.

in the seller. In *Carlos Federspiel & Co SA* v *Charles Twigg & Co Ltd*,[130] sellers manufactured bicycles to the buyers' order. The bicycles were made and packed in containers with the buyers' name and address on them, but before the goods could be shipped, the sellers became insolvent. It was held that the property had not passed to the buyers. After a comprehensive review of the authorities Pearson J summed up the law relating to appropriation in the following passage, the whole of which merits quotation:

> First, Rule 5 of s. 18 of the Act is one of the Rules for ascertaining the intention of the parties as to the time at which the property in the goods is to pass to the buyer unless a different intention appears. Therefore the element of common intention has always to be borne in mind. A mere setting apart or selection by the seller of the goods which they expect to use in performance of the contract is not enough. If that is all, they can change their mind and use those goods in performance of some other contract and use some other goods in performance of this contract. To constitute an appropriation of the goods to the contract the parties must have had, or be reasonably supposed to have had an intention to attach the contract irrevocably to those goods, so that those goods and no others are the subject of the sale and become the property of the buyer.
>
> Secondly, it is by agreement of the parties that the appropriation, involving a change of owner-ship, is made, although in some cases the buyer's assent to an appropriation is conferred in advance by the contract itself or otherwise.
>
> Thirdly, an appropriation by the seller with the assent of the buyer may be said always to involve an actual or constructive delivery[131]. If the seller retains possession, they do so as bailee for the buyer. There is a passage in Chalmers' *Sale of Goods Act*, 12th edn at p. 75 where it is said:
>
>> In the second place, if the decisions be carefully examined, it will be found that in every case where the property has been held to pass, there has been an actual or constructive delivery of the goods to the buyer.
>
> I think that is right, subject only to this possible qualification, that there may be after such constructive delivery an actual delivery still to be made by the seller under the contract. Of course, that is quite possible, because delivery is the transfer of possession, whereas appropriation transfers ownership. So there may be first an appropriation, constructive delivery, whereby the seller becomes bailee for the buyer, and then a subsequent actual delivery involving actual possession, and when I say that I have in mind in particular the cases cited, namely *Aldridge* v *Johnson*[132] and *Langton* v *Higgins*.[133]
>
> Fourthly, one has to remember s. 20 of the Sale of Goods Act, whereby the ownership and the risk are normally associated. Therefore, as it appears that there is reason for thinking, on the construction of the relevant documents, that the goods were, at all material times, still at the seller's risk, that is *prima facie* an indication that the property had not passed to the buyer.
>
> Fifthly, usually, but not necessarily, the appropriating act is the last act to be performed by the seller. For instance, if delivery is to be taken at the seller's premises and the seller has appropriated the goods when they have made the goods ready and identified them and placed them in position to be taken by the buyer and has so informed the buyer, and if the buyer agrees to come and take them, that is the assent to the appropriation. But if there is a further act, an important

[130] [1957] 1 Lloyd's Rep 240, 255–6.

[131] The concept of a 'constructive delivery', though sometimes relied upon in older cases, involves use of a fiction and does not seem particularly helpful. But the concept may be important in some cases concerning the transfer of title by a non-owner – see Chapter 12, and in solving the apparent conflict between the Act's risk provisions and the seller's duty to deliver goods of the right quality, see Chapter 7.

[132] (1857) 7 E & B 885.

[133] (1859) 4 H & N 402

and decisive act, to be done by the seller, then there is *prima facie* evidence that probably the property does not pass until the final act is done.

Probably, the decisive fact in this case was that the sellers were responsible for arranging shipment of the goods. By contrast, in *Hendy Lennox Ltd* v *Grahame Puttick Ltd*[134] the sellers assembled generators which had been ordered by buyers and it was held that the property in the generators passed when they were ready for delivery, and buyers received from the sellers the invoices together with delivery notes, containing the serial numbers of the generators sold. At this stage, the sellers had done everything they needed to do under the contract; the serial numbers enabled the particular generators sold to be identified, and nothing remained except for the buyers to pay the invoices and take delivery.

A New Zealand case has gone so far as to hold that where sellers made rope for the buyers' order and stored it in a warehouse from which deliveries were made as requested, there was an unconditional appropriation.[135] This case is also authority for saying that even if the goods are stored with other similar goods they are sufficiently earmarked if the sellers can identify the particular goods set aside for the buyers. It is immaterial that nobody else could tell which goods were meant for which buyer.[136] However, it is doubtful whether this would be an acceptable rule where the only 'appropriation' is in the seller's mind, and there is no independent objective evidence of the 'appropriation'; for example, in the seller's books or records.

Where goods are in the possession of a third party, such as a warehouse keeper, and the third party sets the goods aside for delivery to the buyer, the goods are unconditionally appropriated at the latest when a delivery order is accepted.[137]

It may well be that what is necessary to constitute an unconditional appropriation will vary according to the type of goods in question and the general circumstances of the case. In particular, where goods are being manufactured by the seller, the courts will not too readily infer that the materials have been appropriated since this might hamper the freedom of the seller to manufacture the goods as they think best. This consideration does not apply in the case of goods to be grown by the seller, and here it might well be held that the property in the goods, if sufficiently designated, passes as soon as they come into existence. So, also, where an unidentified part of a specified bulk is sold, the only thing necessary for appropriation is the separation of the part sold from the rest, with the assent of the parties.[138] In *Aldridge* v *Johnson*,[139] the plaintiff agreed to buy 100 quarters of barley out of a particular parcel of 200 quarters which he had inspected. It was held that as soon as the seller filled some sacks sent by the buyer with the barley, the property passed, even though the sacks were still in the seller's possession.

[134] [1984] 2 All ER 152.

[135] *Donaghy's Rope and Twine Co Ltd* v *Wright, Stephenson & Co* (1906) 25 NZLR 641.

[136] See also *Re Stapylton Fletcher* [1994] 1 WLR 1181, discussed at section 10.2.3 below.

[137] *Wardar's (Import & Export) Co Ltd* v *W Norwood & Sons Ltd* [1968] 2 QB 663. Cf. *Hayman & Son* v *McLintock* 1907 SC 936.

[138] This point concerning appropriation is still valid, but before that occurs the effect of the Sale of Goods (Amendment) Act 1995 in such cases must now be noted – see section 10.2.3

[139] (1857) 7 E & B 885.

Conditional appropriation

As to the qualification that the appropriation must be 'unconditional' if it is to pass the property, the general and most important rule is that the appropriation is not unconditional if the seller only means to let the buyer have the goods on payment.[140] *Prima facie* any express or implied contractual stipulation[141] showing that the seller intends to reserve some rights over the goods themselves (and not just contractual rights) until they have been fully paid makes the appropriation conditional, and prevents the property from passing until that happens.

Some important types of conditional contracts of sale are considered in s. 19, which actually applies to the sale of both specific and unascertained goods, but as, in practice, its application to unascertained goods is far more common it has been reserved for consideration here. Section 19(1) is as follows:

> Where there is a contract for the sale of specific goods or where goods are subsequently appropriated to the contract, the seller may, by the terms of the contract or appropriation, reserve the right of disposal of the goods until certain conditions are fulfilled; and in such a case, notwithstanding the delivery of the goods to the buyer, or to a carrier or other bailee . . . for the purpose of transmission to the buyer, the property in the goods does not pass to the buyer until the conditions imposed by the seller are fulfilled.

The courts have been very ready to find that the seller has reserved the right of disposal and that the buyer does not acquire property in the goods before actual delivery. In *Re Shipton Anderson & Co Ltd and Harrison Bros & Co Ltd*,[142] the owner of a specific parcel of wheat in a warehouse sold it on the terms 'payment cash within seven days against transfer order'. The goods were requisitioned by the government under emergency powers before delivery to the buyer. It was held by the Court of Appeal that the express term quoted above was in effect a right of disposal reserved by the seller, as he was not bound to hand over a delivery order until payment. Consequently, the property had not yet passed and the contract was frustrated by the seizure of the goods.

Section 19(1) is only a generalisation of the specific case dealt with by s. 19(2), which is concerned with goods sent by sea. Under this subsection, a shipper who receives from the carrier bills of lading whereby the goods are deliverable to the shipper or their order is taken to reserve the right of disposal because they can hold on to the bill of lading until they are paid or otherwise satisfied, nobody can obtain the delivery of the goods without the bills of lading (at least without giving the shipping company an indemnity against the possible consequences), and the seller's possession of these, where the goods are deliverable to the seller, therefore enables them to treat the goods as continued security for payment. As this is by far the most important illustration of the reservation of the

[140] *Stein, Forbes & Co Ltd* v *County Tailoring Co Ltd* (1916) 86 LJKB 448; see also *Cheetham & Co Ltd* v *Thornham Spinning Co Ltd* [1964] 2 Lloyd's Rep 17, which could perhaps have been decided on this ground. See too *Mitsui & Co Ltd* v *Flota Mercante Grancolumbiana SA* [1989] 1 All ER 951, discussed in Chapter 13.

[141] Moreover, a condition can be imposed on appropriation, even if not in the contract – see Bradgate [1988] JBL 477.

[142] [1915] 3 KB 676.

right of disposal, more detailed consideration of this question will be postponed until Chapter 13, where export sales are dealt with.[143]

Yet another type of conditional contract is dealt with by s. 19(3):

> Where the seller of goods draws on the buyer for the price, and transmits the bill of exchange and bill of lading to the buyer together to secure acceptance or payment of the bill of exchange, the buyer is bound to return the bill of lading if he does not honour the bill of exchange, and if he wrongfully retains the bill of lading the property in the goods does not pass to him.

In other words, the transfer of the property by the bill of lading in such a case is conditional upon the bill of exchange being honoured, and if, for example, the buyer should become bankrupt with the bill of lading still in their possession, and not having accepted the bill of exchange, the seller will be able to claim the goods. Similarly, if the buyer retains the bill of lading without paying for it, they are in breach of their duties to the seller, for example if they take delivery of the goods or send the bill of lading on to a sub-buyer. In such circumstances, the buyer may be sued either for the tort of conversion or for the price of the goods, and their liability will be precisely the same in either case.[144]

It should be noted, however, that even if the property does not pass to the buyer because of the operation of this section, the seller is at risk in one important respect. Although they may be protected against the risk of the buyer becoming insolvent before they have paid for the goods, the seller is at risk that the buyer may resell the goods to a third party. As will be seen more fully in Chapter 23, the buyer may in this situation be able to pass a good title to a third party under various provisions of the Act, even though property has not yet passed to them because the seller has reserved a right of disposal. If the buyer actually obtains the possession of the goods or of the bill of lading and transfers them to a sub-buyer who takes in good faith and for value, the sub-buyer gets a good title under s. 25(1), s. 47(2), and s. 10 of the Factors Act 1889.[145]

Reference was previously made to Rule 3 under which, in a sale of specific goods, the passing of the property is postponed if the seller is bound to weigh, measure, test or do some other act for the purpose of ascertaining the price. Although this Rule is confined to sales of specific goods, it seems that the position is the same in a sale of unascertained goods. In *National Coal Board* v *Gamble*,[146] the appellants supplied coal as part of a bulk sale to a purchaser by loading it onto the buyer's lorry at a colliery. The coal was loaded by means of a hopper and subsequently driven to a weighbridge, where the weight of the coal was ascertained and the statutory weight-ticket supplied. It was held that the property did not pass until the coal had been weighed and the ticket given to and accepted by the buyer. The court had no doubt that if too much had been loaded onto the lorry the seller could have insisted on the excess being unloaded. It seems (although this was not stated in the judgments) that the correct analysis of the facts was that, although the coal was

143 See Chapter 13.
144 *Ernest Scragg & Sons Ltd* v *Perseverance Banking & Trust Co Ltd* [1973] 2 Lloyd's Rep 101.
145 *Cahn* v *Pockett's Bristol Channel Co Ltd* [1899] 1 QB 643.
146 [1959] 1 QB 11.

appropriated to the contract by being loaded onto the lorry, the appropriation was not unconditional until it was weighed and the weight-ticket accepted by the buyer.

On the other hand, in *Edwards* v *Ddin*[147] (a prosecution under the Theft Act 1968) a different result was arrived at. Here it was said that when a person buys petrol at a filling station, the property passes as soon as it is put in the tank of the buyer's vehicle. There is no reservation of rights by the seller, and the appropriation is unconditional. If the buyer does not pay, they may be guilty of an offence and can, of course, be sued for the price, but the property will have passed. It is perhaps unclear if the seller can detain the buyer's vehicle or attempt to drain the petrol out of the tank in exercise of his lien. (For further discussion of the seller's lien, see Chapter 15.)

Assent

The assent which Rule 5 requires for the appropriation may be express or implied. Where, therefore, the defendant sold some rice to the plaintiff from a specified parcel at a particular place, and sent the plaintiff a note of appropriation, his assent was implied from his failure to reply for a whole month.[148] Consequently, although Rules 2 and 3 only require notice to be given to the buyer of the fulfilment of conditions in a sale of specific goods while Rule 5 requires the buyer's assent, there may often be little difference in practice.

Rule 5(1) says that the assent may be given before or after the appropriation is made, and in some cases the assent may be inferred from the facts which take place when the contract is made, or when or before the appropriation takes place. So it has been held that the dispatch and receipt of invoices and delivery orders which clearly identified the goods being sold were enough to transfer property even though there was no further act or indication of assent to the appropriation by the buyer.[149]

As we have seen, Rule 5(2) states that where the goods are delivered to a carrier for shipment to the buyer the goods are taken to be unconditionally appropriated to the contract. Although this sub-rule does not actually say that the buyer's assent must be taken to have been given in these circumstances, it is nevertheless clear that the customary course of business rests on the assumption that shipment is an unconditional appropriation with the assent of the buyer.[150] The buyer's assent is to be inferred from the nature of the transaction itself. It does not follow that property is always transferred on shipment; whether it is transferred then or later depends on the nature and terms of the contract. These questions are discussed in Chapter 24. Here it is merely desired to stress that the apparent absence of a prior assent to the appropriation does not prevent property passing on shipment.

147 [1976] 1 WLR 943. And see also *Re Charge Card Services Ltd* [1988] 3 All ER 702, 706 where it was accepted by the CA that the contract is made in such a case when the tank is filled.

148 *Pignataro* v *Gilroy & Son* [1919] 1 KB 459. But this is of course subject to the need for the goods to be ascertained.

149 *Hendy Lennox Ltd* v *Grahame Puttick Ltd* [1984] 2 All ER 152.

150 The most explicit authority on this point appears to be in dicta of the Australian High Court – see *James* v *Commonwealth* (1939) 62 CLR 339, 377; *Saffron* v *Société Minière Cafrika* (1958) 100 CLR 231, 242.

Transfer of property without unconditional appropriation

As we have seen under s. 18 Rule 5(1), the usual way in which property in unascertained goods is transferred to the buyer is by the goods becoming unconditionally appropriated to the contract, but it is not the only possible way. In *Karlshamns Oljefabriker* v *Eastport Navigation Corp*,[151] the plaintiffs bought 6,000 tons of copra c.i.f. Karlshamns. The sellers shipped 16,000 tons of copra on one ship, part of which was intended for the plaintiffs and part for other buyers. A small quantity, surplus to all the contractual requirements of the various buyers, was bought by F from the sellers and resold by them to the plaintiffs. The plaintiffs thus obtained bills of lading first for the 6,000 tons, and second for the small extra quantity sold to F. But all the copra was shipped in undivided bulk, and it was held that no property could have passed on shipment, or on the transfer of the bills of lading. The ship called first at Rotterdam and then at Hamburg, discharging all the copra meant for other buyers, so that at this stage the only copra left was that destined for the plaintiffs. It was held by Mustill J that at this stage the property passed to the plaintiffs because the goods had become ascertained by a process of 'exhaustion'. Mustill J went on to hold that it is not always necessary that the goods should be appropriated to the contract under Rule 5, although this is the commonest method by which the goods are ascertained. The essential requirements of the law, he held, are (1) that the goods should be, or have become, ascertained, and (2) that the parties should intend that the property be transferred. There is no independent third requirement that the goods should be unconditionally appropriated to the contract.[152] Appropriation is only one way of ascertaining the goods. Mustill J also held that there was no reason why property should not pass even though it was not possible to say which part of the copra was to be taken to be the 6,000 tons sold by the sellers direct, and which the extra quantity sold through F.[153] The result of this case is confirmed by s. 1 of the Sale of Goods (Amendment) Act 1995, discussed below, which adds s. (3) and (4) to s. 18, Rule 5.

10.2.4 Sale of unidentified part of an identified bulk

We have seen above that, no matter what the intention of the parties may be, the effect of s. 16 in its original form was that the property in goods could not pass until they had been ascertained. We have also seen that this meant that where an unidentified and unascertained part of some bulk or whole was sold, then even though the bulk itself might be identified and ascertained, no property could pass until the part sold had been in some way physically severed or segregated from the remainder of the bulk, or at least earmarked so that the parts appropriated could readily be identified. The effect of s. 16 in this respect caused some concern in certain contexts, and the Law Commissions published a Report on the subject.[154] It is now necessary to say something further by way of explanation of

[151] [1982] 1 All ER 208, following *Wait and James* v *Midland Bank* (1926) 31 Com Cas 172.
[152] This was also accepted by Oliver J in In *re London Wine Co (Shippers) Ltd* (1986) PCC 121.
[153] In other words, the plaintiffs were entitled to the whole, albeit under separate contracts.
[154] 'Sale of Goods Forming Part of a Bulk' (Law Com. No. 215, 1993).

these concerns, and the reforms effected by the Sale of Goods (Amendment) Act 1995 consequential on them.[155]

The legal problems which arise from the sale of an unidentified part of a definite bulk or whole involve two sets of relationships, although only one of them is of direct concern to the subject-matter of this book. These two relationships are: first, that between seller and buyer and, secondly, that between the buyer and the carrier where the goods are in the process of being transported (by sea or air, for instance) from seller to buyer. The relationship which concerns us is that of the seller and buyer.

It often happens that the transaction between seller and buyer is completed in all essentials, even to the extent of the buyer actually paying for the goods, while the goods are still in the possession of the seller themself, or of a carrier. If at that stage the goods were ascertained and identified, the property in them would pass to the buyer and two consequences would follow from this. First, the buyer would be protected from the risk of the seller's insolvency because if the property has passed to the buyer they can simply lay claim to the goods themselves if the seller becomes bankrupt. And secondly, the goods would *prima facie* be at the buyer's risk, so that any subsequent deterioration or damage to the goods would no longer be the responsibility of the seller. But where the goods were an unidentified part of a bulk so that property could not pass as a result of s. 16 in its original form these consequences would not follow, and the results often seemed largely fortuitous. We have already seen one example of these fortuitous results, namely *Healy* v *Howlett & Sons*[156] where the property in the fish being sold to the defendant would in the ordinary way have passed to him and with it the risk of delay and deterioration, when the goods were dispatched to the buyer. But because in that particular case the goods were dispatched with similar goods to other buyers, and were not physically earmarked for the defendant himself, the property could not pass and neither did the risk. That result was somewhat unsatisfactory because the outcome depended on the happenstance of when the railway officials allocated the defendant his boxes. This particular problem is, however, unusual because in most cases of this nature (particularly where the goods are dispatched by sea) there is no doubt that the risk will pass on shipment, even if the property does not or cannot pass, and there is, indeed, one leading authority which suggests that even in other circumstances the risk in an unidentified part of a specified bulk may pass before the property.[157]

A more disturbing consequence of s. 16 was that a buyer might find that although they thought he had obtained the property in the goods and had paid for them, they had no property, and remained vulnerable to the risk of the seller's insolvency because of the purely accidental or fortuitous fact that the goods were not ascertained. This problem was perhaps most acute where part of a large cargo of goods was sold while they were at sea, as happened in the *Karlshamns Oljefabriker* case, which was discussed above. This became a more frequent occurrence as a result of larger ships, capable of carrying bigger cargoes, and buyers therefore often buying proportionately smaller quantities. Buyers

[155] See comments on the Law Commissions' Report and on the Act by Bradgate and White [1994] LMCLQ 315; Ulph [1996] LMCLQ 93; Burns [1996] MLR 260 and Gullifer [1999] LMCLQ 93.

[156] [1917] 1 KB 337 – but see section 10.2.2.

[157] See Chapter 15.

often receive bills of lading from sellers (who have, of course, received the bills from the shipping company concerned) and bills of lading are universally regarded by commercial parties as firm documents of title. So buyers (and also banks) quite happily paid for bills of lading in the belief that the bills give an unqualified right to the possession of the goods, yet in these cases where the bills of lading only cover part of a bulk cargo it was clear that no unqualified title was passed because of s. 16 of the Act.[158]

That these difficulties could also arise in other contexts is shown by the facts of *In re London Wine Co (Shippers) Ltd*.[159] In this case a company sold wine to customers, while retaining possession of the wine. The customers paid for the wine, as well as for subsequent storage charges, and the seller gave the buyers 'certificates of title', but there was no actual earmarking or physical segregation of the wine sold to the different customers. The wine company became insolvent, and the receiver (representing mortgagees or chargees) claimed that all the wine still belonged to the company, a claim which was ultimately upheld by Oliver J in a lengthy and complex judgment.[160]

The situation was further complicated in this case because separate claims were made on behalf of several different groups of buyers. One group claimed that in some cases the buyer had bought the whole stock of a particular description of wine owned by the company, so that the property might have passed by 'exhaustion' as in the *Karlshamns Oljefabriker* case, discussed above. But this claim failed because the wine had not been sold *as part of a particular consignment or bulk*, but had merely been described as 'lying in bond'. So although the sellers may genuinely have intended in their own minds to tie in the sales with a particular stock of wine of that description, they were under no legal obligation to do so. That particular stock of wine belonged to them, not the buyers; the sellers could have disposed of it elsewhere and bought further stocks to satisfy the buyers without any breach of contract.

A second group of buyers who had together bought the whole stock of a particular description of wine argued that between them they could have been treated as co-buyers, so that property could have passed to them jointly. But this claim failed for the same reason as in the case of the first group of buyers. A third group of buyers had actually received acknowledgments (attornments) either from the company itself, or from independent warehouse keepers who held the stock, but their claims also failed because of the basic fact that no ascertainment had taken place under s. 16. However, it must be noted that in *Re Stapylton Fletcher*,[161] in which cases of wine were *separately* stored for a group of customers, it was held that for the purposes of s. 16 property had passed to the customers, the customers taking as tenants in common.[162] Judge Paul Baker QC, citing Staughton J's review of the authorities in *Indian Oil Corp Ltd* v *Greenstone Shipping Co*

[158] A point finally appreciated by a Dutch court applying English law in *The Gosforth, S en S* 1985 Nr 91.

[159] (1986) PCC 121.

[160] Oliver J's judgment was approved by the Privy Council in *Re Goldcorp Exchange Ltd* [1994] 2 All ER 806, in which, however, the facts were not precisely the same – the case involved claims to unallocated stocks of bullion, and the PC was of the view that the parties could not have intended to create an interest in its general stock of bullion which would have inhibited the (now insolvent) bullion company's dealings in it. See also *Mac-Jordan Construction Ltd* v *Brookmount Erostin Ltd* [1992] BCLC 350.

[161] [1994] 1 WLR 1181.

[162] See also *Indian Oil* v *Greenstone Shipping Co SA (Panama)* [1988] QB 345.

SA (Panama),[163] concluded that it was possible to use the tenancy in common as a tool for remedying unforeseen mixing, and that if the creation of a tenancy in common could be brought about by construction of law, it could equally be brought about by agreement express or to be inferred from the circumstances. He concluded that from the evidence it could readily be inferred that the parties intended the property in the goods to pass when they were set aside for storage. It was the separation of the goods from the company's trading assets, whether done physically, or by giving instructions to a bonded warehouse keeper, which caused the goods to be ascertained for the purposes of s. 16.[164]

As a result of these difficulties (as well as difficulties arising from the relations between buyer and carrier, which are not strictly within the subject-matter of this book), the Law Commissions suggested that there should be a new rule on sale of goods out of a bulk which would enable property in an undivided share to pass before ascertainment of goods relating to specific sales contracts.[165] We must now deal with this.

10.2.4.1 The Sale of Goods (Amendment) Act 1995[166]

This Act, which came into force on 19 September 1995 (but had no retrospective effect on any contract concluded before that date),[167] implements the recommendations of the English and Scottish Law Commissions in the Report discussed above. The Act does two things: (1) it puts into statutory form the doctrine of 'ascertainment by exhaustion', and (2) it enables property in an undivided share forming part of an identified bulk to pass before ascertainment of the goods relating to the specific sales contract or contracts. We will deal with these in turn, but first we must consider what is meant by 'bulk' for these purposes.

The definition of 'bulk' for the purposes of these subsections

Section 2 of the 1995 Act provides that in s. 61(1) of the 1979 Act, after the definition of 'action' there shall be inserted the following definition:

> 'bulk' means a mass of goods of the same kind which—
> (a) is contained in a defined space or area; and
> (b) is such that any goods in the bulk are interchangeable with any other goods therein of the same number or quantity; . . .

Ascertainment by exhaustion

As recommended by the Law Commissions, the effect of the doctrine of ascertainment by exhaustion[168] is now confirmed by s. 1 of the Sale of Goods (Amendment) Act 1995. This inserts the following words:

[163] [1988] QB 345.
[164] Compare *Customs and Excise Commissioners* v *Everwine Ltd* [2003] EWCA Civ 953.
[165] As is the case under the Uniform Commercial Code, Art. 2-105(4). See Law Com. No. 215 (1993), para. 2.21.
[166] 1995 c. 28.
[167] So that the old rules set out above still apply to such contracts – 1995 Act, s. 3(2).
[168] See section 10.2.2.

(2) In section 18 of the 1979 Act, at the end of rule 5 there shall be added the following—

(3) Where there is a contract for the sale of a specified quantity of unascertained goods in a deliver-able state forming part of a bulk which is identified either in the contract or by subsequent agreement between the parties and the bulk is reduced to (or to less than) that quantity, then, if the buyer under that contract is the only buyer to whom goods are then due out of the bulk—
   (a) the remaining goods shall be taken as appropriated to that contract at the time when the bulk is so reduced; and
   (b) the property in those goods then passes to that buyer.

(4) Paragraph (3) above applies also (with the necessary modifications) where a bulk is reduced to (or less than) the aggregate of the quantities due to a single buyer under separate contracts relating to that bulk and he is the only buyer to whom goods are then due out of that bulk.

It should be noted that this section applies not only where there is only one contract with one buyer, but also where there is more than one contract with one buyer. It also applies where there is more than one buyer initially, but because of deliveries to the other buyers, there is left only one buyer entitled to the residue of the bulk.

The situation where there is more than one buyer entitled to the identified bulk is dealt with by the next subsection of s. 1 of the 1995 Act.

Undivided shares in goods forming part of a bulk

Section 16 of the Sale of Goods Act 1979 is amended by insertion of the words 'Subject to section 20A below . . . '. After s. 20 of the 1979 Act the following section is inserted:

20A (1) This section applies to a contract for the sale of a specified quantity of unascertained goods if the following conditions are met—
   (a) the goods or some of them form part of a bulk which is identified either in the contract or by subsequent agreement between the parties; and
   (b) the buyer has paid the price for some or all of the goods which are the subject of the contract and which form part of the bulk.

(2) Where this section applies then (unless the parties agree otherwise), as soon as the conditions specified in paragraphs (a) and (b) of subsection (1) above are met or at such later time as the parties may agree—
   (a) property in an undivided share in the bulk is transferred to the buyer, and
   (b) the buyer becomes owner in common of the bulk.

(3) Subject to subsection (4) below, for the purposes of this section the undivided share of a buyer in a bulk at any time shall be such share as the quantity of goods paid for and due to the buyer out of the bulk bears to the quantity of goods in the bulk at that time.

(4) Where the aggregate of the undivided shares of buyers in a bulk determined under subsection (3) above would at any time exceed the whole of the bulk at that time, the undivided share in the bulk of each buyer shall be reduced proportionately so that the aggregate of the undivided shares is equal to the whole bulk.

(5) Where a buyer has paid the price for only some of the goods due to him out of a bulk, any delivery to the buyer out of the bulk shall, for the purposes of this section, be ascribed in the first place to the goods in respect of which payment has been made.

(6) For the purposes of this section payment of part of the price for any goods shall be treated as payment for a corresponding part of the goods.

Thus for the section to apply, three conditions must be satisfied: (1) there must be a sale of a specified quantity;[169] (2) the bulk must be identified;[170] (3) the buyer must have paid for some or all of the goods.[171] The new section is not limited to goods in a deliverable state.[172] It is also concerned with *quantity*, not shares expressed as fractions or percentage. The effect of s. 20A(3) is that the buyer's undivided share is such a share as the goods paid for and due to them bear to the quantity of goods in the bulk *at that time*. Where deliveries have been made to the buyer of some of the goods forming part of the bulk, and the buyer has paid for only some of the goods, the deliveries are to be ascribed in the first place to the goods paid for.[173]

Sections 20A(1)(b), (3) and (5) make reference to the case where a buyer has paid for some only of the goods due from the bulk under the contract. Part-payments would not normally be treated as relating to any particular portion of the goods due under the contract; it was necessary therefore for s. 20A(6) to provide that part-payments are to be treated as payments *for* part.

The aggregate shares of two or more buyers can never exceed the whole of the bulk.[174] In such cases, the undivided share of each buyer is reduced proportionately so that the aggregate of the undivided shares is equal to the whole of the bulk.[175]

Unless otherwise agreed, property in an undivided share passes as soon as the buyer has paid for all, or some, of the contract goods, and the buyer becomes an owner in common of the bulk.[176] This does not seem to address the allocation of risk between buyer and seller. Section 20B(3)(c) provides that nothing in the section shall affect the rights of any buyer under their contract, and the Report indicates that the co-ownership of the bulk is without prejudice to the buyers' contractual rights.[177] They are still entitled to goods which conform to the contract in quantity and quality. Presumably, then, risk passes when property passes under s. 18, Rule 5; though delay on the part of the buyer in taking delivery could affect this.[178]

169 As opposed to a sale of a fraction such as a third of a bulk – see Law Com. No. 215, para. 6.3.

170 1995 Act, s. 2(a) amending 1979 Act, s. 61(1), as indicated above. The Law Commissions give the following illustrations of an identified bulk: (a) a cargo of wheat in a named ship; (b) a mass of barley in an identified silo; (c) the oil in an identified storage tank; (d) cases of wine (all of the same kind) in an identified cellar; (e) ingots of gold (all of the same kind) in an identified vault; (f) bags of fertiliser (all of the same kind) in an identified storehouse; (g) a heap of coal in the open at an identified location. See, ibid., para. 4.3. Thus the seller's general stock is not intended to be an identified bulk – ibid.

171 Section 20A(1)(b), added by 1995 Act, s. 1(3) and ibid., para. 6.4. The reason for this exclusion is that the buyer who has not paid suffers no loss because payment and delivery are concurrent conditions – s. 28. Unfortunately, this appears to have the consequence that a seller's liquidator can decide whether or not to deliver according to whether the market price of the goods is above or below the contract price.

172 Ibid., para. 5.6 – goods forming part of an undivided share would never be in a deliverable state within the meaning of s. 61(5), 1979 Act.

173 Section 20A(5), added by 1995 Act, s. 1(3). The definition of 'delivery' in s. 61(1) is amended by adding the words 'except that in relation to sections 20A and 20B above it includes such appropriation of goods to the contract as results in property in the goods being transferred to the buyer'. As to 'unconditional appropriation'.

174 Section 20A(4).

175 Ibid.

176 Section 20A(2), added by 1995 Act, s. 1(3).

177 Paragraph 4.34.

178 Under s. 20(2) – see *Sterns Ltd* v *Vickers Ltd*, discussed in Chapter 11, at section 11.2

Deemed consent by co-owner to dealings in bulk goods

The effect of creating undivided shares in an identified bulk would be similar to the situation which existed in relation to undivided shares in land in England before 1926: it would require all the part-owners to be joined in order to transfer any part of the bulk, and in turn the tracing of title to each part share.[179] Section 20B deals with this by deeming consent by the other co-owners to a sale by one co-owner:

> (1) A person who has become an owner in common of a bulk by virtue of section 20A above shall be deemed to have consented to—
> (a) any delivery of goods out of the bulk to any other owner in common of the bulk, being goods which are due to him under his contract;
> (b) any dealing with or removal, delivery or disposal of goods in the bulk by any other person who is an owner in common of the bulk in so far as the goods fall within that co-owner's undivided share in the bulk at the time of the dealing, removal, delivery or disposal.
> (2) No cause of action shall accrue to anyone against a person by reason of that person having acted in accordance with paragraph (a) or (b) of subsection (1) above in reliance on any consent deemed to have been given under that subsection.
> (3) Nothing in this section or section 20A above shall—
> (a) impose an obligation on a buyer of goods out of a bulk to compensate any other buyer of goods out of that bulk for any shortfall in the goods received by that other buyer;
> (b) affect any contractual arrangement between buyers of goods out of a bulk for adjustments between themselves; or
> (c) affect the rights of any buyer under his contract.

Subsection (1)(b) above makes it clear that each co-owner can deal with goods within their share without needing the consent of the other co-owners. As noted above, the definition of 'delivery' is amended in relation to this subsection.

The purpose of s. 20B(2) is to protect liquidators and other such persons who step into the buyer's shoes on their insolvency.[180] They are protected against any action by other co-owning buyers who may receive short delivery because the bulk is insufficient to meet all claims, as a result of any dealing with the goods of the sort specified in s. 20B(1)(a) or (b).

Section 20B(3) makes it clear that the rules do not: (a) impose any obligation on a buyer who takes delivery of goods out of a bulk to compensate others who receive short delivery as a result; (b) affect any contractual arrangements between the buyers for adjustments between themselves; or (c) alter or diminish contractual rights of the buyer against the seller. If a seller, having sold 50 tonnes out of an identified bulk of 100 tonnes, were subsequently to sell 60 tonnes to a second buyer who bought in good faith without notice, the second buyer would acquire a good title by virtue of s. 24 of the Act,[181] but the first buyer would still have a remedy against the seller for non-delivery of 10 tonnes. Similarly, any sub-buyer of the first buyer who had been sold 50 tonnes would have a remedy for the shortfall of 10 tonnes against the first buyer.

[179] See Co. Litt. L.3.C.4.S.292; *Williams on Real Property* (23rd edn, 1920), p. 150.
[180] Paragraph 6.7.
[181] See Chapter 12.

The effect of these provisions

Therefore, if a buyer who has agreed to buy 50 tonnes out of a bulk of 100 tonnes has paid 50 per cent of the price, and taken delivery of 10 tonnes, they would be taken to have paid for a further 15 tonnes. The buyer's entitlement as a proportion will necessarily fluctuate as the size of the bulk fluctuates. If the bulk is reduced to such a point that it is the same or less than the buyer's entitlement, the buyer will be entitled to the whole under s. 18, Rule 5(3), introduced by the 1995 Act, s. 1(2).

It was perfectly possible for two or more persons to own goods in common under suitably drafted contracts under the law as it was before the 1995 Act came into force (to own 'undivided shares' as the law puts it).[182] Indeed, it has been held that if a seller appropriates goods to the contract, so that property passes to the buyer, and the seller *thereafter* wrongfully (even accidentally) mixes goods of their own with the goods sold (as where an oil cargo, for instance, is sold and then other oil is placed in the same tanks) the buyer and the seller would thereupon become co-owners of the resulting whole.[183] And presumably it must be possible for one person to sell an undivided share in specific goods to another so that the buyer then becomes a co-owner with the seller. It is, indeed, quite common for several individuals to be co-owners of certain types of property; for example, racehorses, and there seems no reason why one owner cannot sell a share in a horse so that the buyer becomes a co-owner.[184] Similarly, the parties could become co-owners where a buyer or buyers are sold a specified share in an identified bulk expressed as a fraction of the whole,[185] provided it was clear from the terms of the contract or the surrounding circumstances that was the intention of the parties. Any lingering doubts about these matters should be put to rest by the amendments to s. 61 of the 1979 Act effected by the 1995 Act.[186] 'Goods' now includes an undivided share in goods. 'Specific goods' includes an undivided share, specified as a fraction of the goods identified or agreed upon, so that the sale of a quarter share in a racehorse is a sale of specific goods. But such a transaction is different from a sale where the intention is that goods forming part of an unascertained bulk will ultimately be divided and part transferred to the buyer, while parts either remain with the seller or are to be transferred to a different buyer or buyers. This is the situation in which ss. 16 and 17 of the Act prevented the property from passing and which is addressed by the provisions of the 1995 Act discussed above.

[182] See *Re Stapylton Fletcher*, section 10.2.2 above.

[183] *Indian Oil Corp Ltd* v *Greenstone Shipping Co SA* [1988] QB 345.

[184] In *Re Sugar Properties (Derisley Wood) Ltd* [1988] BCLC 146 it was held that a charge of such a share did not require registration under Companies Act 1985 (as was then applicable), same position seems likely under the equivalent provisions in the 2006 Act (see ss. 859A-Q).

[185] Section 2(2) recognises a sale between one part owner and another, but there was nevertheless some doubt whether the sale of an undivided share was a sale of goods. The Law Commissions' Report No. 215 recommended that the point be clarified – para. 5.3.

[186] See the Law Commissions' Report, para. 5.3 et seq.

The position in equity prior to the 1995 Act

While common law insisted on identification of the particular thing sold, equity was apparently less stringent.[187] In *Tailby* v *Official Receiver*,[188] Lord Watson stated the single requirement of equity 'which must be fulfilled in order to make the assignee's right attach to a future chose in action, which is that on its coming into existence it shall answer the description in the assignment, or, in other words, that it shall be capable of being identified as the thing, or as one of the very things assigned'. It seems to have been thought that physical identification or ascertainment might not be required in equity so long as the thing sold belonged to an identified bulk or whole. If the contract was one which a court of equity would enforce by a decree of specific performance, it was thought that an equitable interest in the property might be held to pass as soon as the property came into existence and could be made identifiable, presumably by physical separation.

It was never entirely clear before the passing of the Sale of Goods Act whether (and, if so, to what extent) this equitable doctrine applied to an ordinary sale of unascertained goods. It certainly applied to the assignment of a future chose in action and to a covenant to convey or mortgage real estate. In these cases, the equitable doctrine meant that once the property came into the hands of the seller, or the chose in action became currently due, the assignee or buyer was entitled to the property or chose in preference to judgment creditors or a trustee in bankruptcy of the seller or assignor. But an ordinary contract of sale of goods has never been specifically enforceable in equity, though there are dicta in *Holroyd* v *Marshall*[189] suggesting that a contract for the sale of specific goods or of an unspecified part of a specified bulk may be so enforceable.

For some years after the passing of the 1893 Act it was an open question whether this equitable rule was applicable to contracts of sale of goods, but the question appears settled entirely by the judgment in *Re Wait*.[190] Wait bought 1,000 tons of wheat which was expected to be loaded on a named vessel, the *Challenger*, on 20 November 1925. The following day he contracted to sell 500 tons of this to X. The wheat was shipped in one undivided load, and one bill of lading for the whole load was issued. X paid Wait on 5 February, and Wait went bankrupt on 24 February. The ship arrived on 28 February. Wait's trustee claimed the whole 1,000 tons as assets in the bankruptcy, while X claimed either that he had an equitable assignment or charge on the 500 tons, or that he was entitled to specific performance of the contract under s. 52. A majority of the Court of Appeal decided against X on both grounds.[191] There had clearly been insufficient appropriation at law to pass the property and Lord Hanworth MR was of the opinion that, even if the equitable doctrine of *Tailby* v *Official Receiver* survived the Sale of Goods Act, the goods were not sufficiently identified even in equity. But Atkin LJ went much further than Lord Hanworth. He denied that equity would ever have applied its doctrines to an ordinary sale

[187] *Holroyd* v *Marshall* (1862) 10 HLC 191.
[188] (1888) 13 App Cas 523, 533.
[189] (1888) 13 App Cas 523, 533..
[190] [1927] 1 Ch 606. On the equitable doctrine prior to *Re Wait*, see Pennington (1975) 27 IC Law Q 277.
[191] As to the second ground, see Chapter 17.

of future goods. He went on to say that even if equity would ever have applied its doctrine to such a case, it could not do so now having regard to the Sale of Goods Act. He said:[192]

> The Code was passed at a time when the principles of equity and equitable remedies were recognized and given effect to in all our courts, and the particular equitable remedy of specific performance is specially referred to in s. 52. The total sum of legal relations (meaning by the word 'legal' existing in equity as well as in common law) arising out of the contract for the sale of goods may well be regarded as defined by the Code. It would have been futile in a Code intended for commercial men to have created an elaborate structure of rules dealing with rights at law, if at the same time it was intended to leave, subsisting with the legal rights equitable rights inconsistent with, more extensive, and coming into existence earlier than the rights so carefully set out in the various sections of the Code.
>
> The rules for transfer of property as between seller and buyer, performance of the contract, rights of the unpaid seller against the goods, unpaid seller's lien, remedies of the seller, remedies of the buyer, appear to be complete and exclusive statements of the legal relations both in law and equity.

These are powerful arguments, and they have the support of subsequent authority.[193] Accordingly, the only issue in cases of this kind is whether or not the property in the goods has passed in accordance with the rules set out in s. 18 (as amended) and s. 20A inserted by the 1995 Act.[194]

10.3 Proposed changes for consumer contracts

As discussed in Chapter 19, section 4(2) of the Consumer Rights Act 2015 refers the transfer of ownership back to the provisions on the passing of property under the Sale of Goods Act. The passing of risk is dealt with separately in s. 29 Consumer Rights Act 2015.

However, the difficulties associated with the rules of passing property discussed above are even more stark in the context of consumer contracts. The rules do not align sufficiently with modern consumer expectations, particularly in light of common arrangements regarding prepayments. Moreover, the legal jargon used under the SGA 1979 rules such as 'unconditional appropriation' or 'deliverable state' are not in keeping with the theme of CRA 2015 which is to simplify the consumer rights. In order to address these concerns, the Law Commission published a final report in April 2021.[195]

[192] [1927] 1 Ch 606, 635–6.

[193] In re *London Wine Co (Shippers) Ltd* (1986) PCC 121 Oliver J largely agreed with Atkin LJ on this point. Atkin LJ's views were also substantially supported though only on a 'provisional view' by the House of Lords in *Leigh & Sullivan Ltd* v *Aliakmon Shipping Corp Ltd* (The Aliakmon) [1986] AC 785. This passage was applied by the *Privy Council in Re Goldcorp Exchange Ltd* [1994] 2 All ER 806, and approved in *Re Stapylton Fletcher* [1994] 1 WLR 1181. Accordingly, this point would appear to be settled beyond doubt.

[194] Section 1(3).

[195] Law Commission, *Consumer Sales Contracts: Transfer of Ownership report* (Law Com No 246, 2020). (Law Com No 246 2020, hereafter)

10.3.1 Modernising/simplifying the language

To start with, there is a need to simplify and modernise the language used in the transfer of ownership rules under the current SGA 1979 provisions which originate from the original Sale of Goods Act 1893 and now are considered 'old-fashioned and unclear'.[196]

One of the key objectives of the Consumer Rights Act 2015 was to draft legal provisions in a language which is easily understandable and relatable to a consumer, for example, 'trader' and 'consumer' instead of 'buyer' and 'seller'. Thus, in keeping with this theme, abstract words 'specific' or 'unascertained' as used in SGA 1979 need to be simplified. To achieve this, the draft bill subsequently prepared by the Law Commission distinguishes two types of goods, with 'specific' goods referred to as the actual goods to be used to fulfil the contract selected when the contract is made.[197] Therefore, a contract for the sale of specific goods would be referred to as a contract for goods where the actual goods that are to be used to fulfil the contract have been selected when the contract is made, while unascertained goods would be defined as a contract for goods where the actual goods that are to be used to fulfil the contract have not been selected when the contract is made. This more descriptive distinction would make it easier for consumers to understand.[198]

Furthermore, technical phrases like 'deliverable state' and 'unconditional appropriation', which can lead to 'results which are inconsistent with consumers' expectation' as mentioned above are eliminated.[199] In particular, s. 18 Rule 5 of SGA 1979[200] would be replaced with a non-exhaustive list of circumstances that show a transfer of ownership.[201] This would afford more protection to prepaying consumers as, under the new rules, ownership is connected to the 'selection of goods' rather than 'unconditional appropriation'.[202] As a result the new rules would provide more clarity than the original rules, discussed above.

10.3.2 Proposed changes on rules of transferring ownership

As proposed, the final draft bill, s. 4(2) CRA 2015 would insert new sections 18A and 18B into the Consumer Rights Act 2015 and would contain the rules regulating the transfer of ownership under consumer sale contracts.[203] Like the Sale of Goods Act provisions, these new provisions would only apply to contracts for the sale of goods, with other contracts involving the transfer of ownership governed by the common law instead.

[196] Law Com No 246 2020, para 3.28.
[197] Law Com No 246 2020 at 3.32.
[198] See, Michelle Shean, 'Sale of Goods Legislation Reforms: an End to Confusion Over Transfer of Ownership?' (Fieldfisher, 2 Sep 2020).
[199] As seen in part 1, Sarah Green and Matthew Barry, 'Transfer of Ownership of Goods – Modernising the rules' (25 August 2020).
[200] Sale of Goods Act, s.18 Rule 5.
[201] Law Com No 246, 2020, at 3.47.
[202] Law Com No 246, 2020, at 3.73.
[203] Law Com No 246, 2020, at p.15 – para 3.6.

10.3.3 Proposed changes on rules of transferring ownership in Specific goods, s. 18A CRA 2015

The new rules governing consumer contracts for goods where the actual goods that are to be used to fulfil the contract have been selected when the contract is made would be governed by s. 18A of CRA 2015. Under the proposed rules, transfer of ownership of the goods occurs when the contract is entered into. It is not a requirement (in contrast to s. 18 Rule 1 mentioned above) that the goods must be in a 'deliverable state' for ownership to transfer. The result is that ownership transfers on conclusion of the contract, even if the trader has agreed to do something further to the goods (in contrast to rules 2 and 3 mentioned above.) As a result, this makes the transfer of ownership in consumer contracts for goods agreed at time of contract fairly straightforward and easier for the consumer to understand. This is because the four rules set out in s. 18 Rules 1–4 mentioned above will be replaced by one single rule that applies to these contracts, that is, ownership transfers at the time of contract.

10.3.4 Proposed changes on rules of transferring ownership in unascertained goods, s. 18B of the CRA 2015

As mentioned above under the SGA 1979, for unascertained goods, e.g. bought as future goods or by description, they have to first become ascertained and thereafter s. 18 Rule 5 would apply. Under the proposed rules, unascertained goods that have been identified after the contract is made would be governed by a non-exhaustive list set out in s. 18B (3) CRA 2015 paragraphs (a)–(h), which would list the situations that would lead to the transfer of ownership.. Under paragraphs (a), (b) and (h), if in a manner that is intended by the trader to be permanent, goods are physically labelled with the consumer's name, physically set aside for the consumer, or selected by the trader via other methods, ownership is transferred.[204] In addition, under (c) alteration of goods completed to a specification agreed by both parties and under (d) goods with a unique identifier known to the consumer would also qualify as events in which ownership is transferred.[205] The list also includes other 'ownership transferring' situations such as when goods (identified as those for delivery to consumer) are delivered to the carrier and when the goods are delivered to the consumer or when upon examination of goods (with mere inspection of packaging sufficing)[206] the consumer agrees for goods to be used to perform the contract.[207]

The non-exhaustive list attempts to uphold the 'great objective'[208] of predictability as the list provides set circumstances in which ownership transfers; however, the commission's aims to reflect common practices[209] and benefit clarity[210] may be undermined by

[204] Law Com No 246, 2020, at para 3.47.
[205] Law Com No 246, 2020, at para 3.57–3.61
[206] *Thornett & Fehr* v *Beers & Son* [1919] 1 KB 486.
[207] Law Com No 246, 2020, at paras 3.62-3.68.
[208] *Vallejo* v *Wheeler* [1774] 1 Cowp 143 [153].
[209] Law Com No 246, 2020, at para 3.70.
[210] Law Com No 246, 2020, [3.49]

the limited provisions, which raises concerns of restrictiveness and inflexibility, and the wording of certain components arguably leaves consumers and insolvency practitioners with less clarity but more ambiguity than before.

One might criticise the list for omitting other ways of clearly identifying the goods to be used for the performance of the contract, such as creating electronic links between the precise goods and the consumer. Paragraph (d) would go some way in that direction but would require that the consumer is notified – something which usually only happens on dispatch. Perhaps the 'sweep-up limb'[211] in paragraph (h) which covers the trader's selection of goods in some other way intended to be permanent.

The provisions were supposed simplify the law and create clarity, arguably this has not been achieved as in insolvency cases situations (a), (b) and (h) pose real practical issues due to a lack of clarity and certainty for both consumers and insolvency practitioners, when attempting to determine whether the trader had permanent intentions.[212] For instance, how can one prove that labelling of the goods was intended to be permanent? It was precisely this issue that caused difficulties under s. 18 Rule 5 in *Carlos Federspiel* v *Twigg*. A trader may label goods with a consumer's details in anticipation of delivery, but the consumer is unavailable upon delivery, leading to the label being removed and a new label with a different consumer's details being affixed to that item - a common practice for businesses dealing with a high turnover of goods.[213] The final draft Bill would include a presumption that the trader had an intention to label the goods permanently.[214] This presumption would be rebuttable by the trader, so if the trader can show that they did not intend for any form of labelling to be permanent, there will be no transfer of ownership.

Other situations, such as those in (c) and (d), would be particular relevant if the trader has become insolvent. Paragraph (c) covers consumers who may buy an item from the trader's general stock which requires alterations agreed by the parties and establishes that ownership transfers once alterations are complete.[215] An example would be a consumer who purchases a ring which needs to be engraved. Ownership would transfer to the consumer once engraving is complete. Paragraph (d) covers goods with a unique identifier known to the consumer. This would be something like a serial number which is given to some types of consumer goods, or an IMEI for smartphones. However, even where such numbers exist, they are rarely given to consumers in advance.[216]

Although consumers who have pre-paid for goods would be better protected if a retailer goes insolvent, there is still unfairness as it puts those who buy goods for alterations in physical stores in a better position than those who buy online;[217] however the position of consumers in instances of retailer insolvency would be much improved to toe position under existing law.[218]

[211] Law Com No 246, 2020, 3.70.
[212] See Sarah Green and Matthew Barry, 'Transfer of Ownership of Goods – Modernising the rules' (25 August 2020).
[213] Law Com No 246, 2020, para 3.51.
[214] Law Com No 246, 2020, at 3.52.
[215] Law Com No 246, 2020, para 3.57.
[216] Law Com No 246, 2020, para 3.60.
[217] Law Com No 246, 2020, para 3.58.
[218] See Government Press Release, 'Law change to better protect consumers in event of insolvencies' (27 July 2020).

As mentioned above, unascertained goods bought as part of bulk are currently governed by s. 20A SGA 1979. This will remain as it is[219] as there is no pressing need to change it. This is because consumers rarely purchase goods as part of bulk in practice,[220] and if they do so s. 20A SGA 1979 will protect consumers who have already paid.

10.3.5 A move to mandatory rules

Unlike the present rules under ss. 17 and 19 of the Sale of Goods Act 1979, allowing parties to agree when property will pass, s. 18B(5) of the Consumer Rights Act 2015 would state that the proposed rules guiding the transfer of ownership between a consumer and a trader under s. 18A and B of the CRA 2015 would be mandatory.[221] This mandatory rule can be argued to interfere with party autonomy. As Goode expressed, 'businessmen should be free to make their own way'.[222] However, party autonomy is not absolute and is mainly curtailed in consumer contracts because most consumers in reality cannot negotiate the terms of an agreement. [223] Thus, the mandatory effect prevents traders from imposing unfair terms[224] on consumers.

However, the concern is mandatory rules may lead to unfairness, especially for the trader,[225] particularly, in situations where full payment has not been received and ownership has transferred. In such cases, the trader may be able to only sue (which would incur more cost) and if the consumer becomes insolvent the trader becomes an unsecured creditor. In practice, however, most consumers will be either required to pay in advance or at least to provide payment details at the time of placing an order, so the trader should usually be able to receive payment around the time ownership is transferred.

10.3.6 The effect of the changes

This area has been ripe for reform and modern, simple and more protective rules for consumer sales contracts have been long overdue. However, until there is a commitment by government to implement these changes, consumers will continue to be exposed to the risks of retailer insolvency, and the difficult provisions on the passing of property continue to apply.

[219] *Law Commission, Consumer sales contracts: transfer of ownership* (Law Com No 398, 2021) para 3.109. Law Com No 398, 2021 henceforth.

[220] Law Com No 398, 2021, at para 3.83.

[221] Law Com No 398, 2021, at para 3.111.

[222] Roy Goode, 'The Codification of Commercial Law' (1988) 14 Mon LR 135, 149, *Schroeder Music Publisher Co Ltd* v *Macaulay* [1974] 1 WLR 1308 (HL) 1316 (Lord Diplock).

[223] Robert Bradgate, Commercial Law (3rd edn, OUP 2005) at page 6.

[224] Law Com No 398, 2021, at para 3.111/

[225] Law Com No 398, 2021, at para 3.119.

Part IV

The effects of the contract

11

Risk and frustration

11.1 Risk and frustration distinguished

When a person is bound to bear the accidental loss of, or damage to, goods, they are said to be at their risk. Sometimes, also, a contract for the sale of goods, like any other contract, may be totally frustrated by an extraordinary and (usually) unforeseeable event. Because frustration is sometimes also relevant where goods are destroyed or even severely damaged, the two sets of legal principles are interconnected in various ways. Indeed, the doctrine of frustration is sometimes said to be merely an aspect of the general rules as to risk, but this is not entirely accurate. If an executory contract is frustrated, neither party is under any liability to the other. On the other hand, if the goods are at the seller's risk and they perish or deteriorate, although the buyer is not liable to the seller for the price, it by no means follows that the seller is not liable to the buyer for non-delivery if the buyer can prove that they have suffered loss as a result. The rules as to risk have nothing to say in this case, and if the seller is to be exempted from liability, it must be by the doctrine of frustration. Conversely, if the goods are at the buyer's risk, they are clearly liable for the price even though the goods have perished or deteriorated. But it does not follow that they may not also be liable for damages for non-acceptance if the seller can prove that they have suffered any.[1] Only frustration can discharge the buyer from the liability for non-acceptance.

Nonetheless, the doctrines of risk and frustration are undoubtedly related, and it is convenient to consider them in the same chapter. The next three sections will examine the transfer of risk, frustration and the effects of frustration. As the following pages will demonstrate, the whole subject of risk and frustration is intertwined with the distinction between specific and unascertained goods, and by the failure of the Sale of Goods Act to draw any distinction between different types of unascertained goods. Indeed, it is difficult at times to avoid the conclusion that the draftsmen of both the Sale of Goods Act and the Law Reform (Frustrated Contracts) Act 1943 forgot that there were sales of unascertained goods other than purely generic goods.

11.2 Transfer of risk

The general rule laid down by s. 20(1) is that *prima facie* the risk passes with the property:

> Unless otherwise agreed, the goods remain at the seller's risk until the property in them is transferred to the buyer, but when the property in them is transferred to the buyer, the goods are at the buyer's risk whether delivery has been made or not.

[1] For example, for storage charges: see the Sale of Goods Act, s. 37.

If there is an express agreement that one party is to bear the risk even though they have no property (as, e.g. there always is in contracts of sale subject to reservation of title clauses), effect must be given to the agreement. In the absence of an express contract, it has been said that 'the rule *res perit domino* is generally an unbending rule of law arising from the very nature of property'[2] While this is no doubt largely true in a situation where property remains with one person throughout, it is not necessarily true of the situation where property is being transferred from one party to another. In this situation, there is nothing unusual about separating the transfer of risk from the transfer of property and this commonly happens where goods are shipped under a c.i.f. or an f.o.b. contract.[3] Apart from these cases, two other exceptional cases are established by the authorities, in one of which the risk passes before the property and, in the other, the risk passes after. The best example of the former exception is *Sterns Ltd* v *Vickers Ltd*.[4] The defendants in this case sold to the plaintiffs 120,000 gallons of spirit, which was part of a total quantity of 200,000 gallons in a storage tank belonging to a third party. The plaintiffs obtained a delivery order which the third party accepted, but the plaintiffs decided to leave the spirit in the tank for the time being for their own convenience. The spirit deteriorated in quality between the time of sale and the time when the plaintiffs eventually took delivery of the 120,000 gallons. Despite the fact that the property clearly had not passed because the goods sold had not been ascertained in the technical sense, and therefore there had been no appropriation, the Court of Appeal held that the risk had passed to the buyers.

Although the decision in *Sterns Ltd* v *Vickers Ltd* appears to have been approved by the House of Lords[5] and must therefore be accepted as correct on its particular facts, the case raises many problems which are closely related to the difficulties arising with regard to the passing of property. As we saw in Chapter 10, a sale of an unidentified part of a bulk, as in this case, could not, before the changes effected by the Sale of Goods (Amendment) Act 1995,[6] pass property in the goods because of s. 16. The 1995 Act permits property in an *undivided share* to pass to the buyer, but otherwise, as we have seen, the passing of property, and therefore risk, is governed by s. 18, Rule 5. But although property in the goods could not, and still cannot, pass, the facts of *Sterns Ltd* v *Vickers Ltd* illustrate a situation where, for all practical purposes, the goods 'belong' to the buyers and so it seems desirable that they should be treated as being at the buyers' risk, as the court there held. But of course the problems which prevented the law from treating the property as passing can also affect the question of risk. Suppose, for example, that the spirit had been stored in two separate tanks each containing 100,000 gallons and that the contents of one tank only had deteriorated, would the buyer have been compelled to take all the deteriorated spirit, or would he have been able to claim all the spirit from the other tank? Or should the good and bad spirit be divided between the parties in proportion to their respective interests? This latter solution appeared to be the logical conclusion from *Sterns Ltd* v *Vickers Ltd*, since it gives effect to the holding that the risk is on the buyer and, at the same time, it

[2] See the Scots case, *Hansen* v *Craig & Rose* (1895) 21 D 432, 438 per Lord President Inglis, cited by Lord Normand in *Comptoir d'Achat et de Vente SA* v *Luis de Ridder Limitada (The Julia)* [1949] AC 293, 319.
[3] See Chapter 13.
[4] [1923] 1 KB 78.
[5] In *The Julia*, [1949] AC 293.
[6] See Chapter 10.

offers a fair solution to the problem. The 1995 Act, for the reasons explained above, does not seem to offer any further solution to this problem.[7]

The exceptional nature of this case was emphasised by the House of Lords in *Comptoir d'Achat et de Vente SA* v *Luis de Ridder Limitada (The Julia)*,[8] where Lord Porter said:

> It is difficult to see how a parcel is at the buyer's risk when he has neither property nor possession except in such cases as *Inglis* v *Stock*[9] and *Sterns Ltd* v *Vickers Ltd*[10] where the purchaser had an interest in an undivided part of a bulk parcel on board a ship, or elsewhere, obtained by attornment of the bailee to him.[11]

And Lord Normand observed:

> In those cases in which it has been held that the risk without the property has passed to the buyer it has been because the buyer rather than the seller was seen to have an immediate and practical interest in the goods,[12] as for instance when he has an immediate right under the storekeeper's delivery warrant to the delivery of a portion of an undivided bulk in store, or an immediate right under several contracts with different persons to the whole of a bulk not yet appropriated to the several contracts.[13]

It can be seen, therefore, that the acceptance of the delivery warrant in *Sterns Ltd* v *Vickers Ltd* was regarded as the crucial factor in the case, since it was this which gave the buyer an immediate right to possession.[14] This may serve to distinguish *Healy* v *Howlett & Sons*,[15] which is otherwise very similar on its facts to *Sterns Ltd* v *Vickers Ltd*. Here, it will be recalled, it was held that the risk in 20 boxes of fish, which were dispatched to the buyer as part of a total of 190 boxes, none of which had been earmarked for him, was still on the seller. The court pointed out the difficulties which would have arisen if only some of the boxes had deteriorated or perished. As we have seen,[16] the Law Commissions' proposals on the sale of goods forming part of a bulk and the 1995 Act[17] did not deal with this problem directly. The Report indicated that the buyer should be entitled to delivery of goods which conform to the contract in quantity and quality, and that nothing in the new provisions should affect the buyer's rights under the contract.[18] The Commissions are not intending to affect the result in situations similar to those in the cases discussed above in which it was held that the risk of loss or damage to goods forming part of a bulk *could* pass to a buyer prior to delivery.

[7] See Chapter 12.

[8] [1949] AC 293.

[9] (1885) 10 App Cas 263, an f.o.b. case in which risk was held to have passed on shipment before the goods were specifically appropriated to the contract.

[10] [1923] 1 KB 78.

[11] [1949] AC 293 at p. 312.

[12] But this is not really so as regards c.i.f. contracts, for the seller retains the general property, and the buyer has not even an immediate right to possession. See the remarks of Lord Wright in *Smyth & Co Ltd* v *Bailey & Co Ltd* [1940] 3 All ER 60, at 67.

[13] [1949] AC 293 at p. 319.

[14] Where the goods are still in the possession of the seller themselves, though not yet ascertained, it seems that the risk may pass on the making of the contract, or at least when delivery falls due: see the New Zealand case, *Donaghy's Rope & Twine Co Ltd* v *Wright, Stephenson & Co* (1906) 25 NZLR 641, 651–2.

[15] [1917] 1 KB 337.

[16] See Chapter 10.

[17] Law Commission No. 215 – see above, Chapter 10, at section 10.2.4.

[18] Ibid., para. 4.34.

It should, moreover, be remembered that it is only in the sale of an unidentified part of a specific whole that risk can pass before the property in a sale of unascertained goods. It clearly cannot do so in the case of goods not owned or possessed by the seller, except in the sense that the buyer may conceivably have contracted to pay the price whether or not the goods are delivered.

It is not easy to imagine circumstances in which the risk remains with the seller after the property has passed in the absence of express agreement to this effect, but the decision in *Head* v *Tattersall*[19] may provide an illustration of such a case. The plaintiff in this case bought a horse from the defendant, warranted to have been hunted with the Bicester hounds, and the plaintiff was given a week in which to return the horse if it did not answer the description. The horse was accidentally injured before the week was up, and the plaintiff claimed to return it, having discovered that it had not been hunted with the Bicester hounds. It was held that the plaintiff was entitled to return the horse and recover the price. The risk was thus held to be on the seller although the property had probably passed to the buyer (subject to the possibility of being divested).[20] There is no reason to think that the case would not be decided in the same way today, but in most such cases, of course, the property does not pass until the expiry of the time fixed in accordance with s. 18, Rule 4(b). However, the decision may well illustrate a broader principle of some importance, namely that the risk always remains on the seller when the buyer has a right of rejection. Thus if the seller ships or delivers defective goods (or if there is a shortfall in quantity)[21] so that the buyer is entitled to reject, it seems that the risk remains on the seller unless and until the buyer accepts the goods. Although this rule is not actually spelt out in the Act,[22] it seems to follow from the rules on acceptance.[23] As will be seen later, there is nothing in these rules to prevent rejection simply because the goods have been accidentally lost or damaged, and by exercising their right to reject, the buyer can effectively throw the risk on the seller.

A fairly common instance of an express agreement, under which the property passes before the risk, occurs where the seller agrees to dispatch specific goods at his own risk to the buyer. In this event, the seller is only liable for deterioration or destruction not necessarily incident to the course of transit, for s. 33 provides:

> Where the seller of goods agrees to deliver them at his own risk at a place other than that where they are when sold, the buyer must, nevertheless (unless otherwise agreed), take any risk of deterioration in the goods necessarily incident to the course of transit.

It seems that the words 'any risk . . . necessarily incident to the course of transit' must be confined to risks which would have arisen with any goods answering the contract

[19] (1870) LR 7 Ex 7.

[20] This, at least, appears to have been the view of Cleasby B. Neither Kelly CB nor Bramwell B expressed any view on the matter. Given that the underlying nature of the transaction in that case appears to have been a sale subject to a right of rescission, it is suggested that Cleasby B's view was correct – see Adams, *Essays for Clive Schmitthoff* (1983, Professional Books), pp. 1, 3.

[21] See *Vitol SA* v *Esso Australia Ltd* (The Wise) [1989] 1 Lloyd's Rep 96 – Chapter 17.

[22] Compare Art. 2-510 of the UCC.

[23] See Chapter 17 et *seq*. The Law Commissions regarded the position as doubtful, but decided against recommending any changes – see Final Report, 'Sale and Supply of Goods', para. 5.40.

description.[24] Thus, a risk of deterioration which is only incidental to the course of transit because of the defective condition of the goods at the commencement of the transit is not covered by this provision. Reference has already been made to *Mash & Murrell* v *Joseph I Emmanuel Ltd*,[25] where it was held that the implied condition that the goods are of merchantable quality involves a continuing obligation as to the condition of the goods for a reasonable time after shipment in a c.i.f. contract. A position affirmed by the House of Lords.[26]

These cases prompt the question whether there is any need for a separate 'doctrine' of risk, at least so far as deterioration of the goods is concerned. It seems to accord more with the techniques of the English of sale to approach such questions by asking whether the seller has continuously warranted the condition of the goods. If so, then clearly the seller remains liable for the deterioration in their condition. If not, then the risk is the buyer's, but it is perhaps misleading to think of the risk of deterioration in almost tangible terms as something which 'passes' from seller to buyer. There is no distinction in principle between the risk of deterioration, which is treated by s. 20 as passing with the property, and the ordinary risk which every buyer takes in respect of matters not covered by conditions and warranties imposed on the seller.

It may, indeed, be that a similar analysis could be made of the risk of accidental destruction of the goods. The question which is most likely to arise in such circumstances is whether the buyer remains liable to pay the price or whether the seller's inability to deliver the goods discharges the buyer. *Prima facie*, one would have thought that the latter should be the case because payment and delivery are, under s. 28 of the Act, concurrent conditions. But this is not the law because if the goods are accidentally destroyed after the property has passed, the presumption is that the risk has also passed, and the buyer must therefore pay the price even though the seller cannot deliver the goods. It is, however, far from obvious why the risk of accidental destruction should be on the buyer prior to delivery, except in the case of goods which are shipped for dispatch to the buyer. This is particularly the case in respect of retail sales (albeit never to a consumer). If, for example, a person buys goods in a shop for later delivery and the shop burns down, destroying its stock overnight, the buyer would probably be surprised to learn that they might still be liable for the price.[27] That said, the goods would almost certainly be insured and, if the buyer were required to pay the price, it is possible that the seller would be a constructive trustee of the proceeds of the insurance policy for the buyer.[28]

The question of who should bear the risk of accidental destruction, therefore, is bound up with who should be required to insure them. It is s doubtful whether the current rule,

[24] See (1965) 28 MLR 180, 189 and [1962] J Bus L 352. As suggested above, it is arguable that the risk in non-conforming goods always remains with the seller – see *Head* v *Tattersall* (1871) LR 7 Ex 7. The proposition may gain support from *Kinnear* v *Brodie* (1901) 3 F 540; Gow, *Mercantile Law* (W. Green & Sons, Edinburgh), pp. 149, 184, 185. See also Scottish Law Commission Memorandum No. 25, 'Corporeal Moveables: Passing of Risk and of Ownership' (1976); T. B. Smith, *Property Problems in Sale* (1978, Sweet & Maxwell, London), ch. II.

[25] [1961] 1 All ER 485 – see Chapter 7 et seq.

[26] *Lambert* v *Lewis* [1982] AC 225, 276.

[27] Perhaps a court would hold today that property in such a case does not pass on the making of the contract: see the dictum of Diplock LJ in R *V Ward* v *Bignall* [1967] 1 QB 534, 545.

[28] See s. 47 of the Law of Property Act 1925, and *Maurice* v *Goldsborough Mort & Co Ltd* [1939] AC 452, and cases there cited.

which lays the 'obligation' to insure (or, more strictly, the risk of not insuring) on the party who has the property, is really the most desirable solution. Certainly in retail sales and similar transactions, a powerful case could be made for saying that the most appropriate person to insure would nearly always be the party with physical possession, if only because in practice this is what would normally happen.[29] To take a simple example, in a hire-purchase agreement the person who ought to insure the goods is the person in possession and, of course, all hire-purchase agreements of vehicles impose a corresponding obligation to insure on the person in possession, the hirer.

In bulk sales, it seems doubtful whether the present rule is the most appropriate. It seems probable that the right person to insure normally is the person in physical possession, although it may be that special provision would be necessary in relation to insurance while the goods are in the hands of a carrier for transmission to the buyer. And it may well be that commercial practice would, in many other circumstances, rebut the *prima facie* presumption that the person in possession should insure.

The concept of 'risk' is concerned only with accidental destruction or deterioration and does not cover damage to the goods caused by the fault of either party. Section 20, therefore, has the following further provisions:

> (2) But where delivery has been delayed through the fault of either buyer or seller the goods are at the risk of the party at fault as regards any loss which might not have occurred but for such fault.
>
> (3) Nothing in this section affects the duties or liabilities of either seller or buyer as a bailee . . . of the goods of the other party.

Subsection (2) was applied in *Demby Hamilton & Co Ltd* v *Barden*.[30] Here the seller contracted to sell 30 tons of apple juice to be delivered to the buyer in weekly loads. The seller crushed the apples and stored the juice pending delivery. The buyer was late in taking delivery and some of the juice went bad. Applying s. 20(2), the learned judge held that the buyer was liable. But it is important to note that the party in fault is not liable for all risks, but only for those which 'might not have occurred but for such fault'.[31]

Subsection (3) means that the mere fact that one party is at fault does not discharge the other from his obligations to take due care as a bailee. In particular, the fact that the buyer is late in taking delivery does not mean that the seller is not still bound to take all reasonable care of the goods.[32] If they also are at fault, questions might arise as to the possibility of apportioning the damage between the parties, either by the application of

[29] The Uniform Commercial Code adopts this approach fairly consistently – see generally Art. 2, Part 5, and especially Art. 2-509, Comment 3. This is also the position effectively adopted by the Consumer Rights Act 2015.

[30] [1949] 1 All ER 435. See also *Pommer* v *Mowat* (1906) 14 SLT 373.

[31] It is, however, to be noted that there appears to be no justification in terms of insurance for this rule. Generally, the party in possession of the goods will have them insured, and it makes no difference that the delivery to a particular buyer is delayed. It appears to be a weakness of the Uniform Commercial Code that, having adopted a general principle of placing the risk of loss on the party in possession, it then permits breach to affect the risk of loss – see Art. 2-510.

[32] In the Tasmanian case of *Sharp* v *Batt* (1930) 25 Tas LR 33, 56, it was said that the buyer remained liable in the absence of gross negligence by the seller, but today it is unlikely that a court would require the negligence to be gross. The distinction between negligence and gross negligence, though it finds support in some early nineteenth-century English cases, has in any event no currency in modern law.

the Law Reform (Contributory Negligence) Act 1945,[33] or possibly, in some cases, on the basis of causation at common law.[34] In *Knight* v *Wilson*,[35] the seller of a boat, the property and risk in which had passed to the buyer, negligently caused damage to it while sailing it without permission, and was held liable to the buyer under the custodian's duty of care.

11.3 Frustration

It has already been set out that the doctrine of frustration covers a wider field than the rules regarding risk. The drafting of s. 7 supports this view:

> Where there is an agreement to sell specific goods, and subsequently the goods, without any fault on the part of the seller or buyer, perish before the risk passes to the buyer, the agreement is thereby avoided.

The doctrine of risk simply lays down that *prima facie* if the goods perish before the property passes, the seller must bear the loss and cannot claim the price. Were the doctrine of frustration merely an aspect of the rules as to risk, this section would be an absurdity for it would, in effect, be saying that where the risk is on the seller they must bear the risk of the goods perishing. But s. 7 goes further, providing that in the circumstances set out the contract is avoided. This means that both parties are discharged from their obligations; in other words, not only is the buyer not liable for the price, but the seller is not liable for non-delivery.

11.3.1 Application of s. 7

The scope of s. 7 is comparatively narrow. It only applies to a contract for the sale of specific goods in which neither the property nor the risk[36] has passed but, as we have seen, the general presumption is that a contract for the sale of specific goods passes both the property and the risk at once. Section 7 therefore only applies where s. 18, Rule 1 does not apply for some reason, or where, if it does apply, s. 20 does not apply. Section 7 will *prima facie* apply wherever there is a case of a conditional sale of specific goods under s. 18, Rules 2 and 3.

The meaning of the word 'perish' in s. 7 is presumably the same as in s. 6 and the discussion there may be referred to.[37] Destruction of part only of specific goods also raises similar questions in the two sections. If a person agrees to sell specific goods, part only of which perish before the risk passes to the buyer, does s. 7 operate to frustrate the contract

[33] See *Forsikringsaktieselskapet Vesta* v *Butcher* [1988] 2 All ER 43, in which the Court of Appeal clarified the circumstances in which the 1945 Act may be applicable to an action in contract. (The decision was affirmed on a different point: [1989] 1 All ER 402.) The Act has no application where the defendant is in breach of a strict contractual duty as under the Sale of Goods Act 1979 – *Barclays Bank* v *Fairclough Buildings Ltd* [1988] 2 All ER 43 – see Law Commission Report No. 219 (1993).

[34] See, for an example of such apportionment at common law, *Tennant Radiant Heat* v *Warrington Development Corporation* [1988] EG LR 41 (CA).

[35] 1949 SLT (Sh Ct) 26.

[36] Note that s. 7 only applies 'where there is an *agreement* to sell specific goods', not 'where there is a sale', etc., which shows that it has no application where property passes. See, e.g., *Horn* v *Minister of Food* [1948] 2 All ER 1036.

[37] See Chapter 5 et *seq*.

and discharge the seller? *Barrow Lane & Ballard Ltd* v *Phillip Phillips & Co Ltd*[38] suggests that if the contract is unseverable, it is frustrated by the perishing of part of the goods, whereas if it is severable it is frustrated only as to the part which has perished. But this conclusion seems questionable in the light of *H R & S Sainsbury* v *Street.* [39] This case, although not itself falling under s. 7, suggests that where part only of the goods perish, the seller may well be obliged to offer the remaining goods to the buyer. The buyer, however, may not be obliged to take them.

It is thought that the perishing of the goods cannot frustrate a contract except under s. 7. If the property and the risk have both passed, subsequent destruction of the goods cannot possibly frustrate the contract – frustration cannot apply to a fully executed contract.[40] Nor is it easy to see how the result can be different if the property has passed but the risk has not. If the property has passed, it is hard to see that the object of the contract can be defeated by supervening events.

There remains the possibility that the risk may have passed before the property, and the goods may have perished after the one and before the other. However, once again, frustration cannot be possible here, as the result would be to discharge the buyer's obligation to pay the price, or enable recovering it if already paid, and this would mean that the risk was on the seller and not the buyer.[41]

Whatever the true basis of the doctrine of frustration, it would appear that s. 7 is only a *prima facie* rule of construction and nothing more, so that it does not necessarily apply merely because the facts fall within its purview. Once again, there are at least three possible constructions similar to those which were discussed in connection with *Couturier* v *Hastie*[42] and *Howell* v *Coupland*[43] (and again, in commercial cases yet further constructions may be possible where part only of the goods perish):

1 There may be an implied condition that if the goods perish the contract will be discharged and neither party will be liable, that is, the contract may be frustrated.
2 The seller may contract that the goods will not perish, in which case the seller will not only have to bear the loss of the goods; that is, will be unable to claim the price, but may be liable for damages for non-delivery.
3 The buyer may contract that they will take the consequences of the goods perishing, in which case they will have to pay the price whatever happens to the goods, and they may also be liable for damages.

11.3.2 Frustration of contract of sale at common law

Only the perishing of specific goods is provided for by the Act, but at common law a contract for the sale of specific goods could be frustrated by any event which destroyed the

38 [1929] 1 KB 574.
39 [1972] 1 WLR 834 – see Chapter 5.
40 See *Re Shipton Anderson & Co Ltd and Harrison Bros & Co Ltd* [1915] 3 KB 676, where the CA clearly thought that there could be no frustration if property and risk had both passed.
41 *Horn* v *Minister of Food*, [1948] 2 All ER 1036. Certainly, in c.i.f. contracts, where risk usually passes before property, the perishing of the goods after passing of risk does not frustrate the contract, even though there is then no property to pass.
42 (1856) 5 HLC 673 – see Chapter 5.
43 (1876) 1 QBD 258 – see Chapter 5.

whole basis of the contract and radically altered the obligations of the parties, provided that the event occured before the property and risk passed to the buyer.[44]

The question remains whether a contract for the sale of unascertained goods can be frustrated by perishing of the goods or another supervening event. The answer depends upon the type of unascertained goods in question. It is probable that an agreement to sell purely generic goods cannot be frustrated by the destruction of the goods because it is unlikely that all of the existing goods of a particular type could perish in their entirety.[45] A particular stock of a particular type of goods could perish, but as far as the buyer is concerned it is not material that the seller had a particular stock in mind which is accidentally destroyed after the making of the contract.

> Suppose A has contracted to sell to B unascertained goods by description; for example, 'a' Bentley Mark VI (not 'this' Bentley Mark VI) and the seller expects to acquire the goods from a particular source, which may, be the only source available and that when the time for delivery comes, that source has dried up and that the seller cannot draw on it, does not absolve the seller. They are still, in the absence of some contractual term excusing him, liable for non-delivery.[46]

It does not follow from this that a contract for the sale of unascertained goods of the other two types discussed above[47] cannot be frustrated by the perishing of the goods. For example, if a person agrees to sell a crop to be grown on a particular field, the contract may be frustrated by the failure of the crop,[48] or, if a person agrees to construct machinery in a building owned by another, and the whole building with the machinery is accidentally destroyed before it is completed, the contract may be frustrated.[49]

There also seems to be no reason why, in an appropriate case, a contract for the sale of any type of unascertained goods may not be frustrated by some event other than the perishing of the goods. It may, of course, be more difficult to persuade the court that the event which has occurred has destroyed the basis of the contract where the goods are unascertained and, indeed, in *Blackburn Bobbin Co Ltd* v *Allen & Son*,[50] McCardie J went so far as to say:

> In the absence of any question as to trading with the enemy, and in the absence also of any administrative intervention by the British Government authorities, a bare and unqualified contract for the sale of unascertained goods will not (unless most special facts compel an opposite implication) be dissolved by the operation of [the doctrine of frustration].[51]

This decision was affirmed in the Court of Appeal,[52] but without the caution of the court at first instance. The Court of Appeal treated the case as though the doctrine of frustration might have applied, but that it did not do so because the alleged frustrating

[44] For example, *Re Shipton Anderson & Co Ltd and Harrison & Bros & Co Ltd* [1915] 3 KB 676.
[45] As expressed by the maxim *genus numquam perit*.
[46] *Monkland* v *Jack Barclay Ltd* [1951] 2 KB 252, 258 per Asquith LJ.
[47] See Chapter 3.
[48] *Howell* v *Coupland* (1876) 1 QBD 258.
[49] *Appleby* v *Myers* (1867) LR 2 CP 651.
[50] [1918] 1 KB 540, 550.
[51] See also *CTT Group Inc* v *Transclear SA* [2008] EWCA Civ 856.
[52] [1918] 2 KB 467.

event only affected the way in which the seller was going to perform the contract. As Pickford LJ observed:

> Why should a purchaser of goods, not specific goods, be deemed to concern himself with the way in which the seller is going to fulfil his contract by providing the goods he has agreed to sell?[53]

The effect of the application of this principle can be found in the Suez Canal cases,[54] where the House of Lords held that the closure of the canal did not frustrate c.i.f. contracts for the sale of Sudanese groundnuts to European buyers, despite the fact that the only alternative route was via the Cape of Good Hope, several thousand miles longer. The decisive point may have been that these were contracts for the sale of goods c.i.f. in which the buyers were only concerned with the shipment of the goods at the port of shipment, and their ultimate arrival at their destination. Precisely how the sellers got the goods to the buyers was their own business. Conversely, the unloading of the goods from the vessel at the port of destination in a c.i.f. contract is *prima facie* the sole responsibility of the buyer. If the goods cannot be unloaded because the buyer has not obtained any necessary import licence, they will bear the loss.[55] The inability to unload the vessel is not a frustrating circumstance because the buyer could (for example) have diverted the ship to take delivery elsewhere. Crucially, it is of no concern of the seller. Similarly, the contract is not frustrated just because the buyer is unable to export the goods for resale as they had intended.[56]

Conversely, in *Re Badische Co Ltd*, [57] Russell J held that a contract to supply unascertained goods which both parties knew could only be obtained from Germany was frustrated by the outbreak of war. He said:[58]

> Speaking for myself, I can see no reason why, given the necessary circumstances to exist, the doctrine should not apply equally to the case of unascertained goods. It is, of course, obvious from the nature of the contract that the necessary circumstances can only very rarely arise in the case of unascertained goods. That they may arise appears to me to be undoubted.

It has subsequently been affirmed that there is no legal principle excluding the doctrine of frustration in the case of a c.i.f. contract, though also confirming that the doctrine would only apply rarely in practice.[59] In this case, a seller carrying on business in Malta agreed to sell potatoes c.i.f. London, shipment between 14 and 24 April. In fact, only one vessel called at Malta during this period and the seller was unable to obtain space on it. It was held that the seller took the risk of being unable to get shipping space and was liable.

[53] Ibid., at p. 469. Cf. *Re Thornett & Fehr & Yuills Ltd* [1921] 1 KB 219.

[54] *Tsakiroglou & Co Ltd* v *Noblee Thorl GmbH* [1962] AC 93, overruling *Carapanayoti & Co Ltd* v *E T Green Ltd* [1959] 1 QB 131.

[55] *Congimex* v *Tradax* [1983] 1 Lloyd's Rep 250.

[56] *McMaster & Co Ltd* v *McEuen & Co Ltd* 1921 SC (HL) 24. But where an English company orders goods from a foreign company, both parties being aware that an export licence is necessary, the failure to obtain the licence may frustrate the contract – see *A V Pound & Co Ltd* v *M W Hardy & Co Inc* [1956] AC 588. (*Cf. Peter Cassidy Seed Co* v *Osuustukkukauppa IL* [1954] 2 Lloyd's Rep 586.). See Chapter 13.

[57] [1921] 2 Ch 331.

[58] Ibid., at p. 382.

[59] *Lewis Emmanuel & Son Ltd* v *Sammut* [1959] 2 Lloyd's Rep 629.

11.3.3 *Force majeure* clauses

Although it is difficult to invoke the doctrine of frustration when restrictions are imposed by governments on the export or import of goods sold under c.i.f. and similar contracts, contracts often include *force majeure* clauses to protect against liabilities arising from such governmental intervention, war, strikes, civil unrest, etc. These clauses are usually very strictly interpreted by the courts against those relying on them so that liability is often imposed on the ground that, despite embargoes, prohibitions and the like, the party relying on the clause might still have been able to perform; for example, by buying goods afloat, by shipping earlier (or later) or by making more strenuous efforts to obtain a licence to import or export goods. What is striking about the legal approach to these problems is that the liability in question is nearly always a liability for pure expectation, or loss of bargain, damages. There is surely a case for a less strict form of liability, where the claimant claims damages of this nature, even apart altogether from the presence of *force majeure* clauses. To interpret such clauses very narrowly where these are the only damages claimed suggests that the courts are imposing their own view of commercial morality (or economics) and in doing so, thwarting commercial expectations.[60]

A series of cases, which came before the courts in the second half of the 1970s and early 1980s out of one major commercial embargo, illustrates the extreme stringency with which such clauses are usually interpreted. These cases arose out of the failure of the soya bean crop in the United States in 1973, which led to an embargo being placed on the export of soya beans for a short period late in 1973. Many contracts for the sale of this crop, to the value of millions of pounds, were affected, and sellers relied on *force majeure* clauses in the standard contract used in that trade.[61] But in a whole series of decisions the Court of Appeal, and in one or two cases the House of Lords, approached the clause so strictly that the result was almost always to render the seller liable, despite the *force majeure* clause. Sometimes, the courts held that the burden of proof was on the sellers to show that they could not have found adequate supplies already afloat; sometimes it was held that sellers had failed to give notice, as required by the clause, at the right time; sometimes it was held that the sellers could have shipped before the embargo was imposed, or after it was lifted. The story was reviewed by the Court of Appeal in *André et Cie* v *Tradax*[62] in which the judges acknowledged that the courts had perhaps been too legalistic in their approach, or at least that they had tended to look at the problems from a strictly legal, rather than a more realistic commercial, viewpoint. In particular, the courts had sometimes failed to appreciate the aggregate effects of the embargo as a whole, looking too closely at individual contracts to see whether (for instance) a particular seller might in theory have been able to buy the soya beans for his contract without regard to the fact that hundreds of other sellers were all at the same time desperately looking for any soya beans available for export.[63]

[60] The potential availability of more substantial damages is signalled by the recent decision *Classic Maritime Inc* v *Limbungan Makmur SDN BHD* [2019] EWCA Civ 1102.

[61] The GAFTA form.

[62] [1983] 1 Lloyd's Rep 254.

[63] For a detailed treatment of this see generally Treitel, *Frustration and Force Majeure*, 4th ed. (2021, Sweet & Maxwell).

Two recent decisions,[64] the first in many years, while not sale of goods transactions, show that the commercial realism seen in previously decided cases remains but the approach of the courts is no more friendly to *force majeure* clauses in general than it was previously. Indeed, the effect of a more sharply drawn distinction between 'frustration clauses', which excuse all further performance and 'exceptions clauses', which allow for the agreement to continue but which prevent any action for breach where a specified event has occurred, and the resulting requirements to demonstrate, in the absence of contractual provisions to the contrary, that the frustrating event is respectively the sole cause of non-performance and made performance impossible or made performance impossible and 'but for' it occurring performance would have been possible, places a substantial burden on a party seeking to rely on such a clause and will likely only drive the drafting of more and more wide-ranging and elaborate clauses.

11.3.4 Effects of frustration[65]

In English law, the consequences of frustration of a contract for the sale of goods depend upon whether the Law Reform (Frustrated Contracts) Act 1943[66] applies or not.

11.3.5 Cases to which the Frustrated Contracts Act does not apply

Section 2(5)(c) of the Frustrated Contracts Act excludes from its operation:

> Any contract to which section 7 of the Sale of Goods Act, 1979 . . . applies, or [to] any other contract for the sale, or for the sale and delivery, of specific goods, where the contract is frustrated by reason of the fact that the goods have perished.

With regard to contracts to which s. 7 of the Sale of Goods Act applies this is clear enough, but the interpretation of the second part of this clause is problematic. As we have seen, it is probable that no contract for the sale of specific goods is frustrated 'by reason of the fact that the goods have perished' otherwise than in accordance with s. 7. Yet if this is so, there is little purpose to the second half of s. 2(5)(c) of the Frustrated Contracts Act. Moreover, even if, contrary to the above contention, a contract may be frustrated in such circumstances, it is still not easy to understand the object of this clause. Three cases may be considered.

First, where there is a contract for the sale of specific goods in which the property and the risk have both passed to the buyer. Even if such a contract could be frustrated by the perishing of the goods, which seems highly improbable, the Frustrated Contracts Act does not apply. It may be that this was intended to avoid any possible doubt that in such an event the buyer is still liable to pay the whole price and cannot ask the court for any relief under the Act of 1943.

Secondly, where there is a contract for the sale of specific goods in which the property has not yet passed, but in which the risk has passed to the buyer. While seems inconceivable

[64] *Seadrill Ghana Operations Ltd.* v *Tullow Ghana Ltd* [2018] EWHC 1640 (Comm) and *Classic Maritime Inc* v *Limbungan Makmur SDN BHD* [2019] EWCA Civ 1102. For commentary see Jarvis, *Force Majeure and causation*, IELR (2019), 1, 18–20 and Bridge (2020), 136 LQR 1.

[65] See *Glanville Williams, Law Reform (Frustrated Contracts)* Act 1943, pp. 81–90.

[66] Hereafter referred to as the Frustrated Contracts Act.

that such a contract could be frustrated at all because this would render meaningless the statement that the risk is on the buyer, if such a contract can be frustrated the Act does not apply. The intention here may have been to avoid all difficulty in c.i.f. contracts should the goods perish after the risk has passed but before the bill of lading is transferred. In this event, the buyer is still bound to pay the whole price and cannot invoke the Act of 1943.

Thirdly, where the property has passed but the goods are still at the seller's risk. If such a contract is frustrated by the perishing of the goods, which again seems unlikely, the Frustrated Contracts Act does not apply. Presumably, this is to avoid any doubt that the seller must bear the whole loss and cannot transfer any of it to the buyer.

In considering the cases to which the Frustrated Contracts Act does not apply, therefore, it may be permissible to concentrate on cases under s. 7 of the Sale of Goods Act, that is to say, where there is a sale[67] of specific goods in which neither property nor risk has passed to the buyer and the contract is frustrated by the perishing of the goods. To such a case, the ordinary common law rules of frustration apply. The most important of these are as follows.

In the first place, both parties are discharged from all obligations not yet accrued before the destruction of the goods. In other words, the seller is not liable for non-delivery of the goods and the buyer is not liable for non-payment of the price.

Secondly, if the price, or any part of it, has been paid, it can be recovered if there is a total failure of consideration. This was the law even before the decision in the *Fibrosa* case[68] because the rule in *Chandler* v *Webster*,[69] which was overruled in that case, was never applied to contracts for the sale of goods.[70] In the *Fibrosa* case, buyers paid £1,000 in advance for some machinery to be manufactured by the sellers. The contract was frustrated before the machinery was completed and before any part of it was delivered, although the sellers claimed that they had already incurred considerable expense in performance of the contract. The buyers were entitled to recover their prepayment as on a total failure of consideration, and the sellers were not allowed to set off any of their expenses against the prepayment.

Today the *Fibrosa* case would be subject to the operation of the 1943 Act, but comparable cases may still arise where the common law rules continue to operate, so that if there is a total failure of consideration and the buyer can recover the price, the seller is not entitled to set off anything for expenses which they may have incurred before the frustrating event. For example, suppose that A agrees to buy some goods from B and pays the price, or part of it, in advance, but B is to do something to the goods to put them into a deliverable state. Then the goods are accidentally destroyed after B has done some of the work. This is a case to which s. 18, Rule 2 applies and, therefore, *prima facie* the property and the risk do not pass until the work is completed and the buyer has notice thereof. The case, therefore, falls within the clear wording of s. 7 of the Sale of Goods Act, and the Frustrated Contracts Act does not apply. The common law rule therefore enables the buyer to recover the whole amount paid in advance, and the seller is not entitled to retain

[67] It must also be remembered that s. 7 only applies to contracts of sale of goods, so it does not apply to any contract for services, or to a contract for the supply of goods which is not strictly a sale.

[68] [1943] AC 32.

[69] [1904] 1 KB 493.

[70] *Logan* v *Le Mesurier* (1847) 6 Moo PC 116.

any of it on account of the expenses incurred. It is difficult to see why this should be so, for as a matter of justice there seems no material distinction between such a case and the *Fibrosa* case[71] to which the Frustrated Contracts Act clearly would apply. Moreover, the arbitrary results of s. 2(5)(c) of the Frustrated Contracts Act are all the more apparent when considering that s. 7 of the Sale of Goods Act only deals with frustration through perishing of the goods. If the contract is frustrated by some other event; for example, the outbreak of war or civil unrest, s. 7 has no application and the Frustrated Contracts Act can be invoked. It is submitted that this is unjustifiable, and it is hard to see why s. 2(5)(c) of the Act of 1943 was thought necessary, especially as the workings of the Act are left to the discretion of the court.

The fourth rule at common law is that payments made under a contract which is subsequently frustrated cannot be recovered if there is only a partial failure of consideration. Suppose, for example, A agrees to buy a specific parcel of 100 tonnes of wheat now in a warehouse, the price to be paid in advance, but the goods to remain the property of the seller, B, until delivery, and delivery to be by instalments of 10 tonnes each. One instalment is delivered, and the rest of the wheat is then accidentally destroyed by fire. *Prima facie* the risk remains with the seller until the property has passed, so that this is a case within s. 7 of the Sale of Goods Act. The question whether the goods have perished within the meaning of that section probably depends upon the construction of the contract. *Prima facie* it would appear that the destruction of the undelivered part of the goods avoids the whole contract. To this case, the Frustrated Contracts Act does not apply and the position at common law remains. These common law rules, however, are by no means easy to apply to a case of this kind. At first it may seem that nothing can be recovered because there is only a partial failure of consideration, but in fact it is submitted that the buyer can recover the amount of the price which is to be attributed to the goods which have perished. The reason for this is that the risk in respect of those goods was on the seller when they perished. The same applies if the buyer has not paid the price in advance, so that the buyer should only be liable for a proportionate part of the price.

In these cases, therefore, the Frustrated Contracts Act is not needed and does not apply because the common law can achieve a satisfactory result through the rules as to risk. Yet, illogically, if the contract is frustrated by some event other than the perishing of the goods, the Frustrated Contracts Act does apply.

Finally, the usual common law rule, known as the 'entire contracts rule', is that if a contract is frustrated it is not possible to compel one party to pay for a benefit received where the contract was to perform one indivisible service, and nothing has been paid in advance. So if one party has partly (but not 'substantially')[72] performed their contract and find that they cannot complete it as a result of frustration, they are not entitled at common law to any part of the agreed price, even though some benefit has been received by the other party,[73] and perhaps even if that benefit survives the frustrating event.

But although this is the general rule at common law, it can hardly be applied without qualification to contracts of sale of goods. Even if the party who has received the benefit

[71] [1943] AC 32.
[72] As to substantial performance, see Adams and Brownsword (1990) 53 MLR 536 at 538.
[73] *Cutter* v *Powell* (1795) 6 TR 320; *Appleby* v *Myers* (1867) LR 2 CP 651.

before the frustrating event cannot be made to pay for that benefit under the contract, they may be liable in a restitutionary action, based upon his acceptance of the benefit and his refusal to disgorge it. So, for example, if part of the goods under a contract of sale has been delivered and then a frustrating event prevents the seller from delivering the remainder, the buyer may be liable in a restitutionary claim for the goods delivered, which is based at least in part on the benefit received, and his refusal to return the goods. Hitherto, it has been established law that this restitutionary claim is only available where a new promise is capable of being implied in fact.[74] If, therefore, the buyer still has the goods in his possession when the contract is frustrated, no doubt such a new promise can be implied, but if they have already disposed of them it may be that they cannot be made liable to pay a proportionate part of the price for them.[75] This seems a harsh and unreasonable result which is due to the fact that restitutionary remedies were originally based on the idea of an 'implied' contract or promise, and it is ripe for reconsideration in light of modern ideas about the basis of the law of restitution. Once again, the position is different under the Frustrated Contracts Act, though it is hard to see why sales of specific goods should be distinguished from sales of unascertained goods, or is it easy to see why the result should differ according to the nature of the frustrating event. Yet such is the effect of s. 2(5)(c) of the Frustrated Contracts Act 1943.

11.3.6 Cases to which the Frustrated Contracts Act does apply

The Frustrated Contracts Act applies *inter alia* to all contracts for the sale of unascertained goods, and to contracts for the sale of specific goods which are frustrated by some event other than the perishing of the goods. The Act effects three main changes in the law.

First, it enables a person to recover any payments made under a contract which has since been frustrated even though there has only been a partial failure of consideration. This is the effect of s. 1(2) of the Frustrated Contracts Act:

> All sums paid or payable to any party in pursuance of the contract before the time when the parties were so discharged . . . shall, in the case of sums so paid, be recoverable from him as money received by him for the use of the party by whom the sums were paid, and, in the case of sums so payable, cease to be so payable.

So, for example, if a person agrees to buy 1,000 tons of wheat, payment in advance and delivery by instalments and the contract is frustrated after only one instalment is delivered, this subsection applies. The seller is therefore bound to repay the price paid in advance even though there is no total failure of consideration.

The same result could be reached by applying s. 2(4) of the Act of 1943:

> Where it appears to the court that a part of any contract to which this Act applies can properly be severed from the remainder of the contract, being a part wholly performed before the time of discharge, or so performed except for the payment in respect of that part of the contract of

[74] *Sumpter* v *Hedges* [1898] 1 QB 673.

[75] Section 30(1) (see Chapter 7) probably has no application to such a case because it postulates circumstances in which the delivery of only part of the goods is a breach of contract, and in which the buyer may reject that part at once. The case put here is one in which the delivery of part of the goods is not a breach of contract, and the buyer cannot therefore reject them when delivered.

> sums which are or can be ascertained under the contract, the court shall treat that part of the contract as if it were a separate contract and had not been frustrated and shall treat the foregoing section of this Act as only applicable to the remainder of that contract.

By severing the executed from the frustrated part of the contract, the court can in effect turn a partial failure of consideration in respect of the whole contract into a total failure of consideration in respect of the frustrated part, and in this way enable the payer to recover his payment.

The second main change made by the Act is to enable the seller to retain part or all of a sum which would otherwise be recoverable as on a total (or now, a partial) failure of consideration, if they have incurred expenses in or for the purpose of the performance of the contract. Thus s. 1(2) continues:

> Provided that, if the party to whom the sums were so paid or payable incurred expenses before the time of discharge in, or for the purpose of, the performance of the contract, the court may, if it considers it just to do so having regard to all the circumstances of the case, allow him to retain or, as the case may be, recover the whole or any part of the sums so paid or payable, not being an amount in excess of the expenses so incurred.

Apart from imposing upper limits, the Act leaves the question of the amount of the set-off to the discretion of the court, and one possible consequence of this is that the seller will not be allowed to retain a sum equivalent to the whole of the expenses which they have incurred. The object of the Act was to avoid the injustices which followed at common law of throwing the whole loss on to one party or the other, and it is not likely that the Act merely contemplated shifting this loss from one party to the other. Probably, therefore, the court would, in a suitable case, divide the loss between the two parties and permit the seller to recover accordingly.

The third main change in the law effected by the Act is the creation of a special exception to the 'entire contracts' rule, commonly known as the rule in *Cutter* v *Powell*.[76] This case laid down that, where there is a contract to perform a complete action and nothing is payable in advance, no part of the agreed amount can be recovered if the contract is not completely (or anyhow 'substantially') performed as a result of frustration or any other cause. The position is now regulated by s. 1(3) of the Frustrated Contracts Act:

> Where any party to the contract has, by reason of anything done by any other party thereto in, or for the purpose of, the performance of the contract, obtained a valuable benefit (other than a payment of money to which the last foregoing subsection applies) before the time of discharge, there shall be recoverable from him by the said other party such sum (if any), not exceeding the value of the said benefit to the party obtaining it, as the Court considers just, having regard to all the circumstances of the case . . .

Thus where only part of the goods has been delivered and the contract is then frustrated, we have seen that at common law the seller may be unable to recover anything if the circumstances are such that it is not possible to imply a new promise to pay. Where the Frustrated Contracts Act applies, however, s. 1(3) thus enables the court to compel

[76] (1795) 6 TR 320 – but see Adams and Brownsword (1990) 53 MLR 536, at 538, as to the modification of the strict application of this rule in modern contexts.

the buyer to pay for the part which they have received, although it would not have been possible to imply the existence of a promise to pay at common law.

Many intricate questions, mostly turning on the application of s. 1(3) of the Act, were discussed by Robert Goff J (now Lord Goff) in *BP Exploration Co (Libya) Ltd* v *Hunt*.[77] In his view, this subsection is properly to be regarded as the statutory creation of a restitutionary right for benefits rendered. In the application of s. 1(3), the learned judge held that the key question was the identification and measurement of the benefit rendered before the frustrating event. The value of the benefit is the upper limit of the amount which may be awarded but, subject to that, the amount to be awarded is that sum which the court finds to be just having regard to the circumstances mentioned in the Act. He also held that where goods are delivered and retained until the frustrating event, they must be valued for the purposes of the Act as at the date of the frustrating event. But if the goods have been disposed of by the defendant prior to the frustrating event, then they must be valued at the date of disposal and no allowance can be made for any benefits which the defendant may have had from the proceeds of sale; thus if many years elapse before the frustrating event, the defendant cannot be made to pay for the valuable benefits he may have received as a result of having in his hands the proceeds of sale during that time. Robert Goff J also expressed the view that no sum should be awarded for any benefit conferred if, as a result of the frustrating event, the benefit is in effect completely nullified. For example, if goods are delivered to a buyer which have some value, but a subsequent embargo is placed on all dealings with the goods (before the buyer has the chance to dispose of any of them) then, if this is indeed a frustrating event, the buyer will have been deprived by the frustration of the contract of the whole value of the goods. In this event, no compensation can be awarded to the seller under the Act. If this is right, the decision in *Appleby* v *Myers*[78] would be no different under the Act, but the judge's views on this were *obiter* and the point remains open.

Despite the fact that the Frustrated Contracts Act was passed to mitigate the harshness of the common law rules, it still leaves a substantial area for their operation. The Act only alters the common law where something has been paid in advance or where one party has received a valuable benefit under the contract before the frustrating event (and, if Goff J is right, where that benefit survives the frustrating event). But in contracts for the sale of goods to be manufactured by the seller there is rarely any benefit obtained before the contract is fully executed, so the Frustrated Contracts Act does nothing unless there has been some prepayment. Suppose, for example, that A orders machinery from B, nothing to be paid until delivery. After B has incurred considerable expense in the construction of the machinery, the contract is frustrated by the outbreak of war or the like. Although this is not a case within s. 7 of the Sale of Goods Act and the Frustrated Contracts Act could apply, it provides no remedy to the seller. Yet surely his position is no less meritorious because he has not insisted on being paid in advance. The same result follows where there

[77] [1979] 1 WLR 783; affirmed briefly by the CA [1981] 1 WLR 236, and (on one point only) by the HL [1982] 1 WLR 253.

[78] (1867) LR 2 CP 651.

is a payment in advance, but the seller has incurred expense in excess of this amount.[79] If, for example, in the *Fibrosa* case[80] the sellers had spent well over £1,000 on the machinery before the frustrating event they would not, even under the Frustrated Contracts Act, have been able to recover anything from the buyers over and above the amount of the advance payment. Here again, therefore, the seller's rights depend on the purely fortuitous question of how much has been paid in advance.[81]

It seems, therefore, that although the Frustrated Contracts Act is a useful measure of reform, it still leaves much to be desired. In particular, it is submitted that s. 2(5)(c) could safely be repealed, and provision should be made for the case where the seller has incurred expenditure before the frustrating event, but where nothing has been paid in advance, and where the buyer has had no valuable benefit.

It is, however, possible that the whole question is a somewhat academic one. The strangest aspect of the law relating to the Frustrated Contracts Act is that there is still only one reported case in which it has been applied. The reason for this is not entirely clear, but it is possible that businessmen are less attracted than lawyers by the justice of dividing a loss between the contracting parties.

11.3.7 The COVID-19 pandemic and frustration

In a bid to curb the spread of COVID-19 during the height of the pandemic in 2020 and 2021, governments globally set travel restrictions, issued stay-at-home instructions, and introduced social distancing measures. This resulted in significant delays in the performance of contracts, additional requirements to be fulfilled and associated additional costs, plus other inconveniences involved in selling goods. Some of these contracts would have been frustrated, but in many other instances, frustration would not have been triggered.[82]

In many cases, arguments that contracts were frustrated failed because the contracts allocated the risk associated with the inability to perform a contract to one of the parties. *Wilmington Trust SP Services (Dublin) Ltd* v *Spicejet Ltd*[83] is case in point where this issue was considered. This case involved a ten-year lease of a plane rather than an outright contract of sale, but is nevertheless instructive. The defendant failed to make payments, claiming the use of the aircraft was significantly curtailed by the COVID-19 restrictions. The court held that the contract was not frustrated as the defendant had agreed to undertake all the risks of operating and maintaining the aircraft for that 10-year period, and there was no express provision in the contract that allowed the defendant to refuse to make payment. In *Bank of New York Mellon (International) Ltd* v *Cine-UK*

[79] Unless the seller has incurred expenses at least twice as great as the prepayment the problem may not arise because, as has been suggested, the court would probably divide the loss and not permit the seller to throw the whole of it on to the buyer.

[80] [1943] AC 32.

[81] But if the sum is payable before the frustrating event, the mere fact that it has not been paid will not deprive the payee of his right to sue, subject to appropriate deductions, of course.

[82] Cf. Hugh Beale and Christian Twigg-Flesner, 'COVID-19 and English Contract Law' in Ewoud Hondius, Marta Santos Silva, Andrea Nicolussi, Pablo Salvador Coderch, Christiane Wendehorst, Fryderyk Zoll (eds.), *Coronavirus and the Law in Europe* (Intersentia, 2021).

[83] [2021] EWHC 1117.

Ltd,[84] the court held that there is no such thing as temporary frustration of a contract as a matter of English law. The effect of frustration is to bring the contract to an end, so that it cannot then be revived, after restrictions are lifted. One exception to this would be where a contract is severable; in that case, each severed element might be frustrated. The Court further reiterated that frustration is not to be lightly invoked; that mere incidence of expense or delay or onerousness is not sufficient; and that there has to be as it were a break in identity between the contract as provided for and contemplated and its performance in the new circumstances. It is clear therefore, the even during the pandemic, the courts kept the interpretation of the frustration doctrine very narrow applying in very rarest of circumstances.

[84] *Bank of New York Mellon (International) Limited v Cine-UK Limited, Aew UK Reit Plc v Mecca Bingo Limited, Aew UK Reit Plc* v *Sportsdirect.com Retail Limited* [2021] EWHC 1013 (QB),

12

Transfer of title by a non-owner

12.1 *Nemo dat quod non habet*

The second half of Part I of the Act is entitled 'Transfer of Title' and deals with those cases in which a seller with no right to the goods may nonetheless pass a good title to a third party.[1] In most of these cases, the question that arises is which of two innocent people is to suffer for the fraud of a third. A thief steals goods and sells them to someone who buys in good faith and for value; a person hands goods to an agent to obtain offers and the agent sells them without authority and disposes of the proceeds; a swindler buys goods, induces the seller to let him have them on credit and promptly resells or pledges them for whatever he can get; a person sells goods but retains possession of them and fraudulently resells them to a third party. In all these cases, the law has to choose between rigorously upholding the rights of the owner to their property, on the one hand, and protecting the interests of the purchaser who buys in good faith and for value on the other hand. As Lord Denning once put it:

> In the development of our law, two principles have striven for mastery. The first is for the protection of property: no one can give a better title than he himself possesses. The second is for the protection of commercial transactions: the person who takes in good faith and for value without notice should get a better title. The first principle has held sway for a long time, but it has been modified by the common law itself and by statute so as to meet the needs of our times.[2]

The first of these principles is of course still the general rule, and is affirmed by the Act in s. 21(1):

> Subject to this Act, where goods are sold by a person who is not their owner, and who does not sell them under the authority or with the consent of the owner, the buyer acquires no better title to the goods than the seller had, unless the owner of the goods is by his conduct precluded from denying the seller's authority to sell.

This rule is frequently dignified by the use of Latin in the tag *nemo dat quod non habet*, or more shortly *nemo dat*. Some difficulty has arisen with the words 'where goods are sold' in this section, and it has been held that this does not encompass a mere agreement to sell.[3] But this is a somewhat confusing decision: the first part of s. 21(1) – the negative part stating that a non-owner cannot pass title – is merely a re-enactment of the common law principle so it would seem that part of the subsection, or the common law

[1] The extreme complexity of the law dealt with in this chapter compares unfavourably with the simplicity of Art. 2-403 of the Uniform Commercial Code, which, while less comprehensive, deals effectively with the commonest problems.

[2] *Bishopsgate Motor Finance Corpn* v *Transport Brakes Ltd* [1949] 1 KB 332, 336–7.

[3] *Shaw* v *Commissioner of Met Police* [1987] 1 WLR 1332.

in lieu, is applicable whether there is a sale or a mere agreement to sell. The second part of the subsection (beginning with the word 'unless') has the positive effect of enabling a non-owner to pass a good title, although this also appears to be merely a restatement of the common law doctrine of estoppel. The only substantive question, therefore, is whether a person who has merely agreed to buy the goods can rely upon the doctrine of estoppel. This point is discussed below.[4]

12.2 The consent of the owner

Where the goods are sold with the express authority of the owner, the ordinary rules of principal and agent apply and no special difficulty arises. But s. 21(1) also refers to the 'consent' of the owner, and reference should also be made to s. 47(1):

> Subject to this Act, the unpaid seller's right of lien . . . or stoppage in transit is not affected by any sale, or other disposition of the goods which the buyer may have made, unless the seller has assented to it.

If, therefore, the buyer, not being in possession, resells the goods and the seller assents to such sale, the sub-buyer obtains a good title free from the first seller's lien or right of stoppage in transit. The effect of such assent on the part of the seller is very similar to that of estoppel, but the difference seems to be that whereas estoppel can only operate if the assent is communicated to the sub-buyer, the seller may assent to the resale within the meaning of s. 47 even though they only communicate their assent to the buyer. But the mere fact that the seller has been informed of a resale and has not objected to it does not amount to an assent within s. 47.

In *Mordaunt Bros* v *British Oil & Cake Mills Ltd*,[5] the defendants sold oil to X, who resold part of it to the plaintiffs and gave them delivery orders in respect of that part. The plaintiffs paid X for the oil and sent the delivery orders to the defendants, who accepted them without comment. The defendants delivered instalments of the oil direct to the plaintiffs as and when they were paid by X, but, on X's falling into arrears with the payments, they refused to deliver any more. Pickford J held that the defendants had not assented to the resale within s. 47. 'In my opinion', he said,[6] 'the assent which affects the unpaid seller's right of lien must be such an assent as in the circumstances shews that the seller intends to renounce his rights against the goods. It is not enough to shew that the fact of a sub-contract has been brought to his notice and that he has assented to it merely in the sense of acknowledging receipt of the information.'[7]

On the other hand, in *D F Mount Ltd* v *Jay & Jay Co Ltd*[8] Salmon J came to a different conclusion on the following facts. The defendants were owners of 500 cartons of tinned peaches lying at the wharf of D. The defendants were approached by M at a time when the market was falling, and M told them that he had a customer for 250 cartons.

[4] See below, section 12.4.
[5] [1910] 2 KB 502.
[6] At Chapter 19.
[7] The case might well have been different if the goods had been specific goods because in that case the acceptance might have been an attornment which would have passed property, but no property can pass in unascertained goods. Cf. *Laurie & Morewood* v *John Dudin & Sons* [1926] 1 KB 223.
[8] [1960] 1 QB 159.

He made it clear that he, M, would pay the defendants out of the price he obtained from the sub-purchaser. The defendants agreed to sell the cartons to M and gave him a delivery order. M sent the order to D, who received it without acknowledgment. Later M sold the cartons to the plaintiffs, who paid M. The defendants, never having received the price from M, subsequently claimed to be still entitled to the cartons. Salmon J held that the defendants had assented to the sale within the meaning of s. 47:

> In the present case the defendants were anxious to get rid of the goods on a falling market. They knew that M could only pay for them out of the money he obtained from his customers, and that he could only obtain the money from his customers against delivery orders in favour of those customers. In my view the true inference is that the defendants assented to M reselling the goods, in the sense that they intended to renounce their rights against the goods and to take the risk of M's honesty.[9]

The maxim *nemo dat* has a wider application than s. 21 of the Sale of Goods Act because the latter only applies to a sale of goods by a non-owner, while the maxim also covers those cases where an owner sells goods, but is unable to sell them free from some encumbrance or charge existing in favour of a third party. In fact, this is an unusual situation because the law generally sets its face against the recognition of encumbrances which run with chattels into the hands of third parties[10] and, of course, equitable rights are always subject to those of a purchaser for value in good faith without notice.[11] But there is one not uncommon situation where the law does recognise such encumbrances as binding on third parties. Where a person pledges goods, or the documents of title to goods, and subsequently the pledgee returns the goods or the documents to the pledgor for a limited purpose, for example to obtain clearance of the goods from the warehouseman, any unauthorised disposition by the pledgor will not prejudice the rights of the pledgee.[12] In other words, the seller, although owner of the goods, cannot sell them free from the pledgee's right. It may be that, technically, this result depends upon the pledgee's retention of possession, but since the courts are prepared to hold that the return of the custody of the goods or documents of title does not transfer possession back to the pledgor, this is not much consolation to the innocent third party. It might well be thought that the extension of the rule *nemo dat* to these cases is unjustifiable, for it seems extraordinary that an owner who is in actual possession of their goods with the consent of the pledgee cannot transfer a good title free from the pledge to an innocent third party. The hardship on the third party who buys goods from the admitted owner in actual possession is so obvious as to need no stressing. At all events, there are two limitations on the rule *nemo dat* in this connection.

In the first place, if the pledgee returns the goods to the pledgor with an unrestricted authority to sell them, an innocent buyer from the pledgor obtains a good title free from

[9] At Chapter 7.

[10] *McGruther* v *Pitcher* [1904] 2 Ch 306; *Dunlop Pneumatic Tyre Co Ltd* v *Selfridge & Co Ltd* [1915] AC 847. But see *Lord Strathcona* v *Dominion Coal Co Ltd* [1926] AC 108.

[11] See *Gray* v *Smith, JMPC Sales Limited, and Edwards* [2013] EWHC 4136 (Comm), where an undisclosed agent who had acquired the legal title to a car but held it on behalf of his principal sold it to a bona fide purchaser for value who gained good title to the car.

[12] *North Western Bank* v *Poynter* [1895] AC 56, (1894) 22 R (HL) 1, revsg (1894) 21 R 513; *Reeves* v *Capper* (1838) 5 Bing NC 136; *Official Assignee of Madras* v *Mercantile Bank of India Ltd* [1935] AC 53; *Mercantile Bank of India Ltd* v *Central Bank of India Ltd* [1938] AC 287. For Scots law perspectives on this whole area, see Rodger, 1971 JR 193, and Gretton, 1990 JR 23.

the pledge, even though the pledgor fraudulently absconds with the purchase money.[13] And in the second place, if the pledgor is a mercantile agent, the return of the goods to them by the pledgee will enable the third party to plead that the pledgor was in possession of them with the consent of the owner and consequently that they are protected by s. 2(1) of the Factors Act 1889.[14]

12.3 The exceptions to *nemo dat*

As the opening words of s. 21 indicate, there are a number of exceptions to the general rule *nemo dat* which are of considerable importance, though they do not, of course, abrogate the main rule itself, at any rate so far as the sale of goods is concerned. It is perhaps worth pointing out that the exceptions are all cumulative from the point of view of the party seeking protection against the original owner. They need only bring their case under one of the exceptions to obtain protection against the former owner. Failure to bring their case under this or that exception does not prevent them from succeeding under a different exception. We proceed now to examine the exceptions.

12.4 Estoppel

The first exception is provided by the doctrine of estoppel, which is embodied, in this connection, in the concluding words of s. 21(1) itself, which may be repeated here:

> . . . unless the owner of the goods is by his conduct precluded from denying the seller's authority to sell.

This provision merely throws us back on the common law doctrine of estoppel, for it gives no indication when the owner is by their conduct precluded from denying the seller's authority to sell.[15] It seems that there are two distinct cases where the owner is so precluded. The first is where they have by their words or conduct represented to the buyer that the seller is the true owner, or has the owner's authority to sell, and the second is where the owner, by their negligent failure to act, allows the seller to appear as the owner or as having the owner's authority to sell. These are generally called estoppel by representation and estoppel by negligence respectively. The terminology of the subject is, however, somewhat confusing. On the one hand, estoppel by representation is sometimes subdivided into estoppel by words and estoppel by conduct, while the wording of the Act suggests that estoppel by words is merely a species of estoppel by conduct. But there is

[13] *Babcock* v *Lawson* (1880) 5 QBD 284.

[14] *Lloyds Bank* v *Bank of America* [1938] 2 KB 147. On the Factors Act, see below, section 12.5 *et seq*.

[15] There had been suggestions (to which *Shaw* v *Commissioner of Met Police* [1987] 1 WLR 1332 appeared to give some countenance) that s. 21 actually operates independently of the doctrine of estoppel, and so perhaps the 'duty' requirement of common law estoppel does not then apply. But this idea was rejected by the New South Wales Court of Appeal in *Thomas Australia Wholesale Vehicle Trading Co Pty Ltd* v *Marac Finance Australia Ltd* [1985] 3 NSWR 452, and (at p. 470) McHugh JA specifically endorsed the sentence set out above in the text, then appearing in the 4th edn of this work at p. 180. Note further the Scots law comments in Reid, *The Law of Property in Scotland* (1996, Butterworth/Law Society of Scotland), para. 680, emphasising that the Scottish doctrine of personal bar is not precisely analogous to estoppel and that care is therefore needed in handling the English authorities on this topic. There are no Scottish cases in point, however. See further Carey Miller, *Corporeal Moveables in Scots Law* 2nd edn (2005, W Green & Son Ltd, Edinburgh) para 10.20; Reid and Blackie, *Personal Bar* (2006, W Green & Son Ltd, Edinburgh) chapter 11(II).

also much controversy about the propriety of the term 'estoppel by negligence'. Strictly speaking, it seems there is no such thing as estoppel by negligence.[16] All these estoppels rest in the last resort on a *representation* of some kind.[17]

A person may make a representation by words or by conduct, but how does a person make a representation by negligence? The answer appears to be that this is really a representation through an omission.[18] A person who negligently omits to inform another of certain facts may be said to be representing that the facts calling for report do not exist. Again, a person who omits to correct a misrepresentation made by a third party may in certain circumstances be treated as responsible for that representation. Thus if A stands by while B makes a representation to C which A knows to be incorrect, and which he has a duty to correct, A may be said, loosely, to be guilty of misrepresentation by negligence. In truth, what has happened is that A, by his negligence, has allowed B to mislead C by a misrepresentation. Thus, the correct approach is that this kind of estoppel rests in every case on a representation. The representation may be (1) by words, or (2) by conduct, or (3) by a negligent omission.

Although the point is not free from doubt, it seems that in the first two cases it is unnecessary to show fraud or an intent to deceive or negligence as a foundation for the estoppel.[19] The only requirements are those common to all estoppels, namely that the representation must be one of fact, that it must be unambiguous and that it must be acted upon. But although neither fraud nor negligence needs to be shown the representation must at least be *voluntary*, as that term is used in the law. A person who is induced by violence or duress to sign a piece of paper containing a representation in circumstances where the violence or duress would justify a plea of *non est factum* if the document was a contractual document cannot be held to have made a representation, even where some third party has relied upon it.[20]

In the third type of case referred to above, however, it seems that negligence, in the sense of a breach of a duty of care (or, of course, fraud) must be proved. So where a person is charged with having omitted to correct a misleading statement by a third party, and that is the basis of the alleged estoppel, it must be shown that the defendant had some duty to correct the misstatement.

12.4.1 Estoppel by words

A good example of estoppel by words is the decision of the Court of Appeal in *Henderson & Co* v *Williams*.[21] In this case, G & Co were induced by the fraud of one F to sell them goods lying in certain warehouses of which the defendants were warehousemen. The

[16] See *Saunders* v *Anglia Building Society* [1971] AC 1004, 1038 per Lord Pearson, and also Atiyah, *Essays on Contract* (1986, OUP), pp. 316–19.

[17] This suggestion was approved by Popplewell J in *Lenn Mayhew-Lewis* v *Westminster Scaffolding plc*, 5 March 1999 (unreported).

[18] Ibid.

[19] A good example of the confusion in this branch of the law is provided by *Seton, Laing & Co* v *Lafone* (1887) 19 QBD 68 where the whole discussion was in terms of estoppel by negligence, and yet the only representation was that of the defendant himself. This was a simple example of estoppel by representation, and negligence ought not to have been relevant.

[20] *Debs* v *Sibec Developments Ltd* [1990] RTR 91.

[21] [1895] 1 QB 521.

circumstances were such that the contract between G & Co and F was void for mistake. On the instructions of G & Co, the defendants transferred the goods in their books to the order of F. F sold the goods to the plaintiffs who, being suspicious of the bona fides of the seller, made inquiries of the defendants. The latter supplied the plaintiffs with a written statement that they held the goods to the order of F, and, when this did not satisfy them, they endorsed it with a further statement that they now held the goods to the plaintiffs' order. G & Co, not having been paid by F, instructed the defendants not to deliver the goods to the plaintiffs but to themselves, and they gave them an indemnity against so doing. It was held that both G & Co and the defendants were estopped from denying the plaintiffs' right to the goods, the former because they had represented that F was the owner by ordering the defendants to transfer the goods into his name in their books, and the latter because they had attorned to the plaintiffs, that is represented to them, that they held the goods to their order.[22]

A more modern case of estoppel by words is *Shaw* v *Commissioner of Metropolitan Police*[23] where the plaintiffs agreed to buy a car from one L who had obtained it from the true owner, together with a certificate signed by him saying that he had sold the car to L. In fact this was untrue, as the owner had not sold the car to L – he had merely authorised L to sell it on his behalf. L was a swindler who did not pay for the car, and when suspicions were aroused he disappeared, leaving the title to the car in doubt. The plaintiffs had the effrontery to claim that they had acquired title under s. 21 of the Act even though they had not paid the price to L or anyone else. The Court of Appeal denied the plaintiffs' claim, though on the rather unsatisfactory ground (as noted above) that s. 21 did not apply where the buyer had merely *agreed to buy* the goods, but only where he had bought them. This is unconvincing, because if (as has been submitted) s. 21 is merely a statement of the common law principle of estoppel, it ought to protect anyone who has acted to his prejudice on the representation in question. It would therefore have been better to have held that the plaintiffs' claim failed because they had not acted to their prejudice since they had not paid the price.[24]

12.4.2 Estoppel by conduct

An early leading case on estoppel by conduct is *Farquharson Bros* v *King & Co Ltd*.[25] The plaintiffs here were timber merchants who owned timber housed with a dock company. The plaintiffs' clerk had authority to send delivery orders to the dock company, and the

[22] The position of the warehouseman in this sort of case is unenviable because if he had delivered the goods to the plaintiffs he would have been liable to G & Co for disobeying their instructions: *Rogers* v *Lambert* [1891] 1 QB 318. His proper course is to take interpleader proceedings, under which he disclaims title himself, and leaves the court to sort out the claims of the other contending parties.

[23] [1987] 1 WLR 1332.

[24] A difficulty was caused by the fact that they had given a banker's draft for the price, but this was never cashed, and the bank refunded the money, subject to an undertaking to indemnify them if the draft was later cashed in circumstances in which the bank was liable. It is probable that this was thought sufficient action in reliance to raise an estoppel, which may explain why the court was anxious to avoid placing its decision on estoppel. But the result could perhaps have been avoided by application of the principle in *Société Italo-Belge* v *Palm Oil & Vegetable Oils* [1982] 1 All ER 19 (trifling acts of reliance do not justify estoppel when it would be inequitable).

[25] [1902] AC 325.

latter were instructed to act on the clerk's delivery orders, but the clerk had no authority to sell the timber himself. The clerk fraudulently transferred some of the timber to himself under an assumed name and gave the dock company instructions accordingly. He then sold the timber to the defendants under his assumed name and instructed the dock company to deliver the goods to their order. The plaintiffs, having discovered the clerk's fraud, brought an action for conversion. The House of Lords held that the defence of estoppel failed because the defendants had not acted on any representation made by the plaintiffs concerning the authority of the clerk. Even the dock company would not have needed, or been able to plead, estoppel. As Lord Halsbury pointed out, they would not have been liable simply because they had done nothing more than obey their principal's instructions. Despite the vigorous speeches of Lord Halsbury[26] and Lord Macnaghten in this case, and the expressions of astonishment that the defence should ever have been set up, let alone accepted (as it was by the Court of Appeal), it is by no means easy to lay down what sort of conduct is sufficient to invoke the doctrine of estoppel.

One thing, at any rate, is clear, that merely allowing another person to have possession of goods which they do not own is not *by itself* enough to bring into operation the doctrine of estoppel. There are so many different circumstances in which an owner of goods may allow another to have possession of them that it cannot be claimed that such conduct amounts to an unambiguous representation that the party in possession is the owner or has the owner's authority to sell. Although the Privy Council accepted a proposition of almost this width in *Commonwealth Trust Ltd* v *Akotey*,[27] this case was virtually overruled by the Privy Council itself in *Mercantile Bank of India Ltd* v *Central Bank of India Ltd*.[28] In this latter case, X pledged railway receipts, which in this case were documents of title,[29] with the Central Bank in return for an advance. In accordance with the usual practice, the Bank then returned them to X to enable him to obtain clearance of the goods, but X fraudulently pledged them with the Mercantile Bank in return for an advance from them. It was held that there was no estoppel because the possession of the railway receipts 'no more conveyed a representation that the merchants (X) were entitled to dispose of the property than the actual possession of the goods themselves would have done'.[30] If estoppel by conduct is to be invoked there must be some act which positively misleads the third party beyond merely allowing a non-owner to have possession of the goods.[31]

In *Central Newbury Car Auctions Ltd* v *Unity Finance Ltd*,[32] a swindler called on the plaintiffs and offered to buy a Morris car on hire-purchase terms, leaving with the plaintiffs in part-exchange a Hillman car which, as it transpired, was also let on hire-purchase. The swindler signed hire-purchase forms whereby the Morris was to be sold to a finance

[26] Lord Halsbury's speech was a little too vigorous; for he thought the clerk was guilty of larceny: see the note by Pollock in [1902] AC at p. 329.

[27] [1926] AC 72.

[28] [1938] AC 287. Lord Denning in Central *Newbury Car Auctions* v *Unity Finance Ltd* [1957] 1 QB 371 was willing to support it, but his opinion is inconsistent with a mass of other authority.

[29] In English commercial practice railway receipts are not usually documents of title, but if they were the result of such facts would probably be different in England because of the Factors Act which did not apply in India. See below, section 12.5.1 *et seq*.

[30] At p. 303 per Lord Wright.

[31] *Jerome* v *Bentley* [1952] 2 All ER 114.

[32] [1957] 1 QB 371, followed in *J Sargent (Garages) Ltd* v *Motor Auctions Ltd* [1977] RTR 121.

company and then hired to him, and he was thereupon given the registration book and permitted to drive the Morris away. The finance company refused the hire-purchase proposal and the car was later discovered in the possession of the defendants, who had bought it in good faith from an unknown person, who was presumed to be the swindler. The Court of Appeal (Denning LJ dissenting) held that there was no estoppel and that the plaintiffs were entitled to recover the car. The registration book (now, registration document) of a car is not a document of title,[33] and in fact it contains a warning that the person in whose name the car is registered may or may not be the owner. Hence it was not possible to say that the plaintiffs had in any way represented the swindler to be the owner, or to have the owner's authority to sell. The case for invoking estoppel was based entirely on the fact that the owner had entrusted possession of the goods to another party, and this (as we have seen) is normally insufficient to raise an estoppel. Nevertheless, the result in this kind of case is a serious anomaly, having regard to the fact that a private purchaser from a person in possession under a hire-purchase agreement is now protected by Part III of the Hire-Purchase Act 1964.[34]

On the other hand, in *Eastern Distributors Ltd* v *Goldring*[35] where, in pursuance of a plan to deceive a finance company, one M signed and delivered forms to C which enabled C to represent that he had M's authority to sell a car belonging to him, it was held by the Court of Appeal that M was estopped from setting up his title against the plaintiffs who had bought the car from C. It was also held that the estoppel in fact operated to pass a good title to the plaintiffs not only against M himself, but also against a buyer in good faith from M. It is, however, not entirely clear why the case was not disposed of on the simpler ground that C had M's apparent authority to sell, although in fact he exceeded that authority.[36]

So also, if the owner of goods entrusts the possession of them to a dealer with authority to sell, or to obtain offers or something of that kind, the own7er would normally be estopped if the dealer sold without authority or in excess of their authority. But this form of estoppel is now of little practical importance because it has been largely overtaken by the statutory protection conferred on innocent purchasers by the Factors Act 1889.[37]

There is an important distinction between a representation (or conduct equivalent to a representation) that the seller has authority to sell the goods as agent, on the one hand, and a representation that the seller is himself the owner, on the other hand. Where the true owner represents the seller to be the owner, or enables the seller to represent himself as owner, and knows that the seller will or may sell as an owner, it is immaterial that the seller sells outside the ordinary course of business unless this demonstrates lack of good faith on the buyer's part. In *Lloyds and Scottish Finance Ltd* v *Williamson* ,[38] the plaintiff entrusted his car to a dealer and authorised him to sell at or above a certain price. The dealer sold the car above this price but the price was not paid in cash but set off against a debt owed by the dealer to a friend of the buyer. For this reason, the sale was outside the

[33] *Joblin* v *Watkin & Roseveare (Motors) Ltd* (1948) 64 TLR 464.
[34] See below, *et seq*. See also *Shogun Finance Ltd* v *Hudson* [2003] UKHL 62 – discussed in Chapter 2 *et seq*.
[35] [1957] 2 QB 600.
[36] See per Devlin LJ at p. 606.
[37] See below, section 12.5.1.
[38] [1965] 1 WLR 404.

ordinary course of business but it was held that this was immaterial. Since the owner knew that the seller might very well sell as a principal and not as an agent and had authorised him to do so, it made no difference how he sold the goods.

But if the case is one of ostensible agency the position is different. For it is reasonably implicit that an agent is only authorised to sell in the ordinary course of business and if they do not do so there will be no estoppel. Ostensible agency may arise in one of two ways: it may arise where the owner authorises an agent to sell as agent only, or it may arise where the buyer knows that the agent is not the owner and acts on the assumption that the agent is an agent only. This latter possibility is illustrated by *Motor Credits (Hire Finance) Ltd* v *Pacific Motor Auctions Pty Ltd*.[39] In this case M Ltd, who were dealers in vehicles, sold a number of vehicles to the plaintiffs under a 'display agreement' whereby M Ltd remained in possession of the cars for display in their showrooms. They were paid 90 per cent of the price and were authorised to sell the vehicles as agents for the plaintiffs. M Ltd got into financial difficulties and the plaintiffs revoked their authority to sell the vehicles, but M Ltd nevertheless sold a number of them to the defendants who were bona fide purchasers for value. The sale was outside the ordinary course of business, partly because it took place after business hours and partly because the defendants agreed to sell the cars back to M Ltd in certain events (in fact it is clear that the defendants really wanted the vehicles as security for pre-existing debts owed to them). The defendants knew all about the display plan agreement and could not therefore have supposed that M Ltd were owners, though they did suppose M Ltd to have authority to sell. On these facts, the Australian High Court held that the defendants were not protected; as this was a case of ostensible agency and not ostensible ownership the defendants would only have been protected if the sale had been in the ordinary course of business. This decision was reversed on appeal to the Privy Council,[40] without consideration of this point, on the ground that the defendants were protected by s. 24 of the Act. This aspect of the case is considered later[41]

12.4.3 Estoppel by negligence

As we have already seen, estoppel by negligence may be established where the owner of goods has, by their negligence, allowed a third party to represent himself as owner or as having the owner's authority to sell. But the application of the principle of estoppel by negligence is severely restricted by the fact that, as in the law of tort, there can be no negligence unless there is a duty of care. It is for this reason that:

> If I lose a valuable dog and find it afterwards in the possession of a gentleman who bought it from somebody whom he believed to be the owner, it is no answer to me to say that he would never have been cheated into buying the dog if I had chained it up or put a collar on it, or kept it under proper control. If a person leaves a watch or a ring on a seat in the park or on a table at a cafe and it ultimately gets into the hands of a bona fide purchaser, it is no answer to the true owner to say that it was his carelessness and nothing else that enabled the finder to pass it off as his own.[42]

[39] (1963) 109 CLR 87.
[40] [1965] AC 867.
[41] See below, section 12.9.
[42] *Farquharson Bros* v *King & Co Ltd* [1902] AC at 335–6 per Lord Macnaghten.

Since there is no duty of care on an owner of property to see that it does not get lost or stolen, it is comparatively rare to find a clear case of estoppel by negligence in this connection. The dictum of Ashurst J in *Lickbarrow* v *Mason*,[43] which is frequently quoted in this connection by despairing counsel, that 'wherever one of two innocent persons must suffer by the acts of a third, he who has enabled such third person to occasion the loss must sustain it', has been more qualified than any other case in the books and has been dissented from more often than it has been followed.[44]

The necessity for establishing a duty of care often precludes the operation of the doctrine of estoppel in those cases where an owner is induced to part with goods to a buyer under a contract void for 'mistake'. In those cases, the owner can claim the goods even from a bona fide purchaser from the fraudulent buyer, and it is no defence to say that it was the owner's negligence, however gross, which enabled the buyer to obtain the goods unless a duty to take care can be established.[45] Similarly, just as entrusting goods to another has been held not to amount to a representation that they are the owner or have authority to sell, so also if that party represent themselves to be the owner or to have authority to sell, the owner will not normally be defeated by the plea of estoppel by negligence. Once again, the reason given is that there is no duty of care on the owner of goods to protect the possible interests of third parties.[46] On the other hand, estoppel by negligence was applied in *Coventry Shepherd & Co* v *Great Eastern Rly Co*,[47] where the defendants negligently issued two delivery orders relating to the same load of goods. The person to whom they were issued was thereby able to represent to the plaintiffs (to whom he pledged the goods) that the goods were in fact available after they had already been disposed of.

A more modern case where a duty to take care was established, although on the facts it was held not to be broken, is *Mercantile Credit Co Ltd* v *Hamblin*[48] in which the facts were these. The defendant wished to borrow some money on the security of her car. She consulted a dealer who was apparently solvent and respectable and he gave her some hire-purchase forms to sign in blank. She signed the forms thinking they were some sort of mortgage transaction, but retained possession of her car throughout. The dealer told her that he would find out what sum he could arrange for her to raise and would let her know. He also gave her a blank cheque which she was to fill in for the agreed figure on the scheme being completed. In fact, the dealer completed the hire-purchase forms so as to constitute an offer by himself to sell the car to the plaintiffs, a finance company, and an offer by the defendant to take the car on hire-purchase terms from the plaintiffs. Without further reference to the defendant, he sent the forms to the plaintiffs who purported to accept both offers. The defendant repudiated the alleged agreement and it was held by the Court of Appeal that she was not bound by it because she had not in fact authorised the

[43] (1787) 2 TR 63.

[44] See, e.g., *Farquharson Bros* v *King & Co* [1902] AC at 342 per Lord Lindley, 'Such a doctrine is far too wide'; *London Joint Stock Bank* v *MacMillan* [1918] AC 777, 836 per Lord Parmoor; *Jones* v *Waring & Gillow Ltd* [1926] AC 670, 693 per Lord Sumner; *Wilson & Meeson* v *Pickering* [1946] 1 KB 422, 425 per Lord Greene. The truth is that the dictum is really a statement of *principle*, rather than a *rule*.

[45] See, e.g., *Cundy* v *Lindsay* (1878) 3 App Cas 459; *Ingram* v *Little* [1961] 1 QB 31; *Lewis* v *Averay* [1972] 1 QB 198. The House of Lords reviewed these cases in *Shogun Finance Ltd* v *Hudson* [2003] UKHL 62 – see Chapter 2 *et seq*.

[46] See the *Mercantile Bank of India* case [1938] AC 287, above, section 12.5.2.

[47] (1883) 11 QBD 776.

[48] [1965] 2 QB 242, followed in *Beverley Acceptances Ltd* v *Oakley* [1982] RTR 417.

dealer to make any offer to the plaintiffs and was not estopped from denying that she had done so. Although the court held that the defendant did owe a duty of care sufficient to raise an estoppel, it was held that she had not in fact failed to take care. In the particular circumstances of the case, it was not unreasonable for her to have trusted the dealer.

The importance of the case lies in the fact that the court treated the existence and the nature of the duty of care in such circumstances as the same as those which arise in the ordinary law of negligence. Thus, Pearson LJ found a 'sufficient relationship or proximity' between the defendant and the plaintiffs from the fact that the defendant intended that the documents which she signed should constitute an offer to contract subject to certain conditions being fulfilled, and that she had entrusted the documents to the dealer and was thereby arming him with 'the means to make a contract ostensibly on her behalf'.[49]

On the other hand, a majority of the House of Lords arrived at a different conclusion in the important decision in *Moorgate Mercantile Co Ltd* v *Twitchings*.[50] This case arose out of the activities of a body called HPI (Hire-Purchase Information).[51] It was a private body which kept a register of vehicles which were the subject of hire-purchase agreements, or which had been notified to have been stolen. Any finance company which let a vehicle on such an agreement could register the agreement with HPI, and any dealer who was offered a vehicle for purchase could easily find out from HPI whether the vehicle was registered with them. At the time when this case arose there was no express obligation on the plaintiff (the claimant) as a member of HPI to register agreements,[52] although in practice this was the whole purpose of membership, and the great majority did so. Dealers, in practice, relied on the information given by HPI as there was rarely any other means of discovering whether a vehicle was subject to a hire-purchase agreement. In the case in question, the plaintiffs had omitted to register a particular agreement and this was held to be careless on their part. The hirer under this agreement sold the vehicle to the defendants, who inquired from HPI if the agreement was registered and were told that it was not. The plaintiffs then sued the defendants for conversion and the defendants argued that the plaintiffs were estopped from asserting their title.

The defendants' plea was put in two alternative ways. First, they argued that there was estoppel by actual representation. This argument depended on the assumption that HPI gave the information as agents for the plaintiffs, but it failed in any event because the information which HPI gave the defendants was in fact (as the majority of the House of Lords held) true. HPI said the agreement was not registered; they did not say that there was no such agreement in existence.

[49] [1965] 2 QB 242, 275.

[50] [1977] AC 890; followed in *Cadogan Finance Ltd* v *Keith Lavery* (1982) Com LR 248 (omission to notify registration authorities of finance interest in aircraft).

[51] In the early 1990s HPI was sold. It is now owned by Equifax, a credit referencing organisation. In 1997 it was merged with the independent Mileage Verification Association and it provides information both to the motor industry and to consumers. Information about outstanding hire-purchase agreements is now provided by applying to Equifax or Experian credit reference agency.

[52] In the 7th and earlier editions of this book it was stated that HPI had altered its rules since the *Moorgate Mercantile* case so as to impose an obligation to register agreements on its members. This was an unfortunate error which was based on some remarks in the speeches in the House of Lords, where the judges were clearly labouring under the same mistake. What seems to have happened was that, at the time of the *Moorgate Mercantile* case, some members were under an obligation to register agreements, but not all, and in particular not the plaintiff in that case. Following the decision, the obligation to register was totally removed from the HPI rules so that members were no longer bound to register agreements. Professor Atiyah acknowledged in previous editions that he was obliged to HPI for correspondence on this subject.

The defendants' second argument was more difficult. They argued that the plaintiffs were guilty of an omission (to register) and that this gave rise to an estoppel. It was accepted on all hands that the question to which this led was whether the plaintiffs were under a duty to the defendants to register the agreement, or, more strictly, a duty to take reasonable care to register. By a majority, it was held there was no such duty. Membership of HPI specifically did not impose a duty on the defendants to register agreements and the majority did not see where else such a duty could come from. In earlier editions of this book, it was suggested that the dissenting speeches of Lords Wilberforce and Salmon carried more conviction. As Lord Wilberforce pointed out, in practice everyone in the motor trade relied heavily on the registration of hire-purchase agreements with HPI, and it would not seem unreasonable to hold that a duty to register arose out of these facts. But today, it seems that the majority decision in a sense anticipated the current trend to restrict the growth of liability in negligence, and to reassert the view that tort duties are only to be imposed with great caution on parties who have expressly restricted their contractual obligations.[53]

This case can be contrasted with the more recent High Court ruling in *Chatfields-Martin Walter Ltd* v *Lombard North Central plc.* [54] C bought a van from T, knowing that it was owned by L, a finance company, who had supplied it on hire-purchase. T agreed to pay off the outstanding amount so C could become the outright owner. C checked HPI for the amount outstanding on the hire-purchase agreement. T then issued a cheque for that amount which C forwarded to the finance company. When C checked HPI again three weeks later, the record showed that the outstanding amount was now zero. C assumed that the cheque had cleared and that the hire-purchase agreement had been settled, but this had, in fact, not yet happened. It was held that by changing the entry on the HPI register, L had made a continuing representation to anyone searching HPI that L no longer had any interest in the van. Consequently, L was estopped from asserting its title to the van. In this case, the matter was treated as an estoppel by representation rather than by negligence. Moreover, the fact that C had checked HPI twice and thereby noticed the change in the records regarding the amount outstanding was significant in deciding that an estoppel was present.

12.4.4 Effect of estoppel

It should finally be added that if estoppel does operate it will do so whether the transaction is a sale, pledge or other disposition, but that it will not bind anyone who does not claim under the person estopped. A person claiming under title paramount cannot be bound by an estoppel to which they were not privy.

It is not entirely clear whether the effect of estoppel is actually to pass a title good against the party estopped. On one view, estoppel is merely a rule of evidence which precludes a person from adducing certain evidence before a court – they are not permitted to deny statements which they have previously made where the doctrine operates. On this

[53] So *a fortiori* it has been held there can be no duty on the part of a member of the public to warn the police that a car has been stolen (which information would also normally be passed on to and registered by HPI or now its successors – see section 12.11): *Debs* v *Sibec Developments Ltd* [1990] RTR 91.

[54] [2014] EWHC 1222.

view, the 'real' legal position remains unaffected by estoppel. The former owner remains the owner, but simply cannot claim the goods as against anyone entitled to the benefit of the estoppel.[55] But in *Eastern Distributors Ltd* v *Goldring*,[56] the Court of Appeal said that the effect of estoppel anyhow in some cases relating to the sale of goods is to pass a real title, and not merely a 'metaphorical title by estoppel', though precisely when this is the case remains obscure. Since then it has been asserted that estoppel anyhow cannot help transfer a title in cases where s. 16 prevents property passing because the goods are unascertained.[57]

Somewhat akin to the doctrine of estoppel in this connection are cases in which a person who sells goods without title subsequently acquires the title; for example, by paying off the true owner. In such circumstances, it has been suggested[58] that the seller's subsequent acquisition of title 'goes to feed' the defective title of the buyer and any person deriving title through the buyer. This concept has not, however, been fully worked out and may give rise to some interesting questions; for example, can a title be acquired and 'fed' in goods which have already been consumed?[59]

12.4.5 Relationship between estoppel and other principles

It will be apparent that the doctrine of estoppel is closely connected with other legal principles. The ostensible authority of an agent to transfer the title of goods in excess of their actual authority is based on principles similar to, if not identical with, those in the doctrine of estoppel. It must be admitted that legal theory in these areas is in a state of some confusion and it is not always easy to understand the basis for a decision. Estoppel, in particular, sometimes appears to be invoked to justify decisions which can be explained more simply. For instance, in *Snook* v *London West Riding Investments Ltd*[60] the plaintiff was held estopped from denying the title of the defendant's predecessors to a car, although he had intended to transfer the property to them.

The use of estoppel in such cases seems merely confusing. The whole purpose of the doctrine is to prevent the plaintiff from denying their real intentions when they have misled other parties as to those intentions. Where in fact their real intention was to transfer title it is surely unnecessary to invoke estoppel.

12.5 Sale by agent

This exception may be quickly disposed of.[61] Section 21(1) says, *inter alia*, that if the goods are not sold with the authority or consent of the owner, the buyer acquires no title. But this section is subject to the provisions of the Act, and s. 62 preserves the rules of common

[55] See, e.g., *Simm* v *Anglo-American Telegraph Co* (1879) 5 QBD 188, 206 per Brett LJ. The idea that estoppel is a mere rule of evidence is challenged in Atiyah, *Essays on Contract* (1986, OUP), pp. 306–12.

[56] [1957] 2 QB 600, 611.

[57] *In re London Wine Co (Shippers) Ltd* (1986) PCC 121.

[58] *Butterworth* v *Kingsway Motors Ltd* [1954] 1 WLR 1286; *Anderson* v *Ryan* [1967] IR 34.

[59] See Chapter 5.

[60] [1967] 2 QB 786.

[61] For analysis from a Scots law perspective, see Macgregor, *The Law of Agency in Scotland* (2012, W Green & Son Ltd, Edinburgh), paras 3.07–3.09.

law regarding principal and agent. It follows that, according to the ordinary principles of common law, a sale within the usual or 'ostensible' authority of an agent, even though outside their actual authority, will bind the owner. It is not of course every agent who has a 'usual' authority. Unless the agent belongs to a certain class of agents who usually have a certain authority, it cannot be said that the agent has any 'usual' authority wider than their actual authority.[62]

It is not within the scope of this work to analyse in detail the circumstances in which an agent can pass a title to a third party where they act beyond their actual authority. It seems, however, that in addition to cases in which the agent acts within their 'usual' or 'ostensible' authority, there is an independent principle which, at least in some circumstances, enables an agent to pass a title beyond their actual authority. If, for example, an agent is authorised to sell at a certain price and sells below this price to a bona fide purchaser, it seems that the purchaser gets a good title, irrespective of whether the agent has any usual or ostensible authority or, indeed, whether they are known to be an agent at all. In such circumstances, the courts draw a distinction not unlike that drawn in vicarious liability in the law of tort.[63] If the agent has acted within the course of their employment as an agent, they bind the principal even though they exceed their actual authority; if, on the other hand, they act right outside the course of their employment, they do not bind their principal.[64] Another view, however, is that this line of authorities is an anomaly and should not be extended.[65] On this view, the third party will only be protected if the agent had apparent or usual authority beyond their actual authority. Of course, if the buyer is aware that the agent is exceeding their authority, no property will pass.[66]

A person who is not the owner of goods but sells with the consent or authority of the owner may, of course, sell expressly as agent, in which case the only contract of sale is that created between the owner and the buyer; whether the agent is entitled to sue, or liable to be sued on such a contract depends on ordinary principles of agency. But it can also happen that the party actually arranging the sale sells as principal and not as agent, even though they are not the owner. For example, where goods are sold by S to B1 under a contract with a 'retention of title clause', which provides that property is to remain in S until payment in full, but permits B1 to resell the goods in the ordinary course of business, then a resale by B1 to B2 may create a contract of sale between these two parties. B1 may thus be reselling with the consent of the owner S, but he sells as a principal, not as an agent. S will not be a party to the sale contract between B1 and B2.[67]

[62] *Jerome* v *Bentley* [1952] 2 All ER 114.

[63] Treitel, *Law of Contract* (12th edn, 2007, Sweet & Maxwell), §14–084.

[64] See, e.g., *Brocklesby* v *Temperance Building Society* [1895] AC 173; *Fry* v *Smellie* [1912] 3 KB 282; cf. *France* v *Clark* (1884) 26 Ch D 257. Despite some rather loose dicta in *Mercantile Credit Co Ltd* v *Hamblin* [1965] 2 QB 242, it is thought that negligence is not an essential feature of this type of liability. The question was left open in *Moorgate Mercantile Ltd* v *Twitching* [1977] AC 890.

[65] See *Chitty on Contract* (31st edn, 2012, Sweet & Maxwell), §31–065.

[66] *Cressman & anor* v *Coys of Kensington* [2004] EWCA Civ 47.

[67] See Aluminium Industrie BV v Romalpa Aluminium Ltd [1976] 1 WLR 676; Re Bond Worth Ltd [1980] Ch 228.

12.5.1 Section 2 of the Factors Act 1889

The next exception to the rule *nemo dat* is provided by s. 2 of the Factors Act 1889, which was extended to Scotland by the Factors (Scotland) Act 1890.[68] Section 21(2) of the Sale of Goods Act runs:

> Nothing in this Act affects—
> (a) The provisions of the Factors Acts, or any enactment[69] enabling the apparent owner of goods to dispose of them as if he were their true owner.

At common law, the doctrine of estoppel (or usual or ostensible authority) would normally have protected a third party who bought goods from a dealer in the ordinary course of business, where the goods had been entrusted to the dealer by the true owner.[70] But the common law did not protect a person who lent money on the security of the goods, which is in legal terms a pledgee; the courts took the view that a 'factor' was acting outside the normal course of business if he pledged goods rather than resold them.[71] This was a somewhat unreal approach when applied to the commercial agents of import merchants who regularly pledged imported goods (or documents of title) to banks or other financial institutions in order to provide finance pending the arrival and resale of the goods.[72] Accordingly, Parliament took a hand and passed a series of Factors Acts, beginning in 1823 and culminating in the present Act of 1889. The Acts were partly declaratory of the common law and partly an extension of it,[73] but the present Act specifically declares that it is not to be construed in derogation of the common law,[74] and it now appears that there may be circumstances in which the common law is wider than the Act. Thus (as seen above), a sale by an agent outside the ordinary course of business is protected at common law if the true owner has authorised the agent to sell as an owner, and not merely as an agent.[75]

By a somewhat strange twist, the provisions of the Factors Act are now usually applied to situations quite different from those for which they were enacted. The typical Factors Act case envisaged by Parliament was that of the commercial agent who pledged or resold goods (or documents of title to goods) consigned by foreign merchants to English ports; the typical case to which the Act is applied today concerns a motor vehicle entrusted to a motor dealer for sale or to obtain offers.

Section 2(1) of the Factors Act is as follows:

> Where a mercantile agent is, with the consent of the owner, in possession of goods or of the documents of title to goods, any sale, pledge, or other disposition of the goods, made by him when acting in the ordinary course of business of a mercantile agent, shall, subject to the provisions of this Act, be as valid as if he were expressly authorized by the owner of the goods to make the

[68] For analysis from a Scots law perspective, see Reid, The Law of Property in Scotland (1996, Butterworths/Law Society of Scotland), para. 671.

[69] The words 'any enactment' were thought to refer to the reputed ownership clause of the Bankruptcy Act 1914 (under which goods in the possession of a bankrupt in such circumstances that he was the reputed owner could pass to the trustee in bankruptcy); this clause disappeared with the Insolvency Act 1985.

[70] The leading case was Pickering v Busk (1812) 15 East 38, but there is no doubt that the principle itself was older than this.

[71] *Paterson* v *Task* (1743) 2 Str 1178 was the first of a long line of decisions to this effect.

[72] See Holdsworth, *History of English Law*, vol. XIII, pp. 380–1.

[73] See Cole v North Western Bank (1875) LR 10 CP 354, 362.

same; provided that the person taking under the disposition acts in good faith, and has not at the time of the disposition notice that the person making the disposition has not authority to make the same.

The meaning of this subsection requires the most careful consideration.

12.5.2 Mercantile agent

A mercantile agent is defined by the statutes as 'a mercantile agent having in the customary course of their business as such agent authority either to sell goods or to consign goods for the purpose of sale, or to buy goods, or to raise money on the security of goods'.[76] Whether a person is a mercantile agent or has merely obtained goods on sale or return is sometimes a difficult question. In the ordinary way, it makes no difference to the result because a sale or other disposition by the party entrusted with the goods will be valid in either event. If the party entrusted with the goods is a mercantile agent, a sale by him will be validated by the Factors Act, while, if they are held to have the goods on sale or return, a sale by them will normally be treated, under s. 18, Rule 4, as an act 'adopting the transaction' which passes property to them and through them to the sub-buyer. But in some cases, it does make a difference whether the party with the goods is a mercantile agent or has the goods on sale or return, because it is possible to contract out of s. 18, Rule 4, while it is not possible to contract out of the provisions of s. 2 of the Factors Act 1889.[77]

A person may be a mercantile agent although they are only acting for a single principal,[78] but they must be more than a mere servant or employee. A person who induces another to let them have goods on a representation that they know a third party who will buy them is not, without more, a mercantile agent.[79] 5But a person may be a mercantile agent without carrying on the business of being a mercantile agent. [80] And as every business must have a beginning, a person may be held to be a mercantile agent in respect of the transaction in question even though they have never acted as one before.[81] If the person who obtains the goods is not a mercantile agent at the time they obtain them, the fact that they become such later while the goods are still in their possession will not bring the case within the Factors Act[82] unless, presumably, the owner later consents to their possession as mercantile agent. However, if the evidence shows that the alleged mercantile agent is buying and reselling goods rather than acting as an agent, then there is no mercantile agency.[83]

[74] Section 13 of the Factors Act 1889.
[75] Lloyds and Scottish Finance Ltd v Williamson [1965] 1 WLR 404.
[76] Section 1(1) of the Factors Act, also reproduced in s. 26 of the Sale of Goods Act 1979.
[77] See Weiner v Harris [1910] 1 KB 285 – discussed in Chapter 10.
[78] *Lowther* v *Harris* [1927] 1 KB 393.
[79] *Jerome* v *Bentley* [1952] 2 All ER 114.
[80] *Weiner* v *Harris*, above.
[81] *Mortgage Loan & Finance Co of Australia* v *Richards* (1932) SR (NSW) 50, 58.
[82] *Heap* v *Motorists' Advisory Agency Ltd* [1923] 1 KB
[83] *Tahir Fadallah* v *John Pollak* [2013] EWHC 3159 (QB).

12.5.3 In possession of goods or of the documents of title to goods

The Act requires that the mercantile agent should be in possession of the goods or of the documents of title to the goods. It has been held that they must actually be in possession at the time of the sale, pledge or other disposition if the buyer is to be protected under the Factors Act. In *Beverley Acceptances Ltd* v *Oakley*,[84] O pledged two Rolls-Royce cars to the defendant G for a large loan. The cars were parked in G's locked compound but O borrowed the keys of the compound telling G that it was a matter to do with insurance, but in reality to show the cars to the plaintiffs, who were contemplating advancing money on their security. The keys were duly returned to G. Some days later, the plaintiffs did advance money to G, and G executed a bill of sale in their favour which was duly registered. It was held that, even if G was to be taken to be the 'owner' of the cars[85] and even if O was a mercantile agent, and even if O had been allowed temporary possession when he was lent the keys of the compound, still the buyer was not protected. The sale to the buyer had taken place at a time when any temporary possession obtained by O had long disappeared, and the section only applies where the mercantile agent 'is in possession', not where he once has been in possession.

12.5.4 The consent of the owner

The next requirement of the subsection is that the mercantile agent must be in possession of the goods with the consent of the owner. The meaning of these last words, which also appear in s. 25(1),[86] gave rise at one time to considerable difficulty where a person was induced to part with goods as a result of fraud and, in particular, where he parted with the goods in circumstances amounting to larceny by a trick under the old law of theft. It was at one time thought that in such a case the goods could not be said to be in the possession of the agent with the consent of the owner,[87] but it is probably safe to say that this view would not be accepted since the decision in *Pearson* v *Rose & Young*.[88] In this case, the plaintiff delivered his car to X, a mercantile agent, in order to obtain offers, but with no authority to sell it. The agent obtained possession of the registration book by a trick in such circumstances that the owner had clearly not consented to parting with the possession of it, and then promptly sold the car, as he had intended to do from the first. The Court of Appeal held that the question whether the agent had committed larceny by a trick was quite immaterial and that in each case the only question was whether the goods were in his possession with the consent of the owner. In this case, the mercantile agent had possession of the car with the consent of the owner, but not of the registration book. The court further held that a sale without a registration book would not have been a sale in the ordinary course of business and that the defendants were therefore not protected by the Factors Act.[89]

[84] [1982] RTR 417.

[85] Or at least if O and G were together to be treated as owner under *Lloyds Bank* v *Bank of America* [1938] 2 KB 147, below, section 12.5.4..

[86] See below, section 12.10.

[87] See dicta in *Oppenheimer* v *Frazer* [1907] 2 KB 50.

[88] [1951] 1 KB 275. See also *Folkes* v *King* [1923] 1 KB 282.

[89] See also *Stadium Finance Ltd* v *Robbins* [1962] 2 QB 664. See also *Dreveston* v *Regal Garage Ltd*, 9 October 1997 (unreported). It appears that 'goods' for the purposes of the Factors Act in relation to motor vehicles means the vehicle plus its registration documents – see (1951) 67 LQR 3.

The dicta in *Pearson* v *Rose & Young*[90] were applied by Sellers J in *Du Jardin* v *Beadman*,[91] a case under s. 25(1) of the Sale of Goods Act, where the learned judge held that although the goods were obtained by larceny by a trick, they were nonetheless in the possession of the buyer with the consent of the seller. Since the coming into force of the Theft Act 1968, the offence of larceny by a trick has disappeared from English law, but this does not affect the relevance of these cases as representing current law.

It has been suggested that a purchaser cannot rely on the owner's consent to the mercantile agent's possession if that consent was given under an illegal contract.[92] But this would produce the strange result that the owner of the goods could rely on their own illegal agreement with the agent to defeat the claims of an innocent third party. Moreover, the suggestion bears some resemblance to cases prior to *Pearson* v *Rose & Young* which (as we saw above) gave an artificial meaning to the word 'consent' in s. 2 of the Factors Act. It is submitted that this suggestion is wrong.

Not only the requirement of consent, but also the word 'owner' has given rise to difficulty in this section. First, the 'owner of the goods here referred to is the owner with whose consent the agent is in possession of them'.[93] Clearly, the section does not adversely affect the title of any person except the person who has entrusted the goods or documents of title to the mercantile agent. It does not thus affect the title of a person whose goods have been stolen, and later come into the possession of a mercantile agent from the thief.

Another difficulty arose in *Lloyds Bank* v *Bank of America*,[94] where the plaintiffs lent money to X, a mercantile agent, on the security of documents which were pledged with them. The documents were then returned to X under a 'trust receipt'[95] to enable him to sell the goods as trustee for the plaintiffs, but X fraudulently pledged them with the defendants for an advance. The defendants pleaded that they were protected by s. 2 of the Factors Act 1889, but the plaintiffs argued that as X, the mercantile agent, was himself the owner of the goods, it could not be said that he was in possession with the consent of the owner within the meaning of the Act. The Court of Appeal rejected these arguments, however. In the words of Lord Greene MR:

> Where the right of ownership has become divided among two or more persons in such a way that the acts which the section is contemplating could never be authorized save by both or all of them, these persons together constitute the owner.[96]

In this case, the plaintiffs were the legal pledgees and, in equity, beneficiaries of the proceeds of sale, while X was the legal and beneficial owner, subject to the prior claim of the plaintiffs. Consequently, these two persons together constituted the owner within the Act, and the goods were nonetheless in the possession of X with the consent of the owner, because he was himself one of those two persons.

90 [1951] 1 KB 275.
91 [1952] 2 QB 712.
92 *qBelvoir Finance Co Ltd* v *Harold G Cole & Co Ltd* [1969] 1 WLR 1877.
93 *National Employers Mutual General Insurance Association Ltd* v *Jones* [1990] 1 AC 24, 60 per Lord Goff.
94 [1938] 2 KB 147.
95 A 'trust receipt' (now apparently usually called a 'letter of trust') is a document obtained by a bank or other finance institution which has advanced money against documents in respect (usually) of imported goods, when the documents are released to the buyer before the advance is paid off. See *Sale Continuation Ltd* v *Austin Taylor & Co* [1967] 2 All ER 1092, 1098 per Paull J.
96 [1938] 2 KB 147, 162.

12.5.5 Goods entrusted to the mercantile agent as such

The purchaser from the mercantile agent will not be protected if the goods were entrusted to them for some purpose quite unconnected with their business as a mercantile agent. As Lord Denning once said:

> The owner must consent to the agent having them for a purpose which is in some way or other connected with his business as a mercantile agent. It may not actually be for sale. It may be for display, or to get offers, or merely to put in his showroom; but there must be a consent to something of that kind before the owner can be deprived of his goods.[97]

So if the owner does not even know that the bailee to whom they entrust the goods carries on business as a mercantile agent, their consent to the bailee's possession cannot suffice under the Act.[98] Whilet this interpretation is correct in the context of the Act, it creates a difficulty for the claimant buyer who will only be aware of the mercantile agent's possession of the goods, but not the basis on which consent to that possession was given. The tension between Lord Denning's two principles is clearly apparent.

Subsections (2), (3) and (4) of s. 2 of the Factors Act are also concerned with the meaning of the consent referred to in s. 2(1). Section 2(2) lays down that, if the agent obtains the goods with the consent of the owner, the subsequent withdrawal of the consent will not affect the rights of a purchaser who had no notice of the withdrawal. Section 2(3) provides that, if the agent is in possession of the goods with the consent of the owner and obtains possession of the documents of title by virtue of their possession of the goods, they shall be deemed to have such possession also with the consent of the owner. Finally s. 2(4) enacts that 'For the purposes of this Act the consent of the owner shall be presumed in the absence of evidence to the contrary.'

12.5.6 Sale in ordinary course of business

The purchaser claiming the protection of s. 2 must next prove that the mercantile agent acted in the ordinary course of business. This cannot be read literally because, obviously, in one sense a sale without the authority of the owner can rarely, if ever, be in the ordinary course of business, and it is only in this event that the Factors Act is needed at all. Consequently, this should probably be taken as meaning 'appearing to act in the ordinary course of business'.[99] Alternatively, it may mean that the mercantile agent must act in the ordinary course of business except for the fact that they do not have the owner's authority.

It is immaterial that the third party dealt with the mercantile agent as a principal and did not know them to be an agent; and it is also immaterial that the agent entered into a transaction not normally sanctioned by the custom of the trade unless, perhaps, the custom is so notorious that the third party would normally be taken to have knowledge of it as, for example, if an auctioneer were to pledge goods entrusted to them for sale. In

[97] *Pearson* v *Rose & Young* [1951] 1 KB 275, 288. There is a long line of authority supporting this viewpoint, dating back to *Cole* v *North Western Bank* (1875) LR 10 CP 354. It has also been held that the decision in the *Pacific Motor Auctions* case [1965] AC 867 (see 12.9.1) has not affected the law on this point: *Astley Industrial Trust* v *Miller* [1968] 2 All ER 36

[98] *Henderson* v *Prosser* [1982] CLY 21.

[99] See (1951) 67 LQR 6. Cf. *Oppenheimer* v *Attenborough & Sons* [1908] 1 KB 221.

other words, the phrase 'acting in the ordinary course of business of a mercantile agent' means 'acting in such a way as a mercantile agent in the ordinary course of business as a mercantile agent would act, that is to say, within business hours, at a proper place of business, and in other respects in the ordinary way in which a mercantile agent would act, so that there is nothing to lead the pledgee to suppose that anything is done wrong, or to give notice that the disposition is one which the mercantile agent had not authority for'.[100] So also, if a mercantile agent sells goods on the terms that the price is not to be paid directly to them but to one of their creditors, this may well be outside the ordinary course of business.[101] But a sale is not necessarily outside the ordinary course of business because the price is not paid in cash.[102] Whether the mercantile agent has acted in the ordinary way in which a mercantile agent would act in any particular case is a question of fact.[103]

It seems that the requirement that the agent must act in the ordinary course of business is 7distinct from the requirement that the buyer must take in good faith and without notice.[104] A buyer may be in good faith even though the sale is outside the ordinary course of business. To this extent the dictum above, from Buckley LJ's judgment in *Oppenheimer* v *Attenborough & Sons*, must be modified. For if the agent is only held to act outside the ordinary course of business in circumstances in which the buyer would have notice of their lack of authority, it would seem that the buyer would necessarily fail on the second requirement in any event.[105]

These decisions give rise to the question whether the requirement that the agent must act in the ordinary course of business serves any useful purpose. It would seem that the owner is already adequately protected by the requirement that the buyer must act in good faith and without notice, and this additional requirement could well be dropped in any future reform of the law.[106] Indeed, in *Summers* v *Harvad*,[107] the Court of Appeal, presented with an appeal dealing with both requirements, only considered the good faith and notice requirement, which was sufficient to dispose of the appeal.

12.5.7 Sale, pledge or other disposition

What sort of transaction amounts to a 'disposition' has been dealt with by the courts in relation to s. 24 of the Sale of Goods Act, so the point is discussed in connection with that section.[108]

[100] *Oppenheimer* v *Attenborough & Sons* [1908] 1 KB 221, 230–1 per Buckley LJ.

[101] *Lloyds & Scottish Finance Ltd* v *Williamson* [1965] 1 WLR 404, 408.

[102] *Tingey & Co* v *John Chambers* [1967] NZLR 785.

[103] *Biggs* v *Evans* [1894] 1 QB 88.

[104] *Lloyds & Scottish Finance Ltd* v *Williamson* [1965] 1 WLR 404, 408, *Pacific Motor Auctions Ltd* v *Motor Credits (Hire Finance) Ltd* [1965] AC 867; also *Summers* v *Harvad* [2011] 2 Lloyd's Rep. 283, where the two grounds of appeal concerned both requirements. The case was decided on the second (lack of good faith, and presence of notice).

[105] In both the cases cited in the last note sales were made outside the ordinary course of business, but the buyers were in good faith and were both held to be protected though for different reasons.

[106] The UCC retains the requirement that the sale must be in the ordinary course of business on the ground that purchasers (in the USA) were frequently held to be in good faith in cases where this result outraged common sense. See the Commentary to Art. 2-403(2). But this is of course the result of jury trial and is no longer relevant here where commercial cases are hardly ever tried by jury today.

[107] [2011] 2 Lloyd's Rep. 283.

[108] See below, section12.9.3/

12.5.8 Good faith and notice

The next requirement of s. 2 is that the buyer must prove that they took in good faith and without notice that the sale was made without the owner's authority, and the burden of proof is apparently on them in this respect,[109] although under s. 23 lack of good faith must be proved by the original owner.[110] In *Summers* v *Havad*,[111] two used car dealers had supplied another dealer with cars for resale, with an agreement to share profits. That dealer was in financial difficulties, and Harvard removed all the cars which he thought were his and some others to his premises. Summers was asked to identify which of those cars were his, but Havard then contended that these had been bought in good faith. However, the judge concluded that Havard was not acting in good faith and had notice of the fact that some of the cars would belong to other suppliers, and therefore Summers was entitled to receive a sum constituting the value of the cars belonging to him.

12.5.9 Pledges

Although a pledge is included within the protection of this section, s. 4 of the same Act excludes a pledge made for an antecedent debt. Thus if a mercantile agent pledges goods in their possession with the consent of the owner, the pledgee will have to prove that the pledge was made in return for a loan given at the same time, and not before the pledge was made.

12.6 Special powers of sale

Section 21(2) says that:

> Nothing in this Act affects—
> (b) the validity of any contract of sale under any special common law or statutory power of sale, or under the order of a court of competent jurisdiction.

This provision covers a large number of miscellaneous cases where a non-owner may pass a good title to goods, some of which are considered below.[112]

12.6.1 Common law powers

The most important of these is the power of sale of a pledgee, but if the pledge is made under a 'regulated agreement', that is, it is taken by a provider of credit from a consumer, the power must be exercised under the Consumer Credit Act 1974 (see below).

[109] *Heap* v *Motorists Advisory Agency Ltd* [1923] 1 KB 577; although the reasons given are not convincing, the result seems sensible. It is not difficult for the buyer to prove their good faith, but it is very hard for the owner to disprove it. Hence the Law Reform Committee recommended the endorsement of this case: Cmnd 2958, para. 25.

[110] *Whitehorn Bros* v *Davison* [1911] 1 KB 463. The Law Reform Committee recommended reversal of this decision.

[111] [2011] 2 Lloyd's Rep. 283

[112] For Scots law, see Reid, *The Law of Property in Scotland* (1996, Butterworths/Law Society of Scotland), para. 667.

[113] The buyer acquires a good title even if the goods did not belong to the person against whom execution issues, and even if he knew of the rights of the true owner: *Curtis* v *Maloney* [1951] 1 KB 736; *Dyal Singh* v *Kenyan Insurance Ltd* [1954] 1 All ER 847.

12.6.2 Statutory powers

There are a large number of these. The most important include: the power of a law enforcement offices to sell goods seized under a writ of execution;[113] the power of an innkeeper to sell goods upon which he has a lien under s. 1 of the Innkeepers Act 1878; the powers conferred by the Torts (Interference with Goods) Act 1977; and the powers relating to pawns under the Consumer Credit Act 1974. Under s. 120 of this Act, a pawn for under £75 can be forfeited at the end of the redemption period, but a pawn for a sum exceeding £75 can only be realised in accordance with the procedures laid down in s. 121.[114]

The only one of these provisions calling for any further comment is the Torts (Interference with Goods) Act 1977. Section 12 of the Act confers power on a bailee to sell goods after due notice given in various circumstances specified in the Act. If the bailee is unable to trace the bailor, they may still be able to sell the goods subject to the conditions laid down in the Act. A sale under this Act gives a good title to the purchaser as against the bailor, but not against the true owner if the bailor had no authority to bail them.

12.6.3 Sale by order of the court

The court has a wide jurisdiction under the Civil Procedure Rules 1998 to order the sale of goods which 'for any just and sufficient reason it may be desirable to have sold at once', for example because they are of a perishable nature, or because the market is falling. The court has power to insist on a sale despite the objections of the owner, where such a course seems necessary or desirable.[115]

12.7 Sale in market overt

A further, now historic, exception to the *nemo dat* rule in England and Wales was the case of a sale in market overt (another concept unknown in Scots law). Section 22 of the Act provided:

> (1) Where goods are sold in market overt, according to the usage of the market, the buyer acquires a good title to the goods, provided he buys them in good faith and without notice of any defect or want of title on the part of the seller.

This exception could be explained, but scarcely justified, on historical grounds only, and it may be regretted that it was included in the 1893 codification. Reform of the rule was proposed as long ago as 1966, but not acted upon until much later.[116]

In January 1994, the government produced a Consultation Paper[117] which recommended the abolition of the rule, replacing it with a rule which would confer a good title on bona fide purchasers through retail outlets or auctions. The Sale of Goods (Amendment) Act 1994, however, abolished the rule with effect from 3 January 1995. Accordingly, a good faith purchaser will no longer get a good title even in the limited circumstances provided by the market overt rule.

[114] The figure of £75 was substituted for £25 by the Consumer Credit (Further Increase in Monetary Amounts) Order 1998.
[115] *Larner* v *Fawcett* [1950] 2 All ER 727.
[116] Report of the Law Reform Committee, Twelfth Report (Cmnd 2958, 1966).
[117] 'Transfer of Title: ss. 21–26 of the Sale of Goods Act 1979'.

12.8 Sale under a voidable title

Section 23 confirms the common law rule that a person cannot avoid a voidable contract to the prejudice of third-party rights acquired in good faith and for value:

> When the seller of goods has a voidable title to them, but his title has not been avoided at the time of the sale, the buyer acquires a good title to the goods, provided he buys them in good faith and without notice of the seller's defect of title.

The great practical importance of this rule is that, if a person buys goods by fraud[118] and disposes of them before the other party avoids the contract, a buyer in good faith[119] from the fraudulent party acquires a good title. Where, however, the fraud is such as to nullify the offer or acceptance (or where there is a fundamental mistake) so that no real contract comes into existence, the buyer acquires no title at all and cannot therefore pass anything on to the innocent third party.[120] Consequently, this section does not protect such a buyer and unless they can invoke one of the other exceptions to the *nemo dat* rule, such as estoppel or s. 2 of the Factors Act 1889, they will have no defence to an action of conversion by the owner.

In general, the defrauded party can only rescind the contract by communicating with the other party to the contract and notifying them of the rescission. But in *Car & Universal Finance Ltd* v *Caldwell*,[121] the Court of Appeal held that the seller can rescind the contract by evincing an intention to do so and taking all steps open to them (such as informing the police) where they are unable to communicate with the fraudulent party, at least where this is because the fraudulent party is deliberately keeping out of the way. The court left open the question whether the law would be the same where the innocent party's inability to communicate with the other is not due to the fact that the latter is deliberately keeping out of the way. At first it seemed that this decision had fundamentally affected the protection afforded to the innocent third party by the Act because it had previously been assumed that a contract could not be rescinded without communication. Where the contract is fraudulently induced, it was generally thought that in practice there was little that the innocent party could do to defeat a bona fide purchaser. This view of the law was, moreover, adopted in Scotland in *MacLeod* v *Kerr*,[122] which was decided in the same year as *Caldwell*'s case. The facts in this case were substantially identical with those in *Caldwell*'s case and the Court of Session held that 'by no stretch of imagination' could the seller's conduct amount to rescission of the contract. However, as will be seen later, it is now clear that the decision in *Caldwell*'s case will be of limited application in practice because in the circumstances to which it applies the third party will often get a good title under s. 25(1) of the Act.[123]

[118] Or other invalidating case such as duress, which also renders a contract voidable – see *North Ocean Shipping Co Ltd* v *Hyundai Construction* [1979] QB 705; *Pao On* v *Lau Yiu* [1980] AC 614; *Atlas Express Ltd* v *Kafco (Importers and Distributors) Ltd* [1989] 1 All ER 641. Cf. *Universe Tankships of Monrovia Ltd* v *ITWF* [1983] 1 AC 366; *Dimskal Shipping Co SA* v *International Transport Workers Federation* [1992] 2 AC 152.

[119] The onus of proving lack of good faith is on the original owner: *Whitehorn Bros* v *Davison* [1911] 1 KB 463. But cf. *Thomas* v *Helas*, 27 November 1986, only noted in (1986) 3 CL 295a.

[120] As, for example, in *Cundy* v *Lindsay* (1878) 3 App Cas 459 and similar cases.

[121] [1965] 1 QB 525. It was apparently followed in *Thomas* v *Helas*, (1986) 3 CL 295a.

[122] 1965 SC 253.

[123] See below, section 12.10.

Although s. 23 only refers to the possibility of a sale, the common law rule is the same and presumably still applies to pledges, so a person with a voidable title to goods who pledges them before the other party avoids the title can pass a good title to the pledgee.[124] But a trustee in bankruptcy takes no better title than the bankrupt had, and if the bankrupt had a voidable title the seller can still avoid that title and retake the goods even after they have vested in the trustee.[125]

12.9 Seller in possession

Perhaps the most important two exceptions to the *nemo dat* rule are contained in ss. 8 and 9 of the Factors Act 1889 (extended to Scotland by the Factors (Scotland) Act 1890),[126] which are reproduced with the omission, in each case, of a few words in s. 24 and s. 25(1) of the Sale of Goods Act, though the sections of the earlier Act were not repealed. Because the sections of the Factors Act are wider than those of the Sale of Goods Act, the discussion here will be in terms of the former. Section 8 of the Factors Act is as follows:

> Where a person, having sold goods, continues, or is, in possession of the goods or of the documents of title to the goods, the delivery or transfer by that person, or by a mercantile agent acting for him, of the goods or documents of title under any sale, pledge or other disposition thereof [or under any agreement for sale, pledge or other disposition thereof], to any person receiving the same in good faith and without notice of the previous sale, shall have the same effect as if the person making the delivery or transfer were expressly authorised by the owner of the goods to make the same.

The words placed in square brackets in the text are the words omitted in s. 24 of the Sale of Goods Act.[127]

12.9.1 'A person, having sold goods, continues, or is, in possession'

There was for some years a continuous stream of authority holding that it was not enough that the seller was simply in possession of the goods when they resold them, but that the third party claiming under this section must go further and show that the seller was in possession as seller, and not in some other capacity; for example, as bailee.[128]

However, the authority of these decisions was severely shaken by the decision of the Privy Council in *Pacific Motor Auctions Pty Ltd* v *Motor Credits (Hire Finance) Ltd*,[129] the facts of which have already been given.[130] The Privy Council held that the defendants

[124] See, e.g., *Phillips* v *Brooks* [1919] 2 KB 243.

[125] *In re Eastgate* [1905] 1 KB 465.

[126] For a Scottish perspective, see Reid, *The Law of Property in Scotland* (1996, Butterworths/Law Society of Scotland), paras 681 and 682; Carey Miller, *Corporeal Moveables in Scots Law* 2nd edn (2005, W Green & Son Ltd, Edinburgh), paras 10.21-10.23.

[127] The omitted words in ss. 24 and 25 are one of the oddities of the Sale of Goods Act. If Parliament thought that ss. 8 and 9 of the Factors Act were too wide, why did it not repeal them; and if it did not think they were too wide, why did it leave out these words?

[128] *Staffs Motor Guarantee Ltd* v *British Wagon* Co Ltd [1934] 2 KB 305; *Eastern Distributors* v *Goldring* [1957] 2 QB 600; *Dore* v *Dore, The Times*, 18 March 1953; *Halfway Garage (Nottingham)* v *Lepley, Guardian*, 8 February 1964.

[129] [1965] AC 867.

[130] See above, section 12.4.2.

obtained a good title under a section of the New South Wales Sale of Goods Act identical with s. 24 of the 1979 Act. In delivering the opinion of the Board, Lord Pearce rejected the earlier English decisions as wrongly decided. The Privy Council held that the words 'continues . . . in possession' in the section were intended to refer to the continuity of physical possession, regardless of any private transaction between the seller and the first buyer which might alter the legal title under which the possession was held. Accordingly, unless there is an actual transfer of physical possession, the seller is to be treated as continuing in possession and as able to pass a good title under the section.[131] The Privy Council approved the New Zealand case of *Mitchell* v *Jones*,[132] where the seller sold and delivered a horse to the buyer, but later borrowed it back and wrongfully sold it again. In such a case the second buyer is not protected; the seller is 'in possession' in a literal sense, but the fact that he was a seller originally is no longer relevant. He is a bailee, not a seller.[133]

This decision was later followed by the Court of Appeal[134] and was much to be welcomed. It rid the law of an unnecessary complication for it replaced the previous imprecise criteria for determining whether a seller was in possession 'as seller' by the simpler criterion of whether they remained in physical possession throughout. It is also thought that the result is more equitable than that reached in the earlier cases since, if a buyer chooses to leave the seller in possession, the risk of the seller proving dishonest should rest on them rather than on a bona fide purchaser.

In the application of this provision, it must be borne in mind that there is nothing in the section to alter the usual commercial meaning of the word possession. Consequently, it has been held that goods which were at the seller's disposal though physically in the custody of warehousemen were in the possession of the seller within s. 8 of the Factors Act.[135]

However, if the seller only gained possession after the first sale, then this exception cannot apply. In *Tahir Fadallah* v *John Pollak*,[136] P, a buyer of generating sets sold by E but in the possession of J at the time of entering into the contract of sale, had observed them being disconnected and then transported to E's warehouse for storage. E therefore first came into possession of the generating sets as P's bailee. Later, P decided to sell the generating sets back to E, and E agreed to sell them to F. E then went into liquidation. P argued that he remained the owner because of a retention of title clause, so F raised several of the exceptions, including s. 24. The argument in respect of s. 24 failed, because the first time E gained possession of the generating sets was when they were taken to E's warehouse. E therefore never had possession of the generating sets as a seller. Seymour J commented on the state of law thus:

> It cannot be said that the distinction between a case in which a seller has continued in possession of goods which he has sold a second time, and a case in which, not having had possession of the

[131] *Prima facie* a dealer in possession under such an agreement would be able to pass a title under s. 2 of the Factors Act. (See, e.g., the CA decision in *St Margaret's Trust Ltd* v *Castle*, 28 July 1964 (1964) 10 CL §175a.) But the transaction in this case was not 'in the ordinary course of business' and the buyers were therefore compelled to rely on s. 24.

[132] (1905) 24 NZLR 932.

[133] The words 'or is in possession' give rise to some difficulty, but were explained as covering the case where the seller did not originally have possession of the goods but only acquired it later.

[134] *Worcester Works Finance Ltd* v *Cooden Engineering Co Ltd* [1972] 1 QB 210.

[135] *City Fur Co Ltd* v *Fureenbond* [1937] 1 All ER 239.

[136] [2013] EWHC 3159 (QB).

goods at the time of the first sale, the seller subsequently obtained possession before making the second sale, is particularly satisfactory . . . Whether the distinction is satisfactory or not, it does seem to be clearly established.[137]

12.9.2 The delivery or transfer . . . of the goods or documents of title

On the face of it, the section appears to require that the goods should be *delivered* (or anyhow transferred) to the second buyer if they are to obtain a title binding on the first buyer. So if the seller sells goods to B1, *but retains possession of them*, and then sells them again (whether rightfully or wrongfully is immaterial) to B2, but still retains possession of them, it seems that B2 obtains no title under the section, and B1 has the better claim. In *Nicholson* v *Harper*,[138] a merchant owned some wine stored with warehousemen, the defendants; he sold 250 dozen old port to the plaintiffs who left the wine in the possession of the defendants, and apparently gave them no notice of their purchase, nor obtained any delivery orders or other acknowledgment of their claim. Later, the original seller pledged all his wine to the warehousemen, and he subsequently became insolvent. North J held that the property in the wine had passed to the plaintiffs under the first sale, and that the warehousemen obtained no title under s. 25 (now s. 24) of the Sale of Goods Act. Although the merchant was a seller who had retained possession under that section, there had been no delivery or transfer of possession to the warehousemen after the sale.

However, *Nicholson* v *Harper* was rejected as bad law by the Australian High Court in *Gamer's Motor Centre (Newcastle) Pty Ltd* v *Natwest Wholesale Australia Pty Ltd*,[139] a case concerning the parallel provisions of s. 9 of the Factors Act and s. 25(1) of the Sale of Goods Act. In this case, the defendants agreed to sell eight cars to car dealers under an agreement whereby the sellers retained title until payment. The cars were delivered to the dealers who immediately resold them under a financing plan to the plaintiffs, while retaining possession of them for stock display. It was held (by a bare majority of the High Court) that the plaintiffs obtained a title to the cars, good against the defendants, because they had bought the cars from a buyer who had obtained the possession of the goods with the consent of the seller. Like s. 8, s. 9 of the Factors Act appears only to protect a buyer when there has been a delivery or transfer of the goods to him, but the High Court held that it was already well established at the time that the original Sale of Goods Act was passed that this did not necessarily require a physical transfer of possession. The law recognised the concept of a 'constructive delivery' where the physical possession remained unaltered, but the right to possession was transferred. So if S sells goods to B1, and retains possession of them, and then sells them again to B2, although he may still retain the physical possession of the goods unaltered, there may then be a constructive delivery to B2, at least if B2 has an immediate right to possession. The section would then be satisfied, and B2 would have a better claim than B1.[140]

[137] Ibid., para. 47.
[138] [1895] 2 Ch 415.
[139] (1987) 163 CLR 236. But *Nicholson* v *Harper* was followed in New Zealand: *New Zealand Securities & Finance Ltd* v *Wright Cars Ltd* [1976] 1 NZLR 77.
[140] See *Forsythe International (UK) Ltd* v *Silver Shipping Co Ltd* [1994] 1 WLR 1334.

Constructive doctrines are today often regarded as fictions, somewhat out of fashion,[141] and the High Court's decision in the *Gamer* case may appear, at first sight, inconsistent with the general approach of the Privy Council in the *Pacific Motor Auctions* case, where the continuity of physical possession was stressed as the basis of s. 8 of the Factors Act, and where the Privy Council reversed another decision of the High Court on these statutory provisions. But the two cases are not entirely comparable, if only because the *Gamer* decision protects the bona fide purchaser for value, while the High Court's decision in the *Pacific Motor Auctions* case did not. Furthermore, the policy of the Act suggests that the *Gamer* decision is preferable to *Nicholson* v *Harper* because (in a s. 8 case) the second buyer who pays the price of the goods is acting in reliance on his belief that the original seller retains title, having regard to his continued possession of the goods.[142] Moreover, the other exceptions to the *nemo dat* principle, such as estoppel, s. 23 of the Act and s. 2 of the Factors Act, all appear to operate to protect the buyer as from the moment of the sale to him, provided at least that they have paid the price, or acted to their prejudice so as to constitute themselves a bona fide purchaser for value. None of these provisions appears to require an actual delivery to the person claiming to be protected[143]. What is more, the second buyer is protected although they have only agreed to buy the goods and the property has not yet passed to them[144], so it would seem strange to insist on an actual physical delivery to them. In *Michael Gerson (Leasing) Ltd* v *Wilkinson*[145], counsel for the claimant accepted that delivery in s. 24 includes constructive delivery and that it is not confined to physical delivery. Clarke LJ accepted that both concessions were correctly made. They accorded with the decision of the High Court of Australia in *Gamer's Motor Centre (Newcastle) Proprietary Ltd* v *Natwest Wholesale Australia Proprietary Lt*[146]d which he had followed at first instance in *Forsythe International (UK) Ltd* v *Silver Shipping Co Ltd*[147].

12.9.3 Sale, pledge or other disposition

In most cases, the party claiming the protection of this section will rely on a sale or pledge, but the section also refers to other 'disposition'. In *Worcester Works Finance Ltd* v *Cooden Engineering Co Ltd*,[148] the Court of Appeal held that this was a very wide word, but that it did not cover a mere transfer of possession; there must be some transfer of an interest in the goods to constitute a disposition. In this case, one G bought a car from the defendants, paying the price with a cheque which was not met. He then sold the car to

[141] Though there is modern case law applying the concept of constructive delivery in a different context: *Four Point Garage Ltd* v *Carter* [1985] 3 All ER 12.

[142] In the NSW Court of Appeal, McHugh JA suggested that it was 'curious that the legislature, having penalised the owner for allowing the buyer to have possession, intended the sub-buyer to obtain a good title even though he leaves the same goods in the possession of the same person': *Gamer's Motor Centre (Newcastle) Pty Ltd* v *Natwest Wholesale Australia Pty Ltd* [1985] 2 NSWLR 475, 490. But the answer to this is that the seller has induced the injurious reliance of the second buyer by allowing the first to have possession, while the second buyer has induced no reliance at all.

[143] But as to estoppel, see *Shaw* v *Commissioner of Met Police* [1987] 1 WLR 1332, above, section 12.4.2.

[144] This is the effect of s. 8, differing in this respect from s. 24 of the 1979 Act.

[145] [2000] 2 All ER (Comm) 890.

[146] (1987) 163 CLR 236.

[147] [1994] 1 WLR 1334.

[148] [1972] 1 QB 210. See Preston (1972) 88 LQR 239.

another finance company – the plaintiffs – but retained the possession of the car as he had induced the plaintiffs to accept a hire-purchase proposal for the benefit of an accomplice. Subsequently, the defendants, with the consent of G, retook the car from him. It was held that the defendants were protected as against the plaintiffs. So far as the plaintiffs were concerned, G was a seller who remained in possession. Moreover, the retaking of the car by the defendants was a 'disposition' by G to them inasmuch as it amounted to a rescission of the contract between them and therefore it revested the property in the defendants.

This case is also authority for the proposition that a party relying on s. 8 of the Factors Act need not prove that the seller remained in possession with the consent of the buyer. The difference in wording between ss. 2 and 8 in this respect clearly shows that s. 8 was intended to apply even where the seller wrongfully retains possession after the sale.

12.9.4 Good faith and notice

The second buyer is only protected if they act in good faith and without notice of the previous sale. Notice presumably has its usual commercial meaning here, so that it applies only to actual and not to constructive notice; 'there is no general duty on a buyer of goods in an ordinary commercial transaction to make inquiries as to the right of the seller to dispose of the goods'.[149] There is no independent requirement in this section that the transaction should be made 'in the ordinary course of business', though of course a transaction outside the ordinary course of business may sometimes be sufficient to put the buyer on inquiry.

12.9.5 Application of s. 8

As is to be expected, s. 8 only applies when the property in the goods has passed to the buyer under the contract of sale, because if the property has not so passed, obviously the seller sells by virtue of their property in the goods and no statutory exception to the *nemo dat* rule is needed. Hence, s. 8 only applies where the seller has 'sold' (not 'agreed to sell') the goods.

12.10 Buyer in possession

Section 9 of the Factors Act and s. 25(1) of the Sale of Goods Act contain provisions parallel to those of s. 8 and s. 24. Section 9 is as follows:

> Where a person, having bought or agreed to buy goods, obtains with the consent of the seller possession of the goods or the documents of title to the goods, the delivery or transfer, by that person or by a mercantile agent acting for him, of the goods or the documents of title under any sale, pledge or other disposition thereof [or under any agreement for sale, pledge or other disposition thereof], to any person receiving the same in good faith and without notice of any lien or other right of the original seller in respect of the goods, shall have the same effect as if the person making the delivery or transfer were a mercantile agent in possession of the goods or documents of title with the consent of the owner.

[149] *Feuer Leather Corp* v *Frank Johnstone* (1981) Com LR 251, 253.

The words placed in square brackets in the text are omitted in s. 25(1) of the Sale of Goods Act,[150] so the ensuing discussion is in terms of s. 9 because it is the wider provision. Section 26 of the Sale of Goods Act defines the term 'mercantile agent', but the definition merely repeats that incorporated in s. 1(1) of the Factors Act 1889. This has already been discussed in connection with s. 2 of the Factors Act.[151]

12.10.1 A person 'having bought or agreed to buy goods'

It has already been seen that s. 8 only applies where the property has passed to the first buyer before the second sale because otherwise the special provision is not necessary. But s. 9 applies where the first buyer has 'bought or agreed to buy goods', that is to say, it applies whether or not the property has passed to the first buyer. This is a strange provision for it is not easy to see why there should be any special enactment to protect a person who has bought goods from a buyer in possession when the property has already passed to this buyer. *Prima facie* the buyer can sell the goods in these circumstances and pass a good title by virtue of their own property. It is to be hoped that a court would dismiss as mere surplusage the words 'bought or' in s. 9 even though the section imposes certain restrictions on the buyer's ability to pass a good title to a third party;[152] in fact, (as appears below) it is not easy to envisage circumstances in which these restrictions would become applicable. But possibly they do not matter anyhow because it is arguable that a buyer can always pass property even at common law if it has already passed to him, and therefore s. 9 could be ignored in such a case.

Where a buyer has resold goods supplied under a reservation of title clause,[153] a sub-purchaser can acquire a good title under this provision (as well as s. 2(1) of the Factors Act). But if the goods are in turn supplied by the buyer to the sub-purchaser under the reservation of title clause, it would seem that the words in s. 9 which do not appear in s. 25 of the Sale of Goods Act (in square brackets where the section is set out above) do not serve to defeat the original seller's retention of title clause. Unless and until the sub-purchaser has paid for the goods, or satisfied such other conditions as may have been stipulated by the buyer for the passing of property to the sub-purchaser, the original seller is entitled to repossess.[154]

The fact that s. 9 only applies where a person has bought or agreed to buy goods means that there must be a contract of sale within the meaning of the Act.[155] If a supplier contracts to sell goods to a building contractor who is engaged on building works and the goods are delivered direct to the building site, and the contractor subsequently becomes insolvent without having paid their supplier, title to the goods may be disputed between the original supplier and the owner of the site for whom the work is being done. If the

[150] See *P4 Ltd* v *Unite Integrated Solutions plc* [2006] BLR 150.

[151] See above, section 12.5.1 *et seq.*

[152] See the dicta of Brennan J in the *Gamer* case (1987) 163 CLR 236, 251.

[153] See Chapter 15 *et seq.*

[154] *Re Highway Foods International Ltd* [1995] BCC 271. A similar conclusion was reached in *Hanson (W) (Harrow) Ltd* v *Rapid Civil Engineering & Usborne Developments Ltd* (1987) 38 Build LR 106, which argued on the basis of s. 2(1) of the Factors Act and the narrower s. 25(1) of the Sale of Goods Act. As to circumstances in which the seller can trace their security interest into the proceeds of sale, see Chapter 18 *et seq.*

[155] See the Scots decision in *Archivent Sales & Developments Ltd* v *Strathclyde Regional Council* (1984) 27 Build LR 98, 1985 SLT 154. See also *Thomas Graham & Sons Ltd* v *Glenrothes Development Corp* 1967 SC 284.

goods have been delivered to the site under a contract of sale, title can pass under s. 9 of the Factors Act. The supplier is a seller, the contractor has undoubtedly bought or agreed to buy the goods, and delivery to the site is a delivery to the contractor who is thus in possession of the goods. So their contract with the building owner may be a sale or other disposition which transfers title. But if the first relevant contract is not a contract of sale but (for instance) a contract for services, s. 9 will not apply at all, and the original owner may be able to reclaim the goods. So where a contractor had agreed to do certain building works, and a subcontractor had agreed to supply and fix the roof slates, the delivery of the slates to the site by the subcontractor did not pass title to the building owner under s. 9.[156] The first relevant contract here was that between the contractor and the subcontractor which was not a contract of sale at all, so s. 9 simply did not apply. In practice the position is today often complicated by special conditions of sale as well as special conditions in building contracts which may provide that the title to goods delivered to a site passes forthwith to the building owner.[157]

Other problems which arise from the need to show that there was a contract of sale in the strict sense, before s. 9 can apply, relate to hire-purchase and similar agreements. Because a contract of sale is defined by s. 2(1) of the Act as a contract under which the seller transfers or agrees to transfer the property in goods to the buyer in return for a money consideration, a mere option to purchase cannot be a contract of sale until the option is exercised. It is for this reason, as we have seen, that the ordinary hire-purchase agreement is drafted in the form of a bailment with an option to purchase. A person in possession of goods under such an agreement is not a person who has 'bought or agreed to buy goods' within the meaning of s. 9 of the Factors Act.[158] On the other hand, 'A contract of sale may be absolute or conditional',[159] and a person in possession of goods under a contract in which the transfer of the property is conditional, whether on payment[160] or on the occurrence of some other event,[161] was until 1965 treated as a person who had agreed to buy goods within s. 9. Between 1889 and 1965, then, the law distinguished fundamentally between cases where a person obtained possession of goods under a hire-purchase agreement, to which s. 25(1) of the Sale of Goods Act and s. 9 of the Factors Act did not apply (*Helby* v *Matthews*)[162] and cases where a person obtained possession under a conditional sale agreement, to which those sections did apply (*Lee* v *Butler*).[163]

However, the law on this point was profoundly modified by the Hire-Purchase Act 1964. In accordance with the general assimilation of conditional sale agreements to hire-purchase agreements since that Act, it is now provided that, for the purposes of s. 9 of the Factors Act (and s. 25(1) of the Sale of Goods Act), 'the buyer under a conditional sale agreement is to be taken not to be a person who has bought or agreed to buy goods'.[164]

[156] *Dawber Williamson Roofing Ltd* v *Humberside* CC (1979) 14 Build LR 70.

[157] See, e.g., *Hanson (W) (Harrow)* v *Rapid Civil Engineering & Usborne Developments Ltd* (1987) 38 Build LR 106.

[158] *Helby* v *Matthews* [1895] AC 471; *Belsize Motor Supply Co Ltd* v Cox [1914] 1 KB 244.

[159] Section 2(3).

[160] *Lee* v *Butler* [1893] 2 QB 318.

[161] *Marten* v *Whale* [1917] 2 KB 480.

[162] [1895] AC 471.

[163] *Lee* v *Butler* [1893] 2 QB 318.

[164] Section 25(2)(a) of the 1979 Act.

A conditional sale agreement for the purposes of this provision is an agreement for the sale of goods which is a consumer credit agreement, and under which:

> . . . the purchase price or part of it is payable by instalments, and the property in the goods is to remain in the seller (notwithstanding that the buyer is to be in possession of the goods) until such conditions as to the payment of the instalments or otherwise as may be specified in the agreement are fulfilled.[165]

An agreement in which the price is not payable by instalments is not, therefore, a conditional sale agreement for this purpose and remains within the protection of s. 9 of the Factors Act even though it is conditional upon some other event.[166]

It is important to observe that the provisions of the law relating to conditional sales mentioned above are confined to agreements which are consumer credit agreements within the protection of the Consumer Credit Act 1974. In other words, a buyer in possession under a conditional sale agreement can still pass a good title under s. 9 of the Factors Act if the total credit provided exceeds £15,000 or if the buyer is a corporation.

It is apparent, then, that these Acts have to a large extent done away with the distinction between conditional sale agreements and hire-purchase agreements which formerly existed as a result of the celebrated cases of *Lee* v *Butler*[167] and *Helby* v *Matthews*.[168] In view of the fact that the tendency over the last century has been to widen the circumstances in which a non-owner can transfer a good title, this particular move may seem a retrograde step. The justification for it appears to be that, in practice, conditional sale agreements of this kind have not been commonly used as a method of consumer finance, and that it was desirable to assimilate the law relating to conditional sale and hire-purchase, partly in order to prevent evasion of the Acts and partly in the interests of simplicity. Moreover, the practical effect of this statutory modification of *Lee* v *Butler* is much qualified by the special provisions relating to motor vehicles. As will be seen later, Part III of the Hire-Purchase Act 1964 protects a bona fide private purchaser of a motor vehicle from a person in possession under a hire-purchase or a conditional sale agreement.[169]

A person who obtains goods on 'sale or return' has also been said to be outside the provisions of s. 9 because they also are not a person who has agreed to buy goods, although in a certain sense they have made a conditional contract of sale.[170] We have already seen that in many cases it makes no difference whether a person who has taken goods on sale or return comes within s. 9 or not, because if they sell or pledge the goods they do an act adopting the transaction within s. 18, Rule 4(b) and the property passes to them, with the result that the sub-buyer or pledgee is protected. We have also seen that it is possible to contract out of s. 18,[171] but it is not possible to contract out of s. 9 of the Factors Act, so that in this event it is of vital importance to decide whether the case comes within s. 9 or not.

A person who is entrusted with goods as a mere agent to sell them is not within the section,[172] for the obvious reason that they have not bought or agreed to buy them within

[165] Section 8 of the Consumer Credit Act 1974.
[166] So, for instance, *Marten* v *Whale* ([1917] 2 KB 480) would still be decided in the same way today.
[167] See below, section 12.10.8.
[168] *Edwards* v *Vaughan* (1910) 26 TLR 545. See the doubts expressed about this case at section 12.10.8, below.
[169] See section 12.11 *et seq*.
[170] *Edwards* v *Vaughan* (1910) 26 TLR 545. See the doubts expressed about this case at Chapter 10.
[171] *Weiner* v *Harris* [1910] 2 KB 285.
[172] *Shaw* v *Commissioner of Met Police* [1987] 1 WLR 1332.

the meaning of the section. But if they are a mercantile agent, as defined in the Factors Act, then they can pass a good title under s. 2 of that Act; and it may also be possible for a buyer from them to claim that they have acquired title at common law simply on the ground that the agent sold the goods within their actual, usual or ostensible authority.

12.10.2 The consent of the seller

The protection afforded to a third party by s. 9 is only available if the goods were in the possession of the buyer with the consent of the seller. This is similar to the requirement which appears in s. 2, and, *mutatis mutandis*, the law is the same. Consequently, it is not material that the buyer obtained the goods by a criminal offence, the only question being whether the seller in fact consented to the buyer having possession.[173] Nor is it material that the seller has revoked their consent to the buyer having possession. As we have seen, s. 2(2) of the Factors Act specifically states that the subsequent withdrawal of their consent by the seller does not prevent the operation of the Act. This means that the decision in *Car & Universal Finance Co* v *Caldwell*[174] is of little practical importance. In that case, as we have seen, it was held that a contract of sale induced by fraud could be rescinded without communicating with the fraudulent party. But it is now clear that the only result of this is to force the third party to rely on s. 9 of the Factors Act instead of s. 23 of the Sale of Goods Act.[175]

12.10.3 Possession of the goods

It is clear that the section only applies where the first buyer has actually obtained possession of the goods[176] or documents of title to the goods, and it is not enough that they have merely bought or agreed to buy them. So long as the seller retains possession they cannot be affected by a resale by the first buyer unless they have assented to it in terms of s. 47(1) which we have already examined,[177] or unless they are affected by an estoppel. On the other hand, if the seller, at the request of the first buyer, themselves deliver the goods direct to a sub-buyer, this is enough to bring the second buyer within the protection of the section. There is a constructive delivery to the first buyer, and a constructive delivery by them to the second buyer, and that is sufficient for the section to operate.[178]

It is, however, uncertain if the section will apply whatever the nature of the buyer's possession. For instance, would the section apply if a person agrees to sell a car, but insists on a cash price, and then allows the buyer to take the car to a garage for an emergency repair?[179] Despite some doubts expressed in Australia,[180] it is thought that the

[173] *Du Jardin* v *Beadman* [1952] 2 QB 712; *National Employers' Insurance Ltd* v *Jones* [1990] AC 24 – see section 12.5.4, above.

[174] [1965] 1 QB 525, above.

[175] But there is one important respect in which s. 9 may be narrower than s. 23 – below, section 12.10.8.

[176] Rutherford and Todd (1979) 38 CLJ 346 argue, on the basis of the legislative history of the Acts, that s. 25(1) and s. 9 of the Factors Act were not intended to apply to a buyer in possession of goods (as opposed to documents of title). But the argument is of historical interest only because the wording of the sections and the uniform current of case law extending for almost a century preclude this narrow interpretation today.

[177] See section 12.2, above.

[178] *Four Point Garage Ltd* v *Carter* [1985] 3 All ER 12.

[179] See *Langmead* v *Thyer Rubber Co Ltd* (1947) SR (SA) 29, 34.

[180] Ibid.

section would apply. In *Marten* v *Whale*,[181] it was applied even though the goods were temporarily loaned to the buyer, and the analogy of the *Pacific Motor Auction*[182] case appears virtually conclusive.

It is also important that the buyer obtains possession of the goods after the contract of sale with the seller was concluded, so in *Fadallah* v *Pollak*,[183] where the buyer was in possession of the goods as bailee before agreeing to buy them, it was held that s. 25 of the Sale of Goods Act could not apply. In *Forsythe International (UK)* v *Silver Shipping Co and Petroglobe International (The Saetta)*,[184] the plaintiff had supplied bunkers to the charterer of a vessel under a retention of title clause. The charterer did not pay for the bunkers. The owner subsequently withdrew the vessel from service for non-payment of hire, and used the bunkers. The plaintiff sued in conversion, and it was held that there would be conversion unless there was a delivery to the owner justified by s. 25(1) of the Sale of Goods Act. It was held that 'possession' had the same meaning in the Factors Act 1889 and in s. 25(1), and was not limited to physical possession. However, the owner succeeded because it was held that the transfer of the bunkers was not achieved by a voluntary act on the part of the charterer, but by termination of the charter by the owner.[185]

12.10.4 Documents of title

Where the buyer has obtained the documents of title to the goods with the consent of the seller, the position is a little more complicated as a result of the seller's right of lien and of stoppage in transit, if they are still unpaid. Section 47 of the Sale of Goods Act reproduces in almost identical terms s. 10 of the Factors Act 1889, although the latter is not repealed. Section 47(2) is as follows:

> Where a document of title to goods has been lawfully transferred to any person as buyer or owner of the goods, and that person transfers the document to a person who takes it in good faith and for valuable consideration, then—
>
> (a) if the last-mentioned transfer was by way of sale the unpaid seller's right of lien . . . or stoppage in transit is defeated, and
> (b) if the last-mentioned transfer was made by way of pledge or other disposition for value, the unpaid seller's right of lien . . . or stoppage in transit can only be exercised subject to the rights of the transferee.

It is sometimes suggested that this section is more favourable to the third party than s. 9 of the Factors Act because it says nothing about the requirement that they must not have notice of the rights of the original seller, but it may be doubted whether this really adds anything to the requirement of good faith.

It must be added that s. 19(3) of the Sale of Goods Act is subject to these sections. In *Cahn* v *Pockett's Bristol Channel Steam Packet Co Ltd*,[186] the sellers shipped copper on the defendants' ship and sent bills of lading, together with a draft, to the buyers. The buyers,

[181] [1917] 2 KB 480.
[182] [1965] AC 867. See above, 12.9.1.
[183] [2013] EWHC 3159 (QB).
[184] [1993] 2 Lloyd's Rep 268.
[185] See section 12.10.6.
[186] [1899] 1 QB 643.

being insolvent, did not accept the draft, but they transferred the bills of lading to the plaintiffs in pursuance of a contract previously made. The sellers, learning of the buyers' bankruptcy, stopped the goods in transit. The Court of Appeal held that, although the buyers had acted wrongfully in transferring the bills of lading when they did not accept the draft, this breach of s. 19(3) did not deprive the plaintiffs of the protection afforded by s. 47 of the Sale of Goods Act.[187]

Although s. 47 only talks of a transfer of a document of title, it has been held that it applies also where the documents are issued by the seller to the buyer and transferred by the latter to a third party taking in good faith and for value.[188] On the other hand, s. 47(2) apparently applies only where it is the same document which is transferred (or issued) to the buyer, and by the buyer to the third party.[189] In contrast, s. 9 applies even where there are two separate documents.[190]

12.10.5 Delivery or transfer of the goods[191]

The first buyer, having acquired possession of the goods (or of the documents of title) must make a delivery or transfer of them (or of the documents) before the section can apply. In *Forsythe International (UK)* v *Silver Shipping Co and Petrograde International (The Saetta)*,[192] it was held that 'delivery or transfer' required some voluntary act, though actual physical delivery was not required, so that where the owner of a vessel terminated for non-payment of hire, there was no 'delivery or transfer' within the meaning of s. 25(1) of the Sale of Goods Act. The same would equally apply in relation to s. 8 of the Factors Act 1889.

As we saw in considering the parallel provisions of s. 8 of the Factors Act, there is some uncertainty as to the possibility of recognising a 'constructive delivery' for the purposes of this section.[193] It has at least been held that if the seller, at the request of the first buyer, delivers the goods direct to the second buyer, this is a sufficient constructive delivery to the first buyer and by them to the second buyer.[194] (But it is less clear whether, if the goods are delivered to and remain in the possession of the first buyer, a contract for the sale of the goods to the second buyer can itself be treated as enough to amount to a constructive delivery. The cases in this connection were discussed earlier, when considering s. 8. [195]

There are a number of cases in which it has been assumed, without argument, that a sub-buyer can obtain title under s. 9 even in part of an undivided bulk.[196] But it has been pointed out that this may be inconsistent with s. 16 of the Act, which (as seen above)[197] does not permit a transfer of property in an undivided bulk of goods except

[187] And s. 25(1) and ss. 9 and 10 of the Factors Act, an extraordinary duplication of statutory provisions.
[188] *Ant Jurgens & Margarinefabrieken* v *Louis Dreyfus & Co Ltd* [1914] 3 KB 40.
[189] *D F Mount Ltd* v *Jay & Jay Co Ltd* [1960] 1 QB 159, 168.
[190] Ibid.
[191] See also discussion of the equivalent provision in s. 24 at section 12.11.
[192] [1993] 2 Lloyd's Rep 268.
[193] See above, section 12.12 *et seq*.
[194] *Four Point Garage Ltd* v *Carter* [1985] 3 All ER 12.
[195] See above, section 12.12.
[196] *D F Mount Ltd* v *Jay & Jay Co Ltd* [1960] 1 QB 159; *Ant Jurgens Margarinefabrieken* v *Louis Dreyfus & Co Ltd* [1914] 3 KB 40; *Capital & Counties Bank* v *Warriner* (1896) 1 Com Cas 314.
[197] See Chapter 10.

in the circumstances set out in s. 20A inserted by the 1995 Act.[198] The argument rests on the assumption that a sub-buyer of an undivided part of a bulk cannot sue the seller in conversion because they have no property, and if they cannot sue in conversion, they cannot acquire a title under s. 9. No doubt there may be cases where difficulties arise, but so long as the dispute lies solely between a seller and a sub-buyer (which is the usual case dealt with by s. 9) there seems nothing in policy against (and everything in favour of) recognising a distinction between 'property' in the s. 16 sense, and a right of possession necessary to maintain an action of conversion. If the sub-buyer has an immediate right to possession in the sense that they may demand separation of their share of the goods from the remainder of the bulk, it would be pure pedantry to deny them the right to claim a title under s. 9, merely because as between themselves and the intermediate seller there has not been a separation of the part sold from the rest sufficient to pass property. But it must be admitted that more difficulty may arise where insolvency is in issue, or where there is also a dispute between the sub-buyer and intermediate seller.

It is also important to note that delivery (whether actual or constructive) has to occur after the second contract has been concluded. In *Fadallah* v *Pollak*,[199] the purported constructive delivery to the second buyer had occurred at least two weeks before the contract with that buyer had been concluded, and therefore s. 25 of the Sale of Goods Act would not have applied (the court having already decided that it did not apply because the first buyer had already been in possession before agreeing to buy the goods).

12.10.6 Sale, pledge or other disposition

One difference between the wording of s. 9 and s. 25(1) of the Sale of Goods Act is the presence which we noted at the outset of the words 'or under any agreement for sale, pledge or other disposition' in s. 9. If the buyer were to sell the goods on under a retention of title clause,[200] the sub-buyer could not acquire title under s. 25(1) until title had passed to him.[201] But s. 9 of the Factors Act applies where the goods are obtained under any '*agreement* [emphasis supplied] for sale, pledge or other disposition'. It had been suggested that a sub-purchaser might be able to rely on this provision when in possession under a reservation of title clause.[202] In *Re Highway Foods International Ltd*,[203] it was held that in such a situation the original seller could claim title to the goods, however. The effect of s. 9 is that in favour of a bona fide purchaser an agreement for sale has the same effect as if the person making the transfer were a mercantile agent in possession with the consent of the owner.[204] But s. 2(1) of the Factors Act, which deals with the powers of a mercantile agent in possession, only provides that any *sale* etc. by a mercantile agent in possession with the consent of the owner shall be as valid as if the mercantile agent were authorised by the owner.

[198] See Nicol (1970) 42 MLR 129; Law Commission No. 215, para. 2.8. The sub-buyer may, of course, prevail if the original seller, not having been paid, attempts to exercise the *possessory* rights of an unpaid seller – ibid.
[199] [2013] EWHC 3159 (QB).
[200] As to which see Chapter 15.
[201] *Hanson (W) (Harrow) Ltd* v *Rapid Civil Engineering Ltd* (1987) 38 Build LR 106.
[202] *Benjamin on Sale* (4th edn), §5–128.
[203] [1995] BCC 271.
[204] See section 12.5.1 *et seq*.

What amounts to a sale, pledge or other disposition has been considered in connection with s. 24 of the Act.[205] In the present context it may also be relevant to draw attention to some cases dealing with a delivery of goods by a seller to a building site, where the buyer, a contractor, has contracted to install or incorporate them into a building. The contract between the contractor and the building owner may in this situation not be a strict contract of sale because of the contractor's obligations to install or affix the materials, but it seems that this is at least another 'disposition' within the meaning of the section.[206] This situation must be distinguished from that in which the *first* contract relied upon is not a sale of goods because in that case the section does not apply at all.[207]

12.10.7 Good faith and notice

The third party must take the goods 'in good faith and without notice of any lien or other right of the original seller in respect of the goods'. Clearly, if the seller retains the property in the goods after delivery and the buyer has no right to dispose of the goods pending payment of the price or fulfilment of some other condition, any sub-buyer who takes the goods with notice of the circumstances will not be protected by the section. Notice, as usual in commercial law, means actual and not constructive notice.[208]

So far the effect of the section is clear enough. It is much less easy to understand the effect of the section with regard to two other questions, namely the effect of a sub-sale on the seller's lien, and the possible application of the section where the property in the goods has passed to the buyer. Where the buyer is in possession of the goods with the consent of the seller, it is difficult to see how the seller can have any lien or other right in respect of the goods. Under s. 43(1), the unpaid seller loses their lien:

> (b) when the buyer or his agent lawfully obtains possession of the goods.

If the buyer has obtained possession with the consent of the seller, it seems to follow of necessity that they have lawfully obtained possession and it is submitted that this is still the case if the buyer has obtained possession by a criminal offence. This question was discussed in the New Zealand Court of Appeal in *Jeffcott* v *Andrews Motors Ltd*;[209] here, however, the court bypassed the issue. It was there held unnecessary to decide whether the seller's lien could survive where the buyer obtained possession of the goods by criminal fraud, on the ground that in any event the third party was protected by the terms of s. 9. If the lien survives in such circumstances the survival must be purely academic and, it seems, quite meaningless as it gives the seller no right to obtain possession of the goods from the third party. It is therefore submitted that in whatever capacity the buyer obtains control of the goods, provided it is with the consent of the owner, s. 9 applies and the buyer can pass a good title to an innocent third party free from the seller's claims.

However, if the buyer merely obtains possession of the documents of title to the goods and not of the goods themselves, it may be that in some circumstances the seller could

[205] Above, section 12.9.4.
[206] *Archivent Sales & Developments Ltd* v *Strathclyde Regional Council* (1984) 27 Build LR 98, 1985 SLT 154.
[207] *Dawber Williamson Roofing Ltd* v *Humberside CC* (1979) 14 Build LR 70.
[208] *See P4 Ltd* v *Unite Integrated Solutions plc* [2006] BLR 150.
[209] [1960] NZLR 721.

still have a lien on the goods themselves, and effect could then be given to the section by holding that a purchaser with notice of the lien would take subject to the lien, whether or not the property had passed to the original buyer. This is an unlikely eventuality, however, for possession of the documents of title normally carries with it possession of the goods themselves – this is certainly the case with bills of lading – and it could only be in the most extraordinary circumstances that the seller could transfer the documents to the buyer while retaining a lien on the goods themselves.

Apart from the possibility of the seller retaining their lien, the section also requires that the third party should take without notice of any 'other right of the original seller in respect of the goods'. But where the buyer has already bought the goods so that the property has passed to him, it is again not easy to see of what 'other right of the original seller' the third party can have notice. The mere fact that the price has not been paid to the knowledge of the third party surely cannot bring this clause into operation because it is a common business occurrence for a seller to be paid for goods before they themselves have paid for them, and knowledge of these circumstances can scarcely be held to put the buyers upon inquiry.[210] In any event, this would not seem to be a right 'in respect of the goods' but a personal right in respect of the contract of sale. Moreover, if the property has passed to the buyer it is hard to see how there can be any question of bad faith on the part of the sub-buyer. Even if they are aware that the buyer has not paid the seller and cannot do so because they have become insolvent, it is clear that the original seller cannot impugn the sub-buyer's title on the ground of bad faith; otherwise a person could never safely buy goods which they knew had not been paid for. It is, therefore, submitted that the requirement that the third party must receive the goods 'in good faith and without notice of any lien or other right of the original seller in respect of the goods' can generally only be applicable where the property has not passed to the buyer, and even then it is difficult to see how any question of lien can arise.[211]

12.10.8 Effect of s. 9

There is one curious but important difference in the wording of ss. 8 and 9. The former says that a sale by a seller in possession shall, subject to the conditions laid down, 'have the same effect as if the person making the delivery or transfer were expressly authorised by the owner of the goods to make the same'. On the other hand, s. 9 says that a sale by a buyer in possession shall, subject to the conditions already discussed, have the same effect 'as if the person making the delivery or transfer were a mercantile agent in possession of the goods or documents of title with the consent of the owner'. What exactly is the significance of these last words? If read literally they would appear to create a serious difficulty because, it may be recalled, an unauthorised sale by a mercantile agent in possession of goods with the consent of the owner is only made effective to pass a title by s. 2(1) of the Factors Act 1889 if the mercantile agent is *acting in the ordinary*

[210] See *Forsythe International (UK)* v *Silver Shipping Co and Petroglobe International (The Saetta)* [1993] 2 Lloyd's Rep 268, the facts of which are given at section 12.10.5 above.

[211] On the whole of this difficult question, see a review of the second edition of this book by the late Professor J. C. Smith in the *Journal of the SPTL*, vol. VII, p. 226, to which, in previous editions, Professor Atiyah acknowledged his indebtedness.

course of business. If a person is not a mercantile agent, how can they be said to act in the ordinary course of business of a mercantile agent? As Pearson LJ said in *Newtons of Wembley Ltd* v *Williams*[212] 'It seems on the face of it to be an impossible position.' Nevertheless, the Court of Appeal thought that the buyer must somehow be treated as a notional mercantile agent, and the court has to ask whether the sale would have been in the ordinary course of business had he been a mercantile agent. In this case, the court decided that the sale would have been in the ordinary course, so it may be that the court's view on the main issue could be regarded as *obiter*. But this cannot be said of the earlier and unreported case of *Lambert* v *G & C Finance Corporation Ltd*.[213] In this case, the plaintiff sold his car to X, who offered him a cheque for the price. The plaintiff reluctantly accepted the cheque but insisted on keeping the log book until the cheque was met. In fact, the cheque was worthless and X sold the car to a dealer, who disposed of it to the defendants. The learned judge held that the retention of the log book showed an intention that the property was not to pass until the cheque was met and that the defendants did not obtain a title under s. 9 of the Factors Act. Since X had sold the car without the log book, the learned judge had no difficulty in holding that the sale was not in the ordinary course of business, or rather would not have been in the ordinary course of X's business had he been a mercantile agent.[214]

In the *Lambert* and the *Newtons of Wembley* cases, it may well be that substantial justice was done. But if the dicta in the latter case are followed this may not always be possible. For example, a sale by a mercantile agent outside business premises would not generally be in the ordinary course of business.[215] But if a private individual who is not a mercantile agent were, for example, to sell a second-hand car, the sale would almost certainly take place outside business premises, and a strict application of the *Newtons of Wembley* case would take the case outside s. 9. In the circumstances, it is unfortunate that the court was not referred to dicta in Australia[216] and New Zealand,[217] which take a contrary view. On this view, the effect of a sale by a buyer in possession is the same 'as if' the buyer was a mercantile agent and the sale was in the ordinary course of his business. 'The section operates to validate a sale as if the buyer in possession were a mercantile agent; it does not require that he should act as though he were a mercantile agent.'[218] There is no doubt that this was thought to be the law in *Lee* v *Butler*[219] and was assumed to be the law ever since that case until the *Newtons of Wembley* case. In 1966, the Law Reform Committee recommended that the law be amended to restore the position to what it was formerly thought to be,[220] but nothing has been done to implement this recommendation.

[212] [1965] 1 QB 560, 578.
[213] See (1963) Sol Jo 666.
[214] This issue causes some difficulties with the Scottish cases of *Thomas Graham & Sons Ltd* v *Glenrothes Development Corp* 1967 SC 284 and *Archivent Sales & Development Ltd* v *Strathclyde Regional Council* 1985 SLT 154; on which see Reid, The Law of Property in Scotland (1996), para. 682(5).
[215] *Oppenheimer* v *Attenborough & Sons* [1908] 1 KB 221, above, section 12.5.5.
[216] *Langmead* v *Thyer Rubber* Co Ltd (1947) SR (SA) 29, 39. And see now also the dicta of the High Court in the *Gamer case* (1987) 163 CLR 236, 243 and 252–3, though the point was ultimately left open.
[217] *Jeffcott* v *Andrew Motors* Ltd [1960] NZLR 721, 729 per Gresson P.
[218] Ibid.
[219] [1893] 2 QB 318.
[220] Twelfth Report (Cmnd 2958, 1966), para. 23.

On the other hand, in a case in Northern Ireland[221] the dicta in the *Newtons of Wembley* case were followed by Lord Lowry CJ, who insisted that it would be absurd if a buyer from an ordinary seller was in a better position than a buyer from a mercantile agent because this would make s. 9 of the Factors Act a greater invasion of title than s. 2.

> The key to the meaning of s. 9's 'shorthand' [said Lord Lowry] must be that innocent purchasers can be protected not only (as they were originally meant to be) when dealing with mercantile agents acting in the ordinary course of a mercantile agent's business, but also with ordinary persons acting in the way in which a mercantile agent would be expected to act in the ordinary course of business.[222]

Although Lord Lowry may be correct in suggesting that this was the original intention behind s. 9, the contrary view was acted on for so long (beginning, indeed, with *Lee* v *Butler* in 1893) that it seems very late in the day to return now to that view. Moreover, as a matter of policy, one may disagree with his suggestion that it would be absurd to protect the bona fide purchaser where the intermediate buyer has not acted as though they were a mercantile agent. A seller who actually delivers the goods to a buyer before being paid chooses to trust to that buyer's credit, and there seems every reason why they should take the risk if that buyer wrongfully resells the goods to an innocent purchaser in good faith.

12.10.9 Effect of s. 9 where seller is not the owner

One difficult point remains to be mentioned. What is the effect of s. 9 where the seller was not himself the owner of the goods and had no authority to sell from the owner? For instance, if a thief steals a car and sells it to a car dealer who resells it, does s. 9 apply to the resale? A literal reading of the section might suggest that it would protect the second buyer in this situation, on the ground that the first buyer is a person who has bought or agreed to buy the goods, and that the sale by him to the second buyer is then to have the same effect as if it had been made by a mercantile agent in possession of the goods with the consent of the owner. But this literal reading of the section was rejected by the House of Lords in *National Employers Mutual General Insurance Association Ltd* v *Jones*.[223] The words 'with the consent of the owner' at the end of the section were here interpreted to mean, 'with the consent of the owner who has entrusted him with, or consented to his having the possession of, the goods, or of the documents of title to the goods'. [224] The whole point of these provisions is that they are designed to protect someone who buys from a person who has been entrusted with the goods or documents of title. No rational policy could defend protecting a second buyer after a theft, but not a first buyer.[225]

[221] *Martin* v *Duffy* [1985] 11 NIJB 80.
[222] At p. 84.
[223] [1990] 1 AC 24, upholding the view contended for in earlier editions of this work. See the 7th edn, pp. 302–3 for some Commonwealth cases no longer of importance in England.
[224] For a useful note on this case, see Battersby (1991) 54 MLR 752.
[225] If the views of Battersby and Preston (1972) 35 MLR 268 are correct, the effect of a theft is to create a second title within which the Factors Act would apply in the normal way to defeat the rights of the 'owner' under that title, but not of course the rights of the true owner.

12.11 Part III of the Hire Purchase Act 1964

Part III of the Hire Purchase Act 1964 (as re-enacted by the Consumer Credit Act 1974) provides, in essence, that a bona fide private purchaser for value of a motor vehicle from a person in possession under a hire-purchase agreement or a conditional sale agreement[226] obtains a good title. The simplicity of result contrasts starkly with the complexity of the statutory language. Section 27(1) and (2) of the 1964 Act[227] are as follows:

(1) This section applies where a motor vehicle has been bailed or (in Scotland) hired under a hire-purchase agreement, or has been agreed to be sold under a conditional sale agreement, and before the property in the vehicle has become vested in the debtor, he disposes of the vehicle to another person.

(2) Where the disposition referred to in subsection (1) is to a private purchaser, and he is a purchaser of the motor vehicle in good faith without notice of the hire-purchase agreement or conditional sale agreement (the 'relevant agreement'), that disposition shall have effect as if the creditor's title to the vehicle had been vested in the debtor immediately before that disposition.

Thus, the power of a person in possession under a conditional sale agreement to pass a title which was taken away by the sections already discussed was, so far as concerns motor vehicles, in effect restored by this section. There is, however, one important limitation on this power to pass title and that is that a 'trade or finance purchaser' is not protected. The 'private purchaser' referred to in s. 27(2) is any purchaser other than a trade or finance purchaser, and this term is defined by s. 29(2) to mean a person who carries on a business which consists wholly or partly:

(a) of purchasing motor vehicles for the purpose of offering or exposing them for sale, or
(b) of providing finance by purchasing motor vehicles for the purpose of bailing or (in Scotland) hiring them under hire-purchase agreements or agreeing to sell them under conditional sale agreements.

It will be seen that these provisions do not deprive all business concerns of protection under Part III. A large company which buys an expensive lorry may obtain title under Part III. It is only the car dealer[228] and the finance company that are outside the protection of these sections. It has been held that what matters under these provisions is the status of the buyer and not the capacity in which they buy. Thus, a person who deals in motor vehicles is a trade purchaser and outside the protection of the sections, even though they buy a vehicle for their own private use.[229] Similarly, a company offering loans to individuals with a bad credit history by using the individual's car as security (assigned by means of a bill of sale) was not a private purchaser.[230]

[226] It must therefore be the debtor named in the agreement. So title could not be gained under s. 27 from a rogue masquerading as a real person who was named as the debtor in a hire-purchase agreement – *Shogun Finance Ltd* v *Hudson* [2003] UKHL 62.

[227] Re-enacted with terminological changes in Sched. 4 to the Consumer Credit Act 1974.

[228] This does not require the purchaser to have formally set itself up as a car dealer at the relevant time. It suffices that vehicles are bought as a business venture with a view to selling them at a profit – *GE Capital Bank Ltd* v *Rushton and Jenking* [2005] EWCA Civ 1556.

[229] *Stevenson* v *Beverley Bentinck Ltd* [1976] 2 All ER 606.

[230] *Welcome Financial Services Ltd* v *Nine Regions Ltd (t/a Log Book Loans)* [2010] 2 Lloyd's Rep. 426.

If a trade or finance purchaser, having acquired a vehicle from a hirer in possession under a hire-purchase agreement, proceeds to dispose of it to a third party, the third party will be protected by s. 27(3). The section also deals with the possibility that a vehicle which has been disposed of by a hirer to a finance company is then re-let under a new hire-purchase agreement to a new hirer. In this event, the new agreement is itself a disposition by virtue of the definition in s. 29(1) and the new hirer is protected. Moreover, their protection is not displaced by the fact that, before they exercise their option to purchase, the true facts may have come to light. Section 27(4) provides, in effect, that in such circumstances the time for determining whether the new hirer is in good faith or not is when he enters into the hire-purchase agreement and not when they exercise their option to purchase. It may be noted that the trade or finance purchaser will not itself be better off as a result of the subsequent disposition because it will remain liable in conversion to the original owner under s. 27(6). In Scotland, the trade or finance purchaser is liable to the deprived owner insofar as the former is enriched by the transaction. Arguments that they might also be liable under the doctrine of *specificatio* have been authoritatively rejected.[231]

A trade or finance purchaser, though unprotected by *these* sections,[232] can apply to either Equifax or Experian for information. But, as we have seen, there was no redress where the owner of a vehicle let under a hire-purchase agreement had failed to notify the predecessor of the first of these bodies, Hire Purchase Information, of the agreement. The position would appear to be the same in relation to Equifax or Experian. Accordingly, a purchaser will buy in good faith if they have been told there is no agreement registered with either of them.

The first requirement of these provisions, then, is that the vehicle must have been let under a hire-purchase agreement or been agreed to be sold under a conditional sale agreement. The Act does not, therefore, apply where the vehicle has been let under a simple hiring agreement. Nor does the Act have any bearing on the situation which arose in *Central Newbury Car Auctions Ltd* v *Unity Finance Ltd*,[233] where a dealer allowed a swindler to have possession of a vehicle on his signing hire-purchase proposal forms which were later rejected by the finance company. It seems anomalous that the dealer is not at risk in this sort of case for he clearly takes a much greater chance than a dealer who actually enters into a hire-purchase agreement himself. If the finance company accepts the hirer's proposals in this sort of case, then presumably his power to pass title becomes effective as from the moment when the contract is completed, that is, in most cases, when the acceptance is posted to him.

It is important to note that the Act does not require the hirer to be in possession *under* the hire-purchase agreement.[234] It merely requires that the vehicle 'has been bailed under a hire-purchase agreement' and that the hirer should have disposed of it before the property has passed to him.[235] And the definition of 'debtor' in s. 29(4) makes it clear that even if the agreement has already been determined, the former hirer is still the debtor for the

[231] *North West Securities Ltd* v *Barrhead Coachworks Ltd* 1976 SC 68, overruling *FC Finance Ltd* v *Langtry Investment Co Ltd* 1973 SLT (Sh Ct) 11.

[232] See above, section 12.4.3.

[233] [1957] 1 QB 371.

[234] Though, as noted above, they must be the person named in the agreement – see section 12.4.3, above.

[235] *Carlyle Finance Ltd* v *Pallas Industrial Finance and anor* [1999] RTR 281.

purposes of s. 27. So also is a hirer who is in possession under a time order made under s. 130(4) of the Consumer Credit Act.[236]

The next requirement of these provisions is that there must have been a 'disposition' by the hirer or buyer. This is defined by s. 29(1), from which it appears that a disposition includes a sale, a contract of sale and a letting under a hire-purchase agreement. These provisions are narrower than those of the Factors Act and the Sale of Goods Act in that the definition of 'disposition' is exhaustive, whereas under the other Acts any disposition is protected. This is, however, largely an academic point for ordinary vehicles are unlikely to be pledged, and the only other type of disposition which is likely to be encountered, namely the creation of a lien, would almost inevitably be in favour of a trade or finance purchaser who would not be protected anyhow.[237] In *Rohit Kulkarni* v *Manor Credit (Davenham) Ltd*,[238] the contract with the private individual which qualified as a disposition for the purposes of s. 27 had been entered into *before* the car in question was acquired by the seller, who took it under a hire-purchase agreement entered into fraudulently. As the car in question was unascertained under the contract with the private individual, the Court of Appeal held that property did not pass until either after the car had been put into a deliverable state (once the registration plate had been affixed) or, alternatively, on delivery of the car. Therefore the relevant disposition did not occur until property was intended to pass under the contract, which was *after* the trader had entered into the hire-purchase agreement.

Finally, the purchaser must buy in good faith and without notice of the hire-purchase or conditional sale agreement. For this purpose, it is immaterial that the buyer may know that the vehicle was the subject of a hire-purchase agreement if they believe that the finance company has been paid off.[239]

Section 28 of the 1964 Act contains a number of elaborate presumptions to meet the not uncommon situation where a person in possession of a vehicle which was once the subject of an unfulfilled hire-purchase agreement does not know precisely what has happened to the vehicle before they acquired it.[240] The net effect of these presumptions appears to be as follows. The onus of proof that the defendant (or an earlier purchaser) was himself a purchaser in good faith and without notice lies on the defendant. But once this has been proved, there appear to be only two ways in which the finance company will be able to establish its title against the defendant. One will be to show that the first private purchaser to acquire the vehicle was not a purchaser in good faith. If this can be established, then no subsequent purchaser can acquire a title under s. 27 even if they are themselves in good faith. Secondly, the finance company may be able to establish that the vehicle was not in fact disposed of by the hirer at all, but was, for example, stolen from them, or was disposed of by someone who had obtained temporary control of the car with the hirer's consent.

[236] A 'time order' is an order made by a court which gives the hirer or debtor extra time to pay the instalments.

[237] Similarly, the unusual transaction held to be a disposition in *Worcester Works Finance Ltd* v *Cooden Engineering Co Ltd* [1972] 1 QB 210 is unlikely to occur except in favour of a trade or finance purchaser.

[238] [2010] 2 Lloyd's Rep. 431.

[239] *Barker* v *Bell* [1971] 1 WLR 983.

[240] The presumptions do not operate where it is known what transactions have actually taken place: *Soneco Ltd* v *Barcross Finance Ltd* [1978] RTR 444.

12.12 Proposals for reform

There can be no doubt after the above discussion that the law relating to the transfer of title to goods is in a complex and confused state. It has been complained that 'statutory protection for the bona fide purchaser has developed in a piecemeal and haphazard fashion, and some of the relevant provisions have been so drafted and interpreted as to make their application depend not on principles of equity or justice but on fine technicalities which have little rhyme and less reason'.[241] In his judgment in *Ingram* v *Little*,[242] Devlin LJ, as he then was, suggested that it might be possible to apportion the loss which occurs when an innocent owner and an equally innocent bona fide purchaser are left to dispute over the title to goods after some dishonest middle party has quit the scene. The result of this suggestion was that the whole topic was referred to the Law Reform Committee.[243] The Committee in fact rejected Lord Devlin's suggestion as impractical, largely because of the complications which would ensue where the goods pass through several hands. For example, a thief steals a car belonging to O and sells it to A, who sells to B, who resells to C, and so on. In such circumstances, there would be great difficulty in any system of law which allowed apportionment of the loss: should apportionment be only as between O and A? Or between all the parties? And how should the loss be apportioned?

The Committee did, however, go on to make a number of other recommendations for reform of the law. They rejected the notion of fundamental alteration in the law such as would *prima facie* protect any bona fide purchaser for value, but went on to propose the following detailed changes:

1 The Committee recommended[244] the abolition of the distinction between contracts void for mistake and contracts voidable for fraud. Hence, in cases like *Cundy* v *Lindsay*[245] and *Ingram* v *Little*,[246] it would become immaterial whether the contract is void or voidable. In either event, the third party should be protected.[247]
2 The Committee recommended[248] reversal of the decision in *Caldwell*'s[249] case: rescission of a voidable contract should require communication.
3 The third recommendation[250] is that the dicta in the *Newtons of Wembley*[251] case should be reversed and s. 9 of the Factors Act amended to make it clear that it enables the buyer in possession to pass a good title without requiring them to act as a mercantile agent.
4 The Committee rejected the suggestion that any bailee should be able to pass a good title.[252]
5 The Committee strongly criticised the market overt rule as 'capricious', and recommended that the rule should be replaced by a wider protective provision applicable

[241] See the *Report of the Crowther Committee on Consumer Credit* (Cmnd 4596, 1971), para. 4.2.8.
[242] [1961] 1 QB 31. See discussion of this case in *Shogun Finance* v *Hudson* – see Chapter 2.
[243] Twelfth Report (Cmnd 2958, 1966).
[244] Paragraph 15.
[245] (1878) 3 App Cas 459.
[246] [1961] 1 QB 31.
[247] This result is achieved by Art. 2-403 of the UCC.
[248] Paragraph 16.
[249] [1965] 1 QB 525.
[250] Paragraph 23.
[251] [1965] 1 QB 560.
[252] Paragraph 29.

to a sale at any retail premises. As we have seen, however, this is not the path which Parliament saw fit to follow, as the effect of the Sale of Goods (Amendment) Act 1994 is that bona fide purchasers do not acquire a good title.

Within the context of the existing law, the first three of these recommendations appear to be sensible and would have been unlikely to rouse much opposition, although some scepticism may be felt about whether the first recommendation would actually have achieved very much in practice. The fourth recommendation was more controversial, but the fifth appears to have been the real stumbling block to the implementation of the Report. This recommendation raised fears that it would facilitate the disposal of stolen goods by underworld channels. Generally, the Report was a disappointing document largely because of its complete failure to search for any empirical evidence as to the way in which the law operated.[253] The continuing lack of this evidence makes it very difficult to justify positive proposals for change of a fundamental character. The most important question to which insufficient attention has usually been paid is the likelihood of the original owner of lost or stolen goods being protected by insurance.[254] Where this is the normal situation, there seems good reason for giving greater protection under the law to bona fide purchasers than is done at present. A less drastic approach would, as a minimum, amalgamate some of the existing statutory provisions by reducing them to a common principle. Thus ss. 2, 8 and 9 of the Factors Act could well be replaced by a principle (along the lines of Art. 2-403 of the UCC) enabling any dealer to pass a title to goods which have been entrusted to their possession.[255]

In 1976, the Scottish Law Commission produced some tentative proposals for consideration.[256] It suggested that the law should provide protection for *bona fide* onerous acquirers of another's property, provided that the acquirer had taken possession in good faith and provided that the goods were not infected by a real vice resulting from involuntary dispossession of the owner (e.g., theft). The purchaser should have the onus of proving their own good faith, or facts from which it could be inferred, while the owner should be obliged to prove real vice. The basic principle would be to protect the good faith purchaser where the owner's voluntary parting with possession had facilitated wrongful disposal. But these proposals did not even reach the status of a Law Commission Report, and there has been no legislation in Scotland.

A different, and in some ways far more radical, approach was advocated by the Crowther Committee on Consumer Credit.[257] This Committee proposed that legislation, along the lines of Art. 9 of the American UCC should be enacted to cover all situations in which a security interest is reserved over goods, as a form of mortgage or charge, irrespective of its legal nature. Thus this legislation would replace (*inter alia*) the Bills of Sale Act 1882, s. 25 of the Sale of Goods Act and s. 9 of the Factors Act, and would also cover the post-Crowther development of the *Romalpa* reservation of title clauses. The basic

[253] See Professor Atiyah's criticisms of the Report in (1966) 29 MLR 541.

[254] See Battersby, (1991) 54 MLR 752.

[255] Professor Tettenborn has recently developed the case for adopting a default rule based on entrustment: see Tettenborn, Transfer of chattels by non-owners: still an open problem (2018) 77 CLJ 151.

[256] Memorandum No. 27, *Corporeal Moveables* (1976).

[257] See the *Report of the Crowther Committee* (Cmnd 4596, 1971), paras 5.5.1–5.7.83; and see also Goode (1984) 100 LQR 234.

idea behind such legislation is that the law should not differentiate between different types of transaction which have the same fundamental commercial purpose, merely because a different legal form has been adopted. To a considerable extent, this policy has already been adopted in the Consumer Credit Act, which was the first product of the Crowther Committee recommendations. The second major legislative development envisaged by the Committee – a new Lending and Security Act – was also not pursued. The legislation which the Committee, and a later DTI Consultation Document,[258] envisaged would cover all agreements by which one person attempts to obtain an interest over goods by way of security, irrespective of the form of the agreement, would thus cover hire-purchase agreements, sales under which title is reserved by the seller as a security, bills of sale (which are not designed as outright sales) and other arrangements of a similar character.

Such a law would, to some degree, regulate the rights of borrower and lender *inter se*, by providing, for instance, when and how the security rights of the lender could be exercised, and what kind of limits might be imposed on the freedom of the parties to make their own contract, but more importantly, it would regulate the rights of the holder of the security as against third parties, in particular as against creditors of the borrower. It would also provide for some kind of registration system for certain sorts of security. Legislation along these lines would not replace all the provisions of the Sale of Goods Act dealing with the transfer of title – for instance, s. 24 of the Act (sales by seller in possession) and s. 23 (sale under voidable title) would not necessarily be encompassed within such legislation, nor would s. 2 of the Factors Act. But many other provisions dealt with above would fall within the scope of such a new law. The recent huge growth of reservation of title clauses in commercial sales is rendering reform a matter of some urgency,[259] although that sense of urgency has seemingly still not reached policy-makers.

[258] DTI, Transfer of Title: Sections 21 to 26 of the Sale of Goods Act 1979 (1994); see also Diamond, *A Review of Security Interests In Property* (HMSO, 1989).

[259] See Chapter 15 for further discussion of this topic; see also Sheehan, Registration, re-characterisation of quasi-security and the *nemo datrules* (2018) JBL 584.

Part V

Export sales

13
Export sales

The sale of goods which are to be shipped to their destination gives rise to a host of difficult questions, adequate discussion of which would require a whole volume[1] and is therefore beyond the scope of this work, but because the Sale of Goods Act contains provisions relevant to these transactions the main types of export contract, the problems raised by export and import licences, and payment by bankers' commercial credits will be considered in this chapter. The main provisions of the UN Convention on Contracts for the International Sale of Goods ('CISG') will also be considered in the next chapter.

First, however, INCOTERMS will be considered, with specific focus on Free on Board (FOB) and Cost Insurance Freight contract (CIF) which are the most frequently used INCOTERMS in export and import transactions.

13.1 INCOTERMS

INCOTERMS are standard form contracts that have already been produced and exist in skeleton form by the International Chamber of Commerce (ICC). Their main purpose is to facilitate and make sale of goods transactions easier by setting out the obligations and rights of the parties in sale of goods transactions. INCOTERMS 2020 are almost universally accepted and thus provides some uniformity in the interpretation of rules govern those international sale transaction. The ICC usually updates the INCOTERMS after every 10 years and the latest version is the INCOTERMS 2020 which contains 11 standard form contracts as listed below categorised as those that applies for any mode of transportation and those that applies for sea and inland waterway transportation only.

13.1.1 Rules for any mode of transport

- EXW (EX WORKS)
  Here the seller's duty is to only provide conforming goods at the disposal of the buyer at the seller's place business. This is discussed further discussed below.
- FCA (FREE CARRIER) –
  Here the seller delivers the goods to a named place or vehicle nominated by the buyer.

[1] See for example Bridge, The *International Sale of Goods* (5th edn, 2023, OUP); Murray, Holloway and Timson-Hunt (eds), *Schmitthoff's Export Trade* (12th edn, 2012, Sweet & Maxwell).

- CPT (CARRIAGE PAID TO)
  Here the seller delivers the goods to the carrier or another person nominated by the seller at an agreed place and bears the costs of carriage to carry the goods to the named place of destination nominated by the buyer.
- CIP (CARRIAGE AND INSURANCE PAID TO)
  Here the seller is obliged to arrange contract of carriage to the named destination and obtain insurance to cover the buyer's risk of loss of or damage to the goods during carriage.
- DAP (DELIVERED AT PLACE)
  The seller arranges and bears the cost of delivering goods at the buyer's nominated place of delivery and ensures the goods are at the disposal of the buyer on the transportation vehicle ready for unloading at the place of destination or an agreed point within such place.[2]
- DPU (DELIVERED AT PLACE UNLOADED)
  The seller delivers the goods while transferring the risk to the buyer when the goods are unloaded from the arriving means of transport at the named place of destination or any other agreed point within that place. This replaces the old Delivered at Terminal (DAT) under INCOTERMS 2010, with additional requirements for the seller to unload the goods from the vessel used.
- DDP (DELIVERED DUTY PAID) –
  Here the seller's duty is to bear the cost and risk of transporting the goods to the buyer's address. This is also referred to as the Ex-Ship contract and is further discussed below.

13.1.2 Rules for sea and inland waterway transport only

- FAS (FREE ALONGSIDE SHIP)
  Here the main duty of the seller is to provide the contract goods placed alongside the vessel/ship nominated by the buyer.
- FOB (FREE ON BOARD)
  Here the main duty of the seller is to provide the contract goods placed onboard the vessel/ship nominated by the buyer, this discussed further below.
- CFR (COST AND FREIGHT)
  Here the seller delivers the goods on board the vessel and procures the contract to ship the goods to the final destination.[3]
- CIF (COST INSURANCE AND FREIGHT)
  Here the seller delivers the goods on board the vessel, procures the contract to ship the goods and insurance contract for the benefit of the buyer. This is discussed further below.

[2] See, *Vitol SA* v *Genser Energy Ghana Ltd* [2022] EWHC 1812 (Comm) and *Addax Energy SA* v *Petro Trade Inc* [2023] EWHC 1609 (Comm).
[3] See, *Litasco SA* v *Der Mond Oil and Gas Africa SA & Locafrique Holding SA* [2023] EWHC 2866 (Comm).

13.1.3 Nature of INCOTERMS

However, it should be noted that INCOTERMS 2020 only apply where the parties have chosen for them to apply in their contract. Where an INCOTERMS applies it must be interpreted in a manner that is consistent with the applicable law. They are also confined to matters relating to the duties and rights of the parties to the contract of sale with respect to the delivery of the goods sold. INCOTERMS also dictate the time when risk passes within the transaction. Thus via s.20 SGA 1979, when the parties agree to one of the INCOTERMS to apply within their contract, then they would have accepted that risk to pass as per the rules of that INCOTERM.

Importantly, INCOTERMS do not usually deal with when property in the goods passes, that is matter that is left for national legislations. However, where a certain INCOTERM applies there is usually commercial practice that dictates when property is intended to transfer as discussed below. This usually interpreted to be the intentions of the parties via that s.17 and 19 SGA 1979 which gives parties the autonomy to state when and/or set conditions as when property passes in their contract. Nonetheless, property would not pass if the requirements of passing property for contract goods be it unascertained or specific under s.16-20A SGA 1979 are not satisfied.

Care must also be taken not to assume that a contract which is said to be an ex-works contract, or a CIF or FOB contract, necessarily carries all the incidents which may be associated with these contracts in the absence of a contrary intention. Terms of this kind are often used by businessmen in agreements which contain other terms inconsistent with any such possibility. As was said by Roskill LJ in *The Albazero*:[4]

> It is a trite observation that what is sometimes called a true f.o.b. or a true c.i.f. contract is a comparative commercial rarity. Contracts vary infinitely according to the wishes of the parties to them. Though a contract may include the letters f.o.b. or c.i.f. amongst its terms, it may well be that other terms of the contract clearly show that the use of those letters is intended to do no more than show where the incidence of liability for freight or insurance will lie as between buyer and seller, but is not to denote the mode of performance of the seller's obligations to the buyer or the buyer's obligations to the seller. In other cases, though the letters c.i.f. are used, other terms of the contract may show that the property is intended to pass on shipment and not upon tender of and payment against the documents so tendered, or though the letters f.o.b. are used, other terms may show that the property was not intended to pass on shipment but upon tender and payment, the seller by the form in which he took the bill of lading intending to reserve his right of disposal until he was paid against the shipping documents.

13.2 Ex-works or ex-store contracts

Ex-works or ex-store contracts present few difficulties. In fact, they may not be export sales at all, since it is the buyer's duty to take delivery at the works or store in question, and that may or may not be in a different country or territory and they may or may not export them after taking delivery. The property and risk will, in the absence of any contrary indication, pass when the goods are delivered in most contracts of this kind, since they are

[4] [1977] AC 774, 809.

usually sales of unascertained goods and it is unlikely that there will be any appropriation (except perhaps where provision is made for inspection at an early date) prior to delivery.

There are many reasons why parties in an international sale of goods transaction may choose an Ex- work contract including where there is an experienced buyer while the seller is inexperienced in international sale goods transactions or the seller is not familiar with the foreign law and necessary bureaucratic procedures for export sales. Also, this may be the INCOTERMS of choice for the buyer where they looking to save on costs as the seller has to only provide the goods and/or main control of the goods at the earliest stage possible.[5]

13.3 FOB contracts

There is no universal definition of FOB contracts but generally this contract may be described as an INCOTERM which can only be used where the goods are to be transported via ship across the sea or inland waterway and the main duty of the seller is to provide the contract goods placed onboard the vessel/ship nominated by the buyer. Judicially the FOB contract is defined in a number of cases including in *Stock v Inglis*[6] where Brett MR held that:

> 'The words 'Free on board' according to the general understanding of merchants would mean . . . the shipper was to put [the goods] on board at his expense on account of the person for whom they were shipped; and in that case the goods so put on board under such a contract would be at the risk of the buyer whether they were lost or not on the voyage.'[7]

One of the main reasons why there is no one satisfactory definition of FOB contracts is due to the fact that in practice there are different variants of FOB contract has become a 'flexible instrument'.[8] Under English Law there generally three variants of FOB contracts recognised these were identified by Devlin J in *Pyrene v Scindia*[9] and subsequently recognised & endorsed in subsequent cases including *Ian Stach Ltd v Baker Bosely Ltd*[10] Most notably the three variants were neatly summarised by Donaldson LJ in the *EL Amria and EL Minia*[11] as:

> 'In the first, or classic type, the buyer nominates the ship and the seller puts the goods on board for account of the buyer, procuring a bill of lading. The seller is then a party to the contract of carriage and if he has taken the bill of lading to his order, the only contract of carriage to which the buyer can become a party is that contained in or evidenced by the bill of lading which is endorsed to him by the seller. The second is a variant of the first, in that the seller arranges for the ship to come on the berth, but the legal incidents are the same. The third is where the seller puts the goods on board, takes a mate's receipt and gives this to the buyer or his agent who then takes a bill of lading. In this latter type the buyer is a party to the contract of carriage ab initio.[12]

[5] Lista, A. *International commercial sales : the sale of goods on shipment terms* (Routledge 2017) p. 7.
[6] *Stock* v *Inglis* [1884] 12 QBD 564.
[7] Ibid., at 573.
[8] *Pyrene* v *Scindia* [1954] 2 QB 402, Devlin J at 424.
[9] Ibid.
[10] [1958] 2 Lloyds Rep 127, see also, *NV Handel Ny Smits Import-Export* v *English Exporters* (London) Ltd [1957] Lloyd's Rep 517.
[11] [1982] 2 Lloyds Rep 28.
[12] Ibid., at 32.

From this description, it is clear therefore, that in practice the different variants of FOB contract create different forms of legal relationships between the buyer and the seller as well as their respective relationships with the shipowner.[13] This book will focus on the first or classic FOB variant described above.

13.3.1 Duties of the buyer in FOB contract

In an FOB contract, the seller's duty is to place the goods free on board a ship to be named by the buyer during the contractual shipment period. *Prima facie* at least it seems that 'The expression FOB determines how the goods shall be delivered, how much of the expense shall be borne by the sellers and when the risk of loss or damage shall pass to the buyers. It does not necessarily decide when the property is to pass.'[14] The seller's obligations extend to all charges incurred before shipment, including loading charges, but not freight or insurance.

In the absence of a contrary intention, the buyer has the right and the responsibility of selecting both the port and the date of, and generally making the arrangements for, the shipment of the goods.[15] They must nominate a ship within the shipping period on which the goods may be loaded by the seller and give adequate notice to the seller of that nomination. In practice it is important the buyer nominates an effective ship and give adequate notice to the seller in good time as this allows the seller to perform his obligations of delivering goods at port of loading and loading onboard the nominated vessel within the contractual time for shipment (shipping period). In *J&J Cunningham v Munro*[16] the contract provided that the shipment period is October but buyers nominated a ship that could only load from 28 October. Therefore, the legal issue was the nomination was valid. The court held that the buyers were not in breach of contract because they nominated a ship that could be loaded before end of the shipping period, October.

Importantly, the ship nominated by the buyer must be 'effective' in that, it is capable, to 'legally'[17] (seaworthy) and physically and otherwise, of receiving the cargo. If the buyer nominates a ship which cannot receive the cargo or which cannot load in time, they may, if they still have sufficient time within the shipping period, substitute another vessel in place of the one first nominated. In *Agricultore Federados Argentinos* v *Ampro SA*[18] Shipment was to be between 20 and 29 September. The buyer nominated the Oswestry Grange ship but because of heavy weather could not load until 30 September. So, on 20 September the buyer nominated the Austral ship, which was already at port of loading but the seller argued that was breach of contract. The court held that the re-nomination was valid and if the seller co-operated the loading would have been completed within the shipping period. In particular, Widgery J held that:

> 'As a general law applying in such a contract merely is that the buyers shall provide a vessel which is capable of loading within the stipulated time and if as a matter of courtesy or convenience the

13 Ewan McKendrick and Louise Gullifer *Sale of Goods* (Routledge 2014), at 599.
14 *Mitsui & Co Ltd* v *Flota Mercante Grancolumbiana SA* [1989] 1 All ER 951, 956 per Staughton LJ.
15 *Ian Stach Ltd* v *Baker Bosely* Ltd [1958] 2 Lloyds Rep 127.
16 [1922] 28 Com Cas 42.
17 Scrutton LJ in *HO Brandit & Co* v *HN Morris & CO* [1917] 2 KB 784, at 798.
18 [1965] 2 Lloyd's Rep. 157.

> buyer inform the sellers that they propose to provide vessel A, I can see no reason in principle why they should not change their minds and provide vessel B at a later stage always assuming that vessel B is provided within such a time as to make it possible for her to the buyers' obligation under the contract'[19]

It should be noted though that even if the renomination is within the shipping period the re-nomination must comply with the terms of the sale contract. Indeed, LJ Bingham in *Cargill* v *Continental UK Ltd*[20] held that 'it is impossible to imply a (re-nomination) term' that is 'inconsistent with the express terms' of the contract.[21] In *Ramburs Inc* v *Agrifert SA*[22] a FOB contract for sale of a quantity of maize had a shipment period of between 15 and 31 March 2013. The contract required the buyers to serve on the sellers notice as to, *inter alia*, the name and estimated time of arrival of the nominated vessel for delivery, not less than ten days before delivery. On 20 March 2013, the buyer sent a message nominating a vessel, Puffin, to load the cargo, giving an estimated time of arrival at the loading port of 26/27 March. On 26 March, the buyer sent another message nominating another vessel, Sea Way, in place of Puffin, giving an estimated time of arrival of 28 March. It was held that even though renomination was within the shipping period, the renomination did not comply with the contract terms of giving the seller 10-day notice. Therefore, re-nomination was invalid because an implied term of renomination would have been inconsistent with the express terms the contract.

In general, the duty to nominate an effective ship is a condition of the contract to which a failure would entitle the seller to terminate the contract and sue the buyers for non-acceptance via s.50 SGA 1979. This was the case in *Bunge Corp v Tradax SA*[23] where the buyer nominated a vessel five days late. As a result, the seller avoided the contract for breach of a condition and sold the goods elsewhere but a lower price and sued buyer for damages for the difference.

On receiving the necessary notices from the buyer, in line with *Vitol SA* v *JE Energy Ltd*[24] the seller must be ready to ship the goods within a reasonable time, but they do not necessarily have to have the goods available for immediate shipment.[25] Compliance with the obligation to ship at the port nominated is a condition of the contract.[26] On the other hand, if the nomination is subject to acceptance by the terminal operator, the duty of the seller to obtain this acceptance is an innominate term,[27] but failure to fulfil it timeously will be a ground for repudiation by the buyer.[28]

Once the goods are loaded on board the ship the goods would be delivered and thus via s. 28 SGA 1979 the buyer also has the duty make payment unless agreed otherwise. Where the property in goods has passed the seller can sue seller in event of no-payment via s. 49(1) SGA 1979.

19 Ibid., at 167.
20 LJ Bingham [1989] WL 651193, at para 6.
21 LJ Bingham [1989] WL 651193, at para 6.
22 [2015] EWHC 3548 (Comm).
23 [1981] 1 WLR 711.
24 [2022] EWHC 2494 (Comm).
25 *Tradax Export SPA* v *Italgrani Di Franceso Ambrisio* [1986] 1 Lloyd's Rep 112.
26 *Petrograde Inc* v *Stinnes Handel GmbH*, *The Times*, 27 July 1994.
27 As to which see *Phibro Energy AG* v *Nisshop Iwai Corporation*, The Honam Jade [1991] 1 Lloyd's Rep 38.
28 *Phibro Energy AG* v *Nissho Iwai Corp and Bomar Oil Inc* [1991] 1 Lloyd's Rep 38.

13.3.2 Seller's duties as to contract of carriage

Because it is the seller who makes the contract for the carriage of the goods with the shipowner in the 'classic' FOB contract, they must comply with s. 32(2) of the Act. This provides:

> Unless otherwise authorized by the buyer, the seller must make such contract with the carrier on behalf of the buyer as may be reasonable having regard to the nature of the goods and the other circumstances of the case and if the seller omits to do so, and the goods are lost or damaged in course of transit, the buyer may decline to treat the delivery to the carrier as a delivery to himself, or may hold the seller responsible in damages.

In other words, if this subsection applies the buyer can either reject the goods or accept them and claim damages. It may be observed that this differs from the provisions of s. 20(2), which are in certain respects parallel to this provision. Under the present subsection, it appears that the buyer's remedies for the damage to or loss of the goods operate whether or not the loss or damage was the consequence of the seller's failure to make a reasonable contract with the carrier, whereas under s. 20 if either party is at fault in taking delivery of the goods, the goods are at the risk of the party at fault, but only in respect of damage which might not have occurred but for such fault.

What a 'reasonable' contract is for the seller to make must be judged in the light of the circumstances existing when the contract of carriage is made and not at the date of the contract of sale.[29] For example, contract to carry the goods by an unusual route may be reasonable if the more usual route is unavailable when the contract of carriage is made.[30]

A simple illustration of the workings of s. 32(2) is provided by *Thomas Young & Sons Ltd* v *Hobson & Partners*,[31] where goods were damaged in transit as a result of being insecurely fixed. Had the sellers made a reasonable contract with the carriers, that is, had they sent the goods at the company's risk as was the usual practice instead of at the owner's risk, the loss would not have occurred. The Court of Appeal held that the buyers were entitled to reject the goods. On the other hand, in a later decision (on a CIF contract) it was held that the seller was under no obligation to make a contract for the carriage of oil of an unusual kind providing that the oil was to be heated *en route*; in fact such heating was not necessary for the kind and length of voyage contemplated, although in the event the oil suffered damage which would have been averted if it had been heated.[32]

Where the seller is responsible for shipping the goods, it may be an important question whether they do so on their own account as a principal or simply as agent of the buyer. In particular, if the seller ships as principal, the presumption against property passing on shipment is strong, whereas if they ship as agent, it is more likely that property will be held to pass on shipment.[33] But apart from this crucial distinction, many other ancillary questions may turn on whether the seller acts as principal or agent in shipping the goods. For example, if the seller is unable to secure shipping space despite all reasonable efforts,

[29] *Tsakiroglou & Co Ltd* v *Noblee Thorl GmbH* [1962] AC 93.

[30] Ibid. See also the Australian case, *Plaimar Ltd* v *Waters Trading Co Ltd* (1945) 72 CLR 304.

[31] [1949] 65 TLR 365. The contract here was f.o.r. (free on rail) but the legal results are the same as with an f.o.b. contract.

[32] *The Rio Sun* [1985] 1 Lloyd's Rep 350.

[33] See, for example, *President of India* v *Metcalfe Shipping Co* [1970] 1 QB 289.

they would normally be liable for non-delivery if it was their duty as seller to arrange shipping,[34] whereas they would not be liable if they were required to arrange shipping as the buyer's agent. Other issues may also turn on whether the seller ships as principal or as agent; for example, who is to bear any increase in shipping or insurance charges after the contract of sale is made, or whether the seller is entitled to charge commission on the contract of carriage.

Whether the seller acts as principal or agent in shipping the goods usually depends on whether the parties intend that the seller should retain the bill of lading as security for payment. If this is the intention of the parties, the presumption is that the seller is acting as principal. This in turn may be determined by the bill of lading itself. If it is made out in the seller's name (i.e. if goods are deliverable to, or to the order of, the seller) then the seller is reserving a right of disposal which would suggest that they are acting as principal.

Of course, ultimately, everything depends on the terms of the particular contract and it must not be assumed that every FOB contract is identical in the obligations imposed on the parties. It would, however, be very unusual for the property to pass before shipment in an FOB contract,[35] or for the risk not to pass on shipment.

13.3.3 Passing of risk and property

In this sort of FOB contract, the general rule is that risk passes on shipment as soon as the goods are over the ship's rail, and, if it should be material, the risk in each part of the cargo will pass as it crosses the ship's rail.[36] This is because in this type of contract the seller's duty is to deliver the goods FOB Once they are on board, the seller has delivered them to the buyer and it is natural that they should thereafter be at the buyer's risk.[37] However, so far as the exact point at which risk passes, two views are possible: one is that risk literally passes as the goods cross the ship's rail; the other is that the risk passes when the goods are safely loaded on board the vessel.[38] In *BP Oil International Ltd* v *Vega Petroleum Ltd, Dover Investments Ltd*[39] the interpretation that risk passes to buyer when goods are loaded in a FOB contract was applied.

As regards the passing of property, the position is that *prima facie* property may also pass, like risk, on shipment. The loading of the goods may be an 'unconditional appropriation' which passes the property under s. 18, Rule 5. If the goods are loaded together with other goods of the same description so that an unconditional appropriation of the actual

[34] See, e.g., *Lewis Emmanuel & Son Ltd* v *Sammut* [1959] 2 Lloyd's Rep 629.

[35] See *Carlos Federspiel & Co SA* v *Charles Twigg & Co Ltd* [1957] 1 Lloyd's Rep 240, where the authorities are comprehensively reviewed by Pearson J. See Chapter 10.

[36] *See BP Oil International Ltd* v *Vega Petroleum Ltd, Dover Investments Ltd* [2021] EWHC 1364 (Comm); *Colonial Insurance Co of New Zealand* v *Adelaide Marine Insurance Co* (1886) 12 App Cas 128.

[37] *Frebold* v *Circle Products Ltd* [1970] 1 Lloyd's Rep 499.

[38] See Michael G Bridge *Benjamin's Sale of Goods* (12th ed, Sweet & Maxwell 2024) at 20-180-3. Both INCOTERMS and the UCC, Art. 2-319(1) define the seller's duty as being to load the goods '*on board*'. See In *BP Oil International Ltd* v *Vega Petroleum Ltd*, Dover Investments Ltd [2021] EWHC 1364 – the interpretation that risk passing when goods are loaded in FOB contract was applied.

[39] [2021] EWHC 1364

goods sold then takes place, but the goods subject to the contract are still unascertained, property cannot pass on shipment,[40] but the risk will still do so.[41]

Today, any general presumption that property passes with risk on shipment in an FOB contract has probably largely disappeared. Although this may still be the case if the contract contains no contrary provision, the practice of treating the shipping documents as security for the payment of the price is now so well established in international sales that contractual terms requiring payment against (i.e. in exchange for) the shipping documents is the norm in FOB contracts, just as much as in CIF contracts where this practice may have first originated. Where payment is only to be made against documents, the seller will normally be named as the consignee in the bill of lading (i.e. the goods will be deliverable under the bill of lading to, or to the order of, the seller), so that s. 19(1) and (2) become relevant. Section 19(1) that has already been set out above[42] provides:

> Where goods are shipped, and by the bill of lading the goods are deliverable to the order of the seller or his agent, the seller is *prima facie* to be taken to reserve the right of disposal.

This reservation of the right of disposal makes the appropriation conditional under s. 19(1) so that property does not pass until the condition is satisfied. It is clear that today there is nothing contrary to the nature of the FOB contract in the seller doing this, and indeed, as already said, it is nowadays very common. The result is that the shipment is treated under s. 19 as only amounting to a conditional appropriation, the condition being that the seller must be paid before property passes.

But the terms of the bill of lading are only evidence of the intention of the parties. The fact that the bill of lading is taken in the seller's name is not conclusive proof that the seller is shipping the goods as principal or is reserving the right of disposal. There are cases where the seller does not want or need to keep the documents as security for the price, as where (for instance) seller and buyer are associated companies, or where the seller has agreed to grant the buyer credit. In such a case, the seller may in fact transfer the bill of lading to the buyer as soon as they receive it, which would probably indicate that they were acting as agent all along.[43] And although the taking of the bill of lading in their own name by the seller *prima facie* indicates that the property does not pass on shipment, it does not follow that if the bill of lading is taken in the buyer's name it must be held that the property does pass on shipment. The retention of the bill of lading by the seller may be inconsistent with an intention to pass the property until it is handed over.[44]

It must be stressed that even where property does not pass on shipment, the seller normally retains the property only as security for payment or as a means of obtaining bridging finance to cover the period of shipment.[45] Once the goods are shipped, the buyer

[40] Though the buyer may acquire an undivided share in the bulk under the Sale of Goods (Amendment) Act 1995 – see Chapter 10.

[41] *Inglis* v *Stock* (1885) 10 App Cas 263.

[42] See Chapter 10.

[43] *The Albazero* [1977] AC 774.

[44] Compare the classic f.o.b. described at 13.3 et seq. See The *Kronprinsessan Margareta* [1921] 1 AC 486; cf. *The Parchim* [1918] AC 157, but this case can no longer support any general inference of passing of property merely by reason that risk has passed on shipment; see *Mitsui & Co Ltd* v *Flota Mercante Grancolumbiana SA* [1989] 1 All ER 951, 957.

[45] *Ross T Smyth & Co Ltd* v *Bailey Son & Co* [1940] 3 All ER 60, 68

has an interest in the goods so that the seller must transfer goods to the buyer from that shipment; if the seller transfers them to anyone else so that they cannot supply the buyer from that shipment, they break their contract with the buyer, although today the seller will normally be able to pass a good title to the third party buyer. In the absence of privity of contract,[46] the buyer cannot sue a third party (such as the carrier) in tort for damage to the goods where they have no property, or possessory interest, at the time the damage occurred.[47] On the other hand, the seller may sue and recover damages for the full value of the loss to the amount permitted by the Carriage of Goods by Sea Act 1971,[48] even though the seller had only a limited interest in the goods;[49] any surplus will be held on trust for the buyer.[50]

The above analysis of the way the sections of the Sale of Goods Act fit in with modern commercial practice has been reaffirmed by the Court of Appeal, and applied even to a case in which the buyer had paid 80 per cent of the price by letter of credit before the goods were shipped.[51] In such a case, although property does not pass under s. 19 until the conditions imposed by the seller have been fulfilled, the buyer may nonetheless acquire an undivided share in the part of an identified bulk paid for under the Sale of Goods (Amendment) Act 1995.[52]

13.3.4 Seller's duties as to insurance

It has already been seen that under s. 32(1), delivery to the carrier is *prima facie* deemed to be delivery to the buyer themselves, but despite this it has been held that s. 32(3) applies to FOB contracts. This subsection states that:

> Unless otherwise agreed, where goods are sent by the seller to the buyer by a route involving sea transit, under circumstances in which it is usual to insure, the seller must give such notice to the buyer as may enable him to insure them during their sea transit, and if the seller fails to do so, the goods are at his risk during such sea transit.

The construction of this subsection was the subject of some widely differing views in the Court of Appeal in *Wimble Sons & Co Ltd* v *Rosenberg & Sons*,[53] where the plaintiffs

46 But once the bill of lading is transferred to the buyer, the buyer becomes a party to the contract of carriage under the Carriage of Goods by Sea Act 1992 – see below section 13.4.1.

47 *Leigh & Sillivan Ltd* v *Aliakmon Shipping Co Ltd (The Aliakmon)* [1986] AC 785, and see Chapter 10.

48 Giving effect to the Hague/Visby Rules. The Act applies to all shipments where the contract expressly, or by implication, provides for the issuance of a bill of lading or similar document of title. Its effect is to limit the carrier's liability for loss or damage to a certain amount. Where there is no privity of contract, but the buyer is able to sue by virtue of ownership or a possessory title, it is believed that the limits would nevertheless apply under the rules developed in relation to the law of bailments – see *Southcote's Case* (1601) 46 Co Rep 86a; *Gibbon* v *Payton* (1769) 4 Burr 2298. The baroque complexity of this area of law is due to the over-rigid adherence of the courts to the doctrine of privity of contract. As to the effect of the Sale of Goods (Amendment) Act 1995 (ascertainment by exhaustion), see Chapter 10, section 10.2.3.

49 *Obestain Inc* v *National Mineral Development Corp Ltd* [1987] 1 Lloyd's Rep 465; *Linden Gardens Trust* v *Lenesta Sludge Disposals Ltd* [1994] 1 AC 85, though this is subject to the qualification laid down in *The Albazero* [1977] AC 774. So the effect of *The Aliakmon* ([1986] AC 785) may only be to force the buyer to sue in the shipper's name.

50 See *The Winkfield* [1902] P 42.

51 See under s. 19 chapter 10,. *Mitsui & Co Ltd* v *Flota Mercante Grancolumbiana SA* [1989] 1 All ER 951.

52 See section 13.4

53 [1913] 3 KB 743, followed in *Northern Steel Co Ltd* v *Batt* (1917) 33 TLR 516.

sold goods to the defendants FOB Antwerp. The buyers sent instructions for shipping the goods, leaving it to the sellers to select the ship. The sellers shipped the goods, but did not insure and the cargo was lost at sea. Vaughan Williams and Buckley LJJ agreed that s. 32(3) applied to FOB contracts, differing from Hamilton LJ who thought it had no application at all to such contracts because the seller does not send the goods to the buyer but only puts them on the ship for dispatch to the buyer. The majority thought, however, that dispatch was something different from delivery and that the seller dispatches or sends the goods to the buyer but only delivers them to the ship, and such delivery is deemed to be delivery to the buyer by s. 32(1). This was not the end of the disagreements because Buckley LJ thought that the sellers were not liable in this case since the buyers already had sufficient information to enable them to insure if they wished. They knew what the freight was, they knew the port of loading and they knew the port of discharge. The only information lacking was the name of the ship, which would not have prevented insurance. On the other hand, Vaughan Williams LJ thought that such a construction would destroy the efficacy of the section since it is always possible for the buyer to insure the goods by a general cover policy. However, Buckley LJ answered this by pointing out that in this case the buyer had enough information to make a particular insurance, but he agreed that the mere fact that the buyer can take out a general cover policy would not prevent the operation of s. 32(3).

The net result of this case is that, though the subsection in theory applies to FOB contracts, in practice it will rarely be of much importance because in most cases the buyer will already have enough information to insure the goods specifically.

Seller's duties as to documents

Where a seller under an FOB contract must tender documents, their duties are the same as a CIF seller discussed in the following section and the tender must be made as soon as is reasonably possible.[54]

13.4 CIF contracts

Among the INCOTERMS, the CIF contract is the most 'widely and frequently used for the purpose of seaborne commerce'.[55] In the absence of any provisions to the contrary, the seller in a CIF contract is obliged to load the goods or procures goods already so delivered, procure a contract of carriage to ship the contract goods to the port of destination, and obtain a contract of insurance for the buyer's benefit. Thereafter, he must tender the shipping documents (bill of lading, insurance policy and the invoice) to the buyer.[56]

Judicially, the CIF contract has being defined in a series of cases. In 1872, Blackburn J defined a CIF contract as a contract in which the contract price includes the costs, freight and insurance and is paid after the buyer receives the shipping documents.[57]

[54] *Concordia Trading BV* v *Richco International Ltd* [1991] 1 Lloyd's Rep 475.
[55] Lord Wright *in Ross T Smyth and Co Ltd* v *Bailey, Son and Co* [1940] 3 ALL ER 60, at 67
[56] INCOTERMS 2020 Rules, page 123.
[57] *Ireland* v *Livingstone* [1872] LR 5 HL 395.

In 1911, Hamilton J defined a CIF contract by referring to the seller's duties[58] and this was improved by Scrutton J[59] and Atkin J[60] and was later adopted and summarised by Lord Atkinson in *Johnson* v *Taylor Bros*.[61] The definition was later neatly summarised by, Lord Wright in *Smyth & Co Ltd* v *Bailey Son & Co Ltd*[62] as:

> 'The contract in question here is of a type familiar in commerce, and is described as a CIF contract. The initials indicate that the price is to include cost, insurance and freight. It is a type of contract which is more widely and more frequently in use than any other contract used for purposes of sea-borne commerce. An enormous number of transactions, in value amounting to untold sums, are carried out every year under CIF contracts. The essential characteristics of this contract have often been described. The seller has to ship or acquire after that shipment the contract goods, as to which, if unascertained, he is generally required to give a notice of appropriation. On or after shipment, he has to obtain proper bills of lading and proper policies of insurance. He fulfils his contract by transferring the bills of lading and the policies to the buyer. As a general rule, he does so only against payment of the price, less the freight which the buyer has to pay. In the invoice which accompanies the tender of the documents on the 'prompt' – that is, the date fixed for payment – the freight is deducted, for this reason. In this course of business, the general property remains in the seller until he transfers the bill of lading . . .'[63]

From this definition, it is clear that under a CIF contract s. 28 of SGA 1979 does not apply because delivery of goods is not concurrent to payment. Instead, the seller is entitled to the contract price after the delivery of shipping documents (discussed further below) and goods would arrive after.[64] In addition, S.20 SGA 1979 does not apply in a CIF contract because the property and risk in the contract goods do not pass simultaneously to the buyer. Instead, the risk passes from the seller to the buyer on shipment[65] while the property passes to the buyer after delivery of the shipping documents and payment of the contract price.[66] This is discussed in more detail below.

These unique features characteristic of a CIF contract are vital and embody one of the main reasons the buyers and sellers frequently incorporate it in their contract of sale. This is because it allows the seller to retain the property of the contract goods until the buyer pays the contract price while the buyer gains the right to dispose the goods and/or pledge the goods as security to obtain credit, when the goods are afloat, before they are physically delivered. This is achieved by the delivery of the shipping documents, in particular bill of lading, which in a CIF contract is symbolic and equivalent to the actual delivery of the goods (constructive possession).[67] However, in practice the main concern from the buyer's point of view is that this means they will be paying before they inspect the goods. As result if goods are not in order but documents are, it may create complications especially where the goods are further sold to third parties.

[58] *Biddel Bros* v *E Clement Hort* [1911] 1 KB 214, at 220.
[59] *Lauder & Co* v *Craven & Speeding Bros* [1912] 2 KB 94, at 105.
[60] *SC. Sharpe & Co* v *Nossawa & Co.* [1917] 2 KB, at 818–819.
[61] [1920] AC 144, at 155
[62] [1940] 3 All ER 60
[63] Ibid., at 67–8 see also Lord Porter's CIF definition in *Comptoir d'Achat et de Vente Boerenbond Belge SA* v *Luis De Ridder Limitada*, (The Julia) [1949] 1 AC 293.
[64] Ibid.
[65] McCardie J in *Manbre Saccharine* v *Corn Products* [1919] 1 KB 189, at 203–4.
[66] *Mistui & Co Ltd* v *Flota Mercante Grancolumbiana* [1989] 1 All ER 951
[67] Lord Wright in *TD Bailey, Son & Co* v *Ross T Smyth & Co Ltd* [1940] 56 TLR 825, at 829.

13.4.1 The role of the shipping documents in a CIF contract

The importance of the shipping documents in CIF contract cannot be over-emphasised and this is clearly illustrated in the *Julia case.* [68] In that case, the seller delivered to their agent two certificates of insurance and a delivery order but the bill of lading and insurance policy remained throughout in the possession of the seller. The court held that, since the bill of lading and insurance policy were not tendered, the property and risk remained with the seller until the actual delivery of the goods. Consequently, it was held that the contract of sale in that case was not a CIF contract. Therefore, in a CIF contract it is crucial that the seller tenders the correct shipping documents that are in order and contain accurate particulars about the goods, parties and terms of the insurance cover and the contract of carriage. Since this is the case, this section will critically examine why the bill of lading, insurance policy and invoice are so important in CIF contract.

13.4.1.1 Bill of Lading

Bill of lading can be defined as a document issued by or on behalf the carrier acknowledging that the contract goods are loaded on vessel and headed to the port of destination.[69] In a CIF contract usually most of the bills of lading are required to be shipped, so that it acts as a receipt acknowledging that the goods have been loaded by the ship-owner.[70] In addition, provide cover for the entirety of the transit and as per *Hasson v Hamel & Horley Ltd,* [71] any derogation from this can result in repudiation of the contract of sale. The Bill of lading in most cases is usually required to be in negotiable form so that constructive possession can be transferred to the buyer by the delivery of the bill of lading with any necessary indorsement.[72]

Although the buyer does not sign the bill of lading and thus not an original party of the bill of lading, via s.2 Contract of Carriage of Goods by Sea Act 1992, the buyer becomes privy to the contract of carriage because they gain possession of the bill of lading of goods that will be delivered to them. In this way, the bill of lading in a CIF contract acts as evidence of contract of carriage, receipt and document of title. While the bill of lading is in possession of the seller it is the evidence of the terms of the contract of carriage between the seller and the ship-owner.[73] However, when in possession of the buyer it is the contract of carriage and thus anything that takes place between the seller and ship-owner that is not in the bill of lading, does not affect the buyer.[74]

For the bill of lading to be 'valid and effective' receipt it must also satisfy the minimum duties set out in, International Convention For the Unification of Certain Rules Relating

[68] *Comptoir d'Achat et de Vente Boerenbond Belge SA* v *Luis De Ridder Limitada,* (The Julia) [1949] 1 All ER.
[69] See Lorenzon F *Sasson CIF and FOB Contracts* (7th ed Sweet & Maxwell 2020) at p. 116
[70] In *Diamond Alkali Export Corporation* v. *Bourgeois* [1921] 3 K.B. 443 at 641 McCardie J. held that the document was 'not a bill of lading within the c.i.f. contract' which was before him because it was not shipped and thus did not 'acknowledge the goods to be on board a specific ship, nor [did] it acknowledge a shipment on board at all'
[71] [1922] 2 AC 36.
[72] Michael Bridge *Benjamin Sale of Goods* (12th ed. Sweet & Maxwell, 2024) at 19.041, See also, Ewan McKendrick and Louise Gullifer Sale of Goods (Routledge 2014), at 599.
[73] Roach, L., Baskind, E., & Osborne, G. *Commercial Law* (OUP, 2022), at page 517.
[74] Lord Esher MR in *Leduc* v *Ward* [1888] 20 QBD 475, at 479.

to Bill of lading, Brussels 1924 (The Hague Visby Rules hereafter), where it applies, which is incorporated into English law by the Carriage of Goods Act by Sea Act 1971.

Accordingly, the bill of lading must contain the leading marks which are necessary for identification of the goods and they should be legible until the end of the voyage.[75] As per Article III(4) of the Hague Visby Rules, once the bill of lading is transferred to the buyer, these leading marks are conclusive evidence and therefore, any proof showing that they are inaccurate is inadmissible. However, under common law where these leading marks are immaterial to the identification of the goods, that is, they do not indicate key characteristics necessary to the nature and identity of the goods, the seller can submit 'clear and sufficient evidence' to prove that the bill is erroneous.[76] For example, in *Parsons* v *New Zealand Shipping Company*,[77] the bill of lading stated that the contract goods were shipped bearing the mark 622X. However, upon arrival the buyer found that some of the goods had 522X mark and thus refused to accept them and instead sued the seller for damages for miss-delivery. Collins J held that, the mark was not material as it was primarily set for helping manufactures to trace the goods through their books.[78] Thus the action against the seller was dismissed because the marks were immaterial to the existence or nature, quality, or quantity of the goods.

This case clearly illustrates a legal approach in which emphasis is placed on the goods rather than the legal documents. This is because the fact that the nature of the goods was unaltered was enough to dismiss the action against the inaccurate bill of lading. However, arguably from a commercial practice standpoint, this judgement raises concerns because it disregards the crucial need for document sanctity which is the backbone of international trade and crucial in a CIF contract.[79] A preferable approach would allow the buyer to reject the goods because it would encourage the parties to ensure the bill of lading is accurate.

As per the Hague Visby rules, bill of lading must also state the accurate date, thirdly, the apparent order and fourthly, the quality and condition of the goods loaded on board.[80] These are important elements of a bill of lading and if they are satisfied then the bill of lading is clean. A clean bill of lading was defined by Salmon J as 'one that does not contain any reservation as to the apparent good order or condition of the goods, or the packing'. [81]

However, where these requirements are not met or are falsified the bill of lading is dirty and the buyer may be entitled to reject the documents.[82] Notably though, where the buyer accepts and pays against a dirty bill of lading, he cannot reject the goods on that basis. This was the case in *Panchad Frere S.A* v *Etablissements General Grain Company*[83] where the date of loading on the bill of lading was falsified. In the first instance, the court was of the view that the false dating entitled the buyers to reject the goods.[84] However, on appeal

[75] Article III(3)(a) Hague Visby Rules 1924.
[76] Wright J in *Compania Importadora de Arroces y Kamp SA* v *P&O Steam Navigation Co* [1927] 28 Lloyd's L Rep. 63, at 52.
[77] [1901] 1QB 548.
[78] Ibid., at 565–67.
[79] See Chuah J *Law of International Trade Cross border Transactions* (6th ed Sweet & Maxwell 2019), at p. 243.
[80] Article III(3)(b)-(c) Hague Visby Rules 1924
[81] *British Imex Industries Ltd* v *Midland Bank Ltd* [1958] 1 Q.B. 542 at 551.
[82] Lord Devlin *in Kwei Tek Chao* v *British Traders and Shippers Ltd* [1954] 2QB 459, at 481.
[83] [1970] 1 Lloyd's Rep. 53.
[84] [1969] 2 Lloyds Rep. 109, (at the Queen's Bench Division) (commercial court).

this decision was reversed on the grounds that the buyers by accepting the documents and paying against them precluded them from claiming an action against a defective bill of lading.[85]

This decision however in commercial practice means buyer may have to bear the financial loss when reselling the goods where he unknowingly pays against a defective bill of lading and cannot reject the goods because they conform to the contract of sale.[86] Therefore, arguably the courts earlier decision is preferable in this context because it exhorts the need for documentary sanctity by condoning the root cause of such a case which is the laxity in dating the bill of lading.[87]

The bill of lading also acts as a document of title, and this is discussed further in the property and risk section below.

13.4.1.2 Invoice

As mentioned above the seller in a CIF contract has to invoice the goods and tender a commercial invoice to the buyer. According to Blackburn J in *Ireland* v Livingston[88]

> 'The invoice is made out debiting the consignee with the agreed price (or the actual cost and commission, with the premiums of insurance and the freight, as the case may be), and giving him credit for the amount of the freight which he will have to pay to the ship-owner on the actual delivery.'[89]

Therefore, it is clear that the invoice is a statement made out by the seller indicating the particulars of the shipped goods and the contract price and as result, most governments will use the commercial invoice to value the goods so as to set the import duties. In commercial practice, although the invoice is not a document of title, it is vital that the seller tenders it to the buyer because it will help the buyer to prove ownership of the goods and ins some cases may be required by the banks where the buyer has arranged payment of the contract price especially where the buyer has opened a letter of credit.[90] Therefore, it is also crucial that the invoice is accurate and has proper linkage with the goods and the other shipping documents, if not the buyer is entitled to reject it. This is neatly illustrated in *Berge & Sons* v *Laudauer*[91] where the commercial invoice was misdated as it was dated 1 February instead of 2 February. The court held that, despite the fact that 1 February was within the shipping period, the buyer is entitled to reject the invoice because the date in an invoice is a condition and also the buyer in CIF contract is entitled to documents which inform him accurately of the circumstances relating to the goods.

85 [1970] 1 Lloyd's Rep. 53 at the Court of Appeal (Civil Division).

86 This was the case in *Proctor & Gamble Philippine Manufacturing Corporation v Kurt A Becher GMbH & Co.* KG [1988] 2 Lloyd's Rep. 21.

87 Sassoon, DM *C.I.F and F.O.B Contracts* (7th Sweet and Maxwell 2020), at para 146.

88 [1872] LR 5 HL 395.

89 Ibid., at 406–407.

90 See Lorenzon F Sasson *CIF and FOB Contracts* (7th ed Sweet & Maxwell 2020) at pg 208. Letters of credit are discussed below from section 13.6.

91 [1925] 23 LILR 249

13.4.1.3 Insurance

Further, seller must also send the insurance policy as part of the shipping documents and unless otherwise agreed, usually, an insurance certificate or some other document such as a broker's cover note will not suffice. This is the case because unlike these other documents, the insurance policy usually contains all the terms of the insurance and thus the buyer will be able to ascertain the terms of the insurance cover.[92] Indeed in *Diamond Alkali Export Corporation* v *Bourgeois*[93] McCardie J. held that in CIF contract the 'policy of insurance' is the 'essential document' and that: 'mere written statement by the sellers that they hold the buyers covered by insurance in respect of a specified policy of insurance is not itself a policy of insurance within a CIF contract.'[94]

In terms of other requirements of the insurance cover, it in the absence of express provisions in the contract, the seller must tender such policy as is usual in the trade in question.[95] Further the insurance must cover the entirety of the voyage and must be assignable by indorsement under s. 50(3) of the Marine Insurance Act 1906. The effective of the insurance policy to passing of risk is discussed in the property and risk section below.

13.4.1.4 Property and risk

The bill of lading acts as a document of title[96] in CIF contracts because the delivery of the bill of lading by mercantile custom is internationally recognised as a 'symbolical delivery of the cargo.'[97] Moreover, it is usually the intention of the parties[98] in a CIF contract for the conditional property of the ascertained goods[99] to transfer to the buyer after the buyer pays against the delivery of the bill of lading.[100] Of-course the rules of passing property under SGA 1979, discussed in above in chapter 10, must complied for property to pass. The effect of this commercial practice is that it allows the buyer to obtain the goods from the ship-owner at the port of destination by showing the bill of lading[101] as well as have the right to dispose/resell the goods while they are on transit and/or obtain credit from the bank.

There have been a few unusual cases in which property has been held to pass in a CIF contract at some other time than the transfer of documents. For instance, where the relationship between the parties was such that the seller was not concerned over the immediate payment of the price, then the property was held to pass on shipment or at latest on transfer of the bill of lading, even though no price was then paid. In the *Albazero*, the sellers and buyers were both companies which were members of one corporate group, and the sale was not a genuine arm's length transaction. It was held that property

92 Michael Bridge *Benjamin Sale of Goods* (12th ed. Sweet & Maxwell, 2024) at 19-072
93 [1921] 3 K.B. 443.
94 Ibid., at 454.
95 Michael Bridge *Benjamin Sale of Goods* (12th ed. Sweet & Maxwell, 2024), at 19-078.
96 For definition of document title see s.1(4) The Factors Act 1889.
97 Cotton LJ in *Sanders Bros* v *Maclean* [1883] 11QBD 327, at 341.
98 s. 17 of the Sale of Goods Act 1979.
99 s. 16 SGA 1979.
100 Murray C, Timson-Hunt, D and Holloway, D *Schmitthoff the Law and Practise of International Trade* (12th ed. Sweet and Maxwell 2012), at page 334.
101 *Trucks & Spares Ltd* v *Maritime Agencies (Southampton) Ltd* [1951] 2 All ER 982.

passed on the posting of the bill of lading. Conversely, where a seller sold goods 'CIF' but it was intended that they should store the goods in their warehouse and make deliveries as required, payment being made only after the goods left the warehouse, it was held that property had not passed prior to delivery of bills of lading. This was plainly an unusual case in that the goods were imported by the seller but were not intended for immediate delivery, so it was hardly an ordinary CIF contract.

Another case where property did not pass under a CIF contract on transfer of the bill of lading is the case of the sale of an undivided share of goods carried in bulk. If a seller sold 5,000 tons of a cargo of wheat which totals 10,000 tons, the mere transfer of bills of lading for 5,000 tons could not pass the property because of s. 16 of the Sale of Goods Act which requires the goods to be ascertained before property can pass. In such a case, however, the buyer can now acquire an individual share in the bulk, and the property in the whole subject-matter of the contract will probably pass when the goods are discharged from the ship and appropriated to the particular contract in some way. Such a contract differs in various respects from an ordinary CIF contract and indeed comes to resemble an ex-ship contract in that the seller must deliver the goods at the port of destination. If they procure the ship carrying the cargo to be directed elsewhere and the goods are unloaded there, they are guilty of a breach of contract. In an ordinary CIF contract, however, any action by the seller to divert the ship and cargo after the goods are loaded and the documents delivered would not be a breach of the contract of sale; it might possibly involve a breach of the contract of carriage by the carrier, and the seller could conceivably be liable in tort, but would have performed the contract of sale and so could not be liable for breach of that contract.

More recently, a new problem occasionally surfaced as a result of which property may pass at some other time than the transfer of the documents. This problem is that bills of lading are sometimes issued very late, and cargoes sometimes arrive before the bills of lading are ready for transfer to the buyer. When this happens, the seller may instruct the carrier to deliver the goods to the buyer without the production of bills of lading (agreeing to indemnify the carrier in case any holder of the bills of lading turns up with a right to demand the goods); of course, the terms on which the seller is willing to do this will depend on their arrangements with the buyer – they may agree to give the instructions to the carrier only in return for payment if the contract was originally for cash against documents. If the goods are delivered to the buyer in this way, property will then pass to them, in the absence of some express stipulation by the seller whereby they retain property despite the delivery.

As we saw in the quotation from Lord Wright's speech in *Smyth & Co Ltd* v *Bailey Son & Co Ltd*, in the sale of unascertained goods CIF the seller is often under a duty to give notice of appropriation to the buyer, but this 'is not intended to pass and does not pass the property'.[102] The reason for this is that the notice is not an 'unconditional' appropriation within the meaning of s. 18, Rule 5. It is conditional on the buyer taking up the documents and paying for the goods. The effect of such a notice of appropriation may be to convert the sale into one for specific or ascertained goods, so that it would thereafter be a breach

[102] *Smyth & Co Ltd* v *Bailey Son & Co Ltd* [1940] 3 All ER 60, 65 per Lord Wright.

of contract for the seller to deliver any other goods.[103] Otherwise, if the goods still form part of a bulk, the effect is that it will commit the seller to delivering goods from that bulk.

In terms of risk in CIF contracts the risk passes on shipment, and if the goods are lost at sea the buyer is still bound to pay the price, although they will as a rule have the benefit of the insurance policy. This is because if the goods get damaged during transit the insurance policy will enable the buyer to determine if the cause of the damage is covered by the policy[104] and if so, it will also help them get reimbursement for damages or loss of goods.[105] The effect of this in practice is that , since the insurance policy is among the shipping documents the buyer must pay the contract price against, the buyer must make payment even where at the time of payment the goods are lost or damaged during transit, as they can claim via the insurance policy. This is illustrated by the *Galatia case*[106] where after the contract goods were shipped, a fire broke out and damaged the goods. Despite the damage, the court held that the sellers were still entitled to payment because risk passed upon shipment and the seller had correctly tendered the correct documents and they were in order.

The law is the same even if the seller knows that the goods have been lost when they tender the shipping documents.[107] So also, the inability of the buyer to have the goods discharged at the port of destination (because, for instance, they cannot obtain an import licence) is of no concern to the seller, and cannot be a frustrating event.[108] The delivery of the goods on board the vessel, followed by the delivery of correct documents, is a complete performance by the seller of their duties under a CIF contract; what happens after that is of no concern to him, subject to some special cases (for instance, where goods are shipped in an undivided bulk).

13.4.1.5 Is a CIF contract a sale of documents?

Considering that the seller's obligation ends once the goods are loaded and they tender the documents to the buyer, in commercial reality it can be said that a CIF contract is a sale of documents. This is because the primary obligation of the seller is to ensure the effective 'transfer of symbol rather than the physical property' of the goods and this is be achieved by the delivery of the bill of lading.[109] This is further strengthened by the fact that as we saw in the discussion of the *Julia case* above, if the seller delivers the correct goods but does not deliver the correct documents, it is likely the contract will not be considered as a CIF contract. Additionally, as mentioned earlier the buyer's aim of incorporating CIF contract, is usually to gain the right to dispose the goods and/or obtain credit before they are physically delivered, and they gain this through the delivery of the bill of lading which is symbolic to delivery of the goods. Furthermore, as seen in the *Galatia case* above regardless of the state of the goods while on transit the buyer must pay against the delivery of shipping documents that are in order.

[103] *The Vladimir Ilich* [1975] 1 Lloyd's Rep 322, 328.
[104] McCandie J *Diamond Alkali Export Corporation* v *FL. Bourgeois* [1921] 3 K.B. 443, at 445–456.
[105] See s. 50(2) of the Marine Insurance Act 1906.
[106] *M. Golodetz & Co Inc* v *Czarnikov-Rionda Co. Inc.* [1980] 1 WLR.
[107] *Manbré Saccharine Co Ltd* v *Corn Products Ltd* [1919] 1 KB 198.
[108] *Congimex* v *Tradax* [1983] 2 Lloyd's Rep 250.
[109] McCardie J in *Manbre Saccharine* v *Corn Products* [1919] 1 KB 189, at 203–4.

However, there has been consistent judicial emphasis that the seller has dual obligations in CIF contracts, that is, in relation to the documents and the goods.[110] This is best illustrated in *Hindley* v *East India Produce Company*[111] where a buyer used the bill of lading to resell the goods while they were on transit. However, at the port of destination the second buyers found out the goods had never been shipped. Thus the second buyer sued the first buyer for breach of contract but the first buyer argued that he was not liable because they were not the original shippers, and that a CIF contract was merely a sale of documents or one performed by delivery of documents in particular the bill of lading. Kerr J dismissed the first buyer's argument on the grounds that, regardless of whether a seller is the shipper or not, they have dual obligations under a CIF contract, not only to tender the documents covering the goods but also ensure the goods are shipped and bound to the port of destination.[112]

Therefore, in as much there is emphasis of seller tendering the conforming documents that are in order, in a CIF contract also equally contemplates the transfer of actual and conforming goods. The implied terms under the SGA 1979 discussed in Chapter 7, apply to CIF contracts and thus if the goods delivered are not conforming the buyer can reject the goods. As per Winn J in *Cordova Land Co. Ltd* v *Victor Brothers Inc*[113] appropriate cases the seller would be liable where goods are damaged during transit such that they become unsatisfactory[114] this would be the case particularly where there is deterioration of perishable goods that are as 'venerable as potatoes.'[115] In such a case, the buyer would gain the right to reject the unsatisfactory goods or may sue the seller for the difference between the value of the goods at time of delivery and the value they would have had if they were satisfactory.[116] The effect of this is that in CIF contract the buyer has two rights of rejection, one to reject shipping documents that are not conforming or the other non-conforming goods.[117]

13.4.2 Buyer's duties

The duties of the buyer under a CIF contract are to accept the shipping documents when tendered and to pay the contract price in exchange for the documents. Frequently, the price is payable by means of a letter of credit, in which case the documents are sent to a bank in the first instance, and the bank then passes the documents to the buyer, in exchange for payment or for some other method of satisfaction. Sometimes several banks are involved, and the documents are transferred from one to another, ultimately ending up with the buyer.

Sometimes, the buyer is under a contractual duty to nominate a discharge port because the CIF contract may not have originally specified a single port as the CIF port, but may

[110] Chan, Y and Eric K 'Late Shipments, Forged Documents and Falling Markets: James Finlay v Kwik Hoo Tong Revisited' [1992] 13 The *Singapore Law Review* 209, at 210.
[111] [1957] 2 Lloyd's Rep 515,
[112] Ibid., at 518.
[113] [1966] WLR 793.
[114] s. 14 SGA 1979.
[115] *Cordova Land Co. Ltd* v *Victor Brothers Inc* [1966] WLR 793, at 796.
[116] See s. 53 SGA 1979.
[117] See Devlin J in *Kwei Tek Chao* v *British Traders and shippers* [1954] 2 QB 459 at 481.

have envisaged a range of ports (e.g., any port in Italy), leaving the buyer to select the particular port at a later date. In this situation, the buyer must obviously make their nomination in sufficient time for the vessel to sail to the port specified without interruption or delay.[118]

13.5 DDP (delivered duty paid) – ex ship contract

This may be an appropriate contract where the buyer is inexperienced in general or inexperienced with that the exporting country laws and bureaucratic procedures and thus all duties of transporting goods are on the seller. However, it should be noted in practice the extra cost incurred by the seller to fulfil their duty are usually passed to the buyer.

Generally speaking, in contracts of this kind the property and risk will only pass on delivery. Indeed, in *Yangtsze Insurance Asociation* v *Lukmanjee*,[119] the contract of sale was expressed as an Ex-ship (DAP) contract, and some of the timber being sold got lost on transit and buyer sought to claim from the seller's insurance. The court held that the buyer's claim was unsuccessful because in such contracts property and risk pass to the buyer upon actual physical delivery of the goods and thus they had not passed in this case.

13.6 Export and import licences

Despite numerous treaties and trade agreements which seek to dismantle prohibitions on cross-border trade, some still remain and so the obtaining of an export or import license, or both, is often a necessary prerequisite to the performance of a contract of sale. It is, therefore, important to decide which of the parties is to obtain the licence at the outset, and what happens if they fail to do so. As noted above, many export and import transactions are made subject to INCOTERMS. Where the parties have adopted these, the duties of the parties in this respect are clearly spelled out. These duties are not always in conformity with the rules of English law set out below, which apply in the absence of such specific agreement.

13.6.1 Whose duty?

The courts have refused to lay down any general principles on this question and have insisted that each case must be decided according to its own special circumstances.[120] Nevertheless, some indications may be gleaned from the cases to show the sort of considerations which the courts will treat as relevant. It goes without saying, of course, that if the parties have expressed a clear intention as to who is to apply for a licence or what is to happen if it is not obtained then the courts will give effect to that intention. Difficulties arise when the parties have not expressed any such clear intention.

[118] *The Rio Sun* [1985] 1 Lloyd's Rep 350.
[119] [1918] AC 585.
[120] *A V Pound & Co Ltd* v *M W Hardy & Co Inc* [1956] AC 588.

In ex-works or ex-store contracts, it is almost certain to be the buyers' duty to obtain all necessary permits and licences and they will be irrelevant to the contract of sale, unless there is a clear intention in the agreement to the contrary.

At the other end of the scale, ex-ship contracts also do not give rise to much difficulty. In the absence of any contrary intention, it is plainly the seller's duty to obtain any necessary export licence, but probably the buyer's duty to obtain an import licence if required.

It is FOB and CIF contracts and their many variants which tend to give rise to the difficulties in this connection.[121] So far as FOB contracts are concerned, it was for long thought that, as a result of the decision of the Court of Appeal in *H O Brandt & Co* v *H N Morris*,[122] the obligation to obtain an export licence was generally on the buyer. It is obvious that this would in many circumstances be a highly inconvenient conclusion. Fortunately, it appears from the decision of the House of Lords in *A V Pound & Co Ltd* v *M W Hardy & Co Inc*[123] that *Brandt*'s case is not to be taken as laying down any general rule, and although the House refused to lay down any general rule itself, it is possible to say that *prima facie* in an FOB contract the duty of obtaining the export licence is on the seller. *A fortiori* this is the case in a CIF contract.

The points to which attention must be given in considering whether this is so in any particular case are, *inter alia*, the following. Is the seller exporting the goods from one country to the buyer in another, or are both parties carrying on business in the same country? The latter may, of course, be the position where the buyer is buying for export to a customer abroad, and hence buys the goods on FOB or even CIF terms. In this event, as in *Brandt*'s case, it is much easier to reach the conclusion that the duty to obtain an export licence is on the buyer because the seller is not himself selling the goods for export. It is the buyer who wants to export the goods and, naturally, therefore it is for them to obtain the licence.

Another point to consider is whether there are any particular circumstances making it easier for one party or the other to obtain the licence. If, for example, the buyer and seller are based in different countries, and only a member of a certain trade association may be granted an export licence,[124] or if the licences are granted according to a quota system based on the seller's previous shipments,[125] it is difficult to hold that the buyer must obtain the licence.

A third relevant factor is whether the need for a licence existed when the contract was made (and, if so, whether the parties knew about it) or whether the need for a licence was only imposed after the contract was made by new legislation or controls.

The duty of obtaining an import licence must plainly be on the importer, that is the buyer, in most circumstances, if only because the relevant statutory provisions will generally impose the duty on them, and, in the absence of a contrary intention, 'the contract must be treated as made upon the assumption that the statutory law applicable . . . should

[121] See *Schmitthoff's Export Trade* (11th edn, 2007, Sweet & Maxwell), §2-017 et *seq*.
[122] [1917] 2 KB 784.
[123] [1956] AC 588.
[124] For example, *Peter Cassidy Seed Co Ltd* v *Osuustukkukauppa IL* [1957] 1 All ER 484.
[125] *Partabmull Rameshwar* v *K C Sethia Ltd* [1950] 1 All ER 51, affirmed (but no speeches reported) [1951] 2 All ER 352n.

be observed by the parties to the contract'.[126] This is *a fortiori* the case in an FOB sale for the seller may not even know the destination of the goods. Indeed, in many international contracts the ultimate destination of the goods is of no concern to the seller, who performs their contract by shipping the goods and delivering the requisite documents. Thus, failure by the buyer to obtain any required import licences is solely a matter for the buyer, and it is probably even incorrect to regard the buyer as under a contractual duty to obtain such a licence.[127]

13.6.2 Whether duty absolute or to use best endeavours

When it has been decided whether the duty to obtain a licence is on the buyer or the seller, the next question is whether the duty is absolute; has the party in question warranted that they will obtain the licence, or just that they will use best endeavours to do so? If it is the latter, a failure to obtain the licence despite such best endeavours will generally mean that the contract is frustrated. Alternatively, the party unable to obtain the licence may be excused by an express *force majeure* clause, in which case the contract simply fails, since the detailed provisions of a *force majeure* clause usually leave no room for the application of the common law.[128]

Where a licence is required throughout the period of shipment, the party whose duty it is to obtain the licence must not delay in applying for it or they may be held to have failed to use due diligence to obtain one.[129] Conversely, where the need for a licence is introduced during the shipment period, the party who should obtain the licence cannot be blamed for not having acted before the requirement was introduced, and may still be excused by any later failure to obtain a licence.[130]

In *Re Anglo-Russian Merchant Traders Ltd*,[131] the Court of Appeal held that generally there is no absolute duty to obtain a licence, and where a seller applies for and is refused an export licence, they are not generally liable in damages for non-delivery. In *Peter Cassidy Seed Co Ltd* v *Osuustukkukauppa IL*,[132] Devlin J agreed with this as a general principle.

> The person whose duty it is to apply for a licence may either warrant that he will get it, that is an absolute warranty, or he may warrant that he will use all due diligence in getting it. When nothing is said in the contract it is usually – probably almost invariably – the latter class of warranty which is implied, but each case must be decided according to its own circumstances, and the question of implication must be settled in the ordinary way in which implied terms are settled.[133]

But ultimately it held that in the particular circumstances of the case the sellers had warranted that they would obtain a licence. In this case, the contract stated: 'Delivery: prompt as soon as export licence granted' and the sellers had assured the buyers that this was a pure formality.

[126] *Mitchell Cotts & Co (Middle East) Ltd* v *Hairco Ltd* [1943] 2 All ER 552, 554–5 per Scott LJ.
[127] *Congimex* v *Tradax* [1983] 1 Lloyd's Rep 250.
[128] *Pagnan SpA* v *Tradax Ocean Transportation SA* [1987] 3 All ER 565.
[129] *Agro Export State Enterprise* v *Compagnie Européenne de Céréales* [1974] 1 Lloyd's Rep 499.
[130] *Ross T Smyth & Co Ltd* v *W N Lindsay Ltd* [1953] 1 WLR 1280, though in this case the seller was not discharged. Cf. *André* v *Tradax* [1983] 1 Lloyd's Rep 254.
[131] [1917] 2 KB 679.
[132] [1957] 1 All ER 484.
[133] Ibid., at p. 486.

On the other hand, in *Mitchell Cotts & Co (Middle East) Ltd* v Hairco Ltd[134] Scott LJ took the view that the buyers' duty to obtain a licence (in that case, an import licence) is generally absolute, and in *Partabmull Rameshwar* v *K C Sethia Ltd*[135] the House of Lords held, on somewhat unusual facts, that the sellers had bound themselves to obtain an export licence.

Even an obligation by a party to use best endeavours to obtain a licence is somewhat strictly applied by the courts. In *Brauer & Co (Great Britain) Ltd* v *James Clark (Brush Materials) Ltd*,[136] for instance, sellers had agreed to sell goods for shipment FOB a Brazilian port, 'subject to any Brazilian export licence'. The sellers had applied for a licence, which was refused on the ground that the price was too low. On its appearing that the sellers might have obtained a licence if they had been prepared to pay the extra (some 20 per cent above the contract price) to their own suppliers, it was held that they had not used their best endeavours to obtain a licence. So too, a seller who contracts to ship from one of a number of ports is not excused if export from one only is prohibited, even though they may already have made all necessary arrangements to ship from that port.[137] Where the seller is under a duty to apply for a licence, the buyer may nevertheless be bound to supply the seller with any information (e.g. as to the ultimate destination of the goods) which may be required by the licensing authority.[138] Where a seller, who is under a duty to use their best endeavours, fails even to apply for a licence, they have the heavy burden of proving that any application was foredoomed to failure.[139] A party whose licence is revoked is in the same position as one whose application is refused.[140]

On the other hand, total suspension of a licensing system and the banning of all imports (or exports) is a different matter, and even though a party may *prima facie* have warranted to obtain a licence, they may be more readily excused by a *force majeure* clause in this situation.[141]

There is, perhaps, something slightly misleading in talking of an implied warranty by a party to obtain, or to use best endeavours to obtain, a licence. If there is no mention of the matter in the contract, then the true position is simply this. The seller is bound to deliver the goods to the buyer and the buyer is bound to take delivery from the seller. If either party will not or cannot perform their obligations they are *prima facie* in default, unless they can show that the contract has been frustrated. Often they can show that the contract has been frustrated by proving that a necessary licence has been refused despite best endeavours to obtain one.[142] But where the obligation to deliver (or to take delivery) is construed as an absolute obligation, then the failure to obtain the licence does not

[134] [1943] 2 All ER 552. See also *Congimex* v *Tradax* [1983] 1 Lloyd's Rep 250.

[135] [1950] 1 All ER 51, affirmed [1951] 2 All ER 352n.

[136] [1952] 2 All ER 497.

[137] *Pagnan SpA* v *Tradax Ocean Transportation SA* [1987] 3 All ER 565.

[138] *Warinco AG* v *Fritz Mauthier* [1978] 1 Lloyd's Rep 151; see too *Malik Co* v *Central European Trading Agency Ltd* [1974] 2 Lloyd's Rep 279.

[139] *Phoebus D Kyprianou* v *Cyprus Textiles Ltd* [1958] 2 Lloyd's Rep 60.

[140] *Société d'Avances Commerciales (London)* v *A Besse & Co (London)* [1952] 1 TLR 644.

[141] *Czarnikow Ltd* v *Rolimpex* [1978] 2 All ER 1043.

[142] It is now well established that a party who has failed to obtain a licence must himself prove due diligence: *Brauer & Co (Great Britain) Ltd* v *James Clark (Brush Materials) Ltd* [1952] 2 All ER 497; *Vidler & Co (London) Ltd* v *R Silcock & Sons Ltd* [1960] 1 Lloyd's Rep 509; *Tradax Export SA* v *André & Cie* [1976] 1 Lloyd's Rep 416; *Bremer* v *Vanden Avenne* [1978] 2 Lloyd's Rep 109.

excuse non-performance. Strictly speaking, therefore, it does not seem accurate to talk of a person warranting that 'they will get a licence' or that they will use their best endeavours to get a licence'.

13.7 Bankers' commercial credits

13.7.1 Payment of price by bankers' commercial credit

There are a lot of risks of involved in the payment of the contract price in an international sale of goods transaction. This is because it involves an international transaction and thus there is distance between the buyer and the seller and there may be difference in the currency as well as the laws governing the markets.[143] Moreover, the seller may be unsure of the buyer's creditworthiness and if the buyer rejects the goods after inspection at the port of destination, the seller may have to resell the goods to another buyer in a foreign market and at lower price and thus bears the financial loss.[144]

To minimise these risks, various methods of payments have been developed such as, *inter alia*, payment by bill of exchange[145] or payment on an open account. However, discussion of those methods is beyond the scope of this book instead this section will focus on the most commonly used method of payment used in international sale transactions, which is the use of bankers' commercial credits and it is for this reason it is referred to as the 'life blood of commerce.'[146] Such credits are also often referred to as documentary credits or letters of credit but the terms are synonymous.

LC[147] which usually incorporates the standard terms and conditions of the Uniform Customs and Practise for Documentary Credits (UCP hereafter).[148] In accordance with the latest version, the UCP 600, a LC can be defined as an arrangement which constitutes a definite undertaking by the issuing bank to honour a complying presentation by the seller.[149] This section will aim to identify the benefits and types of LCs and thereafter focus on the nature of irrevocable confirmed LCs.

13.7.2 Nature of Letters of Credit

Where a buyer is to pay the contract price via letters of credit the normal procedure is more or less as follows, although there may frequently be variations of detail. The buyer instructs their bank (the issuing bank) to open a credit in favour of the seller with a bank in the seller's country (the 'intermediary' or 'correspondent' or 'confirming' banker). Almost invariably, the buyer instructs the issuing bank that the seller is only to be allowed to draw on the credit on presentation to the paying bank of documents showing that the goods have been shipped and are on their way to the buyer. The shipping documents will comprise (at least) the seller's invoice for the goods, the bill of lading and, frequently

143 HM Revenue & Customs 'Letters of Credit for Importers and Exporters' (2012) UK Government. Available online at https://www.gov.uk/letters-of-credit-for-importers-and-exporters.

144 Hotchkiss, C *International Law for Business* (Mcgraw-Hill Inc., 1994), at 165.

145 For definition of a bill of exchange see s. 3(1) of the Bill of Exchange Act 1882.

146 Lord Justice Kerr in R.D. *Harbottle (Mercantile) Ltd* v *National Westminster Bank Ltd* [1977] 2 ALL ER 862, at 870.

147 HM Revenue & Customs 'Letters of Credit for Importers and Exporters' (2 March 2021).

148 McGuinness, KP The Law of Guarantee (2nd ed. Carswell 1996), at p. 801.

149 Article 2 of the UCP 600.

(always in CIF contracts), an insurance policy or certificate. The intermediary banker will then notify the seller that instructions have been received to open a credit in their favour and will inform them of the precise terms on which they will be allowed to avail themself of the credit. As soon as the goods are shipped and the seller has received the necessary documents from the carriers or their agents and the insurers, they will present these documents together with an invoice to the intermediary banker.

The bank will check the documents against the terms of the credit to ensure that the goods shipped are (so far as can be seen from the documents) the contract goods and that everything appears to be in order and, if satisfied that this is the case, will permit the seller to draw against the credit. The intermediary bank will then transmit the documents to the issuing bank, which will likewise have to check the documents against the terms of the credit, and which will pay the intermediary bank if satisfied that all is in order. The issuing bank will then inform the buyer that the documents have been received and will be transferred to them against payment. The buyer will also satisfy themself that the documents are in order and will, in due course, pay the issuing bank an amount corresponding to the price paid to the seller, together with the bank's own charges. Of-course the issuing bank may be providing credit to the buyer – that is a matter for the contract between them – in which case it will transmit the documents to them, before receiving payment. Armed with the documents, the buyer will then be in a position to resell the goods and transfer the documents to a sub-buyer or, alternatively, to take delivery as soon as the goods arrive. The holder of the documents is prima facie the person to whom the carrier will deliver the goods.

In practice, therefore, this means that when using letters of credit as a method of payment, the parties will incur extra costs as the banks have to be paid for their services. Nevertheless, it not only effectively minimises the risks involved in payment but also benefits the economic interest of the seller and the buyer. This is because on one hand the seller becomes assured that he will receive the contract price and before he parts with the document of title, the bill of lading[150] (for detailed analysis on this see above). The buyer on the other hand is assured of paying the contract price after the goods are shipped/loaded and bound for the port of destination and the seller is no longer in possession of the document of title.[151] However this means seller will be paid before the buyer physically inspects the goods.

Virtually all bankers' credits are today granted on the terms that they are to be governed by the Uniform Customs and Practice for Documentary Credits, UCP, (and Supplement for Electronic Presentation) prepared by the International Chamber of Commerce.[152] The banks of nearly all the countries in the world use this document (hereafter referred to as 'the Uniform Customs'), which is, therefore, to all intents and purposes a part of the law of bankers' commercial credits.[153] But this document is not a statute, and should not be interpreted as such; for instance, reasonable implications can be read into the Uniform Customs.[154]

[150] HM Revenue & Customs 'Letters of Credit for Importers and Exporters' (2 March 2021).

[151] Ibid.

[152] The current version, UCP 600, formally commenced on 1 July 2007.

[153] Of course, there must be something to justify incorporation of the Uniform Customs in the contract, and this is usually done expressly, but a bare marginal note has been held sufficient to achieve this result: *Forestal Mimosa Ltd* v *Oriental Credit Ltd* [1986] 1 WLR 631.

[154] *Co-operative Centrale Raiffeisen-Boerenleenbank BA* v *Sumitomo Bank Ltd* [1987] 1 FTLR 233 (varied on appeal [1988] 2 FTLR 27).

13.7.2.1 Types of Letters of Credit

There are many variations in the form of commercial credits, the principal distinctions being between revocable and irrevocable credits, and confirmed and unconfirmed credits. In a revocable LC the issuing bank has no real commitment to pay the seller because it can be cancelled or amended without giving prior notice to the seller.[155] This is best illustrated in *Cape Asbestos Co Ltd* v *Lloyd's Bank Ltd*[156] where the bank advised the seller that revocable LC credit had opened but later cancelled the LC without the seller's knowledge. Therefore, after the seller shipped the goods and tendered the documents for payment, the bank refused to pay. As a result, the seller sued the bank on the basis that, the bank was bound to give reasonable notice of the withdrawal of the LC. However, Bailhache J dismissed the seller's argument on the grounds that the bank had 'no legal obligation' to give the seller notice that the LC was revoked.[157] Therefore, in a revocable LC the wise course for a seller is to inquire if the credit has been withdrawn before shipping the goods because he has no assured right of payment.[158] It is for this reason that revocable LCs are rarely used in practice and if used it is where security of payment is not the primary objective, for example, where the seller and the buyer have a well-established business relationship.[159] Nonetheless, it should be noted they are now likely extinct in practice and latest version of the UCP 600 does not apply to them, so where used the previous version, the UCP 500, will be used.

As revocable LCs are not recognised by the UCP 600, where there is no express description of the type of the letter of credit it will be generally considered as an irrevocable LC.[160] Under an irrevocable LC, the issuing bank issues a definite undertaking to honour a complying presentation.[161] Usually in commercial practice, this obligation becomes binding on the bank once the seller receives communication of the credit and accepts it.[162]

An irrevocable LC can be either confirmed or unconfirmed. In an irrevocable unconfirmed LC, the credit is unconfirmed, the intermediary bank merely informs the seller that the credit has been opened in their favour, and the seller will have no right of recourse against the bank in the event of its refusing to pay. Thus, this type of LC is unattractive as it defeats the essence of a LC as seller is not assured of payment. Irrevocable confirmed LCs however, give the seller maximum security because their effect is that if the seller presents the accurate and complete documents at the correct time he is assured of payment by both the issuing bank and advising/conforming bank.[163]

[155] Article 8(a) of the UCP 500. Note that UCP 600 does not recognise revocable credits and therefore when used they are subject to UCP 500.
[156] [1921] WN 274.
[157] Ibid.
[158] Ibid,. at 257.
[159] Ewan McKendrick, *Goode on Commercial Law* (6th ed. Penguin Books, 2020) at para 35.26.
[160] Article 3 UCP 600
[161] Article 2 of the UCP 600.
[162] Donaldson J in *Elder Dempser Lines Ltd* v *ionic Shipping Agency Inc* [1968] 1 Lloyd's Rep 529, at 535.
[163] Lord Diplock in *Ian Statch Ltd* v *Baker Bosley Ltd* [1958] 2 QB 130, at 139.

In accordance with Lord Diplock in the *American Accord* case[164] there are 'four autonomous though interconnected contractual relationships' in an irrevocable confirmed LC.[165]

> (1) The underlying contract for the sale of goods, to which the only parties are the buyer and the seller;
> (2) the contract between the buyer and the issuing bank under which the latter agrees to issue the credit and either itself or through a confirming bank to notify the credit to the seller and to make payments to or to the order of the seller . . .
> (3) if payment is to be made through a confirming bank the contract between the issuing bank and the confirming bank authorising and requiring the latter to make such payments and to remit the stipulated documents to the issuing bank when they are received, the issuing bank in turn agreeing to reimburse the confirming *bank* for payments made under the credit;
> (4) the contract between the confirming bank and the seller under which the confirming bank undertakes to pay to the seller . . . up to the amount of the credit against presentation of the stipulated documents.[166]

To his lordship analysis, a fifth contract can be added between the issuing bank and the seller because the issuing bank in an irrevocable confirmed LC also issues a definite undertaking to the seller to honour a complying presentation. In the past, doubts have even existed as to whether the seller could sue the bank if it refused to honour a confirmed credit, anyhow prior to shipment, on the ground that there is no contract between seller and bank, owing to the absence of any consideration supplied by the seller. There is no difficulty when the goods have been shipped because this is an action by the seller in reliance on the bank's undertaking, and that should suffice as a valid consideration by any modern test. But it is theoretically arguable that, if the bank repudiates the credit before shipment, the seller may be unable to enforce the letter of credit by direct action against the bank. In practice, banks never take this technical point and judicial pronouncements now seem to have put their liability beyond doubt.[167]

13.7.3 Doctrine of Strict Compliance

From Lord Diplock's analysis on irrevocable confirmed LCs in the *American Accord* (above) it is clear that the banks in the LC deal with the documents and not the goods or any other services or performance to which the documents may relate to. This is because generally the banks are not considered to be experts in goods but they are capable of examining whether the presented documents are in order. Moreover, it minimises the risk on part of the buyer for non-shipment and delivery by the seller, since the seller is only assured of payment upon presentation of the documents which can include a shipped bill of lading which is document of title, receipt of the goods as well as evidence of contract of carriage.[168]

164 *United City Merchant Investment Ltd* v *Royal Bank of Canada (The American Accord)* [1983] 1 AC 168.
165 Ibid., at 183.
166 *United City Merchant Investment Ltd* v *Royal Bank of Canada (The American Accord)* [1983] 1 AC 168, at 183.
167 See *Especially Hamzeh Malas & Sons* v *British Imex Industries* 1958 2 QB 127, at 129 per Jekins LJ.
168 Hwaidi, M 'The Story of the English Strict Compliance Principle in Letters of Credit and its Consistency with the UCP' (2014) Journal of International Banking Law and Regulation 71, at 71

Thus it a vital element in this commercial machinery that the seller must not be allowed to draw against the credit unless it is quite clear, so far as can be seen from an examination of the documents, that they have fulfilled their obligations under the contract. It is vital therefore that the buyer should inform the issuing bank precisely what documents are required. It is equally important that the documents presented by the seller to the intermediary bank should correspond exactly with the terms of the credit (which should, of course, represent the agreed terms of sale) for otherwise the bank will refuse payment, or if it pays, it does so at its peril because the buyer (or the issuing bank) may refuse to take up the documents.

The inspection of these documents by the banks is done via the doctrine of strict compliance which in an ordinary case involves the '*visual inspection*' of the documents with the aim of determining if they comply with the terms of the LC.[169] This is case because, as per Lord Diplock, the banks are under 'no legal obligation to take further steps to investigate the genuineness of a signature' on a document which on its face 'purports to be the signature of the person named.'[170] The resulting effect of this, is a strict approach, such that, where the documents do not comply with LC on their face, the bank can reject the documents.[171] This is demonstrated in *JH Rayner & Co Ltd* v *Hambro's Bank Ltd*[172] where the LC required presentation of a bill of lading that described goods as 'coromondel groundnuts' but the seller presented a bill of lading referring to the goods as 'machine-shelled groundnuts Kernel'. Although in commercial practice these descriptions where interchangeable, the court held the bank was entitled to refuse payment. This is because the description was clearly not the same upon visual inspection as was required by the letter of credit and it was impossible to suggest that the banks would have knowledge of every customary term in which they may issue a commercial credit.[173]

This strict approach was further justified by Viscount Sumner in *Equitable Trust Company of New York* v *Dawson Partners Ltd*[174] on the grounds that:

> 'The accepting bank can only claim indemnity if the conditions on which it is authorised to accept are in matter of the accompanying documents strictly observed. There is no room for documents which are almost the same, or which do just as well.'[175] In addition, he held that, the conforming bank, 'which knows nothing officially of the details of the transaction thus financed, cannot take upon itself to decide what will do well enough and what will not.'[176]

However, in recent cases, the courts have taken a more liberal approach.[177] For instance in *Bankers Trusts Co* v *State Bank of India* the seller presented documents that described the buyer's telex as '931310' instead of '981310'. The court held that it was a 'trivial defect' on the documents and thus the banks were not entitled to reject the documents. This

[169] Lord Diplock in *Gian Signh & Co* v *Banque de l'ndochine* [1974] 2 All ER 754, at 757–758.
[170] Ibid.
[171] Article 14 UCP 600.
[172] [1943] 1 KB 37.
[173] Ibid., Mackinnon J, at 40.
[174] [1927] 27 Ll l Rep 49.
[175] Ibid., at 52.
[176] Ibid.
[177] Todd, P 'Discrepancies Between Bills of Lading and Letters of Credit' (1999) Letter of Credit Update (Government Information Services), at page 14–19 as cited in Todd, P Case and Materials on International Trade Law (1st ed. Sweet & Maxwell 2014), at p. 472

approach was further buttressed by Lord Evans J who was of the view that the documents must not be 'in exact literal compliance' but instead the banks should 'exercise their own judgement' as to whether, the requirements are satisfied.[178] This recent approach is further reiterated in Article 14(d) of the UCP 600 which states that the data in the documents when read in context with the LC *'need not be identical'* though it must not be in conflict with other documents or the LC. Interestingly in *Bulgrains & Co Ltd* v *Shinhan Bank*,[179] the discrepancy/defect was on the name of the company in the invoice which referred to the company as Bulgrain & Co Ltd instead of Bulgrain Co Ltd as required by the letter of credit. In this case, the court held that this was a material defect and not simply a typographical error.

In practice, minor discrepancies between the shipping documents and the letter of credit are a common problem. The bank to which the documents have been presented will often seek instructions from the buyer (or from an issuing bank) rather than immediately reject non-conforming documents, and very often the letter of credit will be amended, or the discrepancies will be waived. Although the bank is entitled to seek instructions it must act with speed, and must ultimately either accept or reject the documents.[180] Indeed, Article 14 (b) UCP 600 limits the examination period to a maximum of five banking days following the day of presentation.

On one hand, this liberal approach creates an adaptable approach which can evolve with the developing trade and banking practices. Additionally, it embodies the essence of a LC because it minimises the circumstances in which the banks could refuse to pay the seller.[181] On the other hand, this liberal approach is undesirable because, it creates uncertainties and difficulties in LC because it will depends on case to case basis on whether a defect is 'trivial' and thus one cannot be certain whether or not the banks are entitled to reject the documents.[182] Moreover, it places the financial risk on the bank, because where the bank accepts and pays against a document with what appears to be trivial defect but later it is discovered to be a material defect the bank would have paid against a worthless document.[183] Arguably, therefore, the stricter approach is more desirable because it creates certainty, as it means that where *prima facie* the documents are not compliant with the LC they will not be accepted. It is also preferable because it encourages the use of accurate documents in international trade.

As we have seen, the main documents are the bill of lading, the invoice and any necessary insurance documents. The bill of lading must cover shipment from and to the agreed ports. It was for long a requirement that the bill of lading should be a 'shipped' bill of lading:[184] that is, it had to acknowledge that the goods had actually been shipped and

[178] *Kredietbank Antwerp* v *Midland Bank Plc* [1999] C.L.C. 1108, at 1112.

[179] [2013] EWHC 2498.

[180] *Co-operative Centrale Raiffeisen-Boerenleenbank BA* v *Sumitomo Bank Ltd* [1987] 1 FTLR 233, varied [1988] 2 FTLR 27.

[181] Ellinger, E.P 'New Problems of Strict Compliance in Letters of Credit' (1988) *Journal of Business Law* 320, at 320–321.

[182] Costa, M.L 'The Formalism of Letters of Credit: Dispute or Consecration?' (1993) *International Business Law Journal* 707, at 722.

[183] Parker J in *Banque de l'Indochine et Suez SA* v *JH Rayner (Minicing Lane) Ltd* [1983] QB 711, at 721.

[184] See *Wespac Banking Corpn* v *South Carolina National Bank* [1986] 1 Lloyd's Rep 311; UCP600 Art.14(b).

not merely received for shipment,[185] but new types of commercial documentation (such as combined road and shipping documents) led to an abandonment of this requirement since Art. 27 of the 1994 version of the Uniform Customs (UCP500). But some letters of credit still require 'shipped' bills of lading.[186]

The invoice must describe the goods exactly as stated in the credit.[187] It was formerly held that even the *de minimis* rule was excluded in this situation,[188] but Art. 30 of the Uniform Customs permits a tolerance of 5 per cent more or less than the contract quantity unless the credit stipulates to the contrary.[189] In matters other than quantity the position still is that the *de minimis* rule does not apply.[190] Generally, also, the credit requires 'clean' bills of lading, which means that the bill must 'not contain any reservation as to the apparent good order or condition of the goods or the packing'.[191]

Where the documents are to include insurance policies, a certificate will not suffice unless, as is customary, the credit expressly says so. Additional documents are often required by the contract, such as certificates of quality, or the like, to be provided by independent third parties after inspection of the goods.

13.7.4 Principle of autonomy

Provided that the documents presented by the seller are in order, they are entitled to avail themselves of the credit notwithstanding that the buyer may have some complaint about the quality of the goods.[192] The value of this method of payment would be considerably reduced if a claim by the buyer had the effect of preventing the seller from drawing on the credit. One of the principal purposes of a letter of credit is to assure the seller that they will be paid, leaving for later settlement and, if necessary, litigation any complaints by the buyer. A letter of credit therefore throws the onus of litigation on to the buyer

[185] For the difference between a 'shipped' and a 'received for shipment' bill of lading, see *Wespac Banking Corpn* v *South Carolina National Bank* [1986] 1 Lloyd's Rep 311.

[186] *Wespac Banking Corpn* v *South Carolina National Bank* [1986] 1 Lloyd's Rep 311.

[187] It was formerly held that even the bill of lading had to do this – see *Rayner & Co Ltd* v *Hambro's Bank Ltd* [1943] KB 37. But under Art. 14(e) of the Uniform Customs, it is sufficient if the bill of lading describes the goods in general terms. The invoice is in effect a representation by the seller to the buyer of the very goods they have shipped, so it is natural that this is the document where the goods must be described in precise conformity with the contract.

[188] *Moralice (London) Ltd* v *E D & F Man* [1954] 1 Lloyd's Rep 526.

[189] This does not apply where the credit specifies quantity in terms of packing units or containers or individual items. Nor does it entitle the seller to draw more than the amount of the credit. It simply means that the bank will pay even if the seller ships up to 5 per cent more or less than the contract quantity. (The tolerance is extended to 10 per cent if the contract quantity is qualified by words such as 'about' or 'circa'.) It remains the responsibility of the seller to draw the invoice for the correct amount shipped, of course.

[190] *Soproma SpA* v *Marine & Animal By-Products Corpn* [1966] 1 Lloyd's Rep 367, 390.

[191] *British Imex Industries Ltd* v *Midland Bank* [1958] 1 QB 542, per Salmon LJ. See now Art. 27 of the Uniform Customs. In practice bills of lading usually only acknowledge that the goods are in apparent (not actual) good order and condition. That is enough for a clean bill. See also *Golodetz (M) & Co Inc* v *Czarnikow-Rionda Co Inc* [1980] 1 All ER 501.

[192] *Hamzeh Malas & Sons* v *British Imex Industries Ltd* [1958] 2 QB 127. In many cases the buyer will not even see the goods until the seller has obtained payment, so this question can hardly arise, but sometimes the buyer may have grounds for suspecting non-compliance even before they receive the goods, e.g. because of a previous shipment.

who must pay first and sue afterwards. As Lord Diplock put it in *United City Merchants (Investments) Ltd* v *Royal Bank of Canada*:

> The whole commercial purpose for which the system of confirmed irrevocable documentary credits has been developed in international trade is to give the seller an assured right to be paid before he parts with control of the goods and that does not permit of any dispute with the buyer as to the performance of the contract of sale being used as a ground for non-payment or reduction or deferment of payment.[193]

This general policy gives rise to the fundamental principle expressed in Art. 4 of the Uniform Customs that essentially banks 'deal in documents and not in goods' and the commercial credit is independent and detached from the underlying contract of sale between the buyer and the seller. The bank is therefore expected to confine its attention to the documents and to examine them for regularity on their face. This is neatly illustrated in *Hamzeh Malas & Sons* v *British Imex Industries Ltd*[194] where a buyer agreed to buy steel from the seller and was to pay via a LC. The seller shipped the steel but upon delivery the buyer rejected them because they were defective and he sought an injunction to stop the bank from paying the seller. However, the court dismissed the buyer's claim on the grounds that:

> 'the opening of a confirmed letter of credit constitutes a bargain between the banker and the vendor of the goods which imposes upon the banker an absolute obligation to pay, irrespective of any dispute there may be between the parties as to whether the goods are to contract or not.'[195]

However, the principle of autonomy is not absolute as there are exceptions to it, under English law the illegality and fraud exception have been recognized. In terms of the illegality exception, the English courts recognise this because they would not permit the principle autonomy to be used by a seller in order to benefit from an unlawful act. Thus in the *American Accord*[196] case the English court held that a LC that was intended to manipulate the currency exchange regulations was unenforceable because it was contrary to Article VIII, s. 2(b) of the Brent Wood Agreement 1945 which UK is privy to. This case was recently reaffirmed, in *Mahonia Ltd* v *JP Morgan Chase Bank and Another*[197] where the court added that as a matter of public policy reasons, the illegality exception also applies in cases where the underlying contract of sale is 'unenforceable on grounds of illegality'.[198]

In terms of the fraud exception, as matter of English law the banks may also be entitled to reject payment where the seller presents documents that are fraudulent. In the aim of maintaining the seller's assured right of payment, the English courts have generally very reluctant to grant injunctions – even interim injunctions – to restrain banks from honouring their letters of credit, and a strong case must be made for an injunction against the bank itself. Moreover, an injunction is unlikely to be granted to restrain an issuing bank from paying a confirming bank, where the confirming bank has already paid the seller in good faith and looks to the issuing bank for an indemnity under the issuing bank's own obligations, unless it is apparent that the confirming bank has paid on non-conforming documents, or that it had clear knowledge of fraud by the seller.

193 [1983] AC 168, 183. See also *Nova Jersey (Knit) Ltd* v *Kammgarn Spinneiri* [1977] 1 WLR 713; *Power Curber International* v *National Bank of Kuwait* [1981] 1 WLR 1233.
194 [1958] 2 QB 127.
195 Ibid., Jekins LJ, at 129.
196 *United City Merchant Investment Ltd* v *Royal Bank of Canada* (The American Accord) [1983] 1 AC 168.
197 [2003] EWHC 1927.
198 Ibid. Colman J, at para 68.

Accordingly, the English courts have placed the burden of proof on the banks and interpreted the fraud exception narrowly so that it only applies in 'exceptional cases'.[199] It follows that, in order for the bank to reject paying the seller on grounds of fraud, it must *adduce 'strong corroborative evidence'*[200] that will '*very clearly establish*'[201] that the seller was fraudulent or was privy to the fraud or had knowledge of it. The *American Accord*[202] case is a case in point where the bank refused to pay the seller who had presented a bill of lading that was fraudulently backdated by the loading brokers without the seller's knowledge. The court held that the bank had to pay the seller because he had no knowledge of the fraud. In particular, Lord Diplock held that the fraud exception applies, in situations where the seller fraudulently, seeks to benefit himself, by presenting documents that he knows contain 'material statements of facts' that are untrue.[203] He added that, in such a case the fraud exception would apply through the maxim *ex turpi causa non oritur actio*, that is, 'fraud unravels all' and because the court would not permit their process to be used dishonestly to carry out fraud.[204]

The fraud exception under English law has been hailed for closing a loophole in the law and controlling fraud in international trade.[205] Moreover, the narrow interpretation, strikes a balance between the maintaining the commercial utility of LC and the desire to prevent the inequitable results stemming from the seller intentionally submitting documents containing fraudulent misrepresentations.[206] Additionally, it maintains the trust in LC in commercial practise through protecting banks where the seller is intentionally fraudulent and protecting an innocent seller who submits the documents in good faith without any knowledge of fraud by other intermediaries as was the case in the *American Accord.* [207]

However, this approach can be seen to be undesirable as it is too focused on the innocence of the seller that there is a clear disregard of the importance of the sanctity of the documents in commercial practice.[208] This is because, the effect of the judgment in the *American Accord* is that the banks must pay against fraudulent documents which may even be commercially worthless (null) merely because an innocent seller has presented them in good faith and without knowledge of the fraud.[209] This is exacerbated by the high standard of proof imposed by the English courts which require the banks to very clearly establish fraud and the seller's knowledge of the fraud as an allegation or suspicion is

[199] Kerr J in *RD Harbottle (Mercantile) Ltd* v *National West Minister Bank* [1977] 2 All ER 862, at 870.

[200] *Ackner* L.J *United Trading Corp SA* v *Allied Arab Bank Ltd* [1985] 2 Lloyd's Rep. 554, at 561.

[201] *Lord Denning in Edward Owen* v *Barclays Bank International* [1978] 1 Lloyd's Rep. 166, at 173.

[202] *United City Merchant Investment Ltd* v *Royal Bank of Canada (The American Accord)* [1983] 1 AC 168.

[203] *United City Merchant Investment Ltd* v *Royal Bank of Canada (The American Accord)* [1983] 1 AC 168, at 183.

[204] Ibid.

[205] Williams M 'Documentary Credits and Fraud: English and Chinese law Compared (2004) *Journal of Business Law* 155, at 163.

[206] Browne J 'The Fraud Exception to Standby Letters of Credit in Australia: Does it Embrace Statutory Unconscionability?' (1999) 11(1) *Bond Law Review* 98, at 101–102.

[207] Sappideen, R 'International Commercial Letters of Credit: Balancing the Rights of Buyers and Sellers in Insolvency' (2006) *Journal of Business Law* 133, at 149.

[208] Donnelly, K 'Nothing for Nothing: A Nullity Exception in Letters of Credit?' (2008) *Journal of Business Law* 316, at 321.

[209] Goode R, Kronke, H and Mckendrick, E *Transnational Commercial Law Text, Cases and Materials* (1st ed. OUP 2007), at 362.

not sufficient to justify the refusal to pay the seller.[210] Furthermore, this narrow approach shows a contradiction of the rationale of the of the Fraud exception, that is, 'fraud unravels all' because in practice, only the fraud the seller is aware of unravels all.[211]

Nevertheless, the House of Lords decision in the *American Accord* case was approved in *Montrod*[212] case where the bank was obliged to pay the seller against presentation of a certificate of inspection that was fraudulently signed by the buyer, who had deceived the seller that he has authority to do so, making it commercially worthless. In that case, Lord Porter held that there should not be an extension in the law to create a nullity exception because it would create uncertainty and involve '*making undesirable inroads into the principles of autonomy*'.[213] He added that:

> 'If a general nullity exception were to be introduced as part of English law it would place banks in a further dilemma as to the necessity to investigate facts which they are not competent to do. Further, such an exception would be likely to act unfairly upon beneficiaries participating in a chain of contracts in cases where their good faith is not in question. Such a development would thus undermine the system of financing international trade by means of documentary credits.'[214]

Arguably the commercial utility of the LCs appears to be misconceived by his Lordship. This is because the effectiveness of LC required in commercial practice is that the seller is assured of payment upon presentation of documents that are not fraudulent and with commercial value.[215] In fact, this is reflected in Article 2 of the UCP 600 which requires the presentation to be in accordance with the terms and conditions of the LC. Accordingly, if a document is non-compliant because it is fraudulent it should be treated as such and it should be emphasized that the mere fact an innocent seller presents the fraudulent document does not turn them into a conforming document.[216]

In other jurisdiction such as the America a more liberal approach is adopted with regards to the issue regarding the recognition of the nullity exception. This is clearly demonstrated in *Old Coloney Trust Co.* v *Lawyer's Title & Trust Co*[217] case where the bank refused to pay the seller after presentation of documents that the bank knew were fraudulent. In contrast to *the American Accord* case (above), the American court held that the bank was entitled to refuse to pay the seller because:

> 'When the issuer of a letter of credit knows that a document, although in correct form is in point of fact false or illegal he cannot be called upon to recognize such a document as complying with the terms of credit.'[218]

[210] Lord Diplock, [1983] 1 AC 168 at 185..

[211] Donnelly, K 'Nothing for Nothing: A Nullity Exception in Letters of Credit?' (2008) *Journal of Business Law* 316, at 321.

[212] *Montrod Ltd* v *Grundkotter Fleischvertriebs Gmbh* [2002] 1 WLR 1975.

[213] Ibid., at 1991.

[214] Ibid.

[215] Reza Beheshti and Séverine Saintier and Sean Thomas, *Bradgate's Commercial Law* (4th edn, OUP 2024), at 735.

[216] Goode, R 'Reflections on Letters of Credit' (1980) Journal of Business Law 291, as cited in *Beam Technology (Mfg.) Pte Ltd* v *Standard Chartered Bank* [2003] 1 SLR 597, at para 35.

[217] [1924] 297 F. 152.

[218] Ibid. at 158 This principle was reaffirmed in *Szerjn* v *J. Henry Schorader Banking Corp.* [1941] 31 NYS.2d 631 where the American court held that the bank was entitled to refuse to pay the seller who had presented documents that he claimed covered goods but in reality the seller had fraudulently shipped worthless goods.

Therefore, it is highly likely that if the *American Accord* case (above) was decided in an American court, the bank would have been entitled to reject the documents and to refuse to pay the seller since payment would have facilitated a material fraud on the applicant.[219] Singapore law also departed from the English law and recognised a nullity exception. This is clearly illustrated in *Beam Technology (Mfg.) Pte Ltd* v *Standard Chartered Bank*[220] where the bank refused to pay a seller who presented a document that was commercially worthless because the company it claimed it was issued by, did not exist. In this case, the Singapore Court firstly, distinguished *Montrod* case above on the grounds that the certificate of inspection in that case was 'not an essential document.'[221] Thereafter, the court held that, the document in question in this case, was a material document and since the bank had established that it was forged and null it was obliged not to pay the seller. In addition, the court dismissed Lord Porter's concerns (above) with regards to the dilemma of the banks where there is a nullity exception. It held that, such an exception does not require banks to investigate into the documents but rather 'only permits a bank to refuse payment if it is satisfied that a material document is a nullity.'[222]

[219] See the Court of Appeal decision in *United City Merchant Investment Ltd* v *Royal Bank of Canada (The American Accord)* [1982] QB 208, at 254 (Court of Appeal)

[220] [2003] 1 SLR 597.

[221] Ibid., at para 31.

[222] Ibid. at para 34.

14

International Convention on Sales of Goods ('CISG')

14.1 Introduction

Prior to the adoption of the CISG in 1980, there had been efforts to agree on a treaty to provide a set of legal rules for international sales lasting several decades. An initial attempt was the Convention relating to a Uniform Law on the International Sale of Goods 1964, known as the Hague ULIS, but this failed to gain the support of a significant number of states (although the UK did ratify this convention). After several years of further effort, a diplomatic conference of 62 states approved the United Nation Convention on the International Sale of Goods (CISG) in 1980. The CISG is a cornerstone of International Commercial Law.[1] The Convention came into force on 1 January 1988 following ratification by 11 states. At the time of writing, it is in force in 97 countries.[2] The major trading nations which have not ratified the Convention are India and the United Kingdom, and within Europe, Ireland and Malta. The reason the United Kingdom has not ratified appears to be opposition from a number of influential organisations, lack of public service resources and fear that London would lose its edge in international arbitration and litigation,[3] and possibly the fact that the Sale of Goods Act had, for many years, served as a de facto sales law for international sales transactions. Nevertheless, in view of the importance of the Convention it has been thought appropriate to include this brief account in this book.

14.2 International Convention

The CISG is an international Treaty, which has the force of law in those countries which have ratified or acceded to it. The provisions of the CISG only apply to those contracts which fall within its scope, so it is important to examine the field of application of the Convention first. Moreover, as with any international Convention, there are special rules of interpretation which national courts dealing with a case involving the CISG need to follow.

[1] See generally, Twigg-Flesner, *Foundations of International Commercial Law* (Routledge, 2021).

[2] See list at: https://uncitral.un.org/en/texts/salegoods/conventions/sale_of_goods/cisg/status

[3] See Moss (2005) 1 *Journal of Law and Commerce* 483. There may be different views in Scotland: see Report on Formation of Contract: Scottish Law and the United Nations Convention on Contracts for the International Sale of Goods (Scot Law Com No 144, 1993).

14.2.1 Field of application of CISG

Article 1 provides:

(1) the Convention applies to contracts of sale of goods between parties whose places of business are in different States:
 (a) when the States are Contracting States; or
 (b) when the rules of private international law lead to the application of the law of a Contracting State.

Accordingly, the trigger for the application of the Convention is international diversity of *places of business* of buyers and sellers. Place of incorporation is thus irrelevant for the purposes of the Convention. In the case of multinational enterprises with more than one place of business, or parties which do not have a place of business, Art. 10, CISG provides:

(a) if a party has more than one place of business, the place of business is that which has the closest relationship to the contract and its performance, having regard to the circumstances known to or contemplated by the parties at any time before or at the conclusion of the contract;
(b) if a party does not have a place of business, reference is to be made to his habitual residence.

Although by the terms of Art. 1 (above) the Convention applies to international sales of goods, the Convention contains no definition of 'goods'. Instead, Art. 2 *excludes* certain types of goods from its scope.

(a) of goods bought for personal, family or household use, unless the seller, at any time before or at the conclusion of the contract, neither knew nor ought to have known that the goods were bought for any such use;
(b) by auction;
(c) on execution or otherwise by authority of law;
(d) of stocks, shares, investment securities, negotiable instruments or money;
(e) of ships, vessels, hovercraft or aircraft;
(f) of electricity.

Nor does the Convention contain a definition of 'buyer' or of 'seller'. Contracts for mixed goods and services can fall within the Convention. As in the UK and the majority of jurisdictions in the USA, the Convention has a version of the 'predominant purpose' test.[4] Article 3 provides:

(1) Contracts for the supply of goods to be manufactured or produced are to be considered sales unless the party who orders the goods undertakes to supply a substantial part of the materials necessary for such manufacture or production.
(2) This Convention does not apply to contracts in which the predominant part of the obligations of the party who furnishes the goods consists in the supply of labour or other services.

Although the Convention has no express provision dealing with sales of software, the Landgericht München has held that an international sale of a computer program can

[4] See *Robinson* v *Graves* [1935] 1 KB 579.

be subject to the CISG.[5] Whether the CISG should apply to contracts for the supply of software/digital content is a much-debated matter.[6] In view of the crucial significance software/digital content plays in modern supply transactions, the desire to ensure that an international regime is available to deal with issues of conformity and associated remedies is understandable. However, a regime for tangible items cannot be applied directly to non-tangible items such as software/digital content, and it may be both necessary and appropriate to develop more tailored rules.

As noted above, the Convention contains no definition of 'goods'. There is no equivalent to the definition contained in s. 61 of the Sale of Goods Act but presumably the things included in that definition, that is, emblements,[7] industrial growing crops, and things attached to or forming part of the land which are agreed to be severed before sale or under the contract of sale, would also be 'goods' within the Convention. Contracts for mining and other extraction, on the other hand, seem to be outwith the Convention. This seems to be confirmed indirectly by various Articles of the Convention.[8]

14.2.2 Formalities

Article 11 provides that a contract need not be concluded or evidenced by a writing and is not subject to any other requirement as to form. However, this provision was not acceptable to a number of states involved in the negotiation of the Convention. Accordingly, Art. 12 was added allowing nations to obviate Art. 11 by so declaring at the time of ratification.[9]

14.2.3 Battle of the forms

This refers to the situation where the *pro forma* used by the offeree in purporting to accept an offer differs from the *pro forma* used by the offeror in making the offer. In English law, under the notorious doctrine in *Hyde* v *Wrench*,[10] the 'acceptance' amounts to a rejection of the offer, and a counter-offer from the offeree. CISG modifies this doctrine only in a minor way. Article 19 provides that 'reply to an offer which purports to be an acceptance but contains additions, limitations or other modifications is a rejection of the offer and constitutes a counteroffer'. This is subject to the proviso in Art. 19(2) in respect of terms which do not 'materially alter' the terms of the offer, in which case the acceptance will be effective as such. Article 19(3) makes it clear that terms on matters such as price, payment, quality or quantity of the goods, as well as the place and time of delivery would be treated as material.

5 CLOUT, Case 131, 8 February 1995.

6 See e.g., Diedrich, Maintaining uniformity in international uniform law via autonomous interpretation: software contracts and the CISG (1996) *Pace International Law Review* 303; or Munoz, Software technology in CISG contracts (2019) 24 *Uniform LR* 281.

7 That is, annual growing crops.

8 See Art. 35 (conformity of goods); Arts 31–33 (delivery and shipment), Arts 66–70 (risk of loss).

9 See Art. 96 Nine countries have exercised this option.

10 (1840) 3 Beav 334.

14.2.4 Parol evidence rule

When the terms of a contract have been embodied in a writing to which both parties have assented as the definite and complete statement thereof, parol evidence of antecedent agreements, negotiations, and understandings is not admissible for the purpose of varying or contradicting the contract so embodied.[11] In spite of its name, this is in fact a rule of law, not evidence.[12]

Because Art. 8(3) requires that 'due consideration is to be given to all relevant circumstances of the case', it would seem that CISG overrides any domestic rule of law that would bar a tribunal from considering parol evidence.[13] Nevertheless, it has been argued that the rule could be an appropriate way to discern what consideration is due under Art. 8(3) to evidence of a parol nature.[14]

14.2.5 Interpretation

As noted earlier, the CISG is an international Treaty and as such, there are special rules of interpretation to follow. This has been recognised expressly in Art. 7. According to Art. 7(1),[15] there are three key factors which need to be taken into account when interpreting the provisions of the CISG. First, its 'international character' is important. This means that the CISG should be interpreted autonomously and not on the basis of any particular domestic law, even where a provision might resemble a specific national rule or approach.

In essence, a court needs to ensure that the interpretation of the CISG's terminology is not influenced by how similar (or potentially even identical) terms have been interpreted in a domestic setting.

Secondly, the interpretation adopted should seek to 'promote uniformity in its application': i.e., there should be a high degree of consistency in the way in which courts in the various Contracting States treat comparable factual circumstances. This implies a strong encouragement for courts in one jurisdiction to take note of rulings on similar issues by courts in other jurisdictions. This is facilitated by the provision of the CLOUT database, and the UN's Digest on the Convention.[16]

Finally, regard is to be had to the 'observance of good faith in international trade'. This is a somewhat controversial aspect of Art. 7(1). It reflects the difficult compromises that need to be made when negotiating an international convention. There was disagreement as to whether to impose a positive duty to act in good faith on the parties to an international sales contract or whether to refrain from including any reference to good faith (reflecting a long-running tension between some common law jurisdictions and the civil

[11] *Corbin on Contracts* (1960, West), §§573–96.
[12] Ibid.
[13] See Honnold, *Uniform Law*, §110 at 170–1.
[14] See Moore (1995) BYU L Rev 1347. See also *Beijing Metals & Minerals Import/Export Corp* v *American Business Center Inc* 993 F 2d 1178, 5th Circ (1993); *MCC-Marble Ceramic Center Inc* v *Ceramica Nuova d'Agostino SpA* 144 F 3d 1384, 11th Circ (1998).
[15] See Komarov, Internationality, uniformity and observance of good faith as criteria in interpretation of CISG: Some remarks on Article 7(1) (2005–6) 25 *Journal of Law and Commerce* 75.
[16] UNCITRAL, *Digest of Case Law on the United Nations Convention on Contracts for the International Sale of Goods* (2nd edn, 2012, UNCITRAL).

law jurisdictions), which eventually resulted in the compromise solution to make 'good faith' a relevant factor in the interpretation of the CISG.

Article 7(2) deals with circumstances where an issue before a court does not fall clearly within the provisions of the CISG. This is often referred to as a 'gap'. Some gaps are 'internal': that is, the issue is one not directly addressed in the CISG but it falls within the areas covered by it (e.g., the remedies of a buyer). Here, courts are required to adopt an interpretation which reflects the principles on which the CISG is based (although these are not espoused clearly anywhere) first, and only have recourse to the applicable domestic law as a matter of final resort.[17] Where the gap is 'external',[18] it relates to an issue not covered in the CISG at all (e.g., validity, or passing of property), and such a matter needs to be resolved on the basis of the provisions of the domestic law applicable to the contract, established by applying the private international law rules of the forum.

In addition to the specific rules in Art. 7 CISG, the Vienna Convention on the Law of Treaties, which entered into force in 1980, is also relevant in this regard. Article 31(1) stresses the need to give terms their ordinary meaning, albeit as used in the context of a Treaty and in light of the Treaty's object and purpose, and Art. 32 permits recourse to the preparatory works for that Treaty.

14.3 Comparing the CISG with the Sale of Goods Act 1979

As the focus of this book is primarily on the English law of sale, this chapter will highlight only some aspects of the CISG and contrast them with corresponding provisions in the Sale of Goods Act.

14.3.1 Freedom from third-party claims

Article 41 provides that: 'The seller must deliver goods which are free from any right or claim of a third party.' The absence of the word 'title' from this provision makes it fairly clear that it includes claims by third parties based on intellectual property rights.[19] What is not clear is whether it extends to 'clouds on the title' which, while theoretically not inhibiting dealings in the goods, nevertheless can seriously diminish their commercial value on the market.[20]

14.3.2 Express terms regarding the goods

As the CISG is concerned with international commercial contracts, there will frequently have been considerable negotiation over specifications regarding the goods. Article 35 CISG deals with the general requirement that goods must be in conformity with the

[17] On this, see Lookofsky, Walking the Article 7(2) tightrope between CISG and domestic law (2005-6) 25 *Journal of Law and Commerce* 87.

[18] See McMahon, Differentiating between internal and external gaps in the UN Convention on Contracts for the International Sale of Goods: A proposed method for determining governed by in the context of Article 7(2) (2005–6) 44 *Columbia Journal of Transnational Law* 992.

[19] See *Microbeads* v *Vinhurst Road Markings Ltd* [1975] 1 All ER 529, discussed in Chapter 5, at section 5.2.2.

[20] See *Jeanneret* v *Vichey* 693 F 2d 259, 2nd Circ (1982).

contract, and this includes the seemingly obvious obligation that the goods delivered by the seller are 'of the quantity, quality and description required by the contract and which are contained and packaged in the manner required by the contract' (Art. 35(1)). The requirements as to description under s. 13 of the Sale of Goods Act overlap in part with this Article, but otherwise, these are aspects which would be found in the express terms of the contract.

14.3.2.1 Conformity with the contract: quality and fitness for purpose

Not every contract will contain detailed requirements regarding the goods. Under the Sale of Goods Act, the implied terms as to satisfactory quality (s. 14(2)) and fitness for a particular purpose (s. 14(3)), as well as the requirements as to goods sold by sample (s. 15), fulfil the role of providing a base-line expectation which goods should meet. In the CISG, this objective is achieved through Art. 35(2), which stipulates several requirements goods must meet in order to be regarded as in conformity with the contract, although these requirements are subject to contrary agreement by the parties.

The specific requirements in Art. 35(2) are that the goods should:

(a) be fit for the purposes for which goods of the same description would ordinarily be used;
(b) be fit for any particular purpose expressly or impliedly made known to the seller at the time of the conclusion of the contract, except where the circumstances show that the buyer did not rely, or that it was unreasonable for him to rely, on the seller's skill and judgment;
(c) possess the qualities of goods which the seller has held out to the buyer as a sample or model;
(d) be contained or packaged in the manner usual for such goods or, where there is no such manner, in a manner adequate to preserve and protect the goods.

One can see a parallel with the indicative fitness requirement in the satisfactory quality test, although note that under the CISG, goods should be fit for the purposes for which they would ordinarily be used, whereas s. 14(2B)(a) refers to purposes for which the goods are 'commonly supplied'. There is a subtle but important difference here: ordinary use would seem to take the buyer's perspective, whereas common supply would be considered from the perspective of the seller. Consequently, it is possible that the application of these respective factors to identical facts could lead to different conclusions.

The fitness for a particular purpose criterion in Art. 35(2)(b) will be immediately familiar to anyone who has seen s. 14(3) of the Sale of Goods Act. However, this striking similarity in wording poses a possible trap when interpreting the CISG, because any court tempted to look to the case law under s. 14(3) when dealing with Art. 35(2)(b) would fall foul of the imperative to interpret all the provisions of the CISG autonomously.

Finally, there is an important reference to packaging, which is not surprising as the CISG is concerned with international sales contracts, the performance of which would necessitate that the goods are transported by ship, plane, rail or a combination to the buyer.

14.3.3 Buyer's and seller's remedies

The same provisions, Arts 74–76 apply to buyer's and seller's remedies. For convenience of exposition, however, we deal with buyer's and seller's remedies separately.

14.3.3.1 Buyer's remedies

These are listed in Art. 45(1). This cross-refers to the rights set out in Art 46–52, and the claims for damages set out in Arts 74–77. Article 46 generally enables the buyer to require the seller to perform its obligations, so the primary remedy is performance-focused. This contrasts obviously with the position under English law, where a performance-based remedy is rarely awarded. The buyer can give the seller an additional period of time within which to perform its obligations (Art. 47(1)), during which time the buyer cannot invoke any remedy for breach of contract unless the seller makes it clear that it does not intend to perform (Art. 47(2)). Also, Art. 48 gives the seller a 'right of cure' in certain circumstances where this can be done without unreasonable delay and without causing unreasonable inconvenience to the buyer.

In the case of a non-conformity, Art. 46(3) makes 'repair' the primary remedy, except where repair would be unreasonable. Any request for repair must be made when the buyer notifies the seller of the lack of conformity (see below) or within a reasonable period of time therefrom. Article 46(2) further provides for a right of replacement ('substitute goods'), but this would only be available where the breach of contract constitutes a fundamental breach (discussed next).

Article 49(1)(a) provides that the buyer may declare the contract avoided if the failure by the seller to perform any of their obligations under the contract or this Convention amounts to a 'fundamental breach' of contract. This would include breach of the quality provisions of Art. 35 set out above. 'Fundamental breach' is defined in Art. 25:

> A breach of contract committed by one of the parties is fundamental if it results in such detriment to the other party as substantially to deprive him of what he is entitled to expect under the contract, unless the party in breach did not foresee and a reasonable person of the same kind in the same circumstances would not have foreseen such result.

This requires a careful assessment in each case whether the consequences of the breach as such constitute a substantial deprivation of what the innocent party was entitled to expect under the contract. First, it will be necessary to determine just what the innocent party was entitled to expect and compare this with what the party in breach has actually done. If the discrepancy between expectations and actual performance (to the extent that there has been any performance) is such as to 'substantially deprive' the innocent party of what it expected, there is a fundamental breach. However, the party in breach may yet counter the *prima facie* assumption that there is a fundamental breach when the party in breach, or a reasonable party in its position, would not have foreseen that the consequences of their breach would substantially deprive the innocent party of what it expected. The key point is that the threshold for establishing a fundamental breach is high, which reflects the general desire of the drafters of the CISG to focus on the performance of the contract.

Article 49 provides the instances when a buyer may declare a contract 'avoided' (this is comparable to termination in English law). First, avoidance is permitted where the seller's failure to perform constitutes a fundamental breach (Art. 49(1)(a)). Secondly, in the case of non-delivery, the buyer first has to fix an additional period of time within which the seller must complete its obligation to deliver the goods, and only once this period has expired, or if the seller has declared that it does not intend to deliver the goods, will avoidance be permitted (Art. 49(1)(b)).

In a decision of the Bundesgerichtshof involving a sale of cobalt from a Dutch seller to a German buyer, where the contract required the goods to be of British origin, the buyer purported to declare the contract avoided on the ground that the certificates of origin were wrong and that the goods were of South African origin and of inferior quality. The court held that, since the seller had effected delivery, the buyer could not declare the contract avoided under Art. 49(1)(b), and that there was no fundamental breach within Art. 49(1)(a) since the buyer had failed to show that the cobalt was unsaleable in Germany or elsewhere and that it had failed to show that it was substantially deprived of what it was entitled to expect as required by Art. 25 (above). Nor was the delivery of the wrong certificates a fundamental breach since the buyer could obtain correct certificates. Accordingly, the buyer was obliged to pay pursuant to Art. 58.

Where the contract is avoided, there are particular provisions on damages in the CISG Arts 75 and 76 (these cover damages claims by both seller and buyer). Thus, under Art. 75, if a buyer has bought replacement goods after avoiding the contract due to a breach by the seller, and the goods were more expensive, the buyer is entitled to recover the difference between the contract price under the original contract and the price paid for the substitute goods. Conversely, if the seller has avoided the contract due to a breach by the buyer and has resold the goods but at a lower price than the contract price, that difference can also be recovered. In either instance the substitute transaction must have been effected in a reasonable manner and within a reasonable time after avoidance. Any additional losses can be recovered by way of general damages under Art. 74.

In the absence of a substitute transaction within Art. 75, there is an alternative damages measure under Art. 76. In this case, the measure of damages is the difference between the contract price and the 'current price at the time of avoidance' (Art. 76(1)). By way of exception, if the contract is avoided after the party claiming damages had taken over the goods, the relevant time for establishing the current price is at the point at which the goods were taken over. The determination of the current price should be made with reference to the price at the place where delivery was to be made (Art. 76(2)).

The general measure of damages for other breaches, as well as in the absence of any substitute transactions, and for consequential losses is provided in Art. 74, according to which the measure of damages is 'a sum equal to the loss, including loss of profit, suffered by the other party as a consequence of the breach'. However, this is subject to the requirement that the party in breach 'foresaw or ought to have foreseen at the time of the conclusion of the contract, in the light of the facts and matters of which he then knew or ought to have known' the losses in respect of which damages are claimed.

Does this embody the 'benefit of the bargain' principle which under the Sale of Goods Act is the difference between the value of the goods delivered, and the value they would have had if they had conformed to the contract?[21] Article 76 makes it clear with certain modifications that it does. If the buyer has not covered, damages are measured by the current price for the goods that is the price prevailing for the goods at the place where delivery of the goods should have been made (Art. 76(1)) or, absent such price, at another place

[21] Section 53(3).

that is a reasonable substitute (Art. 76(2)). 'Loss' is broad enough to cover consequential damages but such further damages then are subject to the foreseeability test set out in the second sentence of Art. 74.[22]

As we have seen, CISG does not apply where goods are bought for personal, family or household use,[23] nor does it apply to the liability of the seller for death or personal injury caused by the goods to any person.[24] Professor Honnold has explained the reason for this as follows:

> In UNCITRAL attention was drawn to the development of national legislation and case law designed to protect consumers; it was agreed that the Convention should not supersede these rules. Consideration was given to a provision that the Convention would not override any domestic rule that was 'mandatory' or that implemented 'public policy' (*ordre public*) but it was found that these concepts carried different meanings in various legal systems; the clearest and safest solution was specifically to exclude consumer purchases from the Convention . . .

14.3.3.2 Seller's remedies

These arise when buyers wrongfully declare the contract avoided or, without making a declaration, refuse to accept and pay for the goods.[25] As noted above, the same Articles govern the seller's recovery of damages as govern those of the buyer (set out above).

Article 62 provides for the seller's recovery of the price where the buyer has not paid in accordance with the terms of the contract. The same provision allows the seller to require the buyer to take delivery of the goods, or perform any other obligations. However, the seller will not be able to invoke Art. 62 if the seller has already 'resorted to a remedy which is inconsistent with this requirement', such as avoiding the contract. The recovery of the price is not therefore conditioned on the property having passed to the buyer as it is under s. 49 of the Sale of Goods Act, nor is it conditioned on the seller making a reasonable effort to resell the goods as it is under Art. 2-709(1) of the Uniform Commercial Code.

If sellers have possession and control of the goods and elect not to seek the price, they may claim damages as provided by Arts 74–77.[26] (These provisions are set out above.) Under Art. 74, an aggrieved seller is entitled to a sum equal to the loss, including loss of profit, suffered as a consequence of the breach, but this again is subject to the foreseeability test set out in the second sentence. Moreover, under Art. 77 the seller must take such measures as are reasonable in the circumstances to mitigate the loss, including loss of profit, resulting from the breach. This means that aggrieved sellers in possession of the goods must make reasonable efforts to resell the goods.[27] If the seller has resold the goods, it may recover the difference between the contract price and the (lower) resale price.[28] If the

[22] 'Foreseeability' is not a term used in domestic UK contract law – see *Victoria Laundry (Windsor) Ltd* v *Newman Industries Ltd* [1949] 2 KB 528, as discussed in *Koufos* v *C Czarnikow Ltd* [1969] 1 AC 350, especially Lord Reid's speech at pp. 385–6.
[23] Article 2(a).
[24] Article 5.
[25] Article 61.
[26] Article 61(1)(b).
[27] See Art. 75. See also Art. 76(1).
[28] Article 75.

seller has not resold the goods, it may recover the difference between the price fixed by the contract and the current price at the time of avoidance.[29] 'Current price' means primarily the prevailing price at the place where delivery of the goods should have been made.[30]

The problem of the 'lost volume seller' could in principle arise in international sales subject to the Convention, as it does in domestic sales.[31] The Convention has no specific provision dealing with it. However, Art. 74 is sufficiently widely drafted to cover this, and one learned commentator takes the view that lost volume sellers may have a remedy under the Convention.[32]

14.3.4 Notice of breach

The Sale of Goods Act has no specific provision on notice requirements, but CISG does. Article 39 provides that a buyer has to notify the seller of a lack of conformity within a reasonable time after discovering this, and the notice to the seller has to specify the nature of the lack of conformity. The buyer loses the right to rely on this lack of conformity if they fail to comply with this obligation.

In UNCITRAL CLOUT Abstract 285,[33] it was held that giving notice three weeks after delivery of obviously non-conforming goods was too late. However, failure to give sufficient notice does not result in the buyer being 'barred from any remedy'.[34] Article 44 provides that the buyer might still be able to reduce the price (Art. 50) or claim damages (but not for a loss of profit), provided that the buyer has a 'reasonable excuse' for failing to give notice on time.

This provision is not limited to circumstances in which the price has not been paid. Under Art. 50 the buyer may reduce the price 'whether or not the price has already been paid'.

The time limit for the buyer to serve notice as required by the above provisions is in any event two years from the date on which the goods were 'actually handed over',[35] whether or not the buyer discovered, or ought to have discovered, the non-conformities.[36] This time bar is absolute, and overrides the offset provision of Art. 44.

14.3.5 Execution of sales contracts

The Convention sets out the general obligations of the seller and the buyer. Article 30 requires the seller to deliver the goods, hand over any documents relating to them, and transfer the property in the goods, in accordance with the terms of the contract and any applicable CISG provisions. However, it must be noted that the CISG is silent, beyond the basic obligation to transfer property, as to what the legal conditions for effecting the

[29] Article 76.
[30] Article 76(2).
[31] See Chapter 16, at section 16.2.
[32] See Honnold, *International Sales*, §415.
[33] Oberlandesgericht, Koblenz, Germany, 1998.
[34] Uniform Commercial Code, Art. 2-607(3)(a).
[35] Article 39(2).
[36] Ibid.

transfer of property are. This would therefore be governed by the relevant rules of the national law that applies to the contract (to the extent that the CISG does not apply).

The reciprocal provision governing the buyer's duties is Art. 53, obliging the buyer to pay the price for the goods, and take delivery of the goods, in accordance with the terms of the contract and any applicable CISG provisions.

The seller's obligation to deliver, as under domestic law, is satisfied by putting the goods at the buyer's disposal at the place where the seller has its place of business at the time of the conclusion of the contract,[37] unless the parties knew from the circumstances for example that the goods were to be manufactured or produced at a particular place or that the goods would be placed at the buyer's disposal at another location.[38] If the contract involves the carriage of goods, the seller's obligation to deliver is complied with by handing over the goods to the first carrier for transmission to the buyer.[39] In such cases, absent express agreement, the seller must make such contracts as are necessary for the carriage to the place fixed [*by the agreement*] by means of transportation appropriate in the circumstances and in accordance with the usual terms for such transportation.[40] If the goods are not clearly identified to the contract by markings on the goods, by shipping documents or otherwise, the seller must give the buyer notice of the consignment specifying the goods.[41]

As to the time of delivery, the Convention looks in the first place to the terms of the contract.[42] If a period is fixed or determinable from the contract, the seller can choose to perform at any time within that period unless circumstances indicate that the buyer is to choose a date.[43] If the contract is silent as to the time of delivery, the seller must deliver within a reasonable time after the conclusion of the contract.[44]

In international sales transactions involving carriage of goods by sea, it is often required that the buyer provides that vessel onto which the seller loads in the specified port. In this case, the buyer must give the seller notice specified in the contract, or within a reasonable time, to enable the seller to load. There is no specific Article of the Convention dealing with this, but under domestic law, if due notice is given, the seller must have the goods ready to be loaded at the time specified.[45]

The Convention has no provisions dealing with the performance of contracts for the sale of goods in the hands of a warehouseman or similar.

Unless otherwise agreed, the buyer must pay when the seller places either the goods, or the documents controlling their disposition, at the buyer's disposal in accordance with the contract and the Convention.[46] If the payment is to be made against the handing over of the goods or documents, payment must be made where the handing over takes place.[47] Otherwise payment must be made at the seller's place of business.[48] The Convention does

[37] Article 31(c).
[38] Article 31(b).
[39] Article 31(a).
[40] Article 32(2).
[41] Article 31(b).
[42] Article 33(a) and (b).
[43] Article 33(b).
[44] Article 33(c).
[45] *Compagnie Commerciale Sucres et Denrees* v *C Czarnikow Ltd (The Naxos)* [1990] 1 WLR 1337 (HL).
[46] Article 58(1).
[47] Article 57(1)(b).
[48] Article 57(1)(a).

not deal with the manner of the buyer's payment other than providing that the buyer's obligations include taking such steps and complying with such formalities as may be required under the contract or any laws and regulations to enable payment to be made.[49] This latter could include opening a banker's documentary credit in accordance with the requirements of the contract.[50]

14.3.6 Right of inspection

As under the Sale of Goods Act, s. 34, the buyer has a right to examine the goods, and the buyer is not bound to pay the price until it has had an opportunity to examine the goods,[51] unless the procedures for delivery or payment agreed by the parties are inconsistent with the buyer having such an opportunity.[52]

14.3.7 Risk of loss

The principles governing risk of loss are set out in Chapter IV of the Convention. Article 66 provides that loss or damage of the goods after risk has passed to the buyer will not discharge the buyer from the obligation to pay for the goods, save where the loss or damage was caused by the seller (whether by an act or an omission).

Article 67 deals with contracts involving the carriage of goods. It provides that, unless the contract requires the seller to hand over the goods at a particular place, the risk will pass to the buyer once the goods are handed over to the (first) carrier who will transmit the goods to the buyer. If this handing over is to happen at a particular place, risk will only pass to the buyer once the goods are handed over there. Risk will pass to the buyer in these circumstances even if the seller has the right to retain the documents controlling the disposition of the goods. All of this is subject to the requirement in Art. 67(2) that the goods are 'clearly identified to the contract, whether by markings on the goods, by shipping documents, by notice given to the buyer or otherwise'.

A further rule is Art. 68 on goods sold while they are in transit, which happens frequently in international sales transactions. Here, risk will generally pass to the buyer on conclusion of the contract, except where the seller knew or ought to have known that the goods were already damaged or lost and failed to disclose this to the buyer.

In all other cases, the risk passes to the buyer at the point when they take over the goods. However, if the buyer fails to take delivery at the required time and thereby breaches the contract, risk will be deemed to have passed at the time when the goods were placed at their disposal (Art. 69(1)). This is subject to the requirement that the goods in question were identified to the contract; if this had not yet happened, then risk can only pass once the goods are identified to the contract (Art. 69(3)). Finally, if the buyer is to take over the goods at a place other than the seller's place of business (e.g., where the goods are stored in a warehouse owned by a third party), risk passed when delivery is due, the goods have been placed at the buyer's disposal at that place, and the buyer is aware of this fact.

[49] Article 54.
[50] As to these, see Chapter 13.
[51] Article 58(3).
[52] Ibid.

Article 70 provides that if the seller has committed a fundamental breach of contract, Arts 67, 68 and 69 do not impair the remedies available to the buyer on account of the breach.

14.4 Conclusion

This chapter has given a general flavour of the CISG and how it compares to the Sale of Goods Act. As noted at the beginning of this chapter, the UK is increasingly alone among the leading trading nations of the world in not having ratified the CISG. One wonders whether the UK's reluctance is justified;[53] if parties to an international sales contract would prefer their contract to be governed by the Sale of Goods Act, then they can exclude the CISG altogether under Art. 6 – something which could easily be achieved by a standard choice-of-law clause. By not ratifying the CISG, however, the UK is not giving parties to an international sales contract the option of having their contract governed by the CISG (in combination with any rules from the Sale of Goods Act needed to deal with those matters which are not addressed by the CISG) and, crucially, to take any disputes that may arise to the English courts for resolution. It is to be hoped that some sense will eventually prevail and that Parliament will finally ratify the CISG.

[53] For analysis of the benefits for the UK of ratifying, see Hayward, Zeller and Baasch Andersen, The CISG and the United Kingdom: Exploring coherency and private international law, (2018) 67 *ICLQ*. 607.

Part VI

The remedies of the seller

15

Real remedies

15.1 Seller's rights and powers against the goods

Where the buyer defaults in their principal obligation, that is, in payment of the price, the seller has, of course, their personal action on the contract itself. However, if the seller were limited to this remedy, their position would be in many respects unsatisfactory, in particular if the buyer is not merely unwilling but financially unable to pay. The law has, therefore, developed certain 'real' rights or remedies whereby the seller can still look to the goods as something akin to security[1] for payment of the price. In considering these real remedies, four different fact situations must be distinguished.

First, there may be a sale of specific goods in which the property has passed to the buyer and the goods have been delivered to them. Here, the seller has relinquished all rights to look to the goods if the buyer fails to pay the price, and they are relegated to their personal right of action against the buyer. If the seller attempts to enforce their right to the price by seizing the goods from the buyer's possession, the seller's conduct will be a breach of s. 12 of the Act[2] and will doubtless constitute the tort of conversion in English law as well. It is possible for the parties to provide by express agreement that the property in the goods is to remain in the seller even after they have been delivered, in which case the seller may have the right to seize or reclaim the goods in certain events – for instance, if the buyer becomes insolvent before the price is paid. But such a right to reclaim the goods after delivery cannot be implied since it would be very rare for the property to be retained by the seller after delivery unless there is an express provision to this effect. But the use of such express provisions – reservation of title clauses – is widespread and gives rise to difficult questions. It will therefore be necessary to consider their effect, even though they cannot arise by implication of law in the same way that the other real rights arise.

Secondly, there may be a sale of specific goods in which the property has passed to the buyer, but the goods have not yet been delivered. In this case, whether the goods are still in the possession of the seller or have been dispatched to the buyer (but not yet reached them), the law confers on the seller, subject to certain conditions, (a) the power to resell the goods and pass a good title to a third party as well as some incidental powers, and (b) the right to do so vis-à-vis the first buyer. It must be emphasised that these are two very different things because the seller often has the power to pass a good title to a bona fide transferee without having the right to do so; in other words, the resale may constitute a breach of contract as against the first buyer although it validly transfers the property.

[1] These are not forms of security *stricto sensu*, because there is no obligation to register the rights of the seller under these remedies.

[2] *Healing (Sales) Pty Ltd* v *Inglis Electrix Pty Ltd* (1968) 121 CLR 584.

Indeed, as we have already seen, a seller always has the power to transfer a good title to an innocent third party so long as they are in possession of the goods because of s. 24 of the Sale of Goods Act and s. 8 of the Factors Act 1889, but the right to do so is more severely restricted, as will become apparent in due course.

Thirdly, there may be an agreement to sell specific or unascertained goods in which no property has yet passed, but in which the seller is under a personal obligation to deliver certain particular goods and no others. This is always the case where there is an agreement to sell specific goods, and it may also occur in a sale of unascertained goods when there has been sufficient appropriation to place the seller under an obligation to deliver those particular goods, although there has not been sufficient appropriation to pass the property. This may happen, for example, in a c.i.f. contract when the seller gives notice of appropriation, or in a contract for the manufacture of an article where the personal obligation to deliver the goods may come into being before the property passes.[3] In these cases, the law does not need to confer a power of resale on the seller because they still have the property in the goods and can, simply by virtue of this property, transfer a good title to another buyer. But it does not follow that the seller does not need statutory protection from the consequences of exercising this power. For example, if the buyer defaults in payment of the price on the date agreed, the seller, being still the owner of the goods, has power to resell them (and the incidental powers of retaining them, or recovering them from a carrier), but the exercise of these powers might be a breach of contract. The law, therefore, protects the seller from the consequences of availing themselves of these powers, subject to certain conditions.

Fourthly, there may be an agreement to sell unascertained goods in which no property has yet passed and in which there is no obligation to deliver any particular goods. Here no special provisions are needed at all, because the seller clearly has full power to exercise any control over the goods, and such exercise cannot be a breach of contract. For example, if a seller agrees to sell 1,000 tonnes of a certain type of wheat and procures wheat of that description intending to deliver it in performance of the contract, no property passes before appropriation, nor is the seller bound to deliver that particular 1,000 tonnes. If, therefore, the seller resells this 1,000 tonnes to a third party, they can pass a good title to this party, and their action will not be a breach of contract with the first buyer.

It must be said that the Act fails to draw clearly all the above distinctions, with the natural consequence that confusion results. One does not have to agree with all the conclusions of Hohfeld[4] to acknowledge that there is a world of difference between a power and a right of resale, yet even this clear distinction is obscured by the ambiguity of such phrases as 'the seller has the right to do such and such', or 'the seller may do such and such'.[5] An examination of s. 39, which confers the three real rights of the unpaid seller, illustrates some of these problems:

> (1) Subject to this and any other Act, notwithstanding that the property in the goods may have passed to the buyer, the unpaid seller of goods, as such, has by implication of law—

[3] *Laidler* v *Burlinson* (1837) 2 M & W 602, 610–11 per Parke B; *Wait* v *Baker* (1848) 2 Ex 19, 8–9.

[4] See *Fundamental Legal Conceptions as Applied in Judicial Reasoning* (ed. Cook, 1923, Yale University Press), Ch. 1.

[5] Cf. ss. 39, 41 and 48.

(a) a lien on the goods or right to retain them for the price while he is in possession of them;
(b) in case of the insolvency of the buyer, a right of stopping the goods in transit after he has parted with the possession of them;
(c) a right of resale as limited by this Act.

(2) Where the property in goods has not passed to the buyer, the unpaid seller has (in addition to his other remedies) a right of withholding delivery similar to and co-extensive with his rights of lien and stoppage in transit where the property has passed to the buyer.

The first subsection is not likely to give much difficulty, although it is not so clearly drafted as it might have been. It is clear that its object is to confer on the seller not merely the power to deal with the goods, but also the right so to do as against the buyer. This section is for the benefit of the seller and not of the third party, so that a power without a corresponding right would have been useless in this respect. But the second subsection is not so innocuous and could give rise to trouble. The draftsman seems to have thought it necessary to put in the right of withholding delivery, but not the power of resale, because the seller who is still owner does not need a power of resale. But this appears to be a confusion of the right and the power. If s. 39(2) only means to lay down certain powers, then it is totally unnecessary because the owner of the goods has the power of withholding delivery no less than the power of passing a good title to a third person. On the other hand, if s. 39(2) is meant to confer a right to exercise the power, as one would have thought, it follows that the right to resell the goods should have been included as well. The omission of this right might have the remarkable result that an unpaid seller could, as against the buyer, resell the goods in accordance with the Act where the property had passed to the buyer, but could not do so where the property had not passed. But whatever the literal construction of these provisions may be, the courts have shown no inclination to be too literal-minded. On the contrary, it has been affirmed that the seller's rights of resale cannot be greater where the property has passed to the buyer than where it has not.[6]

The second apparent flaw in s. 39(2) is that it states that the owner-seller's right of withholding delivery is similar to and coextensive with the rights of lien and stoppage in transit where the property has passed. This fails to differentiate those cases where the seller is under a personal duty to deliver a particular lot of goods and those cases where there is no such duty. In the latter event, the seller's right of withholding delivery is by no means coextensive with their right of lien. It is a far wider right because it arises without default on the part of the buyer. Obviously, where the seller's duty has not yet become attached to any particular goods, there can be no question of a breach of contract by them simply because they choose to withhold delivery of some goods which they had intended to use in performance of the contract. It is inconceivable that this section should, by a side wind as it were, alter these fundamentals in the law of sale. In proceeding to examine the three real rights of the unpaid seller, then, it must be borne in mind that we are only concerned with the second and third fact situations put above. In other words, we are concerned with those cases where, but for these special rights, the seller would have a power but no right to deal with the goods by withholding delivery or reselling, and those cases where the seller would have neither the power nor the right to do so.

[6] *R V Ward Ltd* v *Bignall* [1967] 1 QB 534, 545.

15.2 Who is an unpaid seller?

These three real rights may only be exercised by an unpaid seller, and the first question is, who exactly is an unpaid seller within the meaning of the Act? The meaning of 'unpaid' is explained by s. 38(1) as follows:

> (1) The seller of goods is an unpaid seller within the meaning of this Act—
> (a) when the whole of the price has not been paid or tendered;
> (b) when a bill of exchange or other negotiable instrument has been received as conditional payment, and the condition on which it was received has not been fulfilled by reason of the dishonour of the instrument or otherwise.

The seller is therefore 'unpaid' within the meaning of the Act even though they have sold on credit, and they remain unpaid until the whole price has been paid or tendered.[7]

> The meaning of a 'seller', for present purposes, is explained by s. 38(2) as follows:In this Part of this Act 'seller' includes any person who is in the position of a seller, as, for instance, an agent of the seller to whom the bill of lading has been indorsed, or a consignor or agent who has himself paid (or is directly responsible for) the price.

If, for example, the seller sells the goods through an agent and the agent has himself paid the price to the seller, or made themselves liable to pay it, then the agent is entitled to exercise any of the rights of the unpaid seller.[8] A buyer who has rejected goods is not, however, in the position of a seller within the meaning of this section and cannot claim any of the unpaid seller's rights in order to secure repayment of the price.[9] It follows that a buyer who is minded to reject goods on the ground that they do not conform to the contract should, if they have paid the price, be careful to do so only if they are satisfied with the solvency of the seller. The rejection of the goods revests the property in the seller, so if they should prove insolvent the buyer will have worsened their position by the rejection.

We can now pass to examine in detail the three real rights conferred by the Act on the unpaid seller.

15.3 Unpaid seller's lien

The seller's lien in ordinary contracts of sale of goods now depends entirely on the Sale of Goods Act, which is quite inconsistent with any suggestion that there may be any equitable lien differing from that provided for in the Act.[10]

The seller's lien is a right to retain the goods until the whole of the price has been paid or tendered. It does not 'strictly speaking give to the seller any property in the goods subject to it'.[11] At common law, a lien does not confer a power of sale, but the unpaid seller has a statutory power and right of sale subject to certain conditions which will be examined in due course. In practice, the lien is often exercised merely as a preliminary to

[7] See, e.g., *McDowall & Neilson's Trustee* v *Snowball Co* (1904) 7 F 35.
[8] *Ireland* v *Livingston* (1872) LR 5 HL 395, 408; *Cassaboglou* v *Gibb* (1883) 11 QBD 797, 804.
[9] *J L Lyons & Co Ltd* v *May & Baker Ltd* [1923] 1 KB 685.
[10] *Transport & General Credit Corpn Ltd* v *Morgan* [1939] 2 All ER 17, 25 per Simonds J. T.
[11] *Lord's Trustee* v *Great Eastern Rly* [1908] 2 KB 54, 63–4 per Fletcher-Moulton LJ, reversed [1909] AC 109 on grounds not affecting this dictum.

a resale of the goods. The seller's right of lien is a qualification upon the duty to deliver the goods laid down by s. 27 and it only arises if three conditions are satisfied.

In the first place, the seller must be an unpaid seller as defined by s. 38. This section has already been set out and it is only necessary to emphasise here that the whole of the price must be paid or tendered before the buyer can claim to have discharged the lien. This raises important questions in connection with instalment contracts and it has been held that, generally speaking, the seller is entitled to exercise their lien over any part of the goods if any part of the price is outstanding. In other words, they are not confined to claiming a lien over those goods to which the unpaid part of the price may be attributed.[12] Reference should also be made here to s. 42, which is as follows:

> Where an unpaid seller has made part delivery of the goods he may exercise his lien . . . on the remainder, unless such part delivery has been made under such circumstances as to show an agreement to waive the lien . . .

Where, however, there is not one contract, but a number of separate contracts for goods to be separately paid for and delivered, it naturally follows that the seller cannot claim a lien over any part of the goods which have been paid for, merely because some others have not been paid for.[13] This would be a general lien, which may be conferred by express contractual terms, but the lien which the Act confers is only a special or particular lien. It does not follow, of course, from the mere fact that the goods are to be delivered and paid for in instalments that there is not still one contract only. On the contrary, the general rule is that a contract for the sale of goods by instalments is still one contract, and the lien may therefore be exercised over any part of the goods.[14]

In the second place, the seller is not entitled to a lien if the goods have been sold on credit. If a seller agrees to allow the buyer credit, this does not necessarily mean that they are prepared to deliver the goods before the price has been paid. It may only mean that the seller is not insisting on immediate payment to which they are *prima facie* entitled if they are ready and willing to deliver. Oddly enough, the Act appears to assume that an agreement as to credit necessarily means an agreement that the buyer shall be entitled to the goods before payment because s. 41(1)(a) says:

> (1) Subject to this Act, the unpaid seller of goods who is in possession of them is entitled to retain possession of them until payment or tender of the price in the following cases, namely—
>
> (a) where the goods have been sold without any stipulation as to credit . . .

Read literally, this would mean that if a person buys goods and asks the seller for time to pay, which the seller grants, the buyer is forthwith, without more, entitled to demand delivery. Yet in granting credit, the seller may have meant no more than that they would not insist on immediate payment and, in this event, the court would no doubt give effect to the intention.

[12] *Ex parte Chalmers* (1873) 8 Ch App 289; *Longbottom & Co Ltd* v *Bass Walker & Co Ltd* [1922] WN 245.

[13] *Merchant Banking Co Ltd* v *Phoenix Bessemer Steel Co Ltd* (1877) 5 Ch D 205, 220.

[14] *Ex parte Chalmers* (1873) 8 Ch App 289.

Although the seller, therefore, has generally no right of lien if they sell the goods on credit, there are two exceptions to this rule, for s. 41(1) proceeds to add two further cases where the lien may be claimed:

(b) where the goods have been sold on credit, but the term of credit has expired;
(c) where the buyer becomes insolvent.

The first of these exceptions clearly enables the seller to claim a lien on the goods where the buyer has not taken advantage of the sale on credit to take possession of the goods. But it also seems to confer a right of lien even where the seller acts wrongfully in refusing to allow the buyer delivery despite the agreement as to credit, although it may be that the buyer could recover damages for non-delivery in this event.

The second exception requires rather closer examination. This clause enables the seller to refuse delivery even where they have agreed to sell the goods on credit (and *a fortiori*, if they have not) if the buyer becomes insolvent. On the meaning of insolvency, reference should be made to s. 61(4):

> A person is deemed to be insolvent within the meaning of this Act if he has either ceased to pay his debts in the ordinary course of business, or he cannot pay his debts as they become due.

It is important to note that the mere fact that the buyer has become insolvent, or even that the buyer has announced their insolvency, does not necessarily amount to a repudiation of the contract.[15] It is, therefore, open to the trustee in bankruptcy or to a sub-buyer to tender the amount due to the seller and claim delivery of the goods. But although the mere fact of insolvency is not therefore a repudiation of the contract, any clear indication by the buyer that they will not proceed with the contract may amount to a repudiation. 'If a person who has entered into a contract of this kind gives to the vendor before he has parted with the goods that which amounts in effect to this notice, "I have parted with all my property, and am unable to pay the price agreed upon", it is equivalent to a repudiation of the contract.'[16] This may be too rigidly stated. In modern cases, the question whether a party is to be treated as having repudiated the contract has been said to depend upon whether the guilty party has made it quite plain that they will not[17] or cannot[18] perform their obligations.[19] In such a case, the seller can treat the contract as at an end and do as they please with the goods and, if they resell at a loss, they can claim in the bankruptcy for the remainder. For present purposes, the important point is that, even if the seller has sold the goods on credit, they can refuse to deliver them if the buyer becomes insolvent, except on payment of the whole price. The seller cannot be compelled to deliver up the goods and be relegated to a right to claim in the insolvency for the price.

The third essential requirement of the unpaid seller's right to a lien is that the seller must be in possession of the goods. The lien is the right of an 'unpaid seller of goods who is in possession of them . . . to retain possession of them'. It is not a right which enables

[15] *In re Phoenix Bessemer Steel Co Ltd* (1876) 4 Ch D 108; *Ex parte Chalmers* (1873) 8 Ch App 289.

[16] *Ex parte Stapleton* (1879) 10 Ch D 586, 590 per Jessel MR.

[17] See, e.g., *Woodar Investment Devpt Ltd* v *Wimpey Construction UK Ltd* [1980] 1 WLR 277.

[18] *The Hazelmoor* [1980] 2 Lloyd's Rep

[19] And the usual burden of proof in civil cases requires the seller to establish the fact of the repudiation on the balance of probabilities – see *Alfred C Toepfer Int* v *Itex Italgrani Export* [1993] 1 Lloyd's Rep 361, which involved a seller's repudiation, but the point equally applies in relation to a buyer's repudiation.

the seller to regain a possession which has been given up.[20] Possession is always a difficult subject, perhaps largely because it has not always been appreciated that possession means different things in different branches of the law.[21] Indeed, it does not always seem to have the same meaning in the same branch of the law. In *Great Eastern Rly* v *Lord's Trustee*,[22] Lord Macnaghten expressly recognised that the seller's lien differs from other liens in certain respects. It seems highly probable, for example, that the degree of control necessary to retain a seller's lien differs from that necessary to retain an innkeeper's or repairer's lien. An innkeeper does not lose their lien although they permit the owner the most complete control over the goods, provided only that they are not taken out of the inn. A repairer may even retain their lien although they permit the owner to take the goods away for a limited purpose every day, provided they are returned at night.[23] It was, indeed, formerly thought that a seller likewise did not lose their lien if they merely delivered the goods to the buyer as their agent or bailee, but this is probably not so today, even if it ever was.[24] There is, however, no reason to doubt that some element of control over the goods by the buyer is not inconsistent with the seller's retention of their lien.

At common law, a seller was only entitled to the lien if the seller was still in possession in the capacity as seller, and they lost their right of lien if they only retained possession as agent or bailee of the buyer. But the law was altered by the 1893 Act, and s. 41(2) of the 1979 Act provides that:

> The seller may exercise his lien . . . notwithstanding that he is in possession of the goods as agent, or bailee . . . for the buyer.

But if the seller agrees to hold the goods as agent or bailee, it may be held that the seller has waived their lien, the possibility of which is not excluded by this subsection.

The seller's lien is twice said by the Act to be a lien for the price,[25] so presumably the seller is not entitled *as seller* to claim a lien for storage charges or the like. The decision of the House of Lords in *Somes* v *British Empire Shipping Co*[26] is usually cited as laying down that the seller has no lien for storage charges in any circumstances, but in fact the case only decided that the seller cannot claim a lien in respect of storage charges which arise as a result of the seller's exercise of their lien for the price. Indeed, the case also decides that the seller is not entitled to recover from the buyer the cost or expenses incurred by the seller in maintaining their possession for their sole benefit. But the case is not to be taken to decide that such costs or expenses can never be recovered from the buyer where they do derive some benefit from them, and, in particular, where they are incurred before the buyer demands possession, and therefore before the seller is strictly exercising

[20] Scottish courts have held that where the seller retakes possession from the buyer, the former does not necessarily also regain the right of lien: *London Scottish Transport* v *Tyres (Scotland) Ltd* 1957 SLT (Sh Ct) 48; *Hostess Mobile Catering* v *Archibald Scott Ltd* 1981 SC 185. But a lien is not extinguished if the holder is induced to give up possession by improper means: *Goudie* v *Mulholland* 2000 SC 61.

[21] This seems to have been recognised by the House of Lords: see *R* v *Warner* [1969] 2 AC 256.

[22] [1909] AC 109, 115.

[23] *Albermarle Supply Co* v *Hind & Co* [1923] 1 KB 307.

[24] See *Tempest* v *Fitzgerald* (1820) 3 B & Ald 680. But this was a case of a buyer exercising some rights of dominion by permission of and under the supervision of the seller (exercising horse on seller's land).

[25] Section 39(1)(a) and s. 41(1).

[26] (1860) 8 HLC 338.

their lien.[27] However, it is not wholly clear whether the seller has any lien on the goods for such additional costs or expenses. If the goods are actually improved, or at least if they are saved from damage by the expenditure incurred, it seems that in principle a lien could arise for these expenses even though the lien conferred by the Act is confined to a lien for the price. But the general principle is that a bailee cannot claim a lien (except by express contract) unless they have in some way improved the goods, so that mere storage charges would not, in any event, give rise to a lien.[28]

15.3.1 Loss of lien

The seller loses their lien in one of four ways. First, if the price is paid or tendered, the seller ceases to be an unpaid seller and therefore loses their lien. But (apart from any question of waiver to be considered shortly) they are entitled to retain possession until payment or tender. If this is so, it might seem that payment or tender is, strictly speaking, a condition precedent to the buyer's right to claim delivery, but as we have seen s. 28 expressly says that payment and delivery are concurrent conditions. It is usually inferred from this that actual tender of the price is not necessary provided the buyer is ready and willing to pay the price and there is judicial authority to the effect that this at any rate is the limit of the seller's duty to deliver.[29] But if the buyer sues for non-delivery without making tender it would usually be arguable that the seller has waived the need for such a tender by making it quite plain that they are not going to deliver the goods in any event.[30]

The remaining three ways in which the seller loses their lien are set out in s. 43 which runs:

> (1) The unpaid seller of goods loses his lien . . . in respect of them—
> (a) when he delivers the goods to a carrier or other bailee . . . for the purpose of transmission to the buyer without reserving the right of disposal of the goods;
> (b) when the buyer or his agent lawfully obtains possession of the goods;
> (c) by waiver of the lien . . .

We have already seen that for some purposes delivery to a carrier is deemed to be delivery to the buyer, but this section clearly differentiates between these two different possibilities and, as will be seen shortly, the seller's right of stoppage in transit depends on this very distinction. Although the seller loses their lien on delivery to the carrier, they may still have the right of stoppage in transit, but it is all the same important to decide when the goods pass into the possession of the carrier, because the extent of the right of lien differs from that of stoppage in transit. In particular, the seller can only stop the goods if the buyer is insolvent, whereas their right of lien only depends on the absence of a stipulation as to credit. It follows that the seller may well have a right of lien in circumstances in which they will have no right of stoppage once the goods have been delivered to the carrier.

The meaning of a right of disposal has already been discussed in considering s. 19 and, if it means the same thing here as it does in that section, it follows that a seller who takes a bill of lading in their own name will have a right of lien until they transfer the bill. It has, however, been argued that right of disposal means something different here, namely

[27] See *China Pacific SA* v *Food Corpn of India* [1981] AC 939, 962–3 per Lord Diplock.
[28] See, e.g., *Re Southern Livestock Producers Ltd* [1963] 3 All ER 801.
[29] *Levey & Co Ltd* v *Goldberg* [1922] 1 KB 688.
[30] *See Peter Turnbull & Co Ltd* v *Mundas Trading Co Ltd* (1954) 90 CLR 235.

a right of disposal of the *possession*.[31] The point is a difficult one. On the one hand, it would be strange to find a different meaning attributed to the same phrase in a similar context in two parts of the same Act. On the other hand, by s. 39(1)(a) the seller only has a lien while they are in possession of the goods and delivery to a carrier normally means that the seller no longer has possession. Moreover, by s. 39(2) the seller's right to a lien is the same whether or not property has passed, but if the seller is held to 'reserve the right of disposal' within the meaning of s. 43 by taking a bill of lading in their own name, they will not lose the lien on shipment, but only when property passes. The answer to these difficulties probably lies in the principle that possession of a bill of lading (at least where it is in the name of the party in possession) confers possession of the goods. As a practical matter, it seems clear that shipping the goods will not normally deprive the seller of the lien if the goods are deliverable to them (or their order) under the bill of lading. In the absence of any contrary agreement, the seller may decline to transfer the bill of lading except against payment of the price.[32] This difficult point of interpretation has arisen largely because the practice of treating the shipping documents as conferring possession and property has become so much more widespread that it now seems inconsistent with commercial practice to treat shipment of the goods as a delivery to the buyer.

Since possession is essential to the maintenance of a lien, it naturally follows that when the buyer or their agent lawfully obtains possession of the goods the lien is lost. It is submitted that 'lawfully' here means 'with the consent of the seller', so that even if the goods are obtained in circumstances amounting to a criminal offence, provided that it is with the consent of the seller, the lien will be lost. It is only by such an interpretation that the section can be brought into harmony with s. 25(1) of the Sale of Goods Act and s. 9 of the Factors Act which, as we have seen, enable a buyer in possession with the consent of the seller to pass a good title to a third party. Although it may be a little odd to say that a possession obtained in circumstances amounting to an offence may be 'lawfully' obtained, this interpretation seems more consonant with the rest of the Act and would probably be adopted.[33] But if the buyer obtains possession of the goods without the consent of the seller, the lien is not lost and, even if the property has passed to the buyer, it appears that they cannot pass a good title free from the lien to a third party.

It has already been suggested that the seller's lien cannot avail them as against third parties taking in good faith even if they deliver the goods to the buyer merely as their agent or bailee. But it may be that in such a case, the seller will retain the lien as against the buyer, a point which is only likely to assume practical importance in somewhat unusual circumstances.

[31] *Schmitthoff, The Sale of Goods* (2nd edn, 1952, Sweet & Maxwell), pp. 158–9.

[32] If, by the bill of lading, the goods are deliverable to the buyer or their order, it would doubtless be more difficult for the seller to contend that they retained possession sufficient to maintain a lien, but the practice of demanding payment in exchange for the documents in international sales is so well established that, in the absence of a clear contrary intention, it would probably still be held that the seller could do this.

[33] See, e.g., *Du Jardin* v *Beadman* [1952] 2 QB 712, which is inconsistent with any suggestion that the lien would bind a bona fide purchaser to whom the buyer disposes of the goods after having obtained possession by a criminal trick or fraud. This is also confirmed by the New Zealand decision in *Jeffcott* v *Andrews Motors Ltd* [1960] NZLR 721, holding that the bona fide purchaser is protected without deciding whether the lien survives or not. Although it may be argued that this does not preclude the possibility of the lien surviving as between seller and buyer in such circumstances, it is difficult to see how the seller could enforce the lien or what significance the survival of the lien could have. But it is, perhaps, arguable that if the lien does survive, a disposition by the buyer to a third party who takes with notice of the circumstances will not override the seller's lien.

The fourth way in which the seller may lose their lien is by waiver. In a certain sense, delivery of the goods to the buyer on credit is but an instance of waiver of the lien, but the seller may waive their lien without giving up possession at all. If, for example, the seller should ask the buyer's permission to retain possession by way of temporary loan, they may be held to have waived their lien. Although s. 41(2) says that the seller may exercise their lien notwithstanding that they are in possession as the buyer's bailee or agent, the subsection does not say that the seller may exercise their lien notwithstanding that they have impliedly waived their lien. And, if the seller, having originally refused to sell on credit, were later to agree to the buyer taking possession before payment, this would presumably amount to a waiver of the lien and the seller would not be able to change their mind again and insist on the lien after all.[34] Moreover, if the seller wrongly deals with the goods in a manner inconsistent with the buyer's rights, they are held to have waived their lien and cannot therefore plead lack of payment or tender if sued by the buyer in conversion.[35]

Section 43(1)(c), dealing with waiver, is probably to be read subject to s. 41(1)(b) and (c), which confer a lien where the goods are sold on credit but the term of credit has expired, or where the buyer has become insolvent, since both these clauses contemplate a situation in which there is a waiver followed by later events causing the lien to revive. If, therefore, the seller originally refuses credit but later waives their lien, it is probable that the subsequent insolvency of the buyer will cause the lien to revive if the seller is still in possession of the goods. This, at any rate, was the position at common law.[36]

The seller's right of lien is not affected by any sub-sale or other disposition of the goods by the buyer unless they have assented thereto. The meaning of this has already been considered. It must also be remembered that if the seller allows the buyer to have possession of the documents of title or of the goods themselves, a transfer of these to an innocent third party will defeat the right of lien.

A seller who has once lost their lien does not regain it merely because they obtain possession of the goods once more.[37] But a seller who exercises their right of stoppage in transit is in effect restored to their former position and regains their lien.

The exercise of the seller's right of lien does not of itself rescind the contract of sale. This naturally follows from the fact that failure by the buyer to pay the price at the agreed time is not a breach of condition which justifies the seller in repudiating the contract. This question will be more fully examined later.[38]

15.4 Unpaid seller's right of stoppage in transit

The seller's right of stoppage in transit is set out in s. 44:

> Subject to this Act, when the buyer of goods becomes insolvent, the unpaid seller who has parted with the possession of the goods has the right of stopping them in transit, that is to say, he may resume possession of the goods as long as they are in course of transit, and may retain them until payment or tender of the price.

[34] Cf. *Bank of Africa* v *Salisbury Gold Mining Co Ltd* [1892] AC 281, 284 per Lord Watson.
[35] *Jones* v *Tarleton* (1842) 9 M & W 675; *Mulliner* v *Florence* (1878) 3 QBD 484.
[36] *Townley* v *Crump* (1835) 4 M & W 58.
[37] *Valpy* v *Gibson* (1847) 4 CB 837; *Pennington* v *Motor Reliance Works Ltd* [1923] 1 KB 127; London *Scottish Transport* v *Tyres (Scotland) Ltd* 1957 SLT (Sh Ct) 48; *Hostess Mobile Catering* v *Archibald Scott Ltd* 1981 SC 185.
[38] See below, at section 15.4.3.

It makes no difference whether or not the property has passed to the buyer.[39] Where the property has not passed the seller has, by virtue of their ownership, the power to stop the goods, and the Act makes the exercise of this power rightful as against the buyer; where the property has passed, the Act confers both the power and the right to stop.

It had been said that 'the courts look with great favour on the right of stoppage in transit on account of its intrinsic justice',[40] and this is certainly borne out by judicial pronouncements.[41] It seems to accord with commercial morality that the seller should be treated as, in a sense, a secured creditor, looking to the goods as their security, until they have finally passed into the possession of the buyer. In modern times, the development of the system of payment against documents and, in particular, of payment by bankers' commercial credits has greatly reduced the importance of the right of stoppage.[42] Where the price is to be paid in this way, the seller has little to fear from the threat of the buyer's insolvency because the seller will retain the control of the goods through the documents of title until they are paid. The law relating to stoppage in transit is therefore only important where the sale is on credit and there are virtually no modern cases on the subject, though the possibility of the right being needed must sometimes arise.

15.4.1 When right of stoppage arises

Before the seller can exercise their right of stoppage in transit, three conditions must be satisfied: first, the seller must be an unpaid seller within the meaning of the Act; secondly, the buyer must be insolvent; and thirdly, the goods must be in the course of transit. The first two of these have already been considered and it remains now to examine the meaning of the expression 'course of transit'.

Section 45 states that the goods are in transit when they have passed out of the possession of the seller into the possession of a carrier,[43] but have not yet reached the possession of the buyer. Little difficulty is generally encountered with the question, 'When does the transit commence?', but one ambiguity must be cleared up. If the carrier is the seller's own agent no question of the right of stoppage arises at all, for the goods, while in the possession of such agent, are still sufficiently in the possession of the seller to enable them to exercise their lien and they need not invoke the less extensive right of stoppage. The right of stoppage only arises when the carrier is an independent contractor who holds possession of the goods on their own behalf, as carrier.[44]

It is now necessary to examine the question, 'when does the transit end?' In the first place, it must be clearly understood that, although s. 32(1) says that delivery to a carrier

39 Section 39(2).

40 Chalmers, *The Sale of Goods* (13th edn, 1975, Butterworth), p. 124. This passage was excised from later editions.

41 See, e.g., *Booth SS Co Ltd* v *Cargo Fleet Iron Co Ltd* [1916] 2 KB 570, 580.

42 See Chapter 13.

43 It has been held in New Zealand that the Post Office is not a carrier for this purpose and there is no right of stoppage over goods consigned by post: *Postmaster-General* v *W H Jones & Co (London) Ltd* [1957] NZLR 829. The effect of the Regulation of Investigatory Powers Act 2000, s. 1(1) is that an attempt by the seller to intercept the goods once they have come into the hands of the Post Office would be a criminal offence.

44 In *Badische Anilin und Soda Fabrik* v *Basle Chemical Works Bindschender* [1898] AC 200, it was held that the Post Office was the buyer's agent, but, having regard to the rule stated in the previous footnote, even if this view were correct, it is in the present context of academic interest only. The rule for private postal carriers is presumably the same as that for other carriers, namely that the right of stoppage will only be needed when the carrier is the buyer's agent.

is *prima facie* deemed to be delivery to the buyer, this is only a constructive and not an actual delivery, and it is only an actual delivery which ends the right of stoppage.[45] If this were not so, of course, s. 32(1) would be inconsistent with the whole concept of stoppage in transit because this right postulates delivery to a carrier, but not delivery to the buyer. This much is clear from s. 45(1):

> Goods are deemed to be in course of transit from the time when they are delivered to a carrier, or other bailee . . . for the purpose of transmission to the buyer, until the buyer, or his agent in that behalf, takes delivery of them from the carrier or other bailee . . .

Although, therefore, delivery to a carrier is not in itself delivery to the buyer for this purpose, there is no reason why the buyer should not be able to show that, in the particular circumstances of the case, the carrier was their agent and that, therefore, the transit was at an end, just as the seller can show that the carrier was their agent and that the transit had never started. This possibility is expressly recognised by s. 45(1), which refers to the buyer or their 'agent', and by s. 45(5) which says:

> When goods are delivered to a ship chartered by the buyer it is a question depending on the circumstances of the particular case, whether they are in the possession of the master as a carrier, or as agent to the buyer.

If the ship is owned by the buyer, clearly delivery of the goods to the master is a delivery to the buyer's agent which terminates the transit. Likewise, if the ship is demised to the buyer so as to vest complete control over the vessel in the buyer, the master is treated as being employed by the buyer and then delivery to the ship is delivery to the buyer. But if the ship is merely chartered for a voyage or a fixed period, as is the usual case, the master remains the employee of the shipowner and does not become the agent of the buyer, so that delivery to the ship does not end the right of stoppage. If the seller is the owner of the ship no question of the right of stoppage arises at all, of course, because the goods are still in the possession of the seller while on the ship.

The mere fact that the contract is for the sale of goods f.o.b. does not exclude the right of stoppage. Although the seller's duty in a contract f.o.b. may be complete when they have placed the goods on board, this does not mean that they are not still interested in them and that they cannot subsequently stop them if the buyer becomes insolvent.[46]

Similarly, the transit is not at an end merely because it is the buyer who gives the instructions for the dispatch of the goods for part or all of the voyage. 'Wherever it is part of the bargain between the vendor and the vendee that the transit shall last up to a certain time, the transit continues until that time has arrived.'[47] But if the buyer requests delivery to a certain place or person, the transit does not continue merely because the buyer intends ultimately to give, but does in fact give, fresh directions for the dispatch of the goods elsewhere. The law on this point was summed up by Brett LJ (as he then was) in *Bethell & Co Ltd* v *Clark & Co Ltd*:[48]

> Where the transit is a transit which has been caused either by the terms of the contract or by the directions of the purchaser to the vendor, the right of stoppage *in transitu* exists.

[45] *Ex parte Rosevear China Clay Co Ltd* (1879) 11 Ch D 560, 569.
[46] Ibid.
[47] *Kendall* v *Marshall, Stevens & Co Ltd* (1883) 11 QBD 356, 369 per Bowen LJ.
[48] (1888) 20 QBD 615, 617. Cf. *Lyons* v *Hoffnung* (1890) 15 App Cas 396.

> But, if the goods are not in the hands of the carrier by reason either of the terms of the contract or of the directions of the purchaser to the vendor, but are *in transitu* afterwards in consequence of fresh directions given by the purchaser for a new transit, then such transit is no part of the original transit and the right to stop is gone. So also, if the purchaser gives orders that the goods shall be sent to a particular place, there to be kept till he gives fresh orders as to their destination to a new carrier, the original transit is at an end when they have reached that place.

It follows that, in the ordinary way, if the goods pass through successive stages of transit from one carrier to another in pursuance of the contract or of later directions given by the buyer to the seller, the transit continues and the seller retains their right to stop the goods until they reach their ultimate destination.[49] But if the buyer intercepts the goods at some stage in the course of the transit the right to stop is lost. Thus, s. 45(2) says:

> If the buyer or his agent in that behalf obtains delivery of the goods before their arrival at the appointed destination, the transit is at an end.

Where, therefore, the seller of goods contracted to deliver them free of charge at the buyer's premises in London, but the carriers delivered the goods at dock warehouses in accordance with instructions from the buyer, it was held that there was no right to stop.[50]

The transit is normally brought to an end by actual delivery of the goods to the buyer, but the transit is also determined if the carrier in effect attorns to the buyer, or acknowledges to them on arrival at the destination that it holds the goods for the buyer, or if it wrongfully refuses to deliver to the buyer. Thus, s. 45(3) and (6) say:

> (3) If, after the arrival of the goods at the appointed destination, the carrier or other bailee . . . acknowledges to the buyer, or his agent, that he holds the goods on his behalf and continues in possession of them as bailee . . . for the buyer, or his agent, the transit is at an end, and it is immaterial that a further destination for the goods may have been indicated by the buyer.
>
> (6) Where the carrier or other bailee . . . wrongfully refuses to deliver the goods to the buyer, or his agent in that behalf, the transit is deemed to be at an end.

Thus, where goods were sent by rail to a particular station, where the consignee signed a receipt but did not take away the goods, the transit was held to have ended, making a subsequent stop notice too late.[51] If, however, the buyer rejects the goods the transit is not at an end, for s. 45(4) says:

> (4) If the goods are rejected by the buyer, and the carrier or other bailee . . . continues in possession of them, the transit is not deemed to be at an end, even if the seller has refused to receive them back.

It is not clear on the face of the Act whether subs. (4) is to be read subject to subs. (3) or vice versa. If the carrier informs the buyer that the goods have arrived and that it holds them on the buyer's behalf and, subsequently, the buyer inspects the goods and rejects them, does the transit continue or not? As the Act is doubtful, resort may be had to the decisions at common law, and these seem to show that in such a case the transit is not

[49] *Reddall* v *Union Castle Mail SS Co* (1915) 84 LJKB 360.

[50] *Plischke & Sohne GmbH* v *Allison Bros Ltd* [1936] 2 All ER 1009. Cf. *Valpy* v *Gibson* (1847) 4 CB 837; *Reddall* v *Union Castle Mail SS Co*, (1915) 84 LJKB 360.

[51] *Muir* v *Rankin* (1905) 13 SLT 60.

ended because the carrier's attornment (or acknowledgment) to the buyer only transfers the possession to the buyer on the assumption that the buyer assents thereto. Where the buyer rejects the goods, the attornment[52] (or acknowledgment) has no effect and the right to stop continues.

As with the seller's lien, the right of stoppage may generally be exercised over part only of the goods where some other part has been delivered. Under s. 45(7):

> Where part delivery of the goods has been made to the buyer, or his agent in that behalf, the remainder of the goods may be stopped in transit, unless such part delivery has been made under such circumstances as to show an agreement to give up possession of the whole of the goods.[53]

It has been held in a Scots case that if the carrier ignores the stop notice and delivers to the buyer, the stoppage is defeated and the buyer's trustee in sequestration can claim the goods; however, the carrier is liable in damages to the seller.[54]

15.4.2 Transfer of the bill of lading

Somewhat surprisingly, the Act does not make it clear whether the transfer of the bill of lading to the buyer is by itself sufficient to terminate the seller's right of stoppage. It seems implicit in the Sale of Goods Act that mere transfer of the bill of lading to the buyer does not prevent the seller from stopping the goods in transit. Both s. 39(1) (which says that the seller's real rights exist even though property may have passed) and s. 47(2) (which postulates a transfer of the bill of lading to the buyer and further dealings with the bill by the buyer) seem to assume that the right may continue even after the bill is transferred to the buyer. Yet it is surprising that there are no modern cases on the subject, and it may be that in practice, businessmen simply do not believe that they have the right to reclaim the goods from the carrier once they have transferred the bill of lading to a buyer even though they have bought on credit, and become insolvent before paying the price. Despite modern commercial practice, it must still sometimes happen that buyers buy on credit but become insolvent while the goods are at sea, and in this situation the right to stop could still be of practical importance.

But although the mere transfer of the bill of lading to the buyer may not defeat the right to stop the goods, the right may be lost by sub-dealings with the goods (or documents) by the buyer. Considerable difficulties have arisen here and it is essential to keep two points clearly distinct. The first question which arises is whether the sub-buyer or pledgee is entitled to possession of the goods free from the seller's right of stoppage, and the second question is whether, assuming the sub-buyer or pledgee to be so entitled, the seller can exercise their right of stoppage over the money paid by the sub-buyer in the event of a sale, or over the goods subject to the pledgee's rights in the event of a pledge. To take the latter possibility first, there can be no doubt that the seller can still exercise the right of stoppage, notwithstanding that the goods have been pledged, but, of course, the seller can only do so subject to the rights of the pledgee. In other words, the seller

[52] *Bolton* v *Lancs & Yorks Rly* (1866) LR 1 CP 431; cf. *Taylor* v *Great Eastern Rly* (1901) 17 TLR 394.
[53] For an example, see *Mechan* v *North-Eastern Railway* 1911 SC 1348.
[54] Ibid.

can claim the return of the goods from the carrier if the seller is prepared to pay off the pledgee. What is more, even if the pledgee obtains the goods in virtue of their pledge and sells them, the seller is entitled to claim that the balance of the price shall be paid directly to them and not to the insolvent buyer. This was decided by the House of Lords in *Kemp* v *Falk*[55] and the decision has been incorporated in s. 47(2)(b) of the Act, which says that, where the documents of title to goods which the seller would otherwise be entitled to stop have been pledged, 'the unpaid seller's right of lien or stoppage in transit can only be exercised subject to the rights of the transferee'. It is true that this section is mainly concerned to give priority to the rights of the pledgee over those of the seller (hence the word 'only') but it seems necessarily to recognise that the right of stoppage may be exercised in these circumstances.

The problem is more difficult in the case of a sub-sale by the buyer. In *Ex parte Golding Davies & Co Ltd*[56] A sold goods to B and B resold them to C before they were dispatched by A. The bill of lading was taken in C's name, but before it was transferred to C, B became insolvent. C not yet having paid the price, A claimed that he was entitled to intercept the money before it reached B; that is, in effect, A claimed the right of stoppage over the money. It was held by the Court of Appeal that A was entitled to do this.

In *Kemp* v *Falk*[57] Lord Selborne clearly thought that *Ex parte Golding Davies & Co Ltd*[58] was wrongly decided, but the other members of the House in that case expressed no opinion on the point. *Ex parte Golding Davies & Co Ltd* is also not easy to reconcile with *Berndtson* v *Strang*.[59] In this case, the Chancery Court of Appeal held that where goods are damaged in transit, the unpaid seller has no right to the proceeds of an insurance policy covering the goods. The right of stoppage 'is a right to stop the goods in whatever state they are. If they arrive injured and damaged in bulk or quality the right to stop *in transitu* is so far impaired.'[60] Presumably, it follows that if the goods are entirely lost in transit the right to stop is similarly lost, yet there seems no difference in principle between such a case and a resale of the goods.[61] But even if *Ex parte Golding Davies & Co Ltd*[62] was rightly decided at common law, the question must still be answered whether it survives the Sale of Goods Act, and the answer to this, it is conceived, must be 'no'. Section 47(2)(a) says quite clearly that if the bill of lading is transferred by way of resale to a third party taking in good faith and for value, the unpaid seller's right of stoppage 'is defeated'. No mention is made of the possibility of transferring the right from the goods to the money. It should also be borne in mind that even if the above submissions are wrong, and *Ex parte Golding Davies & Co Ltd* does represent the modern law, yet there can be no shadow of a claim of stoppage when the purchase price from the sub-purchaser has actually been paid over to the insolvent buyer. This would be a blatant attempt to obtain full payment of a debt from an insolvent debtor and could not be permitted.

[55] (1882) 7 App Cas 573.
[56] (1880) 13 Ch D 628.
[57] (1882) 7 App Cas 573, 577–8.
[58] (1880) 13 Ch D 628.
[59] (1868) 3 Ch App 588.
[60] Per Lord Cairns at p. 591. But in most c.i.f. and in many f.o.b. contracts, the policy would be taken out by the seller and he would therefore be able to claim the proceeds himself.
[61] Presumably the result would be different if the damage or loss occurred after the seller had given notice of exercise of the right of stoppage.
[62] (1880) 13 Ch D 628.

15.4.3 Position as between vendor and carrier

If a carrier, to whom a notice of stoppage has been sent, wrongly delivers the goods to the buyer, the carrier is liable for conversion to the vendor, so it is of the utmost importance that the relationship between the carrier and the seller should be clearly defined. But the Act does no more than lay down the methods which the seller may adopt of exercising the right of stoppage, and imposes the burden of redelivery on the seller. Section 46 says:

> (1) The unpaid seller may exercise his right of stoppage in transit either by taking actual possession of the goods, or by giving notice of his claim to the carrier or other bailee . . . in whose possession the goods are.
> (2) The notice may be given either to the person in actual possession of the goods or to his principal.
> (3) If given to the principal, the notice is ineffective unless given at such time and under such circumstances that the principal, by the exercise of reasonable diligence, may communicate it to his servant or agent in time to prevent a delivery to the buyer.
> (4) When notice of stoppage in transit is given by the seller to the carrier, or other bailee . . . in possession of the goods, he must redeliver the goods to, or according to the directions of, the seller; and the expenses of such redelivery must be borne by the seller.

The carrier has a lien on the goods for the freight due, and this takes priority over the seller's right of stoppage. Hence, the carrier can refuse to redeliver the goods to the seller unless the latter is first prepared to discharge the amount of the freight. But any general lien which the carrier may have by contract is postponed to the seller's right of stoppage unless the seller was a party to the contract which conferred this general lien.[63] A general lien, that is, a right to retain the goods for other freights due upon other transactions, can only arise by express contract or from general usage, and such a lien, apart from contract, cannot affect the rights of the consignor.[64]

In some respects, the carrier's lien as against the unpaid seller is of a peculiar nature, as it confers on the carrier the positive right of action to recover the amount of the freight. Moreover, an unpaid seller who stops the goods in transit is under a duty to give the carrier instructions as to the disposal or return of the goods and, if the seller fails to do so, the carrier is not responsible for the consequences.[65]

As is the case with the seller's lien, the exercise of the right of stoppage in transit does not of itself rescind the contract of sale. The exercise of the right to stop enables the seller to resume possession of the goods and to retain them until payment or tender of the price.[66] It follows that if the buyer's trustee in bankruptcy chooses to tender the whole price, the seller is bound to accept it and redispatch the goods to them, unless indeed there are grounds for inferring a repudiation of the contract by the buyer.

15.5 Unpaid seller's right of resale

It has already been pointed out that the seller's *power* of resale must be carefully distinguished from their *right* of resale. The seller has the power to resell the goods (a) if they still have the property in the goods, or (b) if, even though the property has passed, they are

[63] See *US Steel Products Co Ltd* v *Great Western Rly* [1916] 1 AC 189.
[64] Ibid.
[65] *Booth SS Co Ltd* v *Cargo Fleet Iron Co Ltd* [1916] 2 KB 570.
[66] Section 44.

in possession of the goods within s. 24 of the Sale of Goods Act or s. 8 of the Factors Act, or (c) if, even though the property has passed, the seller has exercised their right of lien or stoppage in transit. The first case does not call for comment, and the second has already been fully discussed, but the third needs to be briefly considered. Section 48(2) says:

> Where an unpaid seller who has exercised his right of lien . . . or stoppage in transit re-sells the goods, the buyer acquires a good title to them as against the original buyer.

This presumably means that, even though the property has passed to the first buyer, if the seller exercises their right of lien or stoppage, they have the power to resell the goods passing a good title to a third party although they could not have done so under s. 24 of the Sale of Goods Act and s. 8 of the Factors Act. In other words, this subsection envisages the possibility of a resale by a seller not in possession of the goods, and is to that extent wider than these two sections.

It is now necessary to examine the seller's right of resale. The seller is entitled as against the buyer to resell the goods in any of the following circumstances:

1. If the seller's obligation to deliver has not yet crystallised into an obligation to deliver any specific goods. Here it is clear that the seller incurs no liability if they resell the goods for the simple reason that it cannot be said which are 'the goods' which the seller must deliver.

2. If the buyer repudiates the contract, it is again clear on principle that the seller can accept the repudiation and may resell the goods if they choose.[67] It is, of course, immaterial whether or not the property has passed to the first buyer. Refusal to accept the goods by the buyer is *prima facie* a repudiation of the contract, and if the seller accepts that repudiation, the contract is thereby rescinded. Any title which has passed to the buyer will revest in the seller, and the seller may resell the goods and sue for damages for non-acceptance. If, however, the seller refuses to accept the repudiation, then *prima facie* they are not entitled to resell the goods. This is because either the property will have passed to the buyer or the seller will still be bound to transfer it to the buyer. In this situation, the seller can only resell if authorised to do so by s. 48(3) or (4), which are discussed below.[68] As we have seen, the mere fact that the buyer is late in paying the price is not necessarily a repudiation of the contract, but may only amount to a breach of warranty for which the seller may recover damages, so late payment of itself does not justify a resale by the seller unless s. 48(3) or (4) is satisfied, except in cases where time of payment is of the essence.

3. In the third place, the seller has a right of resale if the seller has expressly reserved this right in the original contract, on default by the buyer. In this event, s. 48(4) comes into play:

   > Where the seller expressly reserves the right of re-sale in case the buyer should make default, and on the buyer making default re-sells the goods, the original contract of sale is rescinded, but without prejudice to any claim the seller may have for damages.

[67] See, e.g., *Compagnie de Renflouement* v *W Seymour Plant Sales* [1981] 2 Lloyd's Rep 466, 482.

[68] *R V Ward Ltd* v *Bignall* [1967] 1 QB 534.

As we have seen, s. 48(1) states that:

> Subject to this section, a contract of sale is not rescinded by the mere exercise by an unpaid seller of his right of lien . . . or stoppage in transit.

4. Lastly, the unpaid seller is given a right of resale if the buyer fails to pay the price, and the goods are perishable or, in other cases, if they give notice to the buyer that they intend to resell, and the buyer still does not pay the price due. Section 48(3) states that:

   > Where the goods are of a perishable nature, or where the unpaid seller gives notice to the buyer of his intention to re-sell, and the buyer does not within a reasonable time pay or tender the price, the unpaid seller may re-sell the goods and recover from the original buyer damages for any loss occasioned by his breach of contract.

The first of these four possibilities has already been discussed and the second does not need enlarging upon here. The question what exactly amounts to a repudiation of the contract is never an easy one, but it is a question which belongs more properly to the general law of contract. It is enough here to say that the party claiming that the contract has been repudiated must show that the other party has made it quite plain that they will not[69] or cannot[70] perform their obligations. The third and fourth cases, however, require further consideration.

15.5.1 Resale under s. 48(3) or (4)

It will be noted that s. 48(4) explicitly provides that, where the seller resells in the exercise of an express power of resale in the contract, then 'the original contract of sale is rescinded'. Section 48(3) contains no such provision to cover the case where the goods are perishable or where the seller resells after notice. However, the Court of Appeal in *R V Ward Ltd* v *Bignall*[71] confirmed that the same outcome would arise in this context. In this case, the plaintiffs sold two used cars to the defendant, who almost at once repudiated the purchase and refused to pay or take delivery of the goods. The sellers at first wrote to the buyer insisting that the property in both cars had passed to him and that he was therefore liable for the price. But the sellers also gave notice that if the buyer did not pay the price within five days they would resell the cars. The buyer did not pay and the sellers only succeeded in reselling one car. They therefore sued for the price of the other plus their loss on the resale of the first car. The court held that the sellers were not entitled to the price of the remaining car as the resale of the first had rescinded the original contract. Hence, the buyer was only liable for damages for non-acceptance, assessed in the usual way as the difference between the contract price and the market price of the remaining car.

The court explained away the difference in the wording of s. 48(3) and (4) on somewhat ingenious grounds. Failure by the buyer to pay the price is not *per se* a breach which justifies repudiation, but once the seller has given notice to the buyer to pay, time is made of the essence of the contract. Hence, failure to pay now amounts to repudiation and the seller accepts this by reselling the goods. The resale therefore necessarily amounts to a rescission of the contract, property revests in the seller and the buyer is no longer liable

[69] *Woodar Investments Ltd* v *Wimpey Construction UK Ltd* [1977] 1 WLR 277.
[70] *The Hazelmoor* [1980] 2 Lloyd's Rep
[71] [1967] 1 QB 534.

for the price. If, however, the contract contains an express provision for resale, then such a resale (apart from s. 48(4)) would not necessarily amount to rescission. For in this event, the resale would be an exercise of a contractual right and not an acceptance of repudiation by the buyer. Therefore, s. 48(4) expressly provides that resale is a rescission of the contract. Thus, the reason for the contrast is not that s. 48(3) is intended to have a different result – in both cases the resale rescinds the original contract – but the express provision to this effect is not necessary in s. 48(3), while it was thought necessary in s. 48(4).

In order to avoid confusion, it must now be pointed out that the statutory use of the term 'rescission' in s. 48 is out of line with the modern usage adopted by the House of Lords in *Johnson* v *Agnew*.[72] In this case, a sharp line was drawn for English law between *rescission* of a contract *ab initio* on grounds of contractual invalidity such as fraud or duress, and *termination* of the contract for breach. Only the former is strictly 'rescission' which has retrospective effect.[73] Termination for breach is not retrospective in operation, and leaves standing, not only claims for damages for the breach itself but also claims which have already accrued due at the time the contract is terminated. Now, clearly, a failure to pay the price, and a subsequent resale of the goods by the seller under s. 48(3) or (4), involve termination and not rescission in this terminology. The seller still has a claim for damages for breach of contract, and accrued claims may survive the termination. At the same time, it must be pointed out that even termination must have some retrospective effects in a contract of sale of goods, a point which the House of Lords appears to have overlooked in *Johnson* v *Agnew*, and perhaps even more seriously in *Hyundai Heavy Industries Co Ltd* v *Papadopoulos*.[74] The termination of a contract of sale of goods almost always involves the restoration of the property in the goods from the buyer to the seller if the property has already passed, and to that extent a termination is just as retrospective as a rescission; similarly, if the property has not yet passed when the contract is terminated, the seller's duty to pass the property disappears, even though the duty existed before the contract was terminated.[75]

15.5.2 Who is entitled to profit on resale?

The decision in *R V Ward Ltd* v *Bignall*[76] means that when the unpaid seller resells the goods, either under s. 48(3) or (4), he sells on his own account. This means that if the seller actually succeeds in reselling the goods at a higher price he will retain any profit thereby made. In the ordinary case, that seems a perfectly sensible result; it would be outrageous if a buyer who has defaulted in their obligations was entitled to collect from the seller the additional profit earned by the seller's efforts in reselling the goods.

However, this result may be less absurd and outrageous in one particular type of case. Where the seller sells and delivers goods to the buyer under a 'reservation of title' clause, giving the buyer the right to deal with the goods in the ordinary course of business, but reserving the right to reclaim the goods if the buyer fails to pay or to meet other conditions, the contract clearly envisages the possibility that the seller may sometimes reclaim and then resell the goods. Even in this situation, if the seller first terminates the contract

[72] [1980] AC 367.
[73] Scots law continues to use the term 'rescission' to describe termination for breach.
[74] [1980] 1 WLR 1129 – see Chapter 16, at section 16.1.
[75] For Scots law on this point, see MacQueen [1997] *Acta Juridica* 176, 192–8.
[76] [1967] 1 QB 534.

before reclaiming and reselling the goods, it seems clear that the buyer cannot claim any surplus profit made on the resale.[77]

But in *Clough Mill Ltd* v *Martin*,[78] the Court of Appeal assumed that such a resale of the goods could take place without a rescission (or termination) of the contract, and that the seller would then have to account to the buyer for any surplus made by him on the resale. Unfortunately, no reference was made in this case to s. 48(4) of the Act, which *prima facie* at any rate suggests that this is incorrect because the subsection appears to insist that in this situation the contract is rescinded. Possibly, the analysis in *Clough Mill Ltd* v *Martin* could be supported by arguing that there is in this case an implied term which negatives s. 48(4) and enables the resale to take place without rescission of the original contract. Moreover, there might be good sense in this in the case where the seller reclaims and resells under a reservation of title clause, as the right of the seller to reclaim and resell the goods is very much in the nature of a mortgage or charge. So it is not unreasonable in this case that the first buyer should be entitled to claim the profit on the resale. It is no different, in substance, from the position which arises where the buyer of a house defaults, and the house is sold by the mortgagee: here also the buyer is entitled to any surplus gain made on the resale, even though they may have defaulted in payment of the very first instalment on the mortgage. Paradoxically, though, *Clough Mill Ltd* v *Martin* is the leading authority for saying that a reservation of title clause does not operate like a mortgage or charge but is to be treated as a straightforward sale on special terms. There seems, in truth, to be an irreconcilable conflict at the root of this case, which is discussed further below.

15.5.3 Claim by seller in respect of payments due before rescission

Another difficult problem might arise in connection with the effects of a resale. If the seller resells the goods, can the seller still sue the buyer for any part of the price which was payable before the contract of sale was rescinded? If the seller resells at a loss, this question is not of great importance because the seller is entitled to damages for the buyer's breach, and the damages should fully compensate the seller for their loss anyhow. But if the seller resells at a profit, or if the seller resells at a loss which is less than the sum which should have been paid by the buyer before rescission, the question does assume practical importance.[79]

15.6 Reservation of title clauses

15.6.1 Reservation of title clauses and real remedies

A common feature of modern commercial contracts of sale is 'reservation of title' clauses (sometimes called *Romalpa* clauses, after the first case upholding their utility).[80] Some of these clauses are of considerable complexity, and there are many different versions in use,

[77] See *Clough Mill Ltd* v *Martin* [1984] 3 All ER 982.

[78] [1984] 3 All ER 982.

[79] *Damon Compania Naviera* v *Hapag-Lloyd, (The Blankenstein)* [1985] 1 All ER 475, followed in *Griffon Shipping LLC* v *Firodi Shipping Ltd (The Griffon)* [2014] 1 Lloyd's Rep. 471.

[80] See *Aluminium Industrie* v *Romalpa Aluminium Ltd* [1976] 1 WLR 676. The power to reserve title derives from ss. 17 and 19 of the Sale of Goods Act – Chapter 10.

but the essence of a reservation of title clause is to reserve the property in the goods to the seller until the price is paid in full, notwithstanding that the goods are delivered to the buyer. The purpose of such a clause is, of course, to confer upon the seller some degree of security against the insolvency of the buyer. *Prima facie* at least, if the buyer becomes insolvent before the price is fully paid, the seller will be able to reclaim possession of the goods. From a functional or commercial viewpoint, therefore, reservation of title clauses operate like a more extended version of the real rights of lien and stoppage in transit, and approximate the effect of a registered fixed or floating charge but without the obligation to register.[81] The lien operates while the seller is still in possession, the right of stoppage after they have dispatched the goods but before they have arrived, and a reservation of title clause operates after the goods have actually been delivered to the buyer. But a reservation of title clause must be expressly imposed;[82] there is no implied real right to reclaim goods from the buyer once they have been delivered merely because the price has not been paid. In theory, such a right might exist even without express reservation if there are any grounds for arguing in some particular case that property has not passed on or before delivery, but in the absence of some express provision to this effect it would be rare indeed that property does not pass at the latest on delivery. So it can be assumed for all practical purposes that a reservation of title clause must be expressly imposed if the seller is to retain any title after delivery.

The decision in *The Res Cogitans*[83] has created some difficulties in this field of law. The case involved the supply of fuel bunkers subject to a retention of title clause. It was a common understanding that the bunkers would be consumed before payment is made. The Supreme Court took the view that this constellation meant that the contract was not a contract of sale at all but a *sui generis* contract.[84] This would suggest that any contract where goods are supplied for consumption (or in such a way that their separate identity is lost) are not to be classified as a sale of goods at all, but some other *sui generis* supply transaction. This would take a significant number of contracts outside the scope of the Sale of Goods Act. Quite where the dividing line between cases still within the Act and now outside falls is unclear. All one can say is that this case has introduced a rather unwelcome distinction into the law, and many cases hitherto regarded as being contracts of sale with a retention of title clause might now have to be understood differently, governed by common law principles.

15.6.2 Resale of goods by buyer

In principle, there is nothing new about the possibility of the seller trying to reserve title after delivery, by way of security. Indeed, the hire-purchase contract is a familiar device

[81] In many other jurisdictions, retention of title clauses are treated in the same way as charges and therefore must be registered to be effective.

[82] In contracts for the sale of specific goods the reservation of title clause generally *must* be contained in the contract of sale; otherwise property in the goods will usually pass as provided by s. 18, Rule 1. In the case of unascertained goods, however, s. 19(1) gives the power to impose a reservation in the terms of the appropriation of the goods to the contract – see Bradgate [1988] JBL 477.

[83] *PST Energy 7 LLV* v *OW Bunker Malta Ltd* [2016] UKSC 23.

[84] The wider difficulty created by the Supreme Court's ruling for the scope of the Sale of Goods Act was discussed in Chapter 2.

to achieve the same effect, though the use of such contracts has largely been confined to consumer transactions. But modern reservation of title clauses are being widely used in commercial sales. For example, cases have involved aluminium foil sold to be manufactured into other goods, resin sold for the manufacture of chipboards, leather sold to be made into handbags and so on. Furthermore, these modern clauses often permit or authorise the buyer to use the goods in the process of manufacture, and also to resell the goods in the course of business. Such clauses therefore differ from hire-purchase contracts under which the hirer is not entitled to resell the goods, and, if they do, cannot pass a title to them, except in the case of motor vehicles to which Part III of the Hire-Purchase Act 1964 applies.

A reservation of title clause will not usually restrict the buyer's right to resell the goods in the course of their business because that is not the purpose behind the clause.[85] So such clauses quite often expressly authorise the buyer to resell, though there may be restrictions on their right to resell on credit. And even in the absence of an express authority to resell, such an authority will often be readily implied from the very nature of the transaction as a whole.[86] In *Four Point Garage Ltd* v *Carter*,[87] the sellers were motor dealers who supplied cars to a company under a reservation of title clause. This company was believed by the suppliers to be in the business of letting cars on hire, rather than reselling them, but it was nonetheless held that between two commercial concerns like this, a power of resale would readily be implied, and therefore a buyer in good faith from the company obtained a good title binding on the suppliers even though they had never been paid for the vehicle in question.

Even where the reservation of title clause does impose restrictions on the resale of the goods, they will not be of any avail against a purchaser without notice. As we have already seen, a buyer in possession of the goods has the power to pass a good title to a purchaser for value without notice under s. 25 of the Sale of Goods Act and s. 9 of the Factors Act, and it has been stressed that a sub-buyer is not to be treated as having notice of restrictions on the power of sale contained in a *Romalpa* clause merely because he failed to make inquiry about the buyer's right to resell.[88] In commercial contexts, a buyer is not generally under any duty to inquire into the seller's right to sell the goods. Doubtless there may occasionally be special circumstances putting the buyer on inquiry, or they may have actual notice of a *Romalpa* type clause restricting the seller's power of resale, but in that event the buyer has only themselves to blame if they buy without ensuring that the seller complies with the requirements of the *Romalpa* clause.

The situation where the buyer *resells* is covered by s. 25(1) of the Sale of Goods Act, and s. 2(1) of the Factors Act. But what is the situation where the buyer merely *agrees* to resell? This would be the situation where the buyer sold on to a sub-buyer who took possession under a reservation of title clause. Section 25(1) does not cover that situation, but s. 9 of the Factors Act applieswhere the goods are obtained under any '*agreement* [emphasis supplied] for sale, pledge or other disposition'. But the effect of that provision is that the

[85] See *Fairfax Gerrard Holdings Ltd* v *Capital Bank Plc* [2007] EWCA Civ 1226.
[86] See *Aluminium Industrie BV* v *Romalpa Ltd* [1976] 1 WLR 676.
[87] [1985] 3 All ER 12.
[88] *Feuer Leather Corpn* v *Frank Johnstone* (1981) Com LR 251. See also *Forsythe International* v *Silver Shipping* [1994] 1 All ER 851, 867.

delivery or transfer in favour of a bona fide purchaser has the same effect as if the person making the delivery or transfer were a mercantile agent in possession with the consent of the owner,[89] and s. 2(1) of the Factors Act, which deals with the powers of a mercantile agent in possession, only provides that any *sale* etc. by a mercantile agent in possession with the consent of the owner shall be as valid as if the mercantile agent were authorised by the owner. In *Re Highway Foods International Ltd*,[90] it was held that in such a situation the original seller could claim title to the goods. The sub-buyer would only acquire title on payment of the price to the buyer.

15.6.3 Claims to the goods themselves

In the most straightforward case, the reservation of title clause applies to specific goods which remain identifiable as the goods sold after they have been delivered to the buyer. This sort of clause is effective to reserve title to the seller under ss. 17(1) and 19(1) of the Act. The passing of property in the goods is conditional on the payment of the price, and there is nothing contrary to the law in the parties making a contract to that effect. Nor, as we shall see more fully below, does this case raise any problems as to the need for registration of the clause as a mortgage or charge (though what is being created is practically comparable to a mortgage or charge).[91] In law, the clause is not regarded as a mortgage or charge which might require registration, but simply as an ordinary contractual provision deferring the passing of the property until certain conditions have been complied with. The seller is doing no more than ss. 17(1) and 19(1) permit. A company can create a charge only on its own property, and if it never acquires property in the goods the subject of an agreement for sale, it cannot charge them. In short, the courts have chosen to look at form rather than substance.[92] Usually, these conditions are that the price must have been fully paid, but it is now common to enlarge the conditions by requiring that all outstanding indebtedness of the buyer to the seller should be discharged before the property can pass – the so-called 'all moneys' clause. Thus – assuming always that the goods sold retain their identity and are still in the possession of the buyer – the seller is able to reserve title in all the goods sold by them to the buyer until all the prices due are fully paid. So where a seller makes regular deliveries to the buyer under contracts containing such a clause, the property in the very first delivery may be retained long after the buyer has paid the full price of that delivery, so long as some part of the price of subsequent deliveries is not yet paid.[93] In *Armour* v *Thyssen Edelstahlwerke*,[94] the House of Lords, while upholding an 'all moneys' clause, did not answer, as the facts of the case did not give rise to the problem, what the situation would have been if the seller had used the clause as a basis for repossessing paid-for goods, as well as unpaid-for goods.[95] Arguably, in this situation,

[89] See ibid.

[90] *The Times*, 1 November 1994.

[91] See Ahdar [1993] LMCLQ 382, 382–3.

[92] *Clough Mill Ltd* v *Martin* [1984] 3 All ER 982, 983 per Oliver LJ; and see *Armour* v *Thyssen Edelstahlwerke* [1991] 2 AC 339, 1990 SLT 891; *Accurist Watches Ltd* v *King* [1992] FSR 80.

[93] It is arguable in England and Wales that the effect of such clauses here is to give rise to a floating charge which requires registration under the Companies Act 2006, s. 859A.

[94] [1991] 2 AC 339, 1990 SLT 891.

[95] The previous point was not argued in *Armour* v *Thyssen*.

the seller would be required to refund the price of the paid-for goods, on the ground of a total failure of consideration, so that the clause would be self-defeating. On the other hand, if the clause operated as a charge, the seller would in principle be able to satisfy its debt without an obligation to refund the price of the paid-for goods.[96] In short, this would suggest that such clauses should be treated as charges, but this would mean that they would often be ineffective unless they had been registered.

15.6.4 Claims to the proceeds of resale

Thus far, matters are reasonably simple. Complications start when a seller attempts to draft the relevant clause so as to give them some security even after the goods have been resold. As already mentioned, reservation of title clauses are not designed to prevent the buyer reselling the goods in the ordinary course of their business: to do that would freeze the buyer's business and frustrate the whole point of buying the goods. But a reservation of title clause may attempt to transfer the seller's preferential rights from the goods themselves to the proceeds of sale received by the buyer. For example, the clause may provide that all moneys received by the buyer through disposal of the goods in question are to belong in equity to the seller and to be paid into a separate bank account which is to be held on trust for the seller. In the *Romalpa* case itself, the plaintiffs had sold large quantities of aluminium foil to the defendants on the terms that property was to remain in the plaintiffs until full payment was made. The defendants got into financial difficulties and a receiver was appointed. He found some £50,000 worth of foil still in the possession of the defendants, and he received from sub-buyers a further £35,000, representing the price of goods made out of the foil and sold to sub-buyers. There was no problem as to the £50,000. This represented the foil which still belonged to the plaintiffs, and it could not be disputed that it was their foil. But even the £35,000 was held to be claimable by the plaintiffs on the ground that the defendants had been mere bailees of the foil, which they had sold with the implied authority of the owners, and for which they had therefore to account in equity. At first instance, Mocatta J held that no registrable charge arose and this question was not further discussed on appeal.

The result was in many respects extremely artificial. The decision of the Court of Appeal involved the conclusion that all the money received by the defendants from resale of the goods had to be held on trust for the plaintiffs, including even the profit made by the defendants from making and reselling these goods. Had the plaintiffs strictly enforced their right to have this money paid into a separate bank account, therefore, none of it would have been available for use by the defendants (except to pay the plaintiffs). It is very unlikely that the parties actually contemplated that the money would be used in this way: clearly the plaintiffs did not want to interfere with the daily business activities of the defendants; they merely wanted to be able to step in when the defendants' financial position became precarious and then seize hold of whatever could be found. Furthermore, the equitable ownership of the proceeds of sale which the plaintiffs claimed and which the Court of Appeal upheld was also artificial. Obviously, if these proceeds had actually exceeded the sums due to the plaintiffs, nobody intended that the plaintiffs could keep the

[96] See Goodhart (1986) 47 MLR 96, 97–8. For a contrary view, see Mance [1992] LMCLQ 35.

excess. This fact alone demonstrates that what was really involved here was a mortgage or charge, since the plaintiffs were only entitled to the proceeds of sale insofar as they were necessary to pay off what was due to them. But that conclusion would have involved recognition that the arrangement was registrable as the grant of a mortgage or charge under the Companies Act,[97] the requirements of which are further discussed below, and yet this was not the outcome of the case, partly because the question was not even argued in the Court of Appeal.

The *Romalpa* case itself is therefore a somewhat unsatisfactory authority, and it is not surprising that some subsequent cases should have restricted the authority of that case.[98] These restrictions have so far taken two forms. First, it has been stressed that in the *Romalpa* case it was conceded that the defendants were *bailees* of the aluminium foil, so that there was some justification for the argument that the resale of the goods by the buyer involved a sale of the *plaintiff's* goods, and could therefore give rise to a duty to account for the price, the proceeds belonging in equity to the sellers. But the usual relationship created by a contract of sale, even subject to a reservation of title clause, does not involve a bailment. The mere fact that the seller may in some circumstances be entitled to reclaim the goods does not make the transaction a bailment. The relationship between the parties is simply that of buyer and seller, and if the buyer is authorised to resell the goods, the normal implication is that they have no duty to account for the proceeds or to treat them in any particular way.[99]

Even if the relationship between the parties can be said to be, or to involve, a bailment, it does not follow that there is a fiduciary duty on the buyer which gives the seller the right to claim the proceeds of sale in equity. Not all bailees have such fiduciary obligations; whether such an obligation is to be imposed depends upon the implications to be made in the contract,[100] but *prima facie* at least, it seems that there will be no duty to account for the proceeds unless the contract imposes some obligations on the buyer to deal with them in a particular way,[101] or expressly confers equitable rights to the proceeds of sale on the original seller, as in the *Romalpa* case itself.

In this connection, a claim by the seller runs into certain practical difficulties of proof, unless there are express clauses covering the proceeds of resale. If the seller argues that the buyer was under some implied duty to account for the proceeds in a particular way, they will be faced with the difficulty that it is unlikely that the parties intended the *whole* of the proceeds of sale to be dealt with in this way. Probably, the parties expected the buyer to keep for himself the difference between the sale and the resale prices. But if the seller concedes that the buyer only had to account for a *part* of the proceeds of the resale, this militates against any suggestion of a fiduciary relationship in the first place. It more clearly points to a simple debtor–creditor relationship.

[97] See s. 859A of the Companies Act 2006.

[98] Longmore LJ noted that *Romalpa* was 'a case more distinguished than followed in subsequent authority': *FG Wilson (Engineering) Ltd* v *John Holt & Co (Liverpool) Ltd* [2013] EWCA Civ 123 at para 26.

[99] *E Pfeiffer Weinkellerei-Weinkauf GmbH* v *Arbuthnot Factors Ltd* [1987] BCLC 522, esp. at 530; *Compaq Computers Ltd* v *Abercorn Group* [1993] BCLC 602. In *A M Bisley* v *Gore Engineering & Retail Sales* (1989) 2 NZ BLC 103, 595, Holland J decided that the contractual arrangements between the parties did not create a fiduciary relationship but merely a debtor–creditor relationship.

[100] *Hendy Lennox (Industrial Engines) Ltd* v *Grahame Puttick Ltd* [1984] 2 All ER 152; *Tatung (UK) Ltd* v *Galex Telesure Ltd* (1989) 5 BCLC 325; *Re Weldtech Equipment Ltd* [1991] BCLC 393.

[101] *Re Andrabell Ltd* [1984] 3 All ER 407.

In *FG Wilson (Engineering) Ltd* v *John Holt & Co (Liverpool) Ltd*,[102] a term in the contract stating that 'the buyer shall hold the products as seller's fiduciary agent and shall keep them separate from Buyer's other goods' and entitling the buyer to 'resell or use the products in the ordinary course of business' and requiring the buyer 'to account to the Seller for the proceeds of sale' was held by a majority of the Court of Appeal (Patten and Floyd LJJ, Longmore LJ dissenting on this point) to have the claimed effect and the buyer was treated as acting as the seller's agent when reselling the goods to a sub-buyer. Longmore LJ's strong dissent noted that the contract also contained a separate term expressly denying the creation of an agency relationship between seller and buyer, and, furthermore, that the imposition of a fiduciary relationship was not in line with the commercial relationship between the parties. In *PST Energy 7 Shipping LLC* v *OW Bunker Malta Ltd*, Lord Mance noted *obiter* that 'the interpretation of Holt Liverpool's role as one of agency on behalf of FG Wilson . . . may well merit further consideration in another case in this court',[103] hinting at his lack of agreement with the majority in the Court of Appeal.[104]

Another restriction on the effect of the *Romalpa* case has also become apparent where claims are made against the proceeds of sale. With a bailment that there may be some circumstances in which the bailee is obliged to redeliver the very same goods to the bailor. So if it appears from the nature of the goods that there will never be any such redelivery, the transaction simply cannot be a bailment (no matter what the parties may have called it); it must be a sale, and any attempt by the seller to claim title over the proceeds of resale – even if otherwise valid between the parties – will be a charge or mortgage requiring registration. This point is dealt with again later.

15.6.5 Transferred claims to other goods

Reservation of title clauses frequently give the seller not only the right to treat the very goods sold as still belonging to the seller but also the right to claim any other goods as their property, where those other goods have been made with the goods sold.[105] The question of whether goods which have been used in some manufacturing process still exist in the goods produced by that process is one of fact and degree not susceptible to much exposition.[106] Where yarn was sold to buyers for the purposes of being made into material, the sellers' conditions of contract reserved the title in the yarn until the sellers were paid, but also declared that any material made out of the yarn should belong to the sellers until they were paid.[107] The problem here is that the seller will obtain the benefit

[102] [2013] EWCA Civ 123.

[103] [2016] UKSC 23, para 57.

[104] Lord Mance referred favourably to the analysis of *Holt* v *Wilson* by Louise Gullifer, 'The interpretation of retention of title clauses: some difficulties' [2014] *LMCLQ* 564. Professor Gullifer criticised the Court of Appeal's ruling for upsetting the balance established in the post-*Romalpa* case law on this issue for upholding an 'uncommercial arrangement' flowing from the agency construction and by giving the seller an interest in the proceeds of resale which is unregistrable.

[105] It would seem that in the absence of clear provision, retention of title clauses will be construed narrowly. So where live animals were supplied to an abattoir, the terms 'livestock' and 'goods' applied only to the live animals, not to their carcasses – *Chaigley Farms Ltd* v *Crawford Kaye & Grayshire Ltd (t/a Leylands)* [1996] BCC 957.

[106] *Associated Alloys Pty Ltd* v *Metropolitan Engineering and Fabrications Pty Ltd* (1996) ACSR 205, 209 (Sup Ct NSW) per Sheller, Beazley and Stein JJA.

[107] See *Clough Mill Ltd* v *Martin* [1984] 3 All ER 982.

of the value the buyer has added to the goods. In consequence, such a clause is arguably a charge registrable under the Companies Act. Difficulties can also arise where (as can easily happen) two or more sellers sell materials under similar (or perhaps different) reservation of title clauses, and the goods of all these sellers are ultimately incorporated in some new goods made by the buyers.[108] So far, this particular sort of problem has not come before the courts, but several other difficulties have come to light from these extended reservation of title clauses.

In *Borden (UK) Ltd* v *Scottish Timber Products Ltd*,[109] plaintiffs sold resin to the defendants which the defendants (as the plaintiffs knew) used in the manufacture of chipboard. A simple reservation of title clause provided that the property in the resin was to remain in the sellers until they were fully paid. It was held by the Court of Appeal that the sellers could have no claims to the chipboard in which the resin was incorporated. The resin itself had ceased to exist as an independent commodity. Consequently, there was no property of the sellers which they could claim; no question arose of a charge under the Companies Act. The plaintiffs' claim failed at an earlier point, since there was no property on which they could even claim a charge.

The reservation of title clause in this case did not contain an extended provision declaring that any goods made with, or incorporating, the resin were also to be the property of the sellers, even in equity. It seems, however, that even such a clause is unlikely to save the seller where a significant change in the identity of the goods is contemplated by the parties. In *Re Peachdart Ltd*,[110] sellers sold leather to a company who used it for the manufacture of handbags. The contract contained a reservation of title clause providing that (a) all unworked leather remained the property of the sellers until full payment, (b) the ownership of goods made out of the leather was to vest in the sellers, and (c) the sellers were to have the right to trace the proceeds of sale of the handbags. It was held that, despite the language of the parties, the intention must have been that the sellers should lose their exclusive ownership in each piece of the leather as soon as work on it was commenced by the buyers. The sellers' rights would therefore become, at that point, rights in the nature of a mortgage or charge, and this was therefore registrable, and, being unregistered, it was void.

It follows from the above that use of a reservation of title clause in a repair contract, which purports to give the repairer ownership of the article into which any parts they have supplied have been incorporated, is unlikely to achieve its object. In *Specialist Plant Services Ltd* v *Braithwaite Ltd*,[111] it was held that a clause of this sort created a charge,

[108] The situation may be different where goods of two or more sellers are only co-mingled, and the co-mingled goods form a separate and identifiable bulk. In *Indian Oil Corp Ltd* v *Greenstone Shipping* [1988] QB 345 it was held that where oil was mixed with a quantity belonging to another party already in a ship's hold, the resulting mixture was held in common, and the innocent party was entitled to receive out the same quantity of goods which went in. In *Re Stapylton Fletcher* [1994] 1 WLR 1181 it was held that property in a number of cases of wine, separately stored for a group of customers, had passed as the goods were ascertained for the purposes of s. 16, the customers owning as tenants in common. It would appear to follow from this that each seller of goods under a reservation of title clause would, in a similar situation, have an undivided share in the whole of the resulting product.

[109] [1981] Ch 25. See also the Irish case of *Fried Krupp Huttenwerke AG* v *Quitman Products* [1982] ILRM 551.

[110] [1983] 3 All ER 204. See also *Modelboard Ltd* v *Outer Box Ltd* [1993] BCLC 623; *Ian Chisholm Textiles* v *Griffiths* [1994] BCLC 96; *Chaigley Farms Ltd* v *Crawford, Kaye & Grayshire Ltd* [1996] BCLC 96; but cf. the *Hendy Lennox* case, above.

[111] [1987] BCCL 1.

which was void for non-registration. Where the goods become fixtures on installation, the seller's title is destroyed, because the principle *quicquid plantatur solo, solo cedit* applies.[112]

15.6.6 Charges registrable under the Companies Act

The prime purpose of a reservation of title clause, as we have now seen, is to protect the seller against the insolvency of the buyer. For practical or commercial purposes, it is equivalent to a mortgage or charge upon the goods. However, there are policy arguments against permitting a seller to have the benefit of such a mortgage or charge because its main effect is simply to give the seller priority over other creditors of the buyer in the event of the buyer's insolvency, and the law does not generally permit one creditor to obtain preferential treatment in this way unless the prior charge or mortgage is publicised by some form of registration.

In order to prevent a creditor from obtaining priority in this way, therefore, there are a number of statutory provisions requiring the registration of transactions under which a person grants a mortgage or charge over property while retaining the possession of that property. Under the Bills of Sale Act a person who sells goods and remains in possession, or grants a mortgage or charge over goods by way of security, may have to register the bill of sale under which the transaction is effected or evidenced. In practice, these provisions are today important because they are applied to companies by s. 859A of the Companies Act 2006,[113] which requires particulars of a charge to be delivered to the Registrar of Companies.[114] This includes charges over goods.[115] So a frequent problem arising from *Romalpa* clauses is to know whether they should have been registered under these provisions. If particulars of a charge have not been delivered to Companies House within 21 days of their creation, it is void as against creditors or the liquidator of the company.[116] So even though the reservation of title clause may be effective as between the seller and the buyer, the clause will fail in its main purpose – that is to protect the seller against the risk of the buyer's insolvency – where it should have been registered but was not. Particulars of few of these clauses are actually likely to have been sent to Companies House, so once it is held that the seller's rights are registrable, the result is usually that the seller will fail to get the priority that they seek as against a liquidator or other creditors of the buyers.

A reservation of title clause is clearly an attempt to evade the registration requirements of the Companies Act because its commercial purpose is to grant the seller preferential treatment in the insolvency of the buyer. And any rational system of registration of charges clearly ought to cover reservation of title clauses, as is done, for instance, by Article 9 of the Uniform Commercial Code, but so far this result has not been achieved here. The courts have themselves deprecated any suggestion that these clauses should be narrowly construed or be treated with reserve because they escape the registration requirements.[117]

[112] See *Air-Cool Installations* v *British Telecommunications* [1995] CLY 821.
[113] Companies Act 2006, s. 859A, which is the first section in a new Chapter A1 inserted into Part 25 of the Companies Act by the Companies Act (Amendment of Part 25) Regulations 2013 (SI 2013/600).
[114] Companies Act 2006 s. 859A(2) and (4).
[115] Companies Act 2006 s. 859D.
[116] Companies Act 2006 s. 859H(3).
[117] See *Clough Mill Ltd* v *Martin*, [1984] 3 All ER 982. But see *Chaigley Farms*, [1996] BCC 957.

It has so far been insisted that the parties are entirely free to make whatever contracts they wish on whatever terms they choose and that there is nothing illegitimate about the result if they succeed in evading the requirements of registration.

But all this seems most unsatisfactory. Total freedom of contract is inappropriate where the whole purpose of the contract is to affect the rights of third parties who have no say in the contract.[118]

However, at this time, the law does not generally require reservation of title clauses to be registered. The technical reason given for this, as we have seen, is that the effect of such a clause is simply to prevent the property from passing to the buyer in the first place. They are not in the position of a person who is owner of the goods, and thereafter grants a mortgage or charge over them.[119] The analysis of the situation made by the courts is thus highly formal – the terms of the contract are given full effect, whatever their underlying purpose may be. In this respect, the decisions on these clauses are precisely in line with the law relating to hire-purchase contracts. There also the underlying commercial purpose of the transaction is ignored, and effect is given to the legal form in which the transaction has been cast.

But there are limits to this general approach. In *Re Bond Worth*,[120] sellers sold synthetic fibre to buyers who (as the sellers knew) bought it to spin into yarn together with other fibres, and make carpeting out of the resultant yarn. A retention of title clause provided that the sellers were to retain 'equitable and beneficial ownership' of the yarn, and in the proceeds of sale of goods made with the yarn. Slade J held that this was in substance an outright sale with a mortgage or charge back by the buyer.[121] This 'equitable and beneficial ownership' was plainly not intended to be full ownership, but only a security right because the plain intention of the parties was that (a) the buyers could pay off the sellers at any time the balance of the price due, and thereupon the charge would come to an end, and (b) if the proceeds of resale exceeded the sums due to the sellers they would not have been entitled to the excess. As a result, the transaction was registrable under the Companies Act, and, in default of registration, it was void against the liquidator of the buyers.

There seem to be strong grounds for thinking that any reservation of title clause which gives rights over the proceeds of a sale or sales by the buyer must be vulnerable to this sort of reasoning.[122] Almost always, it would seem, such a clause must carry the two implications (a) and (b) regarded as critical by Slade J.

So also in *Clough Mill Ltd* v *Martin*,[123] there was a reservation of title clause which covered the yarn sold to the buyers, and also any goods into which the yarn was incorporated.

[118] See Bradgate [1987] Conv 434.

[119] See Goff LJ in *Clough Mill Ltd* v *Martin* [1984] 3 All ER 982, 986–9.

[120] [1980] Ch 228.

[121] In reaching this conclusion, Slade J distinguished the Court of Appeal decision in *Re Connolly Bros* (No. 2) [1912] 2 Ch 25. That case, however, was followed by the House of Lords in *Abbey National Building Society* v *Cann* [1990] 1 All ER 1085, which overruled the competing line of authority including *Church of England BS* v *Piskor* [1954] 1 Ch 553. It has been argued that the effect of this is to overturn the 'sale with a mortgage back or charge' analysis – Hicks [1992] JBL 398; Gregory (1990) 106 LQR 550. On this argument, the buyer would merely acquire an equity of redemption, which would not be registrable under Companies Act 2006, s. 859A. However, as Hicks admits, the courts appear to have a policy of striking down clauses which claim rights to new products, or the proceeds of sale.

[122] See *Compaq Computers* v *Abercorn Group* [1993] BCLC 602; *Modelboard Ltd* v *Outer Box Ltd* [1993] BCLC 623.

[123] [1984] 3 All ER 982.

When the buyers went into receivership, the receiver argued that the goods incorporating the yarn sold under the clause were subject to a charge which was void for non-registration under the Companies Act. The Court of Appeal upheld this argument. There was no reason, they held, why the property in these new goods should not be transferred to the sellers if their contract was intended to achieve this result, and the bare fact that the goods had not existed before did not by itself show that this was a transfer by way of charge. But the court went on to say that if these goods were seized and resold by the sellers under the clause it could not have been the intention of the parties that the sellers would be entitled to retain the whole proceeds of sale. Because these goods had never been the sellers' property, and because there might even be additional plaintiffs to the goods under other reservation of title clauses, it must be assumed that the sellers could only keep the sums due to themselves under their own sales, and would have to refund any surplus to the buyers. This meant that the transfer of property in these goods to the sellers must have been intended to operate by way of charge, and not absolutely.

In practice, however, it might have been thought that it would almost always be the case that the parties intend any surplus from the resale of the seized goods over and above the price still due to the seller to belong to the buyer. But while the Court of Appeal in the *Clough Mill* case agreed that this was so with regard to the goods made out of or incorporating the goods sold, they insisted that it was not the case with regard to these goods themselves. They held that a seizure and resale of the actual goods sold might give the buyer the right to claim the surplus proceeds without this showing that the goods were charged. If the seizure and resale of the goods were made under the terms of the contract, it was suggested, the contract could still subsist, and so the resale would be subject to the buyer's rights. However, as we saw earlier, this discussion was conducted without reference to s. 48 of the Act and the decision in *R V Ward Ltd* v *Bignall*[124] which appear to be inconsistent with this analysis. That section makes it clear that if the seller resells the goods, whether under the contract or not, the resale effects a rescission of the original contract. Hence – as decided in *R V Ward Ltd* v *Bignall* – the buyer cannot claim any surplus on the resale. The only way to avoid this conclusion appears to be to hold that s. 48 of the Act is in such cases excluded by a contrary intention, but the only ground for arguing that there is a contrary intention appears to be that the transaction is really not intended to be an outright sale but is intended to operate by way of mortgage or charge. Consequently, if the court in *Clough Mill Ltd* was correct in thinking that the buyer might under the contract in that case be entitled to reclaim the surplus on any resale of the goods by the seller, it would seem they must have been wrong to hold that the actual goods sold were not the subject of a charge.

Many of these more recent decisions represent some move away from the ill-considered *Romalpa* case, though *Armour* v *Thyssen* appears to reaffirm the central point of *Romalpa* on the effectiveness of a simple retention of title clause in relation to the goods supplied.[125] To summarise: a reservation of title clause is effective so far as the original goods are concerned so long as they retain their identity and remain in the possession of the buyer. Conversely, attempts to extend the seller's preferential rights (a) to other goods made with

[124] [1967] 1 QB 534.
[125] See also *Clough Mill Ltd* v *Martin* ([1984] 3 All ER 982).

or incorporating the goods sold, or (b) to the proceeds of sale of the goods by the buyer, are at present highly vulnerable to attack in England as unregistered charges. But (on the present authorities) it appears to be possible to avoid the requirement of registration by a carefully worded clause which stresses that the 'buyer' is not really a buyer but a bailee, which insists that the bailee is only entitled to use the goods to manufacture other goods as a trustee, and on behalf of the seller, and which provides that the proceeds of sale of such goods (or the original goods) are to be held on trust in a separate bank account. Furthermore, it must be made clear that the intention of the parties is that the buyer is not to have any residuary right (in the nature of an equity of redemption) to the balance of the proceeds of sale after payment of the price of the goods (and other goods, supplied by the seller, if the clause so provides). So if the seller reclaims and resells the goods it must be made clear that there will be no liability to account to the buyer for any surplus over and above the price of the goods sold to the buyer under the contract. It is unlikely that many buyers would willingly agree to such a draconian clause if they fully understood its implications; and a clause drafted in this form must raise major doubts as to whether the parties seriously intend it to operate according to its terms, or whether it is in truth a complete sham.

16

Personal remedies

16.1 Action for the price

In addition to the real rights, the seller has, of course, their personal action upon the sale for breach of contract by the buyer. This action may take one of two forms. It may be an action for the price of the goods sold or it may be an action for damages for non-acceptance. The distinction between an action for the price and an action for damages is of considerable importance. In purely monetary terms, there will usually be a substantial difference between the price of the goods and damages for non-acceptance. Moreover, if the property has passed to the buyer and the seller is entitled to sue for the price, they are under no obligation to mitigate the damage[1] by attempting to resell the goods or otherwise.[2] The goods now belong to the buyer and not the seller, and it is the buyer's responsibility to take delivery of the goods or otherwise dispose of them.

The general rule laid down in s. 49(1) and s. 50(1) is that an action for damages is the appropriate remedy where the property has not passed and an action for the price is available when the property has passed. This simple principle is unfortunately complicated by the fact that the property in the goods may pass to the buyer before they have been delivered to and accepted by him. Section 49(1) says:

> Where, under a contract of sale, the property in the goods has passed to the buyer, and the buyer wrongfully neglects or refuses to pay for the goods according to the terms of the contract, the seller may maintain an action against him for the price of the goods.

Section 50(1) says:

> Where the buyer wrongfully neglects or refuses to accept and pay for the goods, the seller may maintain an action against him for damages for non-acceptance.

It is, of course, obvious that the property in the goods may have passed to the buyer, *and* they may have neglected or refused to accept and pay for them because, as we have seen, property in the goods often passes before delivery. In such an event, it seems to follow that the seller has the option of suing for the price under s. 49(1) or for damages under s. 50(1). In other words, the seller has:

1 an action for the price where the property has passed and the buyer has accepted the goods;

[1] As to the normal duty to mitigate, see Chapter 18 at section 18.2.1.

[2] In this sense an action for the price of goods in which property has passed is an illustration of the principle laid down by the HL in *White & Carter (Councils) Ltd* v *McGregor* [1962] AC 413, 1962 SC (HL) 1 – see per Lord Keith at pp. 437 and 19–20 respectively.

2 an action for damages where the property has not passed and the buyer refuses to accept the goods;
3 an action for the price or for damages where the property has passed and the buyer refuses to accept the goods.

It is a pre-condition for the seller's right to bring an action for the price under s. 49 that property must have passed, but where the contract – particularly a contract where goods are delivered in instalments – includes a retention of title clause which has the effect that property cannot pass until full payment, the seller cannot rely on s. 49 to bring an action for the price. The Court of Appeal in *FG Wilson Ltd* v *Holt Ltd*[3] held that s. 49 was of a 'mandatory' character in the sense that an action for the price under a contract of sale would only be possible when one of the circumstances in s. 49 applies. However, in a detailed obiter in *PST Energy 7 LLC* v *OW Bunker Malta Ltd*,[4] the Supreme Court rejected this and effectively over-ruled *FG Wilson* v *Holt* on this point and held that there could be circumstances outside the scope of s. 49 which might permit an action for the price, for example, when goods are already at the buyer's risk but property has not yet passed.[5]

However, as far as s. 49 is concerned, the fact that the property has not passed, owing to some wrongful act of the defendant, does not enable the seller to claim the price, unless the buyer is estopped by their conduct from disputing the fact that the property has passed. So, for instance, if the buyer fails to name an effective ship in a sale f.o.b., the seller's remedy is an action for damages, not for the price.[6] And if the buyer in a c.i.f. contract refuses to take up the shipping documents when tendered, the seller's remedy is once again an action for damages, not for the price.[7]

16.1.1 Price payable on a 'day certain'

There is one exceptional case in which the seller may sue for the price although the property has not passed, for under s. 49(2):

> Where, under a contract of sale, the price is payable on a day certain irrespective of delivery, and the buyer wrongfully neglects or refuses to pay such price, the seller may maintain an action for the price, although the property in the goods has not passed, and the goods have not been appropriated to the contract.

The important point to note about this subsection is that it concerns a case where the price is payable irrespective of delivery. If the price is due on some specified date after delivery, no great difficulty arises.[8] Clearly, the seller can sue for the price as soon as the date arrives. But s. 49(2) also applies to cases where the price is due before delivery, and one can see why this is necessary. If the price is payable before delivery, and the buyer fails to pay, the seller cannot sue for damages for non-acceptance because the date for acceptance has not yet arrived. Indeed, the buyer may very well intend to accept the goods: but they

[3] *FG Wilson (Engineering) Ltd* v *John Holt & Co (Liverpool) Ltd* [2013] EWCA Civ 1232.
[4] [2016] UKSC 23.
[5] [2016] UKSC 23, para [55].
[6] *Colley* v *Overseas Exporters Ltd* [1921] 3 KB 302.
[7] *Stein, Forbes & Co Ltd* v *County Tailoring Co Ltd* (1916) 86 LJKB 448.
[8] See e.g., *Readie Construction Ltd* v *Geo Quarries Ltd* [2021] EWHC 3030 (QB), paras 46–50.

have in the meantime defaulted in their obligation to pay. So the seller clearly needs to be able to sue for the price (or an instalment) due on some date before delivery.

The main difficulty in interpreting the subsection is the meaning of 'a day certain'. Does it mean a named, fixed date, or is it possible to invoke the maxim *certum est quod certum reddi potest*, so that the section could be applied to a contract which contains machinery for ascertaining the date when the price is to be paid without actually fixing any date? In *Workman Clark & Co Ltd* v *Lloyd Brazileno*,[9] it was held that the seller, who was constructing a ship for the buyer, was entitled to sue for the instalments as they became due, although the date on which they became due was ascertained by reference to the stage which had been reached in the construction of the vessel. The Court of Appeal decided both that s. 49(2) applies to instalments payable on a day certain, and that these instalments were payable on a day certain.[10] It does not follow that the price can be sued for whenever the date for payment can be ascertained because in many cases an action for damages would be the more appropriate remedy. But in this case, there would have been no ground for an action for damages and the seller would have been left without any remedy if he could not sue for the price.

But although a seller may need to be able to sue for the price before delivery if the contract provides for advance payment, this is liable to leave open one serious problem: what happens if the goods are never delivered at all? Of course, if this is due to breach by the seller, the buyer will have their own remedy. But suppose the goods are not delivered because the seller treats the non-payment as a sufficient repudiation to justify them in terminating the whole contract, either as a matter of common law or under some specific clause in the contract?

In *Hyundai Heavy Industries Co Ltd* v *Papadopoulos*,[11] which was also a shipbuilding case in which the price was payable by instalments, it was held by the House of Lords that the buyer could be sued for an instalment which fell due on 15 July despite the fact that the seller exercised a contractual right of cancellation on 6 September, with the result that the buyer would have had[12] to pay the instalment even though he would not have received the goods. This holding could have somewhat alarming implications which do not appear to have been wholly thought through by the House of Lords; for it would seem to follow from the decision that even if the entire price had been payable in advance, the seller could have both exercised his right of cancellation, so sparing him the necessity of delivering the ship at all, and still have sued for the price. One factor in the ruling in *Hyundai* seems to have been a desire to maintain what was at the time a newly established distinction between a rescission of a contract *ab initio*, and a mere termination as a result of breach, established by the House of Lords in *Johnson* v *Agnew*.[13] While providing

[9] [1908] 1 KB 968.

[10] On the meaning of 'day certain' see: *Shell Mex Ltd* v *Elton Cop Dyeing Co Ltd* (1928) 63 Comm Cas 29; *Henderson & Keay Ltd* v *AM Carmichael Ltd* 1956 SLT (Notes) 58; *Stein Forbes & Co* v *County Tailoring Co* (1916) 86 LJKB 448.

[11] [1980] 1 WLR 1129. See for Scottish perspectives on this case, *Lloyds Bank plc* v *Bamberger* 1993 SC 570 and MacQueen [1997] *Acta Juridica* 176, 194–5.

[12] 'Would have had' because in fact the case concerned the liability of guarantors, and not the buyers themselves. But one of the two grounds of decision clearly involved the holding that the buyers would have been liable if sued.

[13] [1980] AC 367.

some simplification of the law, the decision concerned land law, and the relationship of a right to specific performance and a claim for damages for breach of a contract to sell land. Applying this decision to the law of sale of goods might overlook the fact that there are special features to a contract of sale of goods, which mean (for instance) that even a termination of such a contract has retrospective effect in certain respects. Moreover, Lord Wilberforce in *Johnson* v *Agnew* (with whom all the other Law Lords concurred) said that:

> If the vendor treats the purchaser as having repudiated the contract and accepts the repudiation, he cannot thereafter seek specific performance. This follows from the fact that, the purchaser having repudiated the contract, and his repudiation having been accepted, both parties are discharged from further performance.[14]

In the context of a simple sale, the vendor cannot both claim to recover the entire purchase price and at the same time insist that the whole contract is terminated because of the purchaser's breach.

The answer may be that the decision in *Hyundai* is confined to contracts which are not straightforward contracts of sale, but contracts which involve the production of goods (here, a ship) over a period of time, requiring both labour and materials. It would therefore go too far if the ruling in *Hyundai* would extend to circumstances where a contract of sale involves payment by instalments and the contract is terminated after one or more instalments have become due. Otherwise, the simple possibility that the duty to pay may be (and normally is) conditional on subsequent performance by the other party would be overlooked.[15]

The ruling in *Hyundai* was applied with approval by the House of Lords in *Stocznia Gdanska SA* v *Latvian Shipping Co.*[16] on similar facts. One important factor was that the contract in both cases was not a simple contract of sale, but effectively one for work and materials which would ultimately have resulted in the transfer of property on completion. The House of Lords stressed the need to distinguish between sales *simpliciter* and contracts for work and materials (or similar). In the latter case, the House held that the question was not whether the 'buyer' had received anything under the contract but rather whether the seller/supplier had performed its contractual obligations in respect of which payment was due. This was so in *Hyundai* and *Stocznia Gdanska*. With regard to sales *simpliciter*, the House stressed that the seller would only be entitled to retain any money paid if the contract was completed, as was held in *Dies* v *British and International Mining and Finance Corporation Ltd.*[17]

This distinction is crucial. In a pure contract of sale, delivery of the goods is the whole consideration for the price, so it would be inconsistent for the seller to claim the price and also the right to cancel or terminate. If the goods are never delivered in such a case there is a total failure of consideration, so the buyer cannot (it seems) be made to pay the price, or, if they have paid it, must be entitled to recover it.[18] But where the contract involves manufacture as well as sale, the manufacture (and preliminary expenses of manufacture)

[14] [1980] AC 367, at 392.
[15] See Beatson (1981) 97 LQR 389.
[16] [1998] 1 W.L.R. 574.
[17] [1939] 1 K.B. 724. There, a distinction was drawn between an instalment payment (which would be recoverable on termination) and a deposit, which would be forfeited on termination due to the buyer's default.
[18] See *Rover International Ltd* v *Cannon Film Sales* [1987] 1 WLR 1597, noted by Beatson (1989) 105 LQR 179.

will be part of the consideration, so the seller would not be acting inconsistently in first suing for instalments, and later cancelling the whole contract. As *Stocznia Gdanska* suggests, this would be on condition that the instalment payment relates to elements of the seller's performance which have been provided (as was the case in *Stocznia Gdanska*).

16.1.2 Critique of present law

Obviously, an action for the price is more favourable to the seller than a mere action for damages for non-acceptance. But where the goods have not been delivered, the law may, in practice, place the seller in a somewhat difficult situation. The seller may choose to take their stand on the argument that the property has passed to the buyer, disclaim all responsibility for the goods and sue for the price. But if they take this course, they run the risk that the court may eventually decide that property had not passed to the buyer and that the seller's only remedy is for damages for non-acceptance. If the court takes this view, it follows that the seller will have been responsible for mitigating the damage by, for example, attempting to resell the goods. Their failure to do so may then reduce the damages to which they would have been entitled. On the other hand, if the seller attempts to mitigate the loss by reselling the goods, or part of them, or by dealing with them in some way, a court may treat this as evidence of an acceptance by the seller of repudiation of the contract by the buyer. The result of this will be that even if the property had originally passed to the buyer, it will now revest in the seller and an action for the price will no longer lie. If, therefore, the seller's efforts to resell the goods have failed, they will have made their own position worse by attempting to dispose of them.[19] And if their efforts to resell succeed, they may make their position worse in another respect. For by reselling these goods they may have lost an alternative sale and (at least in the case of second-hand goods) this will not be a recoverable item of damages.[20]

These difficulties largely stem from the fact that the seller is entitled to sue for the price of the goods where the property has passed but the buyer has refused to take delivery. It is doubtful whether in modern times this is the most sensible approach to the issues which arise. The most important practical problem in this situation is this: whose responsibility is it to resell or otherwise dispose of the goods and to hold them pending resale? If this responsibility should be the buyer's, then an action for the price is appropriate, but if it should rest on the seller, an action for damages for non-acceptance would be more appropriate. Which of the parties should bear this responsibility cannot, it is suggested, be answered simply by asking if the property has passed but should depend on a balance of convenience. For instance, if the seller is a dealer and the buyer is a private consumer (as has happened in several cases concerning the sale of motor vehicles) it seems more sensible that the seller should have the responsibility of reselling the goods, and should be confined to an action for damages. Conversely, there are situations – especially in export sales – where the responsibility for taking possession of the goods and trying to resell them should be on the buyer despite the fact that property has not passed. For instance, if the buyer refuses to accept shipping documents properly tendered in an f.o.b. or c.i.f. sale, it

[19] See, e.g., *R V Ward Ltd* v *Bignall* [1967] 1 QB 534.
[20] See *Lazenby Garages Ltd* v *Wright* [1976] 1 WLR 459.

would be extremely inconvenient for the seller to make arrangements to land, store and dispose of the goods at the place of destination. In this case, it would seem more reasonable if the seller could sue for the price and leave the buyer with the responsibility of dealing with the goods. In practice, if the price is payable by a banker's credit, the seller will probably be able to sue the bank if the documents are wrongly rejected, but there are some situations in which the seller should also have an action against the buyer for the price.

In this connection, it is interesting to note the provisions of Article 2-709 of the Uniform Commercial Code, which seem a considerable improvement on those of the Sale of Goods Act, although the Supreme Court's ruling in *PST Energy 7 LLC* v *OW Bunker Malta Ltd*[21] seems to have moved English law some way towards the position under the UCC.[22] Under Article 2-709(1), the seller can sue for the price if the buyer has accepted the goods, or if the goods have been identified to the contract and 'the seller is unable after reasonable effort to resell them at a reasonable price, or the circumstances reasonably indicate that such effort will be unavailing'. Thus, if the buyer refuses to take delivery of the goods, the seller is in the first instance obliged to try to resell the goods unless it is clear that this will be unavailing. The mere fact that property has passed, therefore, does not entitle the seller to sue for the price. Conversely, once the seller has made reasonable efforts to resell and these have proved unavailing they may sue for the price even though property has not passed. Moreover, once the seller is entitled to sue for the price under Article 2-709(1), Article 2-709(2) enables the seller to resell at any time prior to judgment if such resale becomes possible, without thereby forfeiting their right to sue for the price. They must, of course, give credit for the proceeds of the resale, but their claim will then be for the contract price less the resale price and does not become converted into an action for damages as it does under English law.

16.1.3 Claims for special damage

In addition to the seller's right to sue for the price, or for damages for non-acceptance, they may also have the right to claim special damages under s. 54 and the right to claim for any loss occasioned by the buyer's neglect to take delivery. In both cases, it seems immaterial whether or not the property has passed. A claim by a seller for special damages is likely to arise but rarely in practice,[23] and the principles governing such a claim may be more suitably dealt with when we come to examine the remedies of the buyer. A word needs to be said, however, on the possibility of a claim for loss occasioned by the buyer's failure to take delivery. Section 37 lays down:

(1) When the seller is ready and willing to deliver the goods, and requests the buyer to take delivery, and the buyer does not within a reasonable time after such request take delivery of the goods, he is liable to the seller for any loss occasioned by his neglect or refusal to take delivery, and also for a reasonable charge for the care and custody of the goods.

(2) Nothing in this section affects the rights of the seller when the neglect or refusal of the buyer to take delivery amounts to a repudiation of the contract.

[21] [2016] UKSC 23.

[22] See Saidov, Sales law post-*Res Cogitans* [2019] JBL 1 at 15–18.

[23] For one example, see *Penarth Dock Engineering Co Ltd* v *Pounds* [1963] 1 Lloyd's Rep 359.

Where, therefore, the property in the goods has passed to the buyer and they neglect to take delivery, the seller may either sue for damages or for the price and, in the latter case, they can add a claim under s. 37 for damages to cover the cost of care and custody, and any further loss they may have suffered, for example if the goods have gone bad and tainted other goods not sold to the buyer. If they sue for damages only, their claim will cover these items as a matter of course.

16.1.4 Price payable in foreign currency

Where the price is due in a foreign currency, but the action is brought in England and Wales, judgment can be given in the foreign currency itself.[24] There is, therefore, no need to convert the amount due into sterling, unless and until it becomes necessary to seek leave to enforce the judgment, when the conversion will be made at the rate of exchange prevailing at that date.[25] It has since been held that the buyer can ask that where an order for cost is made in sterling, a court can compensate for any exchange rate loss.[26]

16.2 Action for damages

We have already seen that the seller's only remedy where the property has not passed is an action for damages for non-acceptance, and that such an action is an alternative remedy where the property has passed but the buyer neglects to take delivery. It now becomes necessary to examine the principles on which these damages are calculable, leaving aside for the moment the question of special damages.

It may be convenient, first of all, to recall the general principle of contract law that the innocent party is bound to take reasonable steps to mitigate the damage. This principle applies to contracts of sale of goods as it applies to other contracts, and it applies equally whether the innocent party is buyer or seller. There is no need in a book of this nature to examine this principle at length, but it is mentioned here because the idea behind it underlies many of the detailed rules relating to damages in the law of sale of goods.

Moreover, in practice, breach of contract usually leads to some attempt at negotiating a settlement or finding some alternative way of performing the contract. Thus, a seller who cannot supply the goods contracted for may offer alternatives, or may offer late delivery.[27] A seller who has broken an agreement to supply on credit may offer instead to sell for cash.[28] Generally speaking, at least in commercial contracts, reasonable offers of this kind should be accepted by the innocent party or they may be penalised in damages.

[24] *Miliangos* v *George Frank (Textiles) Ltd* [1976] AC 443. This is also the Scottish position: Commerzbank Aktiengesellschaft v Large 1977 SC 375.

[25] *Miliangos* v *George Frank (Textiles) Ltd*, above, n. 26. See Civil Procedure Rules Part 40, Practice Direction 40B.

[26] *Elkamet Kunststofftechnik GmbH* v *Saint-Gobain Glass France SA* [2016] EWHC 3421 (Pat). See also the Supreme Court's ruling in *Re Lehman Brothers International (Europe) (In Administration)* [2017] UKSC 38, where the court did not apply Miliangos in the context of more recent provisions of the insolvency code.

[27] *The Solholt* [1983] 1 Lloyd's Rep 605.

[28] *Payzu Ltd* v *Saunders* [1919] 2 KB 581.

A second general principle of contract law is also worth noting at this point. In general, where a party has contracted for possible alternative performances, their liability is only to be assessed according to the least onerous or costly of those performances. For instance, in a contract for the sale of 5,000 tonnes, 5 per cent more or less at seller's option, the seller can only be liable for failing to deliver 4,750 tonnes; conversely, if the buyer has the option of choosing whether to take a larger or smaller quantity, they can only be liable for failing to take the minimum which they are obliged to take.[29] It has, however, been held that this principle only relates to the valuation of the defendant's promise; when the question is, 'What promises is he bound by?', it may well be that some term can be implied that the promise should be performed in a reasonable, not a minimal, way. So in *Paula Lee Ltd* v *Robert Zehil Ltd*,[30] where the buyer had agreed to buy at least 16,000 of the seller's dresses, it was held that it was an implied term that the buyer would take a reasonable selection of the dresses, and not 16,000 of the identical cheapest dress.

The general rule for the assessment of damages for the buyer's breach of contract is laid down by s. 50(2):

> The measure of damages is the estimated loss directly and naturally resulting, in the ordinary course of events, from the buyer's breach of contract.

And the general method of computing the loss directly and naturally arising from the buyer's breach is laid down by s. 50(3):

> Where there is an available market for the goods in question the measure of damages is *prima facie* to be ascertained by the difference between the contract price and the market or current price at the time or times when the goods ought to have been accepted or (if no time was fixed for acceptance) at the time of the refusal to accept.[31]

Clearly, resale in an available market is consistent with obligation to take reasonable steps to mitigate one's losses, and s. 50(3) reflects this assumption.[32] The High Court in *Glencore* v *Cirrus*[33] explained that s. 50(3) is not concerned with a loss of profits which the seller might have anticipated, but rather for the loss of the bargain with the buyer. Glencore had agreed to sell 630,000 barrels of blended crude oil to Cirrus, which Cirrus intended to resell, but the sub-buyer did not want blended oil. Cirrus therefore refused to proceed with the sale. Glencore managed to terminate the supply contract with its supplier without any liability, but brought an action for damages under s. 50. Cirrus argued that there was no claim because s. 50 was essentially concerned with lost profits assuming that transactions had proceeded (there was a clause excluding liability for lost profits in the contract). This was rejected by Cooke J, who held that the purpose of s. 50 was to compensate the seller for the loss of his bargain with the buyer, which is done by working out how much worse off the seller would have been if, at the time of the breach, he sold the goods to a substitute buyer. Glencore's claim for damages ($2.5 million) therefore succeeded.

[29] See, e.g., *Laverack* v *Woods of Colchester* [1967] 1 QB 278.
[30] [1983] 2 All ER 390.
[31] This is not, as some suppose, a rule derived from the *Hadley* v *Baxendale* rule, the first limb of which appears in s. 50(2). It is an older rule – see *Dunlop* v *Higgins* (1848) 1 HLC 381, (1848) 6 Bell's App 195. It is regrettable, for the reasons which appear below, that Judge Chalmers chose to codify this rather than the *Hadley* v *Baxendale principle*.
[32] Cf., *Sharp Corp Ltd* v *Viterra BV* [2024] UKSC 14, para 87.
[33] *Glencore Energy UK Ltd* v *Cirrus Oil Services Ltd* [2014] EWHC 87 (Comm).

16.2.1 Meaning of 'available market

The first question to which this subsection gives rise is what is meant by 'an available market'? It is surprising how scanty is the authority on this point. In *Dunkirk Colliery Co Ltd* v *Lever*,[34] there is a dictum by James LJ which suggests that a market necessarily signifies some place where the goods can be sold. In *Marshall* v *Nicoll*,[35] an appeal to the House of Lords from Scotland, it was held, in a somewhat confusing and inconclusive discussion, that there might be a market within the meaning of s. 51(3) – the corresponding section dealing with non-delivery – although the goods were being specially made to order and the market for such goods was extremely limited. Next, in *W L Thompson Ltd* v *Robinson (Gunmakers) Ltd*,[36] the question was fully argued before Upjohn J who thought himself bound to follow the dictum of James LJ in *Dunkirk Colliery Co Ltd* v *Lever*,[37] although that case was decided before the Sale of Goods Act, and although the dictum was manifestly *obiter* and was not expressly concurred in by the other members of the court.[38] But the learned judge gave his own opinion on the matter:[39]

> Had the matter been res integra I think that I should have found that an 'available market' merely means that the situation in the particular trade in the particular area was such that the particular goods could freely be sold, and that there was a demand sufficient to absorb readily all the goods that were thrust on it so that if a purchaser defaulted the goods in question could readily be disposed of.[40]

This opinion seems preferable to that of James LJ as becomes clear when the facts of *W L Thompson Ltd* v *Robinson (Gunmakers) Ltd*[41] are examined. In this case, the buyer contracted to buy a car from the plaintiffs, but failed to take delivery when the car was available. The sellers returned the car to the makers and claimed from the buyer damages for their loss of profit on the sale. It was found as a fact that the supply of cars exceeded the demand in that area when the contract was made. At that time, resale price maintenance was still rigidly enforced in relation to cars and other consumer goods and, consequently, there was rarely any difference between the contract price and the market price in the sense of the fixed retail price.[42] The buyer contended that there was a market and that there being no difference between the market price and the contract price, the sellers were only entitled to nominal damages. Had this contention succeeded, the plaintiffs would have been deprived of damages to which they were clearly entitled in the present state of the law.[43] For even if the sellers had not returned the car to the makers, but resold it to another buyer, they would still have lost one sale. For, with an excess of supply over

[34] (1878) 9 Ch D 20, 25.
[35] 1919 SC (HL) 129.
[36] [1955] Ch 177.
[37] (1878) 9 Ch D 20.
[38] Moreover, two valuable dicta appear not to have been cited. In *The Arpad* [1934] P 189, 191, Bateson J said: 'Market means buyers and sellers'; and in *Heskell* v *Continental Express Ltd* [1950] 1 All ER 1033, 1050, Devlin J said: 'A market for this purpose means more than a particular place. It means also a particular level of trade'.
[39] This definition was in fact adopted by Sellers J in ABD *(Metals & Waste) Ltd* v *Anglo-Chemical & Ore Co Ltd* [1955] 2 Lloyd's Rep 456.
[40] [1955] Ch 177, at 187.
[41] [1955] Ch 177.
[42] Resale price maintenance is prohibited by the Competition Act 1998, s. 2(2)(a).
[43] Which, of course, is based on the assumption that a plaintiff should be entitled to damages for their lost expectations.

demand, the sellers would still have been able to supply the second buyer with a car even had there been no breach, and thereby earned profit on both sales.[44] In the event, Upjohn J avoided this result by holding that, even if there were a market, s. 50(3) only laid down a *prima facie* rule and that this rule could not be applied in this particular case.

This conclusion received the approval of the Court of Appeal in *Charter* v *Sullivan*.[45] This case was the counterpart of *W L Thompson Ltd* v *Robinson (Gunmakers) Ltd* in that, on otherwise identical facts, the claimant was able to dispose of all the cars he could obtain, and he was accordingly held entitled only to nominal damages. The Court of Appeal agreed with Upjohn J that on such facts it was immaterial whether there was an available market or not, but Jenkins LJ disagreed (*obiter*) as to the meaning of the term 'available market'. He did not, however, offer his own definition, but rested content with saying that a market presupposes that prices are fixed by reference to supply and demand, and the goods are not sold at a fixed retail price.

As resale price maintenance is no longer permitted in the UK, this particular point has ceased to be of much importance. Both in retail and in commercial sales the 'market price' is now likely to be the average or mid-point of a number of different prices prevailing in the market in question.

If the meaning of the term 'available market' remains without firm judicial definition, the question whether there is an available market in any particular case seems now to be treated by the courts as a question of fact and, in some cases, even as a question of degree. There may, for instance, be evidence that sales occasionally take the place of the commodity in question, but only rarely, or in small quantities.[46] Or there may be evidence that similar though not identical goods are readily available or disposable.[47] Or again, there may be evidence that it is possible to buy or sell the goods at a different place or in smaller quantities. In all these cases, the courts take a fairly broad and common-sense view of the question. The question which is usually treated as decisive is whether or not it would be reasonable for the seller to dispose of the goods through such market as is in fact available. It has, in fact, been suggested that the market price rule is best seen as an illustration of the rule that the innocent party must mitigate their loss; accordingly, attempts to define 'market' in any narrow or technical sense are to be deplored. The important question is whether the seller can reasonably find a substitute purchaser.

In this regard, the following observations by Lord *Sumption in Bunge SA* v *Nidera BV*[48] are significant:

> 'There are three important things to note about measurement of damages by reference to an available market. First it presupposes the existence of an available market in which to obtain a substitute contract. Secondly, it presupposes that the substitute contract is a true substitute. The claimant is not entitled to charge the defendant with the cost of obtaining superior benefits to those which the defendant contracted to provide. Thirdly (and in the present case most importantly), the purpose of the exercise is to measure the extent to which the claimant is (or would be) financially worse off under the substitute contract than under the original contract.'[49]

[44] Cf. *In re Vic Mill Ltd* [1913] 1 Ch 465.

[45] [1957] 2 QB 117. See also *Lazenby Garages Ltd* v *Wright* [1976] 1 WLR 459.

[46] *Kwei Tek Chao* v *British Traders & Shippers Ltd* [1954] 2 QB 459, 498 (held: a market). Cf. *Garnac Grain Co* v *H M Faure & Fairclough* [1968] AC 1130, 1138 (held: evidence on which judge could find there was a market, although it was not possible to buy the contract quantity in one amount for immediate delivery).

[47] *Hinde* v *Liddell* (1875) 10 QB 265.

[48] [2015] UKSC 43.

[49] Ibid., para 82.

If something needs to be done to the goods to make them saleable on the market, and it would be uneconomic for the seller to carry out such work, it would appear that the contract/market measure would not be the appropriate measure.[50]

16.2.2 Effect of resale by seller on 'available market'

The market price rule is, in principle, based on the loss which the claimant (seller) would have suffered if, on non-acceptance by the buyer, the claimant had sold the goods in the market. It is thus concerned with a notional or hypothetical sale which might reasonably have been made by the seller. The rule then gives rise to problems where the seller actually has gone into the market and resold the goods. If this resale is actually at the market price there will, of course, be no difficulty, but if the resale is made at less than the market price, the seller may wish to claim as damages the difference between the original contract price and the resale price, rather than the market price. Equally, if the resale takes place at a price higher than the market price, the buyer may claim that the damages should only represent the difference between the contract and the resale price. The question then arises whether the actual resale price should be taken into account, or whether the damages must still be calculated by reference to the market price.

In attempting to answer these questions, it is necessary to distinguish between the case where the seller finds a substitute buyer immediately on non-acceptance by the buyer, and the case where the seller chooses to retain the goods for some period before reselling them.[51] If they resell more or less forthwith on non-acceptance by the buyer at less than the market price, the seller will clearly have difficulty in claiming damages based on this resale price. For the obvious question will be why the seller should have resold at less than the market price. *Prima facie*, the requirement that they should mitigate their loss would have required them to sell at not less than the market price and, unless the seller can find some very convincing reason for what they have done, it is difficult to see why they should recover more than the difference between the contract and the market price. If, on the other hand, the seller succeeds in convincing the court that in the particular circumstances, it was reasonable of them (despite the mitigation principle) to resell at the price which they in fact obtained, it seems improbable that the court would find that the resale price actually was lower than the market price. Such findings would be contradictory, in the ordinary way, and a decision that the actual resale price was reasonable would normally connote a finding that there was no available market at which the seller could have disposed of the goods at a higher price.

If the seller resells promptly on breach by the buyer at *more* than the market price, it is not wholly clear whether the buyer can take advantage of this to reduce the damages they would otherwise have to pay. The seller will, of course, face the same evidentiary problem as in the converse situation discussed in the last paragraph. That is to say, the seller may have difficulty in convincing the court that there was an available market in which prices

[50] See *Tharros Shipping Co Ltd and another* v *Bias Shipping Ltd and another* [1994] 1 Lloyd's Rep 533 – this case involved a charterparty, but it would appear to support the point made in the text.

[51] A third possibility is that the seller delays in reselling in the market because they are still trying to persuade the buyer to take the goods.

were lower than the price actually obtained, for this implies that the second buyer made a bad bargain. And although parties do, of course, make bad bargains from time to time, the situation envisaged here is one in which the seller has unexpectedly had the goods left on their hands by non-acceptance by the buyer and in which, therefore, one would have expected the seller to be in a poor bargaining situation. However, let it be assumed that the seller is able to establish that they have resold at more than the market price. As the seller cannot claim for the loss if they sell below the market price, it may seem only fair that they should be able to retain any profit they make by selling at above the market price. But there does seem to be a modern trend to deny recovery for a 'loss' which is in fact counterbalanced by a profit, and it seems probable that a court would hold that the seller is only entitled to the difference between contract and resale price, as this is the true measure of their loss. There seems no clear authority on this point, but the present submission appears to be the correct inference from the decision of the Court of Appeal in *Campbell Mostyn (Provisions) Ltd* v *Barnett Trading Co*[52] where the seller *retained the goods after the breach and subsequently resold them* for more than the market price prevailing at the date of breach. It was held in these circumstances that the seller was entitled to recover the difference between contract and market price and did not have to account for the greater price at which he had in fact sold the goods. Somervell LJ quoted with approval the following passage from Lord Wrenbury's speech in *AKAS Jamal* v *Moolla Dawood*,[53] a Privy Council case dealing with shares:

> If the seller retains the shares after the breach the speculation as to the way the market will subsequently go is the speculation of the seller, not of the buyer; the seller cannot recover from the buyer the loss below the market price at the date of the breach if the market falls, nor is he liable to the purchaser for the profit if the market rises.

It seems a reasonable inference that the position is different where the seller resells immediately upon breach. This conclusion may also be supported by the decision of the Court of Appeal in *R Pagnan & Fratelli* v *Corbisa Industrial Agropacuaria Limitada*,[54] although here the circumstances were rather unusual. This case concerned a breach of contract by the seller rather than the buyer, but in general the same principles are applicable. In this case, the buyers rightly rejected the goods delivered but then, as part of a settlement of the dispute, agreed to buy the same goods at a substantially lower price. This price was lower even than the market price and the buyers consequently made a handsome overall profit which exceeded their loss on the original sale. It was held that the second contract was part of a continuous course of dealing between the parties and not a wholly new and independent event. Consequently, the profit made by the buyers on the second sale had to be set off against their loss on the first, and they were only entitled to nominal damages. While it is not wholly clear whether the result would have been the same if the second purchase had not been from the sellers, the case does illustrate a modern reluctance to award damages for a 'loss' which in one sense is purely notional.

In some cases, the court will lack evidence that the market price on the date when the goods should have been accepted was other than the price at which the seller eventually

[52] [1954] 1 Lloyd's Rep 65.
[53] [1916] 1 AC 175, 179.
[54] [1970] 1 WLR 1306. See also *Lazenby Garages Ltd* v *Wright* [1976] 1 WLR 431, below, p. 413, and *The Solholt* [1983] 1 Lloyd's Rep 605.

sold. In such a case, it will necessarily have to be assumed that the relevant price for the purposes of s. 50(3) is the price at which the seller sold the goods.

16.2.3 Which market?

Where there is an available market in more than one place, the relevant place is *prima facie* the place at which the goods were to be delivered under the contract. So in *Hasell* v *Bagot, Shakes & Lewis Ltd*,[55] where Japanese superphosphate was sold for delivery at Adelaide, it was held by the Australian High Court that the question was whether there was a market at Adelaide and not in Japan. Had there been a market in both places, the market price at Adelaide would have been the relevant price. However, where goods are sold f.o.b. or c.i.f. for shipment to a particular market, then the relevant market would *prima facie* be that at the place of destination.[56] The point to remember in all cases is that if the buyer refuses to accept the goods the seller will ordinarily have to find a substitute purchaser, and the question is where should the seller reasonably be expected to look for such a purchaser? Where the seller's business is limited to a particular local area, the availability of a market in that area and the market price in that area are the only relevant considerations.[57] In other cases, the seller may reasonably be expected to look far afield for a substitute purchaser, where the seller is engaged in international trade, for example.

16.2.4 Market price at what date?

The provisions of the Act dealing with the date at which the damages should be assessed by reference to the market price have given rise to a good deal of trouble, largely because the modern rules as to repudiation and mitigation were not settled when the 1893 Act was drafted. Some points are clear enough. Where the buyer's refusal to take the goods occurs at the time when they should have been accepted, the provisions of s. 50(3) are exactly in point, and the seller recovers the difference between the contract price and the market price at that time. Although it has been argued here that this rule should not be too rigidly applied, this view has apparently not found favour in a recent Supreme Court decision. Lord Hamblen JSC noted that:

> 'Provided there is an available market, the market price establishes the default priceregardless of what the injured party actually does and even if a decision to delay in enteringthe market is a commercially reasonable business decision. A decision to delay is the injuredparty's voluntary and independent commercial decision and its consequences are irrelevant to thedamages payable, however well or badly it works out . . .'[58]

However, in commercial practices, it often happens that a breach by the buyer is not followed by the immediate resale of the goods in the market. Indeed, in practice the seller is much more likely to try to negotiate some alternative arrangement with the buyer, or to

[55] *Lawrence Kostoris & Son Ltd* [1967] 1 Lloyd's Rep 63, 71 per Diplock LJ.
[56] *Aryeh* v *Lawrence Kostoris & Son Ltd* [1967] 1 Lloyd's Rep 63, 71 per Diplock LJ.
[57] *W L Thompson Ltd* v *Robinson (Gunmakers) Ltd* [1955] Ch 177.
[58] *Sharp Corp Ltd* v *Viterra BV* [2024] UKSC 14, para 95.

try to persuade them to take the goods after all. This is reasonable commercial behaviour which ought to be encouraged by the courts, but the Supreme Court's view in *Sharp* v *Viterra* (above) suggests otherwise. It would appear to sit uneasily amongst cases which have accepted that, where commercially reasonable attempts at finding a solution mean that the goods are only resold after some delay, the seller may be entitled to obtain damages based on the market price at this later date.[59]

Where no time for the delivery of the goods has been fixed by the contract, the tendency is for the courts to look to the market price at the time when the goods should have been accepted, i.e., the actual date of delivery,[60] and to ignore the last words of the section which state that the relevant time is the time when the buyer refuses to accept the goods.[61] In *Millett* v *Van Heeck*[62] the Court of Appeal decided that the market price at the date at which the buyer refuses to take delivery is quite irrelevant where his refusal takes the form of an anticipatory breach. In such a case, the seller has the choice of accepting the repudiation,[63] or of continuing to treat the contract as binding, but in either event the damages are *prima facie* assessable by reference to the market price at the date when delivery ought to have been accepted. So, for example, where the buyers failed to give 15 days' notice of readiness to load a vessel as required by the contract, the sellers were entitled to leave the contract open until the last date of the shipment period, and claim damages based on the market price as at that date.[64]

If the action comes on for trial before the date when the buyer was bound to accept the goods, the court must make the best estimate it can of the probable market price at this date. In either event, if the market rises between the date of repudiation and the date when delivery should have been accepted, the relevant market price appears to be that prevailing at the latter date. In other words, the seller is not entitled to receive a higher measure of damages merely because the buyer repudiates the contract at a time when the market is lower than it is on the delivery date.[65] Otherwise, they would receive more as a result of the breach than they would have received if the contract had been performed. This result can be justified by suggesting that where the buyer repudiates before the date for delivery, it must be presumed that the seller will not be able to resell in the market before that date. Even if the seller accepts the repudiation they are entitled to wait until the contractual delivery date, except where it might be expected that the seller's duty to mitigate would oblige the seller to enter into a substitute contract earlier.

Thus, where the market falls between the date of repudiation and the date when the goods ought to have been accepted, the result may be different. Here, it has been held that if the seller does accept the repudiation, the duty to mitigate the damage means that they

[59] This is spelled out quite plainly in the dicta of Lord Wilberforce (speaking for the whole House of Lords) in *Johnson* v *Agnew* [1980] AC 367, 400–1, which were followed in *Suleiman* v *Shahsavari* [1989] 2 All ER 460.

[60] *Bunge SA* v *Nidera SA* [2015] UKSC 43.

[61] See *Tai Hing Cotton Mill Ltd* v *Kamsing Knitting Factory* [1979] AC 91, 104, a case on the equivalent provision dealing with damages for non-delivery, s. 51(3).

[62] [1921] 2 KB 369.

[63] Reselling the goods following the buyer's repudiation can constitute acceptance of the repudiation – see *Vitol SA* v *Norelf Ltd* [1993] 2 Lloyd's Rep 301.

[64] *Lusograin Comercio Internacional de Cereas Ltda* v *Bunge AG* [1986] 2 Lloyd's Rep 654.

[65] *Melachrino* v *Nickoll & Knight* [1920] 1 KB 693.

should resell at once in a falling market, and that if they fail to do this they cannot hold the buyer liable for a greater amount than the difference between the contract price and the market price at the date of the repudiation.[66] However, some justifiable scepticism has been expressed as to the idea that the innocent seller should be able to identify a 'falling market' before it has fallen,*[AM10] and it must be said that it is difficult to justify an assessment of damages at the date of termination on this ground. Of course, it could be argued that once the seller accepts the buyer's repudiation, the contract is at an end, and the damages should be assessed as at the date when the seller should reasonably have resold the goods in the market. But that argument is equally applicable whether the market rises or falls after the termination of the contract, yet, as we have seen, where the market rises it is established that the damages must be assessed as at the contract delivery date and not when the contract is terminated.

Should the seller decline to accept the repudiation, however, as they are perfectly entitled to do,[67] they are under no obligation to mitigate their damage by reselling at once. They can stand by the contract and wait until the delivery date before reselling and, in this case, they are entitled to receive damages assessed in the normal way by reference to the market price at the date when the goods ought to have been accepted.[68] The Court of Appeal's decision in *Millett* v *Van Heeck* was approved by the Privy Council in a case dealing with s. 51(3), the corresponding subsection concerning non-delivery.[69] In this case, the Privy Council accepted that the second limb of the subsection (that damages are to be assessed at the time of refusal to accept where no time is fixed for acceptance) may in fact have no application at all. First, they accepted the decision in *Millett* v *Van Heeck* that the subsection has no application to anticipatory breach, it being the clear assumption of the subsection that the breach has occurred after the date for delivery has passed. But it is also difficult to see how the subsection can apply even if the breach is not anticipatory. If no time for acceptance is fixed by the contract, it must nevertheless be the case that delivery must be made either in a reasonable time or on demand. But if delivery is to be made in a reasonable time, and at the expiry of such a period the buyer refuses to accept the goods, then the first limb of s. 50(3) would apply anyhow. In other words, in this situation, both limbs of the subsection give the same result. The relevant date for assessing the damages is the date when the goods ought to have been accepted, which in this case is also the date when the buyer has refused to accept them. If, on the other hand, the contract provides for delivery on demand, then, as soon as demand is made, a time for the delivery of the goods has been fixed, so once again the subsection would seem to point to the date when the goods should have been accepted as the relevant date, and once again the date of refusal to accept would be irrelevant.

[66] *Roth* v *Tayson* (1896) 73 LT 628.

[67] *Frost* v *Knight* (1872) LR 7 Ex 111. See also *Sudan Import & Export Co (Khartoum) Ltd* v *Société Générale de Compensation* [1958] 1 Lloyd's Rep 310, where the sellers at first refused to accept the repudiation but later agreed to do so.

[68] *Tredegar Iron & Coal Co Ltd* v *Hawthorne* (1902) 18 TLR 716. These principles received the approval of the House of Lords in *Garnac Grain Co* v *H M Faure & Fairclough* [1968] AC 1130.

[69] *Tai Hing Cotton Mill Ltd* v *Kamsing Knitting Factory* [1979] AC 91; see Chapter 18, at section 18.2.2, for the facts.

16.2.5 Cases where market price rule inapplicable

The rule laid down by s. 50(3) is only a *prima facie* method of calculating the damages, and if it would lead to an obviously incorrect assessment of the loss directly and naturally resulting from the breach, it must be discarded and some other method of assessment, based, for example, on the profit lost or expenses incurred (such as sums paid on the cancellation of a charterparty),[70] must be used. We have already seen that problems sometimes arise where specific goods are resold after the buyer has refused to accept them, and the question has arisen whether the seller has, in the result, suffered any loss at all.[71] In the case of new manufactured goods, the answer depends on whether the market situation is such that the seller has lost a sale. But this is not the rule with respect to unique goods. If the buyer refuses to accept goods in this category and the seller resells at (or at more than) the first contract price, they suffer no loss at all, for they could not have made more than one profit from a unique chattel. It has been held by the Court of Appeal that a second-hand car is a unique chattel for this purpose.[72]

Naturally, if there is no market at all the subsection is of no assistance. In these cases, the amount recoverable must depend upon whether the seller has already procured or manufactured the goods for delivery or not. If they have done so, the *prima facie* measure of damages is the difference between the contract price and the value of the goods at the date of breach.[73] Since there is, on this supposition, no market, there will often be practical problems in assessing the value of the goods at the time of breach, but the court must do the best it can on the material available to it, for example, the fact that the seller has managed to re-sell the goods.[74] Where the goods have been manufactured to some special order, it may even be that they have no value at all and the seller will then be able to sue for the full price. But their right to the whole of these damages will, of course, depend upon proof that the goods are useless and unsaleable, not only in their existing form, but even after reasonable alterations. For the seller must always mitigate their damage and, if they can make the goods saleable by small alterations, they should do so.[75] If, on the other hand, the seller has not yet procured or manufactured the goods, they will *prima facie* be entitled to recover the difference between the contract price and the cost to themselves of so procuring or manufacturing the goods, that is to say, their profit.

The mere fact that the non-performance of the contract which has been broken has enabled the seller to make profits on other contracts does not of itself entitle the defaulting buyer to claim that the profits so made should be set off against those which have been lost as a result of their breach, as the seller might have been able to earn both lots of profit.[76]

[70] *Bem Dis A Turk Ticaret S/A Tr* v *International Agri Trade Co Ltd* [1999] 1 Lloyd's Rep 729.

[71] *W L Thompson Ltd* v *Robinson (Gunmakers) Ltd* [1955] Ch 177; *Charter* v *Sullivan* [1957] 2 QB 117.

[72] *Lazenby Garages Ltd* v *Wright* [1976] 1 WLR 459.

[73] *Harlow & Jones Ltd* v *Panex (International) Ltd* [1967] 2 Lloyd's Rep 509, 530.

[74] *McCandless Aircraft LC* v *Payne* [2010] EWHC 1835 (QB), where a second-hand helicopter, which the buyer refused to accept, was resold by the seller at a lower price and damages were calculated on the basis of the difference between the contract price and the sum actually obtained by the seller on resale.

[75] It cannot be said as a general rule that the innocent party cannot be expected to lay out money to mitigate their damages, although this may be so where the suggested expenditure would be highly speculative: *Jewelowski* v *Propp* [1944] KB 510.

[76] *In re Vic Mill Ltd* [1913] 1 Ch 465; *W L Thompson Ltd* v *Robinson (Gunmakers) Ltd* [1955] Ch 177; cf. *Glencore Energy UK Ltd* v *Cirrus Oil Services Ltd* [2014] EWHC 87 (Comm).

But in *Hill & Sons* v *Edwin Showell & Sons*,[77] the House of Lords held that a buyer is entitled to give evidence to show that in fact the seller would not have been able to earn both lots of profit, for example if his factory has been working to capacity the whole time. Although the burden of proof on the buyer in this respect is a heavy one, if they can succeed in establishing the point the seller will only be entitled to recover the difference between the profit they should have made and the profit they actually made.

A relatively recent phenomenon might also necessitate the development of a tailored approach: the increased prevalence of dynamic pricing, enabled by data-driven digital technologies. Prices are adjusted based on a variety of factors, which can include demand but also, in some instance, personal features of a buyer. Where prices are determined on this basis, it might be difficult to have recourse to the market price rule, particularly where dynamic pricing is widespread in a particular business sector.

Damages for non-acceptance can be awarded in a foreign currency where appropriate.[78] For example, where overseas sellers sell goods to English buyers and the buyers wrongfully refuse to accept the goods, it will often be appropriate to award damages in the currency of the seller's business. The appropriate currency may be expressly or impliedly fixed by the contract (e.g. it will often be the currency of the contract itself) or it may be fixed by the court as the currency which best expresses the loss. The rule, it has been said, must be sensibly and flexibly applied so as to produce a just and appropriate result. In some cases, the immediate loss will indicate the appropriate currency; in others, there may be further factors indicating a different currency.

[77] (1918) 87 LJKB 1106.

[78] *The Despina* [1979] AC 685; *Ozalid Group (Export)* v *African Continental Bank* [1979] 2 Lloyd's Rep 231; Civil Procedure Rules Part 40, Practice Direction 40B.

Part VII

The remedies of the buyer

17

Rejection of the goods, rescission and specific performance

17.1 Buyer's right to reject the goods

The buyer's first and primary remedy for a breach of contract by the seller is to reject the goods, and, if appropriate, to repudiate the contract. As we have seen, the remedy of repudiation is available to the buyer only when the seller's breach of contract goes to the root of the agreement, either because it is a breach of condition or because of the nature and consequences of a breach of an innominate term.[1] The right to reject is separate from the right to repudiate the contract, and circumstances giving rise to a right of rejection do not, even if the right is exercised, necessarily put an end to the contract.[2] The seller can usually, until the time of performance has expired, therefore, tender a conforming delivery.[3]

The Sale and Supply of Goods Act 1994 made significant changes to this area.[4] As a result the buyer no longer has the right to reject for breach of the statutory requirements as to quality and quantity where the breach is so slight that it would be unreasonable to reject the goods. This change is implemented by s. 15A to the Act limiting the right to reject for a breach of ss. 13 to 15, and s. 30(2A)–(2E),[5] and where 'the breach is so slight that it would be unreasonable for [the buyer] to reject [the goods]'. In the case of a breach of s. 30, s. 30(2A) likewise limits the buyer's right to reject for a shortfall, or the right to reject all the goods for an excess, if the shortfall or the excess 'is so slight that it would be unreasonable for them to do so'. The right to reject an excess itself is unaffected by these proposals, and remains an absolute right. There are equivalent provisions relating to other contracts for the supply of goods.[6]

The Scottish approach is similar, but easier to state. The buyer may reject only if the breach, whether of an express or an implied term of the contract, is material. The right to reject for excess or shortfall of supply is likewise dependent upon the materiality of the

[1] See Chapter 4 *et seq*. As to the loss of the right of rejection, see section 17.2.1 *et seq*.

[2] See, however, the view expressed by Devlin J in *Kwei Tek Chao* v *British Traders & Shippers* [1954] 2 QB 459, 480. But since the HL decision in *Johnson* v *Agnew* [1980] AC 367 this view is surely incorrect. In [1966] CLJ 192, 194 Lord Devlin pointed out that what creates the breach is failure to tender conforming *goods within the contract time* – see below. Furthermore, where rejection of the goods for breach of condition is a termination of the contract, it is not a rescission *ab initio*. Hence there is no inconsistency in rejecting some of the goods while keeping the rest – see Chapter 19.

[3] See *Borrowman Phillips & Co* v *Free & Hollis* (1878) 4 QBD 500; *E E Brian Smith* (1928) *Ltd* v *Wheatsheaf Mills Ltd* [1939] 2 KB 302; and see Chapter 19.

[4] The Act is based on the proposals contained in the Law Commissions' Report, *Sale and Supply of Goods, paras* 4.1–6.24.

[5] ss. 30(2A) and (2B) do not apply to Scotland, and s. 30(2D) applies to Scotland only.

[6] Schedule 2, para. 6(5) and (9).

excess or shortfall, as the case may be.[7] Again, there are equivalent provisions for other contracts relating to the supply of goods.[8]

As we have previously noted, a regrettable feature of the English provisions is that they only apply to breaches of the seller's statutory duties. They therefore have no application to a breach of a stipulation as to time, or any other express term of the contract which is classifiable as a condition. Presentation of shipping documents one day too late, failure by the buyer to open a letter of credit by the stipulated date and similar breaches of contract will, therefore, continue to be governed by the common law which permits rejection by the buyer (or repudiation by the seller) however reasonable or unreasonable it may be.

Sections 13–15, including the added provisions, being subject to s. 55(1) of the 1979 Act,[9] are excludable by a contrary intention. It might be argued, however, that any contract term purporting to exclude the restrictions on the buyer's right to reject the goods would be subject to a test of reasonableness by virtue of the Unfair Contract Terms Act 1977. However, the application of ss. 3 and 17 is problematic, and the argument could only apply where the contract is made on the *buyer's* written standard terms, when it would have to be argued under s. 3(2)(b) or s. 17(1)(b) that the effect of the term is to allow the buyer to render a contractual performance substantially different from that which was expected of them, or no performance at all. Moreover, s. 6 of the Act, as we have seen, prevents the exclusion of ss. 13–15 and any attempt by the *seller* to exclude the *buyer's* right of rejection would be ineffective by virtue of s. 6 read together with s. 13 or by s. 20 read together with s. 25(3).

These provisions are useful because they preclude rejection on capricious and technical grounds. In particular, rejection on the ground of a technical breach of the statutory implied terms is unlikely to be available now, which will combat instances when the buyer's real motive in rejecting the goods is that market prices had fallen since the contract was made. While these qualifications arguably introduce some element of uncertainty as to when the right of rejection would not be available, this is an acceptable price to pay if it reduces instances of totally unreasonable commercial behaviour.

It is perhaps not entirely clear how far the personal position of the buyer will be relevant in examining the question of reasonableness in this context. Presumably, if the buyer has their own good reasons for needing goods which are in precise conformity with the contract (even if this was not known to the seller) it will not be unreasonable of the buyer to reject them for any slight nonconformity. On the other hand, whether or not the right of rejection arises at all will depend upon there being found a breach of one of the implied terms as to quality; in order to sue for a breach of the implied term as to fitness for purpose, the Act requires the buyer to have made known to the seller the particular purpose for which the goods are required. In consequence, whether or not this situation arises will almost certainly depend upon whether there is found to be a breach of the other quality terms, and in particular the implied term that the goods are of satisfactory quality. It is also unclear whether other personal circumstances of the buyer (his market position, for instance) will be relevant in deciding whether rejection is reasonable.

Two further questions relating to the buyer's right of rejection remain to be discussed here.

[7] Sale of Goods Act 1979, s. 30(2D).

[8] Supply of Goods and Services Act 1982, Pt IA.

[9] See Chapter 5.

17.1.1 Instalment sales

It is first necessary to consider the position which arises in a contract for the sale of goods by instalments, where the seller is guilty of a breach as to one or more instalments. Is the buyer entitled in such circumstances to reject the whole of the contract goods or is the buyer entitled only to reject that part in respect of which there is a breach of contract, or is the only available claim one for damages? The question is posed rather than answered by s. 31(2) as follows:

> Where there is a contract for the sale of goods to be delivered by stated instalments, which are to be separately paid for, and the seller makes defective deliveries in respect of one or more instalments, or the buyer neglects or refuses to take delivery of or pay for one or more instalments, it is a question in each case depending on the terms of the contract and the circumstances of the case, whether the breach of contract is a repudiation of the whole contract or whether it is a severable breach giving rise to a claim for compensation but not to a right to treat the whole contract as repudiated.

17.1.2 Non-severable contracts

Section 31(2), by its express terms, only applies where the goods are to be delivered by instalments and the instalments are to be separately paid for. But this is not an exhaustive statement of the circumstances in which a contract may be severable.[10] As will be seen later,[11] there are cases in which a contract is severable in law even though the goods are not to be delivered by separate instalments or the instalments are not to be separately paid for. But if the contract is not severable, then it is to be treated as an entire contract. Hence, in these cases a partial breach is to be treated in the same way as a total breach and the buyer is *prima facie* entitled to reject all the goods. In this situation, the fact that the goods are delivered in instalments is immaterial once it is found that this does not make the contract severable.[12]

17.1.3 Severable contracts

Where the contract is severable because the goods are to be delivered in instalments and are to be separately paid for, the right of the buyer to reject the whole contract quantity depends, as stated by s. 31(2), on the terms of the contract and the circumstances of the case. If the contract is severable although the goods are not to be delivered in instalments or the instalments are not to be separately paid for, the same rules probably apply as a matter of common law. If the contract is silent as to the events which have occurred:

> The main tests to be considered in applying the sub-section . . . are, first, the ratio quantitatively which the breach bears to the contract as a whole and secondly, the degree of probability or improbability that such a breach will be repeated.[13]

[10] This is expressly stated by Atkin LJ in *Longbottom & Co Ltd* v *Bass Walker & Co Ltd* [1922] WN 245, but it is also implicit in many other cases.

[11] See below, section 17.3 *et seq*.

[12] *Gill & Duffus SA* v *Berger & Co Inc* [1983] 1 Lloyd's Rep 622, reversed on different grounds [1984] AC 382.

[13] *Maple Flock Co Ltd* v *Universal Furniture Products (Wembley) Ltd* [1934] 1 KB 148, 157 per Lord Hewart CJ.

Two cases may be contrasted. In *Maple Flock Co Ltd* v *Universal Furniture Products (Wembley) Ltd*,[14] the plaintiffs contracted to sell 100 tons of rag flock to the defendants, delivery to be at the rate of three weekly instalments of one and a half tons each, as required, and the flock to conform to government standards. The first 15 loads were satisfactory, but a sample from the sixteenth load showed that it did not conform to government standards. In the meantime, the defendants had taken delivery of four more loads, all of which were satisfactory. Applying the above test, the Court of Appeal held that the defendants were not entitled to repudiate the contract, as the breach only affected one and a half tons out of the flock already delivered and it was most improbable that it would recur. On the other hand, in *R A Munro & Co Ltd* v *Meyer*,[15] A agreed to buy 1,500 tons of meat and bone meal, delivery at the rate of 125 tons a month, from B. After more than half of the total quantity had been delivered and discovered to be seriously defective, the buyer claimed to repudiate the contract. Wright J held that he was entitled to do so. 'Where the breach is substantial and so serious as the breach in this case and has continued so persistently, the buyer is entitled to say that he has the right to treat the whole contract as repudiated.'[16]

Another example which concerned an alleged repudiation by the buyers rather than sellers illustrates the delicate position in which commercial parties may find themselves when they claim that a breach in respect of one instalment amounts to a repudiation of the whole contract. In *Warinco A G* v *Samor SPA*, [17] the contract was for the sale of crude rape seed oil in several instalments. The buyers rejected the first instalment, claiming that it was not of the colour required by the contract. The sellers disputed this and, in subsequent proceedings, they were held to be in the right on this point. But the sellers also told the buyers that the next instalment would be identical with the one which the buyers had rejected. The buyers replied, insisting that the instalment must conform to the contract, and the sellers eventually declined to deliver any further instalments, arguing that the buyer's action amounted to a repudiation. Evidently, the sellers feared that, as the second instalment was going to be identical with the first and as the buyers had rejected that one, they would reject the second one as well. Donaldson J held that the sellers had acted wrongly in refusing to tender the second instalment but his decision was reversed on appeal. However, the disagreement related only to the application of the law, and no doubt was cast on Donaldson J's statement of the relevant principles as follows:[18]

> If a buyer under a contract calling for delivery by instalments commits a breach of that contract before all the deliveries have been made and that breach is so serious as to go to the root of the contract – in other words, to destroy the basis of the contract – common sense suggests that the seller should not be expected to go to the trouble and expense of tendering later instalments if he does not want to. The law so provides.
>
> Again, if it becomes clear that the buyer will be unable to accept or to pay for later instalments, common sense suggests that the seller should, if he wishes, be discharged from any obligation further to perform his part of the contract. The law so provides.

[14] [1934] 1 KB 148.
[15] [1930] 2 KB 312.
[16] *R A Munro & Co Ltd* v *Meyer* [1930] 2 KB 312, 331.
[17] [1977] 2 Lloyd's Rep 582; [1979] 1 Lloyd's Rep 450.
[18] [1977] 2 Lloyd's Rep 582, at p. 588.

> Finally, if a buyer acts or speaks in a manner which declares in clear terms that he will not perform his part of the contract, the seller should, in common sense and fairness, have the option of being discharged from further obligation under the contract. And the law so provides. But common sense also suggests that there can be borderline cases in which it is not quite so clear what should happen. The law is at a disadvantage here in that it must draw a line. The line which it draws is indicated by the question: "Has the buyer evinced an intention to abandon or refuse to perform the contract?" In answering this question, the law has regard to such factors as the degree to which the delivery of one instalment is linked with another, the proportion of the contract which has been affected by the allegedly repudiatory breach and the probability that the breach will be repeated. However, these are merely part of the raw material for answering the question. They cannot be conclusive in themselves.

A single contract, though severable, is not the same thing as a number of distinct and separate contracts. If parties enter into distinct contracts, breach of one would very rarely justify repudiation of the others. But a provision in a contract that each instalment or each delivery is to be treated as a separate contract does not mean that there are distinct contracts; it merely indicates that the contract is severable. Hence, such a clause does not deprive a buyer of a right to throw up the whole contract if they would otherwise have such a right.[19]

It will be noticed that s. 31(2) appears to assume that the buyer has one of two possible remedies: repudiation of the whole contract or merely a claim for damages. The subsection does not appear to contemplate the third possibility of allowing the buyer to reject the defective instalments while retaining the rest of the goods. But there is no reason to suppose that the buyer cannot do this, subject to the somewhat complex rules governing the question of partial acceptance.[20] However, this possibility seems to have been overlooked in *Regent OHG Aisenstadt* v *Francesco of Jermyn Street*,[21] a case which nicely illustrates the importance of the distinction between a severable and a non-severable contract. In this case, the contract was for the sale of 62 high-quality men's suits, to be delivered in instalments. The sellers delivered the suits in five instalments, the fourth of which was one suit short. If this had been a non-severable contract, under the law then applicable, the buyer would have been entitled to reject the whole lot because a shortage of one suit was conceded not to be *de minimis* (it exceeded a one per cent shortage). But Mustill J held that the contract was severable and, applying s. 31(2), held that the breach, being unlikely to be repeated and affecting only one instalment, did not give the buyer the right to repudiate the whole contract. He did not, however, consider whether the buyer had the right to reject the whole of the fourth instalment, which it would seem he ought to have had. If the goods had been defective in quality (rather than one suit short), it would seem clear that the buyer would have been able to reject the whole of that instalment. The question would then have arisen whether, in applying s. 31(2), the short delivery ought to have been regarded as a shortage of one suit only or of the whole of the fourth instalment. If the latter had been the correct approach, the result of the case would have been different.

There was one further puzzle about the right of rejection in instalment contracts which affected both severable and non-severable contracts, and which did not seem to have been

[19] *R A Munro & Co Ltd* v *Meyer*, [1930] 2 KB 312.
[20] See below, section 17.3.
[21] [1981] 3 All ER 327.

expressly solved by the courts. The problem was this: if instalments were delivered and accepted – or anyhow not rejected – and a subsequent instalment was then delivered which was defective so that the buyer became entitled to repudiate the whole contract (either because it was non-severable, or because the breach was so serious that s. 31(2) justified the buyer in taking this step), what was to happen to the instalments already delivered and accepted, or not rejected? If the contract was genuinely non-severable, it was clear that the buyer could not accept part and reject part of the goods (see s. 11(4))[22] so their rejection of later instalments must have carried with it the right (and indeed the obligation) to reject the prior instalments as well; and this was presumably still the case even though he might already have accepted the prior instalments. Their acceptance would have to be treated as conditional on the later instalments being satisfactory. Section 35A confers a right of partial rejection, and s. 11(4) is expressly made subject to the new provision, so that problem should no longer arise. This provision is discussed below.[23]

If, on the other hand, the contract is severable, but the defective instalment is sufficiently bad to justify the buyer in throwing up the whole contract under s. 31(2), the buyer does not *have to* reject the prior instalments, but is he entitled to do so? Section 31(2) does not necessarily exclude the possibility that the buyer may have this right, but, by its terms, it deals with the future, so that the buyer can refuse to perform outstanding obligations, but usually their (severable) obligations to accept previous conforming instalments have already been fulfilled and cannot be undone.

It is somewhat surprising that these problems seem never to have been discussed in the cases, though there is a hint of them in *Gill & Duffus SA* v *Berger & Co Inc.*[24] It seems to have been assumed by the Court of Appeal here that rejection of a second instalment retrospectively validated a wrongful original rejection of a prior instalment. The authority of this case is weakened by the fact that the House of Lords held that the second rejection was wrongful, so that the point did not arise.

17.1.4 Consequences of rejection

Where the buyer repudiates the contract, having the right to do so, they can of course decline to pay the price or, if they have paid it, they can recover it. In addition, they may maintain an action for damages, for if the buyer acts within their rights in rejecting the goods tendered, they can normally hold the seller liable for non-delivery.[25] There may be some circumstances in which, after rejection by the buyer, the seller can tender delivery of a new lot of goods if they still have time to do this within the period allowed by the contract,[26] but in general it seems that the buyer is entitled to treat a wrongful delivery as itself a breach of contract which justifies repudiation by them.[27]

[22] See below, section 17.2.

[23] See section 17.2 below.

[24] [1983] 1 Lloyd's Rep 622, reversed on other grounds [1984] AC 382.

[25] *Millar's Machinery Co Ltd* v *David Way & Son* (1934) 40 Com Cas 204.

[26] *Borrowman Phillips & Co* v *Free & Hollis* (1878) 4 QBD 500; *E E Brian Smith (1928) Ltd* v *Wheatsheaf Mills Ltd* [1939] 2 KB 302. Where the seller's breach consists of tendering faulty documents they will usually be able to correct the documents and retender them within the necessary time – see *Empresa Exportadora de Azucar* v *Industria Azucarera Nacional SA (The Playa Larga)* [1983] 2 Lloyd's Rep 171, 184.

[27] Although on one reading, s. 11(3) and (4) may be taken to lay down that rejection of the goods involves repudiation of the contract (or, more accurately, an acceptance of the seller's repudiation), the point made at the outset, that rejection and repudiation are separable, must be borne in mind – see above.

The assumption of the law is that the right of rejection must be exercised in a fairly short period, so that, in practice, no question arises as to any use that the buyer may have had from the goods.[28] The buyer's right to recover the full price after rejecting the goods is based on the supposition that they have received no consideration at all when they reject; in one sense this may not be completely accurate where the buyer may have used the goods before rejecting them. But as a matter of law, it is probably generally correct to treat the rejection as demonstrating a total failure of consideration so that the seller is not entitled to any credit for any use that the buyer may have had from the goods.[29] However, the case may be different if the buyer claims damages in addition to seeking the recovery of their price. It would seem remarkable if the buyer did not have to set off the value of any use they may have had from the goods against a claim for damages.

Where the goods are so rejected, it is not the responsibility of the buyer to return the goods to the seller, for s. 36 states:

> Unless otherwise agreed, where goods are delivered to the buyer, and he refuses to accept them having the right to do so, he is not bound to return them to the seller, but it is sufficient if he intimates to the seller that he refuses to accept them.[30]

As will be seen below,[31] this rule presents some problems where the buyer has redelivered the goods to a sub-buyer before they are discovered to be defective. In this situation, the normal solution is simply to deny the buyer's right to reject altogether.

The acceptance by the seller of the buyer's rejection revests the property in the former if it has passed to the buyer, and also restores to them the immediate right to possession. Consequently, as we have seen, the buyer has no lien on the goods for the repayment of the purchase price.[32] The seller, upon receipt of notice of rejection, is entitled to have the goods placed at their disposal so as to allow their resuming possession forthwith.[33]

As we have already seen, it is not wholly clear whether the risk is to be treated as revesting in the seller on rejection, but the practical position seems to be that the risk does not pass at all where defective goods are delivered and then rejected by the buyer,[34] or even where a short quantity is delivered and the goods are rejected.[35]

[28] Note, however, the Scottish case of *Lamarra* v *Capital Bank plc* 2007 SC 95, where the purchaser's rejection of a car in March 2001 was upheld, although he continued to use the vehicle until the following June; and the sheriff court case of *Fiat Auto Financial Services* v *Connelly* 2007 SLT (Sh Ct) 111 (rejection allowed 10 months after sale).).

[29] Note that Scots law also reaches this position but without reference to total failure of consideration.

[30] In *MacDonald* v *Pollock* [2012] CSIH 12, 2013 SC 22, [2012] 1 Lloyds Rep 425, it was held that the buyer's telephone complaint to the seller about the goods' defects and making demand for repayment of the price amounted to rejection even though the buyer subsequently raised an action for damages only. Where, however, the buyer does return the faulty goods to the seller, that is likely to be taken as effective rejection: see *Durkin* v *DSG Retail Ltd* 2008 GWD 14-254 (Sheriff J. K. Tierney). The latter case was ultimately taken to the UK Supreme Court on other issues: *Durkin* v *DSG Retail Ltd* [2014] UKSC 21, 2014 SC (UKSC) 139, [2014] 1 WLR 1148; and see Chapter 19.

[31] See below, section 17.2.5.

[32] *J L Lyons & Co Ltd* v May & Baker Ltd [1923] 1 KB 685.

[33] *Hardy & Co Ltd* v *Hillerns & Fowler* [1923] 2 KB 490, 496 per Bankes LJ. Cf. *Kwei Tek Chao* v *British Traders & Shippers Ltd* [1954] 2 QB 459, 488 per Devlin J.

[34] See Chapter 11.

[35] *Vitol SA* v *Esso Australia Ltd (The Wise)* [1989] 1 Lloyd's Rep 96.

17.2 Loss of the right to reject

Even though the seller may be guilty of a breach of condition and the buyer may *prima facie* be entitled to repudiate the contract and reject the goods, they may in certain circumstances lose this right, and have to accept the goods and be content with a claim for damages. It is now necessary to examine the circumstances in which this may occur and, first of all, s. 11(4) must be set out in full (although it is to be noted that it does not apply in Scotland). In its present form this reads as follows:

> Subject to section 35A below, where a contract of sale is not severable, and the buyer has accepted the goods, or part of them, the breach of a condition to be fulfilled by the seller can only be treated as a breach of warranty, and not as a ground for rejecting the goods and treating the contract as repudiated, unless there is an express or implied term of the contract to that effect.

17.2.1 Loss of right to reject through acceptance

A few preliminary comments on the concept of acceptance and its relationship to other legal doctrines are necessary. First, the provisions of the Act concerning acceptance must be read against the general common law doctrines of affirmation, waiver and estoppel. The concept of affirmation is in some respects a general common law principle parallel to the concept of acceptance, but there are important differences between them. In particular, it is generally held that an innocent party who wishes to terminate a contract because of a breach of condition (or a repudiatory breach) by the other party cannot be treated as having affirmed the contract unless they knew of the breach, and of their right to terminate.[36] On the other hand, a buyer can be held to have accepted the goods, and so lost their right of rejection under the Sale of Goods Act, even where they did not know of the seller's breach or of their rights. This means that termination for breach is, in principle, often possible long after the breach occurs as the facts may only then come to light, but acceptance is usually something which happens very shortly after delivery in a contract of sale. It is not usually possible to reject goods long after delivery because some latent or hidden defect comes to light months or years after the goods are delivered.[37]

The Law Commissions discussed this question in their Report of 1987,[38] but recommended against any change in the law which would confer a long-term right of rejection on the buyer, where (for instance) serious defects come to light in the goods long after they are delivered. The chief reason for rejecting such a change seems to have been that it would introduce new complications regarding the use and benefit which the buyer may have had from the goods. At present, as rejection must take place within a relatively short period, it is possible for the law to insist that rejection of the goods produces a total failure

[36] See *Peyman* v *Lanjani* [1985] Ch 457. But, as also held in this case, the innocent party may lose their right to terminate even if they do not know the facts or their rights, if they represent (by words or conduct) that they are affirming the contract, and the other relies to their prejudice on that implied representation.

[37] But see *Burrell* v *Harding's Exrs* 1931 SLT 76 (reredos rejected two years after sale after it was found not to be genuine); *MacGill* v *Talbot* 2002 GWD 12-382 (restoration of classic car found to be uneconomical 14 months after purchase); *Cruickshank* v *Specialist Cars (Aberdeen) Ltd* 2002 GWD 25-858 (reasonable for buyer not to test new car's caravan-towing capacity until he went on holiday four months after purchase).

[38] See Law Commissions, *Sale and Supply of Goods* (Cm. 137), paras 5.6–5.13.

of consideration, so that the buyer is entitled to the full repayment of their price. But if the law recognised a long-term right of rejection, it would hardly be possible to maintain this position, and the seller might well expect some credit for the use the buyer has had from the goods, even where the buyer does not seek damages.[39] This would weaken the buyer's bargaining position where they reject (or want to reject) the goods, and introduce complications which the law currently avoids. Of course, nothing said here detracts from the possibility of the buyer being able to pursue a claim for damages where hidden defects come to light long after delivery.

In addition to the common law concept of affirmation, which is largely replaced for contracts of sale by the concept of acceptance, there are also other common law doctrines – such as waiver and estoppel (personal bar) – which are still frequently applied to contracts of sale, especially in commercial situations. Thus, a buyer who makes clear and unequivocal representations (whether by express words, or by implication from conduct) that they will accept the goods, or that they will not reject them on the ground of late delivery or some other ground of that kind, may lose their right to reject them under these common law doctrines.[40] So also a person cannot reject the goods if at the same time they act in a way which is inconsistent with rejection,[41] whether this amounts to an acceptance or not.

A second preliminary comment is that there can be no acceptance of goods which the seller had no right to sell and, in such a case, the mere fact that the buyer has retained and used the goods does not prevent their rejecting them and recovering the full price as on a total failure of consideration.[42] It has been said, however, that 'Clearly the answer would not have been the same if the buyer, with knowledge of the true facts, had continued to use the [goods] for another twelve months or so, and had then found that the market had fallen and that he would like to hand [them] back again.'[43]

Thirdly, a buyer who is entitled to reject goods for breach must, of course, mitigate their damage according to the ordinary rule. However, they cannot, it would seem, be required by this principle to accept goods when they want to reject them (at all events when the goods are defective in quality),[44] nor to reject them when they want to accept them.[45]

Fourthly, it should be observed that the buyer's right to reject defective goods may be, and very often is, qualified by express contractual provisions.[46] In some cases, restrictions on the right to reject may be imposed by making the right conditional on, for example, testing or sampling the goods. In others, there may be stringent time limits within which

[39] This is, in fact, the position under the Consumer Rights Act 2015 where a consumer exercises the final right to reject: see s. 24(8)–(15), and Chapter 19

[40] See Chapter 6.

[41] See *Vargas Pena Apezteguia y Cia Saic* v *Peter Cremer GmbH* [1987] 1 Lloyd's Rep 394.

[42] *Rowland* v *Divall* [1923] 2 KB 500 – see Chapter 5.

[43] *Kwei Tek Chao* v *British Traders & Shippers Ltd* [1954] 2 WLR at 372, a passage omitted from the Report at [1954] 2 QB 459 – see Chapter 5.

[44] *Heaven & Kesterton Ltd* v *Etablissements François Albiac & Cie* [1956] 2 Lloyd's Rep 316. The position is different where there is no physical defect in the goods but the breach is, for example, late delivery: *The Solholt* [1983] 1 Lloyd's Rep 605. The reason for this distinction is that if the buyer proposes to buy in the market it would be reasonable to reject defective goods, but not necessarily reasonable to reject goods proffered by the seller a day or two late if they conform to the contract in quality.

[45] *Kwei Tek Chao* v *British Traders & Shippers Ltd* [1954] 2 QB 459, 483.

[46] For one example, see *W E Marshall & Co* v *Lewis & Peat (Rubber) Ltd* [1963] 1 Lloyd's Rep 562.

notice of rejection may be given, and so forth. In all such cases, the provisions of the contract prevail, though subject, where appropriate, to the reasonableness requirements of the Unfair Contract Terms Act.

The meaning of 'acceptance' depends on the construction of ss. 34 to 35A(1), which are as follows:

> 34 Unless otherwise agreed, when the seller tenders delivery of goods to the buyer, he is bound on request to afford the buyer a reasonable opportunity of examining the goods for the purpose of ascertaining whether they are in conformity with the contract, and in the case of a contract for sale by sample, of comparing the bulk with the sample.
>
> 35 (1) The buyer is deemed to have accepted the goods subject to subsection (2) below—
>
> (a) when he intimates to the seller that he has accepted them, or
>
> (b) when the goods have been delivered to him and he does any act in relation to them which is inconsistent with the ownership of the seller.
>
> (2) Where goods are delivered to the buyer, and he has not previously examined them, he is not deemed to have accepted them under subsection (1) above until he has had a reasonable opportunity of examining them for the purpose
>
> (a) of ascertaining whether they are in conformity with the contract and,
>
> (b) in the case of a contract for sale by sample, of comparing the bulk with the sample.
>
> (3) Where the buyer deals as consumer . . . the buyer cannot lose his right to rely on subsection (2) above by agreement, waiver or otherwise.
>
> (4) The buyer is also deemed to have accepted the goods when after the lapse of a reasonable time he retains the goods without intimating to the seller that he has rejected them.
>
> (5) The questions that are material in determining for the purposes of subsection (4) above whether a reasonable time has elapsed include whether the buyer has had a reasonable opportunity of examining the goods for the purposes mentioned in subsection (2) above.
>
> (6) The buyer is not by virtue of this section deemed to have accepted the goods merely because –
>
> (a) he asks for, or agrees to, their repair by or under arrangements with the seller, or
>
> (b) the goods are delivered to another under a sub-sale or other disposition.
>
> (7) Where the contract is for the sale of goods making one or more commercial units, a buyer accepting any goods included in a unit is deemed to have accepted all the goods making the unit; and in this subsection, 'commercial unit' means a unit division of which would materially impair the value of the goods or the character of the unit.

It will be seen that under these sections there are, in principle, three ways in which the seller can accept the goods and so lose their right to reject them. First, they can expressly intimate that they accept the goods; secondly, they can perform an act 'inconsistent with the ownership of the seller'; and, thirdly, they may simply retain the goods for a reasonable time, without rejecting them. It should be noted that, even if the right to reject is lost under s. 35, the seller's failure to remedy the relevant defects may constitute a repudiation of the contract by the seller which the buyer can accept and in addition seek damages for the losses incurred.[47]

We will now examine these three ways in which the seller can lose the right to reject in turn.

[47] *Gregg & Co (Knottingly) Ltd, Allied Glass Containers Ltd* v *Embart Glass Ltd* [2005] EWHC 804 (TCC).

17.2.2 Acceptance by express intimation

The first way in which the buyer can accept the goods appears simple enough, but the question was discussed by the Law Commissions[48] whether a signed 'acceptance note' which a buyer simply signs without reading when the goods are delivered to them[49] and before the buyer has examined them, or had an opportunity to examine them, can be treated as a true acceptance within the meaning of the sections. It must be appreciated that an express intimation of acceptance for the purposes of s. 35 has a rather special significance and must be interpreted accordingly. Such an acceptance amounts in substance and effect to a waiver of the right to reject the goods; it thus falls mid-way between a mere receipt or acknowledgment of delivery, on the one hand, and a complete waiver of all claims arising out of the sale, on the other hand. A person who simply signs a delivery note when goods are delivered in pursuance of a contract of sale plainly intends to do no more than to acknowledge receipt of the goods; it would be absurd to attribute to the buyer the intention to waive the right to reject. The problem, of course, is that if the buyer signs a printed form placed in front of them without reading it, and the form declares that the buyer accepts the goods within the meaning of s. 35 of the Act, there may be a tendency to treat this as binding on the buyer.[50] It seems unlikely that this in fact would have been held to be the case,[51] but the Law Commissions recommended that the law should anyhow be amended by making it clear that an intimation of acceptance is not in fact a binding acceptance if it occurs before the buyer has had a chance to examine the goods. This is the purpose of subsections (2) and (3) of s. 35. It is also intended that a buyer should not be deemed to have accepted the goods until it has had a reasonable opportunity of examining them, but in this case it will be possible (subject to the Unfair Contract Terms Act) for the parties to agree otherwise.[52]

It is also possible that a buyer accepts the goods in such a manner as to waive, not merely the right to reject, but also any claim for damages which they may have. A buyer who actually examines some specific item and finds it defective in some minor respects, but accepts it without demur, may thus find that they have lost both the right to reject and the right to claim damages. This latter right, however, being more fundamental, is less easily lost. A real waiver or circumstances giving rise to a promissory estoppel may be necessary to deprive the buyer of the right to claim damages where defective goods are 'accepted' by them.[53]

[48] Law Commissions, *Sale and Supply of Goods*, paras 5.20–5.25.

[49] Where the buyer deals as consumer the buyer cannot lose their right of rejection in this way – see s. 35(3) dealt with below.

[50] See *Mechans* v *Highland Marine Charters* 1964 SC 48.

[51] Given the wide interpretation placed on s. 13 of the Unfair Contract Terms Act 1977 by the Court of Appeal in cases such as *Stewart Gill* v *Horatio Myer & Co Ltd* [1992] 2 All ER 257 and *Fastframe Ltd* v *Lohinski* 3 March 1993 (unreported) it might be that such acceptance notes would be held to be subject to that Act. See Chapter 8, at section 8.4.3.

[52] See Law Commissions' Report, paras 5.23 and 5.24.

[53] See *Ets Soules & Cie* v *International Trade Devpt Co Ltd* [1980] 1 Lloyd's Rep 129.

17.2.3 Acceptance by an act inconsistent with the ownership of the seller

The second instance where acceptance can occur is when the buyer does an act in relation to the goods which is inconsistent with the ownership of the seller. This is subject to the precondition in s. 35(2) that the buyer must have had a reasonable opportunity for examining the goods to assess their conformity with the contract.

A difficult instance could be where goods are bought and resold without examination before they are delivered to the sub-buyer. While the sub-buyer would have the right to reject the goods as against the middle buyer, the latter might be thought to have 'accepted' the goods by reselling and delivering them to the sub-buyer and so be deprived of the right to reject. Since the middle buyer cannot reject, in any event, unless they are in a position to restore the goods to the seller,[54] it would seem unfair that the middle buyer should lose the right to reject merely because by reselling them, they have done an act inconsistent with the ownership of the seller and have not availed themselves of the opportunity to examine the goods first. For this reason, s. 35(6)(b) provides that the buyer is not deemed to have accepted goods merely because the goods are delivered to another under a sub-sale or other disposition.

Unfortunately, this leaves a consequential point somewhat unclear. This problem is that it will now be uncertain what is to happen where the sub-buyer rejects the goods without returning them to the buyer. Is the buyer then also to be entitled to reject the goods while they remain physically situated at the premises of the sub-buyer? It will be remembered that under s. 36 of the Act, the buyer is not bound to return the goods to the seller when they reject them; it is sufficient that they intimate to the seller that the goods are at their disposal. Similarly, if the buyer arranges for the retransport of the goods from the sub-buyer, can they charge the seller with the cost of this in addition to rejecting the goods?

Section 35(6)(b) makes it clear that the mere fact of delivery under a subcontract will not now be treated as an act inconsistent with the ownership of the seller; but will the buyer's refusal to recollect the goods from the sub-buyer make any difference? Given s. 36 of the Act, it seems that the answer will probably be 'no', but the results may be somewhat drastic if the goods have (for instance) been shipped to a sub-buyer overseas, who ultimately rejects them on arrival, so that the buyer in turn then rejects them too. Presumably, in this situation it will be the seller's responsibility to arrange for the handling of the goods at their overseas destination, even though the seller is a purely domestic producer who did not sell for export himself, and had no reason to know that the goods were going to be exported.

There are some cases in which the courts are prepared to hold that the place of delivery to the buyer is not a reasonable place to examine the goods,[55] and, in this situation, the buyer does not lose their right to reject when the goods have been resold and delivered. In this case the responsibility for retransporting the goods to the original place of delivery will be the seller's. For instance, in *Molling & Co* v *Dean & Son*, the plaintiffs made

[54] See above, section 17.1.

[55] This is especially true of f.o.b. contracts: see *Bragg* v Villanova (1923) 40 TLR 154; Boks & Co v J H Rayner & Co (1921) 37 TLR 800. But cf. Commercial Fibres (Ireland) Ltd v Zabaida [1975] 1 Lloyd's Rep 27.

40,000 books to the defendants' order, knowing that they were intended for shipment and resale to an American sub-buyer. Indeed, the plaintiffs printed the books with the sub-buyer's imprint and packed them for shipment to him. They were delivered to the defendants, who consigned them to the sub-buyers without examination. The sub-buyers rejected and the defendants brought the goods back to England at their own cost. It was held that they were entitled to reject the goods and also to recover the cost of transport on the ground that the proper place for inspection was on delivery to the sub-buyers. Hence, the buyers had not had a reasonable opportunity to examine the goods. This decision would be the same under the current law: the buyer would be deemed not to have accepted the goods under s. 34 because they had not had a reasonable opportunity to examine them under s. 35. This result anyhow seems perfectly reasonable.

17.2.4 'Act inconsistent with the ownership of the seller'

An unhappy feature is the reference in s. 35 to an act 'inconsistent with the ownership of the seller'. This suggests that the ownership of the goods cannot pass until the buyer has accepted them, but of course this is not so. Furthermore, if the property has already passed to the buyer, how can they be said to do an act inconsistent with 'the ownership of the seller'? One possible answer is to be found in the judgment of Devlin J in *Kwei Tek Chao* v *British Traders & Shippers Ltd*.[56] If the property has passed in circumstances in which the buyer retains the right to reject, the passing is merely conditional:

> He [the buyer] gets only conditional property in the goods, the condition being a condition subsequent. All his dealings with the documents[57] are dealings only with that conditional property in the goods. It follows, therefore, that there can be no dealing which is inconsistent with the seller's ownership unless he deals with something more than the conditional property. If the property passes altogether, not being subject to any condition, there is no ownership left in the seller with which any inconsistent act under s. 35 could be committed. If the property passes conditionally the only ownership left in the seller is the reversionary interest in the property in the event of the condition subsequent operating to restore it to him. It is that reversionary interest with which the buyer must not, save with the penalty of accepting the goods, commit an inconsistent act.[58]

What this comes to can perhaps be put more simply. Although the property in the goods may have passed to the buyer, if the buyer is still entitled to reject them and does reject them, the property will revest in the seller, and they will then become owner of the goods again.

But Devlin J's way of putting the law does not help to decide whether any other sort of act should be held inconsistent with the ownership of the seller. For example, if goods are bought for use or consumption, what kind of use would be inconsistent with the seller's ownership? If the seller's reversionary right is only to receive the goods in the state in which they are when the buyer rejects them, this formula simply gives no answer to the question, what sort of use by the buyer will prevent rejection? The truth is that the phrase 'an act inconsistent with the ownership of the seller' is one with no fixed meaning. The

[56] [1954] 2 QB 459.
[57] The case was concerned with a sale on c.i.f. terms, but the reasoning on this part of the case applies to all sales of goods.
[58] [1954] 2 QB 459, 487.

court is, in effect, empowered to decide whether it thinks that the buyer ought to be entitled to reject the goods according to the circumstances of the case. In order to ascertain what meaning the phrase has, therefore, it is necessary to examine the case law to see what acts the courts have in fact held to be inconsistent with the ownership of the seller.

17.2.5 Documentary sales

In the *British Traders & Shippers* case, Devlin J, after giving his explanation of the phrase 'an act inconsistent with the ownership of the seller', went on to hold that in documentary sales the buyer is not deprived of his right to reject merely by dealing with the documents:

> So long as he [the buyer] is merely dealing with the documents he is not purporting to do anything more than pledge the conditional property which he has. Similarly, if he sells the documents of title he sells the conditional property. But if, as was done in *Hardy & Co* v *Hillerns & Fowler*,[59] when the goods have been landed, he physically deals with the goods and delivers them to his sub-buyer, he is doing an act which is inconsistent with the seller's reversionary interest.[60]

The result of this case appeared to be that in a documentary sale the buyer had two distinct rights of rejection: a right to reject documents not conforming to the contract, and a right to reject the goods themselves if they failed to conform to the contract. A dealing with the documents might deprive the buyer of their right to reject the documents, but could not deprive them of their right to reject the goods. However, it now seems that this is not really a very satisfactory statement of the law. At least three qualifications need to be made to Devlin J's exposition. The first is that if (as sometimes happens) the goods arrive before the shipping documents, and the buyer physically takes delivery or otherwise deals in the goods, they will be held to have accepted them.[61] There will be no separate right of rejection of the documents when they arrive unless perhaps these disclose additional breaches of contract not previously known to the buyer.

The second qualification that needs to be made to Devlin J's statement of the law is that the buyer's acceptance of the documents may very well deprive them of their right to reject the goods where the breach of contract relating to the documents and the breach relating to the goods are in effect one breach only, and not two distinct breaches. Thus, if the goods are shipped late and this fact appears from the documents, the seller is, in principle, in breach of his obligations both as regards the documents and as regards the goods. Nevertheless, it is unreal to treat this as involving two separate breaches, and if the buyer accepts the documents they may well be treated as having waived the seller's breach and thus be bound to accept the goods.[62] Thus, even though acceptance of (or dealing with) the documents may not strictly amount to an act inconsistent with the seller's ownership,

[59] [1923] 2 KB 490.

[60] [1954] 2 QB 459, 487–8.

[61] *Tradax International SA* v *Goldschmidt SA* [1977] 2 Lloyd's Rep 604.

[62] *Panchaud Frères SA* v *Etablissements General Grain Co* [1970] 1 Lloyd's Rep 53; *Bremer* v *Vanden Avenne-Izegen* [1978] 2 Lloyd's Rep 109; *Bremer* v *C Mackprang* [1979] 2 Lloyd's Rep 220. It is controversial whether this is strictly a matter of waiver, or estoppel, or solely the effect of s. 35, but these differences of concept seem largely immaterial except for one point: under s. 35 absence of knowledge of the breach does not preclude a finding of 'acceptance', but it does seem to preclude a finding of waiver. As to estoppel, see Chapter 12.

the buyer may be unable to reject the goods on other grounds in such circumstances, such as waiver or estoppel.

The third qualification that needs to be made to Devlin J's statement of the law in the *British Traders & Shippers* case is that whatever the law may say about dealing with the documents not amounting to a dealing with the goods, in practice such a dealing may affect the buyer's power to reject the goods. If they have resold the documents, for instance, they will hardly be able to reject the goods unless the sub-buyer himself rejects – but equally they are unlikely to want to reject except in this case. In the case of a pledge, however, the position may be more difficult because the buyer may be unable to reject the goods without the consent of the pledgee, who may insist on being paid off first. Certainly this appears to be the effect of the Uniform Customs.[63] Therefore, where the price has been paid to the seller by a banker's credit against documents, the buyer will in practice have to pay off the bank to obtain a release of the documents before they can return them to the seller and so reject the goods.

17.2.6 Goods bought for use

Where goods are bought for use, a somewhat different approach may be necessary in defining the meaning of an 'act inconsistent with the ownership of the seller', though there is little authority directly in point.[64] Probably any substantial or repeated or prolonged use would be held inconsistent with the seller's ownership if it prevented the buyer returning the goods in substantially the same condition as when purchased. In effect, this ground of the loss of the right of rejection merges into the next ground, namely that the buyer has allowed a reasonable time to elapse before rejecting the goods. It is therefore dealt with further under that heading, below.

17.2.7 Acceptance through lapse of reasonable time

The third way in which the buyer can accept the goods within the meaning of s. 35 is to retain them for more than a reasonable time before they inform the seller that they want to reject them.[65] Section 35(5) provides that the questions that are material in determining for the purposes of subsection (4) above whether a reasonable time has elapsed include whether the buyer has had a reasonable opportunity of examining the goods for the purpose mentioned in subsection (2), that is, of ascertaining whether they are in conformity with the contract, and, in the case of a contract for sale by sample, of comparing the bulk with the sample.

[63] See Arts 7 and 8 (UCP 600).

[64] See *Armaghdown Motors* v *Gray* [1963] NZLR 5 (registration of car in buyer's name held inconsistent with seller's ownership). Some older Scottish authorities hold that if the buyer continues to use goods after intimating rejection of them, they cannot insist on their right to reject – *Electric Construction Co* v *Hurry and Young* (1897) 24 R 312; *Croom & Arthur* v *Stewart* (1905) 7 F 563. See also *Morrison & Mason* v *Clarkson Bros* (1898) 25 R 427; *Mechan* v *Bow McLachlan & Co* 1910 SC 750; cf. *Cruickshank* v *Specialist Cars (Aberdeen) Ltd* 2002 GWD 25-858 (Sheriff A. L. MacFadyen); *Lamarra* v *Capital Bank plc* 2005 SLT (Sh Ct) 21 (aff'd on other grounds 2007 SC 95); *Fiat Auto Financial Services* v *Connelly* 2007 SLT (Sh Ct) 111 (use of car as private hire taxi for 10 months, covering over 40,000 miles, not an act inconsistent with seller's ownership where buyer regularly and often complained to seller about vehicle's quality).

[65] Section 35(4).

The question of what is a reasonable time in the case of goods bought for resale was examined by Judge Jack QC in *Truk (UK) Ltd* v *Tokmakidis GmbH*[66] in which a vehicle chassis with a body specially fitted by the claimant was delivered on 14 June 1996. In December 1996, the defendant was informed by the sub-buyer that the body did not correspond to the chassis maker's guidelines. The judge found that the vehicle had been rejected in March 1997. He laid down a number of propositions as to what is a reasonable time to reject the goods: (1) it was necessary to look at the question by balancing the opposing interests of the buyer and the seller; (2) the reasonable time to exercise the right to reject could not be less than the time for the buyer to have a reasonable opportunity to examine the goods; (3) the reasonable time to exercise a right to reject might well be longer than is required to examine the goods; (4) the time could be extended by dealings between the buyer and the seller, in particular as regards the repair of the goods (as had been the situation in the present case);[67] and (5) there was only one reasonable time and not different times for different defects. What mattered in the present case was that the goods were to be resold. This consideration coupled with s. 35(6)(b) led to the conclusion that the reasonable time for rejection would normally be the time taken to resell the goods, together with an additional period in which they could be tested by the sub-buyer.

In the case of goods bought for use, this ground for treating the buyer as having accepted the goods tends to merge, as noted above, with the doctrine of the act 'inconsistent with the ownership of the seller', as, clearly, the longer the buyer retains and continues to use the goods, the more difficult it will be for them to claim that their conduct is not inconsistent with the seller's reversionary rights – circular though that argument tends to be. In these cases, the question will nearly always be one of fact: what is a reasonable time?

Bernstein v *Pamson Motors (Golders Green) Ltd*[68] was something of a test case on this question in relation to the rejection of motor vehicles. Here, the buyer sought to reject a new car for serious defects causing a major breakdown on a motorway after he had had the car for three weeks but only done some 140 miles. While holding that the buyer was undoubtedly entitled to damages, Rougier J held that he had lost the right to reject as a reasonable time for rejection had elapsed. In *Clegg* v *Olle Andersson*,[69] the Court of Appeal held that *Bernstein* v *Pamson Motors* no longer represented the law since the Sale and Supply of Goods Act 1994. Moreover, in *Rogers* v *Parish (Scarborough) Ltd*,[70] the vehicle had travelled over 5,500 miles when the plaintiffs rejected it after the lapse of a period of six months. Nevertheless, it seems not to have occurred to the defendants to argue that the right to reject had been lost.[71] While in several Scottish cases, the sellers' arguments that the buyers' right to reject had been lost through lapse of time were likewise unsuccessful,[72] in a more fully reasoned recent decision it was held that the buyer's use of

[66] [2000] 2 All ER (Comm) 594.

[67] See also *Rogers* v *Parish (Scarborough) Ltd* [1987] QB 933.

[68] [1987] 2 All ER 220.

[69] [2003] EWCA Civ 320.

[70] [1987] QB 933.

[71] Presumably, having regard to the circumstances of the case, the defendants' legal advisers took the view that such an argument was not worth running. It was only on appeal that they attempted to argue this point, and the Court of Appeal declined to deal with it because it had been put forward only at the appeal, having neither been pleaded nor argued at first instance.

[72] *MacGill* v *Talbot* 2002 GWD 12-382 (Sheriff G. J. Evans); *Cruickshank* v *Specialist Cars (Aberdeen) Ltd* 2002 GWD 25-858 (Sheriff A. L. MacFadyen). *Fiat Auto Financial Services* v *Connelly* 2007 SLT (Sh Ct) 11.

a car for over a year before serious defects appeared and subsequent failure to intimate rejection after the seller's failed attempt at repair meant that a reasonable time had passed, making it not possible for the buyer to reject.[73]

One or two earlier cases also indicate a slightly more favourable attitude to the buyer. In *Porter* v *General Guarantee Corpn*,[74] the plaintiff acquired a car at the end of January and by 4 March his solicitors were claiming the right to reject the vehicle; further attempts to put right the defects ensued, but on 20 March the plaintiff finally claimed the right to reject, and this was held not too late. This was, however, a hire-purchase rather than a sale, and there are certain distinctions in the legal position: first, hire-purchase legislation contains nothing equivalent to s. 35 of the Sale of Goods Act, so that the loss of the right to reject is a common law matter and secondly, the supplier in a hire-purchase contract remains the owner and hence continues to have an interest in the condition of the goods after delivery. This means that it may be more reasonable to allow a longer time for rejection in a hire-purchase contract than in a sale. The same comments must apply to another hire-purchase case of a Daimler in which rejection seems to have been permitted several months after the car was first supplied.[75] Indeed, it could, in theory, be argued that since hire-purchase is a contract of hire (plus an option to buy) the supplier should supply goods which would remain fit to be used throughout the period of hire – assuming, of course, that the hirer used them properly. However, the implied terms contained in the Supply of Goods (Implied Terms) Act 1973 (or strictly speaking the Consumer Credit Act 1974) are identical to those contained in the Sale of Goods Act and appear to require the goods to be of the required quality only at the time of supply. The same applies to the terms implied in pure hire contracts by the Supply of Goods and Services Act 1982. In *UCB Leasing* v *Holtom*,[76] the Court of Appeal held that in the case of a finance lease the issue is the fitness of the goods at the time of their delivery. But a finance lease and hire-purchase transactions are functional equivalents of sales of goods, and there may be an argument that, in hiring proper, the situation may be different.

One question is what effect attempts to remedy defects might have on the buyer's right to reject. It is, of course, a normal response, where defective goods are sold, for the buyer to demand that they should be repaired. And in the case of vehicles, there is often a long history of such attempts before the buyer finally tries to reject. In one hire-purchase case, the court seems to have treated the extra time taken up by such repeated attempts at repair as not counting against the buyer in deciding whether a reasonable time had elapsed since the sale,[77] but it is again unclear for the reasons given above whether this kind of reasoning would have been applicable in a contract of sale to which the former s. 35 applied. This point is addressed by s. 35(6)(a), which provides that the buyer is not deemed to have accepted the goods merely because they ask the seller for the goods to be repaired. In *J & H Ritchie Ltd* v *Lloyd Ltd*,[78] however, a purchaser of defective agricultural machinery

[73] *Douglas* v *Glenvarigill Co Ltd* [2010] CSOH 14, 2010 SLT 634 (commented upon by MacQueen, (2011) 15 Edinburgh LR 111). The buyer was held entitled to damages, however. See also *Kelly* v *Andersons House Furnishers (Inverurie) Ltd* 2012 GWD 20-422 (Sheriff J. A. Brown).

[74] [1982] RTR 384.

[75] *Laurelgates Ltd* v *Lombard North Central Ltd* (1983) 133 New LJ 720; see also *Lamarra* v *Capital Bank plc*, (2007) SC (HL) 95; cf. *Lutton* v *Saville Tractors (Belfast) Ltd* [1986] 12 NIJB 1.

[76] [1987] RTR 362.

[77] *Farnworth Finance Facilities Ltd* v *Attryde* [1970] 1 WLR 1053.

[78] 2007 SC (HL) 89; [2007] 1 WLR 670 (HL).

(a harrow) who had accepted the seller's offer of repair was held at first instance unable later to reject the tender of repaired goods that on the evidence were conforming to the contract. The purchaser's difficulty was its inability to obtain from the seller explanations as to what the original problem with the goods had been. For the majority of the court, so long as the contract remained unterminated, the seller had a continuing opportunity to supply conforming goods, and once it had done so, any rejection would be too late. The House of Lords held that the pursuer had not lost the right to reject by allowing the seller the opportunity to repair. This left the question as to whether the pursuer still had the right to reject even after the harrow had been repaired because the seller had failed to explain what the fault had been. The House of Lords held that there was a separate contract to repair the harrow, an implied term of which was that the seller would explain to the pursuer what the defect had been. By failing to do so, the seller had committed a repudiatory breach, which returned the parties to the position before the contract to repair had been made, which meant that the pursuer still had the right to reject.[79]

Where goods are not bought for use but for resale the question of the reasonableness of the time for rejection rarely arises; in practice, either the goods are passed on to sub-buyers who reject forthwith, or they are accepted by the sub-buyers so that the buyers themselves have no need to worry about rejection. But cases can occasionally arise (for instance, where some time elapses before the sub-buyers reject and return the goods to the buyer) in which the reasonableness of the time for rejection can be an issue. In one case[80] it was held that, where the sellers were threatening the buyers that any rejection would be treated as a breach of contract, the buyers were entitled to take particular care to examine the goods, and consult with sub-buyers, before committing themselves to rejection. A seller who insists all along that the goods are in accordance with the contract cannot complain if the buyer takes some extra time to satisfy themselves beyond question that the goods are defective before they reject them.

17.2.8 Acceptance of part of the goods

The question whether the buyer is entitled to accept part and reject part of the goods delivered is one of some difficulty. The opening words of s. 11(4), it will be recalled,[81] are as follows:

Subject to section 35A below, where a contract of sale is not severable, and the buyer has accepted the goods or part of them, etc.

35A. (1) If the buyer –
(a) has the right to reject the goods by reason of a breach on the part of the seller that affects some or all of them, but
(b) accepts some of the goods, including, where there are any goods unaffected by the breach, all such goods he does not by accepting them lose his right to reject the rest.
(2) In the case of a buyer having the right to reject an instalment of goods, subsection (1) above applies as if references to the goods were references to the goods comprised in the instalment.

[79] A somewhat similar outcome was reached in *Zabriskie Chevrolet* v *Smith* 99 NJ Super 441, 240 A 2d 195 (1968) – replacement of transmission of automobile with one of unknown provenance.

[80] *Manifatture Tessile Laniera* v *J B Ashley Ltd* [1979] 2 Lloyd's Rep 28.

[81] See section 17.1.3. Section 11(4) does not apply in Scotland, but s. 35A does.

(3) For the purposes of subsection (1) above, goods are affected by a breach if by reason of the breach they are not in conformity with the contract.
(4) This section applies unless a contrary intention appears in, or is to be implied from, the contract.

Read literally, s. 11(4) only applies to a contract of sale which is not severable; but severability is only relevant where the buyer purports to accept part of the goods, so the paragraph should probably be read as meaning:

> Where the buyer has accepted the goods, or where the contract of sale is not severable and the buyer has accepted part of the goods, [etc.]

Assuming that this is the correct construction, it seems clear that if the contract is severable the buyer is entitled to reject goods not conforming to the contract and to accept the balance of the goods if they choose to do so. (They may also be entitled to throw up the entire contract in the circumstances referred to in s. 31(2), as previously discussed.)[82] Even this proposition may seem open to theoretical objections if the right to reject the goods is merely a species of the right to rescind,[83] and it would seem inconsistent for the buyer to rescind the contract while retaining part of the goods. However, this objection is purely academic; as a matter of practical convenience, it is plainly right that the buyer should be entitled to accept part and reject part of the goods in the case of severable contracts.

A further question arises in relation to the above discussion: what contracts are severable?

17.2.8.1 What contracts are severable?

This is not a question which has been the subject of much judicial discussion. It will be recalled that, under s. 31(2), a contract is severable if the goods are to be delivered in instalments and the instalments are to be separately paid for. But it is clear that a contract may be severable in many other situations also. For instance, a contract for the sale of a quantity of cloth was held to be severable where the cloth was to be delivered in instalments although the price was to be paid by monthly account and not separately for each instalment.[84] And a contract for the sale of some motor accessories was held to be severable purely on the ground that the contract specified 'deliveries as required'.[85] This was interpreted to mean that the goods would necessarily be delivered in instalments and it was assumed that this was enough to render the contract severable. In other cases, a buyer has been held entitled to accept part and reject part of the goods, though it has not always been clear whether this was on the ground that the contract was severable.[86]

Export contracts often provide that the seller is entitled to ship the goods in separate loads and that in this event each shipment is to be considered a distinct contract. Such a clause gives the seller the option to treat the contract as an entire contract by shipping the

[82] See above, section 17.1.
[83] A view which is almost certainly wrong – see Chapter 16.
[84] *Longbottom & Co Ltd* v *Bass Walker & Co Ltd* [1922] WN 245.
[85] *Jackson* v *Rotax Motor & Cycle Co Ltd* [1910] 2 KB 937; see also *Regent OHG Aisendstadt* v *Francesco of Jermyn Street* [1981] 3 All ER 327.
[86] See, e.g., *Molling & Co* v *Dean & Son Ltd* (1901) 18 TLR 217 (sale of 40,000 books printed by plaintiff to defendant's order).

goods in one load, or to treat it as severable and ship different loads.[87] If the seller ships the goods in different lots it may be important for the buyer's right to reject that the contract be treated as severable because different loads involve different shipping documents; hence one load may be resold to X, who may reject the goods, and another load to Y, who does not reject. In this situation, the middle buyer will wish to have the right to reject part and accept part of the total quantity sold to them.

17.2.9 Buyer's right to accept part and reject part of goods in non-severable contracts

Can a buyer accept part and reject part of the goods if the contract was not severable? Earlier editions of this book discussed the pre-1994 situation in some depth, but happily, current law is much simplified. It provides that the buyer should always be entitled to reject part of the goods, even though they have accepted part, so long only as the goods constitute 'different commercial units'.[88] In consequence, s. 11(4) is subject to the right of partial rejection conferred by s. 35A. This means that in severable contracts the law remains unaltered, but the right of partial rejection will in practice probably tend to supersede the provisions about severable contracts.

This right was grafted onto the existing structure of the Act, so that it does not prejudge the question whether the buyer has a right of rejection at all. That question must still be answered first. But if there is such a right of rejection, then, the buyer will only lose it by accepting all the goods, or by accepting goods included in the same 'commercial unit', or (in the case of severable contracts), as at present, by accepting the non-conforming goods which they could otherwise have rejected.

17.3 Relationship with rescission of the contract for an actionable misrepresentation[89]

It is an astonishing fact that the relationship in English law between the right to reject goods for breach of condition and the right to rescind for misrepresentation has not yet been fully explored by the courts.[90] It was at one time thought that 'a right to reject is merely a particular form of the right to rescind'[91] but it has been clear since *Johnson* v *Agnew*[92] that this is not correct. Rescission of the contract *ab initio* differs from mere termination of the contract, as the former is in principle retrospective, while the latter is not. Termination is the appropriate remedy where one of the parties is guilty of a breach of contract. The circumstances in which a rejection of defective goods can amount to termination were discussed above. Nevertheless, the practical distinction between rescission and a termination arising from the rejection of defective goods (or faulty documents) is

[87] For an unusual case in which the goods were shipped on one ship, but as two lots, with separate shipping documents, see *Esmail* v *J Rosenthal & Sons Ltd* [1965] 2 All ER 860.

[88] For definition of this term, see s. 35(7) above section 17.1.3-4.

[89] This book does not deal with the principles surrounding misrepresentation as such. Readers are referred to general books on the law of contract for a fuller treatment of this topic.

[90] This problem arises in relation to Art. 2 of the Uniform Commercial Code because Art. 1-103 preserves the principles of common law and equity. However, there are cases where the effect of a unilateral mistake arising out of an innocent misrepresentation has been discussed – see, e.g., *Harney-Morgan Chevrolet Olds Co* v *Rabin* 37 UCC Rep Serv 50 (1983).

not nearly so great as the conceptual divide between rescission and termination may suggest. In particular, where the buyer rejects the goods or documents, having the right to do so, the effect is very much the same as where the contract is rescinded. The termination of the contract does here have some retrospective results – for instance, if the property has passed to the buyer, it revests in the seller, and if the buyer has paid the price they are entitled to recover it. So the relationship between the right to rescind and the right to reject is very close.

The first question which must be answered is whether the remedy of rescission of a contract of sale of goods for misrepresentation is compatible with the Sale of Goods Act. The point seems never to have been argued in England and the answer depends upon whether the rules of common law saved by s. 62 include the rules of equity. In *Riddiford* v *Warren*,[93] the New Zealand Court of Appeal held, on the construction of an identical statute, that they did not and that the right to rescind for innocent misrepresentation could no longer be applied to contracts for the sale of goods. The judgment of Atkin LJ in *Re Wait*,[94] an extract from which is quoted above, is also very much in point. Atkin LJ there pointed out that a code which only set out the common law rules, and left equitable rights inconsistent with them, would have been futile.

On the other hand, it never seems to have been doubted that the Act leaves the general law relating to fraud unaffected, and the rules concerning fraud include the right to rescind for fraudulent misrepresentation. Then there are a number of cases in which it has been assumed that a contract of sale of goods may be rescinded for innocent misrepresentation in an appropriate case. In *Abram Steamship Co Ltd* v *Westville Shipping Co Ltd*[95] the House of Lords, in a Scots appeal, upheld the rescission of a contract for the assignment of the benefit of a shipbuilding contract. The contract rescinded in this case was treated as a mere assignment of the shipbuilding contract, but since the ship was already under construction it seems that it also involved the sale of the ship itself. Since then, the Court of Appeal has several times assumed that rescission is available for contracts of sale of goods. In particular, in *Leaf* v *International Galleries*,[96] the Court of Appeal clearly thought that the remedy was available in a suitable case, although they denied it there because of unreasonable delay. And again, in *Long* v *Lloyd*,[97] the Court of Appeal seems to have had no doubt that the remedy was available. Finally, in *Goldsmith* v *Rodger*,[98] the Court of Appeal actually rescinded a contract of sale of goods. In this case the misrepresentor was the buyer, but the court held that the remedy of rescission is equally open to either party. It seems certain, therefore, that an English court would not follow the New Zealand Court of Appeal.

Assuming, then, that this remedy is available, it becomes a matter of some importance to decide when exactly it can be invoked, what the relationship is between the right of rejection and the right of rescission, and what the effect is of the Misrepresentation Act 1967.

[91] *Kwei Tek Chao* v *British Traders & Shippers Ltd* [1954] 2 QB 459, 480 per Devlin J.
[92] [1980] AC 367.
[93] (1901) 20 NZLR 572; followed in *Watt* v *Westhoven* [1933] VLR 458. Howard (1963) 26 MLR 272, 282–5.
[94] [1927] Ch 606 – see Chapter 10.
[95] [1923] AC 773, 1923 SC (HL) 68.
[96] [1950] 2 KB 86.
[97] [1958] 1 WLR 753.
[98] [1962] 2 Lloyd's Rep 249.

The first two of these problems were considered at some length in *Leaf* v *International Galleries*[99] and *Long* v *Lloyd*,[100] although neither case can be regarded as wholly satisfactory owing to the many difficult points which were glossed over. But as a result of the provisions of the Misrepresentation Act, these cases can be dealt with quite shortly.

In *Leaf* v *International Galleries*, the plaintiff bought a picture from the defendants, which was stated by them to be a Constable. Some five years later, the plaintiff sought rescission of the contract on the ground that this was an innocent misrepresentation (fraud was not alleged) for which the normal equitable remedy should be available. The Court of Appeal decided that, assuming the plaintiff to have this right, he was in any case too late to rescind since five years was far more than a reasonable time. Similarly, in *Long* v *Lloyd*, the plaintiff bought a second-hand lorry from the defendant on the faith of certain statements made by the latter as to its condition. Despite repeated complaints by the plaintiff to the defendant – which the defendant made some attempt to meet – the plaintiff continued to use the lorry until it broke down more or less completely, though only a few days after he had bought it. Again the plaintiff claimed rescission for misrepresentation, and again the court decided that he was too late, apparently on the ground that the buyer had accepted the lorry.

Two questions which gave rise to difficulties in these cases have been set at rest by the Misrepresentation Act. First, it is not material to inquire whether a statement in this kind of case becomes incorporated into the contract as a contractual term. For by s. 1(a) of the Misrepresentation Act, the fact that a pre-contractual representation has become a term of the contract does not in itself deprive the innocent party of the right to rescind. Secondly, s. 1(b) permits rescission of an executed contract for an innocent misrepresentation. This means that rescission of such a contract will only be barred on one of the other grounds on which rescission may be barred, that is by affirmation, lapse of time, inability to make *restitutio in integrum*, or the acquisition of rights by an innocent third party.[101] It seems probable that, so far as concerns the right of a buyer to rescind, the effect of the Act will be to put rejection for breach of condition and rescission for innocent misrepresentation largely on the same footing. An act which constitutes an acceptance within the meaning of s. 35 will presumably amount to an affirmation of the contract within normal equitable principles.

But there appear to be at least two situations in which the rules governing acceptance in s. 35 differ from the equitable principles governing rescission for misrepresentation. First, we have seen that, under s. 35, if the goods are delivered to the buyer and they do not within a reasonable time intimate that they reject the goods, they are deemed to have accepted them.[102] But in equity it seems that lapse of time by itself does not prevent rescission: it will only do so if it is evidence of affirmation or if the representor is thereby prejudiced.[103] Since it is possible that a reasonable time for rejection may elapse without the seller being prejudiced by the delay, it seems that equity might allow rescission in a case where rejection would be barred under s. 35.

[99] [1950] 2 KB 86.
[100] [1958] 1 WLR 753. See further on this case a note by Grunfeld (1958) 21 MLR 550 and another by Professor Atiyah in (1959) 22 MLR 76.
[101] *Salt* v *Stratstone Specialist Ltd* [2015] EWCA Civ 745.
[102] See above, section 17.2.3.
[103] *Allen* v *Robles* [1969] 1 WLR 1193; *Fenton* v *Kenny* [1969] NZLR 552. It is not clear how this can be reconciled with *Leaf* v *International Galleries*, above.

Another possible divergence concerns the buyer who has had a reasonable opportunity to examine the goods and has resold and delivered them to a sub-buyer. As we have seen,[104] under the 1979 Act this remains a case in which the buyer loses their right of rejection under ss. 34 and 35 of the Act (except insofar as s. 35(6)(b) applies), even though the buyer is willing and able to place the goods at the seller's disposal at the original place of delivery. It seems that a right to rescind for misrepresentation would not be lost in this situation. The buyer would (it seems) only lose their right to rescind if they could not make *restitutio in integrum*.[105] For example, if they cannot get the goods back from the sub-buyer, they plainly cannot rescind their own purchase of the goods. But where they are in fact in a position to restore the goods to the seller, it does not seem that previous dealings by the buyer will deprive them of the right to rescind.[106]

The further question which now arises is the effect of this divergence between the statutory and the equitable principles. In *Leaf* v *International Galleries*,[107] Denning LJ expressed the view that a right to rescind for misrepresentation cannot survive beyond the point when a right to reject for breach of condition is lost because a misrepresentation is 'much less potent' than a breach of condition. But it seems that this reasoning cannot survive s. 1(a) of the Misrepresentation Act, which clearly permits rescission for a misrepresentation even where the misrepresentation has become a term of the contract. This being so, it would be very anomalous if the right to rescind is lost at an earlier date when the misrepresentation does not become a term of the contract.

The conclusion is that, whenever a buyer wishes to reject goods and the seller may wish to contend that the buyer has lost the right to reject, the buyer will be well advised to seek, in the alternative, rescission for misrepresentation. This will not, of course, be possible where the breach complained of was non-performance of a promise and not a misstatement of fact; nor will it always be advantageous to the buyer, particularly as the court may in its discretion refuse rescission under s. 2(2) of the Misrepresentation Act and award damages in lieu. The court has no discretion to deprive a buyer of the right to reject under the Sale of Goods Act.

It seems absurd that where a false representation of fact is made by a seller, the question whether the buyer can reject the goods or rescind the contract will continue to depend on two completely different sets of legal principles, even though they are designed to serve the identical purpose.

17.4 Specific performance or implement

The buyer, but not the seller,[108] may invoke the discretion of the court and ask for a decree that the contract be specifically performed. This is regulated by s. 52 which says:

> (1) In any action for breach of contract to deliver specific or ascertained goods the court may, if it thinks fit, on the plaintiff's application, by its judgment or decree direct that the contract

[104] See above, section 17.2.1.

[105] Note that the courts have indicated that precise restitution may not be necessary where substantive justice could be done by the payment of an appropriate sum: *Salt* v *Stratstone Specialist Ltd* [2015] EWCA Civ 745.

[106] See, e.g., *Abram Steamship Co Ltd* v *Westville Shipping Co* [1923] AC 773.

[107] [1950] 2 KB 86, 90–1.

[108] Although the seller has not in name a right to a decree of specific performance, they do of course sometimes have a right to sue for the price, which is much the same thing. If the seller sues for, and obtains payment of the price, the title to the goods and the right to possession will vest in the buyer by satisfaction, if they have not yet vested in him or her already.

shall be performed specifically, without giving the defendant the option of retaining the goods on payment of damages.

(2) The plaintiff's application may be made at any time before judgment or decree.

(3) The judgment or decree may be unconditional, or on such terms and conditions as to damages, payment of the price, and otherwise, as seems just to the court.

Section 52(4) goes on to say that these provisions are to be deemed supplementary to, and not in derogation of, the right of specific implement in Scotland. The significance of this is that, as a number of cases have affirmed, the basis of specific implement is distinct from that of specific performance. In Scotland, implement is a right and, although this is subject to the equitable control of the court, the exercise of that control is coloured by the different starting point. Thus, the Scottish courts have specifically enforced 'keep open' clauses in leases[109] and have not followed the judgment of the House of Lords in *Co-operative Insurance Society Ltd v Argyll Stores (Holdings) Ltd*.[110] In theory, therefore, there might be enforcement of a contract for unascertained goods, although the courts have generally held against this on the basis that the buyer cannot show any reason for preferring to obtain their goods by this route (*pretium affectionis*) rather than buying replacements on the market at the seller's expense.[111]

Specific goods, as we have seen, are defined by s. 61 as being goods 'identified and agreed upon at the time the contract is made', and it has been said that 'ascertained goods' in this context probably means goods 'identified in accordance with the agreement after the time a contract of sale is made'.[112]

Section 52 applies whether or not the property has passed to the buyer,[113] although if the property has passed the buyer has the option of claiming in the alternative a decree of specific restitution in an action of conversion. But even here they cannot ask for such a decree as of right. This is now expressly provided for in s. 3 of the Torts (Interference with Goods) Act 1977. In other words, the remedy rests entirely within the discretion of the court and will not be granted in respect of chattels of no special importance, where damages would be an adequate remedy. But where a chattel is of peculiar importance and of practically unique value to the claimant, the court will grant the necessary decree.[114]

The English courts still seem most unwilling to use this jurisdiction, still less to extend it.[115] In one case,[116] for example, the Court of Appeal refused to order specific delivery of a machine manufactured by the defendants, although it was over 220 tons in weight, cost some £270,000 and could only be bought in the market with a 9–12 months' delivery date. It was formerly thought that a contract for the sale of a ship would be specifically enforceable almost as a matter of course, as a ship is a pretty unique chattel, but even this

[109] *Retail Park Investments Ltd* v *Royal Bank of Scotland* 1996 SC 227; *Highland & Universal Properties Ltd* v *Safeway Properties Ltd* 2000 SC 297.

[110] [1998] AC 1.

[111] See, e.g., *Union Electric Co* v *Holman* 1913 SC 954.

[112] *Re Wait* [1927] 1 Ch 606, 630 per Atkin LJ; *In Re London Wine Co (Shippers) Ltd* (1986) PCC 121. See also *AstraZeneca UK Ltd* v *Albemarle International Corp* [2011] EWHC 1574 (Comm), paras. 303–4.

[113] *Re Wait* [1927] 1 Ch 606, 617 per Lord Hanworth MR.

[114] *Behnke* v *Bede Shipping Co Ltd* [1927] 1 KB 649.

[115] For a critical comparative discussion see MacQueen, Dauner-Lieb and Tettinger, in Dannemann and Vogenauer (eds), *The Common European Sales Law in Context: Interactions with English and German Law* (2013, Oxford University Press, Oxford), Chapter 18.

[116] *Société des Industries Metallurgiques SA* v *Bronx Engineering Co Ltd* [1975] 1 Lloyd's Rep 465.

proposition was rejected in *CN Marine Inc* v *Stena Line*.[117] According to Parker J in this case, a buyer of a ship is not even *prima facie* entitled to a decree of specific performance, nor does mere inconvenience to the buyer or the possibility of remote loss justify such a decree. It must be shown that the ship was of peculiar importance to the plaintiff, in that the design was especially suited to their needs, or something of that kind.

Although the statutory provisions referred to above seem to make it immaterial whether the property has passed to the buyer or not, it seems that the courts are still more inclined to protect a property owner than someone with a bare contractual right. So where goods were sold and property had clearly passed, but the sellers – though claiming no contractual or proprietary rights over the goods – wanted to use them to satisfy other clients and pay damages to the buyer, the court granted an interim injunction to restrain the sellers from delivering the goods to the other clients.[118] In this case, it was held that it was no defence for the sellers to show that damages would be an adequate remedy, an approach which seems very different from that adopted where the buyer actually seeks a decree of specific performance. Yet the result of this case must surely have been that the sellers actually delivered the goods to the buyer.

Where the property has not passed to the buyer, there can be no question of conversion and the only claim which can be made is on the contract. Until recently, it was generally thought that the court had no power to grant specific performance of a contract for the sale of goods as yet unidentified, and that a contract for the sale of an unidentified part of a specific whole was not a contract for the sale of specific or ascertained goods, of which specific performance could be ordered under s. 52.[119]

But some doubt is thrown on these traditional ideas by *Sky Petroleum Ltd* v *VIP Petroleum Ltd*,[120] where the plaintiffs obtained an interlocutory injunction to restrain the defendants from breaking a contract to supply the plaintiffs with all their petroleum requirements for ten years. Goulding J treated the injunction as in effect a decree of specific performance, but went on to hold that the general rule was inapplicable where damages would clearly not be an adequate remedy. In the case before him there was a real danger that the plaintiffs would be forced out of business if the defendants broke their contract in the very peculiar circumstances then holding. This decision may suggest that a buyer can sometimes obtain a decree of specific performance outside the circumstances contemplated by s. 52, by invoking the residuary equity jurisdiction of the court, but the point remains unsettled.[121]

A buyer who gives the seller reason to believe that they will only claim damages and not specific performance may be estopped from changing their mind if the seller has changed their position by acting to their detriment in reliance on this belief.[122]

[117] [1982] 2 Lloyd's Rep 336.

[118] *Redler Grain Silos Ltd* v *BICC Ltd* [1982] 1 Lloyd's Rep 435.

[119] *Re Wait* [1927] 1 Ch 606; *In Re London Wine Co (Shippers) Ltd* (1986) PCC 121.

[120] [1974] 1 All ER 954.

[121] In *In Re London Wine (Shippers) Co Ltd*, above, (1986) PCC 121, Oliver J was inclined to think that the contract in the *Sky Petroleum* case was not strictly a contract of sale of goods, but 'a long-term supply contract under which successive sales would arise if orders were placed and accepted' (see PCC 121, 149), but he went on to hold that even if *Sky Petroleum* was evidence of a jurisdiction to grant specific performance outside s. 52, it was still not possible to grant a decree where the goods were not ascertained, and the buyer had no proprietary interest in the goods.

[122] *Meng Leong Development Pte* v *Jip Hong Trading Co Pte* [1985] AC 511.

18
Action for damages

18.1 Damages

This chapter considers instances when the Sale of Goods Act provides for a claim for damages. Where the Act is silent, the general rules of the common law will apply. This chapter focuses on damages[1] for non-delivery and for breach of warranty.

18.2 Damages for non-delivery[2]

The buyer's action for damages for breach of contract may take one of two forms. It may be an action for damages for non-delivery[3] or it may be an action for damages for breach of a term in respect of goods which have been delivered.[4] A borderline case is where part of the goods which are part of a global whole has not been delivered. In *Sealace Shipping Co Ltd* v *Oceanvoice*,[5] it was held that the appropriate measure in such a case was damages for non-delivery. First, we shall deal with damages for non-delivery.

Unlike the seller's remedy, the nature of which depends upon whether the property has passed or not, the buyer's action for damages for non-delivery is the same and the damages are assessed in the same way, whether or not the property has passed. In both cases, the buyer's essential complaint is the same, namely that the seller has failed to deliver goods which they ought to have delivered, and the buyer claims damages accordingly. The only difference is that where the property has passed the buyer may have a claim in conversion as well as, or as an alternative to, their action for damages for non-delivery, but, as will be seen, in practice the result is the same in either case.

The main rules for the assessment of damages are laid down by s. 51:

> (1) Where the seller wrongfully neglects or refuses to deliver the goods to the buyer, the buyer may maintain an action against the seller for damages for non-delivery.
> (2) The measure of damages is the estimated loss directly and naturally resulting, in the ordinary course of events, from the seller's breach of contract.
> (3) Where there is an available market for the goods in question the measure of damages is *prima facie to* be ascertained by the difference between the contract price and the market or current price of the goods at the time or times when they ought to have been delivered or (if no time was fixed) then at the time of the refusal to deliver.

[1] For a recent assessment of the law of damages in sale of goods contracts, see Bridge, Marks and damages in sale of goods case (2016) 132 LQR 405.
[2] For a critique of these provisions and their equivalents in the Uniform Commercial Code, see Adams [2002] JBL 553.
[3] Under s. 51.
[4] Under s. 53.
[5] [1991] 1 Lloyd's Rep 120.

18.2.1 The market price rule

If, then, there is a market the *prima facie* rule is the same as in an action by the seller: that is to say, the damages are to be assessed by reference to the market price of the goods at the time when they ought to have been delivered, and by giving the buyer the difference between the market price and the contract price the court puts them in the position they would have been in had the goods been delivered.[6] This reflects the assumption that, in order to comply with their duty to mitigate, the buyer goes into the market to buy substitute goods.[7] If the market price is lower than the contract price it follows, of course, that the buyer is only entitled to nominal damages because they can go into the market and buy replacement goods without extra cost.

The general rule is not displaced merely because the buyer has already contracted to resell the goods to a third party at a price higher or lower than the market price at the date when delivery should be made. This principle was laid down by the Court of Appeal in *Rodocanachi* v *Milburn*[8] and was affirmed by the House of Lords in *Williams* v *Agius*.[9] The resale price is treated as irrelevant because the buyer must, in order to fulfil their sub-sales, buy in the market if the seller fails to deliver. Damages for the non-delivery are intended to compensate for the additional cost of buying in the market.

In option contracts, it would appear that the appropriate measure is a sum which will compensate the buyer for the loss of the opportunity to buy, and in assessing this account must be taken of the fact that the buyer might not have exercised the option.[10]

18.2.2 Market price at what date

We have already seen in dealing with the action for non-acceptance that the concluding words of s. 51(3) have no relevance where there is an anticipatory breach of contract.[11] Should the seller repudiate the contract before the date for delivery arrives,[12] the market price to be taken in the assessment of the damages is not that prevailing at the date of the repudiation but that at the time when delivery might have been expected to be made.[13] In *Tai Hing Cotton Mill Ltd* v *Kamsing Knitting Factory*,[14] the sellers failed to deliver 424 bales of yarn to buyers under a contract without a fixed delivery date. On 31 July 1973, the sellers wrote repudiating the contract. The buyers did not accept this and continued to press for delivery, as they were entitled to do. But eventually they recognised that the sellers would not deliver, and on 28 November 1973, the buyers issued a writ claiming damages. It was held by the Privy Council that right up to that date the buyers could have

[6] See, e.g., *Allen* v *W Burns (Tractors) Ltd* 1985 SLT 252. The buyer also recovered extra financing charges caused by the seller's breach.

[7] *Cf. Sharp Corp Ltd* v *Viterra BV* [2024] UKSC 14 esp. paras [93]–[96].

[8] (1886) 18 QBD 67.

[9] [1914] AC 510.

[10] See *Geogas SA* v *Tramono Gas Ltd* [1993] 1 Lloyd's Rep 215.

[11] *Millett* v *Van Heeck* [1921] 2 KB 369 – see Chapter 16.

[12] An inability to perform can amount to a repudiation by the seller, but the buyer must be able to establish this fact on the balance of probabilities – see *Alfred C Toepfer Int* v *Itex Italgrani Export* [1993] 1 Lloyd's Rep 361, and see Chapter 15, at section 15.3, for the related point in relation to repudiation by a buyer.

[13] *Melachrino* v *Nickoll & Knight* [1920] 1 KB 693; *Attorney-General of Ghana* v *Texas Overseas Tank Ships Ltd* [1993] 1 Lloyd's Rep 471 – action against a carrier for non-delivery.

[14] [1979] AC 91.

demanded delivery on reasonable notice. They went on to hold that one month would have been sufficient notice, and accordingly, they could have demanded delivery up to 28 December, one month after they issued their writ. That, then, was the date when the goods ought to have been delivered within the meaning of the section and the date by reference to which the damages were to be assessed.

It will be observed that the buyer is not bound to accept the seller's repudiation when it is first made. In accordance with the general principles of the law of contract, as affirmed by the House of Lords in *White & Carter (Councils) Ltd* v *McGregor*,[15] the buyer can keep the seller's obligations alive by refusing to accept the repudiation. However, if this principle is combined with that laid down by the Privy Council in the *Tai Hing Cotton Mill* case, it would seem that the buyer could prolong the seller's duty to deliver more or less indefinitely in a contract without a fixed delivery date. If they simply tell the seller that they do not accept the repudiation and then wait five years before issuing their writ, are the damages to be assessed by reference to the market price at that date? This result presumably could be avoided by holding that the intention of the parties was that the goods would be delivered within a reasonable time after the contract was made, and then finding an appropriate date for that purpose.[16]

Of course, the whole situation is changed if the buyer accepts the seller's repudiation,[17] for they must then mitigate their damage, as a 'reasonable man'.[18] And if the market is rising, it seems that the buyer must then buy in the market without delay, although we have also seen that some skepticism has been expressed about the possibility of identifying rising and falling markets in advance.[19] But in any event, according to the *White & Carter* case, the buyer is under no obligation to accept a wrongful repudiation (as long as the seller's performance is still possible[20]), and the duty to mitigate does not arise until and unless they do so accept it, and bring the primary contractual duties of the seller to an end.

Where a contract expressly provides for a period of time during which delivery is to be made – as is very common in commercial sales – the seller is not in breach until the end of the last day of the permitted period. That is the time when the goods ought to have been delivered within the meaning of the subsection, and it is by reference to the market price at that time that the damages must be assessed.[21] In a c.i.f. contract, the time when the goods ought to have been delivered within s. 51(3) is the time when the documents ought to have

[15] [1962] AC 413, 1962 SC (HL) 1. But see also *The Alaskan Trader* [1984] 1 All ER 129. Note that the Scottish Law Commission, *Remedies for Breach of Contract* (Scot. Law Com. No. 174, 1999) has recommended that the decision in *White & Carter* be reversed by legislation imposing a requirement of reasonableness.

[16] The Court of Appeal has held that affirmation of the contract by the innocent party would not be possible where the defaulting party would no longer be able to perform: *MSC Mediterranean Shipping Company SA* v *Cottonex Anstalt* [2016] EWCA Civ 789 (here, performance was no longer possible as the commercial purpose of the contract had been frustrated).

[17] Presumably, on the analogy of *Vitol SA* v *Norelf Ltd* [1993] 2 Lloyd's Rep 301, buying on the market on the basis of the seller's repudiation would be sufficient act of acceptance.

[18] As to what amounts to such acceptance, see *Vitol SA* v *Norelf Ltd* [1993] 2 Lloyd's Rep 301 – acceptance by conduct as well as words.

[19] *Roth* v *Tayson* (1896) 73 LT 628. On the doubts about identifying rising markets in advance, see *Lusograin Comercio Internacional de Cereas Ltda* v *Bunge AG* [1986] 2 Lloyd's Rep 654, 662–3, per Staughton LJ, and on the whole question, see Chapter 16 *et seq.*

[20] *MSC Mediterranean Shipping Company SA* v *Cottonex Anstalt* [2016] EWCA Civ 789.

[21] *Toepfer* v *Cremer* [1975] 2 Lloyd's Rep 118, following *Brown* v *Muller* (1872) LR 7 Ex 319; *Roper* v *Johnson* (1873) LR 8 CP 167.

been delivered[22] and, therefore, if a period of time is allowed, as is usual, it is the last day of the period which fixes the day by reference to which the damages must be assessed.

Although the market price rule is now firmly established in English and Scots law, it may be observed that there are cases in which it would lead to injustice if the rule were rigidly applied (e.g. by over-compensating the buyer[23]). In particular, it is unrealistic to suppose that a buyer will, in practice, be able to buy goods in the market on the very day on which the seller fails to deliver. The buyer will often wish to consider their position, or to negotiate with the seller on breach and some delay before they buy substitute goods is likely to be the rule rather than the exception. In this situation, although it has been stressed that assessment of damages as at the date of breach remains the *prima facie* rule,[24] there are some circumstances in which the relevant market price will be that prevailing on the date when the buyer finally accepts (or perhaps ought reasonably to accept) that the seller is not going to deliver, so that the buyer will have to go into the market and buy substitute goods.[25] Indeed, once this is established as the right approach there seems no real reason why the courts should not adopt the rule of the Uniform Commercial Code[26] – at least as *prima facie* evidence of the buyer's loss – that the price of the substitute goods should be taken as the basis for the assessment of the damages. Of course, care must be taken not to permit the buyer to prejudice the seller's position by delaying for too long their decision to buy in the market, though there is once again some difficulty in reconciling this with the *White & Carter* decision which seems to rule out any duty to mitigate unless and until the repudiation is accepted. Certainly, the buyer will have difficulty in making out a case for higher damages where they have, after the seller's failure to deliver, bought in the market at higher than market prices. There is, perhaps, more likelihood that the damages will be reduced if the buyer has bought at lower than market prices.[27]

18.2.3 Market price at what place

The relevant market for the purposes of the rule is generally that at the place of delivery because that will usually be the market on which the buyer will buy. Any principle requiring the buyer to go into another available market in order to mitigate their loss is of limited applicability because it is the value of the goods at the port of destination for which the buyer is being compensated.[28]

[22] *C Sharpe & Co Ltd* v *Nosawa & Co Ltd* [1917] 2 KB 814; *Garnac Grain Co* v *H M Faure & Fairclough* [1966] 1 QB 650, affirmed [1968] AC 1130.

[23] In *Bunge SA* v *Nidera BV (formerly known as Nidera Handelscompagnie BV)* [2015] UKSC 43, a case involving the interpretation of clause 20 of GAFTA 49, the Supreme Court noted that s. 51(3) was a *prima facie* rule, and – as with clause 20 – the compensatory principle would be the overriding concern. Post-breach events known at the time of arbitration or court hearing could therefore be taken into account, especially where these indicate that the buyer's losses are lower.

[24] *Janred Properties Ltd* v *Ente Nazionale Italiano per il Turismo* [1989] 2 All ER 444.

[25] *Johnson* v *Agnew* [1980] AC 367, 400–1; *Suleiman* v *Shahsavari* [1989] 2 All ER 460; see also *Asamera Oil Corp* v *Sea Oil & General Corp* (1978) 98 DLR (3d) 1.

[26] Article 2-712.

[27] See *R Pagnan & Fratelli* v *Corbisa Industrial Agropacuaria Limitada* [1970] 1 WLR 1306, though the facts here were rather special – see Chapter 16.

[28] *Attorney-General Rep of Ghana* v *Texaco Overseas Tank Ships Ltd* [1993] 1 Lloyd's Rep 471.

18.2.4 Cases where the market price rule is inapplicable

It is now necessary to examine those cases in which the damages are assessed by some other yardstick than that of market price. In the first place, even where there is a market for the goods in question[29] the buyer may in some exceptional cases be able to claim damages representing the loss they have suffered on sub-sales which they have been unable to fulfil. For example, a buyer may contract to buy goods at £10 per tonne and may contract to resell the same goods at £12 per tonne. If the market price at the date of non-delivery to the first buyer is £11 per tonne, the question is whether the first buyer should recover as damages £1 per tonne (the difference between market price and contract price) or £2 per tonne (the difference between market price and resale price). As we have seen, the normal rule is that sub-sales must be ignored in assessing the damages, but this rule only applies to damages arising directly and naturally from the breach under s. 51. The buyer may, in addition, be able to claim special damages, the right to which is reserved by s. 54, and which are based on loss not directly or naturally following from the breach, but on loss arising from special circumstances of which the parties were aware. These two different types of damages correspond to the first and second rules in *Hadley* v *Baxendale*,[30] which were authoritatively restated by the House of Lords in *Koufos* v *Czarnikow Ltd (The Heron II)*.[31] According to this decision, the question in every case is whether on the information available to them at the time the contract was made, the seller should, or a reasonable man in their position would, have realised that such loss was sufficiently likely to result from the breach of contract to make it proper to hold that the loss flowed naturally from the breach, or that loss of that kind should have been within their contemplation.[32]

A simple example of special damage which may be alleged by the buyer is for freight which they have had to pay despite non-delivery of the goods,[33] or sums paid for the cancellation of a charterparty.[34]

But it is one thing to recognise in principle that damages may be given in respect of a resale price. It is another thing to define the precise circumstances in which a buyer is entitled to claim damages in respect of sub-sales. The leading case is the decision of the House of Lords in *Re R & H Hall Ltd and W H Pim (Junior) & Co's Arbitration*,[35] which 'astonished the Temple and surprised St Mary Axe'.[36] In this case, the sellers sold a specific cargo of corn in a specific ship to the buyers at fifty-one shillings and ninepence per quarter. The buyers resold at fifty-six shillings and ninepence per quarter, but when the vessel arrived the market price had fallen to fifty-three shillings and ninepence per quarter. The sellers failed to deliver and the question was whether the measure of damages was the difference between the contract price and the resale price, on the one hand, or the contract price and the market price, at the date when the goods should have been delivered, on

29 On the meaning of 'market', see Chapter 16.
30 (1854) 9 Ex 341.
31 [1969] 1 AC 350.
32 Per Lord Reid, p. 386.
33 *E Braude (London) Ltd* v *Porter* [1959] 2 Lloyd's Rep 161.
34 *Bem Dis A Turk Ticaret S/A Tr* v *International Agri Trade Co Ltd* [1999] 1 Lloyd's Rep 729 – this case involved a seller suing for these expenses, but the principle is the same.
35 (1928) 139 LT 50; [1928] All ER Rep 763.
36 See *James Finlay & Co* v *NV Kwik Hoo Tong Handel Maatschappij* [1929] 1 KB 400, 417. Indeed, the decision seems to have been found so distasteful by some that it was not even reported in the Appeal Cases!

the other. It was held that the former was the appropriate measure of damages but the precise *ratio decidendi* is not easy to state. It seems that there were two critical factors in the case which displaced the general principle: first, the sale was for a specific cargo on a specific ship, and it was this same specific cargo which had been resold and secondly, the contract of sale by its terms actually provided for resale by the buyer in the sense that various provisions of the contract dealt with this eventuality.

It has been suggested that the reason why the buyer can claim a higher measure of damages where these two conditions are satisfied is that the buyer cannot fulfil their sub-sales by buying in the market. If the buyer has contracted to resell the specific goods which they have agreed to buy under the first contract, they will necessarily be unable to fulfil the second contract if the goods are not delivered. Substituted goods bought in the market will not do, and accordingly the market price is irrelevant.[37] The only alternative is to assess the damages by reference to the resale price provided (and this is the second requirement) that it was known or foreseen that the goods were to be resold. The buyer's expectation loss is the difference between the contract price and the resale price. The right of the buyer to recover the higher measure of damages on a sub-sale is surely simply an application of the second limb in *Hadley* v *Baxendale*, and it is clear that the seller must have been aware, or ought to have been aware, of the buyer's intention to resell.[38]

It seems clear that both requirements must be satisfied because the mere fact that sub-sales may be contemplated as a reasonable probability is not enough to displace the general principle. For as Maugham LJ said in *The Arpad*:[39]

> I suppose most vendors of goods and most carriers might be taken to know that if the purchaser or consignee is a trader the goods will probably be sold, or be bought for sub-sale; but the authorities seem to show conclusively that something more than that is necessary to enable the damages to be assessed by reference to a contract of sub-sale entered into before the date of delivery.[40]

But it has been said that the position may differ where 'the seller knows that the buyer is buying the goods in order to fulfil an already existing special contract, and knows that if he fails to deliver the goods the buyer will come under a specific liability to his sub-buyer'.[41]

Where the two conditions are satisfied but the buyer has contracted to resell the goods at *less* than the market price the question arises whether the seller is to be given the benefit of this. All the cases which have arisen so far in which sub-sales have been taken into account have been cases in which the buyer *increased* their damages by proving that this loss was more than the difference between the contract and the market price. A possible reason for this is apparent from the facts of *Williams* v *Agius*. In that case, Agius sold a quantity of goods to Williams at sixteen shillings and threepence per unit. Williams sold to a third party X at nineteen shillings. X sold to Agius at twenty shillings. Agius failed to deliver to Williams, no doubt because the market price had now risen to twenty-three shillings and sixpence. The question to be decided by the court was whether Williams

[37] See, e.g., Ogus on *Damages* (1973, Butterworths), pp. 333–5.

[38] *Seven Seas Properties* v *Al-Esso* [1993] 3 All ER 577.

[39] [1934] P 189, 230.

[40] Cf. *James Finlay & Co* v *NV Kwick Hoo Tong Handel Maatschappij* [1929] 1 KB 400, 411–12 per Scrutton LJ, and 417–18 per Sankey LJ. Cf. also *Horne* v *Midland Rly Co* (1873) LR 8 CP 131.

[41] *Aryeh* v *Lawrence Kostoris & Son Ltd* [1967] 1 Lloyd's Rep 63, 68 per Willmer LJ.

should recover the contract/market difference at the time of non-delivery (seven shillings and threepence), or be limited by the amount of the sub-sale to X to two shillings and ninepence. It was held that Williams should recover the full contract/market difference. After all, in order to fulfil his contract with X, he would have had to pay twenty-three and sixpence on the market. If he did not fulfil his contract with X, or was unable to because this was a specific cargo on a specific vessel as in *Hall & Pim's Arbitration*, he would have had to pay X the difference between X's contract price of nineteen shillings and the market price, that is, four shillings and sixpence, to which there would have to be added his own gain of two shillings and ninepence. Either way, the damages suffered by Williams work out at seven shillings and threepence.

If the buyer can bring themselves within the principle of *Hall & Pim's Arbitration*, they may be entitled to recover not only their loss of profit on sub-sales (for that is what it comes to) but also any damages which they may have had to pay their sub-buyer in respect of their loss of profit and, indeed, that of other sub-buyers in the string. Moreover, if the buyer has been sued by their sub-buyer and has had to pay damages and costs, they are entitled to claim from the seller the total sum they have had to pay as well as a sum in respect of their own costs.[42] The only qualification on this rule is that the buyer must have acted reasonably in defending the action. In string contracts, it may well be easier for the buyer to claim loss of profit than in other sales because, in such a case, if the seller knows that the buyer 'is not buying merely for resale generally but upon a string contract where they will resell those specific goods and where they can only honour their contract by delivering those goods and no others, the measure of profit on resale is the right measure'.[43] This approach was also followed in the context of a 'carousel' of transactions for the supply of oil in *Euro-Asian Oil SA* v *Credit Suisse AG*.[44] Although not string contracts in the strict sense (the oil for the sub-sales could have been sourced from elsewhere), the way in which the various transactions had been set up suggested that it had been in the contemplation of the parties that the buyer would allocate the cargo supplied by the seller to its sub-sales.

Where there is no market for the goods in question, the buyer's damages clearly cannot be assessed in the usual way in terms of the market price. In such a case, the method to be adopted for assessing the damages depends partly on whether the buyer is a trader buying for resale or whether they are buying for use, and partly on what measures the buyer actually adopts to meet the seller's failure to deliver. Where they are a trader, the buyer is entitled to recover the difference between the value of the goods at the time they should have been delivered and the contract price. The value of the goods is *prima facie* to be assessed at the price at which the buyer may have contracted to resell them. Putting it briefly, the buyer is able to recover their loss of profit.[45] And, again, if the buyer can prove special knowledge on the part of the seller, they may also be able to recover in respect of

[42] *Hammond & Co* v *Bussey* (1887) 20 QBD 79.

[43] *Kwei Tek Chao* v *British Traders & Shippers Ltd* [1954] 2 QB 459, 489–90 per Devlin J. In *Aryeh* v *Lawrence Kostoris & Son Ltd* ([1967] Lloyd's Rep 63 at p.72), Diplock LJ suggested that these remarks must be confined to string sales in standard form entered into by dealers on a commodity market where it is contemplated that the buyer may resell on the same terms.

[44] [2018] EWCA Civ 1720; [2019] 1 All ER (Comm) 706.

[45] *J Leavey & Co* v *Hirst & Co* [1944] KB 24; *Patrick* v *Russo-British Export Co Ltd* [1927] 2 KB 535; *Household Machines Ltd* v *Cosmos Exports Ltd* [1947] 1 KB 217.

damages which they have to pay to the sub-buyer.[46] Alternatively, the buyer may choose to buy substitutes with which to fulfil their contracts, and, should these cost more than the contract goods, they can *prima facie* recover this excess cost and is not bound to account for the better quality of the goods so bought.[47] In the case of goods bought for use, the buyer may be able to recover damages to meet the additional cost of buying reasonable alternative goods or of adapting or modifying alternative goods for their purposes. So in *Air Studios (Lyndhurst) Ltd (t/a Air Entertainment Group)* v *Lombard North Central Plc*,[48] involving second-hand equipment used in television and radio post-production, the Court concluded that there was no available market for second-hand goods because although comparable second-hand goods were available, it would have taken around three months to source those. Consequently, the basic rule in s. 51(2) was applied instead, and the yardstick for the quantum of damages would be the cost of procuring equivalent second-hand equipment.

It should be observed that a sub-sale price cannot be taken as conclusive evidence of the value of the goods. In particular, where it is proved that the contract of sub-sale was entered into long before the date at which delivery should have been made and that the price of similar goods has fallen heavily in the meantime, some other mode of assessing the value of the goods must be chosen.[49] So also, where the sub-sale was made on very unusual terms, the buyer cannot claim loss of profit based on the sub-sale price, though it may be possible to adjust the price notionally by eliminating the unusual features, and asking what the sub-sale price would then have been.[50]

Another situation where the market price rule may be inapplicable arises where, even if the seller had delivered the goods, the buyer would not in fact have been able to dispose of the goods in the market. So where goods were sold c.i.f. Beirut, and the sellers failed to deliver, it was held that the damages must be assessed by reference to the value of the goods in the vessel, and not the landed value because the port was closed and the buyer would not have been able to land the goods even if they had been delivered.[51] A similar situation might occur where a buyer orders goods for resale in a particular market into which they cannot be imported due to the existence of a third party's intellectual property rights. Assuming that the seller did not warrant the saleability of the goods in the

[46] In a suitable case the court may grant a declaration that the buyer is entitled to an indemnity in respect of damages and costs they may have to pay their sub-buyer: *Household Machines Ltd* v Cosmos Exports Ltd ([1947] KB 217). But this remedy is sparingly used – see, e.g., *Trans Trust* v *Danubian Trading Co Ltd* [1952] 2 QB 297.

[47] *Hinde* v *Liddell* (1875) LR 10 QB 265.

[48] [2013] 1 Lloyd's Rep. 63.

[49] *The Arpad* [1934] P 230; *Heskell* v *Continental Express Ltd* [1950] 1 All ER 1033.

[50] *Coastal International Trading Ltd* v *Maroil AG* [1988] 1 Lloyd's Rep 92.

[51] *R Pagnan & Filli* v *Lorico* (1981) Com LR 152. But there are puzzling features to this decision. Usually the market price is taken as the yardstick because if the seller fails to deliver, the buyer will have to buy in the market in lieu. Here it seems to have been assumed that the reason why the market price is the yardstick is because, on delivery, the buyer can resell in the market. Perhaps this case would have been better decided on the ground that in a c.i.f. contract the seller fulfils their duty by delivering documents; inability to unload is the buyer's problem, not the seller's – so long at least as the seller has made a proper contract of carriage and supplied proper documents. See also *Sealace Shipping Co Ltd* v *Oceanvoice* [1991] 1 Lloyd's Rep 120. In that case the seller failed to deliver a spare propeller with a vessel. There was no available market in spare propellers, and accordingly the measure of damages fell to be assessed under s. 51(2). In the event, the arbitrator held that the damages suffered by the buyer assessed under that subsection were to be fixed by reference to the scrap value of the spare propeller.

particular market,[52] it would appear that the value of the goods would have to be assessed by some other criterion such as the price at which the buyer could have disposed of the goods in another market (assuming the buyer used reasonable endeavours to get the best price possible).

18.2.5 Damages for breach of condition or warranty

In English law, the seller may deliver the goods to the buyer, but may still be guilty of a breach of a contractual term entitling the buyer to damages, that is to say, a breach of warranty, or a breach of condition or of an innominate term which the buyer chooses, or is compelled, to treat as a breach of warranty. In this event, s. 53 applies:[53]

> (1) Where there is a breach of warranty by the seller, or where the buyer elects (or is compelled) to treat any breach of a condition on the part of the seller as a breach of warranty, the buyer is not by reason only of such breach of warranty entitled to reject the goods; but he may—
> (a) set up against the seller the breach of warranty in diminution or extinction of the price; or
> (b) maintain an action against the seller for damages for the breach of warranty.
> (2) The measure of damages for breach of warranty is the estimated loss directly and naturally resulting, in the ordinary course of events, from the breach of warranty.

18.2.6 Late delivery

Late delivery may, of course, justify the buyer in refusing to take the goods at all. Whether it has this effect depends upon whether time is of the essence so that late delivery is treated as a breach of condition; in cases where time is not of the essence, late delivery may still be so inordinate that eventually the buyer is justified in refusing to take delivery, though they may sometimes have to give notice before they do so.[54] If the buyer does refuse to take the goods, their claim for damages will be a claim for non-delivery rather than, strictly, a claim for late delivery, and the applicable rules will be those relating to non-delivery, considered above. The only additional point to note here is that the mitigation rule may operate in a somewhat strange way in the case of late delivery, in effect undercutting the buyer's claim for non-delivery altogether. In *The Solholt*,[55] for instance, sellers had contracted to sell a ship for $5m, delivery not later than 31 August; in fact, they only tendered the ship on 3 September and the buyers refused to accept it, as they were entitled to do. The market price had actually risen by this time to $5.5m so that *prima facie* it would seem the buyers might have expected to recover half a million dollars in damages. In fact, they recovered nothing because their refusal to accept the ship amounted to a termination of the original contract, as a result of which their duty to mitigate came into operation. Reasonable mitigation demanded that they should have sought some arrangement after the breach, it being found as a fact that they could have negotiated a settlement with the sellers after the breach under which the ship would still have been delivered, albeit a few days late. This

[52] See Cchapter 7 p. 169 *et seq*.
[53] The section does not mention innominate terms, which were, of course, not invented when the Act was first passed. But it can be assumed that the measure of damages for breach of such a term is exactly the same as the measure of damages for breach of warranty.
[54] See Chapter 6.
[55] [1983] 1 Lloyd's Rep 605. See Bridge (1989) 105 LQR 398 at 417–23.

was, of course, a case dealing with a rather special type of goods – a ship; in other cases, late delivery will usually result in the buyer going into the market to buy replacements, and once this has been done it will obviously be too late for the seller to tender delivery and claim that the buyer can best mitigate the damage by taking the goods late. But the case does suggest that a late delivery is worth tendering because if the buyer has not yet made other arrangements their failure to accept even a late delivery may well cut their damages significantly, even perhaps to nil.

If, however, the goods are delivered late and are accepted, the method of assessing the damages may depend on whether the buyer is a trader buying for resale or whether they are buying for use. If they are buying for use, the appropriate damages may be calculated by considering how much it would have cost the buyer to hire substitute goods during the delay, or what additional costs may have been incurred by the buyer as a result of having to make do without the goods during the delay. Much will depend here on what the buyer has actually done to mitigate their loss arising out of the delay and whether their conduct has been reasonable.

Where, on the other hand, the buyer is a trader buying for resale, it seems that the normal rule is that the buyer is entitled to recover as damages the difference between the market price at the time the goods should have been delivered and the market price at the time they were in fact delivered. Oddly enough, there appears to be no clear authority to this effect in the law of sale, but this was the measure of damages awarded by the House of Lords for delayed delivery in a contract of carriage in *Koufos* v *Czarnikow*,[56] and it seems to be generally accepted that the same measure applies in a sale.

Under this measure of damages, it will be observed that the contract price is irrelevant. The rule is based on the assumption that the buyer resells the goods as soon as they are delivered to them; on this assumption, the loss to the buyer which is caused by the delay is the fall in the market between the contract delivery date and the actual delivery date.

A difficult and controversial case is *Wertheim* v *Chicoutimi Pulp Co Ltd*,[57] where A contracted to sell goods to B at twenty-five shillings a ton. With the costs and expenses of transport, the total cost to the buyer was thirty-eight shillings a ton. A was late in delivering the goods. The market price at the date when the goods ought to have been delivered was seventy shillings a ton, but the market price at the date when the goods were in fact delivered was forty-two shillings and sixpence a ton. The buyer, however, resold the goods at sixty-five shillings a ton. It was held by the Privy Council that the buyer was only entitled to the difference between seventy shillings and sixty-five shillings a ton, that is, five shillings, not the difference between seventy shillings and forty-two shillings and sixpence, that is, twenty-seven shillings and sixpence a ton. Although this case was accepted as good law in *Williams* v *Agius*[58] by Lord Dunedin and by Lord Atkinson,[59] it has given rise to a certain amount of criticism[60] on the ground that it conflicts with the general principle that subcontracts are to be ignored unless they were especially contemplated. What seems to have weighed with the Privy Council was that, had the goods been delivered as promised,

[56] [1969] 1 AC 350 (The Heron II).
[57] [1911] AC 301.
[58] [1914] AC 510.
[59] Who delivered the judgment of the Privy Council in *Wertheim*.
[60] See *Slater* v *Hoyle & Smith* [1920] 2 KB 11, especially at p. 24 per Scrutton LJ.

the plaintiff would have made a gain of thirty-two shillings had he resold at seventy shillings. He had in fact resold at sixty-five shillings, and so got back twenty-seven shillings of the potential gain of thirty-two shillings. Thus, giving him five shillings gives him his expectation of gain. If he were allowed to recover twenty-seven shillings and sixpence a ton he would have gained fifty-nine shillings and sixpence (twenty-seven shillings and sixpence plus thirty-two shillings), which is more than he would have got had the goods been delivered timeously, and would be contrary to the principle that damages should be compensatory only. The Privy Council had evidence to support the above analysis, but in many cases the court will not have any such evidence. Thus, in other cases the fact that the buyer did not suffer the full loss which might have resulted from the seller's breach would, in a sense, be due to their own business success in selling goods for sixty-five shillings a ton when the market price was only forty-two shillings and sixpence. The buyer might, if the goods had been delivered on time, have resold those goods at their market price of seventy shillings per ton and bought other goods to fulfil his contract. In this way, they would have made a large profit of which they would have been deprived by the breach of contract.

A number of difficult cases have raised questions as to the buyer's damages where shipping documents have been antedated to conceal a late shipment, and market prices have fallen by the time the goods are delivered. In this situation, the buyer can still find themselves compelled to accept the goods before they are fully aware of the breach which has occurred. As we have already seen, this remains possible even though it is now less likely to occur under the current versions of ss. 34 and 35 of the Sale of Goods Act.[61] In this event, the buyer may feel that it is unreasonable to confine them to the measure of damages prescribed by s. 53(3) because they will have lost the opportunity of rejecting the goods and buying replacements in the market at the now lower market price. They may therefore claim damages based on the fall in the market price of the goods; that is, they may claim damages representing the difference between the contract price and the market price of the goods at the date when they were delivered. This is different from the normal measure of damages for late delivery because that measure would only give the buyer the difference between the market price at the date when the goods should have been delivered, and the market price at the date when they were delivered.

Although it is by no means obvious why any sympathy should be shown to a buyer who has thus lost the opportunity for escaping from a bad bargain, the courts have in fact come to the assistance of the buyer in two cases of this nature. Both cases concerned late shipment under c.i.f. contracts in which the bills of lading were wrongly antedated to make it appear that the goods had been shipped during the contract period. In the first case,[62] it was held that the buyers, who had lost their right to reject before being aware of the late shipment, could recover damages representing the difference between the contract and the market price at the date of delivery. This decision was, it seems, partly based on the argument that the buyers were claiming damages, not merely for the late shipment of the goods, but for the separate breach involved in tendering false bills of lading. It was because of this falsity that the buyers did not discover until too late that the goods had been shipped late and, in a sense, it was therefore true to say that it was the falsity of the

[61] See Chapter 17 *et seq*.
[62] *James Finlay* v *NV Kwik Hoo Tong Handel Maatschappij* [1929] 1 KB 400.

bills of lading which caused the buyers' loss; had the bills of lading been accurate, the buyers would probably have rejected the documents (owing to the fall in the market price) on the ground of late shipment and thus escaped their bad bargain.

In the second case,[63] the buyers were again deceived by false bills of lading, but in this case they knew of the late shipment by the time the goods themselves arrived. Although it was too late for them to reject the documents they could (it was held) have still rejected the goods when they arrived, and the case had to be decided on the supposition that they had accepted the goods with knowledge of facts from which the right to reject arose. Even in this situation, it was held by Devlin J that the buyers could recover the difference between the contract price and the market price at the date of delivery and thus throw onto the sellers the loss caused by the drop in the market. This case seems to push this principle as far as it can be taken, and it was based on Devlin J's view that a buyer who has accepted documents under a c.i.f. contract may have practical difficulties about rejecting the goods, and that their choice to accept them is therefore not a wholly free and unconstrained one. Subsequently, some doubts were expressed in the Court of Appeal about the validity of the argument that there are two rights of rejection, one for the documents and one for the goods, in a c.i.f. contract.[64] Certainly, it would seem wrong to allow a buyer quite freely and voluntarily to accept goods which they are entitled to reject and then try to place themselves in the same financial position that they would have been in if they had rejected. A buyer who wants to do this should reject the goods first and then try to negotiate a new price with the seller based on the fall in the market. However, the two decisions referred to above may be justified because of the seriousness of the practice of antedating bills of lading to conceal a late shipment and the desirability of ensuring that the seller should not be able to retain any advantage as a result.

The above cases were distinguished by the Court of Appeal in *Procter & Gamble Philippine Manufacturing Corp* v *Kurt A Becher GmbH*[65] where the sellers tendered bills of lading falsely dated 31 January, though the goods were shipped in February, which was in fact still during the contractual shipment period. The buyers accepted the documents, not then being aware of the false date, and they also accepted the goods when they arrived, by which time the market price had fallen. They then tried to recover damages in respect of this fall in the market for breach of the contractual duty to tender correctly dated documents, but their claim was rejected. Although the buyers could have rejected the documents if they had known that they were falsely dated (and then they could of course have renegotiated the price to take account of the fall in the market), their acceptance of the goods was not the result of the mis-dating of the documents. If the documents had been correctly dated, the buyers could not have rejected either the documents or the goods, so that the mis-dating of the bill of lading caused the buyers no loss. The earlier cases were different because in both of them the mis-dating of the documents was the cause of the buyers accepting the goods and thus losing their opportunity to reject them and take advantage of the fall in the market. In the result, therefore, the mis-dating of the documents here caused the buyers no loss.

[63] *Kwei Tek Chao* v *British Traders & Shippers Ltd* [1954] 2 QB 459.

[64] *Panchaud Frères* v *Etablissements General Grain Co* [1970] 1 Lloyd's Rep 53; *Vargas Pena Apezteguia y Cia Saic* v *Peter Cremer GmbH* [1987] 1 Lloyd's Rep 394.

[65] [1988] 2 Lloyd's Rep 21.

18.3 Breach of warranty of quality

Different considerations arise again where goods defective in quality are delivered. To such a case, s. 53(3) applies in English law:

> In the case of breach of warranty[66] of quality such loss is *prima facie* the difference between the value of the goods at the time of delivery to the buyer and the value they would have had if they had fulfilled the warranty.

The *prima facie* rule is thus that the buyer is entitled to the difference between the value of the goods actually delivered and the value which the goods would have had if they had conformed to the contract.[67] Of course, this means that if the goods are so seriously defective as to have no value at all, the buyer is entitled to recover the full value which the goods should have had.[68] The market price of the goods is, in principle, irrelevant to an action for damages of this kind, although in some cases (especially in consumer sales) the market price of the goods as warranted may be some evidence of the value of the goods as warranted.

The normal rule here, as elsewhere, is that sub-sales by the buyer are irrelevant to the buyer's claim for damages. In *Slater* v *Hoyle & Smith*,[69] the buyers contracted for the purchase of 3,000 pieces of unbleached cloth of specified quality. Some 1,625 pieces of lower quality than specified were delivered, but the buyer delivered 691 of them under a subcontract he had made for the higher grade material, and obtained payment from his sub-buyer at the full rate. The Court of Appeal held that these facts must be ignored in assessing the damages, and that the buyer was entitled to the difference between the value of the contract goods and the value of the goods actually delivered. A different decision was reached in *Bence Graphics International Ltd* v *Fasson UK Ltd*.[70] The seller had supplied the buyer with vinyl film which was then made into decals for containers. These should have lasted for at least five years, but the film supplied was substandard and lasted only for a considerably shorter period. The buyer brought an action against the seller for breach of warranty and claimed the difference in value. The Court of Appeal considered whether damages should be based on the difference in value between defective and non-defective vinyl, or measured by reference to the buyer's liability to the sub-buyers of the decals. The Court of Appeal decided on the latter, as there had only been one complaint about the defective quality, and applied s. 53(2) instead. It has been observed that *Slater* v *Hoyle & Smith* and *Bence Graphics* v *Fasson* are 'not easy to reconcile'.[71] Nevertheless, until it has been reconsidered, *Bence* remains a relevant authority and continues to be applied.[72]

[66] It is curious that this section refers to a breach of warranty of quality, when all the terms as to quality implied by ss. 13–15 are conditions. This suggests that the draftsman may have thought that a condition becomes a warranty if the buyer claims damages in respect of it, but it has been held that this is not so: *Wallis Son & Wells* v *Pratt & Haynes* [1911] AC 394. Presumably, as already suggested, breach of an innominate term would be treated in the same way as a breach of warranty for this purpose.

[67] For an application of this rule to Certified Emissions Reductions in the context of the European Union Emissions Trading System, see *Deutsche Bank AG* v *Total Global Steel Ltd* [2012] EWHC 1201 (Comm).

[68] See *Argos Distributors* v *Advertising Advice Bureau*, 15 February 1996 (unreported), where, as well as extinguishing the price, the court ordered the seller to compensate the buyer for lost profits on an existing sale and lost profits on expected repeat orders.

[69] [1920] 2 KB 11.

[70] [1998] QB 87.

[71] Andrew Smith J in *Bear Stearns Bank Plc.* v *Forum Global Equity Ltd* [2007] EWHC 1576 (Comm) at para 204. Smith J also concluded that the reasoning in *Bence Graphics* should be confined to s. 53, and not be relevant to the application of the market price rule under s. 51: ibid, para 208.

[72] e.g., the detailed discussion in *BP Oil International Limited* v *Glencore Energy UK Limited* [2022] EWHC 499 (Comm).

A slightly different approach was taken in *Saipol SA* v *Inerco Trade SA*,[73] involving a contract of sale for 3,000 mt of Ukrainian Sunflower Oil. The seller had a total cargo of 16,000 mt on-board a ship co-mingled with oil belonging to others. The cargo was discharged at Dunkirk and the buyer delivered the oil to sub-buyers, but they subsequently complained that the sunflower oil had been contaminated with mineral oil (a widespread problem which triggered an EU-wide recall and import ban). The buyer brought an arbitration claim to recover the difference in value, for its liability to sub-purchasers, and the expenses incurred in disposing of contaminated product. The arbitration panel awarded only the difference in value on the basis of s. 53(3). But the High Court allowed the buyer's appeal because the arbitration panel had applied s. 53(3) rather than starting with s. 53(2). On the facts, a claim for consequential losses was permissible and should have been considered by the panel.[74]

Although it is stated that the relevant date for valuing the goods actually delivered is the time of delivery to the buyer, this does not always work well in practice. It may, for instance, be some time after delivery that the breach of warranty is first discovered. Or the goods may be consigned and delivered to sub-buyers before the defect is discovered. In this last situation, the courts have held that the goods should be valued at the time and place of delivery to the sub-buyer provided that the seller knew or could have foreseen that the goods might be redelivered without examination.

It will be seen that the *prima facie* rule laid down by the two sections treats the market price as irrelevant except insofar as the market price may be taken to be the value which the goods should have had. It is the defects in the goods for which the buyer is to be compensated, and the damages are thus based on the deficiency in their value arising from the defects. If, however, the market price of the goods has fallen significantly since the contract was made, the buyer is likely to reject defective goods, as they are often entitled to do. In this event, the buyer is able to take advantage of the seller's breach to throw onto them the loss flowing from the fall in the market; there is in law no general principle of good faith which prevents the buyer from rejecting for any reason they choose, so long only as there is a right to reject.[75] Likewise, in Scots law the only control is the requirement that the breach be material. But where the buyer, with full knowledge of the defective nature of the goods, chooses to keep them and merely to claim damages for the breach, the normal rule must be applied and the buyer will be able to recover only the difference between the value of the goods and their value as warranted.[76] The buyer cannot accept the goods with full knowledge of the seller's breach, and then claim the damages for the loss they might have avoided by rejecting the goods.[77] But by analogy with the cases discussed above concerning wrongly dated shipping documents, it may be that the buyer would be permitted to obtain damages covering the fall in the market price of the goods if they do not know of the defects when they accept the goods, particularly if they have in some way

[73] [2014] EWHC 2211.

[74] In *Dreyfus Trading* v *Reliance Trading* [2004] 2 Lloyd's Rep. 243, where a damages claim for breach of the implied warranty under s. 12(2) was dealt with by reference to s. 53, the High Court held that the *prima facie* measure of damages was the difference in value but that presumption could be rebutted in favour of applying the general measure under s. 53(2) and a sub-sale taken into account where this was in the reasonable contemplation of the parties – the goods had been bought for the specific purpose of reselling to a specific sub-buyer.

[75] As to which, see Chapter 16 *et seq*.

[76] *Vargas Pena Apezteguia y Cia Saic* v *Peter Cremer GmbH* [1987] 1 Lloyd's Rep 394.

[77] Ibid.

been deceived by misrepresentations by the seller, or by the concealment of defects in the goods. This may happen, for instance, where a clean bill of lading is wrongly issued for goods whose apparent condition is manifestly unsatisfactory.

18.3.1 Goods bought for use

Sections 53(3) does not differentiate between goods bought for use and goods bought for resale, and the same measure of damages is thus *prima facie* applicable in the two cases. The buyer can thus recover the difference between the actual value of the goods and their value as warranted, even where they buy for use. In practice, however, the damages in this case are likely to take a different form, or at least to be calculated in a different manner. One possibility is that the buyer will simply have the goods modified or repaired so as to bring them up to the requisite standard. Clearly, in this event the cost of such work is likely to be treated as equal to the difference in value between the goods delivered and their value as warranted.[78] But what happens if there is no difference in value, but a considerable one in having the goods modified or repaired?[79] In the case of *Ruxley Electronics and Construction Co* v *Forsyth*,[80] the plaintiffs had built a swimming pool in the defendant's garden which was shallower than the depth specified. The trial judge found that the shortfall had not decreased the value of the pool and awarded £2,500 general damages for loss of amenity.[81] The Court of Appeal pointed out that there were two methods of assessing the buyer's loss, namely to assess the difference in value, or, alternatively, to assess the costs of modification or repair. The difference in value method was appropriate when the chattel which was damaged[82] or was not up to specification was of a kind commonly available. But this method was inadequate where the buyer's chattel had some unique quality and could not be replaced. Although it would be unreasonable for a buyer to claim an expensive remedy when a cheaper one would make good their loss, on the facts, it was not unreasonable to award as damages the costs of replacing the swimming pool. The House of Lords, however, unanimously restored the trial judge's decision.[83] The House of Lords took the view that to award the cost of reinstatement was wholly unreasonable.

Peculiarly difficult problems attend the calculation of damages for breach of warranty of quality in respect of profit-earning chattels. This is partly because of the need to avoid duplicating the damages by including the same item as a capital loss and an income loss,

[78] *See Keely* v *Guy McDonald* (1984) 134 NLJ 522 (Rolls-Royce found unmerchantable; held: seller liable for repair costs); see also *Bernstein* v *Pamson Motors (Golders Green) Ltd* [1987] 2 All ER 220.

[79] In the Scots case of *Douglas* v *Glenvarigill Co Ltd* [2010] CSOH 14, 2010 SLT 634, for example, the pursuer was awarded the costs of expert examination and repair of his faulty car, plus storage costs incurred where the vehicle might otherwise have suffered further damage or deterioration; wasted costs of comprehensive insurance and road tax from the date the vehicle was taken in for initial repair until its storage; inconvenience; diminution in the value of the car caused by the seller's initial incompetent repair and depreciation.

[80] [1996] AC 344 (HL); [1994] 3 All ER 801 – on appeal from a decision of Judge Diamond QC in the Central London County Court.

[81] It should be noted that the pool as constructed was perfectly safe for diving.

[82] [1996] AC 344. The swimming pool was not, of course, a chattel, but the Court of Appeal treated this distinction as immaterial. This decision was applied by the House of Lords in *Farley* v *Skinner* [2001] UKHL 49.

[83] [1996] AC 344.

[84] [1954] 1 QB 292.

and partly because there is a large number of ways in which loss of profits may be calculated. Difficulties of this nature led to a divided Court of Appeal in *Cullinane* v *British 'Rema' Manufacturing Co Ltd*,[84] but it is doubtful if any general principle can be extracted from this troublesome case.[85] The case was considered in *A C Daniels & Co Ltd* v *Jungwoo Logic*,[86] which involved a contract for the supply of injection moulding machinery for making plastic bins. It was held that since the buyer had properly rejected the goods, the claim was one for non-delivery under s. 51, and the buyer was entitled to damages which would place it as far as possible in the position it would have been in had the contract been performed. *Cullinane*, properly understood, was not authority for the proposition that damages for breach of contract could be recovered on the basis of restoration of the claimant to the position it would have been in if there had been no contract. The claimant was allowed the return of the price paid to the seller, plus the claimant's wasted expenditure. The court did not allow an alternative claim of loss of profit because, on the evidence, it could not quantify this in a satisfactory way. In *Beoco Ltd* v *Alfa Laval*,[87] a heat exchanger supplied by the first defendant was found to be cracked. It was negligently repaired by the second defendant, as a result of which an explosion occurred causing damage to equipment and loss of production. The plaintiffs were found to be negligent in failing to check the repair before switching the machine back on. It was held, applying the same principles as in tort, that the plaintiffs' damages should be limited to the repair costs and losses incurred due to loss of production on the day the repair was effected.

Where the damage caused by the breach requires the buyer to replace plant or machinery, they will not necessarily be compelled to give credit for the fact that they are replacing worn or partly used plant or machinery with new plant or machinery. But they probably would if the old plant or machinery were so worn that it had little life and would have had to be replaced soon anyhow.[88]

Where the buyer buys goods for the use of members of their family, it seems that they can recover damages in respect of (at least some of) their losses, as well as their own.*[AM12] But it does not seem likely that the buyer could recover in respect of personal injuries suffered by members of their family through defective goods bought by them.

18.3.2 Consequential loss

Claims for damages for consequential loss are more commonly associated with breaches of warranty of quality and the like than with claims for non-delivery. Obviously, the main reason for this is that defective goods can cause damage or injury in use, and this type of claim for consequential loss is therefore more frequently made when the goods have been bought for use. Where personal injury or physical damage to property is caused by defective goods in this way, the damages are assessed in much the same way as in the tort/delict of negligence. In such circumstances, the damages may run into thousands of

[85] See Macleod [1970] Journal Bus Law 19; see also *TC Industrial Plant Pty Ltd* v *Roberts Queensland Pty Ltd* (1964) ALR 1083.
[86] 14 April 2000 (unreported).
[87] [1994] 4 All ER 464.
[88] *Bacon* v *Cooper (Metals) Ltd* [1982] 1 All ER 397.

pounds, although the inherent value of the goods may be only a few shillings, as where a child was blinded by use of a defective catapult,[89] or where a man contracted dermatitis from wearing underpants containing an excess of harmful chemicals.[90]

The general principle remains, of course, that the loss must have been in the contemplation of the parties at the time the contract was made, in accordance with the decision in *Hadley* v *Baxendale*.[91] In recent times, claims for consequential losses in contracts of sale of goods have multiplied, both in commercial and consumer sales. Generally speaking, the courts appear to treat such claims very favourably from the buyer's point of view, although *Transfield Shipping Inc* v *Mercator Shipping Inc (The Achilleas)*[92] (not a sale of goods case) suggest that in some instances, one must first decide whether the loss for which compensation is sought is of a 'kind' or 'type' for which the contract-breaker ought fairly to be taken to have accepted responsibility (which could have the effect of either reducing or increasing[93] the overall amount of damages recoverable).

In *Parsons (Livestock) Ltd* v *Uttley, Ingham & Co Ltd*,[94] the defendants sold a large feeding hopper to the plaintiffs, who were pig farmers. In installing the hopper, the defendants failed to open a ventilator at the top (which was not visible from the ground) with somewhat disastrous consequences. The nuts stored in the hopper became mouldy and some of the pigs became ill; later, this triggered off an attack of a much more serious pig disease and many of the pigs died. The value of these pigs amounted to some £10,000, and, in addition, the plaintiffs claimed for substantial losses of profits. It was held that the former losses were recoverable, but not the latter. Although the gravity of the consequences could not have been foreseen in this case, it was held that the parties could reasonably have contemplated that some of the contents of the hopper would become mouldy from the ventilator being closed and that this might have caused some illness of the pigs. In effect, the court here applied the tort/delict decision in *Hughes* v *Lord Advocat4e*[95] that the general *kind* of damage must be foreseeable, but it is not necessary to show that the precise *extent* could have been foreseen. On the facts, the decision is somewhat remarkable and must stand as a warning against taking the foreseeability test too seriously. It seems absurd to suppose that any person would have foreseen anything remotely resembling what happened here as a result of leaving the ventilator closed. The House of Lords passed up an opportunity to consider *Parsons* in the Scottish case of *Balfour Beatty* v *Scottish Power plc*.[96] Balfour Beatty were building an aqueduct, using a 'continuous pour' of concrete for the purpose. A power failure constituting breach of contract by Scottish Power interrupted the pour and led ultimately to the demolition of the work done and its later reconstruction at considerable expense. The Court of Session held the loss recoverable, on the basis that it was of a foreseeable kind, even if the amount was greater than might have been foreseen. The House of Lords held that the loss was too remote under the first leg

[89] *Godley* v *Perry* [1960] 1 WLR 9.
[90] *Grant* v *Australian Knitting Mills* [1936] AC 85.
[91] (1854) 9 Ex 341. This is also the leading case in Scots law, although the principles were established in Scotland long before 1854 – see MacQueen, 1996 JR 295, 296.
[92] [2008] UKHL 48.
[93] *Supershield Ltd* v *Siemens Building Technologies FE Ltd* [2010] EWCA Civ 7.
[94] [1978] QB 791.
[95] [1963] AC 837, 1963 SC (HL) 31.
[96] 1994 SC (HL) 20.

of *Hadley*, saying that while business people were to be taken as having knowledge of the ordinary course of each other's business, that did not extend to specialist technical aspects such as concrete pours. On the other hand, the test is sometimes used to limit recovery of losses which an ordinary person might think are foreseeable, such as losses consequent on a damaged reputation. In *Amstrad plc* v *Seagate Technology Inc*,[97] the defendants supplied defective hard disk drives for the plaintiff's new range of computers. It was held that the plaintiff was entitled to damages for lost and delayed sales and costs under s. 53(2), but not for lost sales on the plaintiff's successor range as this was not within the contemplation of the parties at the time of the contract.

On the other hand, in a later case (which was not a sale of goods case) where the plaintiff claimed damages falling within the second limb in *Hadley* v *Baxendale*, the Court of Appeal took a markedly more realistic, if less sympathetic stance.[98] Here, the plaintiff had booked a holiday through the defendants, and it had been mentioned that he needed medical insurance because he was liable to attacks of asthma. A breach of contract by the defendants triggered off a serious attack of asthma but the defendants were held not liable for the additional consequences of this, on the ground that the information about the plaintiff's medical condition had been volunteered conversationally, and was not part of the contractual terms. So far as contracts of sale of goods are concerned, damages under the second limb of *Hadley* v *Baxendale* are usually regarded simply as 'special damages' which are recognised by s. 54, though that section merely preserves the common law rule.

A failure by the buyer to take normal or reasonable precautions may be a *novus actus interveniens* which prevents the seller being responsible for the ultimate consequences of their breach. For instance, in *Lambert* v *Lewis*[99] a farmer bought a towing coupling from a retail seller. The coupling was defective so that the seller was guilty of a breach of the implied terms under the Sale of Goods Act. But the farmer continued to use the coupling even though he was or should have been aware that it was defective. When the coupling gave way, causing an accident in which the plaintiff was injured, it was held that the farmer could not claim an indemnity from the seller in respect of his own liability to the plaintiff. If, however, the seller warrants the quality or fitness of the goods in such terms as to indicate that there is no need for the buyer to examine or check upon the continued safety of the goods, and the buyer is (despite this warranty) held liable to a third party for injury caused by the goods so warranted, then the buyer could expect to recover a complete indemnity from the seller.[100]

Again, where a seller delivered some yarn to the buyer at the docks in damaged cartons, it was held that the seller was not responsible for the very much greater damage done to the goods as a result of being shipped in the damaged cartons.[101] The buyer's agents had handled the goods and should have appreciated that the cartons were not fit for shipment. Thus, the buyer's damages were limited to the difference between the value of the

[97] (1997) 86 BLR 34. On the other hand, in *Argos Distributors* v *Advertising Advice Bureaudamages* were awarded for loss of profits on repeated orders. The crucial difference is probably that in that case the supplier knew that the goods were for resale to third parties, whereas the launch of a new product range, although within the buyer's contemplation, is unlikely to be within the seller's.

[98] *Kemp* v *Intasun Holidays Ltd* [1987] 2 FTLR 234.

[99] [1982] AC 225.

[100] *Lambert* v *Lewis*, [1982] AC 225.

[101] *Commercial Fibres (Ireland) Ltd* v *Zabaida* [1975] 1 Lloyd's Rep 27.

damaged cartons and the value of undamaged cartons. He was unable to recover for the damage done to the goods while at sea as a result of being shipped in those cartons. But again, if the seller had warranted the cartons in such terms as to lead the buyer to suppose that there was no need for him to have the cartons further examined or inspected, it would seem clear that the seller would have been responsible for all the ultimate damage.

A different type of consequential loss is encountered where the goods are bought for resale, and that is where the buyer has resold and delivered the goods to a sub-buyer who later has claimed damages against them for the defects in the goods. We have already seen that, in the usual course of events, sub-sales are ignored in claims under ss. 53(3) and claims of this kind therefore are normally treated as claims for 'special damages' under the second limb of *Hadley* v *Baxendale*, which requires proof of special knowledge of the probability of resale. But the buyer's burden of proof here is lighter than where they claim similar damages in an action for non-delivery because they need only show that sub-sales were contemplated as a reasonable probability and need not go on to show (as it seems they must in the non-delivery cases) that they had contracted to resell the specific goods to sub-buyers. Once it is shown that the seller should have contemplated that the goods were bought for resale, any damages and costs paid to the sub-buyer as a result of defects of quality can be properly regarded as special damage recoverable under the second limb of *Hadley* v *Baxendale*.[102] But it has been stressed that in order that the buyer should be able to claim such damages and costs it is an overriding requirement that the subcontracts should have been made on the same terms and conditions as the first contract. For, clearly, if the buyer chooses to resell the goods on more onerous terms or with more extensive warranties, they cannot fix liability on the seller for damages they have had to pay in respect of these more onerous terms or more extensive warranties. The law on this topic was well summed up by Branson J in *Kasler & Cohen* v *Slavouski*:[103]

> If a man has sold goods to another in such circumstances as to fix him with special knowledge of the purpose for which those goods are being bought, and that other sells them on the same terms and conditions and then is subjected to an action because the goods do not come up to the contract quality, or for any other reason entitling him to claim damages upon such contract, the first purchaser is entitled, if he has acted reasonably in defending the action and has yet been cast in damages and costs, to claim from his seller not only the damages but also the costs he has had to pay.[104]

And if the buyer reasonably settles a claim made against them by the sub-buyer, the amount paid under such a settlement is *prima facie* the measure of damages recoverable from the seller, and is in any event the upper limit. But it is open to the seller to contest the amount and to show that the sum paid was excessive, for they are of course not bound by the settlement to which they were not party.[105] Moreover, the buyer still has to show that

[102] But a buyer claiming damages for breach of condition as to quality cannot of course tender as evidence of their loss the amount paid by them to their sub-buyers as damages for non-delivery: *Aryeh* v *Lawrence Kostoris & Son Ltd* [1967] 1 Lloyd's Rep 63; Danecroft Jersey *Mills* v *Criegee, The Times*, 14 April 1987.

[103] [1928] 1 KB 78, 85.

[104] Cf. *Bostock & Co Ltd* v *Nicholsons & Co Ltd* [1904] 1 KB 725; *Dexters* v *Hill Crest Oil Co Ltd* [1926] 1 KB 348, 359 per Scrutton LJ. If the sub-sales are not on exactly the same terms, it is uncertain if the buyer can claim damages paid to the sub-buyer in respect of defects for which the seller would have been liable. According to Devlin J in *Biggin & Co* v *Permanite Ltd* [1951] 1 KB 422 the answer is 'Yes', but with qualifications.

[105] *Fletcher & Stewart Ltd* v *Peter Jay & Partners* (1976) 17 Build LR 38.

there was a breach of contract by the seller; the settlement is only admissible to show the *prima facie* level of damages once liability is proved or established.[106]

Another type of case in which sub-sales may be taken into account, at least indirectly, is illustrated by *GKN Centrax Gears Ltd* v *Matbro Ltd*.[107] Here, it was held that the buyers could recover damages in respect of the loss of repeat orders from customers to whom they had resold defective goods supplied by the sellers. So long as such losses are within the contemplation of the parties, no question of principle is raised by a claim of this nature.

18.4 Damages in tort

In English law, where the property and the immediate right to possession have passed to the buyer they may have, in addition to their remedies in contract, an action in tort for conversion. As between the parties to the contract, the action in tort has no advantages and is rarely used. The buyer cannot get higher damages by suing in tort than in contract, even where the measure of damages in the former case would normally be the higher,[108] or can they obtain a decree of specific restitution except in cases where they could obtain a decree of specific performance.[109] The only advantage to the buyer of the action in tort is that it avails against third parties who have meddled with, or caused damage to, the goods at a time when the buyer had the property in the goods.

A buyer of goods which are imported from overseas is usually entitled to sue the carrier for damage done to the goods at sea, subject to the restrictions on liability contained in the Hague-Visby Rules as laid down in the Carriage of Goods by Sea Act 1971. Even in these cases, however, the buyer will rarely need to rely on their property in the goods as a basis for their claim. The reason for this is that by virtue of the Carriage of Goods by Sea Act 1992, the contract of carriage is actually transferred to the buyer when the bills of lading are transferred to them. This gives the buyer in most cases a right to sue for damage done from the time of the original shipment of the goods, since they would have been covered by the contract of carriage from that time. The buyer will, of course, have their recovery limited to the amount permitted under the Hague-Visby Rules.[110] It has been held by the House of Lords that the buyer cannot sue the carrier in tort in respect of damage done at a time before they became owner of the goods.[111] Nor, presumably, can they avoid the limitations of liability imposed by the Hague-Visby Rules by suing in tort *after* they become owner.[112]

It remains unsettled whether a buyer who does have the property at the relevant time, and sues the carrier for damages in tort, will always find their tort action subject to the

[106] *Fletcher & Stewart Ltd* v *Peter Jay & Partners* (1976) 17 Build LR 38.

[107] [1976] 2 Lloyd's Rep 555.

[108] *The Arpad* [1934] P 189. In Australia a buyer has been held entitled to exemplary damages for wrongful seizure of goods delivered to him (*Healing Sales Pty Ltd v Inglis Electrix Pty Ltd* (1968) 121 CLR 584), but it is doubtful if such damages could be awarded in England under *Rookes* v *Barnard* [1964] AC 1129. And note that (in a different context) the Court of Appeal has indicated that the amount of damages recoverable does not depend on whether the claimant's (pursuer's) course of action is in contract or tort – see *Parsons Ltd* v *Uttley Ingham* [1978] QB 791.

[109] *Cohen* v *Roche* [1927] 1 KB 169.

[110] See Carriage of Goods by Sea Act 1971

[111] *Leigh & Sillivan Ltd* v *Aliakmon Shipping Co Ltd (The Aliakmon)* [1986] AC 785.

[112] See [1986] AC 785, 801.

limitations on contractual liability imposed by the Carriage of Goods by Sea Act 1971. No doubt, where the contract of carriage is transferred to the buyer – as it usually is – the tort action will become subject to the terms of the contract, including the statutory regime in the 1971 Act. But if there should be some rare case in which the contract of carriage is not transferred although the buyer has acquired the property, it may be that the 1971 Act will not restrict the buyer's action in tort. In this event, there would be very clear advantages in suing in tort, but it is certain that a sequence of successful actions of that nature would rapidly lead to legislative amendment of the 1971 Act.

18.5 Damages for misrepresentation

In a work of this nature it is unnecessary to make more than a brief reference to the possibility of an action for damages for misrepresentation. In English law, such an action lay at common law for fraud, but under s. 2(1) of the Misrepresentation Act, damages may be obtained also for a misrepresentation unless the representor proves they had reasonable grounds to believe, and did believe up to the time the contract was made, that the acts represented were true. Moreover, under s. 2(2) of the Act, the court may award damages even for innocent misrepresentation, in lieu of rescinding the contract. There are advantages in making a claim for damages for misrepresentation in the alternative to a claim for breach of express warranty. The remedy created by the Act is tortious, and the damages are to be calculated according to the rules for tort.[113] The claimant can recover the loss (including consequential loss) they incurred by entering the contract.[114] They cannot recover loss of profits, but they can recover the difference between the purchase price and the value the goods should have had if the representation had been true,[115] and they can recover profits which would have been made had the misrepresentation not been made, and the claimant entered into an alternative contract.[116] Moreover, the remoteness rules applicable are those of the tort of deceit, and are thus not limited by foreseeability.[117]

In Scots law, delictual damages may be recovered for fraud and negligent misrepresentation, including pre-contractual negligent misrepresentation, under s. 10 of the Law Reform (Miscellaneous Provisions) (Scotland) Act 1985.

18.6 Remedies available to a buyer in breach

18.6.1 English law

Obviously a buyer who is in breach of contract has no right to sue for damages, but buyers sometimes pay, or agree to pay, part or all of the price of the goods in advance; and important and difficult questions may arise with regard to such advance payments if the

[113] *Sharneyford Supplies Ltd* v *Edge* [1986] Ch 128, 169; *Royscot Trust Ltd* v *Rogerson* [1991] 2 QB 297; *Pankhania* v *Hackney* LBC [2004] EWHC 323

[114] *Davis & Co (Wines) Ltd* v *Afa-Minerva (EMI) Ltd* [1976] 2 Lloyd's Rep 27; a curious decision – see Taylor (1982) 45 MLR 139.

[115] *Naughton and another* v *O'Callaghan* [1990] 3 All ER 191 – it will be necessary to show, however, that the fall in market value is not simply due to a market trend.

[116] *East* v *Maurer* [1991] 2 All ER 733.

[117] *Royscot Trust Ltd* v *Rogerson* [1991] 2 QB 297.

buyer subsequently fails to fulfil their contract and the seller accepts this as a discharge of the whole contract.

If the price, or part of it, has actually been paid in advance and the contract is then abandoned because of the buyer's breach the seller may, of course, claim damages for non-acceptance from the buyer. But the amount paid by the buyer may greatly exceed any damages recoverable by the seller. In *Dies* v *British International Mining etc Corp*,[118] the buyers contracted to buy goods to a total value of £270,000 and paid £100,000 before the agreed delivery date. The buyers then failed to take the goods or pay the balance of the price, and the sellers treated this as discharging the whole contract. The buyers sued to recover their advance payments, and this claim was upheld by Stable J, though the buyers did not dispute that the sellers were entitled to damages which were set off against the £100,000.

On the other hand, it has always been held that payments by way of earnest only, that is by way of forfeitable deposit, are not recoverable by the party in breach. The distinction between a part-payment which is thus recoverable by the buyer, and a deposit which is not, is said to depend on the intention of the parties. Was it the intention that the amount paid in advance should be forfeited if the buyer refused or failed to complete the purchase? In practice, contracts often fail to indicate whether such advance payments are forfeitable or not, so the question has to be answered by looking to the customs of the trade, and also to the amount of the part-payment. Forfeitable deposits of up to 10 per cent of the price are not uncommon (indeed, almost invariable in the case of contracts for the sale of land and houses); and it is well established that *prima facie* deposits of this amount are not recoverable by the buyer if they are in breach, even if the seller resells without loss after the buyer's breach.[119] The law relating to penalties, it has been insisted, has no application to this situation.[120]

But in the *Dies* case, the amount was not only very large in itself but also about 37 per cent of the total price. It seems, therefore, that such very large part-payments will not be regarded as forfeitable deposits, but will *prima facie* be recoverable according to the true construction of the contract, if the buyer fails to complete.

Unfortunately, the position as set out above is greatly complicated by three further problems which often cause difficulty. The first of these difficulties concerns the question whether the above rules also apply where the sum payable in advance is not in fact paid. If the buyer was required by the contract to pay a deposit which would have been forfeited on breach, but they failed to pay it, can the seller sue for the deposit, irrespective of the amount of damage which they have suffered? Although the point is by no means free from doubt, the general view seems to be that nothing turns on the accidental fact of the time of the actual payment: if the money should have been paid before breach, it can be sued for after breach.[121] The result gives cause for unease since an action to recover more than the claimant has lost through the breach of contract must inevitably look penal. The present rules are usually justified by saying that the buyer should not be advantaged by the fact that they have broken their contract and failed to pay the deposit when they should have

[118] [1939] 1 KB 724.
[119] *Howe* v *Smith* (1884) 27 Ch D 89.
[120] *Linggi Plantations Ltd* v *Jagatheesan* [1972] 1 MLJ 89 (PC).
[121] *Dewar* v *Mintoft* [1912] 2 KB 373.

paid it, but this often happens when the buyer fails to pay the price, because *prima facie* the seller's remedy is only an action for non-delivery, and not for the price itself. It must also be remembered that a contract of sale of goods is different from other contracts in that rejection of the goods does to some degree work as a retrospective rescission of the contract – the goods revest in the seller, and their duty to deliver conforming goods can no longer be enforced by the buyer. It is also disturbing that the seller is able to recover damages for a totally non-existent 'loss' in this situation, without any regard to the law relating to penalties. Since there is no real loss, the damages must inevitably be penal – the purpose of the action is to punish the buyer for their breach in not paying the deposit, and the denial of the relevance of the rules as to penalties rests simply on reiteration rather than on any rational justification.

The current rules were pressed even further in *Damon Cia Naviera* v *Hapag-Lloyd (The Blankenstein).*[122] In this case, the buyers had agreed to sign a contract for the purchase of three ships for $2.36m. The written contract, if signed, would have required the buyers to pay a deposit of 10 per cent of the price ($236,000), which was expressly stated to be forfeitable in the event of non-completion by the buyers. The buyers failed to sign the written contract, or to pay the deposit, and the sellers sued for damages. The sellers had resold the ships for $2.295m, and thus suffered a loss on resale of $65,000, which was plainly recoverable once it had been decided that the buyers were guilty of a breach of contract. But the sellers argued that they were entitled to much more than this; they sought damages representing the amount of the unpaid deposit, on the ground that if the buyers had signed the written contract they would have had to pay the deposit, which would have been irrecoverable. Because the written contract here had never been signed, the sellers did not sue for the deposit itself; their claim was for damages for non-payment of the deposit. A majority of the Court of Appeal upheld this claim on the ground that the sellers were entitled to be put in the position they would have been in if the contract had been performed, but Goff LJ dissented on the ground that if the whole contract had been performed the sellers would not have obtained more than the total purchase price. Effectively, the sellers were claiming not to be put in the position they would have been in if the whole contract had been performed, but in the position they would have been in if the buyers had first signed the written contract, and then defaulted. Whatever the merits of these somewhat refined arguments, the net result seems indefensible. The sellers were, in effect, awarded damages far above their loss.

The converse case concerning this point raises no problem. If the amount in question is a genuine part-payment rather than a forfeitable deposit – so that if, as in *Dies*, the money had actually been paid in advance, it would have been recoverable by the buyer – then it must follow *a fortiori* that if the buyer has failed to pay it, the seller cannot sue for it.

The second major difficulty concerning the above rules arises from the possibility of equitable relief. Where a seller sues to recover an agreed penalty payable for breach by the buyer, the buyer may try to set up by way of defence the standard equitable doctrines restricting the enforcement of penalty clauses. Under these rules, which apply, of course, irrespective of the parties' actual intention, and therefore override the freedom of contract of the parties, a clause designed to operate *in terrorem*, rather than to provide for a

[122] [1985] 1 All ER 475. Leave to appeal to the HL was given, but no appeal was pursued.

genuine pre-estimate of the damages, is a penalty clause rather than a liquidated damages clause,[123] and penalty clauses are unenforceable. But as we have already seen, it has several times been insisted that the doctrine of penalties has no application to these clauses for the forfeiture of deposits.[124] Moreover, the House of Lords has shown a strong disinclination to extend the principles of equitable relief to forfeitures in commercial contracts.[125] But there have been suggestions that a different form of equitable relief may be available – that is, relief to enable the buyer to complete the contract late, if they are able to pay in full all the sums due plus any costs incurred by the seller.[126] It is also well established that a forfeiture of a property right is challengeable under the penalty rules,[127] and it seems the barest technicality to insist that a deposit is a contractual right and not a property right.

A third problem arising from the rules about deposits and part payments has been touched on earlier,[128] and it stems from the decision of the House of Lords in *Johnson* v *Agnew*,[129] which laid down a clear and precise demarcation line between *termination* of a contract for breach and rescission *ab initio* for fraud or other invalidating cause. A termination does not operate retrospectively in the same way that rescission *ab initio* does. So it may seem that if the buyer pays part of the price in advance, or is bound to do so and fails, their obligation to do this remains binding on them, despite the subsequent termination of the contract. But if that were the law, then the decision in *Dies* would be wrong, and a buyer who paid part of the price in advance – no matter how large a part, or indeed, even if they paid the whole price in advance – would be unable to recover it if they were subsequently guilty of non-acceptance of the goods.

This was the conclusion which the House of Lords reached in *Hyundai Heavy Industries Co Ltd* v *Papadopoulos*,[130] in the context of an instalments payable by the buyer of a ship while the ship was under construction. The House of Lords held that this remained payable, despite the seller's subsequent decision to treat the non-payment as a repudiation and to terminate the whole contract.[131] It was said that *Dies* only applied to a pure contract of sale and not to a contract to *manufacture* and sell goods.[132] Since then, the House of Lords confirmed this distinction in *Stocznia Gdanska SA* v *Latvian Shipping Co.*[133] on similar facts. The House of Lords highlighted the distinction between sales simpliciter and

[123] The leading case is *Dunlop Pneumatic Tyre Co Ltd* v *New Garage & Motor Co Ltd* [1915] AC 79.

[124] See *Linggi Plantations Ltd* v *Jagatheesan*, [1972] 1 MLJ 89 (PC), but cf. *Public Works Commission* v *Hills* [1906] AC 368.

[125] See, e.g., *Scandinavian Trading Tanker Co* v *Flota Petrolera* [1983] 2 AC 694; *Sport International Bussum* v *Inter-Footwear* [1984] 1 WLR 776.

[126] See *Stockloser* v *Johnson* [1954] 1 QB 476; *Barton, Thompson & Co Ltd* v *Stapling Machines Co* [1966] Ch 499.

[127] *BICC* v *Burndy Ltd* [1985] Ch 232.

[128] See Chapter 2 and Chapter 16.

[129] [1980] AC 367.

[130] [1980] 1 WLR 1129. But another difficulty which did not actually arise in the *Hyundai* case is that the mere fact that the obligation to pay the price is binding on the buyer does not mean they can be sued for the price. The seller's remedy for a breach of the buyer's duty to pay the price is not in general an action for the price, but an action for damages; see s. 49(1), see Chapter 16, at section 16.1, which was not mentioned in the *Hyundai* case, presumably because in that case each instalment was payable on 'a day certain' within the meaning of s. 49.

[131] Of course, on any view, instalments only payable after the date on which the contract was terminated ceased to be payable as a result of termination, or rather, never became payable.

[132] See Chapter 2.

[133] [1998] 1 WLR 574.

contracts for work and materials (or similar). With regard to sales simpliciter, the seller would only be entitled to retain any money paid if the contract was completed, confirming the ruling in *Dies* v *British and International Mining and Finance Corporation Ltd.*[134]

On this view, a prepayment (not being a forfeitable deposit) will be recoverable by the buyer – or not payable – where there is a total failure of consideration, and in an ordinary contract of sale there will be such a total failure of consideration whenever the goods are not delivered or accepted, from whatever cause, even if the seller is also the manufacturer.

134 [1939] 1 KB 724.

Part VIII

Consumer sales

19
Consumer sales contracts

19.1 From the Sale of Goods Act to the Consumer Rights Act

One of the most significant developments in the past decade has been the enactment of the Consumer Rights Act 2015.[1] Many of the provisions in the Sale of Goods Act which previously applied to both consumer and commercial contracts of sale (or specifically to consumer sales) are now limited to non-consumer contracts, particularly with regard to the obligations of a seller, or 'trader' in the language of the Consumer Rights Act (CRA), and the remedies of the consumer. The Consumer Rights Act does more than merely hive-off the regulation of consumer contracts – whilst some provisions previously found in the Sale of Goods Act were re-enacted in substantively unamended form (save for some adjustments to language), there are also some important developments, including a better integration of the existing right to reject goods and terminate a contract for breach of condition with the specific remedies for consumer contracts introduced into the Sale of Goods Act in order to implement the first Consumer Sales Directive (99/44/EC). In addition, the Consumer Rights Act reduces, insofar as possible, the distinction between different forms of supply transaction. of the Consumer Rights Act also introduced specific rules on 'digital content', which to a large extent render obsolete the academic discussion about whether software/digital content ought to be treated as 'goods' for the purposes of the Sale of Goods Act. The parts of the Act dealt with in this chapter generally extend to England and Wales, Scotland and Northern Ireland, and are mostly drafted in jurisdiction-neutral language.

The reform process started in 2004 when the UK government first considered modernising consumer law.[2] A White Paper published in 2009[3] set out concrete plans, notably plans for a Consumer Rights Bill to modernise and simplify UK Consumer Law.[4] At the request of the government, two academic reports were produced which provided detailed options for consolidation and simplification[5] and the possible regulation of digital products.[6] In addition, the Law Commission published an important report on reform of the consumer

[1] 2015, ch. 15.

[2] Department of Trade and Industry, *Extending Competitive Markets: Empowered Consumers – Successful Business* (DTI: London, 2004).

[3] HM Government, *A Better Deal for Consumers – Delivering Real Help Now and Change for the Future* (London: TSO, 2009).

[4] Ibid, pp. 78/9.

[5] Howells and Twigg-Flesner (eds.), *Consolidation and Simplification of UK Consumer Law* (London, BIS, 2010).

[6] Bradgate, *Consumer Rights in Digital Products: A research report prepared for the UK Department for Business, Innovation and Skills* (London: BIS, 2010).

remedies for faulty goods.[7] Specific proposals followed in 2012.[8] The Consumer Rights Bill would deal with the sale and supply of goods, services and digital content, unfair contract terms, damages for breach of competition law rules, and improved enforcement measures. A draft Bill was published in June 2013, and the Bill itself introduced into Parliament on 23 January 2014. It received Royal Assent at the end of March 2015. The Act does not consolidate all areas of consumer law, and for the Consumer Contracts (Information, Cancellation and Additional Charges) Regulations 2013 ('CCR')[9] which implement the Consumer Rights Directive,[10] and the provisions from the Consumer Protection Act 1987[11] remain separate.[12] Also, the Sale of Goods Act has not become entirely irrelevant for consumer sales: the Consumer Rights Act does not contain any provisions on the transfer of property or on the *nemo dat* rule and its exceptions.[13]

In April 2019, the EU adopted two new directives on both the Sale of Goods to Consumers (2019/771/EU) and on Digital Content and Digital Services (2019/770/EU).[14] Both directives became applicable in the EU from January 2022. As this date falls after the completion the UK's withdrawal from the EU at the end of 2020, the directives were not implemented, notwithstanding the fact that both contain provisions on aspects not fully covered in the CRA.

Finally, in 2024, Parliament enacted the Digital Markets, Competition and Consumers Act 2024 (DMCCA). This does not have a direct impact on the law regarding the sale and supply of goods. The DMCCA re-enacts the provisions of the Consumer Protection from Unfair Trading Regulations 2008[15] regarding unfair commercial practices (including marketing and general conduct by traders in their dealings with consumers).[16] Furthermore, the DMCAA introduces new rules on so-called subscription contracts,[17] such as improved pre-contractual information and reminder notices before automatic renewal of a subscription. These provisions have some bearing on contracts for the sale and supply of goods insofar as such contracts are based on a subscription model; however, the core features of sale and supply of goods contracts remain unaffected.

7 Law Commission, *Report 317/Scottish Law Commission Report 216 – Consumer Remedies for Faulty Goods* (London: TSO, 2009).

8 Department for Business, Innovation and Skills, *Enhancing Consumer Confidence by Clarifying Consumer Law – Consultation on the Supply of Goods, Services and Digital Content* (London, 2012).

9 S.I. 2013/3134.

10 Article19 of the Directive was implemented ahead of the other provisions in the Consumer Rights (Payment Surcharges) Regulations 2012 S.I. 2012/3110.

11 Primarily those on product liability – see Chapter 20.

12 See Twigg-Flesner, Some thoughts on consumer law reform – consolidation, codification, or a restatement? in Gullifer and Vogenauer (eds.), *English and European Perspectives on Contract and Commercial Law – Essays in Honour of Hugh Beale* (Oxford: Hart, 2014).

13 See chapters 10 and 11.

14 Directives (EU) 2019/770 of the European Parliament and of the Council of 20 May 2019 on certain aspects concerning contracts for the supply of digital content and digital services (2019) OJ L 136/1 and 2019/771 of the European Parliament and of the Council of 20 May 2019 on certain aspects concerning contracts for the sale of goods (2019) OJ L 136/28. See e.g., Carlvaho, Sale of goods and supply of digital content and digital services – overview of Directives 2019/770 and 2019/771, (2019) EuCML 194.

15 S.I. 2008/1277, as amended by The Consumer Protection (Amendment) Regulations 2014 (S.I. 2014/870).

16 See Part 4, chapter 1 DMCAA.

17 See Part 4, chapter 2 DMCAA. These provisions are expect to enter into force in spring 2026 at the earliest.

The purpose of this chapter is to provide an overview of the CRA and some related measures, particularly as relevant to contracts for the sale and supply of goods.

19.2 Key definitions and scope

For this book, the most relevant part of the Consumer Rights Act is Part 1, dealing with consumer contracts for goods, digital content and services.[18] The part is then divided into separate chapters, dealing with contracts between a trader and a consumer to supply goods, digital content or services respectively. A consumer is 'an individual acting for purposes that are wholly or mainly outside that individual's trade, business, craft or profession',[19] and a trader is 'a person acting for purposes relating to that person's trade, business, craft or profession, whether acting personally or through another person acting in the trader's name or on the trader's behalf'.[20]

There are two issues which have arisen regarding these definitions. The first is in respect of goods which are acquired partly for professional and partly for non-professional purposes. In interpreting the special rules for jurisdiction over consumer contracts under the Brussels-1 Regulation, the CJEU has held that an individual buying goods partly for private and partly for professional purposes would be a 'consumer' for that contract if the professional purpose was negligible.[21] Recently, the Court of Appeal preferred to express this as requiring the private purpose to predominate.[22]

A second issue arises with regard to a growing number of private individuals taking advantage of the many on-line platforms for selling or auctioning goods. Often, such sales are limited to goods no longer required by the individual, but some have developed their activities into an income-generating and profit-making endeavour. In some instances, this will mean that a private individual might have to be treated as a 'trader' and would therefore be subject to the obligations on a trader imposed by consumer law. It is difficult to say with certainty when a private individual would cross that threshold. Some guidance was given by the CJEU in *Karmenova*,[23] where the Court suggested as relevant criteria:

> 'whether the sale on the online platform was carried out in an organised manner, whether that sale was intended to generate profit, whether the seller had technical information and expertise relating to the products which she offered for sale which the consumer did not necessarily have, with the result that she was placed in a more advantageous position than the consumer, whether the seller had a legal status which enabled her to engage in commercial activities and to what extent the online sale was connected to the seller's commercial or professional activity, whether the seller was subject to VAT, whether the seller, acting on behalf of a particular trader

[18] Section 1(1) CRA. Part 2 of the CRA contains rules on unfair terms in consumer contracts which consolidate the provisions previously found in the Unfair Contract Terms Act 1977 and the Unfair Terms in Consumer Contracts Regulations 1999. Part 3 contains a range of provisions dealing with enforcement, private actions in respect of competition law infringements, letting agents and, secondary-ticketing markets.

[19] Section 2(3) CRA, removing the possibility under the previous law that in certain circumstances a company or a partnership could be a 'consumer' – see the 12th edition of this work at p. 229. The definition is modified in respect of most provisions in Chapter 2 on goods to exclude sales contracts for second-hand goods sold at a public auction which individuals have the opportunity of attending in person (s.2(5)/(6) CRA).

[20] s. 2(2) CRA.

[21] C-464/01 *Johann Gruber* v *Bay Wa AG* ECLI:EU:C:2005:32.

[22] *Eternity Sky Investments Ltd* v *Xiaomin Zhang* [2024] EWCA Civ 630, para.34.

[23] C-105/17 *Komisia za zashtita na potrebitelite* v *Evelina Kamenova* ECLI:EU:C:2018:808

or on her own behalf or through another person acting in her name and on her behalf, received remuneration or an incentive; whether the seller purchased new or second-hand goods in order to resell them, thus making that a regular, frequent and/or simultaneous activity in comparison with her usual commercial or business activity, whether the goods for sale were all of the same type or of the same value, and, in particular, whether the offer was concentrated on a small number of goods.'[24]

Ultimately, it will necessitate a case-by-case assessment, and the problem is perhaps more troubling for those individuals than their customers because of the sanctions attached to a failure to act in accordance with the obligations of a trader under various consumer law measures. Following the UK's withdrawal from the EU, these cases continue to be part of domestic law[25] but domestic courts can depart from these judgments.[26]

One of the objectives of the CRA is to ensure that the rules and remedies in respect of all three are as similar as possible (although with regard to services, the CRA continues to apply the requirement that the service must be performed with reasonable care and skill only).[27] More significantly, the CRA overcomes the need to classify transactions to identify which Act applies: so whenever a contract between a trader and a consumer involves the supply of goods, chapter 2 of Part 1 applies; when it involves the supply of digital content, chapter 3 applies, and in respect of services, chapter 4 applies.[28] If the contract involves a combination ('mixed contract'), then all relevant chapters apply.[29] As a result, whenever a contract between a consumer and a trader involves the supply of goods (whether that is a sale, hire-purchase or hire) the same provisions will apply, although there are minor modifications for certain contracts. This is a welcome development in the law, although it heightens the need to consider a similar reform in respect of commercial contracts, where the old distinction between different types of supply transactions and consequently, the application of different Acts of Parliament continues to be an unnecessarily confusing feature of the law.

19.3 Contracts for the supply of goods

Chapter 2 deals with contracts for the supply of goods. In the CRA, goods are defined as 'any tangible moveable items, but that includes water, gas and electricity if and only if they are put up for supply in a limited volume or set quantity'.*[AM1] There are four types of contract included in the umbrella definition of 'contract to supply goods':*[AM2]

(a) a sales contract;
(b) a contract for the hire of goods;
(c) a hire-purchase agreement;
(d) a contract for transfer of goods.

This definition of a contract to supply goods is exhaustive s. 3(2) CRA opens with the words 'it applies only if' the contract is one of the four listed above. This might leave some supply transactions outside the scope of this chapter, and so the definitions of these

24 Para [38].
25 This is now treated as 'assimilated case law' under the Retained EU Law (Revocation and Reform) Act 2023 s.5 (1).
26 See s.6 of the European Union (Withdrawal) Act 2018. Amendments to s.6 to be made by the Retained EU Law (Revocation and Reform) Act 2023 have not yet been brought into force.
27 See s. 49 CRA.
28 s. 1(3) CRA.
29 s. 1(4)/(5) CRA.

contracts in ss. 5–8 CRA are important. Of particular note is the definition of 'sales contract' in s. 5, which states that:

> A contract is a sales contract if under it—
> (a) the trader transfers or agrees to transfer ownership of goods to the consumer, and
> (b) the consumer pays or agrees to pay the price.
> (2) A contract is a sales contract (whether or not it would be one under subsection (1)) if under the contract—
> (a) goods are to be manufactured or produced and the trader agrees to supply them to the consumer,
> (b) on being supplied, the goods will be owned by the consumer, and
> (c) the consumer pays or agrees to pay the price.
> (3) A sales contract may be conditional (see section 3(5)), but in this Part "conditional sales contract" means a sales contract under which—
> (a) the price for the goods or part of it is payable by instalments, and
> (b) the trader retains ownership of the goods until the conditions specified in the contract (for the payment of instalments or otherwise) are met; and it makes no difference whether or not the consumer possesses the goods.

This definition appears clearer than that in s. 2(1) of the Sale of Goods Act 1979, and it contains the clarification that it also covers goods to be manufactured or produced. It is certainly helpful to have this additional clarification in the definition, as there might otherwise have been a loophole in respect of these contracts: although the CRA would apply to mixed contracts involving a service and the supply of goods, a contract to manufacture goods to order would possibly not qualify as one of the four types of supply contracts. However, it seems that the definition of 'contract for transfer of goods' in s. 8, which relates to other contracts involving the transfer of ownership in goods, would ensure that the CRA applies: s. 8(a) of that definition essentially covers contracts of barter or exchange ('consideration otherwise than paying a price'), but s. 8(b) effectively operates as a safety net by including a contract which 'for any other reason, [is] not a sales contract or a hire-purchase agreement'.

A contract for the hire of goods is one under which the trader 'gives or agrees to give the consumer possession of the goods with the right to use them, subject to the terms of the contract, for a period determined in accordance with the contract'.[30] The difference between a sales contract and hire therefore is that the trader only transfers possession but not ownership to the consumer. Moreover, possession is only transferred for a set period and not permanently.

Finally, there is the 'hire-purchase agreement', which, according to s. 7 CRA, has two key features: (i) the trader hires the goods to the consumer, in return for which the consumer makes regular payments to the trader. This is akin to a contract of hire. (ii) Under the contract, ownership will eventually transfer to the consumer, once the terms of the contract have been complied with and either the consumer exercises the option to buy the goods, or any party to the contract does an act specified in the contract, or an event specified in the contract occurs. Under a hire-purchase agreement, ownership will be transferred eventually, but unlike a contract of sale, this does not happen automatically – paying all the instalment payments would not be enough. A contract which would transfer ownership once all the required payments have been made would be regarded as a 'conditional sale' contract (covered by the definition of 'sales contract').[31]

[30] s. 6(1) CRA.
[31] See s. 5(3) CRA.

19.3.1 Transfer of ownership

It was noted earlier that the Consumer Rights Act 2015 does not contain separate rules regarding the transfer of ownership; instead, the provisions regarding the passing of property under ss. 16–19 and ss. 20A/B continue to apply to consumer contracts.[32] In 2016, the Law Commission published a report on *Consumer Prepayments on Retailer Insolvency*[33] which included recommendations for amending the rules on the passing of property in consumer contracts. A draft bill dealing with the transfer of ownership in consumer sales contracts was subsequently published by the Law Commission in 2021.[34] The draft bill proposed adding two new sections to the CRA, ss. 18A and 18B. Section 18A dealt with goods 'actually selected' (a term preferred to the term 'specific goods' in the Sale of Goods Act 1979). Clause 18A(1) and (2) would provide that where the actual goods to be used to fulfil the contract have been selected when the contract of the sale is made, then the contract is treated as including a term that ownership of the goods is transferred when the contract is made. However, clause 18A(3) would render ineffective any term that would delay the transfer of ownership to a later point, so a reservation of title clause requiring payment before ownership is transferred would no longer be effective.

Clause 18B deals with the transfer of ownership in goods not actually selected at the time the contract of sale is made (in the Sale of Goods Act 1979, these would be unascertained goods, i.e., goods with are not specific). Clause 18B(2) would provide that where goods are to be manufactured or produced, ownership would transfer as soon as the manufacture or production for the consumer has been completed. Clause 18B(3) would deal with any other situation involving goods not actually selected, and would provide that ownership would transfer when the first of the events listed in clause 18B(3)(a)–(h) has occurred. It is worth reproducing this list in full here:

(a) the goods are physically labelled with the consumer's name in a way that is intended by the trader to be permanent;
(b) the goods are physically set aside for the consumer in a way that is intended by the trader to be permanent;
(c) the alteration of the goods to a specification agreed between the trader and the consumer is completed;
(d) the consumer is told by the trader that goods bearing a unique identifier will be used to fulfil the contract;
(e) on examining the goods the consumer agrees that they are to be used to fulfil the contract;
(f) the goods, identified as being those for delivery to the consumer, are delivered to a carrier;
(g) the goods are delivered to the consumer;
(h) the goods that are to be used to fulfil the contract are selected by the trader in some other way, and the trader intends the selection to be permanent.

As with clause 18A, a term deferring the transfer of ownership to a later point than would occur under clause 18B(3) would be ineffective.[35] Furthermore, clause 18B(4) would create

[32] s. 4(2) CRA.
[33] *Law Commission, Consumer Prepayments on Retailer Insolvency* (LC Report No.368) (London, TSO, 2016).
[34] Law Commission, *Consumer sales contracts: transfer of ownership* (LC Report No.398 (London, 2021).
[35] Clause 18B(5).

a presumption in respect of paragraphs (a), (b) and (h) that the trader's action is intended to be permanent.

The intention behind the draft Bill would be to provide greater clarity and certainty regarding the point at which ownership is transferred, which would be an improvement compared to the situation under the Sale of Goods Act 1979. Whether these amendments would provide a sufficient improvement might be open to debate. However, following consultation as part of the preparations for the Digital Markets, Competition and Consumers Act 2024, the government confirmed in 2023 that it decided not to proceed with the proposals for the time being, but will keep the situation under review.[36]

19.4 Requirements in respect of goods

Sections 9 (satisfactory quality), 10 (fit for particular purpose) and 11 (description) then essentially re-enact the substance of the provisions previously contained in ss. 13–14 of the Sale of Goods Act. There have been some changes to the layout and wording from the corresponding provisions in the Sale of Goods Act to provide greater clarity, and also to broaden the requirements in some respects. Moreover, there has been a shift in the terminology – the CRA states that under these sections, a 'contract is to be treated as including a term', rather than the 'implied terms' language used in the Sale of Goods Act, and the term is no longer classed as a condition. Apart from making the text jurisdiction-neutral, the thinking behind this is that the CRA contains a detailed set of remedies available if there is a breach of any of these terms, which, as will be seen below, include the right to reject the goods and terminate the contract. This is one step towards recognising that in a consumer contract, the implied terms had become *de facto* statutory rules, and the general common law remedies for breach of contract had already been significantly modified by the notion of 'acceptance'.[37] However, it is somewhat unfortunate that the Consumer Rights Act stops short of making the requirements of quality and fitness fully statutory and continues to adhere to the idea that these are terms of the contract. The only benefit that this might bring is the ability of a consumer to claim damages for any consequential losses (or, indeed, as an alternative to the statutory remedies) on the basis of the general common law rules (see below). One wonders whether it would not have made more sense to use the Consumer Rights Act to provide a complete set of remedies, including rules on available damages, but, as has already been noted, the Act does not quite constitute a full consolidation of the main rules of consumer law.

19.4.1 Satisfactory quality

Section 9(1) specifies that 'every contract to supply goods is to be treated as including a term that the quality of the goods is satisfactory'. S. 9(2)–(4) repeat the familiar test for establishing whether goods are of satisfactory quality (cf. ss. 14(2A)–(2C) of the Sale of Goods Act):[38]

> (2) The quality of goods is satisfactory if they meet the standard that a reasonable person would consider satisfactory, taking account of—
> (a) any description of the goods,
> (b) the price or other consideration for the goods (if relevant), and
> (c) all the other relevant circumstances (see subsection (5)).

[36] *Ministry of Justice, Report on the implementation of Law Commission recommendations* (July 2023), para.137.

[37] s. 35 of the Sale of Goods Act 1979.

[38] See the discussion in Chapter 9.

There is no substantive difference from the provisions in the Sale of Goods Act. One interesting question is the extent to which case law under s. 14 of the Sale of Goods Act will be taken into account when interpreting s. 9 CRA. The near-identical wording will undoubtedly tempt a court to refer to such earlier case law, but if this is done, a court should be mindful that a case which was decided after 1995 (when the satisfactory quality test was first introduced) involving a consumer contract will be a strong authority on the application of the satisfactory test in s. 9 CRA, but any case between two commercial parties should be treated with caution and not followed without due consideration of whether this would be appropriate in a consumer case. Over time, distinct case law under s. 9 CRA will emerge although thus far the number of reported decisions is surprisingly small. Should the Sale of Goods Act itself be revised one day to assess its suitability for contemporary commercial contracts, an altogether different test might be developed for commercial sales.[39]

The general test to be satisfied is in s. 9(2) CRA: goods are satisfactory 'if they meet the standard that a reasonable person would consider satisfactory'. This is an objective test, asking what a reasonable person would think about the quality of the goods supplied. If the same approach as under s. 14(2) of the Sale of Goods Act is taken, then the perspective of the reasonable person should be that of the consumer: the Court of Appeal has stated that the 'reasonable person must be one who is in the position of the buyer, with his knowledge; for it would not be appropriate for the test to be that of a reasonable third party observer not acquainted with the background of the transaction'.[40]

The consumer buyers in *Bramhill* v *Edwards* had some experience of the type of goods (motor-homes) they were buying, and this was taken into account in applying the reasonable person test. Consequently, their knowledge of motor homes meant that they could be expected to know about the applicable road safety requirements. However, the extent to which a consumer's knowledge or expertise in respect of the goods in question should be taken into account remains somewhat unclear. In *Bramhill*, the consumers had relevant specialist knowledge which the general consumer might not have, but this might not always be appropriate.

In considering whether a reasonable person would regard the goods as satisfactory, s. 9(2) states that account should be taken of (i) the description of the goods; (ii) the price or other consideration, if relevant; and (iii) all the other relevant circumstances. Goods sold as 'ex display' might mean that they might be marked or even have minor damage but could still be regarded as satisfactory, whereas this would not be so if they were new. Similarly, a higher price might indicate better quality, although a lower price during a sale period would not suggest lower quality.

Section 9 then lists several factors which are relevant 'in appropriate cases'. It is not necessary to consider all of these factors every time, but only insofar as they related to the problem with the goods encountered by the consumer:

[39] This could, perhaps, be modelled on Article35 of the UN Convention on the International Sale of Goods 1980 – see Chapter 14.

[40] *Bramhill* v *Edwards* [2004] EWCA Civ 403, para [39]. See also the non-consumer case of *Friarwood Ltd* v *Champagne Cattier SA* [2006] EWCA Civ 1105: 'It was common ground that in this case satisfactory quality is to be judged by the standards of a reasonable wine merchant buying non-vintage champagne from a reputable, but not top flight, producer for resale in both the wholesale and the retail market.' (para [5])

> (3) The quality of goods includes their state and condition; and the following aspects (among others) are in appropriate cases aspects of the quality of goods—
> (a) fitness for all the purposes for which goods of that kind are usually supplied;
> (b) appearance and finish;
> (c) freedom from minor defects;
> (d) safety;
> (e) durability.

From these factors, 'durability' is likely to be considered frequently, as consumer goods often work fine when they are delivered and only break down or malfunction some time afterwards. The task for the consumer is to show that goods which have broken down some time after delivery suffered from a latent fault which only materialised at a later point. Establishing this can be difficult, because over time, the effects of normal wear and tear, or the consumer's use of the goods, could also explain the break-down. Examination of the goods by an independent expert will often be necessary. It seems that relevant considerations are (i) the average expected life-span of this type of goods; (ii) break-downs which might be expected due to normal wear and tear; and (iii) the manner in which the consumer has used the goods. If the goods broke down sooner than would have been expected, it would strengthen the case for claiming a lack of durability which could render the goods unsatisfactory.

Section 9(5)–(7) then include the provisions previously contained in ss. 14(2D)–(2F) dealing with the inclusion of public statements within the notion of 'relevant circumstances':

> (5) The relevant circumstances mentioned in subsection (2)(c) include any public statement about the specific characteristics of the goods made by the trader, the producer or any representative of the trader or the producer.
>
> (6) That includes, in particular, any public statement made in advertising or labelling.
>
> (7) But a public statement is not a relevant circumstance for the purposes of subsection (2)(c) ifthe trader shows that—
> (a) when the contract was made, the trader was not, and could not reasonably have been, aware of the statement,
> (b) before the contract was made, the statement had been publicly withdrawn or, to the extent that it contained anything which was incorrect or misleading, it had been publicly corrected, or
> (c) the consumer's decision to contract for the goods could not have been influenced by the statement.

Subsections (5) to (7) reflect the fact that what a reasonable person might regard as satisfactory is also shaped by public statements, particularly advertising. In essence, s. 9(4) confirms that public statements can be taken into account.

The exceptions in s. 9(7) leave some open questions. The wording corresponds with that in the first Consumer Sales Directive (99/44/EC), Article 2(4) (now Article 7(2) of the second Consumer Sales Directive (2019/771/EU). Subsection 7(a) excludes public statements of which the trader was not, nor could reasonably have been, aware. This was presumably intended to reflect that the trader is the only party liable to the consumer; there, a public statement made by a party higher up in the chain of transactions which the trader did not know about should not create liability on the trader because the trader would not have had the opportunity to correct or clarify such statement. However, public statements are only relevant to determining what a reasonable person would regard as satisfactory, and if those expectations were shaped, at least in part, by a public statement regarding the goods then why should they not be a relevant circumstance irrespective of the trader's knowledge? A consumer cannot know whether a particular public statements was known to the trader.

The second exclusion in subsection 7(b) is more defensible: a public statement could be inaccurate or give an incorrect impression about the characteristics of the corresponding goods. If corrected or clarified, then the earlier incorrect public statement should no longer be considered in determining the reasonable person's view as to the goods' satisfactory nature.

On the other hand, the final exclusionary factor in subsection 7(c) asks the wrong question by focusing on the relevance of the public statement on the consumer's decision to buy the goods. However, the focus of s. 9 is on the facts a reasonable person would consider to decide whether the goods are of satisfactory quality. If anything, this exclusion would need to exclude the public statement where it would not influence the satisfactory quality assessment, e.g., where the public statement was clearly exaggerated and could not have been intended to convey a realistic impression of the qualities of the goods.

The various factors in s. 9 CRA are indicative, rather than exhaustive, and other factors can also be relevant in the circumstances of a particular contract. Case law under the Sale of Goods Act had established that inaccurate or misleading instructions may be relevant.[41] A failure of heating boilers to provide satisfactory energy ratings was a relevant consideration in a more recent case (although the boilers were found to be of satisfactory quality overall).[42] Other factors may also be relevant. Indeed, the list of indicative factors included in s. 9, which are those included in the Sale of Goods Act 1979 in 1994 reflect the recommendations made by the Law Commission in 1987. One may therefore query whether the time has come to update the list to reflect the changes to goods and consumer expectations. Here, the criteria of the corresponding requirement in the EU's Consumer Sales Directive (2019/771) are instructive; relevant factors mentioned there include accessories and instructions (both use and installation); technical standards; and packaging. Furthermore, as many consumer goods rely on digital content to operate, factors such as functionality (which partly overlaps with the notion of 'fitness for common purpose' – see above),[43] interoperability,[44] compatibility[45] and security are also listed expressly. Although the same result would be achieved by arguing that these factors are relevant circumstances in a case under the CRA, greater clarity would be provided through a revision and updated of the list of indicative relevant circumstances.

[41] *Wormell* v *R.H.M. Agriculture (East) Ltd.* [1987] 1 WLR 1091.

[42] *Jewson Ltd* v *Boyhan* [2004] 1 Lloyd's Rep. 505.

[43] 'the ability of the goods to perform their functions having regard to their purpose' (Art. 2(9), Directive 2019/771).

[44] 'the ability of the goods to function with hardware or software different from those with which goods of the same type are normally used' ((Art. 2(10), Directive 2019/771).

[45] 'The ability of goods to function with hardware or software with which the goods of the same type are normally used, without the need to convert the goods, hardware or software' (Art. 2(8), Directive 2019/771).

There is a limitation to the scope of the satisfactory quality test in s. 9(4) CRA, excluding matters known to the consumer before entering into the contract:

> (7) The term mentioned in subsection (1) does not cover anything which makes the quality of the goods unsatisfactory—
> (a) which is specifically drawn to the consumer's attention before the contract is made,
> (b) where the consumer examines the goods before the contract is made, which that examination ought to reveal, or
> (c) in the case of a contract to supply goods by sample, which would have been apparent on a reasonable examination of the sample.

It is important that s. 9(4)(b) should only be engaged when a consumer has actually examined the goods before the contract is made and only cover those aspects which the examination which the consumer has actually undertaken should have uncovered. The suggestion by Auld LJ in *Bramhill* v *Edwards*[46] that the consumers who looked around the motor-home should have realised that it might exceed permitted dimensions and should therefore have measured it should not be followed – this might seem appropriate in a commercial context but not in respect of a consumer contract.

19.4.2 Fitness for particular purpose

Section 10 CRA is based on s. 14(3) of the Sale of Goods Act, but what is one sub-section in that Act is now a separate section with several sub-sections. There is no difference in the substantive effect of s. 10 CRA as compared to s. 14(3) of the Sale of Goods Act, but the new provision is more intelligible. It provides that:

> (1) Subsection (3) applies to a contract to supply goods if before the contract is made the consumer makes known to the trader (expressly or by implication) any particular purpose for which the consumer is contracting for the goods.
> (2) Subsection (3) also applies to a contract to supply goods if—
> (a) the goods were previously sold by a credit-broker to the trader,
> (b) in the case of a sales contract or contract for transfer of goods, the consideration or part of it is a sum payable by instalments, and
> (c) before the contract is made, the consumer makes known to the credit-broker (expressly or by implication) any particular purpose for which the consumer is contracting for the goods.
> (3) The contract is to be treated as including a term that the goods are reasonably fit for that purpose, whether or not that is a purpose for which goods of that kind are usually supplied.
> (4) Subsection (3) does not apply if the circumstances show that the consumer does not rely, or it is unreasonable for the consumer to rely, on the skill or judgment of the trader or credit-broker.

The requirements are familiar: a particular purpose has to be made known, and then the goods have to be reasonably fit for that purpose. It will be interesting to see if case law will develop a separate approach to the trader's defence in sub-s. 4 that the consumer did not rely on the trader's skill or judgment, or that it was unreasonable for him to do so. Article 2(2)(b) of the Consumer Sales Directive (99/44/EC) (and its replacement, Art. 6(b)

[46] [2004] EWCA Civ 403.

of Directive 2019/771/EU) adopts a different approach to this issue. It includes within the presumption of 'conformity' that the goods:

> . . . are fit for any particular purpose for which the consumer requires them and which he made known to the seller at the time of conclusion of the contract and which the seller has accepted.

This provision seems to put the matter more succinctly, although there are differences. First, it seems that Art. 2(2)(b) might require absolute fitness, rather than reasonable fitness (although there might be good grounds for having a higher standard in a consumer context) and secondly, the burden of proving that the seller has accepted that purpose is probably with the consumer, unlike the proviso in what is now s. 10(4) CRA, which puts the onus of showing a lack of reliance on the trader. Perhaps some more thought could have been given to how a statutory provision on fitness for a particular purpose should be worded in an Act dealing exclusively with consumer contracts.

19.4.3 Terms included as a matter of custom

Sections 9(8) and 10(5) provide that a term about the quality of goods or fitness for a particular purpose might be treated as included in the contract as a matter of custom.

19.4.4 Goods to match description

Section 11 CRA deals with the requirement that goods have to be as described. Other than a slight change of wording ('match' rather than 'correspond'), the substance of s. 13 of the Sale of Goods Act is retained:

> (1) Every contract to supply goods by description is to be treated as including a term that the goods will match the description.
> (2) If the supply is by sample as well as by description, it is not sufficient that the bulk of the goods matches the sample if the goods do not also match the description.
> (3) A supply of goods is not prevented from being a supply by description just because—
>   (a) the goods are exposed for supply, and
>   (b) they are selected by the consumer.

Thus far, this is familiar material. However, it has not yet been established whether the restrictive approach developed in the case-law under s. 13 of the Sale of Goods Act would also apply here. For s. 13, only those descriptive words which identify the essential commercial characteristics of the goods are relevant in this context,[47] and the description must have had some influence in bringing about the sale, i.e., the buyer must have relied on it.[48]

There is an argument for suggesting that it would be appropriate to depart from this narrow interpretation of 'description' in favour of a broader reading, in line with what would be considered for the purposes of applying the satisfactory quality test in s. 9 CRA. Some support for this argument can be taken from two new sub-sections in s.11 CRA which have no parallalel in s.13 of the Sale of Goods Act:

[47] *Ashington Piggeries Ltd.* v *Christopher Hill Ltd.* [1972] AC 441; *Reardon Smith Lines* v *Hansen Tangen* [1976] 1 WLR 989.

[48] *Harlingdon Leinster Ents.* v *Christopher Hull Fine Arts* [1990] 1 All ER 737.

(4) Any information that is provided by the trader about the goods and is information mentioned in paragraph
  (a) of Schedule 1 or 2 to the Consumer Contracts (Information, Cancellation and Additional Charges) Regulations 2013 (SI 2013/3134) (main characteristics of goods) is to be treated as included as a term of the contract.

(5) A change to any of that information, made before entering into the contract or later, is not effective unless expressly agreed between the consumer and the trader.

As s. 11(4) CRA already covers the 'main characteristics of the goods', one could assume that the 'description' in s. 11(1) might have a wider scope, because otherwise, s. 11(4) would do no more than duplicate what is already the narrow interpretation of 'description'.

As will be seen below, the Consumer Contracts Regulations 2013 impose a range of pre-contractual information requirements. This CRA provision ensures that information about the main characteristics of the goods has contractual force.

This is somewhat exacerbated by s. 12 CRA, which deals with to all the *other* information requirements under the Consumer Contracts (Information, Cancellation and Additional Charges) Regulations 2013. These are also treated as a term of the contract, too.[49] If this information given changes either before or after a consumer has entered into the contract, then such a change would not be effective in the sense of amending these 'implied' terms unless the trader has the express agreement of the consumer.[50] In so far as changes are made to such information after a consumer has entered into the contract, the effect would be a variation of these 'implied' terms which is binding on the basis of the express agreement of the parties. This would be an exception to the requirement of English contract law that any contract variation must be supported by consideration from both parties. If the consumer does not agree but the information is changed anyway[51] and the trader then acts on the basis of the circumstances as are indicated by the new information, the trader would, presumably, be in breach of the 'implied' term and be liable to compensate the consumer for any costs incurred.[52]

19.4.5 Goods to match sample or model

Section 13 CRA is based on s. 15 of the Sale of Goods Act and deals with goods supplied by reference to a sample. It provides that:

(1) This section applies to a contract to supply goods by reference to a sample of the goods that is seen or examined by the consumer before the contract is made.

(2) Every contract to which this section applies is to be treated as including a term that—
  (a) the goods will match the sample except to the extent that any differences between the sample and the goods are brought to the consumer's attention before the contract is made, and
  (b) the goods will be free from any defect that makes their quality unsatisfactory and that would not be apparent on a reasonable examination of the sample.

[49] s. 12(1) CRA.

[50] Section 11(5) and 12(3) CRA respectively.

[51] It seems unlikely that a trader could rely on any express power of unilateral variation granted by the trader's standard terms and conditions, as such a term would be at high risk of being declared unfair under Part 2 CRA.

[52] See s. 19 CRA, discussed below.

There is then a new provision in s. 14 CRA which deals with goods supplied by reference to a model. However, rather than covering both in one section, the new s. 14 provides:

> (1) This section applies to a contract to supply goods by reference to a model of the goods that is seen or examined by the consumer before entering into the contract.
> (2) Every contract to which this section applies is to be treated as including a term that the goods will match the model except to the extent that any differences between the model and the goods are brought to the consumer's attention before the consumer enters into the contract.

The main difference between s. 13 and s. 14 is that there is no corresponding provision to s. 13(2)(b) in s. 14, which seems appropriate as a sample is a part of the actual goods to be supplied (e.g. a fabric swatch), whereas a model is a scale representation of a finished item.

19.4.6 Installation of goods

Section 15 CRA deals with the situation where installation is part of the contract and the seller has installed the goods:

> Goods do not conform to a contract to supply goods if—
> (a) installation of the goods forms part of the contract,
> (b) the goods are installed by the trader or under the trader's responsibility, and
> (c) the goods are installed incorrectly.

In contrast, a complaint based on inadequate installation instructions would need to be brought on the basis of the satisfactory quality test in s. 9 (as a 'relevant circumstance').

19.4.7 Digital content and goods

Section 16 is a provision that can be deployed to address a problem increasingly common with goods which often include digital content (often operating software, but also so-called 'smart goods') to function. There may be instances when goods fail to work satisfactorily, not because of a mechanical problem but because of an issue with the operating software on which the goods depend for their functionality. Increasingly, this may result from an update to the software over the internet. If that digital content does not conform to the contract of supply (see below), then by virtue of s. 16(1), the goods themselves are deemed not be in conformity. This has several consequences: first, a consumer can use the remedies provided under the CRA in respect of non-conforming goods where the problem is caused by the digital content. Secondly, liability falls on the trader who contractually supplied the goods in respect of a non-conformity caused by the digital content, even where access to the digital content is based on a separate contractual agreement between the consumer and a different trader in respect of that digital content. The benefit of s. 16, however, is that it avoids any debate as to whether the non-conformity should be treated as one of the digital content or the goods by clearly stipulating that the goods themselves are non-conforming.

The original intention behind s. 16 might have been simply to deal with digital content supplied on a physical medium (such as a disk[53]), its wording is broad enough to deal

[53] See *Explanatory Memorandum to the Consumer Rights Act 2015*, paragraph 79; however, at paragraph 192, the supply of software on a physical medium and software running the functionalities of a physical product are both referred to as a supply of digital content on a tangible medium.

with goods relying on operational software for their functionalities (smart goods). Alternatively, in the case of smart goods, it might be arguable that a lack of functionality due to a software issue would render the goods themselves non-functional. In either case, a wider problem with smart goods is that updates happen repeatedly after the goods have been supplied to the consumer, and a loss of some functionality might only occur because of such an update. As the trader's obligations regarding the goods is determined at the point of delivery, post-delivery issues caused by software updates might not be covered by the current requirements at all.

19.4.8 Right to supply goods, freedom from encumbrances and right to quiet possession

It was seen in Chapter 5 that s. 12 of the Sale of Goods Act includes a term about the seller's right to sell the goods, that goods must be free from any undisclosed charges or encumbrances, and that the buyer has the right to enjoy quiet possession of the goods. Similarly, s. 7 of the Supply of Goods and Services Act 1982 includes related provisions in respect of contracts of hire. Section 17 CRA is a substantively corresponding provision which deals with both contracts involving the transfer of ownership in goods (ss. (1)–(2)), hire (ss. (3)), and contracts for the transfer of a limited title (ss. (4)–(7)). The problems discussed there regarding smart goods equally apply in the context of s. 17 CRA.

19.5 Remedies (consumer's rights to enforce terms about goods)

The remedies (referred to as 'rights' in the CRA) available for a breach of the terms discussed above are set out in s. 19 CRA. For this purpose, s. 19(1) defines the shorthand phrase 'goods conforming to a contract' as compliance with ss. 9–11 and 13–16, as well as any additional requirements expressly stated in the contract. However, there is a limitation in s. 19(2) which excludes any failure to conform if this has its origins in materials supplied by the consumer.

The remedies available to a consumer depend on the type of breach complained of. The following table summarises the position:

Non-conformity due to breach of:	Rights (remedies):
Satisfactory quality (s.9) Fitness for particular purpose (s.10) Matching description (s.11) Matching sample (s.13) Matching model (s.14) Goods include digital content which does not conform with the contract (s.16)	Short-term right to reject Repair or replacement Price reduction Final right to reject (s.19(3))
Incorrect installation (s.15) Other express contractual requirement	Repair or replacement Price reduction Final right to reject (s.19(4))

Non-conformity due to breach of:	Rights (remedies):
Pre-contractual information duties (s.12)	Recovery from trader amount of any costs incurred by consumer as a result of breach, up to the amount of price paid or value of other consideration given (s.19(5))
Right to supply (s.17(1))	Right to reject (not restricted by time limits) (s.19(6))

Section 19(7) makes these remedies subject to the provisions dealing with the delivery of the wrong quantity,[54] and the availability of the short-term right of rejection or the right to reject for breach of the term under s. 17(1) is subject to the rules on instalment deliveries.[55]

In respect of all the requirements regarding the goods (ss. 9–17 and express terms in the contract), a consumer can seek remedies not provided for in the Act, either in addition to one of the Act's remedies (provided that this would not mean that the consumer recovers twice for the same loss) or instead of, and in respect of, breaches for which the Act itself does not provide any remedies. As s. 19(11) states:

> Those other remedies include any of the following that is open to the consumer in the circumstances—
> (a) claiming damages;
> (b) seeking specific performance;
> (c) seeking an order for specific implement; (d) relying on the breach against a claim by the trader for the price;
> (e) for breach of an express term, exercising a right to treat the contract as at an end.

However, the right to terminate the contract ('to treat the contract as at an end') is not available for any breaches of the terms included in the contract under the Act except as indicated in the table above. The relevance of the right to claim damages is discussed further below.

The availability of repair or replacement, price reduction and the final right to reject benefit from the provisions in ss. 19(14) and (15), which creates a presumption that if goods do not conform to the contract at any time during the six-month period from the date of delivery, they did not conform at the time of delivery. However, a trader can rebut this presumption by showing that the goods did in fact conform to the contract when delivered, or the presumption is incompatible with the nature of the goods,[56] or the type of non-conformity complained of.[57]

The various remedies will be examined in turn below but before doing so, a further observation is appropriate. One of the objectives of the Consumer Rights Act was to integrate the remedies derived from the first Consumer Sales Directive (99/44/EC) with the existing right to reject the goods. In Part 5A of the Sale of Goods Act (now repealed),

[54] s. 25 CRA.
[55] s. 26 CRA.
[56] For example, goods which perish in a short period of time.
[57] For example, a vase shattered into small pieces – which is more likely to have been caused by someone dropping it onto a hard surface.

the link between old and new remedies was so confusing that the Law Commissions were asked to propose appropriate reforms.[58] Although the gist of the Law Commissions' proposals has found their way into the Act, there is one important recommendation which was not followed. To integrate old and new remedies, the Commissions correctly noted that the right to reject the goods and the right to terminate the contract, whilst often exercised together, are two separate stages. Moreover, when a consumer requests repair or replacement he is also, in fact, rejecting the goods, although not terminating the contract. Consequently, the Law Commissions recommended that the primary remedy would be rejecting the goods, with a choice of three follow-on remedies: repair, replacement or termination of the contract. It is regrettable that this particular recommendation was not followed by the government, as doing so would have further simplified the law and ensured a proper integration of all the remedies.

19.5.1 Right to reject

In the Consumer Rights Act, there are three variants of the right to reject:[59] the 'short-term' right to reject, the 'final' right to reject, and right to reject for breach of the term included in the contract by s. 17(1).[60] A consumer can reject the goods and treat the contract as at an end by indicating so to the trader.[61] This can be done by words or action, as long as it is sufficiently clear to the trader that the consumer is rejecting the goods.[62]

One important thing regarding the exercise of the right of rejection where goods are supplied on hire-purchase is that a consumer would have to contact the finance company to exercise their right rather than the trader where the consumer chose the goods. So for a car supplied on HP, rejection should be indicated to the finance company rather than the car dealer. Many consumers will not appreciate the exact legal nature of a hire-purchase arrangement, bringing with it the risk of ineffective rejection. However, a recent county court ruling suggests that, if the car dealer is treated as acting as agent for the finance company in respect of some matters, then indicating rejection to the car dealer might suffice.[63] However, this would depend on the circumstances of each case, and so the risk of ineffective rejection remains.

Following rejection, the trader is under a duty to give the consumer a refund,[64] which normally means that the consumer is entitled to receive back the same amount of money that he paid.[65] If the consumer transferred something else, the consumer is entitled to receive back what was transferred, either the same amount of what was transferred[66] or, in case it is not substitutable, whatever was transferred in its original state.[67] However, in the

[58] Law Commission, Report 317/Scottish Law Commission No 216 – *Consumer Remedies for Faulty Goods* (London: TSO, 2009).
[59] See s. 20 CRA.
[60] Note the provisions on severable obligations in ss. 20(20)/(21).
[61] s. 20(4)/(5).
[62] s. 20(6).
[63] Cf. *Dr William Van Gordon* v *Volkswagen Financial Services (UK) Ltd (t/a Audi Finance)*, Nottingham County Court, 30 April 2019.
[64] s. 20(7)(a).
[65] s. 20(10).
[66] s. 20(11).
[67] s. 20(12).

latter case, there is no right to a refund if it is not possible to return what was transferred in its original state.[68] The consumer is able to claim damages in that situation instead. [69]

A refund has to be given 'without undue delay', and within 14 days from when the trader agrees that the consumer is entitled to a refund[70] (rather than from the date when the consumer has rejected the goods). Unless the consumer agrees otherwise, a refund has to be made using the same payment method as the one used by the consumer, and the trader is precluded from charging any fees for the payment method used.[71]

In contracts of hire, the refund covers only the hire charges for the period of hire not used following termination of the contract.[72] If the consumer transferred something else for the duration of the hire, then the consumer is entitled to receive back whatever reflects the unused period of hire unless it is not possible to return only a part of that.[73]

Conversely, in respect of a hire-purchase or conditional sale contract, any instalments already paid are refunded only.[74] This reflects the different objectives of these supply contracts: a hire contract is a fixed-term agreement for the duration of which the consumer is entitled to use the goods, and up to the point when the contract is terminated, the consumer will have had use of the goods and is therefore required to pay charges accordingly. A hire-purchase or conditional sale agreement ultimately have the objective of transferring ownership, but following termination this will not happen and, consequently, the consumer is entitled to receive back everything he paid.

As far as the consumer is concerned, after rejecting the goods, he has to make the goods available for collection by the trader, or, if it is agreed that the consumer will return them to the trader, to return them as agreed.[75] The consumer's duty to make the goods available is not indefinite, and if the trader fails to collect them then the consumer may be entitled to dispose of them elsewhere: *Christina Tenant Johnston and Peter Johnston* v *R&J Leather (Scotland) Limited*. The consumer in this case had rejected a leather suite which was not of satisfactory quality.[76] The trader failed to react to multiple attempts to contact them so they would collect the leather suite. After some time, the consumer disposed of the leather suite by other means, and sought to recover the price they had paid. The trader argued that the consumer could not reject the goods because the goods were no longer available for collection. It was held that the obligation under s. 20(7) CRA was not without limits and that, depending on factors such as the nature of the goods, a consumer's ability to store them, the number of failed attempts to contact the trader and the length the goods have already been retained, a consumer can dispose of them after an appropriate period of time. Exercising the right to reject also does not preclude the continued use of the goods until they are collected by the trader.[77]

[68] s. 20(12).
[69] s. 20(19).
[70] s. 20(15).
[71] s. 20(16)/(17).
[72] s. 20(13).
[73] s. 20(18)(c).
[74] s. 20(14).
[75] s. 20(7)(b).
[76] [2019] SAC (Civ) 1.
[77] *Alan King* v *Black Horse Limited* [2024] CSIH 3.

Irrespective of how the goods are returned, the trader has to bear any reasonable costs of returning the goods; however, this does not extend to the cost for the consumer of returning the goods to the place where the consumer took physical possession of the goods.[78] Thus, if the consumer bought goods in a shop and took them home, the consumer has to pay for the bus fare, or car parking charges etc., associated with returning to that shop.

Section 21 provides for the partial rejection of goods where the contract covers more than one item. This is familiar from s. 35A of the Sale of Goods Act. The consumer can elect which of the non-conforming goods to reject (although he has to keep those goods which do conform) – whether delivered all at once or in instalments, but if the goods form a commercial unit[79] then all of the goods in that unit have to be rejected (or none). Section 21 then repeats the provisions on exercising the right to reject, providing a refund to the consumer, and making the goods available to the trader already discussed.

In a departure from the vagueness associated with the question of how long the reasonable period of time lasts before a buyer is deemed to have accepted the goods under s. 35 of the Sale of Goods Act 1979, s. 22 of the Consumer Rights Act introduces a clear time limit for the short-term right to reject, although consumer and trader can agree on a longer time period. But if nothing is agreed, the time limit starts to run once ownership in the goods has transferred to the consumer (or, in the case of hire, hire-purchase or conditional sale, possession), the goods have been delivered, and in the case of contracts requiring the trader to install the goods or take some other action before the consumer can use them, the trader has notified that the necessary action has been taken[80] (although the consumer can exercise his right to reject before all of these things have occurred).[81] The time limit ends after 30 days. If goods are reasonably expected to have a shorter life expectancy, then the shorter period applies.

The section then goes on to deal with the impact on the time limit in circumstances where the consumer opts for repair or replacement rather than immediate rejection. If the consumer does so within the 30-day period, time stops on the day the consumer has requested or agreed to repair or replacement and a 'waiting period' starts.[82] The waiting period ends on the day the consumer receives back the repaired goods or a replacement.[83] If the goods still do not conform to the contract, the time limit for exercising the right to reject will be either seven days after the end of the waiting period, or if the unexpired portion of the original time limit is longer, then it is the remaining portion of the time limit (but time only starts to run again after the waiting period has finished).

For example, A has bought a new microwave oven on 1 July. On 15 July, it stopped working (which means it was not of satisfactory quality at the time of delivery). The consumer asked the retailer to replace the oven, and the replacement was received on

[78] s. 20(8).
[79] Defined in ss. 21(4) as a unit 'if division of the unit would materially impair the value of the goods or the character of the unit'.
[80] s. 22(3).
[81] s. 22(5).
[82] s. 22(8)(a).
[83] s. 22(8)(b).

20 July. On 3 August, the replacement oven stops. More than 30 days have passed since delivery, but asking for a replacement started the waiting period. At that time, there were still 16 days of the time limit left. The time limit re-started when the replacement was delivered to the consumer, and there were still two days left to run when the replacement oven failed. The consumer can therefore still exercise the short-term right of rejection.

Another example is as follows. A has bought a new microwave oven on 1 July. On 29 July, it stopped working (which means it was not of satisfactory quality at the time of delivery). The consumer asked the retailer to replace the oven, and the replacement was received on 1 August. On 6 August, the replacement oven stops working. More than 30 days have passed since delivery, but asking for a replacement started the waiting period. At that time, there were only 2 days of the time limit left. The time limit re-started when the replacement was delivered to the consumer. As there were only 2 days remaining, the time limit is extended to 7 days. The consumer can therefore still exercise the short-term right of rejection.

In a third example, A bought a new microwave oven on 1 July. On 29 July, it stopped working (which means it was not of satisfactory quality at the time of delivery). The consumer asked the retailer to replace the oven, and the replacement was received on 1 August. On 14 August, the replacement oven stops working. More than 30 days have passed since delivery, but asking for a replacement started the waiting period. At that time, there were only 2 days of the time limit left. The time limit re-started when the replacement was delivered to the consumer. As there were only 2 days remaining, the time limit is extended to 7 days, but this meant that the time limit expired on 8 August. The consumer can therefore no longer exercise the short-term right of rejection.

19.5.2 Repair and replacement

Instead of rejecting the goods and treating the contract as at an end, a consumer can, in the circumstances set out above, request a repair or replacement. Repair means bringing goods which do not conform to the contract into conformity.[84] Generally speaking, the consumer has the right to choose either repair or replacement, but that choice may not always be available. S. 23 (3) states that the trader cannot be required to repair or replace an item if that is impossible, or if the remedy the consumer has requested is disproportionate to the other of those remedies.[85] So if one remedy is impossible, then the consumer can only request the other, and if both remedies are impossible, the consumer can either rely on the short-term right of rejection (if still available), or alternatively request a reduction of the price or the final right of rejection (see below).

[84] s. 23(8) CRA.

[85] This is a change to the wording adopted in s. 48B(3)(c) of the Sale of Goods Act, which permitted a comparison also with price reduction and rescission (as the final right of reject was known as there). This change is consistent with C-65/09 *Weber* v *Wittmer* and C-87/09 *Putz* v *Medianess Electronics*, para. [68].

In order to establish whether a remedy is disproportionate compared to the other, it is necessary to consider whether it would impose unreasonable costs on the trader, taking into account:

(a) the value which the goods would have if they conformed to the contract,
(b) the significance of the lack of conformity, and
(c) whether the other remedy could be effected without significant inconvenience to the consumer.

Assuming the chosen remedy (repair or replacement) is available then the trader is required to provide this within a reasonable time and without significant inconvenience to the consumer.[86] This is to be determined by considering the nature of the goods and the purpose for which the goods were acquired.[87] The trader is also required to cover the relevant costs of providing the chosen remedy, including postage, materials and labour.[88]

A difficult situation is where goods were supplied by a trader but installed by the consumer, and after installation, the goods turn out to be not in conformity with the contract (where the installation itself was done properly). Can the trader be required to cover the cost of uninstalling the faulty goods and of reinstalling their replacement? The CJEU was faced with this question in two cases, *Weber and Putz*.[89] The goods in these cases were floor tiles and a dishwasher respectively (the latter being easier to uninstall than floor tiles, which would require significant time and labour costs). The CJEU held that the trader could be required to cover the cost of uninstalling the non-conforming goods and reinstalling the replacement goods. This obligation was not affected by the fact that, in the case of the floor tiles, the cost of removing the faulty tiles and laying their replacement exceeded the purchase price by a considerable amount. However, the potential financial impact on a trader was mitigated by the CJEU by making this obligation subject to a separate proportionality assessment with would fix a ceiling to the trader's obligation to cover the cost of uninstalling and reinstalling the goods. In many ways, the ruling seems entirely unnecessary, because this question could, and should, be dealt with by considering an award of damages for consequential losses (see below), and a court faced with such a question now might not follow the reasoning in *Weber and Putz*.

19.5.3 Price reduction and the final right to reject

There are three circumstances when a consumer is entitled to request a price reduction, or exercise the final right to reject (although not both):[90]

> (1) The goods do not conform to the contract after *one* repair or replacement. This requires that the consumer has requested or agreed to repair or replacement, and the trader has delivered or made available goods to the consumer in response.*

[86] s. 23(2)(a).
[87] s. 23(5).
[88] s. 23(2)(b).
[89] C-65/09 *Weber* v *Wittmer* and C-87/09 *Putz* v *Medianess Electronics* ECLI:EU:C:2011:396.
[90] s. 24(5) CRA.

(2) The consumer is neither entitled to repair nor replacement (as per s. 23(3))
(3) The trader is in breach of the requirement to provide the repair or replacement requested within a reasonable time and without significant inconvenience to the consumer.

'Price reduction' means that the price payable is reduced by an 'appropriate amount' (or anything else the consumer is required to transfer under the contract),[91] and if the consumer has already paid more than the reduced amount, that the excess is refunded.[92] It is possible that the price may be reduced to zero.[93]

If the consumer exercises the final right to reject, the trader has to provide a full refund. However, after more than six months from delivery (including installation), it is permissible for a deduction from that refund to be made to reflect the period of time since delivery during which the consumer was able to use the goods, except where the reason this time exceeds six months is because the trader failed to collect the goods at the agreed time.[94] However, where the goods consist of a motor vehicle (or goods defined by order made by the Secretary of State), a deduction for use may be made at any point in time, including during the six months from delivery.

19.5.4 Common Law remedies: damages

As noted above, s. 19(11) preserves the right to claim damages, which would be of particular relevance in respect of consequential losses. It has long been the case that, in consumer cases, damages may cover losses which go beyond the reduced value of non-conforming goods.

In consumer cases, where goods are bought for use, there is no difficulty in obtaining damages for inconvenience and even disappointment and distress in appropriate cases. In *Jackson* v *Chrysler Acceptances Ltd*,[95] the plaintiff bought a new car from the defendants, informing them that he specifically wanted to take it abroad for his holiday. Owing to repeated breakdowns as a result of defects in the car, the plaintiff's holiday was ruined. It was held that he was entitled to damages for this, in addition to normal damages for the defects in the car. In *Bernstein* v *Pamson Motors (Golders Green) Ltd*,[96] where a new car broke down on a motorway, and the plaintiff and his wife had to summon emergency assistance, he recovered as damages: (1) the cost of wasted petrol; (2) the cost of the plaintiff and his wife getting home by alternative transport; (3) damages for vexation and distress for the ruined day's outing and (4) loss of the use of the car while it was being repaired. He would also have been entitled to the cost of the repairs and the emergency services, if these had not already been borne by the defendants.

Although the Court of Appeal denied that damages for breach of contract can never include an item for 'mental distress',[97] damages for vexation and disappointment and

[91] Although note that if whatever the consumer is required to transfer under the contract cannot be divided up to allow the trader to receive only the reduced amount, then the right to price reduction is not available.
[92] s. 24(1).
[93] s. 24(2).
[94] s. 24(8)–(10).
[95] [1978] RTR 474.
[96] [1987] 2 All ER 220.
[97] *Bliss* v *South East Thames Regional Health Authority* [1987] ICR 700.

distress continued to be regularly awarded in minor consumer cases, often in the County Courts, or before County Court District Judges sitting as arbitrators. Moreover, in *Farley* v *Skinner*,[98] where a surveyor was specifically asked to advise whether a holiday property the claimant was proposing to buy could be affected by aircraft noise, the House of Lords held that the claimant was entitled to non-pecuniary damages when it turned out after the claimant had bought the property that it was indeed affected by aircraft noise.[99]

The possibility of claiming damages for consequential losses is often downplayed when considering consumer remedies in respect of faulty goods, but this right should be seen as integral to the set of remedies available to a consumer. Indeed, it would have been preferable had the Consumer Rights Act included a new statutory right to damages for consequential losses as this might have clarified the kinds of losses that would be within the range of recoverable damages.

19.6 Delivery of goods

The Consumer Rights Act contains a number of rules on the delivery of goods. Some of these are based on existing provisions in the Sale of Goods Act 1979; others are new.

Two familiar provisions are found in s. 25 and s. 26 CRA. Section 25 deals with circumstances where the trader has delivered the wrong quantity of goods.[100] The consumer has the choice whether to accept a short delivery or reject this, but if he accepts, the goods delivered must be paid for at the contract rate.[101] If there is an excess delivery, the consumer can accept the whole delivery, or the contract quantity (and reject the excess), or reject the whole delivery, but goods accepted must be paid for at the contract rate.[102] If the consumer rejects the whole delivery and accepts none of the goods, then it will depend on the contract whether the consumer is entitled to treat the contract as at an end,[103] so deciding to reject a delivery of goods of incorrect quantity does not automatically entitle the consumer to treat the contract as at an end.

Section 26 deals with instalment deliveries.[104] There is a presumption against the consumer being required to accept delivery by instalments, unless trade and consumer have agreed to this.[105] Where the contract is also a subscription contract for the regular supply of goods within chapter 2 of part 4 of the Digital Markets, Competition and Consumers Act 2024, the presumption is presumably rebutted implicitly – the DMCCA does not address this point. Section 26 lays down several rules where there is an agreement to deliver goods by instalments, each of which is to be paid for separately. Thus if the trader makes one or several defective deliveries, then a consumer may either be entitled to reject the instalment, or, in some circumstances, exercise the right to reject under s. 19(6) CRA in

[98] [2001] UKHL 49.
[99] Note that in Scotland damages may be awarded for 'trouble and inconvenience', including in commercial cases – see *Webster & Co* v *Cramond Iron Co* (1875) 2 R 752; *Smith* v *Park* 1980 SLT (Sh Ct) 62; *Gunn* v *NCB* 1982 SLT 526; *Douglas* v *Glenvarigill Co Ltd* [2010] CSOH 14, 2010 SLT 634.
[100] Cf. s. 30 of the Sale of Goods Act 1979.
[101] s. 25(1) CRA.
[102] s. 25(2)/(3) CRA.
[103] s. 25(4) CRA.
[104] Cf. s. 31 of the Sale of Goods Act 1979.
[105] s. 26(1) CRA.

respect of the whole contract.[106] Conversely, if the consumer neglects or refuses to accept a delivery or to pay for an instalment, the trader may in some instances be entitled to terminate the whole contract, but if the breach by the consumer is a severable breach the trader will only be entitled to damages.[107]

Section 28 then introduces new rules on delivery specifically for sales contracts (but not all contracts involving the supply of goods). It contains several presumptions. First, each sales contract is treated as including a term that the trader has to deliver the goods to the consumer (subject to agreement to the contrary).[108] Also, if there is no agreement as to the time or period by which the trader has to deliver the goods, the contract is treated as including a term that delivery must occur without undue delay and no more than 30 days after the date of concluding the contract.[109] If the consumer is to take immediate delivery of the goods, then the agreed time will be the time the contract is concluded.[110]

If the trader fails to deliver on time the consumer may, in some circumstances, treat the contract as at an end. This is the case when:

(1) The trader has refused to deliver the goods.
(2) It is essential that the goods are delivered at the agreed time or within the agreed period, taking into account all the relevant circumstances of when the contract was entered into.
(3) The consumer told the trader that delivery by an agreed date, or within the standard 30 day period, was essential before the contract was concluded.

In all other circumstances, the consumer has to set a period 'appropriate in the circumstances' and require the trader to deliver by the end of that period, and if the trader still fails to deliver by then, the consumer may treat the contract as at an end.[111] Once a contract is treated by the consumer as at an end, the trader is obliged to reimburse all payments made by the consumer within undue delay.[112]

A consumer who has ordered a number of goods may wish to keep some but cancel the order in respect of other goods, or reject goods already delivered – but not treat the whole contract as at an end. Section 28(10) CRA permits a consumer to do so, subject to the requirement that a consumer cannot reject only some goods forming part of a commercial unit.[113]

19.7 Passing of risk

The Sale of Goods Act already contained a special provision on the passing of risk in consumer contracts,[114] but this was replaced with a new provision in the Consumer Rights Act; this also only applies to sales contracts. In essence, goods remain at the trader's risk until they come into the physical possession of the consumer, or a person nominated by

[106] s. 26(3) CRA.
[107] s. 26(6) CRA.
[108] s. 28(1) CRA.
[109] s. 28(2) CRA.
[110] s. 28(4)(b) CRA.
[111] s. 28(7)/(8) CRA.
[112] s. 28(9) CRA.
[113] s. 28(11)/(12) CRA.
[114] s. 20(4) of the Sale of Goods Act, revoked by the Consumer Rights Act.

the consumer to take possession of the goods.[115] Somewhat strangely, this is also done by treating a sales contract as including a term to that effect, rather than simply having this as a statutory rule, as was the case under s. 20(4) of the Sale of Goods Act. This seems to unnecessarily complicate matters.

Also, this rule does not apply where the consumer has commissioned a carrier to deliver the goods and that carrier is not among the options given to the consumer. In that case, delivery of the goods to the carrier will mean that risk passes to the consumer at that point.[116] It is important to stress that this will only be the case where the consumer decides to make delivery arrangements which differ from the various options a trader might offer. Many websites offer a range of delivery options, and these might be provided by different carriers. If a consumer selects a particular method from those offered by the trader, then the main rule that risk will not pass until the goods come into the consumer's physical possession will apply.

19.8 Digital content

The Consumer Rights Act introduced dedicated rules for the supply of digital content to consumers. has removed the need to develop complicated arguments about whether software/digital content should be treated as 'goods', and if so, in what circumstances. Often, the main concern was to ensure that a buyer of unsatisfactory digital content would have some recourse. The Consumer Rights Act contains specific provisions dealing with quality and fitness of digital content, as well as appropriate remedies.

'Digital content' is defined in general terms as 'data which are produced and supplied in digital form'.[117] Chapter 3 of Part 1 of the Consumer Rights Act only applies to certain types of contracts for the supply of digital content, which are:

(1) Contracts for the supply of digital content where the consumer pays a price.
(2) Digital content supplied free with goods or services, or other digital content for which the consumer pays a price.
(3) Digital content not generally available to a consumer unless they have paid a price for it or for goods or services or other digital content.

In essence, therefore, the chapter on digital content does not apply to free digital content,[118] such as the many applications ('apps') which are available free of charge, although the immediate challenge here is the question of whether the CRA will apply to apps which can be downloaded free of charge but for which a consumer can purchase additional features, or make so-called 'in-app' purchases. One would certainly expect that any paid-for features are subject to the rules of the Act, and if the effect of accessing paid-for elements is that the digital content as a whole fails to meet the statutory requirements, then the consumer's rights under the Act should extend to the content that was previously free.[119]

[115] s. 29(2) CRA.
[116] s. 29(3)/(4) CRA.
[117] s. 2(9) CRA.
[118] Although note the order-making power in s. 33(5) which permits the Secretary of State to extend the scope of the chapter to other contracts for the supply of digital content. However, there is a threshold test that it must be 'appropriate to do so because of significant detriment caused to consumers' under the relevant contracts.
[119] Cf. s. 33(2)(a).

19.8.1 Requirements in respect of digital content

The provisions on digital content follow the provisions on the supply of goods as closely as possible, and variations only exist insofar as these are necessary because of the inherent differences between a supply of goods and a supply of digital content. Section 34 stipulates that digital content must be of satisfactory quality, and s. 34 largely mirrors s. 9, although the list of indicative factors in s. 34(3) does not include 'appearance and finish'. However, it is debatable whether this close alignment between digital content and goods was really appropriate, because the kinds of factors affecting the quality of digital content may be different. Once again, we may draw a comparison with corresponding EU legislation: Article 8 of the Digital Content and Digital Services Directive (2019/770/EU) lists factors such as performance features, functionality, compatibility, accessibility, continuity and security, as well as the supply of relevant accessories and instructions. Of course, these could be referred to as 'other relevant circumstances', but it might have been preferable to list these, or others, expressly.

S. 35 deals with the requirement that digital content has to be fit for a particular purpose and this follows the corresponding provision for goods (s. 10). The same is true of the requirement that digital content has to match its description in s. 36, although s. 36(2) refers to the consumer examining a 'trial version' of the digital content, rather than a sample. Section 37 then ensures that relevant information provided under the Consumer Contracts (Information, Cancellation and Additional Charges) Regulations becomes a term of the contract, in the same vein as s. 12.

An important provision is found in s. 40, which deals with digital content supplied 'subject to the right of the trader or a third party to modify the digital content'. In other words, this deals with the frequent situation where updates are provided for digital content. Whenever digital content is modified, the modified version of the content must also comply with the various requirements of quality, fitness for purpose and description. Additional features may be added, but the digital content must still match its description, as well as any pre-contractual information (unless any change to that information has been agreed with the consumer). However, the CRA stops short of requiring the provision of regular updates; instead, a consumer would have to argue that a lack of updates, or the availability of updates only for a short period of time, might render the digital content unsatisfactory.

Earlier, we noted the relevance of s. 16 for goods which require digital content in the form of operating software to perform their functionalities (smart goods). If an update to such operating software results in the loss of functionality, a consumer would have to argue that, as result, the digital content is no longer of satisfactory quality. The difficulty with this is that goods must be of satisfactory quality at the time of delivery. If there is a problem with the digital content at that point, then the goods are treated as unsatisfactory. It is unclear whether this would extend to digital content which is rendered unsatisfactory after an update which causes the loss of functionality. Whilst it is arguable that the digital content is no longer satisfactory (as it is no longer fit for its common purpose of providing functionality for the relevant goods), this does not obviously extend to the operation of s. 16. However, it would be logical for the effect of s. 16 to be that goods which become unusable due to an update to the operating software are rendered unsatisfactory too.

Whether a court could be persuaded so to find is uncertain. With smart goods so prevalent nowadays, amendments to the CRA are now needed to clarify the law on this point.

There are then a number of provisions specific to digital content. Thus, s. 39 deals with the supply of digital content where the consumer's access to the content on a device (such as a smartphone) requires that the digital content is transmitted to that device and that this is arranged by the trader. Section 39(2) states that the time of supply is either when the content reaches the device, or, if earlier, if the content reaches another trader who has a contract with the consumer to supply a service by which the digital content reaches the device. The latter would be an internet access provider such as the consumer's broadband supplier; it seems that Parliament thought that any problems in accessing the content on the consumer's device which is caused by the broadband service rather than by the trader supplying the digital content should not lead to liability on the part of that trader.

Sections 39(3)-(7) then deal with the situation where there is a contract to supply digital content, and the contract provides that once the trader has supplied that content, the consumer is to have access to a processing facility (arranged by the trader). A 'processing facility' is defined in s. 39(4) as 'a facility by which [the trader] or another trader will receive digital content from the consumer and transmit digital content to the consumer (whether or not other features are to be included under the contract)'. This relates to situations where the supply of the digital content is not limited to a single act of supply but involves repeated access to the digital content online, such as subscription-style services (e.g., video-streaming facility or games with online multi-player facility). Under s. 39(5), the contract is treated as including a term that this facility must be available to the consumer for a reasonable time or for the time specified in the contract.

Under s. 41, a contract is treated as including a term that the trader will have the right to supply the digital content at the time of supply (which adapts s. 17(1), although note that there are no provisions in respect of digital content dealing with freedom from encumbrances etc.).

19.8.2 Remedies in respect of digital content

Where digital content does not conform to the contract (which, in this context, means the requirements of ss. 34–36 CRA), the available rights are a right to repair or replacement, or the right to price reduction.[120] The remedies are structured similarly to the remedies made available in respect of contracts for the supply of goods. The six-month presumption of non-conformity is also applicable in the case of digital content, if a consumer has requested repair, replacement or price reduction in respect of non-conforming digital content.[121] Additionally, a consumer can rely on remedies provided at common law, either instead of or in addition to the remedies under the Act (subject to the proviso that double recovery is not allowed).[122] However, for a non-conformity and for a breach of the terms in ss. 37 and 41, there is no right for the consumer to treat the contract as at an end,[123] nor is there a right of rejection of digital content.

[120] s. 42(2) CRA.
[121] s. 42 (9) and (10) CRA.
[122] s. 42(6)/(7) CRA.
[123] s. 42(8) CRA.

Section 43 spells out in more detail how the remedies of repair and replacement are intended to operate. Repair is given the same meaning as for goods, i.e., making non-conforming digital content conform.[124] Repairing digital content would usually involve a software update, or patch, which will modify the digital content to fix the non-conformity. This is different from routine updates which are not provided in response to a consumer's request for a remedy but on the basis of the trader's contractual right to modify the digital content. A repair, just like a routine modification, has to ensure that the digital content is in conformity with the contract afterwards.

'Replacement' is not defined, nor is it clear what replacing digital content might mean. Practically speaking, a non-conformity in the digital content might not be solved by acquiring another copy of the same digital content. Goods might be non-conforming because the item supplied to a consumer has a manufacturing defect only affecting that particular item, so a replacement would not have this problem. In the case with digital content, this is either accessed online or a copy of that digital content is supplied to the consumer. Supplying another copy would simply replicate the problem. A replacement might be appropriate if the non-conformity of the digital content was due to the fact that the digital content was corrupted during the process of transmitting it to the consumer. A further download resulting in the 'replacement' of the earlier download might cure the non-conformity. Replacement might also be appropriate when the digital content supplied to the consumer didn't include any features which should have been part of it under the terms of the contract. In that case, the version which does contain all those features could be supplied as a replacement to remedy the non-conformity.

Section 43 CRA largely is similar to s. 23 CRA (for goods). The consumer's choice between repair and replacement is subject to the requirement that the remedy chosen must be possible, and not disproportionate when compared to the alternative remedy. Repair is often more likely to cure the problem, particularly if this can be done by providing the necessary patch to fix the problem which has been identified.

Where both remedies are possible, considering whether the remedy chosen by the consumer is disproportionate requires determination of whether that remedy would impose unreasonable costs on the trader, taking into account:

(a) the value which the digital content would have if it conformed to the contract,
(b) the significance of the lack of conformity, and
(c) whether the other remedy could be effected without significant inconvenience to the consumer.

In the case of generic digital content, it will often be more convenient and effective to provide a replacement to the consumer – provided that this would actually be suitable for curing the non-conformity – because the costs to the trader of supplying the replacement would be low. In most instances, the content can be provided as a download. The difficulties discussed in respect of the uninstallation of non-conforming goods and installation of their replacement do not arise here. For more complex digital content, such as bespoke software, a patch to fix the problem (if this is possible) might be the proportionate solution. In any event, the disproportionality of the remedy chosen by the consumer does not

[124] s. 43(8) CRA.

just require determination of the cheaper of the two remedies; the cost to the trader of providing the chosen remedy would have to be unreasonable compared to the alternative for it to be regarded as disproportionate.

Where it is not possible to repair or replace the digital content, or where the trader has failed to repair or replace the digital content within a reasonable period of time and/or without significant inconvenience to the consumer, the consumer will be entitled to a price reduction instead.[125] This remedy is given effect by reducing the price payable by 'an appropriate amount'[126] which, in some instances, may be the full amount of the price.[127] A reduction to the value of the full amount would be appropriate if the digital content in question fails to work and the consumer is not able to use it at all. A lesser reduction would be appropriate where a minor bug affected an app several months after using it trouble-free and the functionality of the app as a whole was not significantly affected.[128]

Where a consumer is entitled to a refund, the trader must give this without undue delay and within 14 days at the latest. Time begins to run once the trader has agreed that the consumer is entitled to a refund. [129] Unless the consumer agrees otherwise, the trader has to use the same method of payment of the refund as the one that was used for making the original payment.[130] Moreover, the trader must not charge the consumer for the refund.[131] Thus, if the consumer paid for the digital content using a credit card, then the trader has to use the same credit card for making the refund.

For a breach of the term included in the contract by virtue of s. 37 (i.e., a failure to comply with information given under the 2013 Regulations), the remedy is to recover from the trader any costs incurred by the consumer as a result of the breach, up to the amount of the price paid.[132]

19.8.3 Damage to device or other digital content

Section 46 CRA deals with the situation where the trader supplies digital content to the consumer under a contract, and the digital content causes damage to a device or other digital content belonging to the consumer. The damage in question has to be of a kind that would not have occurred, had the trader acted with reasonable care and skill.

Unlike the other provisions in chapter 3, this section applies even where the consumer has not paid a price, and will therefore apply if a consideration other than money (such as data) is provided by the consumer.[133] The potential effect of this is somewhat obscure from the CRA itself, but it has been argued that this section does not only apply in respect of the contract of supply between trader and consumer, but also to the End-User Licence Agreement (EULA) between the consumer and the producer of the digital content, which

[125] s. 44(3) CRA.
[126] s. 44(1) CRA.
[127] s. 44(2) CRA.
[128] See the examples in the Explanatory Memorandum to the Consumer Rights Act 2015, para. 215.
[129] s. 44(4) CRA.
[130] s. 44(5) CRA.
[131] s. 44(6) CRA.
[132] s. 42(4) CRA.
[133] Cf. s. 33(8) CRA, which disapplies the limitation of scope to digital content supplied in return for a price from s. 46 CRA.

would be a separate contract under which digital content is supplied to a consumer (in the sense that the EULA unlocks access to the digital content).[134] This could be particularly important where the consumer has acquired the digital content via a retailer or other intermediary and not from the producer/rights-holder directly, because the kind of damage for which a remedy can be claimed has to be one within the control of the trader in question – the trader will be liable on the basis that insufficient care and skill was exercised to prevent the damage, and the only trader in a position to do so would be the 'producer' of the digital content.

Where s. 46 applies, the consumer can require the trader either to repair the damage, or to compensate the consumer for the damage with an appropriate payment. 'Repair' is handled here in the same way as elsewhere in the CRA, and it has to be provided free-of-charge, within a reasonable time, and without causing significant inconvenience to the consumer.[135]

The alternative is to compensate the consumer for the damage suffered with an 'appropriate payment'. However, beyond establishing the entitlement to receive compensation, s. 46 does not specify how the appropriateness of that payment is to be determined. It is possible to approach this as akin to the way damages from consequential loss arising from a breach of contract would be calculated at common law. Digital content which causes damage to a device or other digital content would almost certainly not be in conformity with the contract in any event, giving rise to an entitlement to damages at common law. However, the common law right to damages is restricted by a remoteness test and the consumer's duty of mitigation. However, as the common law right to claim damages would be available in any event, the purpose of s. 46 might be a different one, and could be interpreted as permitting a claim for compensation without having to apply a remoteness test. The absence of a foreseeability requirement in s. 46 CRA lends further support to this view. However, it cannot be that there is an unrestricted entitlement to compensation for all losses.

Section 46 CRA is expressed in broad terms as covering damage to other digital content or hardware. It is not clear if this would include any losses to the consumer directly resulting from this damage. For example, would it cover data lost from the consumer's computer as a result of the damage caused? Also, would the entitlement to compensation be subject to limitations (e.g., on the basis of contributory negligence) matter where a consumer has failed to keep secure back-up copies of such data? It seems unlikely that Parliament would have intended a broad approach to recoverable losses here without any kind of restriction, but without any case-law on this to date, it is difficult to say which losses would be within the scope of s. 46.

Finally, two procedural points are included in s. 46. First, s. 46(7) states that a consumer can bring an action to enforce the rights under this section in civil proceedings. Secondly, s. 46(8) CRA specifies that the limitation period is the same as for an action based on a breach of contract.

[134] See Beale, Conclusion and performance of contracts: An overview, in Schulze, Staudenmeyer and Lohse (eds.) *Contracts for the Supply of Digital Content: Regulatory Challenges and Gaps* (Nomos, 2017), pp. 48–9.
[135] s. 46(3)/(4) CRA.

19.9 Exclusion of liability

19.9.1 Controls over specific terms seeking to exclude/limit liability

The adoption of the Consumer Rights Act meant that the provisions in the Unfair Contract Terms Act 1977, which previously dealt with the exclusion of the implied terms and the associated remedies in consumer cases, ceased to have effect. For contracts involving the supply of goods, the relevant provision is found in s. 31 of the Consumer Rights Act (rather than in Part 2 of the Act, which deals with unfair terms generally). According to s. 31(1), a contract term which would exclude or restrict the trader's liability arising under ss. 9–17 and ss. 28–29 is not binding on a consumer. By virtue of s. 31(2), any term of a contract which would exclude or restrict a right or remedy in respect of liability under those sections, or make it more difficult to enforce such a right, will also not be binding on a consumer. The same applies in respect of a term which would allow a trader to put a person at a disadvantage for pursuing such a right or remedy, as well as a term excluding or restricting rules of evidence. The upshot is that the rights of a consumer under the Consumer Rights Act are mandatory and therefore non-excludable, and that any attempt to do so will be ineffective. In essence, this means that – as was already the case under UCTA – any exclusion or limitation clause in respect of the supply of goods is blacklisted by the Consumer Rights Act.

With regard to digital content, the same approach is taken for the trader's liability arising under ss. 34–37 and 41, which is non-excludable in the circumstances set out above.[136]

In contracts for the supply of goods, limitation or exclusion of liability under any other contract term is subject the provisions of Part II of the Consumer Rights Act 2015. This is also the case for any exclusion or limitation of the trader's liability for damage caused by digital content to the consumer's device or other digital content under s. 46.[135]

19.9.2 General control over contract terms

All terms in a contract between a trader and a consumer are subject to the unfair terms control in Part 2 of the Consumer Rights Act. This part is an amalgam (and re-working) of the provisions on consumer contracts previously found in the Unfair Terms in Consumer Contracts Regulations 1999 and the Unfair Contract Terms Act 1977, and reflects proposals made in two Law Commission reports.[136] One significant aspect of this consolidation is that the controls over unfair terms in the Consumer Rights Act now extend to all contract terms – the 1999 Regulations applied only to terms which had not been individually negotiated.

[136] s. 47 CRA.
[137] s. 47(6) CRA.
[138] Law Commission, *Unfair Terms in Contracts* (2005) Report No 292/Scottish Law Commission Report No 199; Law Commissions, *Unfair Terms in Consumer Contracts: Advice to the Department for Business, Innovation and Skills* (2013).

There are some limitations to this though. Most significantly, s. 64(1) provides that:

> A term of a consumer contract may not be assessed for fairness under section 62 to the extent that—
>
> (a) it specifies the main subject matter of the contract, or
> (b) the assessment is of the appropriateness of the price payable under the contract by comparison with the goods, digital content or services supplied under it.[139]

The unfairness test in section 62(4) states that a

> A term is unfair if, contrary to the requirement of good faith, it causes a significant imbalance in the parties' rights and obligations under the contract to the detriment of the consumer.

In applying this test, the nature of the subject-matter of the contract needs to be taken into account, and reference is to be had to all the circumstances existing when the term was agreed and to all the other terms of the contract (or any other contract on which it depends).[140] A term found to be unfair under this test is not binding on the consumer,[141] although the consumer can choose to rely on the term even though it is unfair.[142]

The application of the fairness test has given rise to some case law, and domestic courts have taken into account key decisions of the Court of Justice of the European Union (CJEU).[143] A detailed discussion of this case law is not needed for present purposes, but a few observations are appropriate. In the important decision in *Director-General of Fair Trading* v *First National Bank*,[144] the House of Lords had to consider whether a term in a standard-form consumer credit agreement, requiring the borrower to pay interest after judgment at the contract rate, was fair under the Unfair Terms in Consumer Contracts Regulations 1994 (another precursor of the current Part 2). It concluded that it was. Lord Bingham observed:

> A term falling within the scope of the regulations is unfair if it causes a significant imbalance in the parties' rights and obligations under the contract to the detriment of the consumer in a manner or to an extent which is contrary to the requirement of good faith. The requirement of significant imbalance is met if a term is so weighted in favour of the supplier as to tilt the parties' rights and obligations under the contract significantly in his favour.[145]

He considered that substantive unfairness was complemented by the requirement of good faith, which was evidenced by fair and open dealing. Openness required that the terms should be expressed fully, clearly and legibly, containing no pitfalls or traps, with prominence being given to terms which might operate disadvantageously to the consumer.

[139] This is subject to the requirement that such a term is transparent (expressed in plain and intelligible language and legible (if in writing)) and prominent (brought to the consumer's attention in such a way that the average consumer would be aware of the term: see s. 64(2)–(5) CRA. This might mean a different outcome now in a case like *Office of Fair Trading* v *Abbey National plc* [2009] UKSC 6, [2010] 1 AC [696.

[140] s. 62(5) CRA.

[141] s. 62(1) CRA.

[142] s. 62(3) CRA.

[143] In *Eternity Sky Investments Ltd* v *Xiaomin Zhang* [2024] EWCA Civ 630, the Court of Appeal referred to CJEU case-law without discussing its continued relevance (although the contract in question was concluded in 2016, when CJEU case-law was still binding on the UK courts).

[144] [2001] UKHL 52.

[145] Ibid., at para. 17.

Fair dealing required that the supplier should not, whether deliberately or unconsciously, take advantage of the consumer's necessity, indigence, lack of experience, unfamiliarity with the subject-matter of the contract, weak bargaining position, or any other factor listed in, or analogous to, those listed in Sched. 3 to the then Regulations. Although the *First National* case did not concern a sale of goods transaction and it concerned the predecessor of what is now Part 2 of the Consumer Rights Act, it provides useful guidance as to the way in which the application of fairness test is to be approached.

Further guidance may be derived from a number of rulings by the CJEU, notwithstanding that such case law is no longer binding on the courts (but it continues as assimilated case 74 law unless it is overruled). An early ruling was *Freiburger Kommunalbauten*,[146] where the CJEU made it clear that applying the fairness test requires that it is necessary to consider the consequences of the term under challenge within the context of the applicable national law, that is, how does the term alter the consumer's legal rights that would otherwise be applicable? This was further emphasised in *Banco Espanol SA* v *Maria Teodolinda Rivas Quichimbo*,[147] where it was held that determining whether a term causes a significant imbalance to the consumer's detriment necessitates that a court considers the rules of national law that would apply in the absence of that term and how the term alters this. It would be contrary to good faith if a trader, dealing fairly and equitably with a consumer, could not reasonably assume that the consumer would have agreed to term had it been individually negotiated.[148] Finally, in *Constructora Principado SA* v *José Ignacio Menéndez Álvarez*,[149] the CJEU held that the 'significant imbalance' element did not mean that there would have to be a significant economic impact compared to the value of the transaction; rather, it was enough that there consumer's position under national law was impaired to a sufficiently serious degree. This would be the case if the trader's contract terms restricted the rights, or constrained their exercise, or imposed additional obligations on the consumer not ordinarily to be expected, or generally imposed on the trader, by national law.

The leading case in domestic law is the ruling in *ParkingEye Ltd* v *Beavis*.[150] The case itself concerned the fairness of a term in a contract for parking which offered a free period of two hours, followed by a significant fee if the consumer stayed longer. In deciding on the fairness of the term, the Supreme Court adopted the CJEU's interpretation in *Aziz*[151] and held that the 'significant imbalance' element involves enquiry into whether the position of the consumer under the contract is worsened compared to the position in law without the relevant term. The 'good faith' element requires to ask whether a trader dealing fairly and equitably with the consumer could reasonably assume that the consumer would have agreed to the term had it been agreed through individual contract negotiations.

This approach will work well as long as the terms in question are in a standard form contract (which will be the vast majority of consumer contracts), but it will not be easy to

[146] C-237/02 *Freiburger Kommunalbauten GmbH Baugesellschaft & Co. KG* v *Ludger Hofstetter and Ulrike Hofstetter* [2004] ECR I-3403.

[147] C-537/12 & C-116/13 *Banco Popular Español SA* v *Maria Teodolinda Rivas Quichimbo* ECLI:EU:C:2013:759.

[148] The Directive does not apply to individually negotiated terms, unlike Part 2 of the Consumer Rights Act.

[149] C-226/12 *Constructora Principado SA* v *José Ignacio Menéndez Álvarez* ECLI:EU:C:2014:10.

[150] [2015] UKSC 67.

[151] Case C-415/11 *Aziz* v *Caixa d'Estalvis de Catalunya, Tarragona i Manresa* ECLI:EU:C:2013:164.

apply to a contract term which *has* been individually negotiated. As such terms are within the scope of Part 2 CRA, a different test interpretation of the 'good faith' criterion will be needed; otherwise, any individually negotiated term would by definition not violate the good faith requirement in section 62(4).

In many cases, the term under challenge will be similar to a term included in the indicative list of unfair terms found in Schedule 2 of the Consumer Rights Act. This is a 'grey list' of unfair terms, which means that a term which corresponds with one of the terms in the Schedule may be regarded to be unfair, which effectively creates a presumption of unfairness. However, it will depend on the circumstances of the particular contract as to whether the term is actually unfair – it is possible that a term in the indicative list may nevertheless pass assessment under s. 62(4).

In addition to the fairness test, written terms of a consumer contract must be transparent, which means that they must be plain and intelligible, and legible.[152] According to the CJEU, this requirement has to be understood in a broad sense and is not limited to considering whether a term is 'formally and grammatically intelligible';[153] rather, a consumer must be able to evaluate, on the basis of clear intelligible criteria, the economic consequences resulting from the term.[154] Moreover, if a term is ambiguous, the meaning which is most favourable to the consumer prevails.[155]

19.10 Other rules applicable to consumer sales contracts

Thus far, this chapter has focused on the provisions in the Consumer Rights Act 2015 as they pertain to contracts for the sale and supply of goods. It is necessary to mention a number of other measures of consumer law which are of some relevance to consumer sales contracts, although these provisions are of wider application. Of particular relevance here are the Consumer Contracts (Information, Cancellation and Additional Charges) Regulations 2013,[156] and the Consumer Rights (Payment Surcharges) Regulations 2012.[157]

19.10.1 Consumer Contracts (Information, Cancellation and Additional Charges) Regulations 2013

The Consumer Contracts (Information, Cancellation and Additional Charges) Regulations 2013 ('CCR') primarily deal with pre-contractual information duties and the right of cancellation in off-premises and distance contracts. An off-premises contract is defined as

> a contract between a trader and a consumer which is any of these—
>
> (a) a contract concluded in the simultaneous physical presence of the trader and the consumer, in a place which is not the business premises of the trader;
>
> (b) a contract for which an offer was made by the consumer in the simultaneous physical presence of the trader and the consumer, in a place which is not the business premises of the trader;

[152] s. 68 CRA.
[153] C-26/13 *Árpád Kásler, Hajnalka Káslerné Rábai* v *OTP Jelzálogbank Zrt* ECLI:EU:C:2014:282, para.[71].
[154] Ibid., para.[73].
[155] s. 69 CRA.
[156] S.I. 2013/3134.
[157] S.I. 2012/3110.

(c) a contract concluded on the business premises of the trader or through any means of distance communication immediately after the consumer was personally and individually addressed in a place which is not the business premises of the trader in the simultaneous physical presence of the trader and the consumer;
(d) a contract concluded during an excursion organised by the trader with the aim or effect of promoting and selling goods or services to the consumer.*

And a distance contract is

> a contract concluded between a trader and a consumer under an organised distance sales or service-provision scheme without the simultaneous physical presence of the trader and the consumer, with the exclusive use of one or more means of distance communication up to and including the time at which the contract is concluded.[158]

Most of the CCR deal with rules on either off-premises or distance contracts, although there are a few provisions on on-premises contracts (i.e. contracts which are neither off-premises or distance contracts). There are various types of contract which are excluded from the scope of the CCR,[159] but as the present focus is on contracts for the sale and supply of goods only (rather than a full account of the CCR), it is not necessary to consider these exclusions here.

19.10.1.1 Pre-contractual information in on-premises contracts

Although much of the CCR are concerned with off-premises and distance contracts, there is a limited requirement to provide information before an on-premises contract is concluded. This obligation does not arise in respect of day-to-day transactions which are performed immediately at the time the contract is entered into.[160] Reg. 9(1) requires that prior to the conclusion of an on-premises contract the trader must give or make available to the consumer a number of items of information insofar as this information is not already apparent from the context. Any information thus given is treated as a term of the contract,[161] and any change of that information is not effective unless expressly agreed between consumer and trader. The information to be given is:

(a) the main characteristics of the goods or services, to the extent appropriate to the medium of communication and to the goods or services;
(b) the identity of the trader (such as the trader's trading name), the geographical address at which the trader is established and the trader's telephone number;
(c) the total price of the goods or services inclusive of taxes, or where the nature of the goods or services is such that the price cannot reasonably be calculated in advance, the manner in which the price is to be calculated;
(d) where applicable, all additional delivery charges or, where those charges cannot reasonably be calculated in advance, the fact that such additional charges may be payable;
(e) where applicable, the arrangements for payment, delivery, performance, and the time by which the trader undertakes to deliver the goods or to perform the service;
(f) where applicable, the trader's complaint handling policy;

[158] Ibid.
[159] See, e.g., Reg. 7 CCR.
[160] Reg. 9(2) CCR.
[161] s. 11(4) and s. 12 of the Consumer Rights Act, discussed above.

(g) in the case of a sales contract, a reminder that the trader is under a legal duty to supply goods that are in conformity with the contract;
(h) where applicable, the existence and the conditions of after-sales services and commercial guarantees;
(i) the duration of the contract, where applicable, or, if the contract is of indeterminate duration or is to be extended automatically, the conditions for terminating the contract;
(j) where applicable, the functionality, including applicable technical protection measures, of digital content;
(k) where applicable, any relevant compatibility of digital content with hardware and software that the trader is aware of or can reasonably be expected to have been aware of.

As can be seen, some of this information is particularly relevant to sales contracts ((a)–(e), and (g)–(h)), or contracts for the supply of digital content ((j)–(k)).

19.10.1.2 Pre-contractual information for distance/off-premises contracts

A similar approach to the provision of pre-contractual information is taken in respect of off-premises[162] and distance[163] contracts, although here the list of items of information a trader might have to supply is considerably longer. Again, this information is treated as included as terms of the contract. The items of information are:

(a) the main characteristics of the goods or services, to the extent appropriate to the medium of communication and to the goods or services;
(b) the identity of the trader (such as the trader's trading name);
(c) the geographical address at which the trader is established and, where available, the trader's telephone number, fax number and e-mail address, to enable the consumer to contact the trader quickly and communicate efficiently;
(d) where the trader is acting on behalf of another trader, the geographical address and identity of that other trader;
(e) if different from the address provided in accordance with paragraph (c), the geographical address of the place of business of the trader, and, where the trader acts on behalf of another trader, the geographical address of the place of business of that other trader, where the consumer can address any complaints;
(f) the total price of the goods or services inclusive of taxes, or where the nature of the goods or services is such that the price cannot reasonably be calculated in advance, the manner in which the price is to be calculated,
(g) where applicable, all additional delivery charges and any other costs or, where those charges cannot reasonably be calculated in advance, the fact that such additional charges may be payable;
(h) in the case of a contract of indeterminate duration or a contract containing a subscription, the total costs per billing period or (where such contracts are charged at a fixed rate) the total monthly costs;
(i) the cost of using the means of distance communication for the conclusion of the contract where that cost is calculated other than at the basic rate;
(j) the arrangements for payment, delivery, performance, and the time by which the trader undertakes to deliver the goods or to perform the services;
(k) where applicable, the trader's complaint handling policy;

[162] See Reg. 10 CCR.
[163] See Reg. 13 CCR.

(l) where a right to cancel exists, the conditions, time limit and procedures for exercising that right in accordance with regulations 27 to 38;
(m) where applicable, that the consumer will have to bear the cost of returning the goods in case of cancellation and, for distance contracts, if the goods, by their nature, cannot normally be returned by post, the cost of returning the goods;
(n) that, if the consumer exercises the right to cancel after having made a request in accordance with regulation 36(1), the consumer is to be liable to pay the trader reasonable costs in accordance with regulation 36(4);
(o) where under regulation 28, 36 or 37 there is no right to cancel or the right to cancel may be lost, the information that the consumer will not benefit from a right to cancel, or the circumstances under which the consumer loses the right to cancel;
(p) in the case of a sales contract, a reminder that the trader is under a legal duty to supply goods that are in conformity with the contract;
(q) where applicable, the existence and the conditions of after-sale customer assistance, after-sales services and commercial guarantees;
(r) the existence of relevant codes of conduct, as defined in regulation 5(3)(b) of the Consumer Protection from Unfair Trading Regulations 2008, and how copies of them can be obtained, where applicable;
(s) the duration of the contract, where applicable, or, if the contract is of indeterminate duration or is to be extended automatically, the conditions for terminating the contract;
(t) where applicable, the minimum duration of the consumer's obligations under the contract;
(u) where applicable, the existence and the conditions of deposits or other financial guarantees to be paid or provided by the consumer at the request of the trader;
(v) where applicable, the functionality, including applicable technical protection measures, of digital content;
(w) where applicable, any relevant compatibility of digital content with hardware and software that the trader is aware of or can reasonably be expected to have been aware of;
(x) where applicable, the possibility of having recourse to an out-of-court complaint and redress mechanism, to which the trader is subject, and the methods for having access to it.

Note: In the case of a public auction, the information listed in paragraphs (b) to (e) may be replaced with the equivalent details for the auctioneer.

For off-premises contracts, this information must be given on paper or another durable medium (if the consumer agrees), and it must be legible.[164] A trader who fails to give the information required by (g), (h) or (m) above cannot impose those costs or charges on the consumer.[165] Also, for paragraphs (l), (m) and (n), a template is provided in Schedule 3 to the CCR. In addition, Reg. 12 CCR requires that the trader gives the consumer either a copy of the signed contract, or a confirmation of the contract, which has to include all the relevant information (if not already provided on a durable medium before conclusion of the contract), and must either be on paper or on another durable medium.[166]

In a distance contract, this information has to be given in way appropriate to the medium of distance communication used. If such a means of communications only allows limited space or time to display the information then as a minimum, items (a), (b), (f), (g), (h), (l) and (s) have to be given, with the remainder provided in another appropriate way.

[164] Reg. 10(2) CCR.
[165] Reg. 10(4) CCR.
[166] There are special provisions on repair and maintenance contracts in Regulation 11 CCR.

The same rules in respect of charges and costs, and information about cancellation rights mentioned above, also apply to distance contracts.[167] Moreover, the trader must provide the consumer with a confirmation of the contract, which includes all the required information on a durable medium no later than the time of delivery of the goods.[168]

There are special requirements for distance contracts concluded by electronic means (e.g. online via a website), if the contract places the consumer under an obligation to pay (which would seem to be the case with most consumer contracts). Immediately before placing an order, the consumer has to be made aware of items (a), (f), (g), (h), (s) and (t) in a clear and prominent manner.

When placing the order, the consumer must explicitly acknowledge that this implies an obligation to pay, and where placing the order involves clicking on an online button, this has to be labelled such as to make it clear that the consumer will be under an obligation to pay. If the trader does not comply with this the consumer is not bound by the contract.[169]

Even from this brief overview, it can be seen clearly that the requirement for a trader to provide information to a consumer before a contract is concluded has become a very detailed and technical (some might say overly technical) process. Whether this really benefits consumers continues to be a matter of some controversy.

19.10.1.3 Right of cancellation in off-premises and distance contracts

A second major feature of the CCR is the provision of a right of cancellation in respect of distance and off-premises contracts. However, this right is not available in respect of all contracts. Among the contracts for which this right is not available are contracts for:[170]

- the supply of goods for which the price is dependent on fluctuations in the financial market which cannot be controlled by the trader and which may occur within the cancellation period;
- the supply of goods that are made to the consumer's specifications or are clearly personalised;
- the supply of goods which are liable to deteriorate or expire rapidly;
- the supply of alcoholic beverages, where—
  (i) their price has been agreed at the time of the conclusion of the sales contract,
  (ii) delivery of them can only take place after 30 days, and
  (iii) their value is dependent on fluctuations in the market which cannot be controlled by the trader;
- concluded at a public auction.

In addition, even where a right to cancel is available, this is lost where,

(a) in the case of a contract for the supply of sealed goods which are not suitable for return due to health protection or hygiene reasons, if they become unsealed after delivery;

[167] See Regs. 13 (3) and (5) CCR.
[168] Reg. 16(1) and (4)(a) CCR.
[169] Regs. 14(3)-(5) CCR.
[170] See Reg. 28(1) CCR for the full list.

(b) in the case of a contract for the supply of sealed audio or sealed video recordings or sealed computer software, if the goods become unsealed after delivery;
(c) in the case of any sales contract, if the goods become mixed inseparably (according to their nature) with other items after delivery.[171]

The general right to cancel a distance or off-premises contracts is provided in Reg. 29(1) CCR. The consumer can exercise this right at any time during the cancellation period and does not have to give any reason. The right to cancel a contract therefore does not depend on there being a fault with the goods acquired – the consumer is free simply to change his mind.[172]

The cancellation period lasts for 14 days,[173] but it is calculated differently depending on the type of contract. Thus, for a contract for the supply of digital content, the period ends 14 days after the day on which the contract was entered into.[174] For a contract for the sale of goods it will be 14 days after the day on which the goods were delivered,[175] with special provision for goods comprising multiple orders (14 days from the date on which the last item was delivered),[176] orders consisting of multiple lots or pieces delivered on different days (also 14 days from the date on which the last item was delivered),[177] and orders where goods are delivered regularly on a recurring basis (14 days from the date on which the *first* item was delivered).[178]

In order to exercise the right to cancel, the consumer must notify the trader,[179] which can be done by completing a model cancellation form or any other clear statement to the same effect. The trader may also make available an online cancellation form on the trader's website, which the consumer can use, but is not required to use.[180]

Following cancellation the obligations of the parties to perform the contract is brought to an end.[181] The trader is required to reimburse all payments made by the consumer,[182] and has to do so within 14 days.[183] However, with regard to delivery charges, the trader only has to reimburse the equivalent of the least expensive method offered by the trader,[184] so if the consumer chooses a more expensive method (e.g. next-day courier delivery), the consumer cannot recover the additional cost of this delivery service. Also, if the consumer has handled the goods 'beyond what is necessary to establish the nature, characteristics and functioning of the goods',[185] which has resulted in the value of the goods diminishing,

[171] Reg. 28(3) CCR.
[172] It is important to appreciate that this right only exists for off-premises and distance contracts, but not for on-premises contracts (contrary to what some consumers think to be the case). Often, stores will operate a voluntary no-quibble returns policy, but these are not a legal requirement.
[173] Although under Reg. 31 CCR, this period is extended where the trader has failed to provide the consumer with the relevant information about the existence of the right of cancellation.
[174] Reg. 30(2)(b) CCR.
[175] Reg. 30(3) CCR.
[176] Reg. 30(4) CCR.
[177] Reg. 30(5) CCR.
[178] Reg. 30(6) CCR.
[179] Reg. 32(2) CCR.
[180] Reg. 32(4) CCR.
[181] Reg. 33(1) CCR.
[182] Reg. 34(1) CCR.
[183] See Regs. 34(4)–(6) CCR.
[184] Reg. 34(2) CCR.
[185] Reg. 34(9) CCR.

then the trader is entitled to make a deduction from the sums he would otherwise be required to refund. So if a consumer has bought clothing and instead of just trying it on at home to see if it fits, wears it on a night out during which it is stained by food, the consumer will not be entitled to a full refund.

As far as returning the goods is concerned, Reg. 35 contains a number of rules. It is the trader's responsibility to collect them where he has offered to do so, or where, under an off-premises contract, goods were delivered to the consumer's home but they cannot be returned by post due to the nature of the goods (e.g., bulky or heavy items). Otherwise, the consumer may be required to send back the goods to the trader, or hand them over to the trader (or a person authorised by the trader). The consumer is required to bear the costs associated with returning the goods, unless the trader has agreed to do so, or the trader has failed to inform the consumer that the consumer has to bear those costs (cf. item (m), above).

In the case of digital content, the general position under Reg. 37 CCR is that the trader should not supply digital content until the end of the cancellation period. However, if the consumer expressly consents to supply before then and acknowledges that this will mean the right of cancellation is lost, then the trader can supply the digital content sooner.

19.10.1.4 Other rights

Although the CCR primarily deal with pre-contractual information and the right of cancellation, the several other rights relevant to consumer sales contracts are provided. Thus, it is made clear that any additional payments which may be payable in addition to the price for the main obligation need to be expressly consented to by the consumer, and the use of pre-selected options (e.g. 'pre-ticked boxes' on a website) is no longer permitted.[186] So, for example, it would no longer be permitted to pre-select an extended warranty for goods purchased on-line and to require the consumer to deselect that option. Any additional charges to which the consumer has not expressly consented but which have been paid must be refunded.[187] Somewhat strangely, this is done by treating the contract as including a term to that effect, with the consequence that not refunding such charges would be a breach of that term. This might impose the onus on the consumer to act swiftly so as to avoid the risk of having waived the right to receive a refund by delaying steps to enforce that term.

A further provision deals with 'helpline charges', and requires a trader to charge no more than the basic call rate for telephone calls to contact the trader.[188]

Finally, the Consumer Rights (Payment Surcharges) Regulations[189] provide that a consumer who uses a certain payment type, such as a credit card or debit card, cannot be

[186] Reg. 40 CCR.
[187] Reg. 40(4) CCR.
[188] Reg. 41 CCR.
[189] Consumer Rights (Payment Surcharges) Regulations 2012 S.I. 2012/3110.

charged a fee for using this payment method which exceeds the cost to the trader of the consumer choosing to use a particular payment method.

19.10.2 Consumer protection from unfair trading

Finally, the Prior to the changes which resulted in the Consumer Rights Act 2015 and the Consumer Contracts Regulations 2013, consumer law had already been significantly overhauled by the introduction of the Consumer Protection from Unfair Trading Regulations 2008 (CPUTR).[190] These regulations established a broad framework within which to control the manner in which traders deal with consumers both before a contract is made as well as during its performance and beyond. The CPUTR were not limited to consumer sales contracts, but dealt with most transactions consumers might enter into. Until 2014, the CPUTR were only enforced by public bodies (both local Weights and Measures Authorities (often known as Trading Standards Departments) and the Competition and Markets Authority, and the enforcement tools ranged from undertakings, to injunctions to prohibit specific violations of the CPUTR, to enforcement by means of criminal penalties. A detailed discussion of all this is beyond the scope of this book. However, in 2014 the CPUTR were amended to provide consumers with a private right of redress in respect of certain infringements of the regulations, so a brief explanation is appropriate here. The CPUTR were replaced by chapter 1 of Part of the Digital Markets, Competition and Consumers Act 2024 from April 2025; the new provisions are given alongside the provisions from the CPUTR in the discussion below.

19.10.2.1 Regulating commercial practices

The CPUTR deal with 'commercial practices', which are defined as 'any act, omission, course of conduct, representation or commercial communication (including advertising and marketing) by a trader, which is directly connected with the promotion, sale or supply of a product to or from consumers, whether occurring before, during or after a commercial transaction (if any) in relation to a product'.[191] It is clear from this definition that it is a very wide-ranging concept, and effectively almost anything a trader does vis-à-vis a consumer is caught by this definition. In many cases, the focus will be on how goods or services ('products') are marketed to consumers, and it is not necessary that a consumer enters into a contract for the regulations to apply.

Regulation 3(1) (and s.225(1) DMCCA) states in clear terms that 'unfair commercial practices are prohibited', and the remainder of Reg. 3/s.225 DMCCA goes on to set out

[190] S.I. 2008/1277.

[191] Reg. 2(1) CPUTR. Section 225 DMCCA changes this to 'an act or omission by a trader relating to the promotion or supply of (a) the trader's product to a consumer, (b) another trader's product to a consumer, or (c) a consumer's product to the trader or another person'.

the general test for establishing whether a commercial practice is unfair. However, the test itself is not going to be deployed too frequently, as in addition to this general prohibition there are more detailed prohibitions of misleading actions, misleading omissions, and aggressive commercial practices.[192] A particular commercial practice can thus be assessed for its fairness both under these specific provisions and the general test, although in most cases the unfairness will be the result of a consumer either being misled or having been subject to pressure selling (aggressive commercial practice). However, it is also recognised that some types of behaviour should be prohibited outright, and so Schedule 1 to the CPUTR (and Schedule 20 DMCCA) contains a list of commercial practices which are always regarded as unfair (thereby creating *de facto* prohibitions).

19.10.2.2 Private redress

As noted, the CPUTR did not grant individual consumers new rights when they were first enacted, not least because this was not required by the UCPD. However, the Law Commissions were asked to consider whether it would be appropriate to give individual consumers a private right of redress,[193] and its recommendations were enacted through the Consumer Protection (Amendment) Regulations 2014.[194] The effect of these changes was to make available a private right of redress in a narrow range of circumstances, and the following three conditions had to be met:[195]

(1) It applies to three situations: (i) a contract with a trader for the sale or supply to the consumer of a product, (ii) a contract with a trader under which the consumer sells goods to the trader; or (iii) where the consumer makes a payment to a trader for the supply of a product.
(2) The trader engages in a misleading action (under Regulation 5) or an aggressive practice (under Regulation 7).
(3) The misleading action or aggressive practice must have been a significant factor in the consumer's decision to enter into the contract.

So, importantly, the misleading action or aggressive commercial practice must have caused the consumer to enter into a contract – it did not seem to apply where such matters occur during the performance of the contract, or when trying to terminate it.

A consumer had the 'right to unwind' the contract (which right lasts for 90 days if the contract falls within situation (i),[196] and without restriction in situation (ii)),[197] which meant that the contract was brought to an end. A consumer who had made a payment

[192] Regs. 5–7 CPUTR; sections 226-230 DMCCA.
[193] Law Commission, *Report 332*/Scottish Law Commission, Report No 226 – *Consumer Redress for Misleading and Aggressive Practices* (London: TSO, 2012)).
[194] S.I. 2014/870.
[195] See new Reg. 27A CPUTR.
[196] Reg. 27E CPUTR.
[197] Reg. 27G CPUTR.

(situation (iii)) which the consumer was not required to make (in part or full) then the consumer was entitled to receive a refund of that payment.[198]

A consumer who did not exercise the right to unwind could instead have claimed the right to a discount[199] on any sums paid (or which are payable). The discount was measured based on the seriousness of the prohibited practice as follows:[200]

(a) if the prohibited practice is more than minor, it was 25%,
(b) if the prohibited practice is significant, it was 50%,
(c) if the prohibited practice is serious, it was 75%, and
(d) if the prohibited practice is very serious, it was 100%.

In order to establish this seriousness, it was necessary to consider the behaviour of the person engaging in the practice, its impact on the consumer and how much time has passed since it took place (although note the derogation in Reg. 27I(6)/(7)).

Finally, a consumer had a right to claim damages under Reg. 27J if the consumer:

(a) has incurred financial loss which the consumer would not have incurred if the prohibited practice in question had not taken place, or
(b) has suffered alarm, distress or physical inconvenience or discomfort which the consumer would not have suffered if the prohibited practice in question had not taken place.

Damages are to cover that loss or the alarm, distress or physical inconvenience or discomfort in question.

There has been limited evidence of the extent to which these rights have been exercised and effective in practice. The scheme in these provisions seemed rather complicated, and would almost certainly have required the assistance of a court to apply sensibly (particularly with regard to the right to claim a discount and any damages claims). Following these changes, a consumer no longer had the right to claim damages for misrepresentation under s. 2 of the Misrepresentation Act 1967 (in England & Wales)[201] or s. 10 of the Law Reform (Miscellaneous Provisions) (Scotland) Act 1985 (in Scotland).

The DMCCA has not simply re-enacted the provisions as they were. Instead, s. 232 DMCCA provides that a consumer has a right of redress in the circumstances previously required for the application of Part 4A CPUTR. Section 233 DMCCA requires that secondary legislation will be required to provide specific remedies; s. 233(1) refers to the same remedies previously included in Part 4A. Whether such secondary legislation will simply replicate the regime from Part 4A, or take a different approach, has yet to be confirmed at the time of preparing this edition.

[198] Reg. 27I CPUTR.
[199] Reg. 27I CPUTR.
[200] Reg. 27I(4) CPUTR.
[201] See new ss. 2(4) of the Misrepresentation Act 1967.

19.10.3 Additional protection under s. 75 of the Consumer Credit Act 1974

For many consumer sales contracts, a credit card is the main method of payment (whether over the internet or instore). For UK buyers this leads to a useful source of redress against the credit card company where the goods supplied are defective. The key provision is s. 75(1). This provides:

> If the debtor under a debtor-creditor-supplier agreement falling within section 12(b) or (c) has, in relation to a transaction financed by the agreement, any claim against the supplier in respect of a misrepresentation or breach of contract, he shall have a like claim against the creditor, who, with the supplier, shall accordingly be jointly and severally liable to the debtor.

Section 75(3) provides:

> Subsection (1) above does not apply to a claim –
>
> (a) under a non-commercial agreement, or
> (b) so far as the claim relates to any single item to which the supplier has attached a cash price not exceeding [£100] or more than [£30,000].

The upper limit was included because it was felt that purchasers of goods as costly as this did not need the protection of this section. The reason for inserting the lower of these limits was to exclude common cases where the card is simply used as a substitute for cash. Unfortunately, the effect of this is to exclude from s. 75 transactions for goods costing less than £100.

Sections 12(b) and (c) respectively define 'debtor-creditor-supplier agreements' which are 'restricted' and 'unrestricted-use' credit agreements. The exact details of these definitions do not concern us here. The key to them is the definition of 'consumer credit agreement'. Under s. 8(2) this is:

> . . . a personal credit agreement by which the creditor provides the debtor with credit not exceeding [£25,000][202]

Since almost all transactions involving consumers will fall within the upper financial limit, provided the lower financial limit is exceeded, most potentially fall within s. 75(1). Where the seller is within the UK or outside the UK but within a member state of the EEA, the consumer will have the remedies against the seller set out above and in other sections of this book cross-referred to, and, in consequence, will potentially have a remedy against the credit card company under s. 75(1).[203] However, two restrictions on this need to be noted. First of all, some cards which in popular parlance are referred to as credit cards are not credit cards for the purposes of the Act. Whilst Visa and MasterCard offer the option of paying off the monthly debt in full, or partially, and are therefore true credit cards, American Express and Diners Club do not offer this option and require the monthly

[202] As amended by SI 1998/996. As noted above, s. 75(3)(a) further limits its application by requiring the value of the goods to exceed £100 and not to exceed £30,000.

[203] See, e.g., *Office of Fair Trading* v *Lloyds TSB Bank plc* [2007] UKHL 48, [2008] 1 AC 316; *Durkin* v *DSG Retail Ltd* [2014] UKSC 21, 2014 SC (UKSC) 139, [2014] 1 WLR 1148.

debt to be paid off in full. Therefore, they are not credit cards within the meaning of the Act, and are not, therefore, subject to s. 75. On the other hand, the credit limits imposed by both Visa and MasterCard on individual cardholders mean that almost all agreements with these companies will be 'personal credit agreements' within the meaning of the Act.

Moreover, debit cards are also not covered by the s. 75 scheme. However, in the internal arrangements between card issuers (banks) and debit card scheme operators, there is a facility known as 'charge-back', which effectively allows the issuer of a debit card who has refunded a consumer in circumstances similar to s. 75 to reclaim this through the contractual arrangements within the debit-card system. In many cases, this will provide consumers with protection comparable to that offered by s. 75, although this system is not a legal requirement and so this protection is not on particularly solid foundations.[204]

[204] For a useful explanation of this system, see Law Commission, *Consumer Prepayments on Retailer Insolvency*, Report No. 368 (2016), chapter 7.

20

Product liability

The previous chapter considered the extensive changes made to the consumer law landscape through the Consumer Rights Act 2015 and related legislation. This chapter concentrates on an aspect of consumer protection which was in place before the recent reforms, and considers primarily the legal obligations a manufacturer of goods may have towards consumers.

20.1 Product liability at common law

In a claim by a buyer based on breach of the statutory requirements regarding quality and fitness of goods, it is unnecessary, as a rule, to distinguish between a claim for damages arising from defects *in the goods themselves*, and a claim for damages for damage *caused by the goods*; for example, personal injury caused by a dangerous electrical product or a defective car. In this chapter, however, we are concerned with possible complaints in respect of defective goods, arising outside the contract, which may be made *against third parties* (e.g. manufacturers) or which may be brought *by third parties* (e.g. non-buyer users of the goods). In dealing with claims of this nature, it is necessary to distinguish between claims in respect of damage caused by the goods, and claims in respect of defects in the goods themselves. In this and the next sections we are concerned with claims in respect of damage caused by the goods.

We have seen that, in general, a seller/trader who is sued under s. 14(2) or (3) of the Sale of Goods Act or s. 9 or s. 10 of the Consumer Rights Act is liable irrespective of all due care and skill on the part of the seller, and we have also referred to many cases which illustrate that the seller's strict liability extends to consequential loss caused by the defective goods and is not limited to losses arising under the contract itself. Thus, if the buyer suffers personal injury through the use of unsatisfactory goods, they can claim damages from the seller under statutory provisions, despite the fact that the seller has not been guilty of any negligence. In this respect, the buyer is in a privileged position compared to most persons who suffer personal injury. Normally, claims for damages for personal injury must be made in tort or delict and, generally speaking of course, such claims require proof of negligence on the part of the defendant.

20.1.1 Privity of contract: liability confined to the seller

But it will also be seen that the doctrine of privity of contract imposes serious limitations on this form of liability[1] now generally called 'product liability'. The buyer's remedy is only available against the actual seller. If the buyer wishes to sue the manufacturer they

[1] As to the effect of the Contracts (Rights of Third Parties) Act 1999 on this doctrine.

cannot *prima facie* invoke the strict liability involved in a breach of condition or warranty,[2] unless the manufacturer is also the immediate seller of the goods to the consumer. At common law, their principal possible sources of remedies against a manufacturer lay in negligence, showing breach of a collateral contract, or through third party proceedings. [3] However, alongside the common law position, Part I of the Consumer Protection Act 1987 deals with the liability of a producer for defective products resulting in injury or damage. Because the 1987 Act provides remedies *in addition to*, rather than in substitution of, those previously available, it is also appropriate to consider the position at common law.

20.1.2 Negligence or delict

In the famous case of *Donoghue* v *Stevenson*,[4] it was held that the pursuer, who had consumed part of the contents of a bottle of ginger beer which allegedly contained the remains of a decomposing snail, and who as a result suffered physical illness, might sue the manufacturer of the ginger beer, notwithstanding that the bottle had been bought for her at a café by a friend. It is beyond the scope of a work of this nature to deal in detail with the complexities of the tort or delict of negligence; however, its principal problems from the claimant's point of view must be noted.

In the first place, the claimant must establish negligence on the part of the manufacturer. The fact that it can be shown that a defect in the product was the cause of the injury will suffice to throw the onus onto the manufacturer to show that they exercised proper care, but they may be able to discharge that onus. In *Daniels* v *R W White & Sons and Tabard*,[5] the plaintiff's husband bought a bottle of lemonade manufactured by the first defendant from the second defendant's shop. The lemonade contained carbolic acid, and both were injured when they consumed some of it. The husband was able to recover against the shopkeeper for breach of the old merchantable quality warranty (now the satisfactory quality term), but the wife's remedy depended on proof of negligence on the part of the manufacturer, and it was held that the manufacturer had exercised reasonable care and accordingly was not liable in negligence.

The second limitation of the tort of negligence or delict is that in general it permits recovery only in respect of physical damage, not economic loss. The buyer of goods *may* have a claim in tort or delict for economic loss against the manufacturer for the defects *in the goods themselves* where there is some real proximity between the buyer and the manufacturer, but, for the reasons explained below, even this is doubtful. If the manufacturer, for instance, gives advice or information to the owner, it is possible that the owner may be able to establish liability under the *Hedley Byrne*[6] principle. And this also explains why, even on the restrictive view of the law adopted by the Canadian Supreme Court, and approved by the House of Lords in *D & F Estates* v *Church Commissioners*,[7] the plaintiffs

[2] The Contracts (Rights of Third Parties) Act 1999 does not alter this.

[3] And this was generally so even in a system which, like Scots law, recognises the enforceability of benefits arising under contracts for third parties (*jus quaesitum tertio*) if the contracting parties so intended.

[4] [1932] AC 562, 1932 SC (HL) 31. For a discussion of whether this famous case might have been dealt with as an instance of the Scots doctrine of *jus quaesitum tertio* (under which third parties may have rights under a contract between others) rather than negligence in delict, see McBryde, 2012 SLT (News) 45.

[5] [1938] 4 All ER 258.

[6] [1964] AC 465.

[7] [1988] 2 All ER 992.

succeeded in part in *Rivtow Marine* v *Washington Iron Works*.[8] If it is once held that a manufacturer of a product owes a duty to warn owners of any design defects that come to their attention after it has been put into circulation, it may be possible to claim damages on the basis, as in the latter case, that the warning was unreasonably delayed and thereby increased the damage. In the unreported case of *Walton* v *British Leyland*,[9] the rear wheel of a car manufactured by the defendants came off whilst the car was being driven, causing injury to the plaintiff. The cause of the accident was faulty design. The defendants had become aware of the problem because numerous incidents had been reported. They had failed, however, to mount a major recall campaign in case it damaged their sales. It was held that the defendants were liable in negligence for selling cars with a design fault, but it was also said obiter that the failure to recall itself amounted to negligence. A failure to warn can also itself amount to negligence.[10]

One case where a sufficient degree of proximity was established was *The Diamentis Pateras*,[11] where the defendants were manufacturers of ships' furnaces which were installed in the plaintiffs' ship. Defects in the furnaces led to their cracking and replacement at high cost, and Lawrence J would have been prepared to hold that the defendants owed a duty of care in these circumstances, but negligence was not established. It is, however, not clear whether the duty arose out of the advice given by the defendants or perhaps out of the need to replace the boilers to avoid danger.

Beyond this point, it is not possible to go very far. At one point in the evolution of the case law on the tort of negligence, it seemed that the decision of the House of Lords in *Junior Books Ltd* v *Veitchi Co Ltd*,[12] which followed *Anns* v *Merton London Borough Council*,[13] might have heralded a willingness to see a great expansion in the law on this point. In that case, the House upheld a claim for damages by the owner of a building against a subcontractor who had laid a floor so negligently that the work had to be redone. The owner had no direct contractual relationship with the subcontractor so the action had to be an action in delict (tort); furthermore, there was no suggestion that it was necessary to relay the floor in order to avoid danger to persons using the building. The claim thus seems to have been a claim to pure economic loss, and yet it was allowed by a majority of the House of Lords. However, the House of Lords changed course in the *D & F Estates* case, and in *Murphy* v *Brentwood Council*,[14] where Lord Brandon's dissent in *Junior Books* was largely endorsed. *Junior Books* is a case confined to its own facts: a high degree of proximity existed between the parties so as to justify the imposition of a duty of care. The owners, or their architects, had nominated the subcontractors, and thus the relationship between the parties, as the majority held, fell just short of a contractual relationship. It can be argued, therefore, that the case is really an application of

[8] [1974] SCR 1189.
[9] 1976 (unreported).
[10] See the unreported case of *Brocket* v *DSG Retail Ltd*, 26 February 2003.
[11] [1966] 1 Lloyd's Rep 179.
[12] [1983] 1 AC 520, 1982 SC (HL) 244. It is not clear from the Report why the pursuer chose to sue the subcontractor rather than the main contractor, but it appears that the reason for this course was that, before the defects in the floor became apparent, the owner had settled a large number of other claims against the main contractor in such terms as precluded all further action against him.
[13] [1978] AC 728.
[14] [1991] 1 AC 398.

the proximity principle established in *Hedley Byrne & Co* v *Heller & Partners Ltd*.[15] It is clear that a similar result will not be reached in future on such facts unless the relationship between the client and the subcontractor differs substantially from the ordinary commercial relationship between such parties.

Certainly, there is general agreement that the mere fact that a manufacturer has made a defective product which may cause economic loss to a buyer does not, by itself, render the manufacturer liable unless there is a close degree of proximity between the parties. Even in *Junior Books*, this does not seem to have been seriously doubted. But precisely what will be needed to establish the requisite degree of 'proximity' remains in some doubt.[16] If contract and tort/delict liability are getting closer in this area, as seems to be the case, it may well be that proximity will only be found when the facts are sufficient to establish a collateral contract, or at least come very close to doing so. At the very least, it seems certain that some direct contact between the buyer (or their agent) and the manufacturer will be necessary, and mere reliance on the manufacturer's reputation, or perhaps even on their promotional literature, will probably not by itself suffice.[17]

The reason for this refusal of the courts to impose direct manufacturer liability for defective products is that, as was suggested by Lord Fraser in the *Junior Books* case, there appears to be no way of judging what is the appropriate standard to which the goods have to be made except by invoking a contract. Goods may be of high quality or of low quality, but a manufacturer can hardly be guilty of negligence just because they make low-quality goods. Thus, Lord Fraser said:[18]

> A manufacturer's duty to take care not to make a product that is dangerous sets a standard which is, in principle, easy to ascertain. The duty is owed to all who are his 'neighbours'. It is imposed on him by the general law and is in addition to his contractual duties to other parties to the contract. But a duty not to produce a defective article sets a standard which is less easily ascertained, because it has to be judged largely by reference to the contract.

This is no doubt a good reason for not placing liability on a manufacturer for making a product to a low-quality standard which is intended to be sold as such. But it is far from clear why this is an adequate reason for not imposing liability on a manufacturer for making a product which is not of satisfactory quality when the product was *originally* sold as being of satisfactory quality. One explanation may be that what passed for satisfactory quality as between manufacturer and intermediate seller may not be satisfactory as between final seller and end user. However, the search for reasoned argument in this difficult area of the law does not seem to have been carried very far. Perhaps the best reason which can be suggested for the present law is that, leaving aside the possibility of a manufacturer's liability on a consumer guarantee,[19] it is simply easier and less costly if buyers look to their sellers for redress for defective goods. If purchase and sale contracts

15 [1964] AC 465.

16 This has continued to be a challenge in the case law post the landmark ruling in *Caparo Industries plc* v *Dickman* [1990] UKHL 2, which reformulated the requirements to establish a duty of care (of which proximity is one element).

17 See *Muirhead* v *Industrial Tank Specialities Ltd* [1986] QB 507. As to the possibility of such promotional literature giving rise to a collateral contract, see below.

18 [1983] 1 AC 520, 533.

19 See Chapter 21.

in the marketplace are entered into with the appropriate degree of care and foresight by all parties, there should be less need for buyers to look to third parties for redress. This is doubtless a reasonable argument when commercial contracts are in question;[20] it is perhaps less convincing when consumers are under consideration. At all events, in many cases the Consumer Protection Act 1987 will provide consumers with a remedy against, *inter alia*, a manufacturer. This is dealt with below.

20.1.3 Collateral contracts

One common law expedient whereby a buyer may be able to hold a manufacturer strictly liable despite the apparent absence of privity is the collateral contract. For instance, in *Wells* v *Buckland Sand*[21] the plaintiff bought sand for growing chrysanthemums in reliance on an express assurance that the sand was suitable for this purpose. This assurance was not given by the seller but by the manufacturer. It was held that there was a collateral contract, and the buyer was entitled to damages when the sand proved unsuitable and the buyer suffered loss. This was a case in which a specific and personal assurance was given to the buyer by the manufacturer. What is not clear is whether such a claim could be based on statements made in a manufacturer's advertisement. Apart from the famous case of *Carlill* v *Carbolic Smoke Ball Co*,[22] there are hardly any illustrations of this possibility in English law.

But in one English case on this subject, the Court of Appeal declined to hold that statements made by a manufacturer in his brochures could be construed as collateral warranties, on the ground that they were not 'intended' to create contractual liability.[23] This is open to criticism because manufacturers issue their promotional literature plainly intending to influence buyers, and it would seem perfectly reasonable to hold that simple statements of fact relied upon by buyers should be held to create collateral contracts. 'Puffs' and other vague advertising language are a different matter, but simple statements of fact ought to be held to create collateral contracts, when calculated to be relied on and in fact relied upon. In any event, in the case of consumer sales public statements about the specific characteristics of the goods can give rise to liability under the Consumer Rights Act 2015, s. 9, but that liability falls on the trader who sold the goods to the consumer, rather than the manufacturer/producer.

This possible liability is wider in scope than the statutory liability under the Consumer Protection Act because (as we shall see later) that Act only applies to *defective* goods – though the meaning of that expression causes problems. But the common law liability arising under a collateral contract can extend to cases where the goods are in no real sense defective, but are merely unsuitable for the buyer's purposes, or fail to live up to some claim made by the manufacturer. But even so, the collateral contract has serious limitations as a device for holding a manufacturer strictly liable. In particular, it only helps a buyer where they can find some *express* statement or assurance that can be construed

[20] As in the *Muirhead* case, and also in *Simaan & General Contracting Co* v *Pilkington Glass Ltd* (No 2) [1988] 1 All ER 791.

[21] [1965] 2 QB 170. See also *Shanklin Pier Ltd* v *Detel Products Ltd* [1951] 2 KB 854.

[22] [1893] 1 QB 256.

[23] *Lambert* v *Lewis* [1980] 2 WLR 289, [1980] 1 All ER 978; reversed on different grounds [1982] AC 225.

as a warranty,[24] or a public statement on the specific characteristics of goods, within the meaning of the Consumer Rights Act 2015, s. 9, in the case of consumer sales.

There is, as yet, no authority which goes so far as to hold that a manufacturer could be liable for breach of implied terms on the basis of a collateral contract. The step from express to implied warranties would be a momentous one in practice, but in legal theory it seems a small extension. A manufacturer markets their products through retailers; they advertise directly to the public, inviting them to buy their products. It does not seem unreasonable to hold that they are impliedly promising a product of satisfactory quality to a member of the public who buys the product. However, in view of the Consumer Protection Act 1987, it is perhaps unlikely that the courts will feel the need to develop the common law further in this area.[25]

20.1.4 Part 20 (Counterclaims and other additional claims)

The second common law expedient by which strict liability may be effectively imposed on the manufacturer is through third- and (if necessary) fourth-party proceedings. In the interests of making the law more 'user-friendly', under the Civil Procedure Rules 1998 these are now referred to as 'Part 20' proceedings in England and Wales. If the buyer sues the seller for breach of contract, the seller may claim an indemnity from their own supplier, and that supplier (if not themselves the manufacturer) may in turn claim an indemnity from the manufacturer. As between each pair of parties, the relationship will be contractual and liability for breach of contract can be established. For instance, in the old case of *Dodd* v *Wilson*,[26] the plaintiff farmer employed a veterinary surgeon to inoculate his cattle with some serum; it proved to be defective and many of the cattle died or became diseased. The plaintiff recovered damages from the surgeon as on an implied warranty; the surgeon brought in his suppliers as third parties and the suppliers brought in the manufacturers as fourth parties. The surgeon obtained an indemnity from the third parties and they, in turn, obtained an indemnity from the fourth parties. In this way, liability was imposed on the manufacturer for breach of implied warranty from the manufacturer through the intermediaries. Furthermore, the House of Lords has given the existence of such rights of indemnity as itself a good ground for imposing strict liability on a supplier in contracts for work and materials.[27] This is, however, a somewhat clumsy and costly expedient. Why should not the claimant have a direct remedy against the manufacturer for breach of an implied term? Moreover, the expedient may not always work; for example, if one of the intermediaries is insolvent, cannot be found, only carries on business overseas or has gone out of business.

In *Lambert* v *Lewis*,[28] retailers bought a defective coupling through a wholesaler whom they were subsequently unable to identify. In the Court of Appeal, where the retailers were held liable to pay damages to the ultimate buyer of the coupling, they were refused an

[24] See Bradgate (1991) 20 Anglo-Am LR 327, 342.

[25] Even though the Act is much more limited than a warranty of fitness would be, as we shall see below.

[26] [1946] 2 All ER 691.

[27] *Young & Marten Ltd* v *McManus Childs* [1969] 1 AC 454. Furthermore, the House of Lords made it quite clear that the same rule would apply in contracts of sale of goods.

[28] [1980] 2 WLR 289.

indemnity from the manufacturers on the ground that, in the absence of a direct contract between the retailers and the manufacturer, any such claim would have to be made in tort, and tort law did not recognise such a claim as it was a claim for pure economic loss.[29] In the House of Lords, the decision was reversed on a different ground,[30] but the House left open the possibility that such a claim for economic loss might be recognised by the law, where the economic loss consisted of a liability to pay damages in respect of some personal injury (or, presumably, property damage). However, such a development has looked improbable since *Murphy* v *Brentwood District Council*.[31]

20.1.5 Privity of contract: remedy confined to the buyer

The doctrine of privity of contract is also very material in the law of product liability in another major respect. Not only does the doctrine normally restrict liability to the seller; it also normally confines the remedy to the buyer. A sub-buyer, a donee, a member of the buyer's family, an employee of the buyer, a mere bystander – none of these can sue the seller (nor, *a fortiori*, the manufacturer) for breach of condition or warranty, but only for negligence.[32] Thus, if any of these persons should be injured through the use of a defective product they can only sue the retailer or manufacturer if they can establish liability under the Consumer Protection Act 1987 or through negligence. Even in Scots law, which allows third parties to acquire rights under contracts to which they are not privy, by means of its doctrine of *jus quaesitum tertio*, it is rare for a contract of sale to show the necessary irrevocable intention of the parties to confer such an enforceable benefit.[33] Given the limitations of the 1987 Act, and the difficulty of establishing negligence on the part of the manufacturer, such third parties are in a significantly worse situation than buyers. The Contracts (Rights of Third Parties) Act 1999 has done nothing to ameliorate this situation.

In some situations, the courts have struggled against the apparent logic of the doctrine of privity. For instance, in *Lockett* v *A & M Charles Ltd*, [34] a husband and wife went into a hotel for a meal and the wife was made ill by being served infected food. Negligence on the part of the hotel was not made out so the claim had to be made in contract as on a breach of warranty. The hotel argued that the only contract was with the husband as it was a reasonable presumption that he would pay the bill.[35] This argument was rejected by Tucker J who held that, in the absence of evidence to the contrary, both husband and wife were in a contractual relationship with the hotel. He held that the normal inference where a person orders food in a hotel or restaurant is that he makes himself liable to pay for it, whatever

[29] This outcome would be unaffected by the Contracts (Rights of Third Parties) Act 1999.

[30] [1982] AC 225.

[31] [1991] 1 AC 398 and it must be noted that no reference to the dicta in *Lambert* v *Lewis* was made in the case of *D & F Estates* v *Church Commissioners* [1988] 2 All ER 992 which signalled a stop to the expansion of liability for economic loss in that *Junior Books* v *Veitchi Ltd* [1983] 1 AC 20, 1982 SC (HL) 244 was not followed.

[32] As to the application of the Contracts (Rights of Third Parties) Act 1999 in this regard, see below.

[33] But see, e.g., *Cullen* v *McMenamin Ltd* 1928 SLT (Sh Ct) 2 and, possibly, *Scott Lithgow Ltd* v *GEC Electrical Projects Ltd* 1989 SC 412. See further on possible reform Scottish Law Commission Discussion Paper No 157 on Third Party Rights in Contract (2014).

[34] [1938] 4 All ER 170.

[35] Times have perhaps changed in this regard.

the position may be as between the person ordering the food and his companions. But it would be difficult to apply this reasoning (say) where a person ordered a meal for a child. Similarly, if somebody books a private room at a hotel to entertain a large party, it would be clear that only they are in a contractual relationship with the hotel.[36] Or again, where it is plain from the circumstances that the meal is to be paid for by a diner who has brought with them a single guest, the guest will have no claim for breach of warranty.[37]

There is no doubt that the doctrine of privity can lead to some apparently anomalous results in these cases. A man buys a bottle of perfume (say) and gives it to his partner as a present. If the bottle explodes and injures his partner, they cannot sue the seller for breach of warranty (though they might have a remedy under the Consumer Protection Act or possibly in negligence). If, however, he has bought the bottle at his partner's request, and therefore as their agent, the position is different. One possible way of escaping these is under *Jackson* v *Horizon Holidays Ltd*,[38] where the Court of Appeal awarded damages for the inconvenience and disappointment of a ruined holiday, not merely for the inconvenience and disappointment of the plaintiff himself but also for that of his family. Whether this would extend to personal injury cases is still uncertain, but it seems unlikely.[39]

Despite various signs of tentative movement in some directions, then, the broad position remained, until the coming into force of Part I of the Consumer Protection Act 1987,[40] that, unless the plaintiff could sue on a contract, they had to prove negligence to found their cause of action. But, at least in the case of personal injury and death, if such negligence can be proved, there can be no exclusion of business liability by contract or notice.[41]

20.1.6 Assignment and novation

Where goods are sold by the original purchaser to a third party, normally the sale will be treated as a sub-sale, and the third party will have no remedy against the original seller. It would appear, however, that the rights that the original purchaser had against the seller can pass to the third party by assignment, at least where such a sub-sale is contemplated by the original parties.[42] Any burden under the original contract, such as transferring to the purchaser the liability to pay service charges to the original seller, could only pass by novation or, in Scots law, delegation. It would appear that such assignments and novations are not uncommon when complex pieces of commercial equipment are sold. In English law, if no formal assignment has taken place complying with s. 136 of the Law of Property Act 1925, the assignment might nevertheless be effective in equity, but the assignee would have to sue in the name of the original purchaser. In Scots law, neither the agreement to

[36] This situation would seem closer to the Law Commission's second example.

[37] *Buckley* v *La Reserve* [1955] Cr Law Rev 451. But again, the 1999 Act might alter this outcome.

[38] [1975] 1 WLR 1468, approved to a limited extent in *Woodar Investment Ltd* v *Wimpey UK Ltd* [1980] 1 All ER 571.

[39] But see *Donnelly* v *Joyce* [1974] QB 454.

[40] See s. 2 of the Unfair Contract Terms Act 1977. For the meaning of the term 'business liability', see Chapter 8, at section 8.4.4.

[41] See s. 2 of the Unfair Contract Terms Act 1977. For the meaning of the term 'business liability', see Chapter 8, at section 8.4.4.

[42] *Darlington Borough Council* v *Wiltshier Northern Ltd* [1995] 1 WLR 68. This case involved a building contract, but the same point would appear to be relevant in sales of goods.

assign nor the assignation itself need to be in writing, although a simple style of written assignation is available under the Transmission of Moveable Property (Scotland) Act 1862. Intimation of the assignation to the debtor in the obligation assigned is, however, necessary to complete the transfer, although again this need not be in writing.

20.2 Product liability under the Consumer Protection Act 1987

In 1985, the EU (then the EEC) promulgated a Directive on liability for defective products[43]. This introduced a regime of so-called 'strict' product liability. Part I of the Consumer Protection Act 1987 was passed to give effect to this Directive, and it applies equally in Scots law as in English law. So far as the background to this Act is concerned, it will be enough to mention four points. First, one of the main sources of initiative behind the Directive was undoubtedly the view that the previous law created unacceptable anomalies in the way it distinguished between the remedies of a buyer and a non-buyer, the latter generally requiring proof of negligence. Secondly, another major concern was the view that it was anomalous that it was generally much easier to establish liability against a retailer than against the manufacturer, who was often the party primarily responsible for defective goods. Thirdly, American law was thought to have demonstrated that it was possible to impose strict product liability in tort on manufacturers without undue strain[44]. And fourthly, the European involvement arose because it was thought desirable that all manufacturers in member states should face similar legal liabilities so as to avoid distortions of competition which might arise if manufacturers had to bear different liabilities, according to varying laws in the member states[45].

Part 1 of the Consumer Protection Act 1987 ('CPA') remains in force despite the UK's withdrawal from the European Union in 2020 without substantive amendments; changes were made to reflect the fact that the UK is no longer a member of the EU and that obligations regarding the interpretation of domestic law in accordance with EU Law have fallen away.

The CPA and the Directive on which it was based were adopted at a time when products where primarily mechanical, but these days, the integration of physical and digital aspects in many goods, combined with internet or other forms of connectivity, are prevalent. The digital economy has also supported the growth of new distribution and retain models, especially the rise of online platforms and online shopping. More recently, we have seen significant advances in deep-learning artificial intelligence. This has resulted in the replacement of the 1985 Directive by a new Directive[46] that will apply in the EU Member States from 9 December 2026.[47] At the time of preparing this edition, the UK had not proposed specific plans for amending the CPA, although it had consulted on the issue in very broad terms as part of its Product Safety Review.[48] The case for reform is strong,

[43] 85/374/EEC, amended by Directive 99/34/EC.

[44] See in particular s. 402A of the Restatement of Torts, 2d (1965).

[45] Yet there is no uniform product liability law in the United States, where this is a matter left to the law of each individual state; and there are indeed many variations – the Uniform Commercial Code Art. 2-318 has three alternatives, any of which may be chosen by a particular jurisdiction, and some states have introduced their own variations.

[46] Directive (EU) 2024/2853, OJ L 2024/2853.

[47] Ibid., Article 22.

[48] Department for Business and Trade, *Smarter Regulation: UK Product Safety Review* (August 2023).

particularly in view of the novel challenges created by goods relying on software for its functionalities which are regularly updated remotely over the internet. Such updates can affect the performance of a product and can, in extreme cases, turn a once safe product into an unsafe one. For now, this chapter is limited to an overview of the CPA provisions already in force.

The form of legal liability created by Part I of the Consumer Protection Act raises a very large number of difficult and intricate questions, but has generated a moderate number of key cases. Here, it will suffice to offer a summary view of some of the essentials. The basic principle of the statutory product liability is that (1) any person who suffers damage, which is (2) caused by a defective product, is entitled to sue (3) the producer (and various other possible parties) without being required to prove fault.

20.2.1 Claimant or pursuer must show 'damage'

The first requirement to the application of the Act is that the claimant or pursuer must show that they have suffered 'damage'. By s. 5(1) 'damage' means 'death or personal injury or any loss of, or damage to any property (including land)'. There is no particular difficulty here with regard to personal injury. It is defined by s. 45(1) so as to include 'any disease and any other impairment of a person's physical or mental condition'. Presumably, this is wide enough to cover the cases dealt with at common law under the term 'nervous shock'. So far as death is concerned, the new Act is tied in with the existing tort statutes relating to death, so that liability will only arise on behalf of financial dependants under the Fatal Accidents Act 1976, or, in the case of non-dependants, in the very limited cases (and to the very limited extent) provided for by the Law Reform (Miscellaneous Provisions) Act 1934, as amended. In Scotland, the tie-in is with the Damages (Scotland) Act 2011 and Part II of the Administration of Justice Act 1982.

So far as property damage is concerned, there are more complications. First, the Act excludes claims for £275 or less.[49] Secondly, no claims for pure economic loss can be entertained under the Act. It is unclear to what extent consequential economic loss claims can be attached to claims for material loss or damage to property. If the consequential loss does not derive from the value of the damaged goods themselves, or is not parasitic on that damage,[50] it would seem not to be claimable under the Act. If the claim can be said to concern the quantification of the value of the physical damage itself, the consequential loss might be claimable, but that will not generally be the case with goods intended for private use as opposed to business use, and (as we shall see) there are severe limits on the extent of liability for goods intended for business use.

Next, it is made clear by s. 5(2) that damage to the defective product *itself* is not covered by the statutory liability. Nor does the statutory liability cover damage to a product 'which has been supplied with the product in question comprised in it'. So, arguably, if a defective tyre, which has been supplied with a car, bursts causing damage (a) to the tyre itself, and

[49] Section 5(4). If the claimant is awarded £250 damages, nothing will be recovered. But if they are awarded £280, the whole sum, including the first £275, is recoverable. The exclusion applies to the amount to be awarded; so if the claimant/pursuer claims £500, but half is deducted for contributory negligence, nothing will be awarded under the Act.

[50] ee *Spartan Steels & Alloys Ltd* v *Martin & Co (Contractors) Ltd* [1973] 1 QB 27; *Muirhead* v *Industrial Tank Specialities Ltd* [1986] QB 507.

(b) to the car, then neither the damage to the tyre nor the car is covered, assuming that the tyre can be said to be 'comprised in' the car. If the tyre is comprised in the car, would the statutory liability extend to an accessory, such as an expensive sound-system?[51] If the tyre is bought separately from the car, then the damage to the car will be covered.[52] This result is illogical. In order to reach a more rational solution, a distinction might be drawn between those aspects of a product having no reality as articles of commerce apart from forming part of the complete unit such as a motor vehicle, and parts such as, in the case of motor vehicle, tyres, batteries, lamps, steering wheels, etc., which are customarily dealt with as accessories.[53] In practice, such items may be specified by the customer when the car is bought from the dealer, and it seems absurd that the result might be different where on the one hand the customer has requested the item to be fitted when the car is supplied, and on the other if they go back a week later and purchase the item which causes the damage to the car. In other words, it is not stretching things too far to argue that such accessories or 'add-ons' are not really 'comprised in' the item supplied, but are bought *along with* it.

Section 5(3) largely confines the liability for property damage to property which is intended for private use, occupation or consumption. The section disallows an action for damage to property if the property is not:

(a) of a description of property ordinarily intended for private use, occupation or consumption; and
(b) intended by the person suffering the loss or damage mainly for his own use, occupation or consumption.

So the claimant or pursuer must show *both* that the property is ordinarily intended for private use, occupation or consumption, *and* that they did so intend it. The second requirement rules out the property of public authorities and business corporations,[54] and also, presumably, claims by professional firms who could hardly say that their property is intended for 'private' use, etc., even if it is property ordinarily used for private purposes. But the position may be different with a single self-employed professional, such as an author, who could reasonably claim that even goods used for the purposes of their profession (especially if these are kept in their home) are intended for 'private use'.

It must also be remembered that under s. 5(1) 'property' includes land and therefore a house, so damage to a house caused by a defective product will be recoverable under the Act if the house is occupied by the owner (presumably it is intended 'mainly' for their private occupation even if they have a partner and 10 children). On the other hand, if the house is merely rented, the damage will not be recoverable unless the tenant is legally answerable for it under the lease, in which case they will still be the person 'suffering the loss or damage'. Otherwise, the landlord will be the person suffering the loss or damage, and they will not be able to recover it under the Act.

[51] For a discussion of this, and various other points arising on these difficult provisions, see Bradgate and Savage (1987) 137 NLJ 929, 953, 1025 and 1049.
[52] See below, at section 20.2.2.
[53] This suggestion is based on the analogy of registered designs law – see *Ford Motor Company's Design Applications* [1994] RPC 545 (upheld by HL: [1995] RPC 167). The Directive merely excludes 'damage to the defective product itself', which begs the question as to what the product itself is.
[54] Even a company car, it seems, would not be covered because it is not intended by the person 'suffering the loss or damage' (the owner company) mainly for the owner's own use, occupation or consumption.

20.2.2 Damage must have been caused by a defective product

The next requirement is that the claimant or pursuer must show that their loss or damage was caused by a defective product. The term 'product' is defined by s. 1(2) of the Act as 'any goods or electricity';[55] the definition also includes any product which is comprised in another product; for example, as a raw material or as a component part. Next, the word 'goods' is defined by s. 45(1) so as to include:

> . . . substances, growing crops and things comprised in land by virtue of being attached to it and any ship, aircraft or vehicle.

Although there is no express mention that goods are 'tangible', one would expect that this would be the implicit as this mirrors the definition of goods elsewhere.[56] The definition in the CPA is a little wider than the definition of 'goods' in the Consumer Rights Act and the Sale of Goods Act in that it includes things attached to land, but probably not actual buildings – though *damage* to buildings is covered. Presumably, this means that there could be liability under the Act for damage done by defective parts of a new building, as if window glass or roof tiles fall off and injure a passer-by.

A number of questions which arise in the law of sale, and which have previously been considered, may also arise in the present context. For instance, there is the question whether human blood (or plasma) supplied for transfusion is a 'product', which in turn must depend on whether it is 'goods' within the meaning of the Act.[57] Perhaps the inclusion of the word 'substances' in the statutory definition makes it more likely that blood and similar products would fall within the 1987 Act. On the other hand, it may well be that the Act does not affect the general tendency to hold that professional liability is a matter of fault only, and should not be converted into strict liability merely because some product is incidentally supplied.

On the other hand, it is not clear to what extent goods which rely on software to perform their functions are covered by the definition. Standalone software is clearly excluded, but software integral to the functionalities of a product should, in principle, be covered so that a fault in the operating software affects the product itself. However, a difficulty is caused by operating software which is regularly updated remotely over the internet; here, a software update could render a product defective but it would then be debatable whether any subsequent injury or property damage is cause by the *product*, or by the software update. If it is the latter, the fact that purely digital products are seemingly not covered by the definition of product would mean that an injured person could not claim under the CPA.

The next, and vital, requirement is that the claimant or pursuer must be able to show that the product was 'defective'. The meaning of a 'defect' is closely defined in s. 3 of the Act, though subject to an important defence in s. 4, which is considered later. Broadly, s. 3(1) says that a product is defective if 'the safety of the product is not such as persons

[55] For an American example of liability for electricity, see *Ransome* v *Wisconsin Electric Power Co* 275 NW 2d 641 (1979). But cf. *Singer Company, Link Simulation Systems Division* v *Baltimore Gas and Electricity Company* 558 A 2d 419 (1988).

[56] Cf. s. 2(8) of the Consumer Rights Act 2015 ('tangible movable items'), and s. 61(1) of the Sale of Goods Act 1979 ('personal chattels').

[57] See *A* v *National Blood Authority* [2001] 3 All ER 289. This point, however, was passed over no doubt as a result of the defendant's concession in relation to Article 6 of the Directive.

generally are entitled to expect'.[58] Section 3(2) then goes on to say that all the circumstances must be taken into account in deciding what persons generally are entitled to expect,[59] including the way the goods are marketed, their get-up, and any warnings and instructions. In addition, it is necessary to take account of what 'might reasonably be expected to be done with or in relation to the product'. Further, it is provided that the time of supply must be taken into account and that it is impermissible to infer that a product was defective *merely* because later versions of the product are safer (a rather important qualification).[60] However, later versions may provide valuable evidence as to what might have been achieved at the time.

Plainly, the need to show that the product was defective is the heart of this statutory liability. Although the precise cause of a defect need not be established, it is not sufficient that component in a product has failed to conclude that it was defective when the failure could be due to another cause,[61] e.g., overtightening a pivot-bolt on a mountain bike rather than following the maintenance instructions provided by the producer.[62] The burden remains on the claimant to establish their case, and an appellate court will generally not interference with a trial judge's assessment of the evidence unless the judge 'erred in law, made a finding without any basis in the evidence or demonstrably misunderstood, or failed to consider, relevant evidence.'[63]

Equally plainly, it raises similar questions in some respects to some of the requirements of ss. 9 and 10 of the Consumer Rights Act 2015, and (it may be suggested) the statutory definition of a defective product is as open-textured as the definition of 'satisfactory quality'. No doubt there will be many obvious situations where a product will be obviously 'defective' in some very simple way. But there will be some instances where the statutory definition will not provide an easy solution. To suggest that products should be as safe 'as persons generally are entitled to expect' does not help a great deal when the question at issue is: precisely what are persons generally entitled to expect? Nor does it help a great deal when the alleged defect is of an esoteric or complex nature as to which 'persons generally' probably have no expectations at all. Do 'persons generally' expect blood for transfusion (for instance) to be free from unknown and undiscoverable viruses? Again, when the person injured was not the buyer of the product, but (say) some innocent bystander, it is not clear why it should be relevant to ask what persons generally are entitled to expect of the goods in question. So far, the case law on this has been somewhat 'black letter' and unreflective, and, whilst this may accord with continental notions of strict liability, it seems to pay scant regard to economic theory, and it has potentially harmful consequences in that many pharmaceutical products have to be launched with

[58] See Butterworths Common Law Series, *Law of Product Liability* (eds. Grubb and Howells, 2nd edn, 2007, Butterworths), para. 1.13 *et seq*.

[59] In *Richardson* v *LRC Products* [2000] Lloyd's Rep Med 280, the claimant had become pregnant by an act of sexual intercourse during which the condom failed. She sued the defendant manufacturer. After considering expert testimony, the court found in favour of the defendant. No one had ever said that this method of contraception was 100 per cent effective. Fractures happened by chance. There was no evidence of a weakness in the system of testing used, and the condoms were manufactured to the standard required.

[60] Directive, Art. 6.2.

[61] Cf. *Ide* v *ATB Sales Ltd* [2008] EWCA Civ 424. In *Ayannuga* v *One Shot Products Ltd* [2022] EWHC 590 (QB), Yip J stressed that one must not make an inference from the outcome but consider all the evidence (para.46).

[62] *MacDonald* v *Cube Bikes UK Ltd* [2022] E.C.C.2

[63] *Hastings* v *Finsbury Orthopaedics Ltd* [2022] UKSC 19, para 65.

known serious side effects; for example, chemotherapy for terminal cancer patients. Are the manufacturers to be held liable for those known but unavoidable side effects?

For many years, the ruling by Burton J in *A* v *National Blood Authority*[64] was regarded as authoritative on the notion of 'defect'. In that case, the claimants had been infected with Hepatitis C through contaminated blood transfusions, or blood products, administered in the course of surgery. At the time, the risk of infection was known to the medical profession, but it was impossible to detect with the screening tests then available. Burton J held that the avoidability of the harmful characteristic was not a relevant circumstance to take into account in determining whether a product was defective, but that persons generally were entitled to expect that the blood would be free from what was in effect an unavoidable risk.[65] In *Abouzaid* v *Mothercare (UK) Ltd*,[66] where a 12-year-old boy, helping his mother attach a product to a pushchair, was injured in the eye when one of the product's elasticated straps snapped back, the defendants were held liable though the danger had not previously been contemplated. However, the approach by Burton J in *A* v *National Blood Authority* was doubted by Hickinbottom J in *Wilkes* v *Depuy*,[67] who said that 'the ease and extent to which a risk can be eliminated or mitigated may be a circumstance that bears upon the issue of the level of safety that the public generally is entitled to expect.'[68] Burton J had also distinguished between 'standard' and 'non-standard' products,[69] but Hickinbottom J rejected this distinction as 'unnecessary and undesirable',[70] preferring to limit the question whether a particular product is within the producer's intended specifications as being a relevant factor in determining whether the product is of the level of safety persons are generally entitled to expect. Overall, he suggested a number of relevant circumstances in addition to considering whether a product was within the producer's specifications: the overall risk-benefit balance of the product,[71] the ease with and extent to which a risk could be eliminated and reduced, and compliance of the product with relevant mandatory standards or regulations. The approach of Hickinbottom J was preferred in the subsequent group litigation, *Re Depuy Pinnacle Metal on Metal Hip Litigation*[72] and taken as guidance by the Court of Appeal in *The Seroxat Group Litigation (Bailey & Ors* v *GlaxoSmithKline)* [73]

[64] [2001] 3 All ER 289.

[65] It should be noted that the defendants accepted that a producer's liability under Art. 6 of the Directive was irrespective of fault. Accordingly, there was no real discussion in the case of the sort that has taken place in many US decisions of the meaning of 'strict liability'.

[66] [2000] EWCA Civ 348.

[67] *Anthony Frederick Wilkes* v *Depuy International Limited* [2016] EWHC 3096.

[68] Para [89].

[69] At para [36] in *A* v *National Blood Authority*, Burton J said: '. . . [A] standard product is one which is and performs as the producer intends. A non-standard product is one which is different, obviously because it is deficient or inferior in terms of safety, from the standard product: and where it is the harmful characteristic or characteristics present in the non-standard product, but not in the standard product, which has or have caused the material injury or damage.'

[70] Para [94].

[71] Hickinbottom J said that 'any assessment of its safety will necessarily require the risks involved in use of that product to be balanced against its potential benefits including its potential utility' (at para [82]) but also cautioned that 'the fact that risk-benefit may lie at the heart of the question of appropriate level of safety of a medicinal product for the purposes of the Act does not mean that the detailed specific aspects of the doctrine of risk-utility as formulated in the United States will apply – or that the approach of our courts will, or should, be the same' (para [67]).

[72] [2018] EWHC 1208 (QB).

[73] [2019] EWCA Civ 1924 (8 November 2019), para [8].

It must be remembered that many goods are inherently unsafe, in that their use always involves some element of risk. A sharp kitchen knife can cut fingers as well as meat; a ladder is something that people fall off, despite all precautions. The mere fact that such goods are inherently risky does not make them defective under the Act.

One point is, however, made reasonably explicit by s. 3(2)(b), which has already been referred to. Manufacturers must expect that goods will sometimes be misused, or that they will be involved in accidents. So, for instance, goods may be defective if they would be dangerous even if not used strictly as they should have been. A car may be defective in design if it does not stand a crash as well as it should have done because, for instance, the petrol tank is so situated that it is liable to explode in a rear-end collision. It is no defence for the manufacturer to claim that a car is designed to be driven and not to be crashed.

Finally, the claimant or pursuer also has to establish a causal link between the defect and the personal injury or damage suffered. Thus, the fact that serious injury or even death resulted whilst a product was being used does not mean that the product is the cause of injury or death. The sad facts of *Ayannuga* v *One Shot Products Ltd*[74] illustrate this: a drain cleaner had been used and during use, toxic gas emerged from the drains which resulted in the death of one person and catastrophic brain injury to another. Careful consideration of all the evidence showed that the product was not defective and that the death was caused by an escape of sewer gas. The temporal connection between the use of the product and the presence of the gas neither meant the product was defective nor that there was a causal link between the use and the escape of the gas.

20.2.2.1 The 'state of the art' or 'development risks' defence

Section 4(1) provides a number of defences to the producer, including that the product did not exist at the relevant time (s. 4(1)(d), i.e,. the time of supply; or that the defendant did not supply the product to another (s. 4(1)(b)). It is not necessary to explore all the defences here, but one merits further discussion: the so-called 'development risks' defence (also known as 'the state of the art' defence). Section 4(1)(e) says that there is no liability if the defendant can show:

> that the state of scientific and technical knowledge at the relevant time was not such that a producer of products of the same description as the product in question might be expected to have discovered the defect if it had existed in his products while they were under his control . . .

The effect of the defence, as interpreted in the Act, is plainly to reincorporate something very like a no-negligence defence into the statutory cause of action; and it is for this reason that the Act has been seen to be a somewhat illusory piece of reform which largely takes away with one hand what it has given with the other. Clearly, there will be cases in which the statutory defence under this section will enable the defendant to escape liability by proving, in substance, that they were not negligent. However, the onus of proof of this defence is on the defendant, and this may be a very important point in respect of many types of allegedly defective products. Moreover, the defendant may be liable, even though they have not been negligent because the defect in question may anyhow not have arisen

[74] [2022] EWHC 590 (QB).

from a lack of scientific and technical knowledge permitting its discovery, but from the failure to put together obvious facts to appreciate and eliminate (or reduce) a risk.

Finally, depending on the meaning attributed to 'scientific and technical knowledge', the practical impossibilities of perfect quality control at places of production might be relevant. Suppose one heart pacemaker in a thousand fails to work properly, and this failure rate cannot be reduced, not because of a lack of scientific and technical knowledge in the ordinary sense, but because it is impractical (or far too costly) to raise the level of factory quality control to such a point as to eliminate the risk.[75] The actual product which fails is defective under the Act, but could the defendant escape liability under 'the state of the art' defence? The answer is far from clear, though *Richardson* v *LRC Products* suggests that the defendant might escape liability on this ground.[76] Whether a product is defective in this sense under s. 3(1) might depend upon the existence of warnings or general knowledge of these things. If there were no evidence on these matters, a defence on the basis of s. 4(1)(e) would still seem to be available.

However, as observed above, the courts have approached the matter in a somewhat unreflective manner. In *A* v *National Blood Authority*[77] it was held that the defence in Article 4(1)(e) of the Directive did not apply where the existence of the generic defect was known or should have been known in the context of accessible information. Once the existence of the defect was known, there was the risk of that defect materialising in any particular product, and it was immaterial that the known risk was unavoidable in the particular product. It would be inconsistent with the Act if a producer, in the case of a known risk, continued to supply products simply because, and despite the fact that, they were unable to identify in which of their products that defect would occur or recur, or, more relevantly, in a case where the producer was obliged to supply, they continued to supply without accepting the responsibility for any injuries resulting, by insurance or otherwise. The defence also failed in *Abouzaid* v *Mothercare (UK) Ltd.*[78]

20.2.3 Producers and other parties liable

The third essential question under the Act is: who is liable?[79] The answer broadly is that under s. 2 three parties are, in principle, made liable for damage done by a defective product: (1) the 'producer' of the product, (2) anyone who has 'held himself out to be the producer of the product'; for instance, by putting his trade mark on the product,[80] and (3) anyone who has imported the product into a member state from a place outside the

[75] See Newdick [1988] CLJ 455.
[76] [2000] Lloyd's Rep Med 280.
[77] [2001] 3 All ER 289.
[78] [2000] EWCA Civ 348.
[79] Identifying the correct party to claim important can be important, as naming the wrong defendant cannot be corrected once the 10-year limitation period in s.11A of the Limitation Act 1980 has expired: *Holterman* v *Electrium Sales Ltd* [2020] EWHC 3915 (TCC).
[80] Section 2(1)(b). Where a mark is applied by a licensee, it would appear, therefore, that it is the *licensor* who is liable under this provision because by licensing the application of his mark he has 'held himself out to be the producer of the product'. The licensee will be liable as 'the producer' if such he is. But if he is buying in goods and applying the mark, he presumably will not be liable as producer. In such a case the original producer is liable, together with the trade mark licensor.

member states. In addition, any supplier of the goods can also be liable if they fail, on request, to identify to the claimant one of the parties in the first three groups.

On the other hand, any party (including the producer) can escape liability if they can show that they did not supply the goods in the course of business or with a view to profit. 'Supply' is defined in an elaborate way in s. 46: it includes, in particular, selling, hiring or lending, furnishing by way of hire-purchase, supplying the goods under a contract for work and materials, or giving the goods away as a prize or gift. The coverage is fairly wide, but it is not exhaustive. Even a producer of a defective product would not be liable if they did not supply the product at all, but (say) the product was stolen from their factory, and ultimately sold to the claimant (or anyone else). It also means that a party who causes injury while using the goods will not be liable for product defects under the Act because they do not supply the goods to anyone. And this is true even if the user is also the producer – so if (say) the maker of forklift trucks uses them in its own factory, and a defect causes injury to a workman, there will be no statutory liability.

There may be more than one 'producer' of a defective product within the Act. Because of the definition of 'product', the term covers the finished product as well as component parts and raw materials. So if a product is defective because of a defective component, the producers of both the finished product and the component will be liable, assuming each has 'supplied' the relevant product, as will usually be the case.[81] The liability of the producer of the finished product in this particular respect may well be genuinely strict, and may easily extend beyond common law liability for negligence.

20.2.4 Relation of the statutory liability to other forms of liability

The cause of action under the 1987 Act is in addition to, and does not in any way supersede, any other cause of action[82] Further, the Act prohibits any party from contracting-out of (or limiting) their liability under the Act.[83] It is therefore possible, in theory, for a person who acquires goods from a producer of those goods to bring a claim under the Consumer Protection Act which overlaps with their contractual causes of action under the Consumer Rights Act, or otherwise. And occasionally, this may help a buyer because (for instance) the definition of a defective product is wider than the quality requirements under the Consumer Rights Act, or because the prohibition on limiting or excluding liability is wider than that imposed under the Consumer Rights Act. But this will not often be a matter of much practical importance, as consumers rarely buy goods direct from the manufacturers, and businesses which do so will find that there is virtually no liability for business damage under the Act.

So the main practical importance of the Act will lie in the fact that a buyer will sometimes be enabled to sue parties other than the seller without having to prove fault, and

[81] Though there may be good economic grounds for not holding a component manufacturer liable – see *Goldberg v Kollsman Instruments* 191 NE 2d 81 (1963) below.

[82] Section 2(6). However, a claimant who could have brought a claim under Part 1 of the Act but fails to do so within the 10-year limitation period (s.11A Limitation Act 1980) cannot instead try to base a claim on s. 41(1) of the Consumer Protection Act dealing with civil liability for contravening a safety obligation: *Wilson v Beko plc* [2021] 1 W.L.R. 1711.

[83] Section 7.

that a non-buyer will likewise be enabled to sue the producer (though not a mere seller) without proving fault.

20.3 Non-contractual claims in respect of defects in the goods

A person who buys goods which prove defective may wish to claim damages in respect of the defects themselves because, for instance, the goods may have to be repaired, or because they are simply worth less than the buyer had expected, or because they are less efficient in use. As seen, such cases are outside the Consumer Protection Act, which excludes liability for loss or damage to the product itself, or any part of any product which has been supplied with the product in question comprised in it. If the buyer sues the seller, such a claim raises no particular problem and is governed by the same principles as apply to actions for damages in respect of defective goods.[84] But if the buyer wishes to sue the manufacturer or anyone else responsible for the state of the goods, then apart from the possibility of recovering through the device of the collateral contract, or through intermediate suppliers, the action must be brought in tort. And a tort action of this nature is still the subject of very considerable legal difficulty because it appears to be (at least in many cases) a claim for pure economic loss. Moreover, case law suggests that this form of liability will rarely be available in tort or delict to supplement contractual liability.

Since *Murphy* v *Brentwood*, which was mentioned above, the possibility of suing in negligence for economic losses has virtually ceased to exist. This may leave a person under-compensated if, for some reason, an action against the contractual supplier is not/no longer possible.

[84] See Chapter 19 at 19.5.4.

21

Manufacturers' guarantees

21.1 Introduction: a word about the word 'guarantee'

The word 'guarantee' is used in law in four very different senses:

1 It is the promise to answer for the debt or default of another. Under the Statute of Frauds,[1] such contracts must be evidenced in writing, signed by the party to be charged. Guarantees in this sense are commonly met with in consumer credit transactions; for example, where a parent might be required to guarantee his or her child's hire-purchase debt to a finance company. We are not concerned with guarantees in this sense in this chapter.
2 Product guarantees, of which the most common is the manufacturer's product guarantee, commonly found printed as a standard form purporting to take effect as a contract between the buyer of the goods in question and the manufacturer. These are dealt with in the following section.
3 'Extended warranties' or 'guarantees' routinely offered with more expensive consumer electrical goods and the like. In return for a lump sum[2] or regular payments to a company which may be (but is not necessarily) independent of either the retailer or the manufacturer,[3] the costs of repair should the goods break down will be covered. These are dealt with in the section following 'manufacturers' guarantees'.
4 'Satisfaction guarantees': these are typically in a form such as: 'Money back in 30 days if not completely satisfied.'

Here, the focus is on product guarantees, exemplified by the manufacturer's guarantee.

21.2 Manufacturers' guarantees

A useful working definition of the manufacturer's guarantee is as follows:

> . . . a voluntary undertaking given by a manufacturer (the 'guarantor') without charge to provide a remedy, should the product covered by the guarantee become defective as a result of poor workmanship or the use of faulty materials in the manufacturing process during a specified period of time after purchase.[4]

[1] 29 Car. 2 c. 3 (1677), s. 4. For Scots law, see Gloag & Henderson, *The Law of Scotland* (13th edn, 2012, W. Green, Edinburgh), para. 16.07.

[2] Which may be covered by the moneys lent under the credit agreement covering the price of the goods.

[3] Which may be an insurance company – from the consumer's point of view, as explained below, there are certain advantages in it being an insurance company.

[4] This definition is taken from Twigg-Flesner, *Consumer Product Guarantees* (2003, Ashgate), p. 1.

Similar guarantees are offered by some retailers, and these too are within the scope of this chapter, though, to avoid complicating matters, we will, in general, be focusing on manufacturers' guarantees. Since there will be a contractual nexus between the buyer and the retailer, retailers' guarantees will operate either as part of the sales transaction, or as collateral contracts, the consideration for which in English law can be found in the buyer entering into the sales contract.[5]

The popularity of online shopping via marketplace platforms and auction sites means that many consumers will now buy goods via such online platforms, and many platform operators will offer guarantees of some kind or another in respect of transactions concluded via such platforms. Some of these types of guarantees may be within the scope of s. 30 of the Consumer Rights Act 2015 (discussed below), but in any event, such guarantees may be enforceable as a type of collateral contract, for which the consumer provides consideration by concluding a contract for the supply of goods via the platform.[6]

The contractual aspect of manufacturers' guarantees in English law was more problematic. Prior to the implementation of the EU's Consumer Sales Directive (99/44/EC) in the Sale and Supply of Goods to Consumer Regulations 2002[7] (since replaced by the corresponding provisions of the Consumer Rights Act 2015), there was scarcely any English or Scottish authority on the effect of manufacturers' guarantees. Were the buyer of goods aware of the guarantee, then it would be possible to analyse it as a collateral contract, the consideration for which was the purchase of the goods from the dealer.[8] It would, however, be difficult to apply this analysis where the buyer only became aware of the guarantee when they got home and opened the box. In fact, this will commonly be the case, as most consumer (and many non-consumer) goods are either delivered from the retailer's stockroom in sealed boxes after the buyer has selected a model from the samples on display, or more commonly delivered directly by a courier from an online retailer or fulfilment service provider. Thus, the first time that the consumer will see the guarantee is when they open the box at home. Formerly, it was possible to argue that by completing and posting the guarantee, which invariably excluded common law and statutory rights, the consideration was the surrender of these rights in return for the manufacturer's undertakings given under the guarantee. This line of argument might have some validity in non-consumer cases, but because (as we have seen) the consumer buyer cannot surrender their common law and statutory rights,[9] this analysis is not useful in consumer cases. Another possibility is that the English courts may be prepared to hold such guarantees binding as unilateral contracts.[10] This would certainly provide a sensible solution in non-consumer cases, where otherwise the absence of consideration would mean that the buyer has no legal rights

[5] On the analogy of the series of hire-purchase cases starting with *Webster* v *Higgins* [1948] 2 All ER 127, where dealers said, 'If you buy the [*car*] we will guarantee that it is in good condition.' In reliance on this statement, the defendant entered into a hire-purchase transaction with a third party. The car turned out to be in poor condition, and the dealers were held liable on their 'guarantee'. See also *VAI Industries (UK) Ltd* v *Bostock & Bramley & others* [2003] EWCA Civ 1069.

[6] See, e.g. Twigg-Flesner, Legal and policy responses to online platforms, in Blaurock, Schmidt-Kessel and Erler (eds.) *Plattformen* (Nomos, 2018), esp. pp. 152–155.

[7] S.I. 2002/3045.

[8] See *Shanklin Pier Ltd* v Detel Products Ltd [1951] 2 KB 854.

[9] See Chapter 19 at 19.9.

[10] See *Blackpool and Fylde Aero Club Ltd* v *Blackpool Borough Council* [1990] 3 All ER 25 – see Adams and Brownsword (1991) 54 MLR 301.

under the guarantee. This problem did not arise under Scots law, as it has no consideration requirement;[11] manufacturers' guarantees are characteristically seen as unilateral promises rather than contracts.

A further problem with manufacturers' guarantees is whether or not they are limited to the original buyer, or whether they run to persons who subsequently become owners of the goods within the period of the guarantee. The current situation is that manufacturers can limit the guarantee to the first buyer, although it is possible that such a restriction might, in some instances, constitute an unfair term within the meaning of Part II of the Consumer Rights Act 2015 because it undermines the consumer's right to assign a contractual right, although this point remains untested before a court.

A related question is who should be liable to the consumer under the guarantee. Clearly, the manufacturer giving the guarantee is liable on it, subject to the legal questions discussed above in relation to non-consumer sales. It has been suggested, however, that the retailer should additionally be liable, since the manufacturer's guarantee is often specifically mentioned by the retailer as a selling point for the goods in question. However, nothing has been done about this, though, as noted above, many reputable retailers do offer their own guarantees, which may extend for a longer time than the manufacturer's. Obviously, there is a cost in this, and probably the answer is best left to consumer choice. If goods are bought at a low price from online marketplaces or the warehouse type establishments sometimes referred to as 'box shifters', no doubt the price will be lower than from a reputable department store/online retailer, but by buying from the latter type of establishment, the consumer does often acquire additional security in the form of the store's guarantee. This is particularly useful where, as is often the case, it is more convenient to return defective goods to the store than to the manufacturer.

The situation under manufacturers' guarantees so far as the consumer buyer is concerned changed after the Sale of Consumer Goods and Associated Guarantees Directive.[12] Initially implemented through the Sale and Supply of Goods to Consumers Regulations,[13] the relevant provision now is s. 30 of the Consumer Rights Act 2015.

21.2.1 The Consumer Rights Act 2015 and Guarantees

The Directive did not make it obligatory that a manufacturer's guarantee be given, but, if it is, the provisions implementing Art.6 of the Directive are applicable. The definition of 'guarantee' is as follows:

> . . . an undertaking to the consumer given without extra charge by a person acting in the course of the person's business (the "guarantor") that, if the goods do not meet the specifications set out in the guarantee statement or in any associated advertising—
> (a) the consumer will be reimbursed for the price paid for the goods, or
> (b) the goods will be repaired, replaced or handled in any way.

[11] See Cusine, 1980 JR 185.

[12] Directive 99/44/EC on Certain Aspects of the Sale of Consumer Goods and Associated Guarantees, OJ 1999 L177/12. The Directive has since been replaced by Directive 2019/771/EU on certain aspects concerning contracts for the sale of goods, OJ 2019 L136/28, but this has no effect on UK law due to the UK's withdrawal from the EU in 2020.

[13] SI 2002/3045.

Section 30 of the Consumer Rights Act 2015 contains the relevant provisions on guarantees. Section 30(3) lays to rest the doubts (mentioned above) that existed at common law about the effectiveness of manufacturers' guarantees as legal documents. Guarantees now take effect at the time the goods are delivered as a contractual obligation owed by the guarantor under the conditions set out in the guarantee statement and the associated advertising. Because a guarantee is treated as a unilateral promise, rather than as a contract, in Scots law,[14] s. 30(3) does not state that the guarantee forms a contract between the manufacturer and the buyer. Perhaps so far as the law in England and Wales is concerned, the use of the term 'contractual obligation' is also intended to signal that these documents are unilateral contracts, a possibility suggested above for analysing guarantees in non-consumer cases. The effect of s. 30 is to override the common law requirements for a binding contract, and a guarantor would not be able to resist the effects of s. 30 by claiming that the consumer failed to provide any consideration for the guarantee, or that the guarantor did not intend the guarantee to be legally binding.

As was pointed out above, manufacturers are under no legal obligation to provide guarantees, but, if they do, they are legally binding and must comply with the terms of s. 30. In particular, the guarantee must set out in plain and intelligible language the contents of the guarantee and the essential particulars necessary for making claims under the guarantee; notably the duration and territorial scope of the guarantee as well as the name and address of the guarantor.[15] If the consumer requests, the guarantee must be made available in writing or other durable medium available and accessible to them within a reasonable time.[16] Enforcement is by injunction, or in Scotland specific implement, applied for by an enforcement authority[17]

21.3 Extended warranties or guarantees[18]

As noted above, these are usually offered with more expensive types of domestic electrical appliance such as fridges, washing machines and dishwashers. These are known in the trade as 'white goods'. Such warranties or guarantees are also offered with a range of 'brown goods' such as television sets computers/laptops, and other smaller consumer electronics.[19] These contracts cover three types of risk: (1) the risk of product breakdown;[20] (2) the financial risk if an expensive part needs replacing and (3) the risk that a suitable repairer may be difficult to find (the warrantor should offer a network of repairers who can carry out the repair quickly and efficiently). These contracts add to the remedies

[14] See Hogg (2001) 9 ERPL 337; Ervine 2003 SLT (News) 67, 70.

[15] s. 30(4)/(5).

[16] s. 30(6).

[17] The Competition and Markets Authority, a local weights and measures authority in Great Britain, or the Department of Enterprise, Trade and Investment in Northern Ireland: s. 30(10).

[18] For a useful, if now dated, discussion of this sparsely covered topic, see Twigg-Flesner, *Consumer Product Guarantees* (2002, Ashgate), Ch 2.5, and [2002] 4 Web JCLI by the same author.

[19] Leaving aside the situation under extended warranties, an important practical difference between the two categories of goods is that in the case of white goods, the manufacturer will usually have its own repair network, and the consumer will deal with that directly. In the case of brown goods, traditionally the dealer maintained its own repair facilities. Today, not all retailers maintain these facilities, and, where they do not, the manufacturer will provide a list of approved repairers.

[20] This could be due to inherent lack of reliability, accidental damage, or simply wear and tear.

provided to the consumer under the Consumer Rights Act 2015, but how much they add is problematic because obviously at the outset the reliability of goods is unknowable, and many manufacturers' guarantees will cover most breakdowns that are likely to occur, and the retailers are liable for defects existing at the time of sale under the Consumer Rights Act. As noted previously, reputable retailers often themselves offer guarantees equivalent to manufacturers' warranties for a period that may even be longer than the manufacturer's guarantee. Where goods are heavily used by different persons, as will be the case with goods present in furnished lettings, they may well prove to need more repair and maintenance than those in homes under single-family occupation. In this case, these extended warranty contracts can offer a good way of making outgoings predictable, which will usually be what the owners in such cases want. It may also be that those on a tight budget will find that the predictability that these contracts offer is of value. In practice, however, it would appear that these contracts are offered by retailers whose margins on their sale can be very high, as a way of inflating their profits.[21] In fact, the claims made seem to be lower than for insurance generally.[22] In short, for most consumers they offer poor value.

A further cause of concern is that whereas the real nature of these contracts is that of insurance, many are not made with insurance companies. Where, as has happened, the warranty providers become insolvent and unable to provide the contracted services, the consumer has been left without recourse, and the premiums paid are unrecoverable. By contrast, if an insurance company were involved and became insolvent, the Financial Services Compensation Scheme would cover the case.[23] In consequence of these concerns, in July 2002, the Competition Commission was asked to investigate and report on the existence or possible existence of a monopoly situation in relation to the supply of extended warranties for domestic electrical goods in the UK. Its report appeared in 2003.[24] Four overlapping characteristics of market behaviour suggested that, given the point of sale advantage that the offer of such contracts possesses, practices that might otherwise be unexceptionable could act to restrict or distort competition:

(a) Almost all extended warranties are purchased at point of sale; few consumers seek information on extended warranties prior to their purchase;[25] and consumers have little opportunity to consider alternatives to the extended warranty on offer at point of sale.
(b) Extended warranties on offer at point of sale are nearly always all from one provider, usually the retailer (or a third party which is the sole supplier to the retailer).
(c) There is generally no information available at point of sale on prices, or terms and conditions, of extended warranties available from alternative providers (such as manufacturers, insurers, credit card companies or others).
(d) There is generally no information available on domestic electrical goods' reliability, likely repair costs, or the probability of theft or accidental damage.

21 Competition Commission Report, 'Extended warranties on domestic electrical goods: a report on the supply of extended warranties on domestic electrical goods within the UK – Volumes 1, 2 and 3' accessible at website http://webarchive.nationalarchives.gov.uk/+/http:/www.competition-commission.org.uk/rep_pub/reports/2003/485xwars.htm.

22 Office of Fair Trading, 'Extended Warranties on Domestic Electrical Goods' 2002b, para. 4.31.

23 Ibid., para. 4.59.

24 See Competition Commission Report. Extended warranties on domestic electrical goods: a report on the supply of extended warranties on domestic electrical goods within the UK.

25 Or indeed intend to purchase an extended warranty before they go out to buy electrical goods. It is the element of surprise that tends to reinforce the retailer's point of sale advantage.

Based on their consultation on remedies and further consideration, the Competition Commission developed two packages of possible remedies. In the event, it is the first of these packages which is given effect to by the Supply of Extended Warranties on Domestic Electrical Goods Order,[26] which came into force on 6 April 2005. Retailers now have to do the following:

- show the price of the extended warranty alongside electrical goods, in store and in their printed advertising material;
- provide consumers with information about their statutory rights, cancellation rights and details of the warranty, including whether or not the warranty provides financial protection in the event of insolvency and terminates if a claim is made;
- give the consumer 45 days to cancel the extended warranty, including giving the consumer a written reminder of this right and the right to cancel at any time and receive a refund;
- offer any consumers, who do not wish to purchase a warranty immediately, quotations stating that the extended warranty remains available on the same terms for 30 days if the consumer chooses not to buy it at that time. Any discounts tied to the purchase of the extended warranty should also be available for 30 days.

21.4 EU Reforms not implemented in the UK

As noted, s. 30 of the Consumer Rights Act has its origins in EU legislation. That legislation was replaced by the 2019 Consumer Sales Directive (2019/771/EU). This largely restates the earlier provision regarding guarantees ('commercial guarantees' in the language of the new Directive). Article 17(1) holds a manufacturer offering a 'commercial guarantee of durability' directly liable to a consumer for the repair or replacement of the relevant goods throughout the period of durability as a minimum substantial requirement, although a manufacturer could offer more generous terms than those under Art. 14 of the Directive (which broadly reflect the earlier obligations under Art. 3 of the old Consumer Sales Directive, implemented in UK Law via Part 1 of the Consumer Rights Act 2015[27]

The UK declined to make any changes to domestic law in light of the 2019 Directive because the deadline for implementing that Directive only fell after the end of the transition period following EU withdrawal.[28]

[26] SI 2005/37.
[27] See Chapter 19 at 19.4.
[28] Cf. Article 24 of Directive 2019/771/EU.

Part IX

Dispute resolution

22
Dispute resolution

22.1 Introduction

In the absence of any provisions or restrictions on how to resolve disputes arising out of contract of sale of goods disputes under the Sale of Goods Act 1979, the parties to a contract for the sale of goods have two forms of dispute resolution available: traditional litigation (national courts) and alternative dispute resolution (ADR hereafter). Parties will, of course, try to settle their disputes through informal or formal negotiations first, but this is not always successful.

Over recent years there has been significant increase in the use of ADR methods, which has resulted in the development of a legal framework for the various ADR methods and, despite the use of the word 'alternative', they are now very much seen as 'appropriate' methods of dispute resolution between parties to contracts for the sale of goods, and commercial disputes generally.

This chapter briefly considers litigation, ADR mechanisms and ultimately focuses on arbitration as a method of dispute resolution.

22.2 National courts

Traditional litigation of commercial disputes through national courts is often seen as the default method of dispute resolution. In some cases, it can be the only method of dispute resolution available to the parties due to nature of the dispute.[1] However, for settling commercial disputes, it is usually not the only method, as most of these disputes can also be resolved using ADR. As with any other method of dispute resolution, a choice to use litigation must be informed by a consideration of its effects or practical consequences for the parties, overall process and third parties, if applicable.

A choice to use litigation can benefit the parties as usually the final decision of the court process is binding on the parties. If a party fails to comply with the ruling, enforcement can be sought. This is of advantage as it creates certainty that the final ruling will be followed by the parties. In common law jurisdictions, a reasoned judgment can set a precedent for similar disputes in the future. If a party is not satisfied by the court ruling, there will usually be an opportunity to appeal. Even if the case is affirmed on appeal, the parties will be assured no error in the application of the law was made. Of-course, it can be argued that appeals can further prolong the dispute resolution process and the

[1] For more on this see section 22.5.2 below and Ndolo, D. (2023) 'The Role of Public Policy in the Arbitrability of Disputes under US and English law' *Int. A.L.R.* 26(1), 72–87

associated uncertainty. That may be so, but appeals usually require permission (leave to appeal) and significant point of law requiring consideration by the appellate court.

The court process is also formal, institutionalised, and has a number of safeguards and due process requirements in place to ensure that justice can be obtained. One of the safeguards is that the court process is usually public – decisions are reported and third parties can, in some instances, intervene in the process. Parties to a commercial dispute present their cases regarding the facts of the dispute and the associated legal issues.

However, for the resolution of commercial disputes, there a significant number of drawbacks associated with the use of national courts. First, if the dispute is international (i.e., parties are from two different jurisdictions), the foreign party may be concerned that the host judicial system favours the local party. This is because there may be differences in legal systems and rules of civil procedure, and also the fact that the host court is a national institution enforcing local public policy. Importantly also, due to the adversarial nature of the court process, the decision will usually result in one party ending up as the 'winner', which could sour the parties' business relationship.

Additionally, as mentioned above, the court process is public and thus may create an opportunity to clarify disputed facts, but reports of ongoing disputes could result in adverse publicity, and this may, in turn, affect the parties' existing and future clients.

Finally, the formal and institutionalised nature of the court process means that it can be lengthy and costly as well as very rigid. In terms of rigidity, the parties have very limited, if any, autonomy in the process, for instance, in the selection of the adjudicator, time or venue. The selection of the adjudicator affords the parties an opportunity to select someone who is an expert with commercial experience within the subject matter of the dispute, rather than getting an adjudicator who may be expert in law but lacking practical commercial experience. This factor makes ADR methods particularly suitable for complex disputes. What is more, under ADR the parties can choose a number of adjudicators to preside of the case and their role, or may even choose not to have an adjudicator at all. In terms of selection of time of and venue, under ADR parties can adjust their commercial activities to accommodate the dispute resolution process.

22.3 Alternative methods of dispute resolution

One of the main features of ADR methods is that they are voluntary, flexible and private. Voluntary, in this context, refers to the fact that parties will usually have to consent to use the ADR mechanism to resolve their dispute. Flexibility in this context refers to the fact that parties in disputes usually are free to decide, among other things, the procedural rules, the neutral party if there is one, and the time and place of the process. They are private because they do not involve the public national judicial process and, as a result, they are usually less formal.[2]

However, each type of ADR has its own characteristics/features and procedural rules which are different from the others. Therefore, in practice, parties in dispute over a contract for the sale of goods will usually choose their preferred ADR mechanism based on

2 Born, G. (2021) *International Arbitration: Law and Practice* (3rd ed) Wolters Kluwer, at 5.

consideration of their unique circumstances, the nature of the dispute and the nature of the ADR mechanism.[3]

This chapter will provide an overview of mediation, conciliation, negotiation and expert determination with specific consideration of how their unique features can assist parties to a contract for the sale of goods in identifying the appropriate method of dispute resolution. There will then be a more detailed focus on arbitration as a key form of commercial dispute resolution. There are other ADR mechanisms, including private judging, private jury judging, ombudsman etc., but these are beyond the scope of this chapter.

22.3.1 Negotiation

A negotiation involves direct or indirect communication whereby the parties in dispute discuss the dispute and the form of any joint action which they might take to ultimately reach an agreement.[4] A unique feature of the negotiation process is that it involves only the parties in dispute and thus negotiation and the outcome is reached by the parties together without recourse to a neutral third-party. This is particularly advantageous in cases involving sensitive information, and where privacy and confidentiality is of high priority. This feature also makes negotiation suitable for parties with a well-established business relationship and seeking to save cost in dispute resolution process.

However, the absence of a neutral third party to adjudicate or at least facilitate can result in a prolonged dispute resolution process, as the parties may be unable to reach an agreement as they may be incapable of impartially assessing the dispute. Moreover, the absence of a neutral third party may encourage one party to attempt to take advantage of the other, particularly where the parties are of unequal bargaining power. In these cases, negotiation is often seen as a method that is not appropriate, for example in disputes between an established trader and a consumer.

22.3.2 Mediation

Through mediation, the parties in dispute or conflict utilise the assistance of a neutral third-party mediator to attempt to resolve their dispute.[5] The mediator aims to facilitate the negotiation between the parties with the aim of reaching an agreement. Therefore, the mediator seeks agreement between parties and does not make an independent final decision to resolve the dispute. Thus, unlike the court process, a mediator has no power to adjudicate or to decide but only to facilitate, discuss and encourage resolution of the dispute. In addition, unlike the court process, the final agreement between the parties is not binding.[6]

As a result, mediation is appropriate where the parties in dispute want to resolve the matter themselves but with the assistance of a neutral facilitator (mediator). In practice, parties will want a neutral adjudicator if they are in a position to resolve the dispute for themselves,

[3] Ibid.
[4] Michael, P. & Roberts, S.R. (2005). *Dispute Processes: ADR and the Primary Forms of Decision Making* (2nd ed.) Cambridge University Press, at 113.
[5] Spencer, D. (2006) *Mediation law and Practice*. Cambridge University Press, at 3.
[6] Ibid.

or if there is a well-established legal relationship between the parties to the contract of sale such that they can attempt to resolve the dispute. The effect of this is usually that the parties end up with a win–win resolution, which may allow them to continue with their existing business relationship, rather than the win–lose situation that is often achieved in court due to the adversarial nature of the process, which may significantly affect the business relationship.

Another key feature of mediation are the privacy and confidentiality, as well as the 'without prejudice', principles. The latter prevents statements made in a genuine attempt to settle an existing dispute, whether made in writing or orally, from being put before the court as evidence of admissions against the interest of the party that made them unless where parties expressly or impliedly exclude it. These features opens the door to frank and open discussions between the mediator and each of the parties in their private meetings, as well as between the parties during the course of the mediation.

Generally, mediation is seen as a less formal method of resolving disputes as, although there is increasing use of mediation, there are fewer legal formalities and bureaucratic processes in the mediation process than in the national courts, and fewer laws governing the process than in arbitration (discussed below). Indeed, Lord Golf noted that mediation 'is seen as the one means of escaping from the inflexible processes towards which substantial arbitrations seem to gravitate. ADR, if effective, may produce not only a less expensive but, also, a less traumatic resolution of disputes.'[7]

In fact, it was only in 2019, in *Ohpen Operations UK Ltd* v *Invesco Fund Managers Ltd*,[8] that the English High Court clarified instances where they would enforce an agreement to mediate. They held that for the English courts to stay court proceedings in favour of an agreement to mediate, the following is required: First, the agreement should be worded in terms which create an enforceable obligation mandating that parties shall engage in mediation. Secondly, the obligation should be drafted clearly and state unequivocally that it is a condition precedent to court proceedings or arbitration. Thirdly, the agreement to mediate need not be a formal one, but it must be sufficiently clearly and certainly set out, by reference to objective benchmarks, including methods to appoint a mediator or to determine any other imperative actions in the process without the need for any further agreement between the parties. Fourthly, the court holds a discretion to stay court (or arbitration) proceedings which were initiated in breach of that enforceable agreement to mediate.[9] Fifthly, when exercising that discretion, the court will balance (1) the public policy considerations of having to uphold any contractual agreements concluded between parties with (2) any overriding prerogatives within court processes to assist parties in resolving disputes in an efficient and effective manner. In *Ohpen*, the contract between the parties contained the following clause:

> '. . . the Dispute shall be referred for resolution to mediation under the Model Mediation Procedure of the Centre of Dispute Resolution (CEDR) for the time being in force. If the Parties are unable to resolve the Dispute by mediation, either Party may commence court proceedings.'

Therefore, the legal issue was whether it was enforceable. The High Court held that the clause mandated mediation as a condition precedent to starting court proceedings.

[7] Tackaberry (ed) (1991) *International Commercial Arbitration for Today and Tomorrow*. Euro Conferences, at 41.

[8] [2019] EWHC 2246 (TCC)

[9] Senior Courts Act 1981 s.49(3).

Furthermore, the agreement was sufficiently clear and certain to be enforceable because the selection of the procedural rules, CEDR, was enough for mediation to commence as selection of the mediator and conduct of the mediation are set out in therein. As result the court issued stay in favour of the mediation process.

The mediation process is generally flexible, and parties have the autonomy to choose whether to commence and continue the mediation process, the mediator, and the place of mediation; as result, the parties can tailor the mediation process to their needs, for example, to reduce the cost of dispute resolution. In 2023, the UK signed The Singapore Convention on Mediation which when ratified will facilitate the uniform and efficient cross-border enforcement of mediation settlements agreements, almost in the same manner as the New York Convention 1958 (discussed below.).

22.3.3 Conciliation

Conciliation is similar to the mediation process in that it involves a neutral third party, a conciliator, who facilitates the dispute resolution between the parties with the aim that the parties reach an amicable dispute settlement. The main difference between mediation and conciliation is that during the conciliation process the conciliator will be asked by the parties to provide them with a non-binding settlement proposal. A mediator, by contrast, will in most cases and as a matter of principle, refrain from making such a proposal.[10] Therefore, unlike a national judge, conciliators do not have the power to adjudicate and to make a final decision but only to facilitate, and unlike in the mediation process, the conciliator can provide the parties with the a non-binding settlement proposal, which the parties can reject and proceed with their own settlement agreement or adopt.

Due to the similarities between mediation and conciliation, the factors that may affects parties' choice to use mediation mentioned above apply to conciliation *mutatis mutandis*. However, the unique feature of the non-binding proposal is of particular significance to the parties to conciliation, as it gives reassurance that if they cannot resolve the dispute then they will receive a settlement proposal to which they have the freedom to decide whether to adopt or not.

22.3.4 Expert determination

The expert determination process involves a neutral third party with relevant expertise who makes a binding decision on technical rather than legal issues. This process is particularly suitable for disputes that are purely technical nature, such as those within the sale of goods that involve an element of intellectual property. In such a case an expert can be required to assess the value of the intellectual property.[11] Usually, the decision of the expert is final and binding on the specific issue.[12] Expert determination is usually confidential but is not subject to a legislative framework, therefore authority of the independent expert is dependent

[10] For more see Ndolo, D. (2019) 'The Role of the English Courts in the Enforcement of Arbitration Agreements', *Coventry Law Journal*, 24(1), 39–48, at 40.

[11] See Tweeddale, A. &Tweeddale, K. (2007) *Arbitration of Commercial Disputes International and English Law and Practice*. OUP. at 18, para 1.40

[12] Born, G. (2021) International Arbitration: Law and Practice (3rd ed.) Wolters Kluwer, at 5–7.

on the parties. Notably, in *Premier Oil UK Ltd* v *Shell International Trading and Shipping Co Ltd (for and on behalf of Shell Trading International Ltd)*,[13] the English High court provided guidance on the expert determination process in general and more specifically on whether the courts can intervene before the expert makes a decision. The court held that:

> 'If the parties have agreed the principles or procedures pursuant to which an expert is to make their determination, the court does have jurisdiction to decide whether the expert has correctly applied those principles or procedures and can and will set aside a determination made contrary to the agreed principles or procedures, because the expert has acted outside the scope of their authority. The fact that the issue which the expert is required to determine requires the expert to reach conclusions on the proper construction of the contract does not prevent the expert from reaching those conclusions but, subject to the wording of the contract, the expert's conclusions are open to review by the court even if the contract otherwise provides that the expert's decision is to be final and binding on the parties.The court will not usually intervene before an expert has completed their task, even if one or other party fears that the expert may go wrong because, unless there are strong grounds for thinking that the expert is likely to go wrong, the court's intervention is likely to result in a waste of time and the incurring of unnecessary costs.The decision as to whether to intervene before the expert has made their determination is ordinarily one for the discretion of the court. There do not need to be exceptional circumstances to justify the court reaching its conclusions on the issues of construction first, and the court may well do so if the issue in dispute is real, rather than hypothetical, and if it is in the interests of justice and convenience for the court to do so.The fact that one party may face evidential difficulties in establishing that an expert has gone outside their authority is not usually a legitimate reason for the court to give a pre-emptive ruling. The parties have agreed to submit to a particular form of decision-making with whatever evidential difficulties that might entail.The court should be careful not to re-write the terms of the dispute resolution mechanism even if one party may no longer regard that regime to be satisfactory.'[14]

22.4 Arbitration

In the absence of a universal definition of arbitration, an understanding can be drawn from its key features as a dispute resolution process that is non-judicial, flexible, consensual and that resolves disputes in a binding manner.[15] All the elements of this definition are important, as discussed below.

Non-judicial refers to the fact that arbitration is not a national court procedure but rather a private mechanism for resolving disputes. This is one of the key features of arbitration and it refers to two important principles of arbitration: privacy and confidentiality. Privacy in this context means that no third party can attend the arbitral process, while confidentiality means that parties have the advantage of non-disclosure of specific information about the dispute in public.[16] This makes arbitration particularly suitable where the parties in dispute are concerned about the effect of the dispute on their public reputation on existing and future clients.

[13] [2023] EWHC 3269 (Comm)

[14] Ibid., Mr. Nigel Cooper KC at para 35

[15] For more on the definition of arbitration see Ndolo, D. (2019) 'The Role of the English Courts in the Enforcement of Arbitration Agreements', *Coventry Law Journal*, 24(1), 39–48, at 40.

[16] Barkett, J.M., Cruz-Alvarez, F. & Pagliery, S. (2016) 'Perspectives on the New York Convention under the Laws of the United States Forum Non Convenience as a Stopper to Enforcement', Kluwer Arbitration Blog, August.

The non-judicial aspect also refers to the fact that the dispute is resolved by (an) arbitrator(s) chosen by the parties and thus a non-judicial/governmental decision maker. In practice, parties will usually choose an arbitrator (or arbitral panel) who is an expert in subject matter of the dispute. In comparison to the mediation process, the arbitrator gains power from the arbitration agreement to adjudicate and decide the case in final binding manner. This feature makes arbitration suitable for parties in dispute who do not want the publicity of the court process and want the freedom to choose the adjudicator, with practical experience in the sale of goods rather than only expertise in theory and the law.

'Consensual' within the arbitration elements refers to the fact that arbitration is based on the consent of the parties to use arbitration to resolve their dispute which is usually expressed in the form of an arbitration agreement. An arbitration agreement is binding on the parties, and it mandates the arbitrator or the arbitral tribunal to decide the dispute that is covered in that agreement. Article II of the New York Convention 1958 requires each contracting state to recognize and enforce arbitration agreements and as a result, national courts have developed remedies with this effect including arbitration anti-suit injunctions in order to achieve that. Moreover, this provision sets a requirement that all arbitration agreements must be in writing.[17]

Flexibility is one of the main objectives and advantages of arbitration as it refers to party autonomy (similar to that mentioned of mediation above). Party autonomy in this context refers to the flexibility afforded to the parties in the arbitration process such that the parties have the freedom to agree on the procedural rules to govern their dispute resolution.[18] Moreover, the parties have the freedom to choose an arbitrator or arbitral tribunal who/that is sufficiently experienced, which should be able to quickly completely grasp the salient issues of fact or law in dispute. In addition to this, the parties have the freedom to choose the applicable law and the seat of arbitration. In this way, therefore, arbitration promotes neutrality within dispute resolution. This is an important factor because international arbitration usually involves parties from different jurisdictions and these parties may have reservations on being in the other's national courts on basis of *inter alia* bias, incompetency, even costs or complex foreign legal formalities.[19] Therefore, they may get an international arbitration seat that is not in either party's jurisdiction but in a third state which provides a neutral, objective forum for dispute resolution.

Finally, the disputes submitted to arbitration are usually resolved in a final binding manner in which the final decision is given in the form of an arbitration award. Arbitration awards are binding to the parties such that the parties have to abide by the arbitral award. Article III of the New York Convention 1958 requires each contracting state to 'recognize arbitral awards as binding and enforce them in accordance with the rules of procedure of the territory where the award is relied upon'. As will be discussed below, as a result of this national courts have adopted pro-enforcement bias towards arbitral awards and only allow limited grounds for denying recognition or appeal.

17 Brought into English law at by s. 5 AA 1996

18 Born, G. (1994) *International Commercial Arbitration in the United States: Commentary and Materials.* Kluwer Law and Taxation Publishers, at 7.

19 Born, G. (2021) *International Arbitration: Law and Practice* (3rd ed.) Wolters Kluwer, at 5.

22.4.1 The modern role of the courts in the arbitration process

Under English law, before arbitration was accepted as a legitimate ADR mechanism, the English courts followed the ouster rule as confirmed in *Kill* v *Hollister*[20] that 'an agreement to refer all matters in difference to arbitration is not sufficient to oust the Courts of Law or Equity of their jurisdiction'.[21] The main concerns were that arbitration could be used to evade statutory rights and that it would oust the courts from much of their jurisdiction.[22] However in *Scott* v *Avery*,[23] there was significant judicial shift as the Court held that there is 'no principle or policy of the law' which prevents parties from agreeing an arbitration clause that postponed court action until an award is granted.[24] The practical effect of this ruling was to recognise that an arbitration agreement that includes a '*Scott* v *Avery clause*' as not completely ousting the jurisdiction of the courts.[25]

This significant shift in judicial attitude, together with the rapid increase in use of arbitration, led to the passing of national legislation that was pro-arbitration. This led to a gradual transition in the approach of national courts from using the public policy concerns mentioned above to accepting, supporting and supervising arbitration as a legitimate method of dispute resolution.[26]

One of the significant pieces of legislation in the UK arbitration legal framework history was the Common Law Procedure Act 1854, which contained provisions that prevent the English courts from revoking valid arbitration agreements. These provisions were further revised, enhanced and consolidated in the Arbitration Act 1889 (AA 1889 hereafter). The AA 1889 and its subsequent amendments notably in 1950 and 1979 and these Acts were subsequently amended and consolidated in the AA 1996 which presently governs arbitration under English law with current proposed reforms discussed below section 22.5.5.

Internationally, one of the earliest pro-arbitration conventions was the Geneva Protocol of 1923. This mandated that national courts of the countries that ratified it enforce arbitration agreements, but it had a limited effect as it was not ratified widely. This was expanded by the Geneva Convention of 1927 which required the recognition and enforcement of arbitration awards in all contracting states. Although the 1927 Convention was a considerable step forward, there was concern that it no longer entirely met the modern economic requirements.[27] As a result, in 1958, the Convention on the Recognition and Enforcement of Foreign Arbitral Awards, New York 1958 (New York Convention 1958) was signed and has been ratified by over 160 countries in the world including the UK. The main aim of NYC 1958 is to encourage the recognition and enforcement of commercial arbitration agreements and awards.[28] By doing this, the New York Convention 1958 has

[20] [1746] 1 Wils. 129
[21] Ibid., at 40
[22] For more on this see Ndolo, D. (2019) 'The Role of the English Courts in the Enforcement of Arbitration Agreements', *Coventry Law Journal*, 24 (1), 39–48, at 41.
[23] [1856] 5 HL Cas 811
[24] Ibid., at 4
[25] See Blake, S., Browne, J. & Sime, S. (2018) *A Practical Approach to Alternative Dispute Resolution* (5th ed.) OUP, at s.26.48–26.49
[26] Hwang, M. & Muttah, R. (2002) 'The Role of Courts in the Course of Arbitral Proceedings: Singapore and other Asian Perspectives' 68(3) *Arbitration* 223, at 224.
[27] See ICC 'Report and Preliminary Draft Convention adopted by the Committee on International Commercial Arbitration at its meeting of 13 March 1953' (1953) Publication no 174, at page 7 reported at The ICC International Court of Arbitration Bulletin (1998) 9(1).
[28] Justice Stewart in *Scherk* v *Alberto-Culver Co.* [1973] 417 U.S. 506, at 521.

completely revolutionised international arbitration. In fact, it is due to this that it has been hailed as 'the most successful private law treaty in history'[29] and by far 'the most significant contemporary international agreement' in relation to arbitration.[30]

There have been attempts by the United Nations Commission on International Trade Law (UNICITRAL) in particular to harmonise national arbitration laws and to assist states in reforming and modernising their national laws on the arbitral procedure to ensure they take into account the fundamental features and the particular requirements of international commercial arbitration.[31] At time of writing, the UNCITRAL Model Law on International Commercial Arbitration (1985), with amendments as adopted in 2006 (UNICITRA Model Law), is the current unifying tool, and in fact legislations in over 75 states in a total of over 100 jurisdictions are based on it, including *inter alia* Scotland.[32] This model law, however, has not been adopted under English law, because England had already developed a comprehensive body of arbitration laws.[33]

22.4.2 Enforcement of arbitration agreements

An agreement to arbitrate is the founding stone of international arbitration. As mentioned earlier, it records the parties' consent to resolve an existing or future dispute via arbitration.[34] In accordance with s. 5 of AA 1996, the arbitration agreement must be in writing and will be considered as such, if the agreement is made in writing (whether or not it is signed by the parties) or if the agreement is made by exchange of communications in writing, or if the agreement is evidenced in writing even if separate document (s. 6(2), Arbitration Act). Therefore, parties to a contract for the sale of goods can include the arbitration agreement in the underlying contract or in the separate contract or separate contracts. Usually, within the arbitration agreements parties can include, *inter alia*, the scope of the agreement, the arbitral seat, choice of law, arbitration rules and number of arbitrators.[35]

Under s. 7 AA 1996, once the parties enter into an arbitration agreement, even if contained in the underlying contract of sale, this will be treated as a separate and autonomous contract. The main practical purpose of the separability doctrine is to protect the parties' chosen dispute resolution method and arbitrator's jurisdiction even if it is alleged that the underlying contract may be invalid.[36] For instance, in *Fiona Trust & Holding Corp* v *Privalov*,[37] Fiona had purported to rescind the underlying contract on the basis it was

[29] Born, G. (2014) 'Introduction to International Arbitration: A Summary of the Basic Principles and Practices of International Arbitration' (2014) Magna Charter Law

[30] Born, G. (2021) *International Commercial Arbitration in the United States: Commentary and Materials* (Kluwer Law and Taxation Publishers 1994), at page 18 - see also Born, G. B. *International Arbitration.* (3rd ed.) OUP, at 45

[31] UNICITRAL 'AA Guide to UNCITRAL: Basic facts about the United Nations Commission on International Trade Law' (2013) UN, at 13.

[32] For the full list please see UNICITRAL 'Status: UNCITRAL Model Law on International Commercial Arbitration (1985), with amendments as adopted in 2006' Note that not all states have adopted the 2006 amendments.

[33] Rutherford, M. & Sims, J. (1996) *Arbitration Act 1996: A Practical Guide.* Pearson Professional, at 12.

[34] See s. 6 of the AA 1996

[35] Born, G. (2021) *International Arbitration: Law and Practice* (3rd ed.) Wolters Kluwer, at 35.

[36] Blackaby, N., Redfern, C. & Hunter, M. (2015) *Redfern and Hunter on international arbitration* (6th ed.) OUP, at 172.

[37] [2007] UKHL 40

believed to have been procured through bribery and it was argued as a result of this that the arbitration clause contained in it was not binding. The UK Supreme Court held that the arbitration agreement had to be treated as a distinct agreement and could be void or voidable only on grounds that related directly to it. Therefore, Fiona's argument was dismissed because the arbitration agreement was valid and thus it was for the arbitrators to determine if the underlying contract was void as a result of bribery.

However, if there are questions as to the validity, enforceability or scope of arbitration agreements, s. 30 AA 1996 grants the arbitrator(s) jurisdiction to determine the case under the principle of competence-competence. The UK courts have interpreted this doctrine broadly such that mere existence of an arbitration agreements is enough to give the arbitrator this power. [38] Nevertheless, it must be noted that the arbitrator's decision on jurisdiction is not binding because the English courts have the power of reviewing the arbitral determination for example where a party is challenging an arbitral award on grounds of substantive jurisdiction.[39]

22.4.2.1 Remedies for breach of an arbitration agreement

There are a number of remedies the English courts can issue in order to enforce a valid arbitration agreement. This section will discusses stay of proceedings and anti-suit injunction remedies which are granted where a party starts court proceedings in breach of the arbitration agreement.

Stay of legal proceedings

It is well settled that English courts can issue a stay of proceedings under s. 9 of the AA 1996 to enforce an arbitration award where a party to the arbitration agreement starts court proceedings in breach of an arbitration agreement. This specific provision is modelled around Article 8 of the UNICITRAL Model Law and thus written with mandatory and/or commanding terms, with particular emphasis on the use of the word 'shall'. In this way, the section restricts the English court's discretion to decline or approve an application for a stay of proceedings in favour of arbitration, as the conditions set out in the section are satisfied.

The stay of legal proceedings in practice is usually issued as a defence remedy, in that it is usually the defendant seeking this remedy where the court action amounts to a breach of a valid arbitration agreement. In such a case, the defendant, must not admit the court claim but rather seek stay within 14 days,[40] and if the dispute is arbitrable[41] the courts 'shall' (must) issue a stay for the matter to resolve via arbitration the arbitration agreement not unless arbitration agreement is null and void, inoperative, or incapable of being

[38] *HC Trading Malta Ltd* v *Tradeland Commodities SL* [2016] 1 W.L.R. 3120, at 3126-7.

[39] Section 67(1)(a) of the AA 1996 give English courts the power to hear challenges of award on grounds of arbitrator's substantive jurisdiction.

[40] s. 9(3) of the AA 1995

[41] s. 9(1) of the AA 1995 – not all disputes are arbitrable. For more on this see section 22.5.2 below and Ndolo, D. (2023) 'The Role of Public Policy in the Arbitrability of Disputes under US and English law' *Int. A.L.R.* 26(1), 72–87

performed.[42] At the time of writing, s. 9 AA 1996 does not expressly recognise the right to appeal against a court decision under s. 9 AA 1996. This is one matter identified for reform by the Law Commission. This is discussed in more detail below in section 22.5.5.

Arbitration anti-suit injunctions

Anti-suit injunctions are often sought to restrain a party from commencing or continuing with foreign court proceedings in breach of a valid arbitration agreement.[43] The English senior courts have a 'general power' to issue an anti-suit injunctions, under s. 37(1) of the Senior Courts Act 1981, in cases where it appears to the court to be 'convenient' to do so. The courts usually exercise this general power cautiously and 'sensitively' in the arbitration context 'with due regard for the scheme and terms' of the 1996 Act in particular s. 44 of the AA 1996.[44]

Nevertheless, anti-suit injunctions are far from perfect. The central concern is the jurisdictional practicalities of issuing anti-suit injunctions. This is because although they are an equitable remedy and thus directed to the party in breach of the arbitration agreement *in personam*, in practice there is indirect interference with the sovereignty and process of the foreign court.[45] Moreover, in practice this may be interpreted as the issuing court lacking trust in the foreign court submitting the dispute to the appropriate forum. Indeed, it is for these reasons that the Court of Justice of the European Union in the *West Tankers*[46] case, imposed a restriction on European Union (EU) member state courts from granting anti-suit injunctions to parties who have started court proceedings in an EU member state court. The effect of Brexit on this matter is dealt with below.[47]

22.4.3 Enforcement of arbitration awards

The general practice in international commercial arbitration is that arbitral awards are final and binding; therefore the parties must comply with them without any delay.[48] Usually, in practice, most awards would not require either judicial enforcement or confirmation because they are voluntarily complied with. In practice, this is usually the case because the parties voluntarily choose arbitration as their preferred dispute resolution mechanism and the parties usually do not want to break their commercial ties as they may have a continuing commercial relationship or may venture into a future commercial relationship.

Article III of the New York Convention 1958 mandates the national courts of the signatory states to 'recognize arbitral awards as binding'. In addition, under English law,

[42] s. 9(4) of the English AA 1996.

[43] For a detailed discussion on anti-suit injunctions see Ndolo, D. (2017) 'Does the will of the parties supersede the sovereignty of the state? Anti-suit injunctions in the UK post-Brexit', *Arbitration* 83(3), 254–266.

[44] Ust-Kamenogorsk Hydropower Plant [2013] 1 W.L.R. 1889; [2013] Bus. L.R. 1357, at 60

[45] See Ndolo, D. (2019) 'The Role of the English Courts in the Enforcement of Arbitration Agreements' *Coventry Law Journal*, 24(1), 39–48, at 45–46

[46] Allianz SpA (formerly Riunione Adriatica di Sicurta SpA) v West Tankers Inc (C-185/07) EU:C:2009:69; [2009] 1 A.C. 1138; [2009] 2 WLUK 197 (ECJ (Grand Chamber)).

[47] See section 22.5.4 below. A more detailed discussion on this is available in Ndolo, D. (2019) 'The Role of the English Courts in the Enforcement of Arbitration Agreements' *Coventry Law Journal*, 24(1), 39–48, at 45–46

[48] Blavi, F. (2016) 'The Role of Public Policy in International Commercial Arbitration' 82(1), *Arbitration*.

s. 58(1) and 66(1) of the AA 1996 mandates the national courts recognise awards as final and binding and enforce them 'in the same manner as a judgment or order of the court to the same effect'. In light of these statutory mandates, the English have generally adopted 'a pro-enforcement policy for the recognition and enforcement of arbitration awards'.[49] This means that the English courts would generally recognise arbitration awards unless they fall under very limited exceptional circumstances listed under the NYC 1958 and AA 1996, discussed below.

Therefore, although the courts have adopted a pro-arbitration general approach, there are limited exceptions in which the courts may refuse to enforce the arbitration awards. Internationally, the primary source of the exceptional circumstances in which recognition and enforcement of the award may be refused, at the request of the party against whom it is invoked, are contained in Article V of the New York Convention 1958. To this effect, the exceptional circumstances contained in Article 34 and 36 of the UNICITRAL Model law 1985 as amended in 2006 are almost identical to the provision in the New York Convention 1958. Notably, these exceptional circumstances are exhaustive and thus they are the only reasons in which the recognition and enforcement may be refused.[50] Crucially, it must be stressed that Article V of the New York 1958 exceptions apply exclusively outside the country where the arbitration award was granted.[51] As for the awards granted in the UK, parties can rely on s.103 AA 1996 which has identical provisions. In addition, s.66-69 AA 1996 provide that an award can be refused where the arbitrator does not have substantive jurisdiction, or there is a serious irregularity in the arbitration process or there is challenge on point of law, respectively.

Under Article V of the NYC 1958, the exceptional circumstances under which an arbitration award can be set aside are set in such a way that aims to balance between, on the one hand, the need to protect the efficiency of international arbitration and ensuring the finality of arbitration awards and, on the other hand, the need to respect fundamental national judicial sovereignty and principles of fairness and due diligence. They include, *inter alia*, where the arbitration agreement was not valid, where the subject matter was beyond jurisdiction of the arbitrator or where enforcing the award would be contrary to public policy.

It is noteworthy that (aside from the court refusing the arbitration award on its own motion)[52] due to the pro-enforcement policy, the party seeking to challenge the award, bears the burden of proving that one of the limited grounds on refusing to enforcement exists and even if they do prove, the courts retain the discretion on whether or not recognise and enforce the award.[53] Nonetheless, it must be stressed that, despite this discretion, it is highly unlikely that a national court would enforce an award that clearly falls under one of the exceptions.[54] This is because doing this would allow parties to abuse the arbitration procedure and would completely undermine the efficacy of the arbitration procedure.

[49] Lord Collins in *Dallah Real Estate & Tourism Holding Co* v *Pakistan* [2010] UKSC 46: [2010] 3 W.L.R. 1472, at 1510.

[50] Blackaby, C. & Redfern, A. (2022) *Redfern and Hunter on International Arbitration*. (7th ed.) OUP, at 10.33.

[51] Ibid., at 10.30.

[52] Article V(2), New York Convention 1958.

[53] Blackaby, C. & Redfern, A. (2015) *Redfern and Hunter on International Arbitration* (6th ed.) OUP, at 623.

[54] Dicey, Morris and Collins (2017) *The Conflict of Laws* (15 ed.) Sweet and Maxwell, at para 16–137

22.5 Recent Developments in Arbitration Law

22.5.1 Online dispute resolution

Online dispute resolution is not something new – the idea and the technology was available even before the COVID-19 pandemic. For example, where it was practically impossible or unreasonable to get the parties to attend physically, they could provide their evidence virtually. Nevertheless, it was fairly common for opposing counsel to object this and thus most of the arbitration proceedings were held face to face. The COVID-19 pandemic served as a catalyst to hasten the wider awareness and acceptance of virtual arbitrations. This is because governmental restrictions put in place to curb the spread of the pandemic included both travel restrictions and social distancing measures. This meant, in some instances, that it was impossible or even illegal to travel to attend arbitration proceedings and thus parties turned to virtual arbitration.

Although virtual arbitration provided a solution to this, it came with its own challenges, particularly in international arbitration. This is because there were situations where the parties involved were in different time zones and thus proceedings were held at inconvenient times for at least one the parties. Further, there were technological challenges as parties encountered different internet speeds in their respective countries. Some participants may not have the technical know-how or capacity to operate a videoconference. This is of particular concern because, under Article V(1)(b) of the New York Convention, an arbitral award may be challenged if a party against whom the award is invoked is otherwise 'unable to present his case' or s. 68 AA 1996 for a serious irregularity within the proceedings.

Nonetheless, the adoption of virtual hearings has brought great flexibility within the arbitration process from which all parties involved benefit. For example, in most cases it usually results in shorter proceedings and, perhaps more importantly, a more cost-effective process as the parties involved do not have to travel or incur other costs, such as hotels or catering. Furthermore, virtual arbitration means that that there is no need to print documents, and is thus more eco-friendly.

However, virtual hearings, at least at the early stages, presented concerns with confidentiality and privacy, as virtual platforms do not always offer the same level of security as real-life meetings and thus there were concerns over data protection, hacking of electronic document depositories, such as witness statements, sharing of confidential documents, or external parties high-jacking video or audio. Further, in face-to-face cross-examination of witnesses, counsel can exercise their advocacy skills such as observing body language, facial expression, the use of voice, eyes, to test the credibility of witnesses, and in virtual hearings this is not possible.

Nevertheless, as the witness is not in physical attendance it has meant that arbitrators focus on the evidence and this has made it less probable that the arbitrator might be influenced by the physical attributes of a witness when cross-examining them. There are also innovative ways to mitigate issues with privacy, confidentiality and ethical breaches; for instance, a witnesses could be asked to have one camera pointing at them and a second camera into the rest of the room. Alternatively, the witness may be asked to attend a neutral physical venue for examination. Indeed, International Arbitration Centre Alliance, an alliance of arbitral institutions was formed for this specific purpose. Additionally, there are a number of arbitral institutions, including the London Court of International

Arbitration, which have revised their rules and now embrace electronic communications and filings as the default rule, eliminating the need to submit hard copies of documents and allowing for electronic signature of arbitration awards.[55] In 2021, the UK Law Commission announced they are reviewing and reforming the Arbitration Act of 1996 to ensure it is up to date with today's standards of arbitration including allowing, 'electronic service of documents, electronic arbitration awards, and virtual hearings'.[56] The current practice post-COVID 19 pandemic indicates more use of hybrid or virtual hearings than in the pre-pandemic era.

22.5.2 Arbitrability

This non-arbitrability doctrine is recognised in the English Arbitration Act 1996 (AA 1996)[57] and the New York Convention 1958,[58] but they both do not contain any limitations as to the arbitrability of particular disputes. Prohibitions on arbitrability, therefore, are based on other statutes or public policies and thus in absence of statutory prohibition it leaves this matter almost in its entirety to national courts. As a result, whether or not a particular type of dispute is arbitrable under a given legal system is a matter of public policy, and this varies from country to country and changes over time. The effect of this is that there is no universal approach by which disputes are arbitrable. Each state decides which matters can be resolved through arbitration, taking in account its own political social and economic policy. The matter arbitrability in general is dealt with in another context,[59] but for the purposes of this book, we examine recent developments on this area, relating commercial disputes.

Traditionally there was reluctance to resolve commercial disputes involving aspects of intellectual property, such as patents, privately through arbitration. This was mainly because they are granted by national authorities, and so it was argued that disputes regarding such rights should be resolved by a public national institution. However, over the last few decades, there has been a significant and marked trend towards the arbitration of IP disputes. The advantage of arbitrating these disputes is that the confidentiality of the proceedings as well as the flexibility of arbitration, which allows the parties to select a neutral arbitrator who has specific knowledge of the subject matter as well as a neutral venue to resolve the dispute.[60] The Court of Appeal in *Nokia Technologies OY* v *Oneplus Technology (Shenzhen) Co Ltd*,[61] acknowledged how the supranational nature of arbitration can aid in avoid jurisdictional issues and deter parties from forum shopping in IP disputes.

[55] See Article 26.2 of the LCIA Arbitration Rules 2020, see also Article 2 of the UNICITRAL Arbitration Rules 2021.

[56] Law Commission 'Law Commission to review the Arbitration Act 1996 (30 November 2021)' – the reform of the current Arbitration Act 1996 is discussed below in section 22.5.5

[57] For instance, see s. 9 AA 1996 – in one of the conditions the court must satisfy to issue stay in proceedings is that that the dispute must be arbitrable.

[58] For instance, one of the grounds to challenge an award under Article V(2)(b) is if the subject matter of dispute cannot be settled via arbitration.

[59] Ndolo, D. (2023) 'The Role of Public Policy in the Arbitrability of Disputes under US and English law' *Int. A.L.R.*, 26(1), 72

[60] Ibid., at 79–80

[61] [2022] EWCA Civ 947

With regards to insolvency/bankruptcy disputes, the court in *Riverrock Securities Ltd* v *International Bank of St Petersburg*[62] considered the extent to which such disputes are arbitrable. The court held that insolvency claims are generally arbitrable where they:

> 'do not engage the interests of third parties save to the extent that any creditor of an insolvent company will benefit from its success in arbitration, those claims are arbitrable'.[63]

It is well settled that in English law arbitrators do not have the power to convict a person of a criminal offence.[64] However, for commercial disputes involving aspects of crime such as bribery and fraud, the position under English law was rather controversially confirmed by the English Court of Appeal, in *London Steam Ship Owners Mutual Insurance Association Ltd* v *Spain*,[65] that arbitrators have jurisdiction to find that a criminal offence has been committed for instance bribery or fraud. In that case, Moore-Bick LJ held that:

> 'It was not disputed that in the ordinary way an arbitrator has jurisdiction to find facts which constitute a criminal offence (fraud being an all-too-common example) or that in an appropriate case an arbitrator also has jurisdiction to find that a criminal offence has been committed.'[66]

Such an approach is controversial particularly because it is not clear how such a criminal offence must be proved in arbitration proceedings. It is not clear what burden of proof would be applied, whether this would be the usual criminal standard beyond reasonable doubt or the civil standard on the balance of probabilities. Also, due to privacy and confidentiality of arbitration, the arbitrator may not have all the necessary tools to determine criminal liability as compared to the courts, for instance, a jury or records of bad character.[67]

22.5.3 Separability

DHL Project and Chartering v *Gemini Ocean Shipping*[68] is a case in point that dealt with the scope of the separability and competence-competence principle discussed above. The facts of the case were that, in August 2020, the charterers and the owners negotiated the terms of a fixture through the intermediary of a broker (MIT). On 25 August 2020, MIT circulated a 'recap' email. The email included an unsigned proforma charterparty for the owners' vessel to carry a goods from Australia to China. The email stated that the fixture was 'subject shipper/receiver's approval', but the shipper never approved it. Clause 17 of the recap provided for English law and London arbitration and clause 20 provided that the terms were 'Otherwise as per attached charterer's proforma'. The owners contended there was breach of contract and thus commenced an arbitration in which the charterers did not participate and thus the arbitrator awarded damages to the owners.

62 *Riverrock Securities Ltd* v *International Bank of St Petersburg* [2020] EWHC 2483 (Comm); [2020] 2 C.L.C., at 547

63 Ibid., Foxton J, at 580.

64 Davies, R. (2015) 'England and Wales: Arbitrability of Claims which Involve Alleged Criminal Conduct'. Kluwer Arbitration Blog, May.

65 [2015] C.P. Rep. 31.

66 Ibid., at para 78.

67 See Ndolo, D. (2023) 'The Role of Public Policy in the Arbitrability of Disputes under US and English law'. *Int. A.L.R.* 26(1), 72, at 77–78

68 [2022] EWHC 181 (Comm)

The charterers challenged the award under s. 67 AA 1996 on the basis that the arbitrators did not have jurisdiction because by virtue of the doctrine of separability, the question of whether there was a binding arbitration agreement was not the same as whether there was a binding underlying contract. The defendant, the owners, argued that there was a valid arbitration agreement as per s. 7 AA 1996, and that the arbitration agreement is a separate contract that can survive disputes between the parties relating to the underlying contract as per in *Fiona Trust & Holding Corp* v *Privalov*[69] discussed above. Therefore, the legal question was whether s. 7 AA 1996 applies where there is no underlying contract.

The English High court held that s. 7 AA 1996 does not apply where there is no valid agreement. An arbitration agreement is not a mini-agreement which is in some way divorced from the main agreement. Instead, an arbitration clause was part of the bundle of rights and obligations under negotiation. The fact that the recap and the arbitration agreement were contained in the same document (contract that did not come into force) reinforced the conclusion that in this case they would stand and fall together.

This decision is very controversial because s. 7 of the AA 1996 specifically states that arbitration clauses will not be held to be invalid where the matrix contract 'did not come into existence' and thus it is difficult to reconcile that provision with this decision. In addition, the decision appears to be at odds with the well-established principle from the *Fiona* case discussed above that to challenge the validity of the arbitration agreement evidence has to be brought against that agreement not the underlying contract. Furthermore, it also affects the competence-competence principle discussed above under s. 30 AA 1996. This is because, as per this principle, the arbitrator should have jurisdiction to determine the validity of the underlying contract where there is a valid arbitration agreement. But the effect of this decision in practice is that it takes away the power to determine the validity/existence of the underlying contract in such cases from the arbitrators. This potentially opens the floodgates of challenges of arbitration awards on substantive jurisdiction ground where arbitrator decides that underlying contract was not valid.

Upon appeal in November 2022, the English Court of Appeal confirmed and agreed with the High Court ruling[70] and permission to appeal to the Supreme Court was denied in June 2023. Therefore, the DHL case remains good law restricting the scope of s. 7 AA 1996.

22.5.4 Brexit (anti-suit injunctions)

Before Brexit, in 2010, the Court of Justice of the European Union held in *West Tankers*[71] (ECJ (Grand Chamber)] that anti-suit injunctions of the nature described above[72] run counter to the principle of mutual trust among the EU member states as required by the EU jurisdictional law, the Brussels I Regulation.[73] The resulting effect was that national

[69] [2007] UKHL 40

[70] [2022] EWCA Civ 1555

[71] *Allianz SpA (formerly Riunione Adriatica di Sicurta SpA)* v *West Tankers Inc* (C-185/07) EU:C:2009:69; [2009] 1 A.C. 1138; [2009] 2 WLUK 197 (ECJ (Grand Chamber)).

[72] See section 22.4.2

[73] Council Regulation (EC) No 44/2001 of 22 December 2000 on Jurisdiction and the Recognition and Enforcement of Judgments in Civil and Commercial Matters.

courts within the European Union, including the English courts at the time, could issue an anti-suit injunction in favour of arbitration where a party starts foreign court proceedings in an EU state.

In 2015, the Brussels I Recast[74] replaced the Brussels I Regulation, and expressly removed arbitration from its scope. This has led to further debate as to whether the Recast can accommodate anti-suit injunctions. Interestingly, in *Gazprom*,[75] Advocate General Wathelet held that, if *West Tankers* had been decided under the Brussels I Recast, anti-suit injunctions in favour of arbitration would not have been held to be incompatible with the Regulation. However, the CJEU affirmed the ban by West tankers and emphasized it still good law protecting the principle of mutual trust.

In *Nori Holdings Ltd* v *Bank Financial Corp*,[76] the claimant sought an anti-suit injunction under the Brussels l Recast relying on the opinion of advocate General Wathelet. Justice Males held that 'the opinion of the Advocate General on this issue was fundamentally flawed' for, *inter alia*,[77] the CJEU did not adopt the AG's approach; instead, it reaffirmed the decision in *West Tankers*. In doing it clears up most of the confusion that had been brought up by the AG opinion in the *Gazprom* case in relation to the arbitration exception in the Recast.[78]

Following the EU referendum in 2016, the UK parliament passed the European Union Withdrawal Act 2018 (EUWA) and it repealed the European Communities Act 1972 such that the full effect of EU law will no longer apply in the UK from the exit day (31 January 2020).[79] Instead, the EUWA 2018, as amended by the Retained EU Law (Revocation and Reform) Act 2023, transferred all EU laws, including previous CJEU case law, into UK domestic law. As a result, the first and second instance English courts remain mostly bound by previous CJEU cases. The UK Supreme Court, however, via s. 6(4) of the EUWA, will have the power to depart from previous CJEU decisions in the same way it can depart from its own earlier case law.

In relation to anti-suit injunctions, this means that, the UK Supreme Court has the power to depart from the CJEU ruling in *West Tankers*, removing the restriction on UK courts to issue anti-suit injunctions to parties in EU state national courts. However, at time of writing no such ruling has been made yet. Of course in such an instance, even if the UK courts would revert to full power to grant anti-suit injunction the legal issue then is whether this would be enforceable and complied with in state where West Tankers remains good law? In the *Re enforcement of the English anti-suit injunction*[80] the Court of Appeal in Germany refused to serve an anti-suit injunction that UK High Court had issued (before CJEU's decision in *West Tankers*) directed a German party from proceeding with court proceedings in the German Courts. The German courts emphasised the fact

[74] Regulation 1215/2012 on the Jurisdiction and the Recognition and Enforcement of Judgments in Civil and Commercial Matters.

[75] [EU:C:2014:2414]

[76] *Nori Holdings Ltd* v *Bank Financial Corp* [2018] EWHC 1343 (Comm).

[77] Ibid., at, at 91–98.

[78] For more on this case see Ndolo, D. (2018) 'Judicial Clarification on Anti-suit Injunctions: The Right Approach?' Kluwer Arbitration Blog, July.

[79] ss. 1 and 2 of EUWA.

[80] Decision of 10 January 1996, file no. 3 VA 11/95, EuZW 1996, 351 as cited in Baker & McKenzie (2013) *International Arbitration Yearbook* 2012–2013 (6th ed.) Juris Publishing Inc., at 95.

that the anti-suit injunction is not directed directly to the German state or the German courts is immaterial. This is because the anti-suit injunction has the effect of infringing the sovereignty of the German courts and thus refused to comply with the anti-suit injunction under Article 13 of the Hague Service Convention 1965. The legal consequence of such an approach is undesirable because that the EU state courts (German courts as per case above) would issue a ruling despite the anti-suit injunction, but such a ruling would not be enforced under English law following the *Philip Alexander Securities and Futures Limited* v *Bamberger and others*.[81] In that case, the German court refused to serve an anti-suit injunction issued by English courts so the English court had to consider whether it would recognise the decision of the German courts. The English court held that:

> 'It would seem to me prima facie that if someone proceeds in breach of and with notice an (anti-suit) injunction granted by the English court to obtain judgements abroad those judgements should not as a matter of public policy be recognised in the UK.'[82]

It would be unsurprising if the UK Supreme Court overturns *West Tankers* case and reverts to its full power of issuing antisuit injunctions because the English courts highly value this power.[83] Indeed, in *Turner* v *Grovit*,[84] the court referred to anti-suit injunctions as an 'important valuable weapon' giving to the London seat of arbitration an advantage over its competitors. In addition, the UK Supreme Court has also twice ruled in favour of the court's power to issue anti-suit injunction in *West Tankers*[85] and *Turner* v *Grovit*,[86] as not being contrary to the principle of mutual trust under Brussels Regulation 1, albeit that its decisions were not endorsed by the CJEU. Moreover, despite the CJEU ruling in *West Tankers*, the English courts have continued to grant anti-suit injunctions in favour of arbitration proceeding directed to parties who started foreign proceeding in non-EU national courts. For instance, in 2020, in *Enka Insaat Ve Sanayi AS* v *OOO Insurance Company Chubb*[87] it held that English law governed the arbitration agreement and granted an anti-suit injunction restraining the appellant from continuing the Russian proceedings. Similarly in 2024, in *UniCredit Bank GmbH* v *RusChemAlliance LLC*[88] the UKSC issued an anti-suit injunction to restrain one party to a contract from pursuing proceedings in Russia against the other in breach of an arbitration agreement.

22.5.5 Reform of the Arbitration Act 1996

After two years of consultation, on 21 November 2023, The Arbitration Bill was introduced in parliament. In summary the final report of the law commission recommended the following changes, significant changes and minor corrections:

[81] *Times*, 22 July 1996, [1997] Eu LR 63
[82] Ibid., at 115.
[83] For more see Ndolo, D. & Liu, M. (2018) 'A Departure from West Tankers after Brexit? Anti-suit Injunctions in the UK directed to Parties in EU National Courts' 21(1) *Irish Journal of European Law* 55.
[84] [2001] UKHL 65.
[85] [2007] UKHL 4.
[86] [2001] UKHL 65.
[87] [2020] UKSC 38.
[88] [2024] UKSC 40.

Significant changes

- Codification of an arbitrator's duty of disclosure of any circumstances likely to give rise to justifiable doubts as to their impartiality or independence. Generally, s. 33 AA Act 1996 requires the arbitrator to act fairly and impartially, as was noted in *H1 and another* v *W*,[89] where an arbitrator was removed under s. 24 AA 1996 on the basis that his statements about the expert witness raised justifiable doubts as to his impartiality. Despite this, there is no express provision on disclosure prior to appointment. The arbitrator's duty to disclose prior appointment was however recognised and applied in *Halliburton Co* v *Chubb Bermuda Insurance Ltd*[90] by the UK supreme court as an implied term. Thus the aim was to codify this. It should be mentioned though that this is usually a matter covered under Arbitration procedural rules, e.g. under Article 11-13 UNICITRAL Arbitration Rules 2021 and Article 5 of the London Arbitration Rules 2020.
- Strengthening arbitrator immunity around resignation and applications for removal. Although, s. 29 of the AA Act 1996 provides the arbitrator with immunity while discharging their duties in good faith, the arbitrator can still be liable for resignation or cost of their removal even if the challenge is unsuccessful.[91] In order to offer better protection to the arbitrator, the Law Commission recommends arbitrators should incur no liability, including costs liability, in respect of an application for removal unless acting in bad faith and no liability for resignation unless such was unreasonable.
- A revised framework for challenges under section 67 AA 1996 which allows a party to arbitration award to challenge the award on grounds that the tribunal lacked jurisdiction to decide the matter. On this matter the law commission recommend legislating to provide the power to make rules of court to limit what evidence and grounds of objection can be put before the court when the challenging party has already made a similar challenge before the tribunal.[92]
- A new rule on the governing law of an arbitration agreement. This point of reform is stirred by somewhat controversial majority Supreme court decision in *Enka* v *Chubb*[93] that the general rule is that where parties have chosen a governing law for the main contract, that law will apply to the arbitration agreement, or if not it would be the law to which it is most connected to in the main contract. The issue with the rule is complex where you have parties of different nationalities involved plus restricts party autonomy, e.g. power to select applicable law in practice. As a result, the Law Commission aims to provide a default rule, to be inserted under s. 6, that applicable law will be the law of the seat, unless otherwise agreed. The intended impact of this to simplify this issue plus encourage and further promote use of English law and London as the seat.
- In addition to this, the report recommends clarification of court powers in support of arbitral proceedings and in support of emergency arbitrators.

[89] [2024] EWHC 382.
[90] [2020] UKSC 48, [2021] AC 1083.
[91] See *C Ltd* v *D* [2020] EWHC 1283 and Halliburton Co v Chubb Bermuda Insurance Ltd [2020] UKSC 48, [2021] AC 1083 at [111] by Lord Hodge.
[92] Law Commission 'Review of the Arbitration Act 1996: Final report and Bill', 5 September 2023 at chapter 9, para 9.3
[93] [2020] UKSC 38, [2020] 1 WLR 4117

Minor corrections

- Making appeals available from an application to stay legal proceedings. Section 9 of the AA 1996 mandates the English courts to issue a stay in proceedings where a defendant files for it in response to court proceedings in breach of arbitration agreement, provided all requirements are met, i.e. agreement is valid and operative plus there is an arbitrable dispute. The issue is that currently s. 9 AA 1996 does not expressly mention whether one can challenge the court's decision on this. The Law Commission thus recommends addition of express right to appeal following court decision on this.[94]
- Simplifying preliminary applications to court on jurisdiction and points of law and clarifying time limits for challenging awards. On this point the Law Commission aims to clarify when the 28 days limit to bring challenge an award set out in s. 70 AA 1996 starts. The Law Commission recommends that s. 70(3) of the Arbitration Act 1996 be amended to be in line with s. 57 AA 1996, i.e. if there has been a request, under s. 57 or an alternative regime agreed by the parties, for a correction or additional award material to the application or appeal, the time runs from the date of the correction or additional award.[95]
- Finally, repealing s. 85–88 AA 11996 as they are unnecessary and have yet to come into force. These unused provisions seek to distinguish between domestic and international arbitration and, according to the Law Commission, are superfluous.

These changes were anticipated to come into force by end of 2024, however rather disappointingly the progress through parliament was interrupted by the announcement of an early general election. However, in July 2024 the Bill was reintroduced, and the Arbitration Act 2025 received royal assent on 24 February 2025. However, this came too late for a discussion of the final version of the Act for this edition.

[94] Law Commission 'Review of the Arbitration Act 1996: Final report and Bill', 5 September 2023 at chapter 11, at 11.26

[95] Law Commission 'Review of the Arbitration Act 1996: Final report and Bill', 5 September 2023 at chapter 11, at 11.97

Index

A

B

C

D

F

G

J

K

L

M

Q

S

T

U

V

W